Communications in Computer and Information Science 697

Commenced Publication in 2007
Founding and Former Series Editors:
Alfredo Cuzzocrea, Dominik Ślęzak, and Xiaokang Yang

More information about this series at http://www.springer.com/series/7899

Carlos Jaime Barrios Hernández · Isidoro Gitler
Jaime Klapp (Eds.)

High Performance Computing

Third Latin American Conference, CARLA 2016
Mexico City, Mexico, August 29 – September 2, 2016
Revised Selected Papers

 Springer

Editors
Carlos Jaime Barrios Hernández
Universidad Industrial de Santander
Bucaramanga
Colombia

Isidoro Gitler
Centro de Investigación y de Estudios
  Avanzados
CINVESTAV-IPN
Ciudad de México
México

Jaime Klapp
Instituto Nacional de Investigaciones
  Nucleares
La Marquesa, Estado de México
México

ISSN 1865-0929   ISSN 1865-0937 (electronic)
Communications in Computer and Information Science
ISBN 978-3-319-57971-9   ISBN 978-3-319-57972-6   (eBook)
DOI 10.1007/978-3-319-57972-6

Library of Congress Control Number: 2017939120

Printed on acid-free paper

This Springer imprint is published by Springer Nature
The registered company is Springer International Publishing AG
The registered company address is: Gewerbestrasse 11, 6330 Cham, Switzerland

Preface

High-performance computing (HPC) or supercomputing has become an essential tool for modern science and technology. In addition to basic science and experimentation, HPC has become an essential tool for advancing our understanding of nature, for the analysis of society's behavior, and for technological advancement.

Today, current research in many branches in science and engineering relies more and more on supercomputing, allowing us to expand basic research and experimentation. Supercomputing has proven to be equally essential for developing and understanding a wide range of advanced science and technology topics that are directly related to our daily lives. HPC enables the design of models and running computer simulations of phenomena before passing through an experimental phase, with great economic savings, but more importantly allowing us to provide results within days or weeks when months or even years were required in the past.

The Latin American High-Performance Computing Conference, CARLA (http://www.ccarla.org), is a joint conference of the High-Performance Computing Latin America Community – HPCLATAM – and the Conferencia Latino Americana de Computación de Alto Rendimiento – CLCAR. In 2016 both major HPC Latin-American workshops came together again at CARLA 2016, and were held in the recently created Abacus Laboratorio de Matemática Aplicada y Cómputo de Alto Rendimiento (Laboratory for Applied Mathematics and High Performance Computing) of CINVESTAV that since early 2015 has been hosting one of the largest supercomputers in Latin America, where scientists and engineers in Mexico and other countries are able to develop computational projects that require very large HPC facilities. Furthermore, with the Abacus-CINVESTAV supercomputer, Mexico returned in 2016 to the Top 500 list of the 500 most powerful supercomputers in the world.

HPCLATAM (http://hpclatam.org) gathers a young but growing community of scientists and practitioners in the HPC area in Latin America. Past events proved that the HPC community in the region is steadily growing. HPCLATAM aims to bring together researchers, developers, and users of HPC to discuss new ideas, experiences, and problems. The main goal of HPCLATAM is to provide a regional forum fostering the growth of the HPC community in Latin America through the exchange and dissemination of new ideas, techniques, and research in HPC.

The CLCAR (http://www.cenat.ac.cr/) conference has been held since 2007 and is driven by a group of researchers from universities and research centers in Latin America that seek to promote a space for discussion of new knowledge and trends in the area. A further aim is to coordinate initiatives and efforts toward the development of technologies for HPC that can contribute to solving common problems of social and economic relevance to the region. CLCAR is an event for students and scientists and is dedicated to the areas of HPC, parallel and distributed systems, e-science and its applications to real-life problems, but especially focused on Latin American researchers.

The CARLA 2016 symposium featured invited talks from academia and industry speakers, with short- and full-paper sessions presenting both mature work and new ideas in research and industrial applications in HPC.

This book contains the best papers from CARLA 2016, which is organized in three parts. In Part I the contributions are related to supercomputer infrastructure and applications, Part II includes works on algorithms and applications, and finally in Part III you can find interesting papers on HPC applications and simulations applied to various fields of science and engineering.

The book is aimed at scientists in the fields of computer science, mathematics, physics, engineering, chemistry, biology and many other fields that have an interest in HPC, infrastructure, algorithms, and a variety of applications. It is also aimed at senior and graduate students who are in some way involved in HPC. The material includes recent advances in HPC and is suitable for both teaching and research.

We thank Estela Hernández Juárez and Adriana Aranda for their valuable contribution in the production of this book.

March 2017

Carlos Jaime Barrios Hernández
Isidoro Gitler
Jaime Klapp

Acknowledgments

The production of this book was sponsored by the Consejo Nacional de Ciencia y Tecnología (Conacyt), the Consejo Mexiquense de Ciencia y Tecnología (Comecyt), the Instituto Nacional de Investigaciones Nucleares (ININ), and the Laboratorio de Matemática Aplicada y Computo de Alto Rendimiento of the Centro de Investigación y de Estudios Avanzados of the Instituto Politécnico Nacional through the "ABACUS" CONACyT grant EDOMEX-2011-C01-165873.

Organization

General Chair

Isidoro Gitler — ABACUS: Laboratorio de Matemática Aplicada y Cómputo de Alto Rendimiento, CINVESTAV-IPN, México

Co-chairs

Carlos Jaime Barrios Hernández — Universidad Industrial de Santander, Colombia

Jaime Klapp — Instituto Nacional de Investigaciones Nucleares, México

Gonzalo Hernández — USACH & CCTVal, Chile

Salma Jaliffe — CUDI, Mexico

Esteban Mocskos — Universidad de Buenos Aires/CONICET, Argentina

Phillippe Navaux — Universidade Federal do Rio Grande do Sul, Brazil

Technical Program Committee

Tracks Coordinators

Cyber-Infrastructures, Storage, Networking and HPC Data Centers

Moisés Torres Martínez — Universidad de Guadalajara, Mexico

Big Data, Data Analytics and Data Visualization

Raúl Ramos — Universidad Industrial de Santander, Colombia

Scientific and Industrial Applications

Nicolás Wolovick — Universidad Nacional de Córdoba, Argentina

Education and Outreach in HPC and Advanced Computing

Esteban Clua — Universidade Federal Fluminense, Brazil

Towards Advanced and Scientific Computing and HPC

Sergio Nesmachnow — Universidad de la República, Uruguay

Technical Program Committee Members

Andrés Avila — Universidad de la Frontera, Chile

Javier R. Balderrama — Inria Rennes, France

Carlos J. Barrios Hernández	Universidad Industrial de Santander, Bucaramanga, Colombia
Lola Bautista	Universidad Industrial de Santander, Colombia
Carlos Bederián	Universidad Nacional de Córdoba, Argentina
Cristiana Bentes	Universidade do Estado do Rio de Janeiro, Brazil
Cristina Boeres	Universidade Federal Fluminense, Brazil
Rossana Bonasia	ESIA-IPN, Mexico
Francisco Brasileiro	Universidade Federal de Campina Grande, Brazil
Carlos Buil Aranda	Pontificia Universidad Católica de Chile, Chile
Víctor Calo	King Abdullah University of Science and Technology (KAUST), Saudi Arabia
Néstor Calvo	CIMEC, Argentina
Luis Fernando Castillo	Universidad de Caldas, Colombia
Marcio Castro	Universidade Federal de Santa Catarina, Brazil
Harold Castro	Universidad de los Andes, Colombia
Gerson Cavalheiro	Universidade Federal de Pelotas, Brazil
Marcia Cera	Universidade Federal de Santa Catarina, Brazil
Andrea Charao	Universidad Federal Santa María, Brazil
Esteban Clua	Universidade Federal Fluminense, Brazil
Daniel Cordeiro	Universidade de Sao Paulo, Brazil
Alvaro Coutinho	Universidade Federal do Rio de Janeiro, Brazil
Fernando Crespo	Universidad Central de Chile, Chile
Marcela Cruchaga	Universidad de Santiago de Chile, Chile
Jesús Cruz	UNAM, Mexico
Alvaro de la Ossa	CENAT Laboratory, San José, Costa Rica
Claudio Delrieux	Universidad Nacional del Sur, Argentina
César Díaz	Universidad de los Andes, Bogotá, Colombia
César Díaz	Instituto Potosino de Investigación en C y T, Mexico
Gilberto Díaz	Supercomputación y Calculo Científico, Universidad Industrial de Santander, Colombia
Bernabé Dorronsoro	Universidad de Lille 1, France
Nicolás Erdody	Multicore World Conference Organizer, New Zealand
Pablo Ezzatti	Universidad de la República, Uruguay
Ricardo Farías	Universidade Federal do Rio de Janeiro, Brazil
Verónica Gil Costa	Universidad Nacional San Luis, Argentina
Isidoro Gitler	ABACUS: Laboratorio de Matemática Aplicada y Cómputo de Alto Rendimiento, CINVESTAV-IPN, México
Brice Goglin	Inria Bordeaux, France
Antonio Gomes	Laboratorio Nacional de Computacional Científica, Brazil
Jose L. Gordillo	Universidad Nacional Autónoma de México, Mexico
Benjamín Hernández	Oak Ridge National Laboratory, USA
Gonzalo Hernández	USACH & CCTVal, Chile
Tiberio Hernández	Universidad de los Andes, Bogotá, Colombia
Salma Jaliffe	CUDI Initiative, Mexico

Jaime Klapp	Instituto Nacional de Investigaciones Nucleares, México
Alejandro Kolton	Centro Atómico de Bariloche, Argentina
Roberto León	Universidad Nacional Andrés Bello, Chile
Francisco Luna	Universidad Carlos III de Madrid, Spain
Rafael Mayo	CIEMAT, Spain
Ricardo Medel	Intel Corporation, Argentina
Wagner Meira Jr.	Universidade Federal de Minas Gerais, Brazil
Alba Melo	Universidade de Brasilia, Brazil
Esteban Meneses	Costa Rica Institute of Technology, Costa Rica
Renato Miceli	CENAI-CIMATEC, Brazil
Pablo Mininni	Universidad de Buenos Aires, Argentina
David Monge	Universidad Nacional de Cuyo, Argentina
Sergio Nesmanowch	Universidad de la Republica, Uruguay
Luis Nuñez	RedCLARA/Universidad Industrial de Santander, Colombia
Julio Paciello	Universidad Nacional de Asunción, Paraguay
Elina Pacini	Universidad Nacional de Cuyo, Argentina
Jairo Panetta	CPTEC, Brazil
Johnatan Pecero	Luxembourg, Researcher, Mexico
Gabriel Pedraza	Universidad Industrial de Santander, Bucaramanga, Colombia
Guilherme Peretti Pezzi	University of Turin, Italy
Jorge Pérez	EuroNova, Belgium
Carlos Piedrahita	Universidad de Antioquia, Colombia
Laercio Pilla	Universidade Federal de Santa Catarina, Brazil
Carlos Hernán Prada Rojas	STMicroelectronics, France
Javier Príncipe	CIMNE/Universidad Politécnica de Catalunya, Spain
Marcela Printista	Universidad Nacional de San Luis, Argentina
Juan Manuel Ramírez Alcaraz	Universidad de Colima, Mexico
Raúl Ramos Pollan	Universidad Industrial de Santander, Bucaramanga, Colombia
Vinod Rebello	UFF, Brazil
Olivier Richard	LIG Laboratory Grenoble, France
Genghis Ríos	Pontificia Universidad Católica del Perú, Peru
Robinson Rivas	Universidad Central de Venezuela, Venezuela
Ascanio Rojas	Universidad de Los Andes, Venezuela
Isaac Rudomin	Barcelona Supercomputing Center, Spain
Alfredo Cristóbal Salas	Universidad Veracruzana, Mexico
Afonso Sales	Pontificia Universidad Católica do Rio Grande do Sul, Brazil
Liria Sato	USP, Brazil
Lucas Schnorr	INRIA MESCAL/CNRS LIG, France
Hermes Senger	Universidade Federal de São Carlos, Brazil
Alejandro Soba	CNEA-CONICET, Argentina

Contents

HPC Applications and Simulations

HPC Infrastructure and Applications

Efficient P2P Inspired Policy to Distribute Resource Information in Large Distributed Systems

Paula Verghelet[1] and Esteban Mocskos[1,2(✉)]

[1] Departamento de Computación, Facultad de Ciencias Exactas y Naturales,
Universidad de Buenos Aires, C1428EGA Buenos Aires, Argentina
{pverghelet,emocskos}@dc.uba.ar
[2] Centro de Simulación Computacional p/Aplic. Tecnológicas/CSC-CONICET,
Godoy Cruz 2390, C1425FQD Buenos Aires, Argentina

Abstract. The computational infrastructures are becoming larger and more complex. Their organization and interconnection are acquiring new dimensions with the increasing adoption of Cloud Technology and the establishment of Federations of cloud providers.

These large interconnected systems require monitoring at different levels of the infrastructure: from the availability of hardware resources to the effective provision of services and verification of terms of the established agreements.

Monitoring becomes a fundamental component of any Cloud Service or Federation, as the up-to-date information about resources in the system is extremely important to be used as an input to the scheduler component. The way in which the different members of such a distributed system obtain and distribute the resource information is what is known as *Resource Information Distribution Policy*.

Moving towards the obtention of a scalable and easy to maintain policy leads to interaction with the Peer to Peer (P2P) paradigm. Some of the proposed policies are based on establishing a ranking according to previous communications between nodes. These policies are known as learning based methods or Best-Neighbor (BN). However, the use of this type of policies shows poor performance and limited scalability compared with defacto Hierarchical or other hybrid policies.

In this work, we introduce *pBN* which is a fully distributed resource information policy based on P2P. We analyze some reasons that could produce the poor performance in standard BN and propose an improvement which shows performance and bandwidth consumption similar to Hierarchical policy and other hybrid variations. To compare the different policies, a specific simulation tool is used with different system sizes and exponential network topology.

Keywords: Distributed systems · Monitoring · Resource distribution policy

© Springer International Publishing AG 2017
C.J. Barrios Hernández et al. (Eds.): CARLA 2016, CCIS 697, pp. 3–17, 2017.
DOI: 10.1007/978-3-319-57972-6_1

1   Introduction

The computational infrastructures are moving towards a new level of complexity and computing power in terms of organization and interconnection. Cloud Federations represent the implementation of the utility computing model that was once incarnated in the Grid Computing paradigm. Large distributed systems play a fundamental role in an increasing number of scientific projects [3,33,37] and virtualization and Internet ubiquity are becoming more and more important.

These large interconnected systems require monitoring at different levels of the infrastructure: from the availability of hardware resources to the effective provision of services and verification of terms of the established SLA [19].

In this scenario, monitoring becomes a fundamental component of any Cloud Service or Federation [9–11,31]. In particular, the up-to-date information about resources in the system is extremely important as it can be used by the scheduler to select the target for each job [16,27].

The *Resource Information Distribution Policy* dictates the way in which resource information is obtained and distributed. In the Grid architecture described by Foster et al. [13], the discovery mechanisms are included in the *Resource Layer*. In another view of this architecture [23], the state information of resources is managed by the component named *Collective Subsystem*. In Cloud platforms, this service needs to be pervasive, is required by several components of the Cloud service, cuts across the layers of the Cloud System, and needs to be established between all the members of any Cloud Federation.

In this work, we focus on the monitoring of resources that represent hardware or software components. They can be characterized in two main classes [30]:

(i) *Static attributes*: the type of attributes which show a very slow rate of change. For example operating system, processor clock frequency, total storage capacity or network bandwidth.
(ii) *Dynamic attributes*: in this class, we can find the attributes related with the use of the system which change as the usage evolves, for example free memory, processor usage, available storage or network usage.

Having a centralized component to manage the resource information presents several drawbacks [30] (for example, is a single point of failure). Furthermore it is difficult to be adopted in a Federation of Clouds as all the members of the Federation should manage their own information and should be able to provide services independently of the rest of the members. Manually assembling a static hierarchy has become the defacto implementation in grid information systems [12]. However, in medium-to-large scale environments, the dynamics of the resource information and system members cannot be managed using a static hierarchy [23,34]. This approach has similar drawbacks to the centralized one, such as the point of failure and poor scaling for large number of users/providers [28,29]. Therefore, it results necessary to design new distributed policies for discovery and propagation of resource information.

The ideas based on the Peer to Peer (P2P) paradigm could help towards obtaining scalable solutions [21,34]: (i) very dynamic and heterogeneous environment and (ii) creation of a virtual working environment by collecting the resources available from a set of distributed, individual entities [29].

Iamnitchi et al. [16,17] proposed a P2P approach for organizing the information components in a flat dynamic P2P network. This decentralized approach envisages that every administrative domain maintains its information services and makes it available as part of the P2P network. Schedulers may initiate look-up queries that are forwarded in the P2P network using flooding (a similar approach to the unstructured P2P network Gnutella [32]).

Other scenarios in which the resource information is central to an efficient system performance are Volunteer and Mobile Cloud Computing. For example, Ghafarian et al. [14] presents a protocol for resource discovery with QoS restrictions in P2P based volunteer computing systems. Liu et al. [20] focuses on the integration of mobile computing resources in a cloud environment. They introduce an energy-efficient method of adaptive resource discovery to solve the problem of finding how available resources in nearby devices are discovered, it transforms between centralized and flooding modes to save energy.

The most common resource information distribution policies are:

- **Random**: Every node chooses randomly another node to query information from. There is no structure at all. Usually this policy is used as baseline behavior to be compared with.
- **Hierarchical:** In this kind of policy, a hierarchy is established beforehand and the resource information is sent using this fixed structure. In this way, the nodes at the top of the hierarchy exchange information with the ones below them. This is the standard actually used by Grids.
- **Super Peer:** Some nodes are defined as *super-peers* working like servers for a subset of nodes and as peers in the network of super-peers. In this way, a two level structure is defined in which the *peers* nodes are only allowed to communicate with a single super-peer and the cluster defined by it.
- **Best-Neighbor**: Some information about each answer is stored and the next neighbor to query is selected using the quality of the previous answers. At the beginning, the node has no information about its neighbors, thus it chooses randomly. As information is collected, the probability of choosing a neighbor randomly is inversely proportional to the amount of information stored.

Mastroianni et al. [22] evaluate the performance of these policies and analyze the pros and cons of each solution, concluding that Super Peer Policy (SP) presents interesting and competitive results. Cesario et al. [8] study the performance of a framework oriented to execute applications for distributed data mining combining volunteer computing and P2P architecture. SP policy is used to discover the available resources obtaining an important performance gain compared with a standard policy. These policy was also analyzed by Verghelet and Mocskos [35], who proposed an improvement to its communication protocol.

Meshkova et al. [24] provide a classification for policies according to structured or unstructured architecture. Structured architectures are further subdivided into centralized (client-server) or decentralized ones. Following this idea,

SP is classified as hybrid (unstructured-structured), Random as an uninformed search method and BN as an informed search method.

Iamnitchi et al. [16] show the best performance is obtained using Learning Based policies, while the work by Agrawal et al. [1] presents a distributed protocol based on the history of previous answers. Hasanzadeh and Meybodi [15] propose using a distributed learning automata (DLA) based on multi-swarm discrete particle swarm optimization approach for Grid resource discovery, while Olaifa et al. [26] follow a similar approach for discovery and scheduling.

Verghelet et al. [36] compare the performance obtained by several policies including the fully distributed BN policy. The improvements proposed lead this policy to be competitive against SP. However, they show that there is space for further improvements to reach the performance of Hierarchical or Centralized policies.

In this work, we focus on the way each node in the system uses the information that is obtained during the communications with its neighbors. We show that the strategy to select the node to communicate has a strong impact on the quality of resource information and this could lead to an overall better system performance and more efficient use of resources. The proposed improvements to BN leads to a fully distributed policy named pBN which shows performance similar to Hierarchical and SP, with a similar use of bandwidth (i.e. control messages).

The rest of the work is organized as follows: in the next section we focus on some details about the procedures followed to simulate the system, their construction and the type of messages used to interchange resource information. In Sect. 3 we describe BN and the function used to rank the neighbors based on the provided information, while Sect. 4 shows the results obtained by the proposed policy and explains the reasons behind the obtained performance improvements. The scalability of this policy is the analyzed in Sect. 4.1 comparing it with other presented policies. Finally, some conclusions are drawn in Sect. 5.

2   Methodology

Grid Matrix is used to analyze the evolution of the resource information in systems with an increasing number of nodes and different underlying network topology. Grid Matrix uses SimGrid2 [7] as the simulation engine.

As a simplification, normally the impact of time is discarded in the evaluation of this kind of systems, hiding the dynamical nature of the system behavior. Mocskos et al. [25] propose a new set of metrics (Local Information Rate (LIR) and Global Information Rate (GIR)) that incorporates the notion of time decay of information in the evaluation of the system performance:

- **LIR**: captures the amount of information that a particular host has from all the entire system in a single moment. For the host k, LIR_k is:

$$LIR_k = \frac{\sum_{h=1}^{N} f(age_h, expiration_h) \cdot resourceCount_h}{totalResourceCount} \qquad (1)$$

where N is number of hosts in the system, $expiration_h$ is the expiration time of the resources of host h in host k, age_h is the time passed since the information was obtained from that host, $resourceCount_h$ is the amount of resources in host h and $totalResourceCount$ is the total amount of resources in the whole system.
- **GIR**: captures the amount of information that the whole grid knows of itself, calculated as the mean value of every node's LIR.

The underlying network topologies used in this work are generated using a custom exponential network generator. The amount of connections of each node follows an exponential distribution law, commonly seen in the Internet or collaborative networks [2,4].

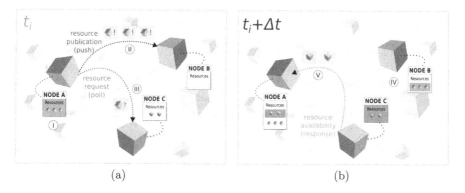

(a)   (b)

Fig. 1. Resource information interchange: `push` (publication of available resources) and `poll` (request of information). Node `A` has information about three available resources (I). It publishes its information sending a `push` to B (II). `A` requests resource information sending a `poll` to C, it includes its own resources in the message (III). B merges the received information (IV). C answers the poll request sending its resource information (V) to `A`.

To inform the state and availability of resources, two strategies can be used: `push` (Proactive) and `poll` (Reactive) [24]. The protocol related with each type of message interchanged to inform the state and availability of resources is shown in Fig. 1. In step I, the node A has information about three resources. When this node sends a `push` message to node B at time t_i (step II), all the information about the resources it knows is communicated to the other node, including the resources belonging to other nodes. At $t_i + \Delta t$, node B receives the information (the amount of time depends of the network topology and latency of each link) and merges the new information in his own database (step IV). The other type of message starts at step III in Fig. 1(a): node A contacts C to obtain information using a `poll` message. In this message, A also packs its resource information to take additional advantage of sending the request. After receiving the message (step V), C answers the request with a message containing all the information it knows about resources in the system.

As SP needs to partition the system in disjoint sets, `metis` [18] is used to generate these subsets using one heuristic to minimize the frontier between them. In each partition, the super-peer is selected minimizing the total distance to the rest of nodes in the partition. In the work by Verghelet and Mocskos [35] new variations of SP were presented: N-SP and A2A-SP. N-SP shows good performance and a balanced trade-off in the use of network bandwidth. A2A-SP gets very interesting results, even better than Hierarchical policy, but the cost lies in an increment of used messages and consumed bandwidth. Finally, a three level hierarchy is generated for the Hierarchical policy.

3   Best Neighbor Policy

There are three remarkable aspects that impact on the performance of BN:

1. The part of the system that is known or was already contacted by each node.
2. The function used to generate the ranking to select the best neighbor or neighbors to communicate.
3. The way in which each node gets information from the rest of nodes and updates its own database (i.e. the way the generated ranking is used).

When using BN, each node goes through two well differentiated stages:

(i) *Learning Stage*: as the nodes have discovered only a small fraction of the system, a random selection is used to select the next to communicate.
(ii) *Operative Stage*: with a populated database using the information received during previous messages, the *best* neighbor is selected according to a ranking generated using a *scoring function*.

During the learning stage, the system operates in similar way to Random policy. The length of this stage could compromise the performance of the system, as Random policy presents poor results, specially in medium to large systems [36]. Shortening of this stage was already proposed using a list merging (LM) mechanism [36], but this approach was not directly reflected in an improvement of the policy performance.

The scoring function that is used during the operative stage is defined as [36]:

$$f_{\text{scoring}}(h) = a \cdot \texttt{INFO\_RES}_h + b \cdot \texttt{RTT}_h + c \cdot \texttt{FAILED\_RESP}_h + d \cdot \texttt{OWN\_RES}_h \quad (2)$$

where $\texttt{INFO\_RES}_h$ is the amount of information about resources that has a neighbor host h, $\texttt{RTT}_h$ is the round trip time with h, $\texttt{FAILED\_RESP}_h$ accounts the amount of communication failures with h and $\texttt{OWN\_RES}_h$ is the amount of local resources owned by h. The constants a, b, c and d are parameters that can be used to adjust the relative weight of each component of the scoring function. Finally, to allow the comparison between different systems, the weighting parameters are normalized. This BN variant is named *fBN* [36] and represents the base of comparison for the improvements introduced in this work.

4   Results

Figure 2 introduces the evolution of system wide GIR for different variations of fBN policy. The underlying network corresponds to systems with 200 nodes Fig. 2(a) and 500 nodes in Fig. 2(b) generated following an exponential topology. The `poll` message is kept without changes: periodically asks for information to the neighbor selected using the scoring function.

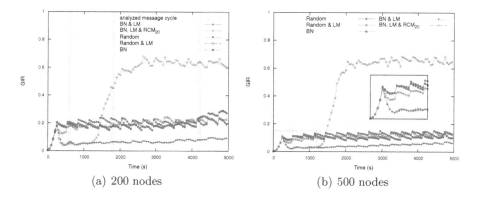

(a) 200 nodes   (b) 500 nodes

Fig. 2. GIR evolution in systems of (a) 200 and (b) 500 nodes (exponential topology). The strategy to select the target for `poll` is based on the BN scoring function in all the cases. Different strategies for selecting the `push` target are tested to overcome the poor performance obtained by BN, but only the repeat control mechanism (RCM) shows a strong improvement. The gray horizontal bars correspond to the interval in which the nodes send the message number 10, 30 and 70 (referenced later during the analysis).

The variations corresponds to the `push` message (a node sends it own information to a selected node):

- `push Random`: the target for pushing its information is selected randomly.
- `push Random & LM`: similar as before, but the list merging mechanism (LM) is used. The nodes aggregates all the known information about the rest of the system in each message shortening the learning stage.
- `push BN`: the target is selected using the scoring function, each node sends only the information about its own resources (not the information it knows about its neighbors).
- `push BN & LM`: the selection is based on the scoring function, each node sends all the information about the system (including neighbors), the receiver uses the list merging mechanism (LM) to shorten the learning stage.
- `push BN, LM and RCM`$_{20}$: similar as before, but it enables target repetition control (RCM) after the first 20 messages. This mechanism consists in avoiding the successive selection of the same node.

The first four variations show a poor performance in both systems. These results were confirmed running additional simulations over the same system and

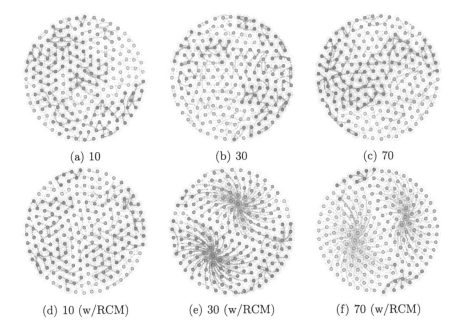

(a) 10   (b) 30   (c) 70

(d) 10 (w/RCM)   (e) 30 (w/RCM)   (f) 70 (w/RCM)

Fig. 3. Emergent communities or modularity classes observed at different moments of the system evolution: 10 (600s), 30 (1800s) and 70 (4200s) message cycles. The first row corresponds to fBN policy (all the variations present similar behavior) and the second row shows the effect of using the Repeat Control Mechanism (RCM).

in different systems presenting minimum deviation (data not shown). Selecting the push target using the scoring function or doing it randomly, using or not the list merge mechanism present similar poor behavior in terms of global information knowledge. As can be seen in the figure, only avoiding the target repetition leads to an strong improvement in the policy performance, we will next analyze this situation.

The analysis of the sequence of target selection for each node in the system shows the establishment of small communities. These small clusters are formed by only a few nodes that contact always the same best neighbor. Moreover, the results obtained by the scoring function in those cases show a strong difference in terms of obtained value for the first node in the ranking compared with the second one. The difference between the best neighbor and the second in the ranking enlarges over the duration of the simulation, which explains why the small clusters persists over the time. Even though, BN selects randomly a target for communication with a small probability (trying to avoid the establishment of these small communities), it results insufficient to overcome the obtained position and the scoring function keeps selecting the same node.

Figure 3(a) to (f) present the emerged communities at three different stages of a system with 200 nodes. These stages are marked at Fig. 2 as gray horizontal bars and correspond to the sending of messages number 10, 30 and 70

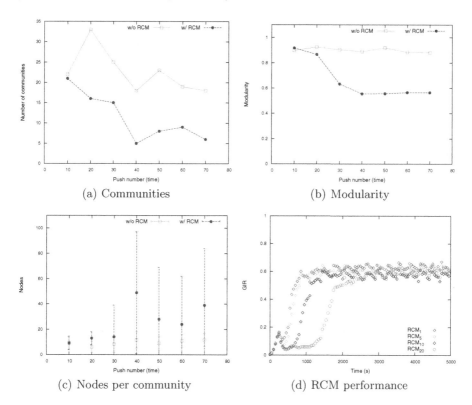

(a) Communities   (b) Modularity

(c) Nodes per community   (d) RCM performance

Fig. 4. Evolution of a 200 node system focusing on its internal structure when using RCM: (a) the number of emerged communities, (b) modularity (higher value means more communities), and (c) number of nodes per community. In (d) the evolution of GIR is shown while activating RCM at different starting messages.

respectively. In these figures, each point represents a node in the system. An edge between two points is included if one point selects the other as the communication target (`poll` or `push`). The color depends of its modularity class, which is computed following the work of Blondel et al. [6] implemented as a module in Gephi suite [5]. All the points with the same color are in the same modularity class. The edges with the same color correspond to messages interchanged between nodes belonging to the same community.

Figure 3(a) to (c) are obtained using fBN policy selecting the `push` target randomly (similar results are obtained with the other variations). On the other hand, Fig. 3(d) to (f) present the evolution of same system but with RCM active. In the first row, the communities slightly change during the simulation, some nodes change from one community to the other, but no strong evidence of change in the number of total communities can be concluded. This view leads to an almost stable number of small communities during all the simulated time. The second row of Fig. 3 presents a different behavior as the system has a similar configuration at message cycle 10, but this situation strongly changes after 30 message cycles, where the system moves towards a few number of larger communities. This scenario is also reflected in an intense increment of GIR in Fig. 2(a), this change in the clusters are reflected in a stable improvement of the policy performance.

Figure 4 seeks to clarify the change produced in the system behavior when RCM is active focusing on the 200 nodes system (similar results are obtained with larger systems). In Fig. 4(a), the number of communities is shown during the evolution of the system using or not RCM. In the first case, after an initial period in which there is a large number of communities, it stabilizes near 20 communities. The behavior of the number of communities when RCM is active differs: after this initial period, it quickly falls to near 5.

The modularity of a network shows how well it decomposes into modular communities. A high modularity value indicates a community structure, namely the network is compartmentalized into sub-networks. Figure 4(b) presents the evolution of modularity when RCM_{20} is active and not. The use of this mechanism after the message number 20 produces a strong decrement in modularity, which means that the system is less compartmentalized and the information is more shared.

The amount of nodes per community can be used to confirm the evolution of the system after the activation of RCM. Figure 4(c) shows that when RCM is inactive, the system presents a low number of nodes per community (near 10 nodes). While when RCM is active, the size of the communities increases, but still some small communities can be found, shown by the large deviation. The Fig. 3(e) and (f) exemplifie this situation as can be seen large communities, but a low number of small communities subsists.

One aspect to consider is whether the message after which RCM is activated has an impact on performance. Figure 4(d) clarifies this aspect showing the evolution of GIR for different starting messages to activate RCM. As can be observed in the figure, the sooner the activation of RCM, the sooner is the increment of the GIR. Notwithstanding, once this increment is produced, all the variations reach the same stable values.

As the main contribution of this work, we introduce *pBN*. This policy is based on BN with these special details:

(i) The targets for `poll` and `push` messages are selected using the scoring function introduced in Eq. 2.
(ii) Usage of the list merging mechanism (LM) to reduce the learning stage.
(iii) The use of the repeat control mechanism (RCM) to avoid the establishment of a large number of small communities.

4.1   Scalability

The efficiency of this policy in terms of used network bandwidth will be treated in this section. As any control protocol, it is a design goal to minimize the use of bandwidth.

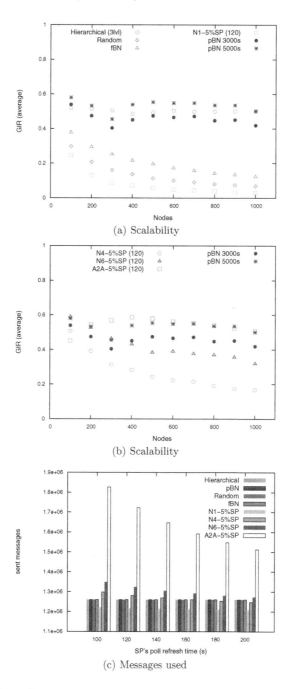

(a) Scalability

(b) Scalability

(c) Messages used

Fig. 5. Scalability of different policies for system size from 100 to 1000 nodes with exponential topology. (a) and (b) compares proposed pBN policy with other previously introduced policies. The bandwidth consumption is shown in (c) in terms of control messages sent during 14 h for the same policies.

Figures 5(a) and (b) show mean GIR for different system sizes from 100 to 1000 nodes. In both figures, we compare pBN with other previously proposed policies.

In Fig. 5(a), pBN is compared with 3-level Hierarchical Policy, Random, SP (5% of super-peers varying the communication protocol between super-peers), and fBN. As pBN improves its performance with the time (due to its learning nature), we show the mean GIR for the initial 3000s and 5000s. Two groups of policies are clearly identified, one consists of Hierarchical Policy and both pBN options showing higher and stable GIR while increasing the size of the system. The other group is composed of fBN, Random and the N1-5%SP variation (super-peers selects randomly other super-peers to communicate). In this case, these policies present poor GIR values, specially for larger systems.

Same pBN policy is included in Fig. 5(b) to be compared with variations of SP policy. Similarly, pBN presents high GIR values with almost same behavior of A2A-5%SP clearly surpassing the other SP variations.

From the point of view of information about the system, our proposed pBN policy shows similar behavior as other policies and presents interesting scalability in the studied range of system sizes. Notwithstanding this, special care should be taken with the amount of interchanged messages as it is a critical aspect of this kind of protocols. Figure 5(c) introduces the number of messages sent during 14 h by the analyzed policies. SP has another key parameter which determines the behavior of the policy: the frequency of message interchange between super-peers. As is expected, the amount of messages decreases with the frequency, only A2A-5% consumes more messages than the rest of policies. The bandwidth usage by pBN is similar to Hierarchical, Random and fBN.

5   Conclusions

The computational infrastructures are moving towards a new level of complexity, with cloud Federations representing the implementation of the utility computing model that was once incarnated in the Grid Computing paradigm.

The interaction with the P2P paradigm tries to reach scalable solutions in a very dynamic and heterogeneous scenario and having to collect information about resource state from a set of distributed and individual entities.

In spite of introducing several improvements to the fully distributed BN policy, it is still not competitive compared with Super Peer Policy (SP). However, there are still space to push towards a policy comparable to Hierarchical or Centralized policies in terms of performance.

The evolution of the communication pattern for different variations of BN policy shows that its poor performance is based on the establishment of small communities, which produces an isolation of the information interchanged in each one. With the inclusion of the Repeat Control Mechanism (RCM), we strongly improve the performance obtained. This BN based policy is named *pBN*.

The evolution of the systems using this new policy shows that larger communities emerged with some small ones still present, which leads to more information interchange. This is confirmed by the number and size of communities.

The bandwidth usage is compared with previously presented policies. Our proposal shows an efficient use of bandwidth, comparable to Hierarchical Policy and much better than some variations of SP while maintaining remarkable performance.

The results included in this work, support that pBN could combine the advantages of a fully distributed policy with the efficiency of a manually established hierarchy.

Acknowledgments. E.M. is researcher at the CONICET. This work was partially supported by grants from Universidad de Buenos Aires (UBACyT 20020130200096BA), CONICET (PIP 11220110100379 and PIO 13320150100020CO), and ANPCyT (PICT-2015-2761 and PICT-2015-0370).

References

1. Agrawal, D., Giles, J., Lee, K.W., Voruganti, K., Filali-Adib, K.: Policy-based validation of san configuration. In: Proceedings of Fifth IEEE International Workshop on Policies for Distributed Systems and Networks, POLICY 2004, pp. 77–86, June 2004
2. Albert, R., Jeong, H., Barabási, A.L.: Internet: diameter of the world-wide web. Nature **401**, 130–131 (1999). http://adsabs.harvard.edu/abs/1999Natur.401.130A
3. Assunção, M.D., Calheiros, R.N., Bianchi, S., Netto, M.A., Buyya, R.: Big data computing and clouds: trends and future directions. J. Parallel Distrib. Comput. **79–80**, 3–15 (2014). http://www.sciencedirect.com/science/article/pii/S0743731514001452, special Issue on Scalable Systems for Big Data Management and Analytics
4. Barabási, A.L., Albert, R.: Emergence of scaling in random networks. Science **286**(5439), 509–512 (1999)
5. Bastian, M., Heymann, S., Jacomy, M.: Gephi: an open source software for exploring and manipulating networks. In: Proceedings of AAAI Conference on Weblogs and Social Media, May 2009. http://www.aaai.org/ocs/index.php/ICWSM/09/paper/view/154
6. Blondel, V.D., Guillaume, J.L., Lambiotte, R., Lefebvre, E.: Fast unfolding of communities in large networks. J. Stat. Mech: Theory Exp. **2008**(10), P10008 (2008). http://stacks.iop.org/1742-5468/2008/i=10/a=P10008
7. Casanova, H., Legrand, A., Quinson, M.: SimGrid: a generic framework for large-scale distributed experiments. In: 10th IEEE International Conference on Computer Modeling and Simulation, pp. 126–131. IEEE Computer Society, Los Alamitos, March 2008
8. Cesario, E., Mastroianni, C., Talia, D.: Distributed volunteer computing for solving ensemble learning problems. Future Gen. Comput. Syst. (2015, in press). http://www.sciencedirect.com/science/article/pii/S0167739X15002332
9. Clayman, S., Toffetti, G., Galis, A., Chapman, C.: Monitoring services in a federated cloud: the RESERVOIR experience. In: Achieving Federated and Self-Manageable Cloud Infrastructures: Theory and Practice, pp. 242–265. IGI Global, May 2012
10. Ergu, D., Kou, G., Peng, Y., Shi, Y., Shi, Y.: The analytic hierarchy process: task scheduling and resource allocation in cloud computing environment. J. Supercomput. **64**(3), 835–848 (2013). http://dx.doi.org/10.1007/s11227-011-0625-1

11. Foster, I., Zhao, Y., Raicu, I., Lu, S.: Cloud computing and grid computing 360-degree compared. In: Grid Computing Environments Workshop, GCE 2008, pp. 1–10, November 2008
12. Foster, I., Kesselman, C.: The Grid 2: Blueprint for a New Computing Infrastructure. The Morgan Kaufmann Series in Computer Architecture and Design. Morgan Kaufmann Publishers Inc., San Francisco (2003)
13. Foster, I., Kesselman, C., Tuecke, S.: The anatomy of the grid: enabling scalable virtual organizations. Int. J. High Perform. Comput. Appl. **15**(3), 200–222 (2001). http://portal.acm.org/citation.cfm?id=1080667
14. Ghafarian, T., Deldari, H., Javadi, B., Yaghmaee, M.H., Buyya, R.: Cycloidgrid: a proximity-aware P2P-based resource discovery architecture in volunteer computing systems. Future Gen. Comput. Syst. **29**(6), 1583–1595 (2013). Including Special sections: High Performance Computing in the Cloud & Resource Discovery Mechanisms for P2P Systems. http://www.sciencedirect.com/science/article/pii/S0167739X12001665
15. Hasanzadeh, M., Meybodi, M.R.: Distributed optimization grid resource discovery. J. Supercomput. **71**(1), 87–120 (2015)
16. Iamnitchi, A., Foster, I., Nurmi, D.: A peer-to-peer approach to resource discovery in grid environments. In: Proceedings of the 11th IEEE International Symposium on High Performance Distributed Computing HPDC-11 (HPDC 2002), p. 419. IEEE, Edinbourgh, July 2002
17. Iamnitchi, A., Foster, I.: A peer-to-peer approach to resource location in grid environments. In: Nabrzyski, J., Schopf, J.M., Weglarz, J. (eds.) Grid Resource Management: State of the Art and Future Trends, pp. 413–429. Kluwer Academic Publishers, Norwell (2004)
18. Karypis, G., Kumar, V.: A fast and high quality multilevel scheme for partitioning irregular graphs. SIAM J. Sci. Comput. **20**(1), 359–392 (1998)
19. Kertesz, A., Kecskemeti, G., Oriol, M., Kotcauer, P., Acs, S., Rodríguez, M., Mercè, O., Marosi, A.C., Marco, J., Franch, X.: Enhancing federated cloud management with an integrated service monitoring approach. J. Grid Comput. **11**(4), 699–720 (2013)
20. Liu, W., Nishio, T., Shinkuma, R., Takahashi, T.: Adaptive resource discovery in mobile cloud computing. Comput. Commun. **50**, 119–129 (2014). Green Networking. http://www.sciencedirect.com/science/article/pii/S0140366414000590
21. Mastroianni, C., Talia, D., Verta, O.: A super-peer model for resource discovery services in large-scale grids. Future Gen. Comput. Syst. **21**(8), 1235–1248 (2005). http://www.sciencedirect.com/science/article/pii/S0167739X05000701
22. Mastroianni, C., Talia, D., Verta, O.: Designing an information system for grids: comparing hierarchical, decentralized P2P and super-peer models. Parallel Comput. **34**(10), 593–611 (2008)
23. Mattmann, C., Garcia, J., Krka, I., Popescu, D., Medvidovic, N.: Revisiting the anatomy and physiology of the grid. J. Grid Comput. **13**(1), 19–34 (2015)
24. Meshkova, E., Riihijärvi, J., Petrova, M., Mähönen, P.: A survey on resource discovery mechanisms, peer-to-peer and service discovery frameworks. Comput. Netw. **52**(11), 2097–2128 (2008). http://www.sciencedirect.com/science/article/pii/S138912860800100X
25. Mocskos, E.E., Yabo, P., Turjanski, P.G., Fernandez Slezak, D.: Grid matrix: a grid simulation tool to focus on the propagation of resource and monitoring information. Simul.-T. Soc. Mod. Sim. **88**(10), 1233–1246 (2012)

26. Olaifa, M., Mapayi, T., Merwe, R.V.D.: Multi ant LA: an adaptive multi agent resource discovery for peer to peer grid systems. In: Science and Information Conference (SAI), pp. 447–451, July 2015

27. Pipan, G.: Use of the TRIPOD overlay network for resource discovery. Future Gen. Comput. Syst. **26**(8), 1257–1270 (2010). http://www.sciencedirect.com/science/article/pii/S0167739X1000018X

28. Plale, B., Jacobs, C., Jensen, S., Liu, Y., Moad, C., Parab, R., Vaidya, P.: Understanding grid resource information management through a synthetic database benchmark/workload. In: Proceedings of the 2004 IEEE International Symposium on Cluster Computing and the Grid, CCGRID 2004, pp. 277–284. IEEE Computer Society, Washington, April 2004

29. Puppin, D., Moncelli, S., Baraglia, R., Tonellotto, N., Silvestri, F.: A grid information service based on peer-to-peer. In: Cunha, J.C., Medeiros, P.D. (eds.) Euro-Par 2005. LNCS, vol. 3648, pp. 454–464. Springer, Heidelberg (2005). doi:10.1007/11549468_52

30. Ranjan, R., Harwood, A., Buyya, R.: Peer-to-peer-based resource discovery in global grids: a tutorial. IEEE Commun. Surv. Tutor. **10**(2), 6–33 (2008)

31. Ranjan, R., Zhao, L.: Peer-to-peer service provisioning in cloud computing environments. J. Supercomput. **65**(1), 154–184 (2013)

32. Ripeanu, M.: Peer-to-peer architecture case study: Gnutella network. In: Proceedings of First International Conference on Peer-to-Peer Computing, pp. 99–100, August 2001

33. Shiers, J.: The worldwide LHC computing grid (worldwide LCG). Comput. Phys. Commun. **177**(1–2), 219–223 (2007)

34. Trunfio, P., Talia, D., Papadakis, C., Fragopoulou, P., Mordacchini, M., Pennanen, M., Popov, K., Vlassov, V., Haridi, S.: Peer-to-peer resource discovery in grids: models and systems. Future Gen. Comput. Syst. **23**(7), 864–878 (2007)

35. Verghelet, P., Mocskos, E.: Improvements to super-peer policy communication mechanisms. In: Osthoff, C., Navaux, P.O.A., Barrios Hernandez, C.J., Silva Dias, P.L. (eds.) CARLA 2015. CCIS, vol. 565, pp. 73–86. Springer, Cham (2015). doi:10.1007/978-3-319-26928-3_6

36. Verghelet, P., Slezak, D.F., Turjanski, P., Mocskos, E.: Using distributed local information to improve global performance in grids. CLEIej **15**(3), 8 (2012). http://www.clei.cl/cleiej/papers/v15i3p7.pdf

37. Williams, D.N., Drach, R., Ananthakrishnan, R., Foster, I., Fraser, D., Siebenlist, F., Bernholdt, D., Chen, M., Schwidder, J., Bharathi, S., et al.: The earth system grid: enabling access to multimodel climate simulation data. Bull. Am. Meteorol. Soc. **90**(2), 195–205 (2009)

Performance Evaluation of Multiple Cloud Data Centers Allocations for HPC

Eduardo Roloff[1(✉)], Emmanuell Diaz Carreño[1],
Jimmy K.M. Valverde-Sánchez[1], Matthias Diener[1], Matheus da Silva Serpa[1],
Guillaume Houzeaux[2], Lucas M. Schnorr[1], Nicolas Maillard[1],
Luciano Paschoal Gaspary[1], and Philippe Navaux[1]

[1] Informatics Institute, Federal University of Rio Grande do Sul - UFRGS,
Porto Alegre, Brazil
{eroloff,edcarreno,jkmvsanchez,mdiener,msserpa,schnorr,nicolas,
paschoal,navaux}@inf.ufrgs.br
[2] Department of Computer Applications in Science and Engineering,
Barcelona Supercomputing Center (BSC-CNS), Barcelona, Spain
guillaume.houzeaux@bsc.es

Abstract. This paper evaluates the behavior of the Microsoft Azure
G5 cloud instance type over multiple Data Centers. The purpose is to
identify if there are major differences between them and to help the users
choose the best option for their needs. Our results show that there are
differences in the network level for the same instance type in different
locations and inside the same location at different times. The network
performance causes interference in the applications level, as we could
verify in our results.

Keywords: Cloud Computing · HPC · Azure · MPI · NAS

1 Introduction

Cloud Computing offers an interesting alternative for High Performance Computing (HPC) applications, due to the pay-per-use cost model and the elasticity [7] to provide any amount of resources in little time. However, due to the virtualized environment, there are some aspects of the Cloud that still remain as a barrier for the large adoption of Cloud Computing by the HPC community. It is clear that the CPU virtualization is not a problem, because the CPU performance in the Cloud is the same as in a traditional machine. Memory accesses and disk I/O are in an earlier stage of development to be used in the cloud, but they do not represent a big issue at this time. The main bottleneck of Cloud Computing is network performance, a very important aspect for HPC.

In this paper, we provide an extensive evaluation of network performance in the Microsoft Azure public Cloud. Since MPI is an important standard for HPC communication [10], we evaluate its performance using three different communication patterns: Single Transfer, Parallel Transfer and Collective Communications. We used the same type of virtual machine (VM) instance among four

© Springer International Publishing AG 2017
C.J. Barrios Hernández et al. (Eds.): CARLA 2016, CCIS 697, pp. 18–32, 2017.
DOI: 10.1007/978-3-319-57972-6_2

different Azure Data Centers and used the machines at different times, during working hours and during the night. The purpose was to verify if the time of the day of each allocation causes a performance impact in the machines and if they have different performance levels among different Data Centers. We used a traditional cluster as a baseline for comparison purposes.

Our results show that the execution during the night has lower performance than when executed during the day. We also conclude that there is a small difference in the application performance when compared the execution times between the different Data Centers.

2 Motivation

The Cloud Computing model offers an interesting alternative as an environment for HPC applications, due to the pay-per-use cost model and the elasticity of resources. The public Cloud could provide any amount of resources in little time, without upfront costs. Theoretically, when the user sends his applications and data to the cloud, they could be stored anywhere on earth, the user does not have control over this. Moreover, the major cloud providers give the user the option on which Data Center location the application and data will be stored. This is necessary because there are some situations where the user needs to know and decide where his application is, due to regulations or data confidentiality.

However, the same VM instances could present different performances when executing in different locations. This could be caused by the different behavior of the users of the Data Center, more or less load, or even by the Data Center configuration itself. There is a lack of research that compares the same VM instances among the same provider.

Our proposal is to provide a comparison among different Data Centers to verify if they present significant differences when executing the same application using the same type of VM instance. This is important to help the user that could execute his application anywhere as well as could help the user with location restrictions. We intend to help the users to choose the machines and locations with the best performance among all available in Microsoft Azure.

3 Methodology

This section describes the hardware and software environments as well as the MPI and NAS benchmarks that were used in our evaluation. The scientific HPC application used is explained as well.

3.1 Cluster and Cloud Environments

We performed experiments on one traditional cluster system as well as four Data Center locations of Microsoft Azure using the G5 VM instance. The G5 instance is a VM with 32 cores, composed of a E5-2698v3 CPU running at

Table 1. Configuration of the cluster and cloud environments used in the experiments.

Machine name	Processor model	Freq.	Cores per instance	Network	Location	Price/hour ($) for all instances
Econome	E5-2660	2.2 GHz	16	10 Gbit/s	France	—
G5	E5-2698 v3	2.3 GHz	32	—	4 DCs	69.52

2.3 GHz with 448 GB of RAM, there is no precise information about the network interconnection. The traditional cluster is the *econome* machine from *GRID 5000* and is composed of two 8-core processors, the network interconnection is 10 Gbit Ethernet.

In all environments, we create systems with 128 cores in total to maintain a comparable baseline. The total number of nodes were four, for the G5 machines, and 8 for the econome cluster. The locations of Microsoft Azure used were: West Europe (WEU), West USA (WUS), East USA (EUS) and Southeast Asia (SAS). To the best of our knowledge, all systems are running without Hyper-Threading. All environments use Intel processors of recent generations, at least the Sandy-Bridge family.

Table 1 contains an overview of the machines used in the evaluation. Although main memory sizes vary between different instance sizes, all amounts were sufficient for our experiments and are therefore not mentioned in the table.

All the tests were executed using two allocations in the cloud to compare the differences among the day. We allocated the machines and executed the tests around 2 AM and 2 PM on business days. The cluster was evaluated just once, because it consists of isolated machines that did not show significant variability during the day.

3.2 Intel MPI Benchmarks

We use the Intel MPI Benchmark communication tests. This benchmark allows us to measure the performance of the most important MPI functions. There are three classes of benchmarks named single transfer, parallel transfer and collective benchmarks. We have selected the PingPong benchmark of the single transfer class, this benchmark entails just two process into communication. The Sendrecv of the parallel transfer class was used, this is based on the MPI_Sendrecv function. For the Sendrecv, each process of a periodic communication chain sends a message to its right neighbor and receives one from its left neighbor. For the collective benchmark, the Reduce and AllToAll were used, the first based on the MPI_Reduce function performs a reduction operation on all processes, and the second based on the MPI_AllToAll function which is a data movement operation, where each process sends data from all to all processes [4]. Each one of the experiments was performed with different message sizes, 0, 1, 2, 4, 8, 16, 32, 64, 128, 256, 512, 1024, 2048, 4096, 8192, 16384, and 32768 bytes.

3.3   NAS

The NAS Parallel Benchmarks (NPB) are a set of benchmarks developed to help evaluate the performance of parallel environments. The benchmarks are derived from computational fluid dynamics (CFD) applications and consist of nine applications with different needs. They cover all major aspects of parallel systems. We used the MPI version of NAS.

3.4   Alya

Alya is a simulation code for multi-physics problems, based on a variational multi-scale finite element method for unstructured meshes. It is used in areas, such as wind energy, aerospace, oil and gas, biomechanics and biomedical research, environment and automotive industry, among others. Developed at Barcelona Supercomputing Center, written in Fortran 90/95 combining MPI and OpenMP. Parallelization of the work is mainly performed using MPI, the original mesh is partitioned into sub-meshes that are executed for MPI processes [8,9].

4   Results

We classified the results of our experiments into two parts. The first subsection has the MPI results, to analyze the network performance. The second subsection has the applications results, then we could analyze the performance of the NAS benchmarks and the application Alya.

4.1   MPI Benchmarks

The MPI results are divided into three different groups: Single Transfer, Parallel Transfer, and Collective Communications. The single transfer results shows the measured performance between two nodes. The parallel transfer shows the results of all the nodes communicating at the same time. Finally, the collective communications results show the behavior of MPI collective operations. These three groups cover the majority of communication patterns used in HPC applications.

Single Transfer. Single Transfer tests are communication between two different processes, all other processes in the cluster wait. We executed the PingPong test from the Intel MPI benchmarks, running each process in a different machine. The purpose was to identify the network performance of a point-to-point communication without interference of other communications. We present results for both Latency and Bandwidth of this test.

Figure 1 shows the latency results of the PingPong test. The line in the lower part of the Figure show the cluster results, as we can see there is practically no latency when varying the package size from 0 bytes to 32 KB. In the other hand, we could conclude that latency in the cloud is less predictable, because there is

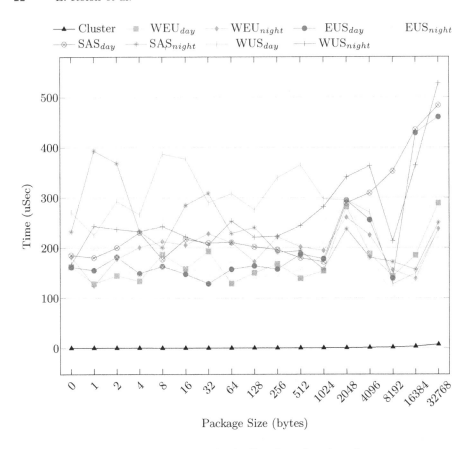

Fig. 1. Latency results for PingPong benchmark.

no such clear tendency for all clouds. In some cases, when the package size was increased, the latency in the cloud decreased and we expect the opposite, using the cluster results as the baseline. Almost all the clouds have a spike when the package size was changed to 2 KB, this could mean that in the cloud infrastructure exists some kind of network optimization for smaller packages. Most of the cloud instances showed the same pattern, with acceptable variability. However the EUS day, SAS day and WUS night executions exhibited some undesirable high latency for the 16 KB and 32 KB packages sizes.

Figure 2 shows the bandwidth results for the PingPong test in logarithmic scale. We could observe that in this case, the cloud instances have the same pattern with little variation between them. The growth of the bandwidth usage is following the pattern of the cluster as well. However, the instances were able to achieve a bandwidth (for package size of 32 KB) of just 140 Mb/sec and the cluster achieved a bandwidth of 4,248 Mb/sec. This points out the network bottleneck of the cloud compared to physical clusters. Despite performance itself,

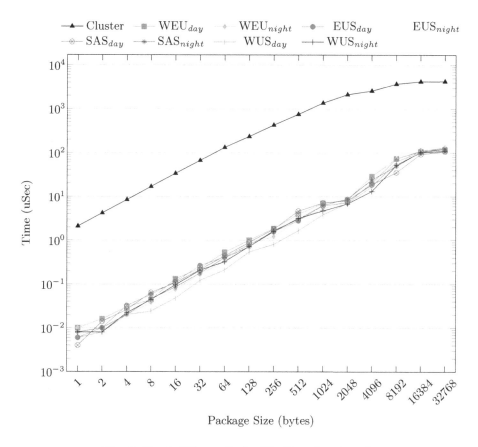

Fig. 2. Bandwidth results for PingPong benchmark.

the user could use the predictable pattern of the cloud network bandwidth to create an application to take advantage of this characteristic.

Parallel Transfer. Parallel Transfer tests measure the communication between more than two processes, in our case we used one process per node. We executed the SendRecv test from the Intel MPI benchmarks. With this test, we are able to identify the network performance when the network has a much higher utilization rate than on the Single Transfer test. We show both Latency and Bandwidth results for SendRecv test.

Figure 3 shows the latency results for the SendRecv test. It is possible to verify that the cluster latency is slightly different from the PingPong test, because in this test the latency has a small increase when the package size increases. This behavior could mean a level of network contention, the reason could be that this test performs a lot more concurrent communication in the network. On the other hand, the cloud results are better than in the PingPong test, they showed less latency and a more predictable behavior, all the cloud instance allocations

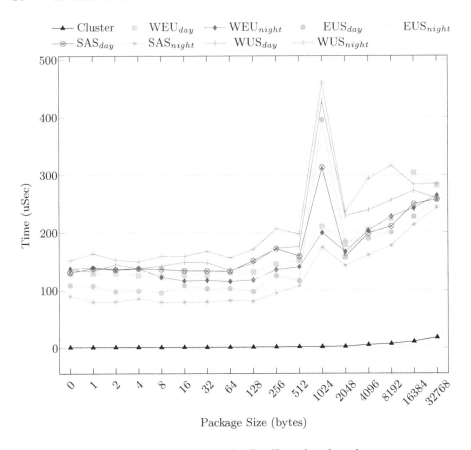

Fig. 3. Latency results for SendRecv benchmark.

displayed the same pattern. It is interesting to note that all of the cloud allocations present a spike when the package size is 1 KB, and then all of them return to the standard pattern. This could be explained for a possible SDN network configuration. The network is configured to handle a certain number of bytes at same time, for optimization, and when this number is reached the switches need to go to the controller to get a new configuration. This took same time, then the latency increases a little and in the next interaction, with the new configuration, the latency returns to the normal behavior.

Figure 4 shows the bandwidth results of the SendRecv test in logarithmic scale. As in the PingPong test, the cloud instances have the same pattern of increasing the bandwidth when the package size increases. We could observe that we have a small decrease of the bandwidth when the package reaches 1 KB. This remarks the explanation of the latency behavior with the same package size. The bandwidth achieved by the cluster was 3,451 Mb/sec when the cloud allocations were around 250 Mb/sec for a 32 KB package. Comparing these numbers with the PingPong test, we could observe that the cluster achieved a lower bandwidth

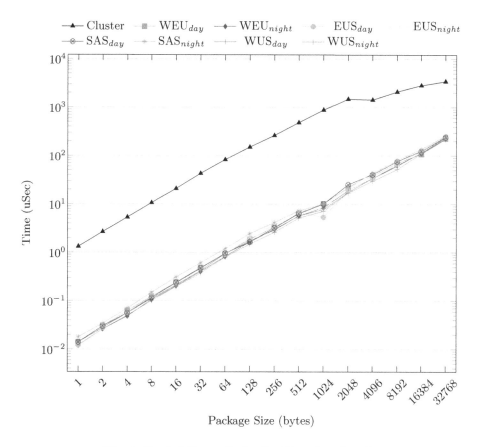

Fig. 4. Bandwidth results for SendRecv benchmark.

in this test and the cloud allocations attained a higher bandwidth. This indicates that the cloud network scales better than the cluster network when there is more communication in the network.

Both the predictable latency behavior and the bandwidth increase of the cloud allocations could benefit the user when configuring his application to be executed in the cloud.

Collective Communications. The Collective Communications tests are designed to measure the performance of the MPI collective operations. There are several collective operations in the MPI standard, due to space restrictions we present the results of the Reduce and AlltoAll tests from Intel MPI Benchmarks.

Figure 5 shows the results of the Reduce test, it measures the performance of the MPI_Reduce operation. The results are displayed in time, showing the average time of an operation. We could observe that the cluster has a time for this operation close to zero and the cloud allocations present a higher time. The

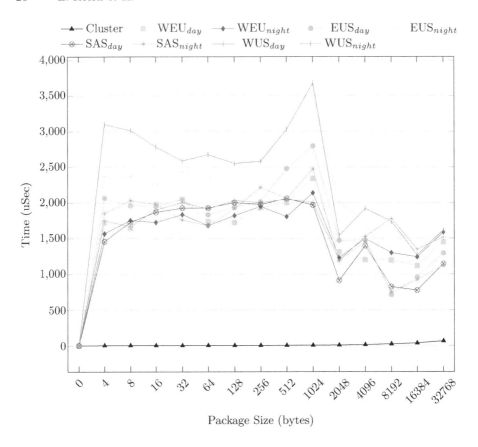

Fig. 5. Results for reduce benchmark.

cloud allocations have the same behavior with decreasing the time when the package size reaches 2 KB. The WUS during the day presented slightly lower performance then the other instances, but this did not impede the usage of this Data Center. According to the results we obtained, it is difficult to recommend using the MPI_Reduce function often in applications in the cloud, because the execution time of the application will be affected.

Figure 6 shows the results of the AlltoAll test, the vertical axis shows the time to execute the operation. In this test, all the processes send a message to all other processes and receive a message from all the other processes. The test was performed varying the package size. The time needed for the cluster to perform this operation is very short. The cloud allocations are very predictable and showed a good performance as well. Using a package size from 4 Bytes up to 8 KB, the time for all cloud allocations is around 200 uSec, that is acceptable. The package size has a key role in this operation.

For package sizes up to 8 KB, both the cluster and the cloud allocations presented the same behavior, with a constant time. When the package was increased

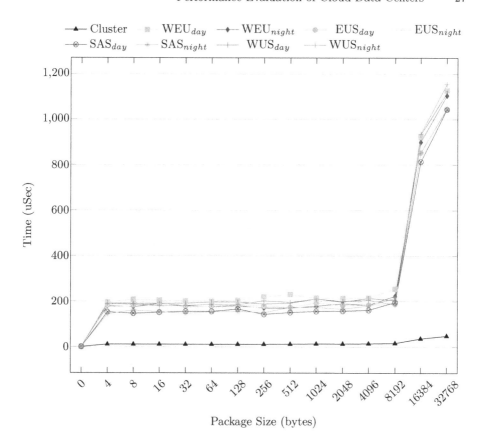

Fig. 6. Results for all to all benchmark.

from 8 KB to 16 KB, the time in the cluster was increased 3 times and the cloud allocations increased the time by 4 times. The reason for this could be the TCP frame used in the network or some aspect of the MPI implementation. Despite the reason, it is clear that this operation presents good performance until a certain package size. If the application uses several MPI_AlltoAll operations, it is necessary that the user measures the performance of this operation in his network to optimize the application performance by adjusting the package size.

4.2 Applications

We used both NAS benchmarks with the sizes B and C, that represents medium input sizes, and Alya application to measure the performance in the Cloud allocations against the physical cluster execution.

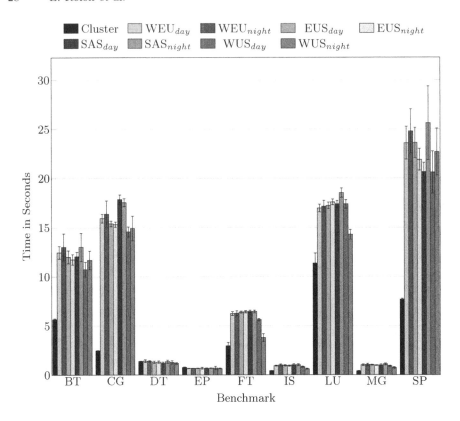

Fig. 7. Performance results for NAS class B.

NAS

Figure 7 shows the performance results of NAS-MPI benchmark class B, for multiple nodes on a cluster and four Microsoft Azure data centers. Cluster was faster than Azure's data centers in most cases. The cluster was faster for all the benchmarks, except for DT and EP. These two benchmarks have little communication and they are CPU-bound, as the CPU of the cloud instances is faster then in the cloud.

Comparing the execution during day and night, we did not observe much variability between these experiments. We can conclude that there is no difference between executing HPC applications during day or night in the Azure Cloud. Additionally, we did not observe a huge variation among the four different data centers. We could conclude again that a user could use any data center that he wants, or needs, without significant performance loss.

Figure 8 shows the results for NAS class C. The behavior was practically the same as in the class B results, without big changes.

The conclusion that we have is that the G5 instances of the Azure Cloud present an excepted performance degradation according to the size of the

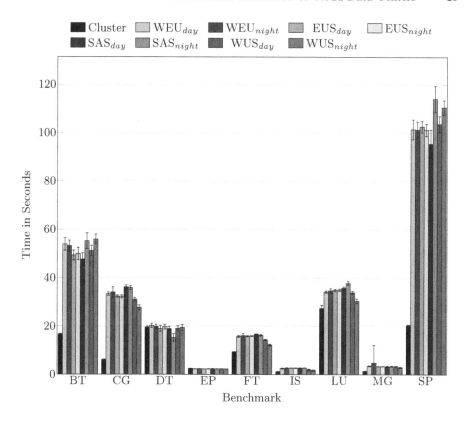

Fig. 8. Performance results for NAS class C.

problem. Also, we could conclude that the main bottleneck of these instances, and possibly in the whole provider, is the network interconnection. This is supported by the network results and the knowledge of the NAS applications. The applications with little communication, DT and EP, presented better performance in the cloud and all the other presented a performance loss in the cloud, because they all depend on the network performance in different levels.

Alya

Figure 9 illustrates the results of the Alya application among four Azure Data Centers. Due to the NAS results, we decided to not execute Alya during night and day, because the differences between them are low. The results present low variability among the four Azure locations, showing that a real HPC application with a heterogeneous behavior does not depend of the Data Center configuration. Compared with the cluster results, the clouds presented 2 times performance loss. This was expected and it is similar to the NAS performance results.

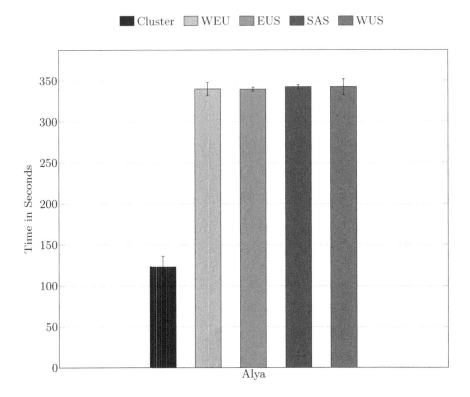

Fig. 9. Performance results for Alya

5 Related Work

Marathe et al. and Awad et al. [1,6] compare a virtualized cloud cluster against a physical cluster. However, the authors do not provide a comprehensive evaluation of public clouds, because they only used a single Data Center and do not provide a evaluation of the behavior of the different locations of the same provider. Since scientists may have the need to execute their applications in their country, due to legal restrictions, an evaluation of multiple locations is necessary.

The work of He et al. and Iosúp et al. [3,5] provide a comparison between three public clouds and compare the results against a physical machine. However, the authors compared aspects of the machines and does not provide a comparison with focus in HPC needs.

Ekanayake and Fox [2] compared several different applications with a focus on communication patterns. They observed that the applications with more communication presented more degradation when executed in the cloud, which echoes our analysis of the network performance. Our work provides a deeper analysis, because we explore the possibilities inside the cloud providers Data Centers, using the same VM among Data Centers and using two different allocations for each one.

6 Conclusions and Future Work

With our results, we could notice that the network is still the main bottleneck in the Cloud. We saw that there is little variability between the executions during day and night in the same Data Center, with slowdowns during the night execution. Among different Data Centers, we did not observe much variation between them. Regarding to the real HPC application, Alya, we observed that the variation is low among the four Data Centers and it performed well on all of them.

As future work, we intend to compare more aspects of the machines, such as disk I/O and memory bandwidth, that are important components of HPC environments.

Acknowledgments. This research received funding from the EU H2020 Programme and from MCTI/RNP-Brazil under the HPC4E project, grant agreement no. 689772. Experiments presented in this paper were carried out using the Grid'5000 testbed, supported by a scientific interest group hosted by Inria and including CNRS, RENATER and several Universities as well as other organizations (see https://www.grid5000.fr). Additional funding was provided by CAPES and Microsoft.

References

1. Awad, O.M.O., Artoli, A.M.A., Ahmed, A.H.A.: Cloud computing versus in-house clusters: a comparative study. In: 2014 World Congress on Computer Applications and Information Systems (WCCAIS), pp. 1–6, January 2014
2. Ekanayake, J., Fox, G.: High performance parallel computing with clouds and cloud technologies. In: Avresky, D.R., Diaz, M., Bode, A., Ciciani, B., Dekel, E. (eds.) CloudComp 2009. LNICSSTE, vol. 34, pp. 20–38. Springer, Heidelberg (2010). doi:10.1007/978-3-642-12636-9_2
3. He, Q., Zhou, S., Kobler, B., Duffy, D., McGlynn, T.: Case study for running HPC applications in public clouds. In: Proceedings of the 19th ACM International Symposium on High Performance Distributed Computing, HPDC 2010, pp. 395–401. ACM, New York (2010). http://doi.acm.org/10.1145/1851476.1851535
4. Intel MPI Benchmarks: User Guide and Methodology Description (2014)
5. Iosup, A., Ostermann, S., Yigitbasi, M.N., Prodan, R., Fahringer, T., Epema, D.: Performance analysis of cloud computing services for many-tasks scientific computing. IEEE Trans. Parallel Distrib. Syst. **22**(6), 931–945 (2011)
6. Marathe, A., Harris, R., Lowenthal, D.K., de Supinski, B.R., Rountree, B., Schulz, M., Yuan, X.: A comparative study of high-performance computing on the cloud. In: Proceedings of the 22nd International Symposium on High-Performance Parallel and Distributed Computing, HPDC 2013, pp. 239–250. ACM, New York (2013). http://doi.acm.org/10.1145/2462902.2462919
7. da Rosa Righi, R., Rodrigues, V.F., da Costa, C.A., Galante, G., de Bona, L.C.E., Ferreto, T.: Autoelastic: automatic resource elasticity for high performance applications in the cloud. IEEE Trans. Cloud Comput. **4**(1), 6–19 (2016)

8. Vázquez, M., Houzeaux, G., Rubio, F., Simarro, C.: Alya multiphysics simulations on Intel's Xeon Phi accelerators. In: Hernández, G., Barrios Hernández, C.J., Díaz, G., García Garino, C., Nesmachnow, S., Pérez-Acle, T., Storti, M., Vázquez, M. (eds.) CARLA 2014. CCIS, vol. 485, pp. 248–254. Springer, Heidelberg (2014). doi:10.1007/978-3-662-45483-1_18

9. Vázquez, M., Houzeaux, G., Koric, S., Artigues, A., Aguado-Sierra, J., Arís, R., Mira, D., Calmet, H., Cucchietti, F., Owen, H., Taha, A., Burness, E.D., Cela, J.M., Valero, M.: Alya: multiphysics engineering simulation toward exascale. J. Comput. Sci. **14**, 15–27 (2016). The Route to Exascale: Novel Mathe-matical Methods, Scalable Algorithms and Computational Science Skills. http://www.sciencedirect.com/science/article/pii/S1877750315300521

10. Zounmevo, J.A., Kimpe, D., Ross, R., Afsahi, A.: Using MPI in high-performance computing services. In: Proceedings of the 20th European MPI Users' Group Meeting, EuroMPI 2013, pp. 43–48. ACM, New York (2013). http://doi.acm.org/10.1145/2488551.2488556

Communication-Aware Affinity Scheduling Heuristics in Multicore Systems

Diego Regueira, Santiago Iturriaga[✉], and Sergio Nesmachnow

Facultad de Ingeniería, Universidad de la República, Montevideo, Uruguay
siturria@fing.edu.uy

Abstract. This article presents the application of heuristic algorithms to solve the affinity scheduling problem in multicore computing systems. Affinity scheduling is a technique that allows efficient utilization of heterogeneous computing systems, by assigning a set of tasks to cores, taking into account specific efficiency and quality-of-service criteria. The heuristics proposed in this article are useful methods to solve realistic instances of the communication-aware affinity scheduling problem, which account for the different speed of communication and data transfer between tasks executing in different cores on a multicore system. The experimental analysis demonstrates that the proposed heuristics outperform the results computed using traditional scheduling techniques up to 12.3% when considering both the communication and synchronization times between tasks.

Keywords: Scheduling · Affinity · Communications · Multicore · NUMA

1 Introduction

The paradigm of *heterogeneous computing* is based on the simultaneous utilization of multiple computing resources with different computing capabilities [3]. Modern multiprocessor and multicore architectures provide support for heterogeneous computing. Although multicore processors are composed of a set of identical processing units (*cores*), in practice they are a special case of a heterogeneous computing system, called Non-Uniform Memory Architecture (NUMA). In NUMA systems, different cores can complete the same task at different speed because of the heterogeneous memory access. The main causes for this are the presence of the processed data in the local cache of the core, or the different speeds of communication and synchronization operations between tasks that cooperate to solve a given problem.

A key problem when using heterogeneous computing systems is to find an appropriate planning (*scheduling*) strategy for assigning computing resources to a set of tasks to execute, for example, in a parallel application. The main goal of the scheduling problem consists in assigning the computing resources in order to fulfill specific efficiency criteria, usually related to the total execution time of

© Springer International Publishing AG 2017
C.J. Barrios Hernández et al. (Eds.): CARLA 2016, CCIS 697, pp. 33–48, 2017.
DOI: 10.1007/978-3-319-57972-6_3

the set of tasks, the utilization of resources, or other quality-of-service metrics. Scheduling problems have been extensively studied in operation research [7], and the variants related to heterogeneous computing systems have been studied since the popularization of parallel computing in the mid-1990s [3].

Affinity scheduling [8] is a planning strategy for assigning tasks or light processes (*threads*) to specific computing resources in multiprocessor and multicore systems. The strategy is based on taking advantage of the capabilities of tasks to execute faster in certain computing resources, due to data locality, cache utilization, or communications with other tasks. This approach is relevant, considering that the access to certain type of resources (cache, RAM, I/O ports, etc.) has different time costs for different computing units, especially for NUMA [14]. In these computing systems, affinity scheduling is useful for reducing the negative impact of the overheads that appears in parallel computing, mainly due to task communication and synchronization, dynamic resource management, and load balancing [16].

Traditional scheduling problems are NP-hard, thus exact resolution techniques are only useful to solve small problem instances (i.e., few tasks, few resources). Heuristics and metaheuristics [11] are efficient alternatives to compute accurate solutions in reasonable execution times. In this line of work, this article studies the application of heuristic and metaheuristic methods to solve the assignment problem related to affinity scheduling in multicore NUMA systems.

We aim to develope an efficient and real-time scheduling tool that allows integrating topological information from both the computational platform and the applications to execute, in order to provide useful suggestions for task planning taking advantage of hardware and software affinities. This way, the improved scheduler will offer an efficient method for executing real-world applications on modern multicore systems. We propose using the *hardware locality* (hwloc) tool [4] to automatically detect the main features of the underlying hardware architecture, defining the hardware topology and hierarchies. In addition, specific benchmarks are applied to evaluate the costs (in time) of communications and synchronizations between different cores in the system. Finally, we propose using a topological characterization of parallel applications to account for different communication and synchronization patterns between tasks.

The main contributions of the research reported in this article are: (*i*) a description of the scheduling problem with affinities, focused on minimizing the communication and synchronization times; (*ii*) the design and implementation of heuristic and metaheuristic methods for affinity scheduling in multicore systems; (*iii*) a topological characterization for parallel applications, in order to study the efficacy of the proposed scheduling methods over realistic problem classes; and (*iv*) the experimental evaluation of the proposed scheduling methods considering realistic multicore systems and different numbers of tasks.

The article is organized as follows. Next section introduces the affinity scheduling problem considering communications and synchronizations. Section 3 describes the heuristics and metaheuristics considered in the study and the proposed topological characterization of parallel applications. The implementation details of the proposed methods are described in Sect. 4. Section 5 reports the experimental evaluation of the proposed heuristics over realistic infrastructures and using real applications. Finally, Sect. 6 presents the conclusions and the main lines for future work.

2 Formulation of the Affinity Scheduling Problem in Multicore NUMA Systems

The affinity scheduling problem considers a multicore NUMA system comprised of a set of processing cores and a parallel application comprised by a set of tasks to be executed concurrently in the system. Tasks collaborate with each other using communication and synchronization primitives to cooperatively solve a given computing intensive problem. The number of cores in the system must be larger than or equal to the number of tasks, allowing each task to be assigned to a core and executed without delay. This is a reasonable assumption when executing both CPU-bounded and memory-bounded tasks in High Performance Computing scenarios.

The affinity scheduling problem consists in finding the assignment of tasks to cores that minimizes the time required for all communication and synchronization operations between tasks. Formally, the mathematical model of the affinity scheduling problem considering communications and synchronizations (ASP-CS) is presented below.

Considering the following elements:

- A multicore system with a set of cores $N = \{n_1, \ldots, n_a\}$.
- A set of tasks $T = \{t_1, \ldots, t_b\}$ to be executed on the system.
- A *communication function* $C : T \times T \rightarrow \mathbb{N}^+$, where $C(t_i, t_j)$ evaluates the number of communications between two tasks t_i and t_j, $1 \leqslant i, j \leqslant b$.
- A *synchronization function* $S : T \times T \rightarrow \mathbb{N}^+$, where $S(t_i, t_j)$ evaluates the number of synchronizations between two tasks t_i and t_j, $1 \leqslant i, j \leqslant b$.
- A *communication cost function* $CC : N \times N \rightarrow \mathbb{R}^+$, where $CC(n_h, n_k)$ is the time required to communicate tasks executing in cores n_h and n_k, $1 \leqslant h, k \leqslant a$.
- A *synchronization cost function* $SC : N \times N \rightarrow \mathbb{R}^+$, where $SC(n_h, n_k)$ is the time required to synchronize tasks executing in cores n_h and n_k, $1 \leqslant h, k \leqslant a$.

The ASP-CS problem proposes finding a scheduling function $f : T \rightarrow N$ to assign tasks to cores in the system. Its goal consists in minimizing the total time demanded for communication and synchronizations between tasks, as given in Eq. 1, where $f(t_i) = n_h$ indicates that task t_i is assigned to execute on core n_h, $1 \leqslant i \leqslant b$ and $1 \leqslant h \leqslant a$. The ASP-CS problem follows a non-preemptive model: each task is considered as an atomic processing unit, which cannot be divided nor interrupted.

$$\sum_{t_i \in T} \sum_{t_j \in T} C(t_i, t_j) \times CC(f(t_i), f(t_j)) + S(t_i, t_j) \times SC(f(t_i), f(t_j)) \qquad (1)$$

2.1   Related Work

Affinity scheduling has been widely used in shared-memory multiprocessor systems. In those environments, it is sometimes beneficial to schedule a task on a certain processor that contains relevant data in its local cache or in a processor that is able to provide a faster communication with other tasks [14].

Early approaches studied cache-affinity scheduling policies for parallel loops and heuristics for grouping tasks in NUMA systems [8]. Subramaniam and Eager [16] proposed two partitioning heuristics to maximize the cache hits. Wang et al. [18] proposed a heuristic that takes into account a hierarchical affinity organization to model hierarchical NUMA systems. Two variants of the proposed heuristic were studied on realistic systems with up to 50 processors.

Torrellas et al. [17] evaluated several affinity strategies using a number of realistic applications. The main results showed that cache affinity techniques were able to reduce the execution times: about 4–6% for scientific computing applications and up to 8% for applications using frequent synchronizations. Hamidzadeh and Lilja [5] studied strategies for affinity scheduling of generic tasks, according to a task-to-processor affinity matrix. Two heuristics based on Branch and Bound are introduced and evaluated on a test suite including problem instances with up to 500 tasks and 20 processors. More recently, Sibai [13] proposed a heuristic for scheduling threads in NUMA-based multicore systems considering affinity for computations and using thread migration. Six variants of the proposed heuristic were analyzed over a NUMA system with 16 processors, and the results demonstrated that the best option is to include the full computation affinity data.

The agent-based strategy by Muneeswari and Shunmuganathan [9] schedules two types of tasks: *critical* and *non-critical*. Critical tasks are scheduled using a hard affinity policy to minimize cache re-utilization. A Round Robin scheduler is used for non-critical tasks, which can or cannot have cache affinity. The experimental evaluation indicated that average response time can be reduced around 30% when compared to traditional scheduling algorithms.

Ortiz et al. [12] presented a scheduling heuristic for processing network packets in multicore systems considering core affinity. The heuristic was evaluated using realistic communication workloads from both a scientific high performance computing application using MPI and a web server application. Packet throughput improved up to 35% for the MPI workload, and up to 100% for the web server.

Related works show that affinity is key for efficiently scheduling parallel tasks in modern multicore systems. Most previous works considered cache utilization/reutilization for affinity scheduling. Very diverse results were reported, with improvements ranging from 4% up to 100% depending on the system and the applications. However, previous work considered uncharacterized applications and have not dealt with network communications. The main novel issues addressed in our work are: (i) we consider the affinity scheduling problem taking into account network communications between tasks, (ii) we characterize the most representative types of parallel applications, and (iii) we design simple and effective heuristics for affinity scheduling. These heuristics are evaluated using real NUMA systems and a comprehensive analysis of the results is presented.

3 Heuristics and Metaheuristics for Affinity Scheduling

This section describes the methods applied in the study and the proposed characterization for parallel applications used in the scheduling problem.

3.1 Heuristics and Metaheuristics Applied in the Study

The heuristics and metaheuristics studied in this article are:

– *Round Robin* (RR), a classic scheduling heuristic that assigns the computing resources in circular order, without considering priorities for tasks.
– *Greedy heuristic* (GH), a constructive method that builds solutions taking locally optimal decisions (e.g., minimum cost, maximum benefit). In each step, the component having the lower heuristic cost is included in the solution. The process is repeated until a valid solution is built.
– *Descent Local Search* (DLS), a local improvement heuristic from the family of local search (LS) methods [1]. LS methods try to improve a solution iteratively, searching for a better solution in its neighborhood. The neighborhood is defined via a single transformation of the solution or *movement*. Regarding the exploration pattern, DLS methods are classified in: (*i*) *simple descent*, which applies a single step search, choosing the first best solution found in the neighborhood of the current one; and (*ii*) *steepest descent*, which explores all candidate solutions and selects the best one among them.
– *Iterated Local Search* (ILS), a metaheuristic that extends LS methods by including a perturbation operator to escape from local optima. In each iteration, the current solution is perturbed and improved using a LS, until a stopping criteria is met (see the schema of ILS in Algorithm 1). The *acceptance criterion* is applied to decide if continuing the search from the former solution or the best one found in the neighborhood of the perturbed solution.

Algorithm 1. Schema of the ILS algorithm.

1: $s_0 \leftarrow$ GenerateInitialSolution()
2: $s^* \leftarrow$ LocalSearch(s_0)
3: **repeat**
4:    $s' \leftarrow$ Perturbation(s^*)
5:    $s'' \leftarrow$ LocalSearch(s')
6:    $s^* \leftarrow$ AcceptanceCriterion(s^*,s'')
7: **until** stop criterion is met
8: **return** s^*

3.2 Topological Characterization of Parallel Applications

In this section we introduce a classification for parallel applications, taking into account communication and synchronization patterns used for collaboration. This characterization is useful to create synthetic workloads of real-world applications for evaluating the proposed affinity scheduling methods. Three different application patterns are proposed: *flat topology*, *application-driven topology*, and *hierarchical topology*.

Flat Topology. This topology includes all applications following the master-slave model for parallelization, where a distinguished process (the *master*) controls a set of subordinate processes (the *slaves*). The master sends a set of data to slaves for processing, then slaves compute and send back the results to the master, which reduces the results. We consider two types of flat master-slave topologies for the application characterization: flat without communications between slaves (Fig. 1a) and flat with communications between slaves (Fig. 1b).

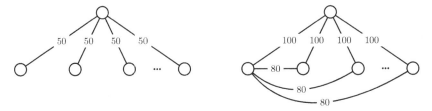

(a) No communications between slaves.   (b) Communications between slaves.

Fig. 1. Flat topology

Application-Driven Topology. This topology characterizes workflow-based applications, where data are distributed and processed by many independent units (*tasks*) according to a specific flow. The data partitioning can be either static or dynamic, applying different domain-decomposition strategies (e.g., row-based, column-based, etc.). Communications and synchronizations are defined according different patterns, e.g. uniform synchronization (Fig. 2a) or level-based synchronization (Fig. 2b).

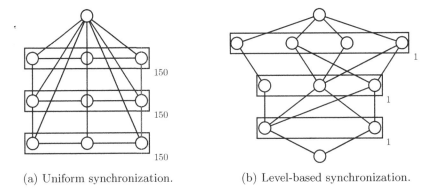

(a) Uniform synchronization.   (b) Level-based synchronization.

Fig. 2. Application-driven topology

Hierarchical (Tree) Topology. This topology describes applications with a hierarchical order defined between tasks. Each task communicates exclusively with tasks in the nearest levels in the hierarchy. Synchronizations are performed between tasks in the same level. The most popular hierarchical topology is the tree topology. In a tree-based application, the communications are performed between parent and children and synchronizations are between siblings (Fig. 3a) or level-based (Fig. 3b).

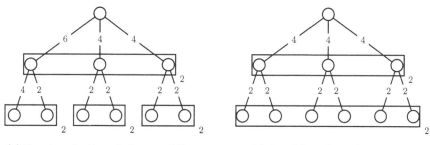

(a) Synchronizations between siblings. (b) Level-based synchronization.

Fig. 3. Hierarchical (tree) topology

In this work we evaluate three parallel applications, one for each characterized topology: a heat transfer application with a master/slave topology, a generic workflow application with an application-driven topology, and a quicksort application with a hierarchical topology. These applications are presented in detail in Sect. 5.2.

4 Methodology and Implementation Details

This section describes the methodology applied for building real-work scheduling scenarios and the implementation details of the proposed schedulers.

4.1 The Procedure for Building Real-World Scheduling Scenarios

A scheduling scenario is described by two main components: (i) the interaction pattern (communications and synchronizations) for the studied application; and (ii) the multicore architecture of the system in which the application is executed. The interaction pattern of an application is defined by its communication matrix (C) and its synchronization matrix (S). These matrices define the number of communications and synchronizations that the application performs during its execution. Likewise, a multicore architecure is described by its communication cost matrix (CC) and its synchronization cost matrix (SC). These matrices define the cost (in time units) of executing a communication or a synchronization operation between two tasks executing in different cores.

Regarding the application patterns, we defined three sets of matrices C and S, in order to model three different real-world parallel applications, following the three categories defined in the topological characterization (see Sect. 5.2). By analyzing the source code of these applications, we estimated the values in C and S matrices when using different numbers of parallel tasks for each application.

To characterize a working set of multicore architectures we created a number of ping-pong benchmark tests. Ping-pong is a point-to-point test which is commonly used for measuring the latency of a communication or synchronization operation. An effective MPI-based ping-pong benchmark suite was applied for estimating CC and SC matrices. We have used this approach in previous articles about performance analysis [2] and affinity scheduling [6].

4.2 Solution Encoding

Schedules are represented as vectors with length a, being a the number of cores available in the multicore architecture, according to the mathematical formulation presented in Sect. 2. In this core-oriented encoding, each position represents a core and each element represents a task assigned to that core. Figure 4 presents an example of scheduling for a parallel application using b tasks, executing in a computer with a cores.

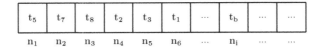

Fig. 4. Core-oriented solution encoding.

4.3 Proposed Schedulers

This section presents the implementation details of the proposed schedulers.

Round Robin. A straightforward implementation was developed for RR, based on the one presented by Stalling [15].

Greedy Heuristic. Tasks are assigned to cores in order, sorted by their total number of interactions with other tasks, such that the task with most interactions is assigned first. Each task is assigned greedily to the core which minimizes the total interaction cost.

Descent Local Search. A *steepest descent* search strategy is implemented. The neighborhood is defined by a *swap* movement that exchanges the assignments for two tasks: given a solution s, for two tasks t_i and t_j, assigned to cores n_k and n_l, respectively, a neighboring solution is constructed by assigning $s[n_k] = t_j$ and $s[n_l] = t_i$.

Iterated Local Search. The same swap movement defined for DLS is applied to define the neighborhood in the ILS algorithm. The perturbation operator is defined to modify a predefined number of task-to-processor assignments.

5   Experimental Analysis

This section describes the experimental evaluation of the proposed heuristics and metaheuristics for affinity scheduling considering communications and synchronizations. We focus on analyzing both the solution quality (i.e., improvements on the execution time when using the proposed schedulers) and the computational efficiency of each method.

5.1   Development and Execution Platform

The proposed heuristics were implemented in C language using MPICH 3 library for MPI support. The experimental evaluation was performed on a HP ProLiant DL585 G7 server, AMD Opteron Processor 6272 at 2.10 GHz, 48 GB of RAM, and the CentOS operating system, from Cluster FING, the High Performance Computing infrastructure at Universidad de la República, Uruguay [10].

5.2   Problem Instances

The problem instances used for the experimental evaluation include a set of multicore architectures, three real parallel applications, different values for the number of tasks in the parallel application, and different input sizes for the applications. A total number of **240** evaluation instances are used in the experimental evaluation. All evaluation instances and their visual representation can be downloaded from https://www.fing.edu.uy/inco/grupos/cecal/hpc/PPSH/data/instances.tar.gz.

Multicore Architectures. Three real multicore architectures from Cluster FING were selected for the experimental evaluation of the proposed heuristics:

- a_1: Multicore server HP ProLiant DL385 G7, having two sockets with two NUMA nodes each. Each node has six cores and three cache levels. The server accounts for 24 cores and 28 GB RAM.
- a_2: Multicore server HP ProLiant DL385p Gen8, having two sockets with two NUMA nodes each. Each node has eight cores and three cache levels. The server accounts for 32 cores and 32 GB RAM.
- a_3: Multicore server HP ProLiant DL585 G7, having four sockets with two NUMA nodes each. Each node contains eight cores and three cache levels. The server accounts for 64 cores and 64 GB RAM.

Parallel Applications. Three parallel applications were used to evaluate the proposed heuristics for communication aware affinity scheduling. These applications are representative examples of the three topologies identified in the classification defined in Sect. 3. Next, we describe each application. Their source code can be downloaded from https://www.fing.edu.uy/inco/grupos/cecal/hpc/PPSH/data/source.tar.gz.

- *Heat transfer.* Describes the evolution of temperature in a bar, solving the differential equation governing the heat transfer process using a master/slave parallel model.
- *Workflow.* Describes a generic workflow application, having a number of tasks and dependencies between them.
- *Quicksort.* Sorts a set of integer numbers applying the quicksort strategy.

5.3   Parameter Setting

Next, we present the parameter settings used for the descent local search and iterated local search. These parameters were configured taking into account the quality of the computed solutions and the computational efficiency of the scheduler. The greedy heuristic and round robin schedulers are not presented in this section because they do not have any configurable parameters.

Descent Local Search. Two stopping criteria are considered: the search stops when no better solution is found in the neighbourhood or when a maximum number of iterations is reached. We defined the maximum number of iterations as $\lfloor \frac{a}{b} \rfloor$, where a is the number of cores in the architecture and b is the number of tasks in the application.

Iterated Local Search. A fixed-effort stopping criterion is used: the main cycle stops after performing 10 iterations. As for the perturbation operator, each task-to-processor assignment is modified with a probability of $p_m = \frac{1}{6}$.

5.4   Numerical Results

This subsection reports the numerical results in the experimental analysis of the proposed schedulers. All the reported results correspond to average values computed in 40 independent executions performed for each method over each problem instance. The traditional RR scheduler is used as a reference baseline for comparing the results computed by each heuristic.

Comparative Analysis. Table 1 reports the improvements in the execution times when solving the affinity scheduling problem using GH, DLS, and ILS for each one of the three applications in the benchmark suite over different multicore architectures (a_i) and using different number of tasks $(\#p)$. The improvements are computed regarding the traditional RR scheduler used as a reference baseline. The best improvements found are marked in bold font.

From the results in Table 1, we conclude that the three evaluated schedulers are consistently better than the RR scheduler. The average improvements over RR are of 9.1% for GH, 11.1% for DLS, and 11.3% for ILS. When comparing the proposed heuristics, results show DLS and ILS compute more accurate schedules than GH for all applications and all architectures. DLS and ILS perform approximately with the same scheduling accuracy, and ILS is slightly more

Table 1. Average improvements of GH, DLS, and ILS over the baseline RR results for each application and architecture.

Instance	Heat transfer			Workflow			Quicksort		
$(a_i \times \#p)$	GH	DLS	ILS	GH	DLS	ILS	GH	DLS	ILS
$a_1 \times 6$	**19.3%**	**19.3%**	**19.3%**	9.3%	**13.2%**	**13.2%**	**16.4%**	**16.4%**	**16.4%**
$a_1 \times 12$	18.0%	**18.4%**	**18.4%**	2.0%	8.0%	**9.7%**	3.9%	5.5%	**5.9%**
$a_1 \times 24$	6.6%	**8.4%**	**8.4%**	8.5%	9.3%	**10.0%**	3.9%	5.1%	**5.4%**
$a_2 \times 8$	15.1%	**19.5%**	**19.5%**	1.5%	6.6%	**7.8%**	3.9%	**7.0%**	**7.0%**
$a_2 \times 16$	10.7%	**12.4%**	**12.4%**	5.3%	9.0%	**10.5%**	6.3%	8.1%	**8.3%**
$a_2 \times 32$	4.3%	**5.9%**	**5.9%**	8.2%	**9.0%**	8.9%	5.0%	**6.6%**	**6.6%**
$a_3 \times 16$	18.8%	**18.9%**	**18.9%**	10.4%	14.9%	**16.1%**	10.3%	10.8%	**11.0%**
$a_3 \times 32$	14.4%	**15.2%**	**15.2%**	10.3%	13.6%	**13.9%**	9.3%	10.3%	**10.5%**
$a_3 \times 64$	5.2%	**6.1%**	**6.1%**	11.7%	**14.0%**	13.2%	6.7%	7.2%	**7.4%**

accurate than DLS. Both DLS and ILS compute the best results when scheduling the heat transfer application. However, ILS computes slightly more accurate schedules than DLS for the workflow and quicksort applications, with average improvements of 0.6% and 1.4% over DLS, respectively.

A graphical comparison of the improvements grouped by application type is presented in Fig. 5. The reported values correspond to average improvements considering the three studied architectures. The graphic clearly shows that the heat transfer application and the workflow application have the largest improvement values, outperforming RR for up to 11.9% and 12.3%, respectively. On the other hand, the improvements achieved for the quicksort application are lower, barely reaching 8.4% over the RR scheduler in the best case.

Computational Efficiency. We also studied the computational efficiency of the proposed methods, taking into account that one of the main goals of the research is to design online scheduling strategies to be used in real time in current multicore systems. Table 2 summarizes the average execution times (in miliseconds) for the proposed affinity scheduling techniques.

The execution times reported in Table 2 shows that all the studied methods have a very low overhead (below 5 ms, except for ILS on the a_3 architecture and the largest number of tasks). GH is the fastest scheduler. This is because the iterative nature of DLS and ILS demands larger execution times than a simple constructive method such as GH. DLS is almost always one order of magnitude slower than GH, except when addressing the smaller instances for each architecture. Likewise, ILS is always one order of magnitude slower than DLS, making it two order of magnitude slower than GH in the largest architecture and using the largest number of tasks.

Figure 6 reports the average improvement achieved by each scheduler for each architecture, and the running time of the scheduler when computing it

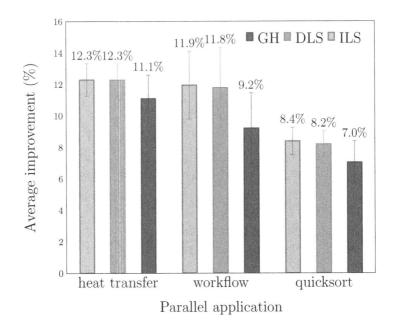

Fig. 5. Average improvements of GH, DLS, and ILS over the RR scheduler.

Table 2. Average execution time of GH, DLS, and ILS for each architecture.

Instance	Execution time ($\times 10^{-1}$ ms)		
$(a_i \times \#p)$	GH	DLS	ILS
$a_1 \times 6$	0.2	0.4	1.4
$a_1 \times 12$	0.5	2.0	16.5
$a_1 \times 24$	1.2	8.9	77.7
$a_2 \times 8$	0.4	0.9	5.0
$a_2 \times 16$	0.9	5.1	42.7
$a_2 \times 32$	2.5	20.4	179.9
$a_3 \times 16$	1.9	8.0	58.4
$a_3 \times 32$	5.7	41.3	362.0
$a_3 \times 64$	16.3	167.3	1517.7

(x-axis, in logarithmic scale). This trade-off analysis is very useful to determine the convenience of applying the proposed methods in real process management systems. The best solutions are on the upper left (as indicated by the blue arrow), having the best execution time improvements and the lower execution times for the scheduler.

The results reported in Fig. 6 indicate that DLS is a very competitive scheduler, performing approximately with the same scheduling accuracy as ILS, but

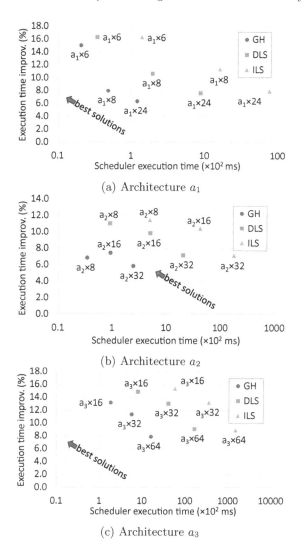

Fig. 6. Trade-off between the average improvement of the execution time of all applications compared to the scheduler execution time for each architecture.

significantly faster. On the one hand, GH is the fastest method (with a significantly lower execution time than DLS and ILS), but the accuracy of its computed schedules is much lower than the ones computed by DLS and ILS, especially when addressing applications executing in architecture a_3. On the other hand, ILS is always the most accurate scheduler, but significantly slower than GH and DLS.

The comparative analysis allows us to conclude that all the studied schedulers have minimum overhead. In addition, DLS provides an excellent trade-off between execution time improvement and execution time demanded to run the scheduling algorithm. For some time-consuming applications, it would be worth applying ILS, as the additional improvements in execution time over DLS could impact significantly on the overall wall-clock time.

Comparison Against Lower Bounds. The proposed heuristics are conceived to execute in real time (*online scheduling*). Lower bounds for the problem can be computed by executing the best method (ILS) with a different (unrealistic in practice) stopping criterion, allowing ILS to execute for a significantly larger time. Figure 7 summarizes the comparison against lower bounds, which demonstrate the capabilities of the proposed methods to compute accurate schedules in very short execution times (dark grey bars indicate the potential improvements).

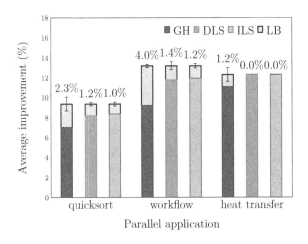

Fig. 7. Average improvement gap of GH, DLS, and ILS compared to the Lower Bound (LB) for each application type.

The results in Fig. 7 suggest that there is still room to improve the execution time for the quicksort and workflow applications. Schedules computed by DLS and ILS could be improved between 1.0% and 1.4%. On the other hand, the results for the heat transfer application demonstrate the high quality of the proposed schedulers, as they reach results that cannot be improved in 10 min of execution time (DLS and ILS always compute the lower bound).

6   Conclusions and Future Work

In this article we address the problem of effective scheduling of parallel applications in multicore systems. We show that the execution time of a parallel application can be significantly reduced by considering affinities when scheduling the task to execute in the system. To this end, we introduce a simple and yet effective mathematical formulation for the affinity scheduling problem and a characterization of parallel applications and multicore architectures. Using these elements, we build a realistic set of instances of the affinity scheduling problem.

Next, we design and implement three affinity scheduling heuristics, based on greedy, descent local search, and iterated local search strategies, and taking into account communication and synchronization patterns for applications. We evaluated the efficacy and efficiency of the heuristics for solving real problem instances and compared the results with a classic round robin scheduler.

Results show ILS and DLS are the most accurate schedulers, improving the average execution time of the applications by 11.3% and 11.1% respectively. GH is less accurate, improving barely 1.5% in average. However, GH is the fastest scheduler with an average execution time of 0.3 ms, while DLS requires an average of 2.8 ms. ILS is the slowest method, with an average of 25.1 ms.

We conclude that affinity scheduling is indeed an effective approach for reducing the execution time of parallel applications with many communications and synchronizations. DLS is the best scheduler overall, with an adequate trade-off between efficacy and efficiency. The main lines for future work are related to designing new scheduling algorithms, characterizing a larger number of applications and architectures, and characterizing applications using automatic profiling tools. We also propose to extend our model by considering applications with dynamic communication and synchronization patterns, and by considering collective communication and synchronization operations involving multiple tasks.

References

1. Aarts, E., Lenstra, J.K.: Local Search in Combinatorial Optimization. Wiley, New York (1997)
2. Alaniz, M., Nesmachnow, S., Goglin, B., Iturriaga, S., Gosta, V.G., Printista, M.: MBSPDiscover: an automatic benchmark for MultiBSP performance analysis. In: Hernández, G., Barrios Hernández, C.J., Díaz, G., García Garino, C., Nesmachnow, S., Pérez-Acle, T., Storti, M., Vázquez, M. (eds.) CARLA 2014. CCIS, vol. 485, pp. 158–172. Springer, Heidelberg (2014). doi:10.1007/978-3-662-45483-1_12
3. Eshaghian, M.: Heterogeneous Computing. Artech House, Norwood (1996)
4. Goglin, B.: Managing the topology of heterogeneous cluster nodes with hardware locality (hwloc). In: High Performance Computing and Simulation, pp. 74–81 (2014)
5. Hamidzadeh, B., Lilja, D.: Dynamic scheduling strategies for shared-memory multiprocessors. In: International Conference on Distributed Computing Systems, pp. 208–215 (1996)
6. Iturriaga, S., Nesmachnow, S.: Evolutionary algorithms for affinity scheduling heuristics in heterogeneous computing systems. In: XL Latin American Computing Conference, pp. 1–12 (2014)
7. Leung, J., Kelly, L., Anderson, J.: Handbook of Scheduling: Algorithms, Models, and Performance Analysis. CRC Press, Boca Raton (2004)

8. Markatos, E., LeBlanc, T.: Using processor affinity in loop scheduling on shared-memory multiprocessors. IEEE Trans. Parallel Distrib. Syst. **5**(4), 379–400 (1994)
9. Muneeswari, G., Shunmuganathan, K.: Agent based load balancing scheme using affinity processor scheduling for multicore architectures. WSEAS Trans. Comput. **10**(8), 247–258 (2011)
10. Nesmachnow, S.: Computación científica de alto desempeño en la Facultad de Ingeniería, Universidad de la República. Revista de la Asociación de Ingenieros del Uruguay **61**, 12–15 (2010)
11. Nesmachnow, S.: An overview of metaheuristics: accurate and efficient methods for optimisation. Int. J. Metahe. **3**(4), 320–347 (2014)
12. Ortiz, A., Ortega, J., Díaz, A., Prieto, A.: Affinity-based network interfaces for efficient communication on multicore architectures. J. Comput. Sci. Technol. **28**(3), 508–524 (2013)
13. Sibai, F.: Nearest neighbor affinity scheduling in heterogeneous multi-core architectures. J. Comput. Sci. Technol. **8**(3), 144–150 (2008)
14. Squillante, M.: Affinity scheduling. In: Padua, D. (ed.) Encyclopedia of Parallel Computing, pp. 11–16. Springer, Heidelberg (2011)
15. Stallings, W.: Operating Systems - Internals and Design Principles. Pitman, London (2011)
16. Subramaniam, S., Eager, D.L.: Affinity scheduling of unbalanced workloads. In: ACM/IEEE Conference on Supercomputing, pp. 214–226 (1994)
17. Torrellas, J., Tucker, A., Gupta, A.: Evaluating the performance of cache-affinity scheduling in shared-memory multiprocessors. J. Parallel Distrib. Comput. **24**(2), 139–151 (1995)
18. Wang, Y., Wang, H., Chang, R.: Hierarchical loop scheduling for clustered numa machines. J. Syst. Softw. **55**(1), 33–44 (2000)

Penalty Scheduling Policy Applying User Estimates and Aging for Supercomputing Centers

Nestor Rocchetti[1(✉)], Miguel Da Silva[1], Sergio Nesmachnow[1], and Andrei Tchernykh[2]

[1] Universidad de la República, Julio Herrera y Reissig 565,
11300 Montevideo, Uruguay
{nrocchetti,mdasilva,sergion}@fing.edu.uy
[2] CICESE Research Center, Carretera Ensenada-Tijuana 3918,
Zona Playitas, 22860 Ensenada, B.C., Mexico
chernykh@cicese.mx

Abstract. In this article we address the problem of scheduling on realistic high performance computing facilities using incomplete information about tasks execution times. We introduce a variation of our previous Penalty Scheduling Policy, including an aging scheme that increases the priority of jobs over time. User-provided runtime estimates are applied as in the original Penalty Scheduling Policy, but a realistic priority schema is proposed to avoid starvation. The experimental evaluation of the proposed scheduler is performed using real workload logs, and validated using a job scheduler simulator. We study different realistic workload scenarios to evaluate the performance of the Penalty Scheduling Policy with aging. The main results suggest that using the proposed scheduler with the aging scheme, the waiting time of jobs in the high performance computing facility is significantly reduced (up to 50% in average).

Keywords: High performance computing · Scheduling · Execution time estimation · Aging scheme · Penalty scheduling policy

1 Introduction

Job scheduling has become a critical issue in supercomputing. When dealing with large and complex problems, small differences in scheduling policies can result in great improvements in resource utilization, performance, and energy consumption [1]. One of the most popular scheduling policies is first-come, first-served (FCFS), which is often used in combination with the EASY-Backfilling method [2]. Backfilling systems rely on job runtime estimates provided by users to accomplish the task planning.

Scheduling strategies based on estimations provided by users are popular. However, the inaccuracy of user estimates impacts on the general performance of the system, worsening its overall performance [3]. Some studies in the literature have proposed strategies to improve runtime estimates to help improve the overall performance of High Performance Computing (HPC) systems [4, 5].

© Springer International Publishing AG 2017
C.J. Barrios Hernández et al. (Eds.): CARLA 2016, CCIS 697, pp. 49–60, 2017.
DOI: 10.1007/978-3-319-57972-6_4

In our previous work [4] we introduced the Penalty Scheduling Policy (PSP) for supercomputing centers. PSP consists of assigning a priority to a recently submitted job. This priority is assigned according to the historical accuracy of job runtime estimations from the task owner, computed in a given window of previously completed jobs. The priority is assigned from a set of five priority groups, in which the priority goes from 1 to 5. In that previous work, we studied the performance of PSP with automatically generated workload logs.

In this article, we contribute with a new version of the PSP scheduler proposed on [4]. We also contributed with an extended analysis of the impact of user runtime estimates on the system utilization in HPC infrastructures using real parallel workload data and simulations.

The new version of PSP presented in this article (PSP+AGING) includes a new approach for defining the intervals of accuracy, and an aging scheme that increases the priority of jobs over time to prevent starvation. Finally, we report results on the performance of PSP under scenarios based on workload logs obtained from the Parallel Workload Archive (PWA) [6] and compared with an experimental evaluation of these scenarios using a traditional FCFS scheduling policy.

The paper is organized as follows. Next section presents a review of related work about scheduling using runtime estimates in supercomputing centers. Section 3 describes the proposed PSP+AGING algorithm. Section 4 introduces the workload analysis and the main features of the problem instances considered in the study. Then, the experimental evaluation of PSP+AGING over realistic HPC scenarios is presented in Sect. 5. Finally, Sect. 6 presents the conclusions and formulates the main lines for future work.

2 Related Work

In this section, we review the related work about analysis of user runtime estimates on parallel supercomputers, its impact on job scheduling, and proposed job scheduling techniques.

According to the seminal work by Lee et al., "it is a well-documented fact that user-provided runtime estimates are inaccurate" [5]. In that article, the authors reviewed the results of previous studies by Cirne and Berman [1], Ward et al. [7], and Chiang et al. [8], in which the previous statement was confirmed. Lee et al. conducted an experiment in which they asked users to estimate their jobs runtime the best they could, and also asked to rate their confidence in the estimation provided with a number from 1 to 5. After the experiment, the results reported by Lee et al. showed that only slight improvements are detected on the job runtime estimates, despite users making their best effort to perform accurate predictions.

Hirales-Carbajal et al. [9] performed an experimental study of scheduling strategies on grid systems. The authors proposed a scheduling approach considering users runtime estimations and multiple optimization criteria. An offline version of the scheduling problem was solved, i.e., considering all information about tasks and resources is known in advance. The proposed scheduling strategies include the following stages: (i) labeling jobs according to users runtime estimates; (ii) allocate resources based on optimization criteria; and (iii) prioritize jobs. The experimental analysis was carried out using a parametric workload generator and the performance of the proposed scheduler was compared with known single workflow algorithms. The authors considered machine heterogeneity in realistic grid systems, nevertheless a specific model is assumed in order to perform the scheduling evaluations in a repeatable and controllable manner.

Ramírez-Alcaraz et al. [10] showed that user runtime estimates do not help to improve the performance of schedulers in cluster systems. The authors stated that "... an appropriate distribution of job processor requirements over the grid has a higher performance than an allocation of jobs based on user runtime estimates ...". Similar conclusions, but related to scheduling to optimize energy consumption, were also found by Iturriaga et al. [15].

In our previous article [4], we introduced the PSP scheduling technique. The main idea of PSP is to integrate user estimates in order to improve the resource utilization and reduce the waiting times of jobs. In PSP, we assign a priority to a job according to the historical accuracy of the runtime estimates of the job owner. In this previous work, user runtime estimates are employed to build a history-based prediction model that is later used by the job scheduler. In this way, user runtime estimates were used as kill times, whereas the predicted time is used to build the schedule. In this previous work, we also assigned a priority from 1 to 5 according to the historical accuracy. The prediction model in PSP uses a history window size. For each newly arrived job, the priority is assigned according to the accuracy of runtime estimates for the owner, which is computed as the average accuracy considering only the last ten completed jobs. The history window approach was originally presented in the article by Tsafrir et al. [11], where authors selected the previous two jobs submitted by the same user. Applying this strategy, the results of Tsafrir et al. showed that taking into account the more recently submitted jobs allows computing improved schedules, as these jobs provide more useful information than older ones.

Regarding the experimental evaluation, in our previous article [4] we created workloads according to the main characteristics of user estimates and jobs submitted to the Cluster FING HPC facility at Facultad de Ingeniería, Universidad de la República [12]. The main results of our previous work showed that using PSP in an environment where some users improve their job runtime estimates over the time is a promising approach to reach the important goal of every user experiencing a decrease on the waiting time of his jobs.

In this article, we improve our previous work by considering a new approach for defining the intervals of accuracy for users estimations, and an aging scheme that increases the priority of jobs over time to prevent starvation.

3 The Proposed Penalty Scheduling Policy with Aging

The main idea of the penalty policy applied in PSP is based on affecting the priority of jobs according to the historical precision of runtime estimates provided by the users on previous job submissions. The proposal we introduce here extends the method in our previous work [4], for dealing with low accuracy in user jobs estimates.

In our previous work [4], the accuracy of the job runtime estimate by users was defined as $A = \frac{t_{run}}{t_{req}}$, where t_{run} is the real runtime of the job, and t_{req} is the time requested by the user during job submission. The accuracy values are between 0.0 and 1.0, thus, the average accuracy for all submitted jobs is also between these values. The bigger the average accuracy, the better the user estimates the runtime of his jobs, and the PSP scheduling method will assign higher priority to new jobs submitted by the user.

In this article, we propose defining ten levels of accuracy (g1–g10). The levels of accuracy are defined by the intervals shown in Table 1. The priority is a number between one and forty-nine, where a higher number means that the job is closer to the head of the queue of pending jobs. For example, a job whose owner has an accuracy of 0.17 will have an initial priority of 25. We use these levels of accuracy to assign the initial priority to the submitted jobs. After that, the priority is updated by applying an aging scheme.

Table 1. Accuracy intervals of estimates and priorities for each tag name.

Tag name	Accuracy interval	Priority
g1	(0.00,0.05)	1
g2	[0.05,0.10)	10
g3	[0.10,0.15)	20
g4	[0.15,0.20)	25
g5	[0.20,0.30)	30
g6	[0.30,0.40)	35
g7	[0.40,0.52)	40
g8	[0.52,0.64)	43
g9	[0.64,0.78)	46
g10	[0.78,1.00]	49

PSP calculates the current accuracy of a user by computing the average accuracy for an amount of completed jobs per user. Below, we report results on problem instances in which the accuracy of user at estimating job runtime is calculated for the last ten jobs that were completed.

We use an aging scheme to increase the priority of the jobs over time. The purpose of the aging scheme is to prevent the starvation of jobs. The aging scheme is recursively computed by the expression in Eq. 1.

$$\begin{cases} priority_{j,i+1} = g_j + \left(priority_{j,i} \times \dfrac{t\_waiting_{j,i}}{t\_estimated_j}\right) \\ priority_{j,1} = g_j \end{cases} \tag{1}$$

In Eq. 1, the new value for the priority of a job is calculated based on the priority of that job in the previous time step. When job j is submitted, the value of the priority in time step i = 1 is calculated using PSP. The new value of the priority for task j in time step $(i + 1)$ is priority$_{j,i+1}$; g_j is the level of accuracy of task j; and $\frac{t\_waiting_{j,i}}{t\_estimated_j}$ is the normalized waiting time for job j in time step i. No further historical information is used.

Figure 1 presents an example of the application of the aging scheme on four different jobs that were submitted at the same time. The new priority for each pending job is calculated at each time step. In this work, we set the time step to 150 s, according to the analysis explained in the next paragraph.

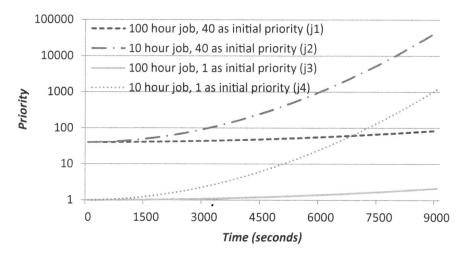

Fig. 1. Example of priority functions for four different types of jobs with a time step of 150 s.

The graphic in Fig. 1 shows the increment in the priority values for each job over time. The horizontal axis represents the time in seconds, and the vertical axis represents the priority [in logarithmic scale]. The priority of small jobs increases faster than the priority of large jobs. This happens due to the fact that priority is calculated using the normalized waiting time of jobs. The larger the job (in terms of time requested) the slower the increment of its priority. In Fig. 1 we compared the increment of jobs priority over time. With a time step of 150 s job j4 has a priority of 58 after 6750 s. Job j1 has a priority of 61 after 6750 s. Job j4 waits 18.8% of the requested time before having higher priority than job j1.

In a 1-h job a 150 s time step is 4.2% of its requested time. This length of time step does not impact negatively on user experience. It is a reasonable tradeoff between CPU usage to perform the planning and the length of the jobs in the workloads. Therefore, we decided to use a time step of 150 s for the rest of the experimental evaluation.

The proposed PSP+AGING scheduling method was coded and included in the multifactor implementation of SLURM Scheduler Priority Plugin API [14]. The priority API is used by the SLURM job manager, which is the component that accepts jobs requests and includes pending jobs in a priority ordered queue.

The priority calculation process is shown in Fig. 2. When a new job arrives, its initial priority is calculated using the PSP+AGING scheduling method. Every time the

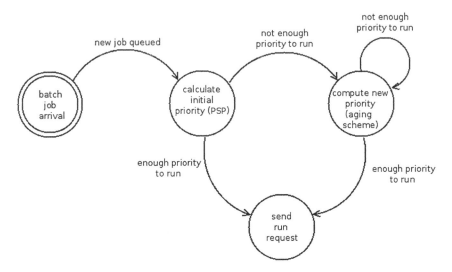

Fig. 2. Diagram of the process for priority calculation in PSP+AGING.

SLURM priority algorithm is executed, the job priorities are increased according to the aging scheme proposed. When the priority is high, and the resources are available, the job will change its state to running and the job and will leave the queue of pending jobs.

4   Workload Analysis and Problem Instances

We built several problem instances based on real workload traces, to be used in the experimental evaluation of the proposed scheduler. This section summarizes the main findings of the workload characterization study, with special focus on job runtime estimates, and also describes the problem instances generated.

4.1   Workload Analysis

We based our analysis in two workload logs taken from the Parallel Workload Archive (PWA) [6]. One of the workload logs was taken from the Curie Supercomputer (Atomic Energy Commission, France) [from February 2011 to October 2012]. The other workload log was taken from the University of Luxembourg Gaia Cluster [from February 2011 to October 2012]. Both workload logs were provided by Joseph Emeras and are publicly available to download at PWA. In addition, the versions used on our simulations were sanitized according to the procedure described by Feitelson and Tsafrir [13].

The log from CEA Curie Supercomputer has 312,826 jobs and 582 users. A total number of 11,808 Intel processors and 288 NVidia GPU cards are available. According to the information available at PWA, the log from the Gaia Cluster at University of

Luxembourg has 51,987 jobs submitted by 84 users and started its operations in 2011. Regarding both workload logs, we built problem instances using a subset of the total number of jobs of each log. The problem instances are specific to each supercomputing infrastructure. In addition, we took into account only jobs that use more than one core.

Table 2 shows the proportion of jobs in the workload logs according to the number of cores requested for the CEA Curie and the Gaia clusters. In this table, it can be seen that 60% of the jobs submitted for the CEA Curie cluster requested between 2 and 16 cores. In the case of the Gaia cluster, 87% of the jobs submitted requested 2 and 16 cores.

Table 2. Cores requested proportions for the CEA Curie and the Gaia clusters.

Cores requested	Proportion	
	CEA Curie	Gaia
2 to 16	0.60	0.87
17 to 64	0.07	0.11
65 to 256	0.18	0.02
257 to 1024	0.14	0.00
1025 or more	0.01	0.00

We computed the initial priority of each submitted job applying the model described in Sect. 3. Table 3 shows the proportions of jobs for each initial priority group. It can be seen that the accuracy for 18% of CEA Curie cluster users is between 20% and 30%. In the case of Gaia cluster, the accuracy for 27% of the users is between 0% and 0.05%. The priority values and the accuracy interval associated to each tag name are shown in Table 1 of Sect. 3.

Table 3. Job priority groups and its proportions of the CEA Curie and the Gaia clusters.

Tag name	Proportion	
	CEA Curie	Gaia
g1	0.14	0.27
g2	0.07	0.08
g3	0.09	0.10
g4	0.10	0.05
g5	0.18	0.15
g6	0.16	0.15
g7	0.11	0.15
g8	0.07	0.00
g9	0.04	0.00
g10	0.04	0.05

4.2 Problem Instances

Using the information gathered in the workload analysis, we extracted a set of representative jobs from each workload log in order to make the workload instances. We also created six scenarios to simulate different scheduling policies and user behavior. The set of jobs and the scenarios were chosen to evaluate the proposed scheduler.

The jobs included in the set of jobs are in the order they appear in the workload log and they were chosen so that it was possible to stress the simulated infrastructure. Periods of less intense jobs arriving are also contemplated. The scenarios are characterized by a combination of scheduling policy applied and job runtime estimation considered.

Three scheduling policies are evaluated: (a) FCFS, (b) PSP without job aging and (c) PSP+AGING. Two type of job run time estimations are considered: perfect estimations and real user estimations. Table 4 shows the configurations assigned to each scenario.

Table 4. Scheduling policy and job estimates accuracy configured for each scenario.

Scenario	Scheduling policy	Job estimates
1	FCFS	Perfect estimates
2	PSP without aging	
3	PSP+AGING	
4	FCFS	Real user estimates
5	PSP without aging	
6	PSP+AGING	

We considered scenarios with perfect estimations in order to have best-case situations for each scheduling policy.

Scenarios 1 and 4 are used as the baseline for the comparison with scenarios 2, 3, 5, and 6.

According to information in the PWA, in the workload logs of CEA Curie and Gaia the utilization of the clusters was 29.3% and 47.9%, respectively. Taking into account the low system utilization, and in order to have a considerable number of jobs in the pending job queue, we configured a simulated infrastructure for each cluster that has a subset of the total number of processors available. It was chosen so that jobs are not necessarily executed as soon as they are submitted.

A total number of 4096 cores comprise the simulated infrastructure for CEA Curie Supercomputer. It was achieved using 1024 CPUs with 4 cores each. For the Gaia Cluster the simulated infrastructure contains 1024 cores. It was achieved using 256 CPUs with 4 cores each. No data about memory capacity of each CPU and memory demand of each job was available when preparing the simulations. Thus, these characteristics are not taken into account in order to run the simulations.

5 Experimental Analysis

In this section we report the experimental analysis of the proposed PSP+AGING algorithm. We explain the metrics used to perform the comparison between the six scenarios defined for each workload. Then, we show the characteristics of the computational platform used to run the simulations. We end the section presenting and comparing the numerical results obtained after the simulations.

The goal of the experimental analysis is to evaluate the efficacy of PSP+AGING. We achieve this goal by computing the makespan and the average waiting time for all the scenarios defined in Sect. 4. Then, we compared the results obtained between scenarios, and also between scenarios of different workloads.

All the simulations were performed in a dual-core machine with 8 GB RAM, running Ubuntu 14.10. We used the SLURM Simulator to run the simulations for each workload log. SLURM is free software and can be downloaded from [14]. We installed the software in Ubuntu OS as it was recommended by the developers of the tool.

Regarding the average waiting time, Table 5 shows the numerical results obtained after performing the simulations with the CEA Curie workload and the Gaia Cluster. It is shown the average waiting time in minutes for each scenario (from scenario 1 to 6). For the CEA Curie workload, in scenario 1 (FCFS with perfect estimates) the average waiting time is 4,569 min (i.e., 76.15 h), whereas in scenario 6 (PSP+AGING with real estimates) the average waiting time is 2,336 min (i.e., 38.93 h). The waiting time in scenario 1 for the CEA Curie workload is 1.956 times higher than in scenario 6. For the Gaia Cluster we computed similar results: the waiting time between scenario 1 (i.e., 4,358 min) and scenario 6 (i.e., 2,421 min) is 1.800 times higher than in scenario 6.

Table 5. Ratio of waiting time between the six scenarios of both workloads. Average waiting time of jobs in the simulation, reported in minutes.

Scenario	1	2	3	4	5	6
Average waiting time (minutes) CEA Curie	4,569	3,785	2,617	4,609	3,706	**2,336**
Average waiting time (minutes) Gaia cluster	4,358	3,716	2,641	5,153	3,354	**2,421**

Figure 3 shows the Average waiting time for each scheduling policy and each job runtime estimates model for the CEA Curie supercomputer workload.

According to the results reported in Fig. 3, users of CEA Curie, in the simulated scenario with a FCFS scheduler and perfect job run time estimates, had a waiting time 1.21 times higher than in the scenario with PSP scheduler and perfect estimates. In the scenario with real estimates, the waiting time in the scenario with FCFS was 1.75 times higher than in the scenario with PSP. In the case of the PSP+AGING and real job run time estimates scenario, the average waiting time is 1.97 times, and 1.57 times lower than in the scenarios with FCFS scheduler and PSP scheduler respectively.

Figure 4 reports the average waiting times for the Gaia cluster.

The results reported in Fig. 4 are similar to the ones for the Curie supercomputer. In this sense, the scenario with PSP+AGING and perfect user estimates had an average waiting time that was 1.80 times and 1.54 times lower than the scenarios with PSP scheduler and FCFS scheduler respectively.

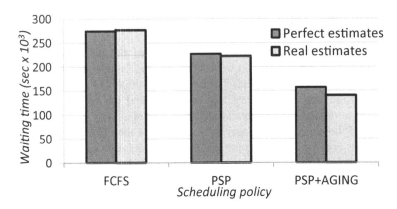

Fig. 3. Average waiting time for each scheduling policy and each job runtime estimates model for the CEA Curie supercomputer workload.

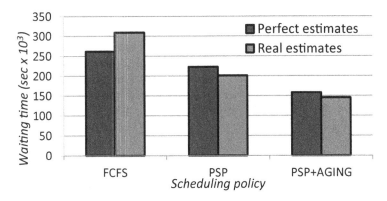

Fig. 4. Average waiting time for each scheduling policy and each job runtime estimates model for the Gaia cluster workload.

Results on both workload logs showed the same trend, in the scenarios with PSP+AGING and real user estimates. Jobs have between 1.5 times and 2.13 times the waiting time in average than scenarios without both PSP and aging.

Table 6 shows the makespan of the each scenario for the subset of jobs selected and simulated of the CEA Curie and the Gaia workload logs. The makespan in the case of the CEA Curie supercomputer varied from 15.33 days in the scenario using FCFS and real user estimates, and 17.71 days in the scenario with PSP+AGING and real user estimates. In the case of the Gaia cluster, the makespan varied between 27.62 and 29.08.

For both workloads used in the simulations, the makespan was higher when using PSP compared to FCFS, and even higher when using PSP+AGING as the scheduling policy. Moreover, the scenario with lower makespan was the one with the simplest scheduling policy and the real (and inaccurate) user estimates By using PSP and aging we achieved lower waiting times. On the other hand, we undertook the makespan of the workloads.

Table 6. Total makespan for the simulated scenarios.

Scenario	CEA Curie makespan (days)	Gaia makespan (days)
1	16.19	27.82
2	15.33	27.62
3	17.19	27.79
4	16.17	27.85
5	17.04	28.03
6	17.71	29.08

6 Conclusions and Future Work

In this paper, we present the new scheduling strategy PSP+AGING, that is a variation of the Penalty Scheduling Policy. The new algorithm includes changes in the granularity of accuracy groups and the initial priority of jobs that belong to each group. We also introduced an aging scheme that increments the priority of the jobs in each iteration of the scheduler according to the waiting time normalized with respect to the user estimation of runtime for the job.

We measure the makespan of the workloads to evaluate the benefits of the variation of PSP and the proposed aging scheme for the overall system performance. We also measured the average waiting time of jobs for each workload.

We presented an experimental evaluation in a simulated computer system environment, developed using the SLURM simulator. However, our strategies can be easily included in other popular resource management systems such as Maui.

We analyze the PSP+AGING performance of part of two real workload logs with six scenarios each varying the user runtime estimates and the scheduling policy. The main results show that introducing job priority according to the accuracy of runtime estimation and applying an aging scheme, every user experiences a drop on the waiting time of their jobs. On the other hand, the makespan is not improved.

The lines for future work include extending the experimental analysis with workloads containing a larger quantity of jobs. We also plan on running the simulations with other workloads of the PWA. In this line of work we plan on performing an experimental evaluation on a real environment: the Cluster FING at Facultad de Ingeniería of Universidad de la República.

Regarding the aging scheme we plan on extending the investigation in order to propose new algorithms to compute job aging.

References

1. Cirne, W., Berman, F.: A comprehensive model of the supercomputer workload. In: IEEE International Workshop on Workload Characterization, pp. 140–148 (2001)
2. Tsafrir, D.: Using inaccurate estimates accurately. In: Frachtenberg, E., Schwiegelshohn, U. (eds.) JSSPP 2010. LNCS, vol. 6253, pp. 208–221. Springer, Heidelberg (2010). doi:10. 1007/978-3-642-16505-4_12

3. Tsafrir, D., Etsion, Y., Feitelson, D.G.: Modeling user runtime estimates. In: Feitelson, D., Frachtenberg, E., Rudolph, L., Schwiegelshohn, U. (eds.) JSSPP 2005. LNCS, vol. 3834, pp. 1–35. Springer, Heidelberg (2005). doi:10.1007/11605300_1

4. Rocchetti, N., Iturriaga, S., Nesmachnow, S.: Including accurate user estimates in HPC schedulers: an empirical analysis. In: XXI Congreso Argentino de Ciencias de la Computación, pp. 1–10 (2015)

5. Lee, C.B., Schwartzman, Y., Hardy, J., Snavely, A.: Are user runtime estimates inherently inaccurate? In: Feitelson, D.G., Rudolph, L., Schwiegelshohn, U. (eds.) JSSPP 2004. LNCS, vol. 3277, pp. 253–263. Springer, Heidelberg (2005). doi:10.1007/11407522_14

6. Feitelson, D.: Parallel Workloads Archive. http://www.cs.huji.ac.il/labs/parallel/workload/. Accessed 12 July 2016

7. Ward Jr., W.A., Mahood, C.L., West, J.E.: Scheduling jobs on parallel systems using a relaxed backfill strategy. In: Feitelson, D.G., Rudolph, L., Schwiegelshohn, U. (eds.) JSSPP 2002. LNCS, vol. 2537, pp. 88–102. Springer, Heidelberg (2002). doi:10.1007/3-540-36180-4_6

8. Chiang, S.-H., Arpaci-Dusseau, A., Vernon, M.K.: The impact of more accurate requested runtimes on production job scheduling performance. In: Feitelson, D.G., Rudolph, L., Schwiegelshohn, U. (eds.) JSSPP 2002. LNCS, vol. 2537, pp. 103–127. Springer, Heidelberg (2002). doi:10.1007/3-540-36180-4_7

9. Hirales-Carbajal, A., Tchernykh, A., Yahyapour, R., González-García, J.L., Röblitz, T., Ramírez-Alcaraz, J.M.: Multiple workflow scheduling strategies with user runtime estimates on a grid. J. Grid Comput. **10**, 325–346 (2012)

10. Ramírez-Alcaraz, J.M., Tchernykh, A., Yahyapour, R., Schwiegelshohn, U., Quezada-Pina, A., González-García, J.L., Hirales-Carbajal, A.: Job allocation strategies with user run time estimates for online scheduling in hierarchical grids. J. Grid Comput. **9**, 95–116 (2011)

11. Tsafrir, D., Etsion, Y., Feitelson, D.G.: Backfilling using system-generated predictions rather than user runtime estimates. IEEE Trans. Parallel Distrib. Syst. **18**, 789–803 (2007)

12. Nesmachnow, S.: Computación Científica de Alto Desempeño en la Facultad de Ingeniería, Universidad de la República. Rev. Asoc. Ing. Urug. **61**(1), 12–15 (2010)

13. Feitelson, D., Tsafrir, D.: Workload sanitation for performance evaluation. In: IEEE International Symposium on Performance Analysis of Systems and Software, pp. 221–230 (2006)

14. Slurm simulator web page. https://www.bsc.es/marenostrum-support-services/services/slurm-simulator. Accessed 12 July 2016

15. Iturriaga, S., García, S., Nesmachnow, S.: An empirical study of the robustness of energy-aware schedulers for high performance computing systems under uncertainty. In: Hernández, G., Hernández, C.J.B., Díaz, G., Garino, C.G., Nesmachnow, S., Pérez-Acle, T., Storti, M., Vázquez, M. (eds.) CARLA 2014. CCIS, vol. 485, pp. 143–157. Springer, Heidelberg (2014). doi:10.1007/978-3-662-45483-1_11

Accelerating All-Sources BFS Metrics on Multi-core Clusters for Large-Scale Complex Network Analysis

Alberto Garcia-Robledo[1]([✉]), Arturo Diaz-Perez[1],
and Guillermo Morales-Luna[2]

[1] Information Technology Laboratory, Cinvestav-Tamaulipas, Cd. Victoria, Mexico
`algarcia@tamps.cinvestav.mx`
[2] Cinvestav-IPN, Mexico City, Mexico

Abstract. All-Sources BFS (AS-BFS) is the main building block in a variety of complex network metric algorithms, such as the average path length and the betweenness centrality. However, AS-BFS calculations involve as many full BFS traversals as the total number of vertices, rendering AS-BFS impractical on commodity systems for real-world graphs with millions of vertices and links. In this paper we present our experience with the acceleration of AS-BFS graph metrics on multi-core HPC clusters by outlining hybrid coarse-grain parallel algorithms for computing the average path-length, the diameter and the betweenness centrality of complex networks in a lock-free fashion. We report speedups of up to $171\times$ on a heterogeneous cluster of 12-core Intel Xeon and 32-core AMD Opteron multi-core nodes; as well as resource utilizations of up to 75%.

Keywords: Network Science · Complex networks · Multi-core HPC clusters · All-Sources BFS · Complex network metrics · Betweenness centrality

1 Introduction

Recent years have witnessed the rise of Network Science [5], defined as "the study of network representations of physical, biological, and social phenomena leading to predictive models of these phenomena." Such representations are known as *complex networks*. The measurement of complex networks and their application in Social Network Analysis, biological network analysis and link analysis have renewed the interest in classical graph problems like Breadth-First Search (BFS). A variation of BFS, All-Sources BFS (AS-BFS), appears as a recurrent building block in the implementation of shortest-path-based metrics such as the average path length, the graph diameter, and the betweenness centrality [6]. AS-BFS metrics have been used for the analysis of errors caused by attacks to the structure of a national airport network, the analysis of the vulnerability of the Internet, to identify key proteins in protein interaction networks and to reveal important agents in terrorist social networks.

© Springer International Publishing AG 2017
C.J. Barrios Hernández et al. (Eds.): CARLA 2016, CCIS 697, pp. 61–75, 2017.
DOI: 10.1007/978-3-319-57972-6_5

The calculation of AS-BFS metrics involves as many full BFS traversals as the total number of vertices, requiring $O(nm)$ time, where n is the number of vertices and m the number of links of the graph. This makes AS-BFS calculations unfeasible on commodity systems for large-scale real-world graphs with millions of vertices and links. We have estimated, for example, that obtaining a single measurement of the betweenness centrality of a citation network with 3M vertices and 16M links would take 6 months on a high-performance AMD Opteron processor when exploiting an efficient sequential algorithm. One solution is to approximate AS-BFS measurements, but this is not always possible. The betweenness centrality, for example, is hard to estimate, and the quality of the approximation depends on the selected source vertices [1].

AS-BFS exhibits different levels of parallelism that can be exploited to tackle large execution times by means of parallel computing. The predominant architecture in the TOP500 supercomputing index is the HPC cluster: a collection of complete and independent commercially-available systems connected through high-speed specialized networks. As of June 2016, the top 10 fastest systems in the index are HPC clusters powered by general-purpose multi-core processors such as the Intel Xeon, the AMD Opteron, and the IBM Power BQC. However, some of the current works that parallelize AS-BFS metrics, like the betweenness centrality, propose schemes for specialized and not widely-available (sometimes discontinued) multi-threaded architectures, such as the Cray MT-2 and the Cray XMT [2,8]. Other works only experiment on single-system multi-core platforms [3,9].

We believe that previously proposed multi-grain parallel algorithms designed for custom architectures like the Cray XMT are not suitable for modern multi-core cluster architectures. In this work we present our experience with the experimentation of a hybrid (process- and thread-level) coarse-grain parallel scheme for accelerating a variety of AS-BFS-based algorithms on HPC clusters of commercial multi-core processors. We span as many tasks as the number of vertices in the graph, each task consisting of a single full BFS traversal. Tasks are first distributed among the available computing nodes. Then, in each node, tasks are further distributed among the node's cores. All task groups are then executed in parallel in a lock-free fashion, requiring only an aggregation step at the final stage. We outline coarse grain parallel algorithms for calculating the average path length, the diameter and the betweenness centrality metrics. The parallel implementations are tested in HPC clusters of AMD Opteron and Intel Xeon processors. We report estimated speedups of up to two orders of magnitude and resource usage efficiencies of up to 75%.

2   Preliminaries

Let $G = (V, E)$ be a graph or complex network with a vertex set V and an edge set E. Let $n = |V|$ and $m = |E|$. Let d_{uv} denote the shortest-path-length between vertices u and v. The *diameter* D is defined as the length of the longest shortest-path in G:

$$D = \max_{u \neq v}\{d_{uv}\}. \tag{1}$$

In their seminal work, Watts and Strogatz [11] found that the majority of the vertex pairs in complex networks are only a few steps away, in spite of their elevated number of vertices. This property can be mathematically characterized by the *average shortest-path length L*:

$$L = \frac{1}{n(n-1)} \sum_{u \neq v} d_{uv}, \tag{2}$$

which grows logarithmically with n in a variety of real-world graphs [6]. The larger the number of shortest-paths in which a vertex participates, the more the importance of that vertex. It is possible to quantify the importance of a vertex u in terms of the proportion of shortest-paths that pass through u. This proportion is known as *vertex betweenness centrality BC(u)*:

$$BC(u) = \sum_{v,w \in V, v \neq w} \frac{g(u,v,w)}{g(v,w)}, \tag{3}$$

where $g(v,w)$ is the total number of shortest-paths between v and w and $g(u,v,w)$ is the number of shortest-paths between v and w that pass through u, for all $v, w \in V$, $v \neq w$.

AS-BFS consists on performing n full BFS traversals, starting each traversal from a different source vertex. AS-BFS is used to implement these and other distance-based metrics, given its efficiency on sparse graphs. BFS can be easily implemented with the help of a queue, and takes only $O(n + m)$ time. AS-BFS performs n full BFS traversals. Thus, AS-BFS time complexity is $O(n(n + m)) \approx O(nm)$. To alleviate large execution times of AS-BFS on large graphs, any combination of the following levels of parallelism can be exploited:

1. *Coarse-grain parallelism.* The parallel algorithm spans n concurrent tasks. Each task consists of a full BFS traversal. All tasks proceed in parallel with no synchronization operations involved.
2. *Medium-grain parallelism.* For each BFS frontier[1], the parallel algorithm spans as many tasks as vertices in the frontier. Thus, each task consists of exploring the neighborhood of a single vertex in the current BFS frontier. In the presence of common neighbors, synchronization operations might be required.
3. *Fine-grain parallelism.* For each BFS frontier in a single-source BFS, the parallel algorithm spans as many tasks as the edges outgoing from the vertices in the current frontier. Thus, each task consists of the exploration of a single edge going out of the current BFS frontier.

The selection of the appropriate parallel granularity depends on the target hardware architecture. Regardless of the level of parallelism, AS-BFS poses challenges in parallel processing, including dynamic and non-contiguous memory access, unstructured parallelism, and a low amount of arithmetic operations [10].

---

[1] The BFS frontier keeps the nodes of the recently visited BFS level, being the ith frontier the set of nodes at (shortest) distance i from the source node.

3   Related Work

Bader et al. [2] proposed the first parallel BC algorithm, designed for the IBM p5 570 and the Cray MTA-2 shared-memory architectures. They propose a multi-grain coarse + fine-grain scheme that parallelizes the BFS computation, as well as the outer level to saturate the MTA-2 multi-threaded architecture.

The approach in [2] is used in [3] to accelerate the BC, closeness centrality and D algorithms, among other metrics. Bader and Madduri experimented with large-scale Protein Interaction Networks on a 8-core Sun UltraSPARC T1 and a 2-core multi-threaded Intel Xeon. Near-to-linear speedups are reported. However experiments were conducted only on a single multi-threaded CPU at a time. In [8] it is presented another multi-grain coarse + fine-grain parallel BC algorithm for the Cray XMT with the Thread-storm processor. Unlike the work in [2], the new proposed algorithm is performed without locks by considering alternate representations for the predecessor multi-sets. However, atomic addition operations are still required to protect the increments to the path count and the predecessor multi-set in the fine-grain algorithm.

In [9] it is reported a low-space complexity parallel algorithm that "eliminates access conflicts to the shared memory cells" by utilizing "an edge-numbering strategy" and a "triple array data structure recording the shortest path for eliminating conflicts to access the shared memory." Experiments were conducted on the Intel Clovertown and Sun Niagara 1 single-node multi-core systems. In [7] it is outlined a distributed BC parallel algorithm that exploits parallelism within the shortest-paths computation through "label-correcting single-source shortest-path algorithms" while "maintaining low space complexity." They experiment on random Erdös-Rényi and synthetic R-MAT graphs on a cluster of 128 nodes. The architecture of nodes is not provided.

Overall, multi-grain strategies like the one reported in [2] are suitable for custom architectures like the MTA-2, but the fine-grain parallelization of single-source BFS's would incur into high overheads in modern multi-core architectures. Also, note that the MTA-2 and the IBM System p5 570 are not longer available in the market, and that the Cray XMT supports a specialized threading hardware model that is not necessarily compatible with current multi-core CPU architectures. Besides [7], none of the reviewed works exploit clusters of the experimented architectures. For the BC it is theoretically possible to perform the BFS traversals concurrently with no synchronization costs: processing units compute their own partial sums of the centrality value [3,10], and then all the sums are aggregated by exploiting an efficient reduction operation [3]. Current works avoid this level of parallelism since it requires a copy of all data structures in memory for each thread [9].

Nonetheless, we claim that the coarse-grain parallel AS-BFS is the best-suited approach for state-of-the-art multi-core clusters that are readily equipped with enough system memory to handle large-scale complex networks and AS-BFS-related data structures.

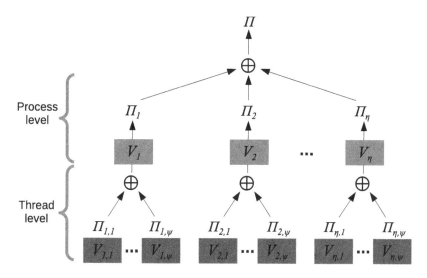

Fig. 1. Hybrid coarse-grain parallel algorithm for accelerating aggregable AS-BFS complex network metrics. η and Ψ are the number of processes and threads per process, respectively. V_p and $V_{p,h}$ are the partitions of V mapped to processes and threads, respectively. Π_p and $\Pi_{p,h}$ are partial measurements calculated by processes and threads, respectively. Π is the final aggregated complex network metric value.

4 Hybrid Coarse-Grain Parallel AS-BFS Scheme

Let Π be a complex network metric measurement that can be calculated by aggregating partial AS-BFS measurements over subsets $V_i \subseteq V$ of the vertex set, i.e. $\Pi = \Pi_1 \oplus \Pi_2 \oplus \ldots$ with $V = V_1 \cup V_2 \cup \ldots$, where $\oplus$ is an aggregation operator, such as max ($\vee$), sum ($+$), or vector sum[2] ($\boxplus$).

We call such metrics *AS-BFS aggregable metrics*. Examples include (but are not limited to): the graph diameter D, the average path-length L, and the betweenness centrality BC. The calculation of all partial Π_i measurements can be performed concurrently, with no locks or inter-process synchronization operations. The granularity of the partitioning of the vertex set $V = V_1, V_2..$ for parallel processing depends on the parallel hardware characteristics. We describe a general hybrid coarse-grain parallel scheme that exploits the parallelism inherent to AS-BFS aggregable metrics and that is suitable for modern multi-core clusters, in order to accelerate a series of distance-based metrics on large complex networks without the need of locks.

Let P be the set of launched processes and $\eta = |P|$ be the number of such processes. Let H_p be the set of threads of process p and $\Psi = |H_p|$ be the number of threads per process. Let $B = \{\beta_1, \beta_2..\beta_\eta\}$ be the load distribution vector,

---

[2] Given two sets $X = x_1, x_2, x_3..$ and $Y = y_1, y_2, y_3..$, $|X| = |Y|$, a vector sum is defined here as $X \boxplus Y = x_1 + y_1, x_2 + y_2, x_3 + y_3 \ldots$.

with $\beta_i \in [0,1]$ and $\sum_{i=1}^{\eta} \beta_i = 1$. The hybrid coarse-grain parallel scheme can be divided into three steps (Fig. 1):

- *Step (1) Vertex partitioning and distribution.* First, the parallel scheme distributes the vertices of the network in a hybrid hierarchy of processes and threads. At the process level, it distributes the vertices among the processes: $V_1, V_2..V_\eta$, $\bigcup_i V_i = V$, such that $|V_1|, |V_2|..|V_\eta| \approx \beta_1 n, \beta_2 n..\beta_\eta n$. At the thread level, for each process p the parallel scheme distributes the vertices V_p among p's threads in an evenly fashion: $V_{p,1}, V_{p,2}..V_{p,\Psi}$, $\bigcup_i V_{p,i} = V_p$.
- *Step (2) Partial measurements calculation.* Once all vertex partitions have been distributed, all threads of all processes are run in parallel. Each thread h of process p performs its BFS traversals starting from the sources in its partition $V_{p,h}$ in a fully lock-free fashion, with no inter-process synchronization involved. Each thread calculates the partial metric value $\Pi_{p,h}$ corresponding to its vertex partition.
- *Step (3) Partial measurements aggregation.* Once threads have finished their BFS traversals, their partial metric measurements $\Pi_{p,h}$ are aggregated at the thread's level as follows: $\Pi_p = \Pi_{p,1} \oplus \Pi_{p,2} \oplus \ldots \Pi_{p,\Psi}$. Then, at the process's level, the final metric value is calculated by aggregating the processes partial values $\Pi = \Pi_1 \oplus \Pi_2 \oplus \ldots \Pi_\eta$.

The parallel time of the described scheme is $O(nm/\eta\Psi) + O(Q)$, where $O(Q)$ is the aggregation time, which can be neglected (no sync costs are involved [2]) if aggregations are trivial or if efficient message-passing reduction operators are used. From a process perspective, the spatial complexity is $O(\Psi n + n + m)$ since each process only needs to keep a single copy of the whole graph structure[3]; and each process's thread uses its own local BFS data structures to avoid the need for locks. Assuming that each process runs on its own processing node, the linear-space requirements become reasonable on high-end modern multi-core systems.

4.1 Parallel Metrics Algorithms

We now describe how to adapt the hybrid coarse-grain parallel scheme for the calculation of three aggregable AS-BFS complex network metrics: the graph diameter D, the average path-length L, and the betweenness centrality BC. For each metric, two algorithms are presented:

- *Hybrid coarse-grain parallel algorithm.* Includes the three steps exposed before; and indicates how to aggregate the partial measurements $\Pi_{p,h}$ at the thread level and the partial measurements Π_p at the process level. To calculate the values $\Pi_{p,h}$, each launched thread runs a per-thread lock-free algorithm on its assigned vertex partition $V_{p,h}$.
- *Lock-free thread algorithm.* The details of this algorithm depends on the AS-BFS metric that is being measured. In general, every thread performs BFS traversals starting from $s \in V_{p,h}$ by using a queue Q. The shortest distance

---

[3] The $O(n + m)$ graph data structure can be shared among all the process's threads.

Input: $G = (V, E), P, B$
Output: D
1: partitioning of V for load-distribution according to B
2: **for** process $p \in P$ **in parallel do**
3:     $V_p \leftarrow$ partition of V of process p
4:     $H_p \leftarrow$ threads of process p
5:     **for** thread $h \in H_p$ **in parallel do**
6:         $V_{p,h} \leftarrow$ partition of V_p of thread h
7:         $D_{p,h} \leftarrow$ run per-thread algorithm with parameters $G, V_{p,h}$
8:         $D_p \leftarrow$ **threads reduce max** $D_{p,h}$
9:     **end for**
10:     $D \leftarrow$ **processes reduce max** D_p
11: **end for**
12: **return** D

(a) Hybrid parallel algorithm for D

Input: $G = (V, E), V_{p,h} \subseteq V$
Output: $D_{p,h}$
1: $D_{p,h} \leftarrow 0$
2: **for** $s \in V_{p,h}$ **do**
3:     $Q \leftarrow$ empty queue
4:     $d[w] \leftarrow -1$ **for** $w \in V$; $d[s] \leftarrow 0$
5:     enqueue s in Q
6:     **while** Q is not empty **do**
7:         $v \leftarrow$ dequeue from Q
8:         **if** $d[v] > D_{p,h}$ **then**
9:             $D_{p,h} \leftarrow d[v]$
10:         **end if**
11:         **for** each neighbor w of v **do**
12:             **if** $d[w] < 0$ **then**
13:                 enqueue w into Q
14:                 $d[w] \leftarrow d[v] + 1$
15:             **end if**
16:         **end for**
17:     **end while**
18: **end for**
19: **return** $D_{p,h}$

(b) Lock-free thread algorithm for $D_{p,h}$

Fig. 2. Hybrid coarse-grain parallel algorithm for the diameter D

Input: $G = (V, E), P, B$
Output: L
1: partitioning of V for load-distribution according to B
2: **for** $p \in P$ **in parallel do**
3:     $V_p \leftarrow$ partition of V of process p
4:     $H_p \leftarrow$ threads of process p
5:     **for** $h \in H_p$ **in parallel do**
6:         $V_{p,h} \leftarrow$ partition of V_p of thread h
7:         $\gamma_{p,h}, \phi_{p,h} \leftarrow$ run per-thread algorithm with parameters $G, V_{p,h}$
8:         $\gamma_p \leftarrow$ **threads reduce sum** $\gamma_{p,h}$
9:         $\phi_p \leftarrow$ **threads reduce sum** $\phi_{p,h}$
10:     **end for**
11:     $\gamma \leftarrow$ **processes reduce sum** γ_p
12:     $\phi \leftarrow$ **processes reduce sum** ϕ_p
13: **end for**
14: $L \leftarrow \frac{\gamma}{\phi}$
15: **return** L

(a) Hybrid parallel algorithm for L

Input: $G = (V, E), V_{p,h} \subseteq V$
Output: $\gamma_{p,h}, \phi_{p,h}$
1: $\gamma_{p,h} \leftarrow \phi_{p,h} \leftarrow 0$
2: **for** $s \in V_{p,h}$ **do**
3:     $Q \leftarrow$ empty queue
4:     $d[w] \leftarrow -1$ **for** $w \in V$; $d[s] \leftarrow 0$
5:     enqueue s in Q
6:     **while** Q is not empty **do**
7:         $v \leftarrow$ dequeue from Q
8:         **for** each neighbor w of v **do**
9:             **if** $d[w] < 0$ **then**
10:                 enqueue w into Q
11:                 $d[w] \leftarrow d[v] + 1$
12:                 $\gamma_{p,h} \leftarrow \gamma_{p,h} + d[w]$
13:                 $\phi_{p,h} \leftarrow \phi_{p,h} + 1$
14:             **end if**
15:         **end for**
16:     **end while**
17: **end for**
18: **return** $\gamma_{p,h}, \phi_{p,h}$

(b) Lock-free thread algorithm for $\gamma_{p,h}$ and $\phi_{p,h}$

Fig. 3. Hybrid coarse-grain parallel algorithm for the average path-length L

$d[w]$ from s to the current visited node w and the partial measurement $\Pi_{p,h}$ are updated as the algorithm traverses the graph. Each thread has its own copy of partial data structures such as Q, $d[1..n]$ and $\Pi_{p,h}$. No locks are required.

Input: $G = (V, E), V_{p,h} \subseteq V$
Output: $BC_{p,h}[1..n]$
1: $BC_{p,h}[v] \leftarrow 0$ for $v \in V_{p,h}$
2: for $s \in V_{p,h}$ do
3:      $Q \leftarrow$ empty queue
4:      $S \leftarrow$ empty stack
5:      $R[1..n] \leftarrow$ empty list
6:      $g[w] \leftarrow 0$ for $w \in V$; $g[s] \leftarrow 1$
7:      $d[w] \leftarrow -1$ for $w \in V$; $d[s] \leftarrow 0$
8:      enqueue s in Q
9:      while Q is not empty do
10:        $v \leftarrow$ dequeue from Q
11:        push v into S
12:        for each neighbor w of v do
13:          if $d[w] < 0$ then
14:            enqueue w into Q
15:            $d[w] \leftarrow d[v] + 1$
16:          end if
17:          if $d[w] = d[v] + 1$ then
18:            $g[w] \leftarrow g[w] + g[v]$
19:            append v into $R[w]$
20:          end if
21:        end for
22:      end while
23:      $\delta[w] \leftarrow 0$ for $w \in V$
24:      while S is not empty do
25:        $w \leftarrow$ pop from S
26:        for $v \in R[w]$ do

Input: $G = (V, E), P, B$
Output: $BC[1..n]$
1: partitioning of V for load-distribution according to B
2: for $p \in P$ in parallel do
3:      $V_p \leftarrow$ partition of V of process p
4:      $H_p \leftarrow$ threads of process p
5:      for $h \in H_p$ in parallel do
6:        $V_{p,h} \leftarrow$ partition of V_p of thread h
7:        $BC_{p,h} \leftarrow$ run per-thread algorithm with parameters $G, V_{p,h}$
8:        $BC_p \leftarrow$ threads reduce vector sum $BC_{p,h}$
9:      end for
10:    $BC \leftarrow$ processes reduce vector sum BC_p
11: end for
12: return BC

27:        $\delta[v] \leftarrow \delta[v] + \frac{g[v]}{g[w]}(1 + \delta[w])$
28:      end for
29:      if $w \neq s$ then
30:        $BC_{p,h}[w] \leftarrow BC_{p,h}[w] + \delta[w]$
31:      end if
32:    end while
33: end for
34: return $BC_{p,h}$

(a) Hybrid parallel algorithm for BC

(b) Lock-free thread algorithm for $BC_{p,h}$

Fig. 4. Hybrid coarse-grain parallel algorithm for the betweenness centrality BC

Diameter. Algorithms in Fig. 2 show the hybrid coarse-grain parallel approach for $\Pi = D$. Each thread performs its share of BFS traversals to calculate the partial diameter $D_{p,h}$, which is the longest shortest-path found from any source in $V_{p,h}$. For the thread-level aggregation step, values $D_{p,h}$ are reduced (max operation) to obtain $D_p = D_{p,1} \vee D_{p,2} \vee ..D_{p,\Psi}$ for all p, respectively. Finally, in the process-level aggregation step, values of D_p are reduced (max operation again) to obtain the final measurement $D = D_1 \vee D_2 \vee ..D_\eta$.

Avg. Path Length. Let γ be the sum of the shortest-path lengths between any pair of vertices in G, and ϕ be the number of such paths. L can be calculated in parallel by computing $\Pi = \gamma$ and $\Pi' = \phi$ separately, and then obtaining the ratio $L = \gamma/\phi$. Algorithms in Fig. 3 show the hybrid coarse-grain parallel approach for L. All threads perform their shares of BFS traversals in parallel to

Table 1. Experimented road, Wikipedia, Internet, and citation complex network instances. The edge traversals column shows the number of edge traversals needed to execute an AS-BFS-based metric like D and L. For BC the number of traversals is twice the value shown in the table, since the Brandes algorithm traverses the BFS trees twice.

Graph	Type	n	m	Edge traversals
roadNet-CA	Road	1,965,206	$5,533,214$	2.17×10^{13}
WikiTalk	Wikipedia	2,394,385	$5,021,410$	2.4×10^{13}
as-skitter	Internet	1,696,415	$11,095,298$	3.76×10^{13}
cit-Patents	Citation	3,774,768	$16,518,948$	1.24×10^{14}

calculate their partial $\gamma_{p,h}$ and $\phi_{p,h}$. In the thread-level aggregation step, values $\gamma_{p,h}$ and $\phi_{p,h}$ are reduced (sum operator) to obtain $\gamma_p = \gamma_{p,1} + \gamma_{p,2} + ..\gamma_{p,\Psi}$ and $\phi_p = \phi_{p,1} + \phi_{p,2} + ..\phi_{p,\Psi}$ for all p, respectively. In the process-level aggregation step, measurements of γ_p and ϕ_p are reduced (sum operation again) to obtain $\gamma = \gamma_1 + \gamma_2 + ..\gamma_\eta$ and $\phi = \phi_1 + \phi_2 + ..\phi_\eta$. The ratio $L = \gamma/\phi$ is then calculated in the master process to obtain the final graph average path-length.

Avg. Betweenness Centrality. The betweenness centrality vector $\Pi = BC$ can be calculated partially by performing BFS traversals from different sets of vertices. Partial vectors can be then summed up to obtain the final vector BC. Algorithms in Fig. 4 show the hybrid coarse-grain parallel approach for BC. All threads perform their shares of single-source BFS's in parallel to calculate the partial betweenness vectors $BC_{p,h}$. To this end, each thread runs the Brandes algorithm [4] for its share $V_{p,h}$, which calculates the centrality in two steps: single-source BFS traversals and backtrack accumulation. Next, in the thread-level aggregation step, vectors $BC_{p,h}$ are reduced (vector sum operation) to obtain $BC_p = BC_{p,1} \boxplus BC_{p,2} \boxplus ..BC_{p,\Psi}$ for all p. Finally, in the process-level aggregation step, vectors BC_p are reduced (vector sum operation again) to obtain the final betweenness vector $BC = BC_1 \boxplus BC_2 \boxplus ..BC_\eta$.

5 Experimental Setup

In this section we list the studied real-world complex network instances, present the specifications of the experimented hardware platforms, offer commentaries on load balancing across processing nodes, and describe our methodology for estimating sequential times in order evaluate the performance of the presented hybrid coarse-grain parallel scheme.

5.1 Graph Instances and Hardware Platforms

We experimented the three metric algorithms on four real-world complex networks listed in Table 1. We considered all the connected components of the undirected version of each graph. Note that the diameter of the roadNet-CA network is up to two orders of magnitude larger than the diameter of the other graphs.

Experiments were performed on two hardware platform settings:

1. *Opteron cluster.* Homogeneous multi-core cluster of seven 32-core nodes powered by AMD Opteron 6274 (Interlagos) CPU's at 2.2 GHz and 64 GB of RAM (for a total of seven nodes and 224 cores). The parallel algorithm for BC on the cit-Patents graph, and the parallel algorithms for D and L on all complex networks ran on this cluster.

2. *Opteron-Xeon cluster.* Heterogeneous multi-core cluster of six 32-core nodes powered by AMD Opteron 6274 CPU's and 64 GB of RAM + three 12-core nodes powered by Intel Xeon X5675 CPU's at 3.06 GHz and 48 GB of RAM (for a total of nine nodes and 228 cores). The parallel BC algorithm on the roadNet-CA, WikiTalk and as-skitter graphs ran on this cluster.

5.2   Load Balance and Data Aggregation

For the Opteron cluster we evenly distributed the vertices among the processing nodes, i.e. $b_p \in B \approx \lceil n/\eta \rceil$ for all p, since all nodes had the same computing characteristics. For the Opteron-Xeon cluster we first profiled the performance of the Opteron nodes and the Xeon nodes, separately, by running a predefined number of multi-threaded single-source BFS's. Then, based on the observed times, we manually tunned the vector B by trial and error until achieving a reasonably good observable load balance between the Opteron and Xeon nodes in the first stage of execution.

Reported parallel times do not include the aggregation times at the process-level since this aggregation is trivial for the diameter and average path-length[4]. Although the aggregation step for the betweenness centrality is more involved and may have a higher impact[5], such an impact has a negligible effect on the overall performance since the bottleneck remains in the AS-BFS step.

5.3   Single-Core Performance Estimation

To measure the benefits of the proposed parallel scheme, we first needed to obtain the total execution time of sequential implementations. Since AS-BFS sequential execution times are prohibitively large for the experimented graphs, specially for the betweenness centrality, we instead estimated these times as follows.

For estimating how long a single sequential BFS takes, we first profiled the performance of a single thread on an AMD Opteron processor by running 5,000 single-source BFS's from random sources. Times that were several orders of magnitude lower than the mean time were considered as outliers and

---

[4] It only requires the communication of $O(\eta)$ integers to the master process, with $\eta = 7$ and $\eta = 9$ for the Opteron cluster and the Opteron-Xeon cluster, respectively.

[5] It requires the communication of $O(\eta)$ vectors of size $O(n)$ to the master process.

Table 2. Statistics on the 5,000 single-thread BFS time measurements (in seconds) and estimated total AS-BFS time (in days) on an AMD Opteron 6274 processor. Time $\mu_T - 3\sigma_T$ represents the estimated time needed by a single thread to perform a single BFS traversal, whereas t_{est} represents the estimated time needed by a single thread to complete the AS-BFS traversal and to produce the final metric value.

Metric	Graph	Min (s)	Max (s)	μ_T (s)	σ_T (s)	$\mu_T - 3\sigma_T$ (s)	t_{est} (days)
Diameter D	roadNet-CA	0.309	0.573	0.500	0.085	0.246	**5.606**
	WikiTalk	0.320	0.660	0.379	0.010	0.348	**9.638**
	as-skitter	0.385	0.641	0.563	0.028	0.479	**9.408**
	cit-Patents	1.879	2.262	1.990	0.056	1.822	**79.613**
Path-length L	roadNet-CA	0.302	0.740	0.534	0.129	0.146	**3.313**
	WikiTalk	0.345	0.607	0.371	0.009	0.344	**9.533**
	as-skitter	0.410	0.796	0.620	0.043	0.491	**9.650**
	cit-Patents	1.897	2.783	2.199	0.118	1.845	**80.587**
Betweenness BC	roadNet-CA	0.039	1.850	1.295	0.215	0.650	**14.787**
	WikiTalk	0.735	1.583	1.111	0.074	0.889	**24.625**
	as-skitter	1.249	3.111	2.030	0.210	1.399	**27.468**
	cit-Patents	0.073	8.876	6.608	0.728	4.423	**193.217**

as such discarded. Then, given the set of single-thread time measurements T (in seconds), the *estimated total AS-BFS sequential time* t_{est} was calculated as $t_{est} = n(\mu_T - 3\sigma_T)$, where μ_T is the average time and σ_T is the standard deviation of T. Three standard deviations were subtracted to avoid overly-pessimistic estimations of the sequential AS-BFS times that could lead to overly-optimistic (e.g. super-linear) speedup values of the parallel implementations[6]. Table 2 shows statistics on the 5,000 single-thread time measurements and the estimated AS-BFS sequential times. The highest estimated t_{est} time corresponds to the sequential BC algorithm on the cit-Patents graph, which would take 193.217 days (6.4 months), followed by the sequential L and D algorithms on the same graph, with estimations of 80.587 days (2.68 months) and 79.613 days (2.65 months), respectively.

6 Experimental Results

Similarly to the Graph500 benchmark, we report raw processing rates measured in Traversed Edges Per Second (TEPS). Let k_w be the degree or number of neighbors of node w. A BFS traverses all the neighbors of each vertex, this is $\sum_{w \in V} k_w = 2m$ edge traversals. Since AS-BFS performs n BFS traversals, the estimated rate of traversed edges per second for AS-BFS on a single-thread is given by $\text{TEPS}_{est} = \frac{2Cnm}{t_{est}}$, while the observed rate of traversed edges per second by the parallel implementations is given by $\text{TEPS}_{par} = \frac{2Cnm}{t_{par}}$, where $C = 1$ for

---

[6] According to the 3-standard deviation rule of thumb, $\pm\mu_T - 3\sigma_T$ accounts for 99.73% of the time measurements, assuming that T is normally distributed.

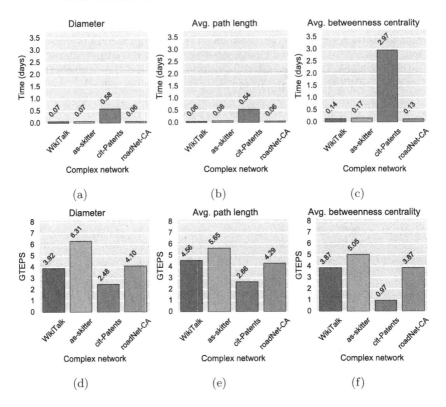

Fig. 5. Observed execution times in days (a, b, c) and traversed edges per second in GTEPS (d, e, f).

the D and L metrics, $C = 2$ for the BC metric (BFS traversals and backtrack accumulation), and t_{par} is the observed execution parallel time on the multi-core clusters (in seconds).

Figure 5(a–c) show the parallel execution times t_{par} in days. All metrics are of the same computational complexity and showed similar running times. Note, however, that the performance was dependent on the complex network instance. Times on the cit-Patents network is several times longer than for the other three networks for the three complex network metrics. This is caused in part by the higher number of edges of this graph (16M edges for cit-Patents vs. 5.02, 5.35M and 11M edges for WikiTalk, roadNet-CA and as-skitter, respectively).

The performance of BFS is strongly influenced by the diameter D of graphs. However, the diameter did not play an important role in our case: times for the high-diameter roadNet-CA network were comparable to other complex networks with lower diameter. This can be explained by the fact that, unlike fine-grain parallel BFS implementations, the coarse-grain AS-BFS does not require the synchronization of the processing units for each BFS frontier. This makes coarse-grain AS-BFS performance less sensitive to large D. In [2] it is noted that the execution time is highly dependent on the size of the giant component of

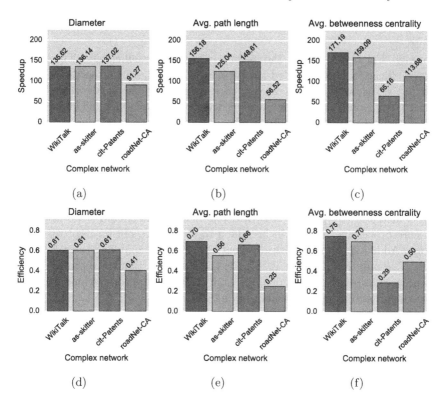

Fig. 6. Speedups over the single-thread estimated time (a, b, c) and estimated efficiencies (d, e, f).

real graphs. However, the giant component of the cit-Patents and the as-skitter graphs accounts for at least 99% of the vertices, yet the observed parallel times for these graphs were noticeably different despite the fact that their sizes are comparable.

Figure 5(d–f) show the observed parallel data throughput TEPS$_{par}$ in GTEPS (1×10^9 TEPS). Highest observed GTEPS corresponded to the as-skitter graph: 6.31, 5.65 and 5.05 GTEPS for D, L and BC, respectively. In contrast, lowest observed GTEPS corresponded to the cit-Patents graph: 2.48, 2.66 and 0.97 GTEPS for D, L and BC, respectively. Again, the cit-Patents appeared as the "hardest" graph to process for all evaluated complex network metrics.

Figure 6(a–c) show the speedups of the parallel algorithms over the estimated throughput of the single-thread performance. The highest observed speedup corresponded to the parallel BC algorithm on the WikiTalk graph (171.19×), whereas the lowest one corresponded to the L algorithm on the roadNet-CA (56.52×). The effect of the large diameter was more noticeable here: the roadNet-CA caused the lowest speedup for the D and L algorithms, and the second lowest speedup for the BC algorithm as well. Nonetheless, our parallel implementations showed average speedups[7] of 125.01×, 121.58× and 127.27× for D, L and BC, respectively.

Finally, Fig. 6(d–f) show the resource utilization efficiency. The highest observed efficiency corresponded to the parallel BC algorithm on the WikiTalk graph (0.75), whereas the lowest one corresponded to the L algorithm on the roadNet-CA graph (0.25). Average efficiencies[8] were 0.56, 0.54 and 0.56 for D, L and BC, respectively. Lowest efficiencies can be attributed to insufficient memory bandwidth when running the algorithms for 32 and 12 threads in each Opteron and Xeon node, respectively, given that BFS is memory-bounded in large complex networks due to its irregular memory access patterns.

Although the betweenness centrality computation is much more involved[9], observed TEPS, accelerations and efficiencies were comparable to that of simpler AS-BFS metrics. The presented hybrid parallel scheme should scale well: more multi-core processing nodes can be added to clusters to obtain improved accelerations. Additional nodes with different computing capabilities can be added as well. The only requirement is to tune the load distribution vector B to balance the work properly. Additional research is needed to produce an on-line load balance algorithm to perform this tunning dynamically.

7   Conclusions

We presented hybrid coarse-grain parallel algorithms for evaluating AS-BFS complex network metrics on clusters of commercially available multi-core nodes. The approach distributes the BFS traversals hierarchically among the processing nodes and then the process's threads, run the BFS traversals in parallel in a lock-free fashion to calculate partial measurements, and aggregates the partial measurements in the final step. Experiments on two multi-core clusters with Intel Xeon and AMD Opteron multi-core processors showed speedups of up to 171× and an utilization efficiency of up to 75%.

As of future work, the load distribution vector can be tuned algorithmically in a way that work is distributed as evenly as possible in face of dynamic workload variations induced, for example, by graphs with unbalanced connected components on heterogeneous clusters. The proposed parallel scheme can be extended to accelerate other AS-BFS aggregable metrics, such as the edge betweenness centrality, the stress centrality, the closeness centrality, and the central point dominance. Further study is needed to go deeper into the correlation between different network properties and the AS-BFS parallel performance to identify key features of complex networks to help us to improve performance.

The presented parallel AS-BFS scheme will be used to develop a Web repository of complex network measurements and analysis of compute intensive graph features on publicly available complex network datasets, by exploiting the Cinvestav's ABACUS multi-core cluster architecture.

---

[7] Average of speedups of the four experimented graphs for a given algorithm.

[8] Average of efficiencies of the four experimented graphs for a given algorithm.

[9] It requires maintaining a BFS stack, a queue and a predecessor list.

Acknowledgments. The authors acknowledge to the General Coordination of Information and Communications Technologies (CGSTIC) at Cinvestav for providing HPC resources on the Hybrid Cluster Supercomputer "Xiuhcoatl", that have contributed to the research results reported within this document.

References

1. Bader, D.A., Kintali, S., Madduri, K., Mihail, M.: Approximating betweenness centrality. In: Bonato, A., Chung, F.R.K. (eds.) WAW 2007. LNCS, vol. 4863, pp. 124–137. Springer, Heidelberg (2007). doi:10.1007/978-3-540-77004-6_10

2. Bader, D.A., Madduri, K.: Parallel algorithms for evaluating centrality indices in real-world networks. In: Proceedings of 2006 International Conference on Parallel Processing, August 2006

3. Bader, D.A., Madduri, K.: A graph-theoretic analysis of the human protein-interaction network using multicore parallel algorithms. Parallel Comput. **34**(11), 627–639 (2008)

4. Brandes, U.: A faster algorithm for betweenness centrality. J. Math. Sociol. **25**(2), 163–177 (2001)

5. Committee on Network Science for Future Army Applications: Network Science. National Academies Press, Washington, DC (2005)

6. Costa, L.F., Rodrigues, F.A., Travieso, G., Boas, P.R.V.: Characterization of complex networks: a survey of measurements. Adv. Phys. **56**(1), 167–242 (2007)

7. Edmonds, N., Hoefler, T., Lumsdaine, A.: A space-efficient parallel algorithm for computing betweenness centrality in distributed memory. In: Proceedings of 2010 International Conference on High Performance Computing, December 2010

8. Madduri, K., Ediger, D., Jiang, K., Bader, D.A., Chavarría-Miranda, D.: A faster parallel algorithm and efficient multithreaded implementations for evaluating betweenness centrality on massive datasets. In: Proceedings of 2009 IEEE International Parallel and Distributed Processing Symposium, May 2009

9. Tan, G., Tu, D., Sun, N.: A parallel algorithm for computing betweenness centrality. In: Proceedings of 2009 International Conference on Parallel Processing, September 2009

10. Tu, D., Tan, G.: Characterizing betweenness centrality algorithm on multi-core architectures. In: Proceedings of 2009 IEEE International Symposium on Parallel and Distributed Processing with Applications, August 2009

11. Watts, D.J., Strogatz, S.H.: Collective dynamics of small-world networks. Nature **393**(6684), 440–442 (1998)

Exploration of Load Balancing Thresholds to Save Energy on Iterative Applications

Edson L. Padoin[1]([⊠]), Laércio L. Pilla[2], Márcio Castro[2],
Philippe O.A. Navaux[3], and Jean-François Méhaut[4]

[1] Department of Exact Sciences and Engineering,
Regional University of Northwest of Rio Grande do Sul (UNIJUI),
Ijuí, RS, Brazil
padoin@unijui.edu.br
[2] Department of Informatics and Statistics,
Federal University of Santa Catarina (UFSC),
Florianpolis, SC, Brazil
{laercio.pilla,marcio.castro}@ufsc.br
[3] Institute of Informatics, Federal University of Rio Grande do Sul (UFRGS),
Porto Alegre, RS, Brazil
navaux@inf.ufrgs.br
[4] Laboratoire d'Informatique de Grenoble (LIG) Grenoble University,
Grenoble, France
jean-francois.mehaut@imag.fr

Abstract. The power consumption of High Performance Computing systems is an increasing concern as large-scale systems grow in size and, consequently, consume more energy. In response to this challenge, we proposed two variants of a new energy-aware load balancer that aim at reducing the energy consumption of parallel platforms running imbalanced scientific applications without degrading their performance. Our research combines Dynamic Load Balancing with Dynamic Voltage and Frequency Scaling techniques in order to reduce the clock frequency of underloaded computing cores which experience some residual imbalance even after tasks are remapped. This work presents a trade-off evaluation between runtime, power demand and total energy consumption when applying these two energy-aware load balancer variants on real-world applications. In this way, we can define which is the best threshold value for each application under the total energy consumption, total execution time or the average power demand focus.

1 Introduction

Several load balancers are able to reduce the total energy consumption of an application by reducing its total execution time (as energy = time × power). Load balancers can improve the performance of imbalanced iterative applications by making a better load distribution among the available processors. However, they can take suboptimal decisions that result in some load imbalance still

© Springer International Publishing AG 2017
C.J. Barrios Hernández et al. (Eds.): CARLA 2016, CCIS 697, pp. 76–88, 2017.
DOI: 10.1007/978-3-319-57972-6_6

remaining after task migrations. This can happen due to characteristics of the application that prevent a perfectly balanced mapping to be achieved, and due to limitations of load balancing heuristics, as the problem that they are trying to solve is NP-Hard [15].

Our proposed algorithms, FG-ENERGYLB and CG-ENERGYLB [17] try to reduce the total energy consumption by exploiting residual imbalance left by load balancing algorithm. The first one, called *Fine-Grained Energy Load Balancer* (FG-ENERGYLB), is suitable for platforms composed of few tens of cores that allow per-core Dynamic Voltage and Frequency Scaling (DVFS). The second one, called *Coarse-Grained Energy Load Balancer* (CG-ENERGYLB) is suitable for current HPC platforms composed of several multi-core processors that feature per-chip DVFS. They identify the possibility of reducing the processors clock to achieve better gains better than other load balancing algorithms that they employ. In this form, energy improvements are achieved due to the reduction of average power during the runtime and also by reducing the application execution time by reducing the number of tasks migrated. The main idea of the ENERGYLB is to exploit the existence of residual imbalances on iterative applications to adjust the clock frequency of underloaded cores/processors through DVFS.

Nevertheless, the definition of the interval between calls to the load balancer is decisive to reduce the load balancing overhead. If the load balancer is invoked in long time periods, the load imbalance may increase too much and result in loss of performance, which consequently increases the total energy consumption. On the other hand, if the strategy is performed very frequently, it also may incur in a reduction of performance, since the load balancing overhead may exceed its benefits. In this context, aiming to decrease the load balancing overhead, recent strategies have adopted a threshold value to determine if load balancing or DVFS must be performed.

In this context, in this paper we focus on a trade-off evaluation between runtime, power demand, and total energy consumption when using different threshold values in the two variants of our energy-aware load balancer (ENERGYLB) on two imbalanced real-world applications. Our results show that FG-ENERGYLB can achieve energy savings of up to 17.1% with an average of 16.3%, and CG-EnergyLB of up to 31% with an average of 23% through the reduction of the average power demand. However, we observed that the total execution time of the applications may be reduced or increased according to threshold value chosen.

The remaining sections of this paper are organized as follows. Section 2 discusses related works on DVFS and energy-aware load balancing. Then, Sect. 3 presents the evaluation methodology and the applications used to evaluate the efficiency of our energy-aware load balancer. Our experimental results are discussed in Sect. 4. Finally, Sect. 5 concludes this paper.

2   Related Work on Energy Consumption

Different techniques have been proposed to reduce the runtime and power demand and thus improve the energy efficiency of platforms while running parallel applications. Among them, we highlight in this section DVFS and load balancing strategies.

Dynamic Voltage and Frequency Scaling (DVFS). Recent studies demonstrate that an idle host may consume more than half of its peak power [7]. Because of that, DVFS has been used in different contexts as a means to save energy. Gerards *et al.* [4] analyze the use of global DVFS in the context of multi-core processors. They proposed a theoretical method to transform the problem of finding an optimal clock frequency on global DVFS systems to a single core problem by using the amount of parallelism of applications. Their main goal is to minimize the energy consumption of nontrivial real-time applications. Spiliopoulos *et al.* [19] extended the gem5 simulator to support full-system DVFS modeling. This extended version is then used to study the behavior of different DVFS governors (interactive, on-demand and performance). They concluded that the interactive governor is faster than on-demand to adapt to the workload changes and thus achieves better performance at about the same energy consumption. Kin *et al.* [14] proposed a realistic DVFS performance prediction method and a practical DVFS control policy (eDVFS) that aims to minimize total energy consumption in multi-core processors. Their experimental results show that eDVFS can save a substantial amount of energy compared with Linux on-demand. Isci *et al.* [9] proposed to fine-tune the processor's clock frequency by using workload characteristics to maintain a chip-level power below a specified budget without degrading the performance significantly. The proposed approach can come within 1% of the performance of an ideal oracle, while meeting a given chip-level power budget.

Energy-Aware Load Balancing. Load balancing is a challenging problem and has been studied extensively in the past to improve the performance of parallel applications [11,21]. However, few works have made some efforts to further improve the energy consumption. Aupy [1] proposed energy-aware scheduling models to schedule tasks under reliability and makespan constraints. They designed and evaluated them using simulations with different heuristics based on the failure probability, the task weights, and the processor speeds. These heuristics aim at minimizing the energy consumption while enforcing reliability and deadline constraints. Sarood *et al.* [18] proposed a load balancing strategy that limits the processors' temperatures to reduce the energy spent in cooling and to prevent hot spots. Their results achieved energy savings of up to 63%, with a timing penalty from 2% to 23%. Goel *et al.* [5] proposed a model that uses CPU performance counters and CPU temperature to generate accurate per-core power estimates in real-time. They showed that the model can be used to guide scheduling decisions in power-aware resource managers. Hartog *et al.* [6] studied the relationship between CPU temperature and energy consumption in clusters and provided a method of estimating the power consumption of the system. This method was then used to implement a MapReduce framework that can evaluate the current status of each node and dynamically react to estimated power usage without having to rely on readings from expensive power monitoring hardware affixed to each node in the cluster.

As opposed to these works, our energy-aware approach performs load balancing along with DVFS to improve the performance and to reduce the energy consumption by exploiting residual imbalances of parallel applications [17]. In addition, we also reduce the cost of task migrations, since we only migrate tasks between processors when necessary. The performance, power demand and total energy consumption of our energy-aware load balancers are here analyzed on a set of real-world application running on top of a real platform without the need of simulations.

3 Evaluation Methodology

This section describes the methodology used in our trade-off study. We first present the execution environment, followed by the applications used in our experiments.

3.1 Experimental Environment

The experiments were conducted on an Altix UV 2000 platform designed by SGI. The platform is composed of 24 NUMA nodes. Each node has an Intel Xeon E5-4640 Sandy Bridge-EP x86-64 processor with 8 physical cores running at 2.40 GHz. There are 14 clock frequency levels available in this processor, allowing us to vary the clock frequency of the processor from 1.2 GHz up to 2.4 GHz.

Each core of the Intel Xeon E5-4640 has 32 KB instruction and 32 KB data L1 caches and 256 KB of L2 cache. All the 8 cores share a 20 MB L3 cache. Each node has 32 GB of DDR3 memory, which is shared with other nodes in a cc-NUMA fashion through SGI's proprietary NUMAlink6. Overall, this platform has 192 physical cores and 768 GB DDR3 memory.

The platform runs an unmodified SUSE Linux Enterprise Server operating system with kernel 3.0.101-0.29 installed. All applications as well as the CHARM++ programming model were compiled with GCC 4.8.2. The CHARM++ version used in our experiments was linux64-6.5.1. The results presented in Sect. 4 are the average of at least 10 runs. The relative error was less than 5% using a 95% statistical confidence by Student's t-distribution.

3.2 Applications

To evaluate the trade-off between run time, power demand and total energy consumption of our proposed variants of ENERGYLB, we selected different real-world applications. They were chosen due to their varied range of communication patterns and workload characteristics. The description of the applications is given below:

- **Ondes3D** is a seismic wave propagation simulator employed to estimate the damage in future earthquake scenarios [3]. In *Ondes3D*, seismic waves are modeled as a set of elastodynamics equations. These equations are then solved by applying a finite difference method. In our experiments, we used a version recently adapted to Adaptive MPI [8,10] that profits from CHARM++'s load balancing framework [20]. In this version, the application is overdecomposed into multiple virtual MPI processes per core. *Ondes3D* presents load irregularity due to the boundary conditions producing additional work, and load dynamicity from the simulation of waves spreading through space;

– **Lulesh** simulates a variety of science and engineering problems requiring hydrodynamics modeling, which describes the motion of materials relative to each other when subject to forces. The Livermore Unstructured Lagrange Explicit Shock Hydrodynamics (LULESH) application was originally developed as one of the five challenge problems in the DARPA Ubiquitous High Performance Computing (UHPC) program. *Lulesh* solves one octant of the spherical Sedov problem using Lagrange hydrodynamics [2,12,13].

Input Parameters. Table 1 summarizes the characteristics of the applications and parameters used in our experiments. Different load balancing frequencies have been chosen for different applications in order to strike a balance between the benefits of remapping tasks and the overheads of moving tasks and computing a new task mapping. Deciding the optimal moment to call a load balancer is a challenging problem [16] and is out of the scope of this paper.

Table 1. Summary of the input parameters of applications.

Application	Tasks	Iterations	LB Frequency
Ondes3D	128	500	20
Lulesh	729	1000	50

3.3   Load Balancers

CHARM++ provides a set of load balancing algorithms that can be used to migrate tasks among processors and to reduce the load imbalance. Thus, to analyze which is the best threshold value for each application under the total energy consumption, total execution time or the average power demand focus, we have selected the GREEDYLB load balancer available on CHARM++ platform.

4   Experimental Results

This section presents a trade-off between run time, power demand and total energy consumption achieved by our energy-aware load balancer.

The Intel Xeon E5-4640 processors, available on our experimental platform, there are 14 clock frequency levels available, which allow us to vary the clock frequency of the processor from 1.2 GHz up to 2.4 GHz. So, we vary the threshold (*thrld*) parameter of the algorithm from 0 up to 5 and execute the applications, in order to make a trade-off. In the following sections we first evaluate the results achieved with FG-ENERGYLB on applications. Then, we perform a similar evaluation using the CG-ENERGYLB.

4.1   Fine-Grained EnergyLB Evaluation

Aiming to reduce the effects of load imbalance and load balancing overhead to save energy, this section provides a trade-off between run time, power demand and total energy consumption when used FG-ENERGYLB over real applications with different threshold values. The application run time depends on several issues, among them, the number of parallel tasks and their load, the duration of each timestep, and the selected load balancing strategy. The impact of load balancing is directly related to the load balancing frequency once load balancing overhead can overcome the gains achieved with load balancing.

In this way, to FG-ENERGYLB, in each call of the load balancer, the algorithm verifies if the weighted load of each processor exceeds or not the *threshold*, makes decisions to adjust the frequencies (determining so that the frequency will be decreased or increased) or invokes other load balancer to migrate tasks. However, the load balancer generates an overhead and when this cost exceeds its benefits, the total execution time is increased, i.e., calling load balancing strategies incurs timing penalties to applications.

Our proposed load balancers take three input parameters in their execution. The first one, is the load balancer that is used to migrate tasks when the imbalance is high. The second one, is the maximum frequency available by processors that can be set to a core, and the last one, is a threshold value, used to decide whether call the load balancer or perform DVFS strategy.

Running the applications with FG-ENERGYLB configured with different threshold values, we obtain different amounts of DVFS performed or load balancers called, what determines different frequency settings of cores or migration tasks. In this way, we can analyze which is the best threshold value for each application under the total energy consumption, total execution time or the average power demand focus as shown in the Fig. 1.

– *Ondes3D* Application

Experiments with *Ondes3D* were performed using 128 tasks, which run for 500 iterations. Total energy spent to run this application without a load balancer is 550.4 kJoules and its total execution time is 645.8 s. In this way, during the execution, the average power demand is 35.5 W. These values are taken as reference in the analysis and represent the NOLB value in the Fig. 2(a).

In the tests with FG-ENERGYLB, the load balancer is called at every 20 iterations, resulting in a total of 24 calls. Using threshold values equal to 0.5 and 1.0, FG-ENERGYLB does not perform DVFS, calling GREEDYLB at every opportunity to migrate tasks. In this context, the average power remains constant around of 35.5 W. However, performing migrations in this application is

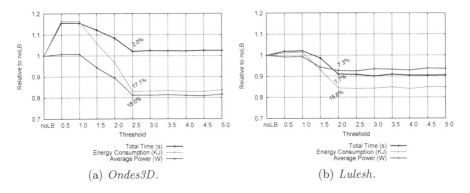

(a) *Ondes3D*.   (b) *Lulesh*.

Fig. 1. FG-ENERGYLB comparison with different threshold value on real applications

very costly, which incurs in an increase of 15.5% in run time and total energy consumption. This increase is the result of the overhead of migrations undertaken by GREEDYLB.

Using a threshold equal to 1.5, FG-ENERGYLB adjusts the clock frequency through DVFS 18× and only 6× calls the other load balancer to migrate tasks. In this way, it is able to reduce the average power in 5.7%. Reducing the number of migrations, the run time suffers a small reduction to 724.38 s, which is still 12.2% longer than with no load balancer, and spends 5.82% more energy.

With the threshold value equal to 2.0, gains in both execution time, power demand and, consequently energy consumption, are achieved. DVFS was performed 18× during the execution, which reduced the average power in 10.6%, but the run time was still 8.32% larger than the baseline. Nevertheless, using this threshold, the total energy consumption is reduced in only 3.15%.

For thresholds from 1.0 up to 2.5, the increase of threshold value also increases the number of calls of DVFS. For these values, the run time has a reduction near to linear. The total execution times is reduced from 15% to 2% larger than the baseline. Similarly, for this threshold range, the average power demand of the parallel platform is reduced by up to 19%. In this way, both run time and power demand reductions contribute to reduce the total energy spent.

The greater energy saving for this application is achieved using the threshold value equal or greater than 2.5. Using these values FG-ENERGYLB is able to reduce in up to 17.1% the total energy consumption in relation to baseline NOLB. These gains are achieved through a reduction in the overhead, which is only 2%, and the average power is reduced in 18%, once that in all calls DVFS was performed, which resulted in a greater amount of energy saving, as shown in Fig. 2(a).

– *Lulesh* Application

Lulesh was executed with 1000 iterations in each one of its 729 processes mapped in 24 cores. This application spent 100.6 kJoules of energy and takes

84.7 s when executed without a load balancer. In this execution the average power demand is 35.1 W. Similar to *Ondes3D*, these values are taken as baseline (NOLB) in Fig. 2(b)) to examine the threshold variation of the *Lulesh* application.

Load balancing call is configured with a frequency of 50 iterations so, in this test, our load balancer are called 19 times during the execution. When thresholds equal to 0.5 and 1.0 were used, FG-ENERGYLB did not perform any time adjustment in clock frequency. So, using these thresholds the average power is not changed. In addition, in these tests the load balancing overhead increases the run time and consequently, the total energy consumption in up to 2%.

A greater amount of DVFS is performed when the value of threshold is increased. For a threshold equal to 1.5, FG-ENERGYLB calls DVFS 17×. Thus, it reduces the run time in up to 1.33%, which also contributes for the reduction of the total energy spent. FG-ENERGYLB achieves a reduction of up to 5.6% in average power demand. In this way, reducing both, the power demand and run time, the total of energy spent is reduced in up to 6.91%.

The energy saving further increases when using thresholds equal to 2.0 or greater. For these values, the run time reduction is greater than the reduction of the average power demand. In every call of the load balancer, DVFS was performed, which resulted in reductions of 7.3% in average power demand and an average performance improvement of 7.74% compared to NOLB. In this way, FG-ENERGYLB is able to save energy by up to 15.6% to *Lulesh*.

For this application, the threshold variation from 1.0 up to 2.0 presented the more significant reduction in execution time. When these values were used, the run time was reduced in up to 11%, while the average power demand is reduced in up to 6%. Similarly to *Ondes3D*, both run time and power demand reductions contribute to the reduction of the total energy consumption.

In the tests with threshold values greater than 2.0, a greater amount of DVFS is performed, resulting in lower average power demands. However, such reductions cause an equivalent increase in the total execution time, thus maintaining the energy consumption constant.

In the execution with threshold equal to 5.0, FG-ENERGYLB adjusts the frequency 8×, which resulted in a reduction of the power in 23.36% and reduction of energy in 21.50%. However, the run time exceeds the baseline by 2.42%.

4.2   Coarse-Grained EnergyLB Evaluation

These scientific applications present a dynamic behavior, as the load of theirs tasks change through the iterations, which provides a more challenging scenario for energy aware load balancing. Since all the 192 cores will be used, different parameters are used in the evaluation of the CG-ENERGYLB, as shown in Table 2.

– *Ondes3D* Application

Experiments with CG-ENERGYLB over *Ondes3D* were performed using 1024 tasks mapped on 192 cores, which run 500 iterations each. Total energy spent to

Table 2. Summary of the input parameters of real applications.

Application	Tasks	Iterations	LB Frequency
Ondes3D	1024	500	20
Lulesh	5832	1000	50

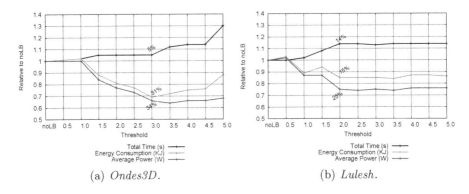

(a) *Ondes3D*.   (b) *Lulesh*.

Fig. 2. CG-ENERGYLB comparison with different threshold value on real applications

run this application without load balancer is 263.1 kJoules and its total execution time is 200.41 s, which represent an average power demand of 54.71 W. These values are taken as reference (NOLB in Fig. 2(a)) in our analysis.

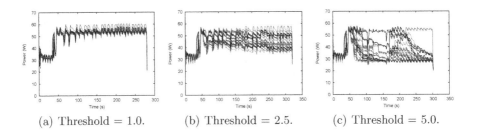

(a) Threshold = 1.0.   (b) Threshold = 2.5.   (c) Threshold = 5.0.

Fig. 3. Power evaluation to different threshold value on *Ondes3D*

Figure 3(a) depicts the instantaneous power of the execution when CG-ENERGYLB uses a threshold value equal to 1.0. In this execution any times DVFS is performed, in all the 24 load balancer calls tasks were migrated by REFINELB. In this way, during execution the power of all processors is always high, resulting in an average power of 54.7 W.

Using threshold equal to 2.5 the processors power is differently reduced as shown in the Fig. 3(b). For this threshold, 17 times DVFS is performed and only 7 calls migrate tasks by REFINELB. This form, the power is reduced in great majority of the processors, which result in a total reduction of 16.08%, leaving the average power in 43.4 W.

A different amount of energy is saved when using threshold equal to 5.0 (Fig. 3(c)). In this execution in all call (24) adjusts in clock were performed, leaving only one processor using its maximum power. For this threshold value, the power demand follows the increase of application needs, once the increases from the second 160 and reduces again from the second 212. This form, in this test the average power is reduced in 32.39%, resulting in an average of 35.0 W.

For *Ondes3D*, the least amount of energy spent is achieved using threshold value equal to 3.0. Using this value CG-ENERGYLB is able to reduce in up to 31% the total energy consumption in relation to baseline NOLB. This reduction is achieved through of the reduction of the average power demand in 34%, which overcome the time overhead of 5%, as shown in the Fig. 2(a).

– *Lulesh* Application

Lulesh was executed with 1000 iterations in each one of its 5832 processes mapped in 192 cores. This application spent 840.6 kJoules of energy and takes 688 s when executed without load balancer. Thus, in this execution the average power demand is 50.9 W. These values are taken as reference (baseline) and shown in column NOLB of the Fig. 2(b)) to examine the threshold variation of the *Lulesh* application.

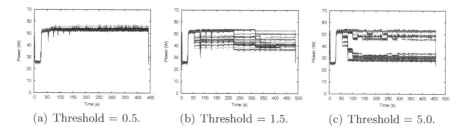

    (a) Threshold = 0.5.   (b) Threshold = 1.5.   (c) Threshold = 5.0.

Fig. 4. Power evaluation to different threshold value on *Lulesh*

Instantaneous power measured when the application is executed with threshold equal to 0.5 is depicted in the Fig. 4(a). Using this value, in all load balancing calls (19 times) were migrated tasks through do REFINELB. Similar to *Ondes3D* execution, for this threshold all processors running using a high power during all execution, which result in an average of power of 50.9 W.

On the other hand, using a threshold equal to 2.5, CG-ENERGYLB is able to reduce the power demand to intermediate levels as shown in the Fig. 4(b). With this threshold, in this execution are performed 4 times DVFS, which reduced the power of the processors in 12.7%, to 43.4 W.

For threshold equal to 5.0 (Fig. 4(c)) were adjusted 19 times the clock frequency of cores. This way, the power of most of the processors is reduced to minimum levels saving more energy. The total reduction was of 24%, which reduced the average power demand to 38.7 W.

The threshold variation from 0.5 up to 2.0 present the reduction more significant in energy consumption for this application. Differently from *Ondes3D*, when used these threshold values in CG-ENERGYLB load balancer, the runtime increases in up to 14%, while that the average power demand reduces in up to 25%. In this way, the least amount of energy spent for *Lulesh*, is achieved using threshold value equal to 2.0. For this value, CG-ENERGYLB reduces the total energy consumption in up to 15% if compared to baseline NOLB. This reduction is achieved through of the reduction of the average power in 25%, which overcome an overhead of 14%, as shown in the Fig. 2(b).

5   Conclusions

The exponential increase in power consumption related to a linear increase in the clock frequency and a higher complexity involved in the processors' design changed the course of development of new processors. Power consumption has become a critical aspect to the development of both large and small scale systems. This concern is now enough to warrant the research on techniques to improve the energy efficiency of parallel applications running on top of HPC platforms.

In this paper, we focused on analyzing the trade-off between run time, power demand and total energy consumption of the variants of our energy-aware load balancer which aim to reduce the energy consumption and power demand of parallel applications without considerably degrading their overall performance.

Our results demonstrated that FG-ENERGYLB can achieve energy savings of up to 17.1% with an average of 16.3%, and CG-ENERGYLB of up to 31% with an average of 23% on real-world applications through the reduction of the average power demand. On the other hand, the total execution time happens to be reduced or increased according to threshold value. In this way, we can analyze which is the best threshold value for each application under the total energy consumption, total execution time or the average power demand focus.

This work can be extended in different directions. One possibility would be to develop a new load balancer that performs load balancing and DVFS at the same time in each load balancing step. For that, it would be necessary to create a heuristic that takes into account the cost of task migrations between cores/processors that operate in different clock frequencies. Another possibility would be to develop a hierarchical energy-aware load balancer that performs task migrations between cores of the same processor and only migrate tasks between processors when needed. In this scheme, only the processors involved in task migrations would need their clock frequencies to be adjusted, reducing overhead of performing DVFS on all processors at each load balancing step. Finally, we also intend to evaluate the benefits of FG-ENERGYLB and CG-ENERGYLB on other real-world applications and platforms.

Acknowledgments. This work was supported by CNPq, CAPES, FAPERGS and FINEP. This research has received funding from the European Community's

Seventh Framework Programme (FP7-PEOPLE) under grant agreement number 295217, funding from the EU H2020 Programme and from MCTI/RNP-Brazil under the HPC4E Project, grant agreement number 689772 and STIC-AmSud/CAPES scientific-technological cooperation program under EnergySFE research project grant 99999.007556/2015-02.

References

1. Aupy, G., Benoit, A., Robert, Y.: Energy-aware scheduling under reliability and makespan constraints. In: Proceedings of International Conference on High Performance Computing (HiPC), pp. 1–10. IEEE Computer Society (2012)
2. Dosanjh, S., Barrett, R., Doerfler, D., Hammond, S., Hemmert, K., Heroux, M., Lin, P., Pedretti, K., Rodrigues, A., Trucano, T., et al.: Exascale design space exploration and co-design. Future Gener. Comput. Syst. **30**, 46–58 (2014)
3. Dupros, F., Aochi, H., Ducellier, A., Komatitsch, D., Roman, J.: Exploiting intensive multithreading for the efficient simulation of 3d seismic wave propagation. In: Proceedings of International Conference on Computational Science and Engineering, pp. 253–260. IEEE, July 2008
4. Gerards, M.E., Hurink, J.L., Holzenspies, P.K., Kuper, J., Smit, G.J.: Analytic clock frequency selection for global DVFS. In: Proceedings of Euromicro International Conference on Parallel, Distributed, and Network-Based Processing (PDP), pp. 512–519 (2014)
5. Goel, B., McKee, S.A., Gioiosa, R., Singh, K., Bhadauria, M., Cesati, M.: Portable, scalable, per-core power estimation for intelligent resource management. In: Proceedings of International Green Computing Conference (IGCC), pp. 135–146. IEEE Computer Society (2010)
6. Hartog, J., Dede, E., Govindaraju, M.: Mapreduce framework energy adaptation via temperature awareness. Cluster Comput. **17**(1), 111–127 (2013). http://dx.doi.org/10.1007/s10586-013-0270-y
7. Hosseinimotlagh, S., Khunjush, F., Hosseinimotlagh, S.: A cooperative two-tier energy-aware scheduling for real-time tasks in computing clouds. In: Proceedings of Euromicro International Conference on Parallel, Distributed, and Network-Based Processing (PDP), pp. 178–182 (2014)
8. Huang, C., Lawlor, O., Kalé, L.V.: Adaptive MPI. In: Rauchwerger, L. (ed.) LCPC 2003. LNCS, vol. 2958, pp. 306–322. Springer, Heidelberg (2004). doi:10.1007/978-3-540-24644-2_20
9. Isci, C., Buyuktosunoglu, A., Cher, C.Y., Bose, P., Martonosi, M.: An analysis of efficient multi-core global power management policies: Maximizing performance for a given power budget. In: Proceedings of International Symposium on Microarchitecture (MICRO), pp. 347–358. IEEE Computer Society, December 2006
10. Kalé, L.V., Bohm, E., Mendes, C.L., Wilmarth, T., Zheng, G.: Programming Petascale Applications with Charm++ and AMPI, pp. 421–441. Chapman & Hall/CRC Press (2008)
11. Kalé, L.V., Bhandarkar, M., Brunner, R.: Load balancing in parallel molecular dynamics. In: Ferreira, A., Rolim, J., Simon, H., Teng, S.-H. (eds.) IRREGULAR 1998. LNCS, vol. 1457, pp. 251–261. Springer, Heidelberg (1998). doi:10.1007/BFb0018544

88 E.L. Padoin et al.

12. Karlin, I., Bhatele, A., Chamberlain, B.L., Cohen, J., Devito, Z., Gokhale, M., Haque, R., Hornung, R., Keasler, J., Laney, D., Luke, E., Lloyd, S., McGraw, J., Neely, R., Richards, D., Schulz, M., Still, C.H., Wang, F., Wong, D.: Lulesh programming model and performance ports overview. Technical report LLNL-TR-608824. http://www.osti.gov/scitech/servlets/purl/1059462

13. Karlin, I., Bhatele, A., Keasler, J., Chamberlain, B.L., Cohen, J., DeVito, Z., Haque, R., Laney, D., Luke, E., Wang, F., Richards, D., Schulz, M., Still, C.: Exploring traditional and emerging parallel programming models using a proxy application. In: Proceedings of 27th IEEE International Parallel & Distributed Processing Symposium (IEEE IPDPS 2013), May 2013

14. Kim, S.g., Eom, H., Yeom, H., Min, S.: Energy-centric DVFS controlling method for multi-core platforms. In: Proceedings of High Performance Computing, Networking, Storage and Analysis (SCC), pp. 685–690. IEEE Computer Society, November 2012

15. Leung, J.Y.T.: Handbook of Scheduling: Algorithms, Models, and Performance Analysis. Chapman & Hall/CRC, Boca Raton (2004)

16. Menon, H., Jain, N., Zheng, G., Kalé, L.: Automated load balancing invocation based on application characteristics. In: Proceedings of IEEE International Conference on Cluster Computing (CLUSTER), pp. 373–381. IEEE Computer Society (2012)

17. Padoin, E., Castro, M., Pilla, L., Navaux, P., Mehaut, J.F.: Saving energy by exploiting residual imbalances on iterative applications. In: Proceedings of 21st International Conference on High Performance Computing (HiPC), pp. 1–10, December 2014

18. Sarood, O., Meneses, E., Kalé, L.V.: A 'cool' way of improving the reliability of HPC machines. In: Proceedings of International Conference on High Performance Computing, Networking, Storage and Analysis (SC), pp. 58:1–58:12. ACM (2013)

19. Spiliopoulos, V., Bagdia, A., Hansson, A., Aldworth, P., Kaxiras, S.: Introducing DVFS-management in a full-system simulator. In: Proceedings of International Symposium on Modelling, Analysis & Simulation of Computer and Telecommunication Systems (MASCOTS), pp. 535–545. IEEE Computer Society (2013)

20. Tesser, R.K., Pilla, L.L., Dupros, F., Navaux, P.O.A., Mehaut, J.F., Mendes, C.: Improving the performance of seismic wave simulations with dynamic load balancing. In: Proceedings of Euromicro International Conference on Parallel, Distributed and Network-Based Processing (PDP), pp. 196–203. IEEE Computer Society, February 2014

21. Zheng, G., Bhatelé, A., Meneses, E., Kalé, L.V.: Periodic hierarchical load balancing for large supercomputers. Int. J. High Perform. Comput. Appl. **25**(4), 371–385 (2011)

Parallel Algorithms and Applications

Design of a Task-Parallel Version of ILUPACK for Graphics Processors

José I. Aliaga[1], Ernesto Dufrechou[2(✉)], Pablo Ezzatti[2],
and Enrique S. Quintana-Ortí[1]

[1] Dep. de Ingeniería y Ciencia de la Computación, Universidad Jaime I,
12.701, Castellón, Spain
{aliaga,quintana}@icc.uji.es
[2] Instituto de Computación, Universidad de la República,
11.300, Montevideo, Uruguay
{edufrechou,pezzatti}@fing.edu.uy

Abstract. In many scientific and engineering applications, the solution of large sparse systems of equations is one of the most important stages. For this reason, many libraries have been developed among which ILU-PACK stands out due to its efficient inverse-based multilevel preconditioner. Several parallel versions of ILUPACK have been proposed in the past. In particular, two task-parallel versions, for shared and distributed memory platforms, and a GPU accelerated data-parallel variant have been developed to solve symmetric positive definite linear systems. In this work we evaluate the combination of both previously covered approaches. Specifically, we leverage the computational power of one GPU (associated with the data-level parallelism) to accelerate each computation of the multicore (task-parallel) variant of ILUPACK. The performed experimental evaluation shows that our proposal can accelerate the multicore variant when the leaf tasks of the parallel solver offer an acceptable dimension.

Keywords: ILUPACK · Graphic processors · Multi-core processors · Sparse linear systems · High performance

1 Introduction

In several scientific applications, the solution of large sparse systems of equations arise as one of the most important stages. Some examples appear in circuit and device simulations, quantum physics, large-scale eigenvalue computations, nonlinear sparse equations, and all kind of applications that involve the discretization of partial differential equations (PDEs) [6].

ILUPACK[1] (incomplete LU decomposition PACKage) is a numerical package that contains highly efficient sparse linear systems solvers, and can handle large-scale application problems of up to millions of equations. The solvers are based

---

[1] http://ilupack.tu-bs.de.

© Springer International Publishing AG 2017
C.J. Barrios Hernández et al. (Eds.): CARLA 2016, CCIS 697, pp. 91–103, 2017.
DOI: 10.1007/978-3-319-57972-6_7

on Krylov subspace methods [9], preconditioned with an inverse-based multilevel incomplete LU (ILU) factorization, which keeps a unique control of the growth of the inverse triangular factors that determines its superior performance in many cases [7,10,11].

Despite the remarkable mathematical properties of ILUPACK's preconditioner, it has the disadvantage of a costly computation and application, in comparison with more simple ILU preconditioners like ILU0. In [4] and [5] we proposed the exploitation of task-level parallelism in ILUPACK, for shared and distributed memory platforms, focusing on symmetric positive definite systems (s.p.d.), by using the preconditioned Conjugate Gradient (PCG) method. More recently, in [1] we used graphics accelerators to exploit data-level parallelism in the application of ILUPACK's preconditioner without altering its mathematical and numerical semantics, by off-loading the computationally-intensive kernels to the device.

In this work we evaluate the combination of both previous approaches, i.e. shared memory and co-processor data parallelism. Specifically, we leverage the computational power of one GPU (associated with the data-level parallelism) to accelerate the individual tasks – i.e. the operations that compose the application of the multilevel preconditioner – of the multicore (task-parallel) variant of ILUPACK. The experimental evaluation shows that our proposal is able to accelerate the multicore variant when the leaf tasks of the parallel solver offer an acceptable dimension.

The rest of the paper is structured as follows. In Sect. 2 we review the s.p.d. solver integrated in ILUPACK and we offer a brief study about the application of both parallel techniques (task and data-level). This is followed by the detailed description of our proposal in Sect. 3, and the experimental evaluation in Sect. 4. Finally, Sect. 5 summarizes the main concluding remarks and offers a few lines of future work.

2   Overview of ILUPACK

Consider the linear system $Ax = b$, where $A \in \mathbb{R}^{n \times n}$ is sparse, $b \in \mathbb{R}^n$, and $x \in \mathbb{R}^n$ the sought-after solution. ILUPACK integrates an "inverse-based approach" into the ILU factorization of matrix A, in order to obtain a multilevel preconditioner. In this paper, we only consider systems with A s.p.d., on which PCG [9] is applied. Although each iteration of the PGC also involves a sparse matrix-vector product (SpMV) and several vector operations, in the remaining part of this section we mainly focus on the computation and application of the preconditioner, which are by far the most challenging operations.

2.1   Sequential (and Data Parallel) ILUPACK

Computation of the Preconditioner. This operation of ILUPACK relies on the Crout variant of the incomplete Cholesky (IC) factorization, yielding the approximation $A \approx L \Sigma L^T$, with $L \in \mathbb{R}^{n \times n}$ sparse lower triangular and

$\Sigma \in \mathbb{R}^{n \times n}$ diagonal. Before the factorization commences, a scaling and a reordering (defined respectively by $P, D \in \mathbb{R}^{n \times n}$) are applied to A in order to improve the numerical properties as well as reduce the fill-in in L. After these initial transforms, the factorization operates on $\hat{A} = P^T DADP$. At each step of the Crout variant, the "current" column of $\hat{A}$ is initially updated with respect to the previous columns of the triangular factor L, and the current column of L is then computed. An estimation of the norm of the inverse of L, with the new column appended, is obtained next. If this estimation is below a predefined threshold κ, the new column is accepted into the factor; otherwise the updates are reversed, and the corresponding row and column of $\hat{A}$ are moved to the bottom-right corner of the matrix. This process is graphically depicted in Fig. 1. Once $\hat{A}$ is completely processed in this manner, the trailing block only contains rejected pivots, and a partial IC factorization of a permuted matrix is computed:

$$\hat{P}^T \hat{A} \hat{P} \equiv \begin{bmatrix} B & F^T \\ F & C \end{bmatrix} = \begin{bmatrix} L_B & 0 \\ L_F & I \end{bmatrix} \begin{bmatrix} D_B & 0 \\ 0 & S_c \end{bmatrix} \begin{bmatrix} L_B^T & L_F^T \\ 0 & I \end{bmatrix} + E. \qquad (1)$$

Here, $\|L_B^{-1}\| \lesssim \kappa$ and E contains the elements dropped during the IC factorization. Restarting the process with $A = S_c$, we obtain a multilevel approach.

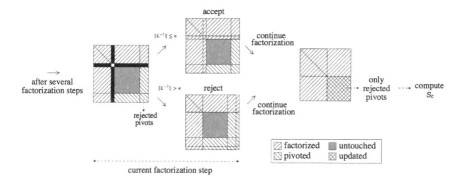

Fig. 1. A step of the Crout variant of the preconditioner computation.

Application of the Preconditioner. The application of the preconditioner in the PCG algorithm consists in the solution of the linear system $z := M^{-1}r$, where M is the preconditioner and r is the current residual. From (1), the preconditioner can be recursively defined, at level l, as

$$M_l = D^{-1} P \hat{P} \begin{bmatrix} L_B & 0 \\ L_F & I \end{bmatrix} \begin{bmatrix} D_B & 0 \\ 0 & M_{l+1} \end{bmatrix} \begin{bmatrix} L_B^T & L_F^T \\ 0 & I \end{bmatrix} \hat{P}^T P^T D^{-1}, \qquad (2)$$

where $M_0 = M$. Operating properly on the vectors,

$$\hat{P}^T P^T D^{-1} z = \hat{z} = \begin{bmatrix} \hat{z}_B \\ \hat{z}_C \end{bmatrix}, \quad \hat{P}^T P^T Dr = \hat{r} = \begin{bmatrix} \hat{r}_B \\ \hat{r}_C \end{bmatrix}, \qquad (3)$$

and applying $L_F = FL_B^{-T}D_B^{-1}$ (derived from (1)), we can expose the following computations to be performed at each level of the preconditioner [1]:

Before: $\hat{r} := \hat{P}^T P^T Dr$, Solve $L_B D_B L_B^T s_B = \hat{r}_B$ for s_B,

$$
\begin{aligned}
&t_B := F s_B, &&y_C := \hat{r}_B - t_B, \\
\text{Recursive step:}\ &\text{Solve}\ M_{l+1}\hat{z}_C = y_C\ \text{for}\ \hat{z}_C, \\
\text{After:}\ &\hat{t}_B := F^T \hat{z}_C, &&\text{Solve}\ L_B D_B L_B^T \hat{s}_B = \hat{t}_B\ \text{for}\ \hat{s}_B, \\
&\hat{z}_B := s_B - \hat{s}_B, &&z := DP\hat{P}\hat{z}.
\end{aligned}
\tag{4}
$$

To conclude this subsection, we emphasize that the data-parallel version of ILUPACK proceeds exactly in the same manner as the sequential implementation and, therefore, preserves the semantics of a serial execution.

2.2   Task Parallel ILUPACK

Following, we summarize the main ideas behind the task parallel version of ILUPACK. A more detailed explanation can be found in [4].

Computation of the Preconditioner. The task parallel version of this procedure employs Nested Dissection [9] to extract parallelism. To illustrate this, consider a ND partition, defined by a permutation $\bar{P} \in \mathbb{R}^{n \times n}$, such that

$$
\bar{P}^T A \bar{P} = \begin{bmatrix} A_{00} & 0 & A_{02} \\ 0 & A_{11} & A_{12} \\ A_{20} & A_{21} & A_{22} \end{bmatrix}.
\tag{5}
$$

Computing a partial IC factorizations of the two leading blocks, A_{00} and A_{11}, yields the following partial approximation of $\bar{P}^T A \bar{P}$

$$
\begin{bmatrix} L_{00} & 0 & 0 \\ 0 & L_{11} & 0 \\ L_{20} & L_{21} & I \end{bmatrix} \begin{bmatrix} D_{00} & 0 & 0 \\ 0 & D_{11} & 0 \\ 0 & 0 & S_{22} \end{bmatrix} \begin{bmatrix} L_{00}^T & 0 & L_{20}^T \\ 0 & L_{11}^T & L_{21}^T \\ 0 & 0 & I \end{bmatrix} + E_{01},
$$

where

$$
S_{22} = A_{22} - (L_{20}D_{00}L_{20}^T) - (L_{21}D_{11}L_{21}^T) + E_2,
\tag{6}
$$

is the approximate Schur complement. By recursively proceeding in the same manner with S_{22}, the IC factorization of $\bar{P}^T A \bar{P}$ is eventually completed.

The block structure in (5) allows the permuted matrix to be decoupled into two submatrices, so that the IC factorizations of the leading block of both submatrices can be processed concurrently, with

$$
A_{22} = A_{22}^0 + A_{22}^1, \begin{cases} \begin{bmatrix} A_{00} & A_{02} \\ A_{20} & A_{22}^0 \end{bmatrix} = \begin{bmatrix} L_{00} & 0 \\ L_{20} & I \end{bmatrix} \begin{bmatrix} D_{00} & 0 \\ 0 & S_{22}^0 \end{bmatrix} \begin{bmatrix} L_{00}^T & L_{20}^T \\ 0 & I \end{bmatrix} + E_0 \\[2ex] \begin{bmatrix} A_{11} & A_{12} \\ A_{21} & A_{22}^1 \end{bmatrix} = \begin{bmatrix} L_{11} & 0 \\ L_{21} & I \end{bmatrix} \begin{bmatrix} D_{11} & 0 \\ 0 & S_{22}^1 \end{bmatrix} \begin{bmatrix} L_{11}^T & L_{21}^T \\ 0 & I \end{bmatrix} + E_1, \end{cases}
\tag{7}
$$

and

$$S_{22}^0 = A_{22}^0 - \left(L_{20}D_{00}L_{20}^T\right) + E_2^0; \quad S_{22}^1 = A_{22}^1 - \left(L_{21}D_{11}L_{21}^T\right) + E_2^1.$$

Once the two systems are computed, S_{22} can be constructed given that

$$E_2 \approx E_2^0 + E_2^1 \;\rightarrow\; S_{22} \approx S_{22}^0 + S_{22}^1. \tag{8}$$

To further increase the amount of task-parallelism, one could find a permutation analogous to $\bar{P}$ for the two leading blocks following the ND scheme. For example, a block structure similar to (5) would yield the following decoupled matrices:

$$
\begin{bmatrix}
A_{00} & 0 & 0 & 0 & A_{04} & 0 & A_{06} \\
0 & A_{11} & 0 & 0 & A_{14} & 0 & A_{16} \\
0 & 0 & A_{22} & 0 & 0 & A_{25} & A_{26} \\
0 & 0 & 0 & A_{33} & 0 & A_{35} & A_{36} \\
A_{40} & A_{41} & 0 & 0 & A_{44} & 0 & A_{46} \\
0 & 0 & A_{52} & A_{53} & 0 & A_{55} & A_{56} \\
A_{60} & A_{61} & A_{62} & A_{63} & A_{64} & A_{65} & A_{66}
\end{bmatrix}
\quad
\begin{aligned}
\bar{A}_{00} &= \begin{bmatrix} A_{00} & A_{04} & A_{06} \\ A_{40} & A_{44}^0 & A_{46}^0 \\ A_{60} & A_{64}^0 & A_{66}^0 \end{bmatrix} \quad \bar{A}_{11} = \begin{bmatrix} A_{11} & A_{14} & A_{16} \\ A_{41} & A_{44}^1 & A_{46}^1 \\ A_{61} & A_{64}^1 & A_{66}^1 \end{bmatrix} \\[1.2em]
\rightarrow & \\
\bar{A}_{22} &= \begin{bmatrix} A_{22} & A_{25} & A_{26} \\ A_{52} & A_{55}^2 & A_{56}^2 \\ A_{62} & A_{65}^2 & A_{66}^2 \end{bmatrix} \quad \bar{A}_{33} = \begin{bmatrix} A_{33} & A_{35} & A_{36} \\ A_{53} & A_{55}^3 & A_{56}^3 \\ A_{63} & A_{65}^3 & A_{66}^3 \end{bmatrix}
\end{aligned}
\tag{9}
$$

Figure 2 illustrates the dependency tree for the factorization of the diagonal blocks in (9). The edges of the preconditioner *directed acyclic graph* (DAG) define the dependencies between the diagonal blocks (tasks), which dictate the order in which these blocks of the matrix have to be processed.

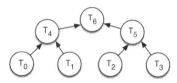

Fig. 2. Dependency tree of the diagonal blocks. Task T_j is associated with block A_{jj}. The leaf tasks are associated with the subgraphs of the leading block of the ND, while inner tasks are associated to separators.

Thus, the task-parallel version of ILUPACK partitions the original matrix into a number of decoupled blocks, and then delivers a partial IC factorization during the computation of (7), with some differences with respect to the sequential procedure. The main change is that the computation is restricted to the leading block, and therefore the rejected pivots are moved to the bottom-right corner of the leading block; see Fig. 3. Although the recursive definition of the preconditioner, shown in (2), is still valid in the task-parallel case, some recursion steps are now related to the edges of the corresponding preconditioner DAG, therefore different DAGs involve distinct recursion steps yielding distinct preconditioners, which nonetheless exhibit close numerical properties to that obtained with the sequential ILUPACK [4].

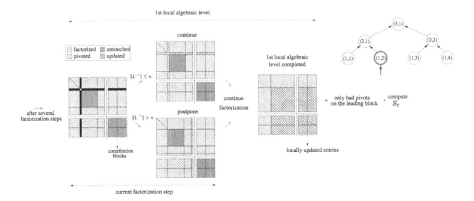

Fig. 3. A step of the Crout variant of the parallel preconditioner computations.

Application of the Preconditioner. As the definition of the recursion is maintained, the operations to apply the preconditioner, in (4), remain valid. However, to complete the recursion step in the task parallel case, the DAG has to be crossed two times per solve $z_{k+1} := M^{-1}r_{k+1}$ at each iteration of the PCG: once from bottom to top and a second time from top to bottom (with dependencies/arrows reversed in the DAG).

3   Proposal

In this section we present our strategy to enable GPU acceleration in the multicore version of ILUPACK. We analize two different approaches. The first one entirely off–loads the leaf tasks of the preconditioner application phase to the GPU, while the second one uses a threshold to use the GPU only when there is enough work to take advantage of the accelerator.

Our solution is designed for multicore platforms equipped with one GPU, using different streams to queue work that belongs to different tasks, but the idea is easily extensible to a multi-GPU context.

3.1   All Leafs in GPU, GPU$_{all}$

The task-parallel version of ILUPACK is based on a ND, that results in a *task tree* where only leaf tasks perform an important amount of work. Inner tasks correspond to the separator subgraphs in the ND process, and hence have much less work than their leaf counterparts. For this resason we only consider leaf tasks from here on.

The leaf tasks are independent from each other and can be executed concurrently provided sufficient threads were available. Therefore, we associate each of these tasks with a different GPU stream. Also, each task has its own data structure, both in CPU and GPU memory, containing the part of the multilevel preconditioner relevant to it, together with private CPU and GPU buffers. At the beginning of the application, where these buffers are allocated, our GPU-enabled versions make this memory non-pageable in order to perform asynchronous memory transferences between the CPU and the GPU.

For the GPU_{all} version of the preconditioner application, the computation on each node of the DAG is based on the data-parallel version presented in [1]. It proceeds as described in Sect. 2.1, with the difference that, in this case, the forward and backward substitution are separated and spread upon the levels of the task-tree. Now, entering or leaving the recursive step in Eq. (2) sometimes implies moving to a different level in the task tree hierarchy. In these cases, the residual r_{k+1} has to be transferred to the GPU at the beginning of the forward substitution phase, and the intermediate result has to be transfered back to the CPU buffers before entering the recursive step. This communication can be broken down into several asynchronous transfers from the device to pinned host memory, given the nature of the multilevel forward substitution. Furthermore, it can be overlapped almost entirely with other computations. Once the inner tasks compute the recursive steps, the backward substitution proceeds from top to bottom until finally reaching the leaf tasks again, where the z_{k+1} vector has to be transferred to the GPU, on which the last steps of the calculation of the preconditioned residual $z_{k+1} := M^{-1}r_{k+1}$ are performed. Upon completion, the preconditioned residual z_{k+1} is retrieved back to the CPU, making asynchronous transfers for each algebraic level of the preconditioner.

The computational cost of the preconditioner application corresponds mostly to two types of operations, the solution of $(LD^{\frac{1}{2}})$ and $(D^{\frac{1}{2}}L^T)$ linear systems and SPMVs. The rest of the operations involve vector scalings, reorderings, and substractions, which have relatively lower cost. We employ the CUSPARSE library kernels for the first two operations, while the lower cost operations (i.e. a diagonal scalings, vector permutations and a vector updates) are performed by *ad-hoc* kernels. The optimal block size for this kernels was determined experimentally, and was set to 512 threads.

This version aims to accelerate the computations involved by the leaf tasks while keeping a low communication cost, relying on the results obtained for the GPU acceleration of the serial version, and the streaming capabilities offered by the new GPU architectures. However, this version has serious drawbacks. The division of the work in various leaf tasks reduces the size of each independent linear system, and the multilevel ILU-factorization of the preconditioner produces levels of even smaller dimension. This can have a strong negative impact on the performance of massively parallel codes [8], and specifically on the CUSPARSE library kernels. It should be noted that the amount of data-parallelism available in the sparse triangular linear systems is severely reduced, leading to a poor performance of the whole solver. Additionally, the work assigned to the CPU in this variant is really minor, impeding the concurrent use of both devices.

3.2   Threshold Based Version, GPU_{thres}

In order to deal with the disadvantages of the previous version, we propose a threshold-based strategy, that computes the algebraic levels in the GPU until certain granularity, and the remaining levels in the CPU. This aims to produce two effects. On one hand, allowing the smaller and highly data-dependent levels to be computed on the CPU while the first levels, of larger dimension and higher data-parallelism, run on the GPU, implies that each operation is performed in the most convenient device. On the other hand, this strategy also improves the concurrent execution of both devices, increasing the overlap of the CPU and GPU sections of the code.

Regarding data transfer, in this approach the working buffer has to be brought to the CPU memory at some point of the forward substitution phase, and it has to be transferred to the GPU before the backward substitution of the upper triangular system ends. Moreover, these transfers are synchronous with respect to the current task or GPU stream, since the application of one algebraic level of the multilevel precondioner cannot commence until the results from the previous level are available.

In this variant we determine the threshold value experimentally. Our on-going work aims to identify the best algorithmic threshold from a model capturing the algorithm's performance.

4   Numerical Evaluation

In this section we summarize the experiments carried out to evaluate the performance of the proposal. Our primary goal is to assess the use of the GPU in the task-parallel version of ILUPACK. In order to do so, we compare our two GPU-accelerated versions with the original task-parallel ILUPACK, which exploits shared-memory parallelism via the OpenMP interface. All experiments reported were obtained using IEEE double-precision arithmetic.

4.1   Experimental Setup

The performance evaluation was carried out in a server equipped with an Intel(R) Xeon(R) CPU E5-2620 v2 of six physical cores, running at 2.10 GHz, with 132 GB of DDR3 RAM memory. The platform also features a Tesla K40m GPU (of the Kepler generation) with 2,880 CUDA Cores and 12 GB of GDDR5 RAM.

The CPU code was compiled with the Intel(R) Parallel Studio 2016 (update 3) using the -O3 flag. The GPU compiler and the CUSPARSE Library correspond to version 6.5 of the CUDA Toolkit.

The benchmark utilized for the test is a s.p.d. case of scalable size derived from a finite difference discretization of the 3D Laplace problem. We generated 4 instances of different dimension; see Table 1. In the linear systems, the right-hand side vector b was initialized to $A(1, 1, \ldots, 1)^T$, and the preconditioned CG iteration was started with the initial guess $x_0 \equiv 0$. For the tests, the parameter that controls the convergence of the iterative process in ILUPACK, *restol*, was set to 10^8. The drop tolerance, and the bound to the condition number of the inverse factors, which control ILUPACK's multilevel incomplete factorization process, where set to 0.01 and 5 respectively.

Table 1. Matrices employed in the experimental evaluation.

Matrix	Dimension n	nnz	nnz/n
A126	2,000,376	7,953,876	3.98
A159	4,019,679	16,002,873	3.98
A171	5,000,211	19,913,121	3.98
A200	8,000,000	31,880,000	3.99
A252	16,003,008	63,821,520	3.99

4.2   Results

Each test instance was executed with 2 and 4 CPU threads with $f = 2$ and $f = 4$ respectively. The parameter f is related with the construction of the task tree. The algorithm that forms this tree relies on an heuristic estimation of the computational cost of each leaf task and divides a leaf into two whenever its correspondent subgraph has more edges than the number of edges of the whole graph divided by f. The parameter f is chosen so that, in general, there are more leaf tasks than processors. In [2,3] the authors recomend choosing a value between p and $2p$, where p is the number of processors.

Table 2 summarizes the structure of the multilevel preconditioner and the linear systems corresponding to leaf tasks that were generated using the aforementioned parameters. For each one of the tested matrices, the table presents the number of leaf tasks that resulted from the task tree construction for $f = 2$ and $f = 4$, and next to it shows the average dimension of the algebraic levels of the corresponding multilevel preconditioner, the average number of nonzeros, and the average row density of the levels, with their respective standard deviation. It can be easily observed that a higher value of f results in more leaf tasks of smaller dimension. Regarding the algebraic levels of the factorization, the table shows how the average dimension of the involved matrices decreases from one level to the next. It is important to notice how, in the second algebraic level, the submatrices already become about one third smaller in dimension, and have five times more non zero elements on each row. In other words, the subproblems become dramatically smaller and less sparse with each level of the factorization, causing that, in this case, only the first algebraic level is attractive for GPU acceleration.

Table 3 shows the results obtained for the original shared-memory version and the two GPU-enabled ones for the matrices of the Laplace problem. In the table, the total runtime of PCG, as well as the time spent on the preconditioner application stage and the SpMV are presented. The table also shows the number of iterations taken to converge to the desired residual tolerance, and the final relative residual error attained, which is calculated as

$$\mathcal{R}(x^*) := \frac{||b - Ax^*||_2}{||x^*||_2},$$

where x^* stands for the computed solution.

Table 2. Number of leaf tasks and average structure of each algebraic level of the preconditioner using $f = 2$ and $f = 4$. To represent the structure of the levels, the average dimension, the number of non-zeros and the rate of non-zeros per row is presented, toghether with the respective standard deviations.

Matrix	# th./f	# leaves	Level	Avg. n	$\sigma(n)$	Avg. nnz	$\sigma(nnz)$	$\frac{nnz}{n}$	$\sigma(\frac{nnz}{n})$
A159	2	3	0	1,006,831	345,798	6,193,794	2,183,862	6.1	0.1
			1	317,362	113,151	9,682,114	3,486,401	30.5	0.2
			2	2,875	736	10,099	2,014	3.6	0.6
	4	6	0	502,108	159,044	3,116,629	1,005,408	6.2	0.1
			1	156,048	50,647	4,685,500	1,537,905	30.0	0.2
			2	1,251	437	4,095	1,754	3.2	0.4
A171	2	2	0	1,881,030	16,604	11,421,390	123,868	6.1	0.1
			1	598,152	1,384	18,490,583	154,695	30.9	0.2
			2	6,304	984	23,444	7,247	3.7	0.6
	4	4	0	937,998	6,011	5,764,461	71,397	6.1	0.1
			1	294,702	1,310	8,967,985	72,180	30.4	0.2
			2	2,845	506	10,885	3,768	3.7	0.7
A200	2	3	0	2,003,212	795,192	12,207,556	4,592,834	6.1	0.1
			1	636,895	253,696	19,665,756	8,089,987	30.8	0.4
			2	6,466	3,316	23,189	12,912	3.5	0.2
	4	7	0	856,365	186,595	5,283,746	1,141,907	6.2	0.1
			1	268,523	595,53	8,155,375	1,842,559	30.3	0.2
			2	2,449	525	8,552	2,032	3.5	0.4
A252	2	3	0	4,004,955	1,694,044	24,271,087	9,856,575	6.1	0.1
			1	1,283,180	543,882	39,965,828	17,408,294	31.0	0.3
			2	14,762	7,162	57,168	28,744	3.8	0.1
	4	6	0	1,998,470	494,294	12,196,071	3,070,313	6.1	0.1
			1	635,612	159,942	19,603,140	4,936,718	30.8	0.1
			2	6,523	1,429	23,807	5,758	3.6	0.3

First, it should be noted that there are no significant differences, from the perspective of accuracy, between the task-parallel CPU variant and the GPU-enabled ones. Specifically, the three versions reach the same number of iterations and final relative residual error for each case, see Table 3.

From the perspective of performance it can be observed that, on one hand, GPU$_{all}$ only outperforms the multi-core version for the largest matrices (A252) and in the context of 2 CPU threads. This result was expected, as the GPU requires large volumes of computations to really leverage the device and hide the overhead due to memory transfer. On the other hand, GPU$_{thres}$ is able to accelerate the multi-core counterpart for all covered cases, see Fig. 4. This result reveals the potential benefit that arise from overlapping computations on both devices. Hence, even in cases where the involved matrices presented modest dimension, this version outperforms the highly tuned multi-core version. Additionally, the benefits related with the use of the GPU are similar for all matrices of each configuration, though the percentage of improvement is a bit higher for the smaller cases. This behavior is not typical for GPU-based solvers and one possible explanation is that the smaller cases are near to the optimal point (from the threshold perspective) while the largest cases are almost able to

Table 3. Runtime (in seconds) of the three task-parallel variants.

# threads	Matrix	Version	Iters	Total SpMV	Total prec	Total PCG	$\mathcal{R}(x^*)$
2	A159	CPU_{omp}	88	2.30	29.55	32.86	1.39E-08
		GPU_{all}			44.33	47.46	
		GPU_{thres}			20.46	23.83	
	A171	CPU_{omp}	97	3.07	39.43	43.87	1.52E-08
		GPU_{all}			48.02	52.36	
		GPU_{thres}			30.62	35.19	
	A200	CPU_{omp}	107	5.83	71.58	79.98	2.45E-08
		GPU_{all}			84.37	92.61	
		GPU_{thres}			47.73	56.26	
	A252	CPU_{omp}	131	13.86	175.66	195.67	3.23E-08
		GPU_{all}			153.48	173.62	
		GPU_{thres}			120.19	140.50	
4	A159	CPU_{omp}	88	1.30	22.72	24.55	9.96E-09
		GPU_{all}			44.82	46.40	
		GPU_{thres}			15.21	17.15	
	A171	CPU_{omp}	95	1.58	22.43	24.76	2.20E-08
		GPU_{all}			57.84	59.78	
		GPU_{thres}			17.50	19.87	
	A200	CPU_{omp}	108	3.13	40.34	45.03	1.06E-08
		GPU_{all}			108.37	112.41	
		GPU_{thres}			33.80	38.60	
	A252	CPU_{omp}	130	8.25	104.21	116.37	2.16E-08
		GPU_{all}			193.19	204.74	
		GPU_{thres}			90.05	104.60	

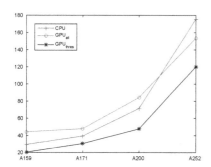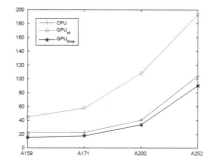

Fig. 4. Execution time (in seconds) of preconditioner application for the three task parallel variants, using two (left) and four (right) CPU threads. CPU version is the blue line with crosses. GPU_{all} version is the red line with circles. GPU_{thres} is the black line with stars. (Color figure online)

Table 4. Runtime (in seconds) of GPU_{thres} adjusting the threshold to compute 1 and 2 levels in the GPU.

# threads	Matrix	GPU_{1lev}	GPU_{2lev}	GPU_{all}
2	A159	23.83	43.79	44.33
	A171	35.19	47.52	48.02
	A200	56.26	84.16	84.37
	A252	140.50	153.79	153.48
4	A159	17.15	44.54	44.82
	A171	19.87	57.21	57.84
	A200	38.60	108.70	108.37
	A252	104.60	185.72	193.19

compute 2 levels in GPU. This can be noticed in Table 4, were we add a variant that computes the first 2 levels on the accelerator. As the multilevel factorization generates only 3 levels, with the third one very small with respect to the other two, it is not surprising that the runtimes of this version are almost equivalent to those of GPU_{all}. The table shows how the penalty of computing the second level in the GPU decreases as the problem dimension grows.

Finally, GPU_{thres} also offers higher performance improvements for the 2-threads case than for its 4-threads counterpart.

5   Final Remarks and Future Work

In this work we have extended the task-parallel version of ILUPACK so that leaf tasks can exploit the data-parallelism of the operations that compose the application of the multilevel preconditioner, i.e. SPMV and the solution of triangular linear systems, along with some minor vector operations. We presented two different GPU versions, one that computes the entire leafs in the accelerator (GPU_{all}) and an alternative that employs a threshold to determine if a given algebraic level of the preconditioner presents enough granularity to take advantage of the GPU (GPU_{thres}). Both variants are executed on a single GPU, asigning a GPU stream to each independent leaf task.

The experimental evaluation shows that the division of the workload in smaller tasks makes difficult the extraction of enough data-parallelism to fully occupy the hardware accelerator, and this results in poor performance for GPU_{all}. However, GPU_{thres} is able to execute each operation in the most convenient device while mantaining a moderate communication cost, outperforming the original multicore version for all the tested instances.

As part of future work we plan to advance towards the GPU acceleration of the distributed task-parallel version of ILUPACK. An intermediate step of this process involves the study of integrating a multi-GPU scenario in the current task parallel versions. Additionally, we plan to develop a mathematical model for the GPU-offload threshold, which was determined empirically in the present work.

Acknowledgments. The researchers from the *Universidad Jaime I* were supported by the CICYT project TIN2014-53495R of The researchers from *UdelaR* were supported by PEDECIBA and CAP-UdelaR Grant.

References

1. Aliaga, J.I., Bollhöfer, M., Dufrechou, E., Ezzatti, P., Quintana-Ortí, E.S.: Leveraging data-parallelism in ILUPACK using graphics processors. In: 2014 IEEE 13th International Symposium on Parallel and Distributed Computing, pp. 119–126. IEEE (2014)
2. Aliaga, J.I., Bollhöfer, M., Martín, A.F., Quintana-Ortí, E.S.: Parallelization of multilevel preconditioners constructed from inverse-based ILUs on shared-memory multiprocessors. Parallel Comput. Archit. Algorithms Appl. **38**, 287–294 (2007)
3. Aliaga, J.I., Bollhöfer, M., Martín, A.F., Quintana-Ortí, E.S.: Design, tuning and evaluation of parallel multilevel ILU preconditioners. In: Palma, J.M.L.M., Amestoy, P.R., Daydé, M., Mattoso, M., Lopes, J.C. (eds.) VECPAR 2008. LNCS, vol. 5336, pp. 314–327. Springer, Heidelberg (2008). doi:10.1007/978-3-540-92859-1_28
4. Aliaga, J.I., Bollhöfer, M., Martín, A.F., Quintana-Ortí, E.S.: Exploiting thread-level parallelism in the iterative solution of sparse linear systems. Parallel Comput. **37**(3), 183–202 (2011)
5. Aliaga, J.I., Bollhöfer, M., Martín, A.F., Quintana-Ortí, E.S.: Parallelization of multilevel ILU preconditioners on distributed-memory multiprocessors. In: Jónasson, K. (ed.) PARA 2010. LNCS, vol. 7133, pp. 162–172. Springer, Heidelberg (2012). doi:10.1007/978-3-642-28151-8_16
6. Barrett, R., Berry, M.W., Chan, T.F., Demmel, J., Donato, J., Dongarra, J., Eijkhout, V., Pozo, R., Romine, C., Van der Vorst, H.: Templates for the Solution of Linear Systems: Building Blocks for Iterative Methods, vol. 43. SIAM, New Delhi (1994)
7. George, T., Gupta, A., Sarin, V.: An empirical analysis of the performance of preconditioners for SPD systems. ACM Trans. Math. Softw. **38**(4), 24:1–24:30 (2012)
8. Kirk, D.B., Hwu, W.W.: Programming Massively Parallel Processors: A Hands-on Approach. Newnes, Boston (2012)
9. Saad, Y.: Iterative Methods for Sparse Linear Systems, 2nd edn. SIAM Publications, New Delhi (2003)
10. Schenk, O., Wächter, A., Weiser, M.: Inertia-revealing preconditioning for large-scale nonconvex constrained optimization. SIAM J. Sci. Comput. **31**(2), 939–960 (2009)
11. Schenk, O., Bollhöfer, M., Römer, R.A.: On large scale diagonalization techniques for the anderson model of localization. SIAM Rev. **50**, 91–112 (2008)

A Taxonomy of Workflow Scheduling Algorithms

Fernando Aguilar-Reyes and J. Octavio Gutierrez-Garcia[✉]

Department of Computer Science, ITAM, Río Hondo 1,
01080 Mexico City, Mexico
faguilarr@comunidad.itam.mx, octavio.gutierrez@itam.mx

Abstract. A workflow is a set of steps or tasks that model the execution of a process, e.g., protein annotation, invoice generation and composition of astronomical images. Workflow applications commonly require large computational resources. Hence, distributed computing approaches (such as Grid and Cloud computing) emerge as a feasible solution to execute them. Two important factors for executing workflows in distributed computing platforms are (1) workflow scheduling and (2) resource allocation. As a consequence, there is a myriad of workflow scheduling algorithms that map workflow tasks to distributed resources subject to task dependencies, time and budget constraints. In this paper, we present a taxonomy of workflow scheduling algorithms, which categorizes the algorithms into (1) best-effort algorithms (including heuristics, metaheuristics, and approximation algorithms) and (2) quality-of-service algorithms (including budget-constrained, deadline-constrained and algorithms simultaneously constrained by deadline and budget). In addition, a workflow engine simulator was developed to quantitatively compare the performance of scheduling algorithms.

Keywords: Workflow scheduling · Distributed computing · Scheduling algorithms

1 Introduction

Complex computing applications involving massive data or multimedia processing demanding powerful computing resources are increasingly common. For instance, there are financial institutions that handle millions of transactions, which are queued for execution during the day, and processed during the night. The transactional negotiation engine of the Mexican Stock Exchange can manage up to 100,000 transactions per second [4]. Another instance is the Large Hadron Collider of the European Organisation for Nuclear Research, which each year generates 15 petabytes of data to be analyzed [20].

Workflow applications are commonly constrained by time, budget and quality-of-service parameters. For this reason, it is of vital importance to *schedule* workflow tasks on multiple computing resources.

We define a *schedule* as a function that maps workflow tasks to computing resources (services) with appropriate hardware and software specifications to

© Springer International Publishing AG 2017
C.J. Barrios Hernández et al. (Eds.): CARLA 2016, CCIS 697, pp. 104–115, 2017.
DOI: 10.1007/978-3-319-57972-6_8

successfully execute the tasks taking into account workflow constraints [24], e.g., task ordering constraints. Most of the workflow scheduling approaches focuses on minimizing makespan (i.e., workflow execution time) by optimizing the schedule. However, with the emergence of the Cloud computing paradigm, in addition to minimizing makespan, both deadline-constrained and budget-constrained workflow scheduling algorithms have been designed.

Nevertheless, due to the existence of numerous and different workflow management systems using proprietary workflow specifications, there is no consensus for a common definition of workflow [9]. This lack of consensus causes that a workflow can be interpreted from multiple perspectives and results in a confusion of what a workflow represents. Therefore, it is necessary to establish a reference for workflow specification to enable the design of workflow algorithms with various objectives, such as minimizing makespan or making an efficient use of a given budget.

The paper is organized as follows: in Sect. 2 we formally define the workflow scheduling problem. In Sect. 3 we present a taxonomy of workflow scheduling algorithms. Also, in Sect. 4 we present a quantitative comparison of commonly used workflow scheduling algorithms by using our workflow engine simulator. In Sect. 5 we describe other taxonomies and software platforms for executing workflow applications. Finally, in Sect. 6 we present some concluding remarks.

2   The Scheduling Problem

Scheduling is the process of mapping workflow tasks to computing resources taking into account ordering constraints of tasks and multiple sets of available computing resources. In this section, we define a fundamental form of the scheduling problem in order to study its properties.

2.1   The Fundamental Scheduling Problem

Ullman et al. [22] define the *fundamental scheduling problem* as a composition of the following elements:

1. A set of tasks $\mathcal{J} = \{J_1, J_2, \ldots, J_n\}$
2. A partial ordering $\prec$ over $\mathcal{J}$
3. A cost function $U : \mathcal{J} \mapsto \mathbb{Z}^+$ that maps an execution time to a task in $\mathcal{J}$
4. A set of k computing resources (processors)

In [22], the main goal of the fundamental workflow scheduling problem is to *minimize* the makespan denoted by t_{max} and subject to a partial ordering $\prec$ by mapping tasks from $\mathcal{J}$ to k computing resources. Also, it is worth mentioning that all the tasks are assumed to be executed without any errors or interruptions.

Hence, the number of combinations of tasks and possible sets of computing resources becomes prohibitively large and leads to different makespans. In fact, Ullman et al. proved that the fundamental scheduling problem belong to the NP-complete complexity class [22].

2.2   The Workflow Scheduling Problem

Workflows as Directed-Acyclic Graphs (DAGs). Mair et al. [14] propose an intermediate workflow representation language based on a DAG structure in order to parse XML-based definitions of Grid workflow applications. This is evidence of the usefulness of representing workflows with DAGs.

As we described in Sect. 1, a workflow can be interpreted from multiple perspectives. However, by using a DAG as a workflow representation, we can represent tasks as nodes and ordering constraints as edges. That is the reason why we make use of DAGs for modeling workflows.

Furthermore, by using the *abstract Grid workflow language*, it is possible to model workflows with conditional execution paths using if, while, for and parallel constructions. With these features, it is possible to represent a wide variety of workflows. However, in order to study workflows with conditional execution paths, it is necessary to use branch prediction mechanisms, which are out of the scope of this paper.

Workflow Scheduling Problem Statement. Using a DAG workflow representation, we define the workflow scheduling problem based on Wieckzorek-Prodan's definitions [23].

Definition 1. *A **workflow** is a DAG $w \in \mathcal{W}, w = (\mathcal{V}, \mathcal{E})$ with a set of nodes $\mathcal{V}$ representing tasks $\tau \in \mathcal{T}$ and a set of edges representing data transferences $\rho \in \mathcal{D}$.*

In the definition stated above, graph edges not only represent data dependencies between tasks, but they could also represent ordering constraints between workflow tasks. Next, we define the computing resources in which workflow tasks are executed.

Definition 2. *A **service** is a computing entity that can execute a workflow task $\tau \in \mathcal{T}$. The set of all available services for executing a workflow is denoted as $\mathcal{S}$.*

Thus, we can define scheduling as a mapping function between services and workflow tasks.

Definition 3. *A **workflow schedule** is a function $f : \mathcal{T} \mapsto \mathcal{S}$ that maps services to tasks of a workflow w. The set that contains all possible schedules is denoted as $\mathcal{F}$.*

Each possible schedule over a workflow w has an execution cost. Then, a workflow execution has an associated cost model.

Definition 4. *A **cost model** $C = \{c_1, \ldots, c_n\}$ is a set of criteria that are used to represent constraints on workflow execution, e.g., deadlines, budget limitations, among others.*

Definition 5. *For each criterion $c_i \in C$, there exists a **partial cost function** $\Theta_i : \mathcal{S} \mapsto \mathbb{R}$ that maps a cost to services, which execute the workflow taking into account the constraints in c_i.*

It should be noted that partial cost functions determine task-related costs.

Definition 6. *For each criterion $c_i \in C$, there is a **total cost function** $\Delta_i : \mathcal{W} \times \mathcal{F} \mapsto \mathbb{R}$, that assigns a workflow w with a schedule f a cost composed by partial costs related to the resources specified in f for executing the workflow.*

Therefore, the main goal of the workflow scheduling problem is to find the schedule f that minimizes the total cost functions Δ_i, $1 \leq i \leq n$.

3   Taxonomy of Workflow Scheduling Algorithms

Nowadays, there are numerous workflow scheduling problems. Then, there are several research efforts aiming at classifying them [21,28] in order to grasp the basic idea behind the algorithms.

According to Yu et al. [28], workflow scheduling algorithms can be divided in two groups: (1) best-effort algorithms and (2) quality-of-service algorithms. The first category includes algorithms that minimize only one criterion, e.g., makespan, by making use of all the available resources. The latter category includes algorithms that look for a schedule that complies with the constraints specified in a given cost model.

In addition, each group of algorithms has subdivisions. Figure 1 shows the taxonomy proposed in this work.

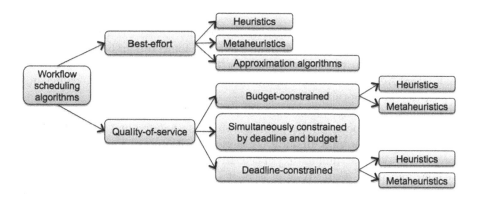

Fig. 1. Taxonomy of workflow scheduling algorithms

3.1 Best Effort Scheduling Algorithms

These algorithms try to minimize a criterion by making their best effort with the available resources. Usually, best-effort algorithms are designed to minimize makespan.

In addition, best-effort algorithms can be classified into heuristic algorithms, metaheuristic algorithms, and approximation algorithms. Heuristic algorithms exploit knowledge on a specific workflow pattern that may find near-optimal schedules under certain conditions [28]. Metaheuristic algorithms include algorithms that select or generate heuristics that produce the best schedules using a search methodology. Approximation algorithms are polynomial-time algorithms that guarantee a suboptimal solution within an approximation ratio.

Best-Effort Heuristic Algorithms. The best-effort heuristic algorithms can be divided into the following groups: (a) immediate algorithms (also known as individual task scheduling algorithms [28]), (b) list-based algorithms, (c) task clustering and (d) task duplication.

The most well-known immediate algorithm is the myopic algorithm [17]. The main idea behind the myopic algorithm is to assign tasks to the least loaded computing resource. List-based algorithms, such as MaxMin, MinMin and Sufferage [13], establish a priority list of tasks, and then, tasks from the priority list are assigned to a computing resource in order to optimize a criterion. In the case of task clustering algorithms, e.g., TANH [2], they create 1-element sets with one task, and then, they optimize the schedule by merging those sets to reduce costs associated to data transfers between tasks. Finally, task duplication algorithms (e.g., Hybrid [18] and TANH [2]) duplicate the execution of certain tasks to reduce communication costs between computing resources.

Best-Effort Metaheuristic Algorithms. In this group, algorithms are classified according to their search method. There are four types of best-effort metaheuristic algorithms, which are as follows: (a) genetic algorithms, (b) Greedy Randomized Adaptive Search Procedure –GRASP–, (c) simulated annealing and (d) particle swarm optimization.

Workflow scheduling algorithms based on genetic algorithms simulate the natural selection process for the selection of the best individual (schedule) that optimizes a given criterion. In addition, these algorithms use a mutation process in order to avoid local minima [27]. The GRASP algorithm [3] generates random schedules and using a greedy approach, it chooses local optimal solutions [3]. Simulated annealing algorithms emulate a crystal formation process, enhancing the quality of the solution with each iteration [25].

Best-Effort Approximation Algorithms. Approximation algorithms are poly-nomial-time algorithms that guarantee a suboptimal solution within an approximation ratio. However, very few approximation algorithms for workflow scheduling have been proposed [10]. Furthermore, most of them assume a constant performance of computing resources and are mostly focused on minimizing makespan, see, for instance [1, 7].

3.2 Quality-of-Service Scheduling Algorithms

These algorithms look for schedules that comply with a set of constraints that represent the quality-of-service requirements that must be fulfilled. Usually, these requirements involve deadline and/or budget constraints as well as task-level constraints.

Quality-of-service scheduling algorithms can be divided into budget-constrained algorithms, deadline-constrained algorithms, and algorithms simultaneously constrained by deadline and budget. Budget-constrained algorithms include algorithms that find schedules that execute workflows staying within a given budget. Deadline-constrained algorithms include algorithms that look for schedules that execute workflows meeting a given deadline. Finally, algorithms simultaneously constrained by deadline and budget include algorithms that look for schedules that execute workflows meeting both a given deadline and a given budget simultaneously.

Budget-Constrained Scheduling Algorithms. Budget-constrained scheduling algorithms are divided into: (a) heuristics and (b) metaheuristics.

On the one hand, budget-constrained workflow scheduling algorithms based on heuristics exploit knowledge about the workflow structure in order to reduce the search space and find feasible solutions, see for instance the LOSS/GAIN algorithm [19]. On the other hand, budget-constrained workflow scheduling algorithms based on metaheuristics keep the best feasible solutions, see for instance the genetic algorithm proposed by Yu et al. [27] whose fitness function favors schedules that stay within a given budget with low makespans.

Deadline-Constrained Scheduling Algorithms. In a similar manner to budget-constrained scheduling algorithms, deadline-constrained scheduling algorithms are divided into: (a) heuristics and (b) metaheuristics.

An instance of a deadline-constrained scheduling algorithm based on heuristics is the back-tracking algorithm proposed by Menascé et al. [15]. An instance of a deadline-constrained scheduling algorithm based on metaheuristics is the genetic algorithm proposed by Yu and Buyya [27] whose fitness function favors solutions meeting deadlines and capable of executing workflows with a minimal budget.

Scheduling Algorithms Simultaneously Constrained by Budget and Deadline. Whereas the majority of workflow scheduling algorithms are either deadline-constrained or budget-constrained, there have been also research efforts focused on executing workflows constrained by budget and deadline simultaneously. For instance, Yu et al. [29] propose a deadline distribution algorithm that partitions workflow tasks into branches, which are modeled as Markov decision processes. Then for each partition branch, an optimal policy is computed by using dynamic programming. In the same vein, Brandic et al. [5] propose a graphical quality-of-service specification and a service-oriented architecture in order to execute workflows while meeting both deadline and budget constraints. Brandic et al. solve the workflow optimization problem using integer programming. Also making use of a mathematical model, namely the multidimensional multi-choice knapsack problem, Kofler et al. [11] propose a *branch and bound* algorithm to optimize workflow execution based on a set of quality-of-service parameters.

4   Workflow Engine Simulator

In order to provide the scientific community with a platform for studying workflow scheduling algorithms on Cloud-computing environments, we built a workflow engine simulator that generates synthetic workflows and schedules them in simulated computing resources. The workflow scheduling algorithms implemented are MaxMin, MinMin and myopic. The simulator was written in Java.

Using the workflow engine simulator, we conducted experiments to compare the performance of the MaxMin, the MinMin and the myopic algorithm. The algorithms were evaluated using 50 randomly generated workflows, each with 10 homogeneous tasks and 12 dependencies (i.e., ordering constraints). It should be noted that the size of the randomly generated workflow instances was sufficient to show differences on the performance of the evaluated scheduling algorithms. The algorithms generated schedules for each workflow taking into account 3 resources with velocity factors of $r1 = 7.373924, r2 = 2.540241$ and $r3 = 4.530177$. It should be noted that the computing powers were calculated using a uniform random distribution $U[1, 10]$. It is acknowledged that in order to ease the analysis

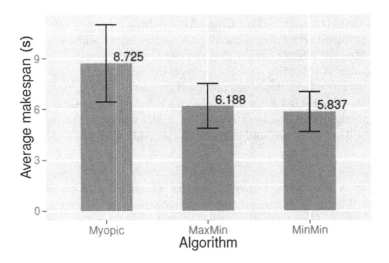

Fig. 2. Average makespan for each scheduling algorithm.

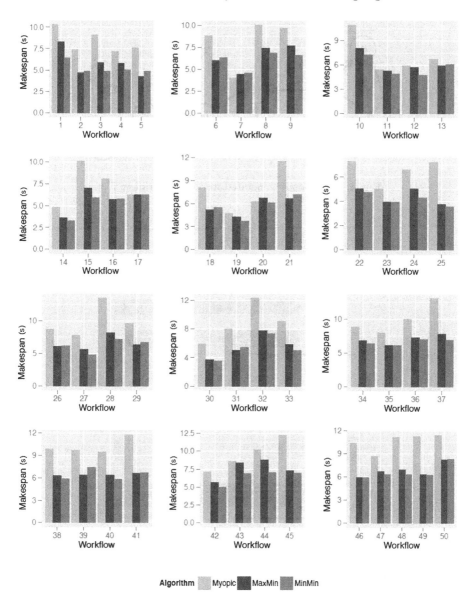

Fig. 3. Makespans attained by the workflow scheduling algorithms.

of results (see Figs. 2, 3, 4 and 5), a relatively small size of workflow instances and a relatively small number of resources were used.

Figure 2 shows the average makespan attained by the scheduling algorithms. The error bars in the graph indicate the standard deviation of the makespan. The results indicate that the MinMin algorithm attained the lowest average makespan, followed by the MaxMin algorithm and the Myopic algorithm.

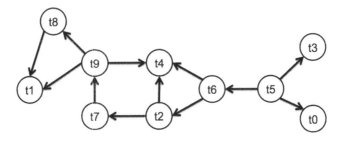

Fig. 4. A randomly generated workflow: workflow 7.

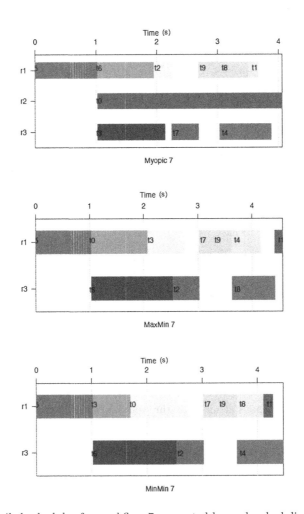

Fig. 5. Detailed schedules for workflow 7 generated by each scheduling algorithm.

However, the error bars indicate that there is a high variability in the results, which suggests that no algorithm completely outperforms the remaining two. In some cases, even the myopic algorithm attained better makespans than the MaxMin and MinMin algorithms. This fact can be seen in Fig. 3, where the myopic algorithm attained the best makespan for workflow 7 (Fig. 4).

Figure 5 shows the schedules for workflow 7 produced by each algorithm. The makespans attained by the Myopic, the MaxMin and the MinMin algorithms were 4.06, 4.47 and 4.57, respectively.

Figure 5 shows that the myopic algorithm assigned task $t0$ to the slowest resource $r2$, whereas the MaxMin and MinMin algorithms did not assign any task to resource $r2$. This can be explained by the fact that MaxMin and MinMin algorithms computes the *Earliest Completion Time* $ECT(t, r)$, defined as the time taken by a resource r to execute a task t. Resource $r2$ has a very high ECT becoming an unfeasible option for the MaxMin and the MinMin algorithms.

5   Related Work

The rising emergence of workflow scheduling algorithms resulted in the creation of comprehensive taxonomies and classifications. For example, Yu et al. [28] propose a taxonomy of Grid scheduling algorithms in conjunction with a review of workflow management systems. Yu et al. [28] introduced the idea of classifying workflow scheduling algorithms according to the objective optimized. Another taxonomy is proposed in [23], which made an exhaustive classification of workflow scheduling algorithms using the subject-verb-predicate notation of the resource description framework. Furthermore, Yu et al. [26] classify workflow management systems according to their functionality. Additionally, van Der Aalst et al. [9] identify workflow patterns based on their structure. Furthermore, there are taxonomies based on the fundamental scheduling problem, see [16].

6   Conclusion

This paper contributes a taxonomy of workflow scheduling algorithms. In addition, we discussed the workflow scheduling problem on distributed computing approaches. We first analyzed the workflow scheduling problem statement based on the generalized definitions proposed by Wieczorek et al. [23] and the fundamental scheduling problem [22]. We extended the taxonomy proposed by Yu et al. [28] by (1) rethinking the functionality of metaheuristics subject to deadline and budget constraints and (2) adding additional categories, e.g., approximation algorithms. Finally, we developed a workflow engine simulator and conducted experiments in order to compare three best-effort workflow scheduling algorithms. Future work will be centered on surveying workflow management systems (such as Pegasus [8], WOHA [12], LiSIs [6]) in order to map state-of-the-art scheduling algorithms on current workflow management systems.

Acknowledgements. This work has been supported by *Asociación Mexicana de Cultura A.C.*

References

1. Agrawal, K., Benoit, A., Magnan, L., Robert, Y.: Scheduling algorithms for linear workflow optimization. In: 2010 IEEE International Symposium on Parallel and Distributed Processing (IPDPS), pp. 1–12. IEEE (2010)
2. Bajaj, R., Agrawal, D.: Improving scheduling of tasks in a heterogeneous environment. IEEE Trans. Parallel Distrib. Syst. 15(2), 107–118 (2004)
3. Blythe, J., Jain, S., Deelman, E., Gil, Y., Vahi, K., Mandal, A., Kennedy, K.: Task scheduling strategies for workflow-based applications in grids. In: IEEE International Symposium on Cluster Computing and the Grid, CCGrid 2005, vol. 2, pp. 759–767. IEEE (2005)
4. Bmv, G.: Informe Anual 2012. Technical report, Bolsa Mexicana de Valores (2012)
5. Brandic, I., Pllana, S., Benkner, S.: Amadeus: a holistic service-oriented environment for grid workflows. In: Fifth International Conference on Grid and Cooperative Computing Workshops, GCCW 2006, pp. 259–266. IEEE (2006)
6. Kannas, C.C., Kalvari, I., Lambrinidis, G., Neophytou, M.C., Savva, G.C., Kirmitzoglou, I., Antoniou, Z., Achilleos, K.G., Scherf, D., Pitta, A.C., et al.: Lisis: an online scientific workflow system for virtual screening. Comb. Chem. High Throughput Screen. 18(3), 281–295 (2015)
7. Chekuri, C., Bender, M.: An efficient approximation algorithm for minimizing makespan on uniformly related machines. J. Algorithms 41(2), 212–224 (2001)
8. Deelman, E., Blythe, J., Gil, Y., Kesselman, C., Mehta, G., Patil, S., Su, M.H., Vahi, K., Livny, M.: Pegasus: mapping scientific workflows onto the grid. In: Grid Computing, pp. 11–20. Springer, Heidelberg (2004)
9. van Der Aalst, W.M., Ter Hofstede, A.H., Kiepuszewski, B., Barros, A.P.: Workflow patterns. Distrib. Parallel Databases 14(1), 5–51 (2003)
10. Dong, F., Akl, S.G.: Scheduling algorithms for grid computing: state of the art and open problems. Technical report (2006)
11. Kofler, K., Haq, I.U., Schikuta, E.: A parallel branch and bound algorithm for workflow QoS optimization. In: International Conference on Parallel Processing, ICPP 2009, pp. 478–485. IEEE (2009)
12. Li, S., Hu, S., Wang, S., Su, L., Abdelzaher, T., Gupta, I., Pace, R.: Woha: deadline-aware map-reduce workflow scheduling framework over hadoop clusters. In: 2014 IEEE 34th International Conference on Distributed Computing Systems (ICDCS), pp. 93–103. IEEE (2014)
13. Maheswaran, M., Ali, S., Siegal, H., Hensgen, D., Freund, R.F.: Dynamic matching and scheduling of a class of independent tasks onto heterogeneous computing systems. In: Proceedings of Eighth Heterogeneous Computing Workshop, (HCW 1999), pp. 30–44. IEEE (1999)
14. Mair, M., Qin, J., Wieczorek, M., Fahringer, T.: Workflow conversion and processing in the ASKALON grid environment. In: 2nd Austrian Grid Symposium, pp. 67–80. Citeseer (2007)
15. Menasce, D.A., Casalicchio, E.: A framework for resource allocation in grid computing. In: MASCOTS, pp. 259–267 (2004)
16. Pinedo, M.L.: Scheduling: Theory, Algorithms, and Systems. Springer Science & Business Media, Berlin (2012)
17. Ramamritham, K., Stankovic, J.A., Shiah, P.F.: Efficient scheduling algorithms for real-time multiprocessor systems. IEEE Trans. Parallel Distrib. Syst. 1(2), 184–194 (1990)

18. Sakellariou, R., Zhao, H.: A hybrid heuristic for DAG scheduling on heterogeneous systems. In: Proceedings of 18th International Parallel and Distributed Processing Symposium, p. 111, April 2004
19. Sakellariou, R., Zhao, H., Tsiakkouri, E., Dikaiakos, M.D.: Scheduling workflows with budget constraints. In: Gorlatch, S., Danelutto, M. (eds.) Integrated Research in GRID Computing, pp. 189–202. Springer, Heidelberg (2007)
20. Shiers, J.: The worldwide LHC computing grid (worldwide LCG). Comput. Phys. Commun. **177**(1), 219–223 (2007)
21. Topcuoglu, H., Hariri, S., Wu, M.Y.: Performance-effective and low-complexity task scheduling for heterogeneous computing. IEEE Trans. Parallel Distrib. Syst. **13**(3), 260–274 (2002)
22. Ullman, J.D.: NP-complete scheduling problems. J. Comput. Syst. Sci. **10**(3), 384–393 (1975)
23. Wieczorek, M., Hoheisel, A., Prodan, R.: Taxonomies of the multi-criteria grid workflow scheduling problem. In: Wieczorek, M., Hoheisel, A., Prodan, R. (eds.) Grid Middleware and Services, pp. 237–264. Springer, Heidelberg (2008)
24. Wieczorek, M., Hoheisel, A., Prodan, R.: Towards a general model of the multi-criteria workflow scheduling on the grid. Future Gener. Comput. Syst. **25**(3), 237–256 (2009)
25. Young, L., McGough, S., Newhouse, S., Darlington, J.: Scheduling architecture and algorithms within the ICENI grid middleware. In: UK e-Science All Hands Meeting, pp. 5–12. Citeseer (2003)
26. Yu, J., Buyya, R.: A taxonomy of scientific workflow systems for grid computing. ACM Sigmod Rec. **34**(3), 44–49 (2005)
27. Yu, J., Buyya, R.: Scheduling scientific workflow applications with deadline and budget constraints using genetic algorithms. Sci. Program. **14**(3), 217–230 (2006)
28. Yu, J., Buyya, R., Ramamohanarao, K.: Workflow scheduling algorithms for grid computing. In: Xhafa, F., Abraham, A. (eds.) Metaheuristics for Scheduling in Distributed Computing Environments, pp. 173–214. Springer, Heidelberg (2008)
29. Yu, J., Buyya, R., Tham, C.K.: Cost-based scheduling of scientific workflow applications on utility grids. In: 2005 First International Conference on e-Science and Grid Computing, p. 8. IEEE (2005)

An Efficient Implementation of Boolean Gröbner Basis Computation

Rodrigo Alexander Castro Campos[1(✉)], Feliú Davino Sagols Troncoso[2],
and Francisco Javier Zaragoza Martínez[3]

[1] Posgrado en Optimización, Universidad Autónoma Metropolitana Azcapotzalco,
Mexico City, Mexico
racc@correo.azc.uam.mx

[2] Departamento de Matemáticas,
Centro de Investigación y de Estudios Avanzados del Instituto Politécnico Nacional,
Mexico City, Mexico
fsagols@math.cinvestav.edu.mx

[3] Departamento de Sistemas, Universidad Autónoma Metropolitana Azcapotzalco,
Mexico City, Mexico
franz@correo.azc.uam.mx
http://sites.google.com/site/rccuam,
http://www.math.cinvestav.mx/fsagols, http://academicos.azc.uam.mx/franz

Abstract. The computation of boolean Gröbner bases has become an
increasingly popular technique for solving systems of boolean equations
that appear in cryptography. This technique has been used to solve some
cryptosystems for the first time. In this paper, we describe a new concurrent algorithm for boolean Gröbner basis computation that is capable of
solving the first HFE challenge. We also discuss implementation details,
including optimal runtime parameters that depend on the CPU architecture. Our implementation is available as open source software.

Keywords: Gröbner basis · Boolean ideals · Concurrent algorithms

1 Introduction

Gröbner bases are useful tools for solving multivariate, non-linear systems of
equations. The Gröbner basis of a system allows us to efficiently list the set of
all its solutions, but since Gröbner bases can be used to solve SAT problems,
computing them is NP-Hard [23]. However, the algebraic algorithms used for
computing Gröbner bases are sometimes capable of finding and exploiting otherwise hidden structural properties of the given system. Recent improvements in
the implementation of such algorithms have rendered Gröbner bases practical.

While the high-level descriptions of the fastest Gröbner basis algorithms have
been known for more than a decade, there are very few efficient implementations.
For example, we could find only three implementations that claim to solve the
first HFE Challenge of Patarin, a cryptographic system in 80 binary variables
over $\mathbb{F}_2$ that is of historical importance as it was first solved using Gröbner bases

© Springer International Publishing AG 2017
C.J. Barrios Hernández et al. (Eds.): CARLA 2016, CCIS 697, pp. 116–130, 2017.
DOI: 10.1007/978-3-319-57972-6_9

[16,24]. Worse yet, one of those implementations is not publicly available while the other two are closed source with one requiring a license fee.

In this paper, we describe a new variant of the F4 algorithm for computing Gröbner bases that is also capable of solving the first HFE Challenge. It includes a novel concurrent implementation of the Buchberger criteria for detecting redundant work and an improved handling of pending polynomials. The strong correlation between the CPU architecture being used and the performance of our algorithm under certain runtime parameters is also discussed. The source code of our implementation is available at https://sites.google.com/site/rccuam/ together with the set of instances used for benchmarking.

2   Preliminaries

In this section we introduce the necessary concepts to understand what are boolean Gröbner bases and why are they useful. We then explain how to compute them using the classic Buchberger algorithm along with the Buchberger criteria for detecting redundant work.

2.1   Boolean Gröbner Bases

Definition 1. *A boolean polynomial is an element of $\mathbb{Z}_2[x_1, x_2, \ldots, x_n]/\langle x_1^2 - x_1, x_2^2 - x_2, \ldots, x_n^2 - x_n \rangle$, which is also called the boolean polynomial ring and is denoted by $\mathbb{B}(x_1, x_2, \ldots, x_n)$.*

The field equations $x_i^2 - x_i = 0$ imply that $x_i \in \{0, 1\}$ and $x_i^k = x_i$ for $k \geq 1$. Hence the maximum degree of a boolean monomial is bounded above by n.

Definition 2. *Let m_1, m_2, m_3 be boolean monomials. A monomial order $<$ is a total order such that 1 is the minimum element and $m_1 < m_2 \Rightarrow m_1 m_3 < m_2 m_3$ when m_2 and m_3 are coprime.*

Definition 3. *Let p be a polynomial and $<$ a fixed monomial order. The leading monomial of p is denoted by $lm(p)$ and is defined as the greatest monomial of p.*

Definition 4. *Let $P \subseteq \mathbb{B}(x_1, x_2, \ldots, x_n)$. The ideal generated by P is defined as the set $\mathcal{I} = \{p_1 q_1 + \cdots + p_k q_k : p_i \in P \wedge q_i \in \mathbb{B}(x_1, x_2, \ldots, x_n)\}$. Any set that generates $\mathcal{I}$ is said to be a basis of $\mathcal{I}$.*

Definition 5. *Let $G \subseteq \mathbb{B}(x_1, x_2, \ldots, x_n)$ be a basis of $\mathcal{I}$. G is a Gröbner basis of $\mathcal{I}$ if for all $p \in \mathcal{I}$, there exists $g \in G$ such that $lm(g) \mid lm(p)$.*

A Gröbner basis under the lexicographical order is said to possess the elimination property: its elements are such that the method of back substitution is applicable in order to find all the solutions of the system [9]. However, algorithms for computing Gröbner bases are usually much faster using other monomial orders [2]. In practice, this is not an issue as there are efficient algorithms for converting a Gröbner basis in one monomial order to another in a different order [12].

2.2   The Buchberger Algorithm

In 1965, Buchberger introduced an alternative characterization of Gröbner bases which led to the first algorithm for computing them [6]. For correctness in the boolean case, the field equations must be considered as part of the input system.

Definition 6. *Let* $p, q \in \mathbb{B}(x_1, x_2, \ldots, x_n)$. *We say that* p *is reducible by* q *if* $lm(q) \mid lm(p)$. *The reduction of* p *by* q *is defined as* $red(p, q) := p - \frac{lm(p)}{lm(q)}$.

Definition 7. *Let* $p \in \mathbb{B}(x_1, x_2, \ldots, x_n)$ *and* $Q \subseteq \mathbb{B}(x_1, x_2, \ldots, x_n)$. *The reduction of* p *by* Q *is defined as* $red(p, Q) := red(red(p, q_i), Q \setminus q_i)$ *if it is possible to choose some* $q_i \in Q$ *as a valid reductor and* p *otherwise.*

Definition 8. *Let* $p_1, p_2 \in \mathbb{B}(x_1, x_2, \ldots, x_n)$. *The s-polynomial of* p *and* q *is defined as* $sp(p, q) := \frac{\lambda}{lm(p)} p + \frac{\lambda}{lm(q)} q$ *where* $\lambda = LCM(lm(p), lm(q))$.

Definition 9. *Let* $G \subseteq \mathbb{B}(x_1, x_2, \ldots, x_n)$ *be a basis of* $\mathcal{I}$. G *is a Gröbner basis of* $\mathcal{I}$ *if* $\forall g_i, g_j \in G, red(sp(g_i, g_j), G) = 0$.

The main idea of the Buchberger algorithm is to enlarge G with the nonzero remainders coming from reductions of s-polynomials, as they belong to the ideal but do not have a reductor. Buchberger also devised two criteria that predict whether an s-polynomial will reduce to zero [7]. Reductions to zero do not contribute to G and their computations are best avoided if possible. The first is called the *relatively prime criterion* and the second is called the *chain criterion*.

Theorem 1. *Let* $p_1, p_2 \in G$ *and* $G \subseteq \mathbb{B}(x_1, x_2, \ldots, x_n)$. *The polynomial* $sp(p, q)$ *will reduce to zero if* $lm(p_1)$ *and* $lm(p_2)$ *are coprime.*

Theorem 2. *Let* $p_1, p_2 \in G$ *and* $G \subseteq \mathbb{B}(x_1, x_2, \ldots, x_n)$. *The polynomial* $sp(p, q)$ *will reduce to zero if* $\exists g \in G : lm(g) \mid lm(sp(p_1, p_2))$ *and* $red(sp(p_1, g), G) = red(sp(p_2, g), G) = 0$.

Even though the field equations $x_i^2 - x_i = 0$ would collapse under the boolean identity $x_i^2 = x_i$, the s-polynomials between them and other elements of the basis must be considered as if no substitutions were applied to the field equations. The boolean substitution can be applied to the s-polynomial afterwards.

Lemma 1. *Let* $p \in \mathbb{B}(x_1, x_2, \ldots, x_n)$. *The s-polynomial* $sp(p, x_i^2 - x_i)$ *is boolean equivalent to* $x_i p$.

Algorithm 1.

   function BUCHBERGER($G \subseteq \mathbb{B}(x_1, x_2, \ldots, x_n)$)
       $Q \leftarrow \{(p_i, p_j) : p_i, p_j \in G \wedge i < j\}$
       while $Q \neq \emptyset$ **do**
          $q \leftarrow select(Q), Q \leftarrow Q \setminus q$
          if $\neg criterion_1(q_1, q_2) \wedge \neg criterion_2(G, q_1, q_2)$ **then**
             $r \leftarrow red(sp(q_1, q_2), G)$

> if $r \neq 0$ then
> $\qquad Q \leftarrow Q \cup \{(r, p) : p \in G\}$
> $\qquad G \leftarrow G \cup r$
> return G

The *select* subroutine may choose any element of Q, which acts as a queue of pending polynomial pairs whose s-polynomial needs to be considered.

3   State of the Art

In this section we study the implementation of the Buchberger criteria and we discuss PolyBori and BooleanGB, popular open source implementations of the Buchberger algorithm for computing boolean Gröbner bases. Later we introduce the F4 algorithm, which is based on linear algebra, and the F5 algorithm, which became the first signature based Gröbner basis algorithm. We end the section by briefly discussing the first HFE Challenge.

3.1   Implementations of the Buchberger Criteria

The relatively prime criterion can be easily implemented by inspecting the leading monomials of a polynomial pair. However, the chain criterion needs to determine whether other related pairs have been already processed. A direct implementation of the chain criteria requires to mantain a table, indexed by a polynomial pair, which stores whether that pair has been already processed. An implementation which uses a triangular bit matrix is presented in [25].

Unfortunately, a direct implementation of the chain criteria has another disadvantage besides the need to store a table: it may happen that many already redundant pairs are kept in the queue for too long before being popped and discarded, wasting memory unnecessarily. In [18], Gebauer and Möller implemented the chain criteria without an extra table, purging the queue on the fly.

Algorithm 2.
> **function** GEBAUER-MÖLLER$(G, Q \subseteq \mathbb{B}(x_1, x_2, \ldots, x_n), p \in G)$
> $\quad C \leftarrow \{(p, g) : g \in G : g \neq p\}$
> $\quad$ **for all** $p, g \in C : \neg criterion_1(p, g)$ **do**
> $\qquad$ **if** $\exists p, g' \in C : g' \neq g \wedge LCM(lm(p), lm(g')) \mid LCM(lm(p), lm(g))$ **then**
> $\qquad\quad C \leftarrow C \setminus (p, g)$
> $\quad C \leftarrow C \setminus \{c \in C : criterion_1(c_1, c_2)\}$
> $\quad Q \leftarrow Q \setminus \{q \in Q : lm(p) \mid LMC(lm(q_1), lm(q_2))$
> $\qquad\qquad \wedge LCM(lm(p), lm(q_1)) \neq LMC(lm(q_1), lm(q_2))$
> $\qquad\qquad \wedge LMC(lm(p), lm(q_2)) \neq LMC(lm(q_1), lm(q_2))\}$
> $\quad$ **return** $Q \cup C$

3.2 Implementations of the Boolean Buchberger Algorithm

Simplified boolean polynomials are multilinear, i.e. no variable occurs to a power greater than one. This allows us to use specialized representations for them. In [21], BooleanGB is presented as an implementation of the boolean Buchberger algorithm where monomials are represented by word sized bitmaps. Monomial multiplication is translated into a single native processor instruction and the same occurs for the monomial divisibility test and monomial division operations. Boolean polynomials are viewed as sets of monomials, so polynomial addition is implemented as a symmetric difference. BooleanGB is implemented in C++ and an interface is available in the free computer algebra system Macaulay2 [19].

A boolean polynomial is also equivalent to a boolean formula written in algebraic normal form, i.e. products of variables connected by XOR operators. As such, the corresponding boolean function can be represented in other ways. In [5], PolyBori is presented as an implementation of the boolean Buchberger algorithm where polynomial structures are represented by zero-suppresed decision diagrams. In the worst case, decision diagrams have exponential size in the number of variables. While the worst case is not common, PolyBori attempts to further reduce its memory consumption by caching subdiagrams and sharing them between polynomials. PolyBori is implemented in C++ and an interface is available in the free computer algebra system SageMath [10].

3.3 The F4 Algorithm and Linear Algebra Strategies

In 1999, Faugère presented the F4 algorithm [13] which is based on two observations. On the one hand, it is not clear what is the optimal implementation of the *select* subroutine in the Buchberger algorithm, so one possibility is to reduce a (not necessarily proper) subset of the elements of the queue by the current basis at the same time. On the other hand, polynomial reduction can be simulated via Gaussian elimination by mapping polynomials into rows and monomials into columns, with the cells becoming the monomial coefficients appearing in the polynomials. This allows us to take advantage of the high performance, concurrent algorithms and implementations already available in linear algebra.

How to produce the matrix to echelonize is fundamental to the correctness of F4. Since row addition is equivalent to polynomial addition, this single operation is equivalent to the polynomial reduction $red(p, g)$ only when g is a divisor of p and $lm(g) = lm(p)$, as the leftmost nonzero cell of both rows are in the same column. When $lm(g)$ strictly divides $lm(p)$, there must be a row in the matrix that is equivalent to a multiple of g. The F4 algorithm checks which leading monomials are missing and may be needed during reduction. It then generates one row for each one that may be produced as a multiple of an existing row. Its main disadvantage is that the generated matrices may be prohibitively large.

Algorithm 3.

> **function** F4($G \subseteq \mathbb{B}(x_1, x_2, \ldots, x_n)$)
> $Q \leftarrow \{(p_i, p_j) : p_i, p_j \in G \land i < j\}$

while $Q \neq \emptyset$ **do**
    $Q' \leftarrow select(Q), Q \leftarrow Q \setminus Q'$
    $S \leftarrow \{sp(q_1, q_2) : q \in Q' \wedge \neg criterion_1(q_1, q_2) \wedge \neg criterion_2(G, q_1, q_2)\}$
    $M \leftarrow preprocess(G, S)$
    $R \leftarrow echelonize(M \cup S\}) \setminus M$
    for all $r \in R : r \neq 0$ **do**
        $Q \leftarrow Q \cup \{(r, p) : p \in G\}$
        $G \leftarrow G \cup r$
return G

To select which elements are popped from the queue, Faugère suggests to use the degree truncated strategy which consists in having a degree limit such that all s-polynomials with smaller or equal degree are selected. The limit is increased when no s-polynomial can be selected within the current limit. For simplicity, the degree of an s-polynomial is taken as the degree of its leading monomial, so monomial orders where $degree(m_1) > degree(m_2) \Rightarrow m_1 > m_2$ holds are used.

3.4 The F5 Algorithm and Signature Strategies

In 2002, Faugère presented the F5 algorithm which focuses on avoiding reductions to zero as much as possible [14]. In this algorithm, the polynomials are annotated with signatures which partially denote how the polynomial was produced, i.e. if the polynomial came from the input or was produced as a linear combination of other polynomials. During the execution, the signature of a would be s-polynomial is examined in order to predict its reduction to zero.

The F5 algorithm is incremental in the sense that it computes the Gröbner basis of the first $k - 1$ input polynomials before considering the kth input polynomial. Faugère also proved that F5 avoids all reductions to zero in the case of homogeneous polynomials. However, it often underperforms in the inhomogeneous case [11]. Homogenization of the system is usually considered, but computing the Gröbner basis of the resulting system may be harder. It is an area of active research how to improve and parallelize signature based algorithms.

3.5 The First HFE Challenge

The Hidden Field Equations or HFE is a cryptosystem introduced by Patarin [24]. The main idea of HFE is as follows. Let $p \in \mathbb{F}_{2^n}[x]$. If the maximum degree of p is bounded by an integer d and d is not very large, it is possible to quickly find a solution of p since it is univariate. However, it is possible to transform p into a public system of quadratic polynomials in $\mathbb{B}(x_1, x_2, \ldots, x_n)$ such that the original structure of p is hidden and the system appears to be random. Solving a system of random quadratic boolean equations is NP-Hard [1].

The first HFE challenge was proposed in 1996 and consists on solving a quadratic boolean system coming from a secret polynomial with parameters $n = 80$ and $d = 96$. It was first solved in 2002 by Faugére's F5 algorithm, implemented in the C language and included in the FGb library [15,16]. Magma quickly followed, solving it in 2004 with an implementation of the F4 algorithm which was around three times faster than Faugére's F5 implementation [26].

It is reported that the MXL3 algorithm can also solve the first HFE challenge [22]. This algorithm uses linear algebra but does not rely on s-polynomials. Instead, it refines the XL algorithm which blindly generates multiples of existing polynomials in an attempt to eventually find a Gröbner basis [8]. Unfortunately, the implementation of MXL3 is not publicly available and the time and memory needed for solving the challenge are not disclosed. It is only mentioned that, despite being slower than Magma 2.15, the matrix generated by MXL3 has fewer rows than those from FGb and Magma.

4   Contributions

In this section we present the algorithmic and implementation details of our F4 variant. We begin by giving a general overview of our algorithm plus a list of assumptions that determine crucial implementation decisions. Then we describe the handling of the s-polynomial queue together with our concurrent implementation of the Buchberger criteria.

We continue by introducing a high performance compression scheme for read-only boolean polynomials that greatly reduces the memory consumption of our algorithm in a wide variety of situations. We end the section by giving thorough explanation of our concurrent polynomial reduction implementation, which covers how to tune its runtime parameters for optimal performance depending on the CPU architecture being used.

4.1   General Overview and Assumptions

As most implementations of the F4 algorithm, our variant uses the degree truncated strategy. We use the graded reverse lexicographical monomial order which is the most popular choice, but any other graded monomial order also works. Individual monomials are represented by bitmaps as in BooleanGB. However, BooleanGB cannot represent monomials in more than W variables where W is the number of bits in a word. By contrast, our representation uses as many words as needed to represent the number of variables in the system.

Monomials in a polynomial are represented as positions in the monomial order. Our implementation can also convert monomials between the bitmap and the position representations using dynamic programming. However, a position is represented with only 32 bits for several reasons. Graded monomial orders very effectively bound the numerical values of the positions of low degree monomials. Additionally, the degree truncated strategy aims to find a Gröbner basis at the smallest possible degree, since the size of the matrices increases exponentially as the degree increases. In fact, in the case of systems with too many variables, a computation that does not finish at a low degree will be deemed infeasible both in time and space. Thus, it makes no sense to use too many bits per position, as 32 bits are enough to represent entries in matrix rows with 2^{32} columns.

4.2   Handling of the S-Polynomial Queue

The degree truncated strategy constrains which s-polynomials are popped from the queue, but it does not constrain the queue insertions. To reduce the memory consumption of the queue, efficient implementations like Magma provide a parameter that statically constrain the degree of the s-polynomials that will be inserted into the queue [4]. However, for correctness it must be true that a Gröbner basis can be found at some point of the computation such that all the excluded s-polynomials would become redundant.

Our implementation can achieve the same goal without the use of an special parameter and without compromising correctness, although a small amount of repeated work must be performed. Our approach is to use the dynamic degree limit used for constraining queue extractions to also constrain queue insertions. When the degree limit is increased, all current polynomial pairs are concurrently retested for queue insertion, except that we ignore s-polynomials with degree less than the new limit, as they should have been processed at a previous limit.

4.3   Concurrent Implementation of the Buchberger Criteria

Although the Gebauer and Möller installation is widely considered the best implementation of the chain criteria, it presents some issues. On the one hand, when there exists a pair of pending s-polynomials such that one of them can be ignored as long as the other is reduced, the algorithm discards one in a sequential fashion: once discarded, such s-polynomial cannot be a member of another pair that would otherwise be in the same situation. On the other hand, the algorithm explicitly constructs and temporarily stores polynomial pairs that can be discarded by the relatively prime criterion, as they may be needed by the chain criterion for the detection of other redundant s-polynomials.

Our implementation solves both problems. To do this, we assign a unique increasing index to each polynomial of the basis such that it is possible to induce a total order between pairs. An s-polynomial will be discarded if two related s-polynomials appear before it in the total order. A polynomial pair that meets the relatively prime criterion will come before those that do not. Additionally, this can be determined on the fly without storing those useless pairs. In the degree truncated strategy, an extension of a degree based partial order can be used.

Algorithm 4.

    function CRITERION$_2$($G \subseteq \mathbb{B}(x_1, x_2, \ldots, x_n), g_1, g_2 \in G$)

        $\lambda_{1,2} = LCM(lm(g_1), lm(g_2))$

        $t_{1,2} \leftarrow (true, degree(\lambda_{1,2}), sort_>(index(g_1), index(g_2)))$

        for all $g_3 \in G : lm(g_3) \mid \lambda_{1,2}$ **do**

            $\lambda_{1,3} = LCM(lm(g_1), lm(g_3))$

            $\lambda_{2,3} = LCM(lm(g_2), lm(g_3))$

            $t_{1,3} \leftarrow (\neg criterion_1(g_1, g_3), degree(\lambda_{1,3}), sort_>(index(g_1), index(g_3)))$

            $t_{2,3} \leftarrow (\neg criterion_1(g_2, g_3), degree(\lambda_{2,3}), sort_>(index(g_2), index(g_3)))$

            if $t_{1,2} > t_{1,3} \wedge t_{1,2} > t_{2,3}$ **then return** $true$

        return $false$

The previous function assumes that G is immutable during the execution of the algorithm, but does not need to know which other pairs are being concurrently tested. It also assumes that G is irreducible, but the same approach can be made to work if this is not true. Our implementation prefers to discard polynomial pairs with high degrees or, in case of a tie, those involving the newest polynomials.

4.4   Compressed Representation of Immutable Polynomials

A polynomial in the current basis will remain unmodified until a reductor is found, and when such situation occurs it will be simply replaced by its remainder, which comes from a recently echelonized matrix. In our implementation, we use large bitmaps to manage the rows of the matrix that are nonpivotal and will be modified during echelonization. For polynomials that will not change during the execution of the algorithm, better representations exists.

If we treat monomials in a polynomial as positions in the monomial order, a boolean polynomial becomes a sorted sequence of unique integers. In fact, Faugère suggests to use delta encoding for the compression of such sequences. In our implementation, we use prefix trees of octets instead. See Fig. 1.

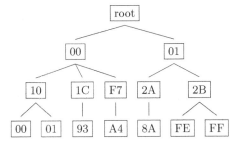

Fig. 1. Example of a prefix tree for a set of seven 24 bit integers (octets in hexadecimal)

In the actual implementation, the stored tree is pointerless. Conceptually, we traverse the tree in pre-order while dumping its contents into a binary stream. For each group of nodes sharing a common parent, we store the number of nodes and then we list their octets, one byte each. By design, a group cannot contain more than 256 nodes. When a group has 32 nodes or more, we switch its representation to a bitmap of 256 bits in order to bound its memory consumption. In practice, we do not explicitly traverse a prefix tree, as we emulate the opposite traversal directly over the sequence of positions and then we reverse the binary output. We achieve significant compression ratios over sparse polynomials.

4.5   Concurrent Implementation of the Polynomial Reduction

The polynomial reduction process consumes most of the total execution time. As such, most algorithmic and implementation decisions become important. Curiously, it is easiest to explain how we achieve concurrency. Using what is called structured Gauss-Jordan, the pivotal and nonpivotal rows of the matrix are identified and the nonpivotal rows are reduced concurrently, one thread each [17]. The reduction of a row stops when no current pivotal row can further reduces it (itself becoming a new pivotal row) or when it becomes empty. To prevent data races when several rows try to become pivotal for the same leading column, atomic compare and swap operations are used.

It is important to mention that our structured Gauss-Jordan and row addition implementations follow a sparse strategy, which is adequate for sparse matrices but asymptotically slower than specialized algorithms for dense matrices. Additionally, our implementation leaves the matrix in some echelon form and not in the reduced echelon form, where pivotal rows are interreduced. This final reduction is only computed until the Gröbner basis has been found.

The main differentiation aspect of our F4 variant comes from the observation that the F4 matrices do not need to be completely constructed in one pass. In fact, it is true in practice that the vast majority of the rows are both pivotal and monomial multiples of the input polynomials. By precomputing how the pivotal rows are induced by the polynomials in the basis, it is possible to construct the pivotal rows on the fly as they become necessary during the echelonization.

The direct application of this idea would be closer to the Buchberger algorithm, but we should mention that the product of a polynomial by a monomial is not a cheap operation and that, in the case of several independent threads requiring to construct the same pivotal row, it may be subject to become repeated work. A crude implementation of memorization would solve this problem, but an adequate solution should not keep the induced rows in memory for too long, as it would reintroduce the problem of storing the whole matrix.

To minimize the amount of repeated work, we construct the pivotal rows in parts, reducing the nonpivotal rows by the current active part. More in detail, we construct the pivotal rows within a certain window of possible leading monomials (the largest monomials first) and then we perform the echelonization with the nonpivotal rows included. We then slide the window downwards, repeating the process for the nonpivotal rows that did not become pivotal or empty within the previous window. This emulates the echelonization of the whole matrix.

Algorithm 5.
    function REDUCTION$(G, Q \subseteq \mathbb{B}(x_1, x_2, \ldots, x_n), d, w \in \mathbb{N})$
    Assume: $\forall q \in Q, \neg criterion_1(q_1, q_2) \wedge \neg criterion_2(G, q_1, q_2)$
        $S \leftarrow \{sp(q_1, q_2) : q \in Q\}$
        for $i \leftarrow \binom{n}{d} ; i > 0 ; i \leftarrow i - min(i, w)$ **do**
            $M \leftarrow preprocess_{[i-min(i,w):i-1]}(G, S)$
            $S \leftarrow echelonize(M \cup S) \setminus M$
    return S

It is easy to see that the echelonization task needs to work on a matrix with $|Q| + w$ rows where w is chosen as the maximum size of the windows. When there are too many pending polynomial pairs, it may be a good idea to partition Q into subsets of at most m elements each, such that the number of rows in the matrix becomes $m + w$. This reduces the memory consumption related to the construction of the matrix, although we would need to perform the reduction process until all the subsets are processed.

The choice of w has been found to strongly affect the runtime performance of the algorithm. Since there is only one active window at the same time, the implementation allocates the memory for w pivotal rows and reuses it. When the w rows fit in the L3 cache of the processor, spatial locality takes effect. This makes sense since the L3 cache, typically the largest cache available in current processors, is usually shared across all the CPU cores and the cores will need to constantly read the pivotal rows in a concurrent fashion. In fact, we recommend that $w + c$ rows fit in the L3 cache where c is the number of cores of the CPU, since c additional rows will be active during the reduction process.

5   Benchmarks

In this section we present the results of a series of benchmarks. First we will present how much time does our implementation take to solve the first HFE challenge under a varying number of cores and different values of the window size w. Then we will compare our implementation against PolyBori, FGB, and Magma. The second set of benchmarks also includes some instances coming from the Unbalanced Oil and Vinegar cryptosystem [20]. Theses instances have the property that their Gröbner bases are relatively large and of high degree.

5.1   Experimental Behavior of the F4 Variant Implementation

Compared to the sequential Gebauer and Möller implementation, our concurrent implementation of the chain criterion easily achieves a linear speedup. Unfortunately, the polynomial reduction procedure, which accounts for more than 90% of the total execution time, is memory bound. After several analysis, we tuned the window size in order make better use of the L3 cache. We present two tests, one that measures the performance impact of the L3 cache saturation in function of the window size, plus another one that measures the impact of the number of cores under an optimal window size. In both tests, the queue is partitioned into sets of at most 2048 polynomials each. A set is reduced in a single pass. The tests were performed on an Intel i7-5820K Haswell processor, which has 15 MB of L3 cache and 6 physical cores with hyper-threading enabled (for a total of 12 logical cores) running at 3.3 GHz. See Fig. 2.

The optimal window size for the tested hardware is $w = 48$, which together with the memory used by the polynomials assigned to each core, will use around 13 MB of the L3 cache. The stack usage and other trivial costs must also be taken into account. The slow performance that happens for very small windows is explained as follows. Each time a CPU core finishes the partial reduction of a polynomial by the current window, another polynomial is assigned to it and read from main memory. This cost is not amortized for very small windows. Decreasing the partition size of the queue to allow the set to also fit in the L3

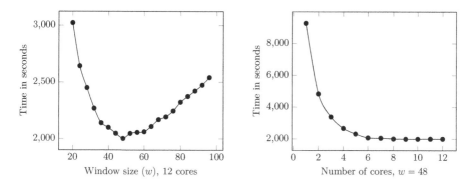

Fig. 2. Execution times for the first HFE Challenge.

cache does not help, since the number of passes would increase considerably and the generation of a window also needs to read from main memory.

The Intel Haswell architecture supports the AVX2 instruction set, which allows us to perform 256 bit vector operations in a single cycle. Our implementation uses them and thus the calculations are performed really fast once the data has been loaded. However, doubling the number of logical cores via hyper-threading does not help if memory is the bottleneck, as many related hardware resources are shared between logical cores inside the same physical core. For example, a line buffer must be allocated each time a memory request cannot be served by the L1 cache, but the hardware only has ten line buffers per physical core.

5.2   Comparison Against Other Gröbner Basis Implementations

We compare the execution time and memory consumption of our implementation against PolyBori, FGb, and Magma. The test cases are the first HFE challenge and the Unbalanced Oil and Vinegar polynomial systems PK15, PK16, PK17, PK18, and PK19, where the number suffix denotes the number of binary variables in the system. While we consider BooleanGB to be a great source of inspiration, its implementation as currently available in Macaulay2 is too slow to be included in the benchmarks, requiring hours of computation even for the smallest test case. The situation worsens if we use Macaulay2 without the module.

Our implementation along with FGb 1.68 and PolyBori 0.8.3 were tested on the Intel i7-5820K processor with 8 GB of RAM. However, the unavaibility of Magma forced us to rely on external reports or to test on unknown hardware with software limits. For the first HFE Challenge, Magma 2.20 was reported to run on a Intel Xeon E5-1650 processor [26]. The PK systems were solved on unknown hardware via the free Magma Calculator, which imposes an execution limit of 120 s and 380 MB of memory consumption [3]. See Table 1.

Our implementation is very fast and consistently consumes the least amount of memory. The memory consumption could be further reduced if we partitioned

Table 1. Benchmarks (* means that the program quickly runs out of memory)

Instance	PolyBori	FGb	Magma (Sparse)	Magma (Dense)	F4 Variant (Sparse)
PK15	60.69 s	2.40 s	1.5 s	1.3 s	0.8 s
	350 MB	108 MB	64 MB	32 MB	15 MB
PK16	518.09 s	18.1 s	7.2 s	5.7 s	5.3 s
	991 MB	202 MB	256 MB	62 MB	18 MB
PK17	1169.41 s	30.2 s	*	20.6 s	15.4 s
	2140 MB	247 MB	>380 MB	128 MB	32 MB
PK18	2976.46 s	70.3 s	*	37.1 s	41.9 s
	4229 MB	359 MB	>380 MB	155 MB	50 MB
PK19	5366.50 s	388.5 s	*	>120 s	101.2 s
	6829 MB	856 MB	>380 MB	>225 MB	122 MB
HFE80	*	>9000 s	3477.1 s	447.4 s	2002.4 s
	>8192 MB	>8192 MB	14029 MB	5836 MB	5981 MB

the queue in smaller sets like Magma does (512 elements per set instead of 2048). However, the dense variant of Magma is the fastest at the first HFE challenge by a considerable margin. This is because the HFE system is dense and Magma uses asymptotically faster algorithms for the dense case, while we always use a sparse strategy. Magma also reports that its F4 algorithm runs on a single core, but we do not know if this holds for the whole algorithm or just for the Gröbner related code surrounding the linear algebra phase. We believe that, aside from using faster algorithms for dense matrices, Magma's implementation is L1 and L2 cache aware. By reworking our polynomial reduction procedure we might considerably improve our timings, but Magma's implementation of dense linear algebra is famous for being one of the fastest available.

6 Conclusions

Understanding the high level descriptions of Gröbner basis algorithms is not enough to produce a highly efficient implementation. In this paper we have presented the algorithmic and implementation details of an F4 variant that is capable of performing Gröbner bases computations that are out of reach for most other implementations. We hope that these descriptions and explanations, plus the available source code of our program, are of help for researchers in the area of Gröbner bases. In a similar way, we also hope that the open source community and its end users are benefited by the availability of this work.

References

1. Bardet, M., Faugère, J.C., Salvy, B., Spaenlehauer, P.J.: On the complexity of solving quadratic Boolean systems. J. Complex. **29**(1), 53–75 (2013)

2. Bayer, D., Stillman, M.: A theorem on refining division orders by the reverse lexicographic order. Duke Math. J. **55**(2), 321–328 (1987)
3. Bosma, W., Cannon, J., Playoust, C.: Magma calculator (2016). http://magma. maths.usyd.edu.au/calc/
4. Bosma, W., Cannon, J., Playoust, C.: Magma computer algebra documentation (2016). https://magma.maths.usyd.edu.au/magma/handbook/text/1207
5. Brickenstein, M., Dreyer, A.: PolyBori: a framework for Gröbner basis computations with Boolean polynomials. J. Symb. Comput. **44**(9), 1326–1345 (2009). Effective Methods in Algebraic Geometry
6. Buchberger, B.: An Algorithm for Finding the Basis Elements in the Residue Class Ring Modulo a Zero Dimensional Polynomial Ideal. Ph.D. thesis (2006)
7. Buchberger, B.: A criterion for detecting unnecessary reductions in the construction of Gröbner-bases. In: Ng, E.W. (ed.) Symbolic and Algebraic Computation. LNCS, vol. 72, pp. 3–21. Springer, Heidelberg (1979). doi:10.1007/3-540-09519-5_52
8. Courtois, N., Klimov, A., Patarin, J., Shamir, A.: Efficient algorithms for solving overdefined systems of multivariate polynomial equations. In: Preneel, B. (ed.) EUROCRYPT 2000. LNCS, vol. 1807, pp. 392–407. Springer, Heidelberg (2000). doi:10.1007/3-540-45539-6_27
9. Cox, D.A., Little, J., O'Shea, D.: Ideals, Varieties, and Algorithms: An Introduction to Computational Algebraic Geometry and Commutative Algebra. Undergraduate Texts in Mathematics, 3rd edn. Springer, New York (2007)
10. Developers, T.S.: SageMath, the Sage Mathematics Software System (2016). http://www.sagemath.org
11. Eder, C.: An analysis of inhomogeneous signature-based Gröbner basis computations. J. Symb. Comput. **59**, 21–35 (2013)
12. Faugère, J., Gianni, P., Lazard, D., Mora, T.: Efficient computation of zero-dimensional Gröbner bases by change of ordering. J. Symb. Comput. **16**(4), 329–344 (1993)
13. Faugère, J.C.: A new efficient algorithm for computing Gröbner bases (F4). J. Pure Appl. Algebra **139**(1–3), 61–88 (1999)
14. Faugère, J.C.: A new efficient algorithm for computing Gröbner bases without reduction to zero (F5). In: Proceedings of the 2002 International Symposium on Symbolic and Algebraic Computation, NY, USA, pp. 75–83. ACM, New York (2002)
15. Faugère, J.-C.: FGb: a library for Computing Gröbner bases. In: Fukuda, K., Hoeven, J., Joswig, M., Takayama, N. (eds.) ICMS 2010. LNCS, vol. 6327, pp. 84–87. Springer, Heidelberg (2010). doi:10.1007/978-3-642-15582-6_17
16. Faugère, J.-C., Joux, A.: Algebraic cryptanalysis of Hidden Field Equation (HFE) cryptosystems using Gröbner Bases. In: Boneh, D. (ed.) CRYPTO 2003. LNCS, vol. 2729, pp. 44–60. Springer, Heidelberg (2003). doi:10.1007/978-3-540-45146-4_3
17. Fayssal, M.: Faugére-Lachartre Parallel Gaussian Elimination for Gröbner Bases Computations Over Finite Fields. Master's thesis, Pierre and Marie Curie University (2012)
18. Gebauer, R., Möller, H.M.: On an installation of Buchberger's algorithm. J. Symb. Comput. **6**(2–3), 275–286 (1988)
19. Grayson, D.R., Stillman, M.E.: Macaulay2, a software system for research in algebraic geometry. http://www.math.uiuc.edu/Macaulay2/
20. Herrera García, J.L.J.: Autenticación y Cifrado Basado en Ecuaciones Cuadráticas de Varias Variables. Ph.D. thesis, Instituto Politécnico Nacional (2015)
21. Hinkelmann, F., Arnold, E.: Fast Gröbner basis computation for boolean polynomials. CoRR (2010)

22. Mohamed, M.S.E., Cabarcas, D., Ding, J., Buchmann, J., Bulygin, S.: MXL3: an efficient algorithm for computing Gröbner bases of zero-dimensional ideals. In: Lee, D., Hong, S. (eds.) ICISC 2009. LNCS, vol. 5984, pp. 87–100. Springer, Heidelberg (2010). doi:10.1007/978-3-642-14423-3_7

23. Nguyen, T.H.: Combinations of Boolean Gröbner Bases and SAT Solvers. Ph.D. thesis, University of Kaiserslautern (2014)

24. Patarin, J.: Hidden fields equations (HFE) and isomorphisms of polynomials (IP): two new families of asymmetric algorithms. In: Maurer, U. (ed.) EURO-CRYPT 1996. LNCS, vol. 1070, pp. 33–48. Springer, Heidelberg (1996). doi:10. 1007/3-540-68339-9_4

25. Roune, B.H., Stillman, M.: Practical Gröbner basis computation. In: Proceedings of the 37th International Symposium on Symbolic and Algebraic Computation, ISSAC 2012, NY, USA, pp. 203–210. ACM, New York (2012)

26. Steel, A.: A dense variant of the F4 Gröbner basis algorithm (2013). http://magma. maths.usyd.edu.au/~allan/densef4/

Accelerating Hash-Based Query Processing Operations on FPGAs by a Hash Table Caching Technique

Behzad Salami[1,2(✉)], Oriol Arcas-Abella[1], Nehir Sonmez[1],
Osman Unsal[1], and Adrian Cristal Kestelman[1,2,3]

[1] Barcelona Supercomputing Center (BSC), Barcelona, Spain
{behzad.salami, oriol.arcas, nehir.sonmez, osman.unsal,
adrian.cristal}@bsc.es
[2] Universitat Polytecnica de Catalunya (UPC), Barcelona, Spain
[3] IIIA-Artificial Intelligence Research Institute-Spanish National Research
Council, Madrid, Spain

Abstract. Extracting valuable information from the rapidly growing field of Big Data faces serious performance constraints, especially in the software-based database management systems (DBMS). In a query processing system, hash-based computational primitives such as the hash join and the group-by are the most time-consuming operations, as they frequently need to access the hash table on the high-latency off-chip memories and also to traverse whole the table. Subsequently, the hash collision is an inherent issue related to the hash tables, which can adversely degrade the overall performance.

In order to alleviate this problem, in this paper, we present a novel pure hardware-based hash engine, implemented on the FPGA. In order to mitigate the high memory access latencies and also to faster resolve the hash collisions, we follow a novel design point. It is based on caching the hash table entries in the fast on-chip Block-RAMs of FPGA. Faster accesses to the correspondent hash table entries from the cache can lead to an improved overall performance.

We evaluate the proposed approach by running hash-based table join and group-by operations of 5 TPC-H benchmark queries. The results show $2.9\times$–$4.4\times$ speedups over the cache-less FPGA-based baseline.

1 Introduction

In the era of Internet of Things (IOT) and Big Data, fast query processing is a crucial requirement of the modern DBMS. In an attempt to move the computation closer to the storage, many previous studies have looked into accelerating database operations in the hardware platforms. Examples include employing vector architectures [9], ASICs [18], GPUs [10], or hybrid [25]. Other approaches either used FPGAs statically [3, 8, 15, 17, 26], or leveraged dynamic reconfigurability characteristic of FPGAs to better fit the requirements of the queries [6, 13]. The industry hasalso invested in products such as IBM Netezza [2] and Teradata Kickfire [14].

The hash-based operations, i.e. hash join and group-by are the most time-consuming operations of databases query processing systems. Previous studies have demonstrated

© Springer International Publishing AG 2017
C.J. Barrios Hernández et al. (Eds.): CARLA 2016, CCIS 697, pp. 131–145, 2017.
DOI: 10.1007/978-3-319-57972-6_10

that these operations account for more than 40% of total execution time while running queries from the TPC-H benchmark [9].

The hash join operation combines two data tables S and T together with a common key. The algorithm consists of *(i)* a build phase to construct a hash table using the rows of the table S, and *(ii)* a probe phase, where all keys in the table T are looked into the hash table to find whole the possible matches. Similarly, the group-by operation groups the rows of a given table based on common values of the *key* column, which can also be implemented using hash tables. The main issue that can degrade the performance of a hash engine is the hash collision, which is the situation of mapping two distinct keys into the same hash index. By design and in practice, these cases are inevitable for database applications and need to be handled appropriately. Among the possible solutions, software fallback mechanisms [17] or rehashing [7] can cause additional latencies that reduce the performance. On the other hand, collision resolution in the hardware implies chaining the hash table entries that can also undermine the hash table performance, especially under DDR memory latencies.

Due to the scarcity of on-chip BRAM resources that cannot guarantee to locate the entire hash table, previous FPGA implementations envisioned building the hash table in the off-chip DDR memory [17, 20]. Alternatively, in this work we propose a hash table caching technique, exploiting the on-chip BRAMs of FPGAs to mitigate the memory latencies. Also, our design resolves hash collisions without reverting to software fallbacks. For the evaluations, we run the hash join and group-by operations of 5 queries of the TPC-H benchmark suite and demonstrate up to 4.4× performance speedups, compared to a hardware baseline that does not employ any caching technique. The hardware baseline is an improved version of Ibex [17]. Despite Ibex that uses software fallbacks to resolve the hash collisions, in our baseline, we follow a pure hardware-based pointer chasing method.

In a nutshell, trading off the size and the latency of on/off-chip memories, we *(i)* can support large datasets using a hash table located in the off-chip memory, and *(ii)* avoid the high memory latencies by utilizing the on-chip BRAMs of FPGAs as the hash table cache. The contributions of this paper can be summarized as below:

- We propose a hash table caching mechanism that efficiently exploits the on-chip BRAMs of FPGA to serve some of the hash table inquiries. This method can be significantly faster than the conventional way to retrieve the hash table entries from the off-chip memories.
- We investigate the proposed technique for the hash-based operations of query processing systems, i.e. hash join and group-by. Hash collisions are resolved purely in the hardware, which taking advantage of the hash table caching method. We design the proposed method by leveraging Bluespec, a high-level synthesis (HLS) tool. The design is implemented on a Virtex 7 FPGA development board (VC709). We achieved up to 4.4× speedup, compared to the hardware baseline.

The rest of the paper is organized as follows: Sect. 2 includes the background information, as well as an illustration of the hash table caching technique. The proposed architecture is elaborated in Sect. 3. Section 4 introduces the evaluation methodology. Section 5 includes discussions the experimental results. In Sect. 6 we review related work and finally, Sect. 7 concludes the paper.

2 Background

Conventionally, data can be organized in either structured or unstructured management systems. Although, the proposed hash table caching technique can be customized in both the systems, our focus will be on the relational DBMS, as a common type of structured data management systems.

In an RDBMS, data is organized into tables using a model of vertical columns and horizontal rows. The rows represent entries in the database and columns define the data types. Data in the tables are formed as a pair of (*key, value*), where *key* points to one of the columns that play the main role in the query analysis such as sort key, hash join key, etc. Other columns are merged into the *value*. In order to access the data into the tables, query languages such as Scripting Query Language (SQL) have been introduced. In a typical SQL query, several language elements such as **SELECT**, **GROUPBY**, **ORDERBY**, etc., can exist. These operations can be semantically mapped to specialized hardware accelerators such as filtering, aggregation, hash join, sorting, etc. The hash-based operations, i.e. hash join and group-by are considered in this work because they are the most time-consuming DBMS operations.

2.1 Hash Join Background

One common type of join operation is the equijoin or θ-join. It means combining rows from two or more tables with a common cell. The hash-based join or hash join is the most common type of table join algorithms.

The objective in the hash join is to reduce the search space using a hash function over the common cell, or *key*. It consists of building and probing phases. In the building phase, the hash table is constructed using the input table (S). In this phase, for each tuple (k_s, v_s) a hash index is calculated using a hash function and correspondingly, a hash table entry is created in that given index of the hash table. In the probe phase, the hash table is being scanned in the hash index. The corresponding hash index is generated by the hash function applied on the each input tuple (k_T, v_T) of data table (T). If any match is found the resulting 3-tuple (k, v_S, v_T) is output, where $k = k_S = k_T$. Otherwise, it means that the current input tuple does not exist in the hash table and it is skipped. It is worth noting that as the hash table construction is more costly operation than the probing of the hash table, the smaller input table is used in the build phase $(|S| < |T|)$.

2.2 Group-by Background

Group-by is another query processing operation that can be implemented using the hash tables, as well. It is usually used in conjunction with an aggregation function to produce the aggregation of the rows in the same group, called group-by aggregation [24]. For a given table S with rows (k_{S1}, v_{S1}) and (k_{S2}, v_{S2}), the group-by and group-by aggregation operations will produce tuples with (k, v_{S1}, v_{S2}) and $(k, aggrFunc(v_{S1}, v_{S2}))$ fields, respectively $(k = k_{S1} = k_{S2})$. The aggregation function can be **SUM**,

AVERAGE, MAX, COUNT, etc. It is worth noting that constructing the hash table on *key* consists of adding the grouped data into the hash table. Another word, data in the hash table are already grouped.

2.3 Collision in the Hash-Based Operations Including Hash Join and Group-by

In practice, in the hash-based query processing operations an ideal hash function to generate a unique hash index for every input data tuple scarcely exist. Thus hash collisions inevitably happen, particularly for DBMS applications, and need to be appropriately handled. In order to resolve this issue, various mechanisms on FPGAs are proposed. Software fallback mechanisms [17] facilitate the hardware design. However, it may cause additional latencies due to the transfer time between the FPGA and the software. Rehashing [7] is another method, which could also cause extra overheads due to additional rehashing costs. On the other hand, supporting collision management in the hardware implies chaining the hash table entries. It means that the next address to be jumped to can only be determined after the previous line is read. Under DDR latencies it can adversely diminish the overall performance.

2.4 Illustrating the Hash Table Caching

The data/instruction caching is a widely used optimization mechanism to cover the speed gap between the storage and the processor. This paper is motivated by the fact that caching can also be employed to improve the performance of the hash-based operations of the query processing systems. As far as we know, this is the first work to design a hash join/group-by engine equipped with a caching mechanism.

For convenience, we illustrate the proposed technique using an example in the probe phase of the hash join operation to show how does this operation can take advantage of the hash table caching technique? The data tables that include the input dataset for probing, the hash table, and the contents of the cache are shown in Fig. 1c–e,

Step	Cycle	Operation	Step	Cycle	Operation
0	0	lookupHT i0	0	0	lookupC i0
1	1	lookupHT i1	1	1	lookupC i1, respC i0, missC, lookupHT i0
2	2	lookupHT i2	2	2	lookupC i2, respC i1, hitC, match k1
3	3	lookupHT i0	3	3	lookupC i0, respC i2, missC, lookupHT i2
4	35	respHT i0, match k0	4	4	respC, missC, lookupHT i0
5	36	respHT i1, match k1	5	31	respHT i0, match k0
6	37	respHT i2, mismatch k2	6	32	respHT i2, mismatch k2
7	38	respHT i3, collision k3, lookupHT p0	7	33	respHT i0, collision k3, lookupC p0
8	69	respHT i0, match k3	8	34	respC i0, hitC, match k3
		(a)			(b)

k0	i0
k1	i1
k2	i2
k3	i0

(c) Dataset

i0	k0	p0
i1	k1	--
p0	k3	--

(d) Hash Table

i1	k1	--
p0	k3	--

(e) Cache

Fig. 1. An example hash probe, baseline (a) vs. cache (b). Example dataset (c), the content of hash table (d) and the cache (e).

respectively. The hash table and cache are already filled in the build phase. The cache has the corresponding hash indexes of only *k1* and *k3*.

The dataset that needs to be probed in the hash table is shown in Fig. 1c, with four keys and their corresponding hash indexes. The hash collision requires scanning a pointer chain from *i0* to *p0*. As it can be seen in this table, there is a hash collision for *k0* and *k3*, both having the same hash index *i0*. There are totally two directly matched key, one matched key after a collision, and one mismatched key.

In this example, the latency of the cache in the on-chip BRAM and the hash table in the off-chip DDR are assumed to be 1 and 30 cycles, respectively. The cycle-by-cycle execution of the cache-less baseline and cache-based hash probe are depicted in Fig. 1a, and b, respectively. Several terms are used to describe the example clearer: *lookup* (to send read request for the hash table –HT or the cache -C), *resp* (to get response from the hash table –HT or the cache -C), *(mis-)match* (to show that an input key is (mis-)matched from the hash table or from the cache), *collision* (to show a detected hash collision), and *hit/miss* (to show a cache hit/miss).

As described in Fig. 1a, in the baseline execution, all the accesses are served from the hash table in DDR (*lookupHT*). The responses arrive 30 cycles later (*respHT*). In contrast, as it can be seen in Fig. 1b, in the cache-based version, all the inquiries are being looked up from the cache, first (*lookupC*). The successful requests (cache hit-*respC*) are being processed in the probe engine, and the unsuccessful (missed) ones are being forwarded to the hash table (*lookupHT*). Serving some of the requests from the cache reduces the total cycles to probe the example dataset from 69 to 34.

In this example, we showed both the cache hit and miss scenarios, to demonstrate the efficiency of the hit requests against the overhead of missed cache inquiries. However, in the real datasets other events such as a chain of colliding keys, redundancy chaining, the irregular latency of DDR, the complexity of the write requests in the build phase, etc., may appear.

3   The Overall Architecture of the Proposed Engine

The overall layout of the proposed accelerator is shown in Fig. 2. The connection of FPGA with the host and the off-chip DDR-3 is through the high-speed PCI-3 and DDR-3 interfaces, respectively. The host initializes DDR-3 with the input data tables.

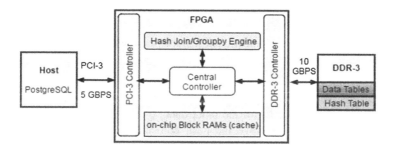

Fig. 2. The overall layout of the accelerator including Host, FPGA, and DDR-3.

DDR-3 memory locates the hash table, as well. FPGA is comprised of several components: *(i)* device drivers to manage the off-chip data transfer, *(ii)* a central controller to manage the computations and data movements, *(iii)* the accelerator engine (hash join and group by), and *(iv)* finally, the on-chip Block RAMs, which are configured as the cache of the hash table.

The detailed structure of the accelerator is shown in Fig. 3. Its overall architecture is comprised of several components: *(i)* a *(Linear Feedback Shift Register) LFSR-based hash function:* It generates the hash index of the input *key* in a fully pipelined fashion. The generated hash indexes are used as the index of the corresponding hash table/cache entries. *(ii) The logic of the accelerator, i.e. hash join build, hash join probe, and group-by:* As a part of their functionality, the hash collisions of the colliding keys are resolved by chained together in a linked list fashion. The similar method is used to organize the repetitive keys in the hash table. *(iii) The hash table in the off-chip DDR-3:* In order to efficiently support pointer chasing in the aforementioned special cases, we partitioned the hash table into two distinct parts. The first half part of the hash table can be directly indexed by the hash function in normal cases. The second half part, which is excluded from the range of the hash function, is used for only the chains of the entries. This part of the memory is consecutively being accessed. *(iv) A cache of the hash table in the on-chip BRAMs:* The entries of the cache are exact copies of some of the hash table entries. The hash table inquiries will be served from the cache. Only the missed requests from the cache will be forwarded to the hash table.

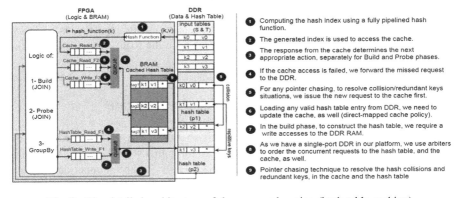

Fig. 3. The detailed architecture of the proposed engine (hash table caching).

In order to support the aforementioned features, each entry of the cache/hash table has several fields, including:

- *valid* bit to show the validity of the entry.
- *key* field to store the input data *keys*.
- *value* field to store the *value* of the input data.
- *pointer$_c$* that is used to resolve the hash collisions by storing the index of an allocated hash table entry, following the pointer chaining mechanism.

- *pointer$_r$* that is used to manage the repetitive keys in the hash table. Similar to the hash collision, it uses the pointer chaining mechanism. The exception is the group-by aggregation, where instead of storing key itself, we compute an aggregation of the keys. Thus, there is no need for pointer chasing in this particular case.
- *cache tag* field to discard false positives in the cache.

Consequently, having any successful inquiries from the cache correspond to skip of the hash table accesses in the off-chip DDR-3 memory. In addition, similar to Ibex [17], we use a Content Addressable Memory (CAM) to remove read-after-write hazards.

3.1 Hash Join: Build Phase- Constructing the Hash Table

In order to insert a new (k_s, v_s) pair into the hash table, first, a hash index of k_s is generated by the hash function. This index points to the corresponding index in the hash table/cache. We use an LFSR-based hash function to generate pseudo-random hash indexes. Later on, the content of the corresponding entry of the cache is retrieved. Due to the retrieved entry, *(i)* if it is not valid or is an undesirable (false positive) entry, a cache miss occurs. The false positive situations of the cache can be recognized by checking the cache tag. In these situations, we forward the same inquiry to the hash table. Or, *(ii)* if the cache hits, or we get the corresponding entry from the hash table, three different cases can occur:

- If the retrieved entry is not valid, a new entry is added to the corresponding index of both the hash table and the cache.
- If the accessed entry is valid, with the same k_s, it needs to allocate a new entry and appropriately update the pointer fields, to manage repetitive keys in a linked-list fashion. Accordingly, the hash table and cache are updated.
- If the accessed entry is valid, but with a different k_s, a hash collision occurs. Similar to the case of repetitive keys, a new hash table entry is allocated. Both the new and old entries are updated in the cache and the hash table, to preserve the linked-list behavior. Following this chaining method, nested hash collision can be resolved, as well.

Our engine can deal with an unlimited number of hash collisions/repetitive keys, as long as the hash table is not full.

3.2 Hash Join: Probe Phase- Scanning the Hash Table

In order to scan the hash table, first, we compute the hash index for the new k_T. Later on, retrieving the corresponding index from the cache, *(i)* if it is not a valid entry or is not the desired entry (false positive), thus, a cache miss occurs. Therefore, the same inquiry is forwarded to the hash table. And, *(ii)* if the cache hits or the response from the hash table arrives, three cases can occur:

- If keys do not match and there is no valid collision *pointer$_c$* field in the retrieved entry, there is no entry in the hash table which matches with k_T.

- If keys do not match, but there is a valid collision *pointer$_c$* field in the retrieved entry, a hash collision occurs. Therefore, we first scan the subsequent hash table entries, retrieving them from the cache, first. This process may lead to a mismatch, if and only if no match can be found until the end of the chain. Never the less, at any point of the chain, it is possible to find a match.
- If keys match, their combination will produce a junction row. This match can be found directly, or after a pointer chasing process. Accordingly, all the v_s in the chain must orderly be read to generate the tuples of the junction table, (k, v_s, v_T) that $k = k_S = k_T$.

In the probe phase, the cache is updated by each valid response from the hash table.

3.3   Group-by Aggregation: Constructing a Hash Table to Group Data

Group-by operation intrinsically is similar to the build phase of the hash join operation, as data in the hash table are already grouped based on the *key* field. The main difference is that *(i)* usually in the SQL queries the group-by operation is accompanied by an aggregation function, such as **SUM**, MAX, **COUNT**, **AVERAGE**, etc. Consequently, instead of storing *key* itself in the hash table, an aggregation of the *key* needs to be stored, without any necessity for pointer chasing to manage the repetitive keys. *(ii)* As the number of groups is usually quite smaller than the size of the input dataset, there are often accesses to the same hash table entries. This can significantly take advantage of the hash table caching technique, as the repetitive accesses can be served from the cache.

In order to perform a group-by operation, similar steps to the hash join build phase are followed, except the step 2, where the input *key* is matched with an entry in the hash table/cache. In this particular case, we perform the aggregation on the *value* field and skip allocation a new hash table entry to store the *key* field.

3.4   Policies of the Cache

Various accessing methods to the cache and its different Read/Write policies can impact the performance. The cache policies in the proposed technique are as below:

- *Cache Contents:* The cache contains a number of the recently accessed valid entries of the hash table. Each cache entry is an exact copy of the corresponding entry in the hash table.
- *Cache Replacement Policy:* The hash table in the off-chip DDR memory is significantly larger than the cache. Thus, a replacement policy is required to substitute the new with the old entries of the cache. We use a direct-mapped policy, where all the valid retrieved entries from the hash table are overwritten into the cache.
- *Cache access policy:* For all the required hash table entries, first, we look up the cache. Any cache hit leads to skipping the DDR-3 accesses, but in contrast, the missed requests need to be forwarded to the hash table. In order to discard false positives, the cache has an additional field, the *cache tag*.
- *Cache Indexing:* We use the Least-Significant Bits (LSB) of the hash table index as the cache index. The Most-Significant Bits (MSB) are stored as the *cache tag* field.

4 Experimental Methodology

We used Xilinx ISE version 14.1 and Bluespec System Verilog compiler [1] in the development phase. Bluespec is a commonly-used cycle-accurate modern HLS tool, desired for control-oriented designs such as hash join. Our system was designed to work at 200 MHz on a VC709 development board with a Virtex-7 FPGA and a 4 GB DDR-3 memory channel. Our device has about 50 MBit on-chip BRAMs that are employed as the cache. The PCI-3 controller works at 150 MHz. Thus, the synchronizing FIFOs are exploited to exchange data among different clock domains properly. We have made all our modules fully parametrizable. We validated the experimental result by checking with the software (PostgreSQL [22]) runs of the same DBMS operations. (*key*, *value*) pairs are 64 bits, each of which is 32-bits.

4.1 Hardware and Software Comparison Baselines

In the hardware baseline, only DDR-3 RAM is exploited to store the hash table, without any caching mechanism. Many FPGA implementations follow the similar design point. For instance, recently Ibex [15] is presented that uses the DDR-3 to locate the hash table but unlike our baseline, it falls back software for the hash collisions. Thus, our hardware baseline is efficient, cache-less, and pure hardware FPGA-based implementation of the corresponding operations, i.e. the hash join and the group-by.

The second comparison case is a state-of-the-art software-based DBMS (PostgreSQL) that is running in the warm cache setup on a server with 64 GB RAM and a Xeon E5-2630 CPU. PostgreSQL does not support multi-threading. Thus, we use the single-thread execution times of the queries for the comparisons. In order to get the warm execution time, we run PostgreSQL two consecutive times. The second run is supposed to be from its internal buffers, where data tables are already located into the system memory. There are no disk I/O transactions in the warm cache mode of the software runs.

It is worth noting that the execution model in the software baseline is different with the FPGA-based solutions, including the proposed cache-based method and the hardware baseline. We follow a dataflow execution model in the FPGA-based accelerators, which allows deep pipelining and data streaming capabilities to achieve the peak performance. In contrast, PostgreSQL runs on the scalar processor with a control-flow execution model, which suffers from its conventional implications.

4.2 The Structure of the Benchmarks

In order to evaluate the proposed engine, we run a set of complex queries from the TPC-H benchmark suite [23]. Specifically, we selected Q03, Q04, Q12, Q13, and Q14, because they have different table sizes and also different join selectivity (the size of the output data table divided by Cartesian product of the two input tables). However, as the given queries are composed of several other operations, such as sorting, aggregation, etc., we made a sub-query to extract only their hash join and group-by part.

Furthermore, some of the queries such as Q03 are composed of multiple hash-based operations. For these cases, we extract different sub-queries for each hash join/group-by operation, run them separately, and get their distinct execution times. Later on, in order to compute the total execution time of the given query, we sum up all those separate parts.

The general format of the generated subqueries is shown in Table 1, separately for the hash join and the group-by operations. We assumed two data tables S and T with data tuples (k_S, v_S) and (k_T, v_T), respectively. In addition, we used various sizes of data tables in the experiments, including 1 GB and 10 GB scales. We repeat the query runs 10 times. The reported total execution time of each given query is the average of the execution times of its various runs.

Table 1. The general format of the sub-queries used in the benchmarks.

Hash join		Group-by	
SELECT	v_S, v_T	SELECT	SUM(v_S)
FROM	S, T	FROM	S
WHERE	$k_S = k_T$	GROUPBY	k_S

5   Experimental Results

In this section, we evaluate the proposed cache-based engine for the hash join and group-by operations. Due to the size of the each entry of the cache and also the size of the available BRAMs in our device, the cache can cope with about 256K entries. Thus, in 1 GB scale, we observed that BRAMs could entirely store the corresponding hash tables without any need for accessing the off-chip DDR memory. Followingly, in 1 GB scale, we exploited the on-chip BRAMs as the hash table (not as the cache). In contrast, for 10 GB scale, as the sizes of hash tables are larger than the BRAMs, we follow the proposed hash table caching technique.

5.1   Analyzing the Hash Table Caching

Table 2 includes the experimental results for 10 GB scale. In this table, *table size* refers to the number of the rows (key-value pairs) of the input data tables. The total *number of the collisions* is also shown in this table. Another important parameter is the *number of lookups* for the cache and for the hash table, as well. The *hit ratio (H.R)* of the cache that is an important metric to determine the performance achievement can be computed as the Eq. 1:

$$H.R = \frac{\#cach\_lookup - \#ht\_lookup}{\#cache\_lookup} \tag{1}$$

For convenience, we describe a sample result of Table 2, probe phase of Q03. For this particular case, we observed that *(i)* totally 44.2M cache read requests are issued;

Table 2. The experimental results of hash table caching, 10 GB scale.

Query	Operation	Table size (M)	#cache_lookup (M)	#ht_lookup (M)	Collision (M)	H.R (%)
Q03	Build	1.4	1.7	1.49	0.3	12.3
	Probe	32.1	44.2	29.4	8.4	33.4
	Groupby	0.3	0.35	0.05	0.02	85
Q04	Build	0.56	0.69	0.56	0.13	18.8
	Probe	37.2	57.1	41.2	13.2	27.8
	Groupby	0.52	0.52	~ 0	0	100
Q12	Build	0.3	0.35	0.3	0.05	14.2
	Probe	15	16.2	15	1.2	7.8
	Groupby	0.31	0.31	~ 0	0	100
Q13	Build	1.5	1.8	1.56	0.3	13.3
	Probe	14.8	19.5	11.9	2.6	38.9
	Groupby	1.5	1.5	~ 0	0	100
Q14	Build	0.7	0.78	0.7	0.08	10.2
	Probe	2	2.2	2	0.2	9

32.1M read requests of the original dataset and 12.1M additional requests (37.6% of the table size) for pointer chasing cases that 8.4M of them are as the result of hash collisions and the rest 3.7M as the result of repetitive keys. Furthermore, *(ii)* 33.4% of cache read requests are successfully served from the cache and the rest are forwarded to the hash table. Thus, the *H.R* is 33.4%.

The experimental results show that the *H.R* is on average 34.75%. It ranges from 7.8% to 100%. More specifically, about the hash join cases, we observed that:

- The average *H.R* in the build phase of the given queries is 13.7% that is significantly less that the total average *H.R* (34.75%). For all of the studied queries, the hash join *key* in the build phase is a primary (no repetitive) key. Thus, the cache is not efficiently utilized as a consequence of the less data locality in the hash table accesses, for this case.
- Probe keys of Q12 and Q14 are the primary keys, as well. Thus, we observed less *H.R* for these queries compared to others (8.4% vs. 24.8%).
- Input data tables in the probe phase are significantly larger than in the build phase, on average 30×. Thus, although, the hash table construction in the build phase is amore expensive operation, we observed that the execution time of the probe phase is dominant.

Although, the cache misses incur additional overheads, the substantial improvement of the cache hits, in terms of mitigating the latency of the memory, covers its side effects and leads to better performance compared to the cache-less hardware baseline.

In addition, most of the studied queries, except Q14, are composed of a group-by aggregation operation. For instance, in 10 GB scale of Q03, 300K tuples are grouped into about 100K individual groups, or 520K tuples of Q04 are grouped into only 5 groups. The experimental results in Table 2 show that the *H.R* of the cache for the queries with a small number of the groups is 100%, which is the consequence of the small enough hash tables that can be entirely located in the cache. In addition, in the group-by aggregation operation, each hash table/cache entry points to an individual group. Thus, repetitive keys that are located in a same group are also served from the same indexes of the hash table/cache. This situation leads to a high hit ratio of the cache.

5.2 The Overall Performance Analysis

The total execution time of the studied queries is shown in Fig. 4. It includes the execution time of *(i)* the BRAMs-based design, where BRAMs are either used as the main hash table in 1 GB scale or as the cache in 10 GB scale, *(ii)* cache-less FPGA-based hardware baseline, and *(iii)* the software baseline.

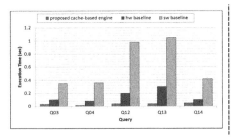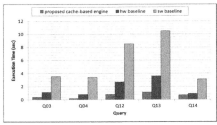

Fig. 4. The overall performance, comparing the proposed engine with a cache-less hardware and also software baselines for (left) 1 GB and (right) 10 GB scales.

For 1 GB scale we achieved on average 4.6× and 18.9×, and for 10 GB scale the speedup is on average 3× and 9.7×, comparing proposed hash join engine against hardware and software baselines, respectively. More specifically, we observed that:

- For 1 GB scale that we could run all the studied benchmarks by exploiting BRAMs as the hash table, the speedup ranges from 2× to 7.5×, comparing proposed architecture to the hardware baseline.
- For the cache-based version in 10 GB scale, the speedup ranges from 1.2× (Q14) to 4.4× (Q04). In Q14, the *H.R* of the cache is 9.6% on average, while it is 45.9% on average for the other queries. The main reason of having less *H.R* in Q14 is that it has no group-by operation, where the cache efficiently works.

Furthermore, comparing the proposed hash join engine to the software baseline, the achieved throughput improvement is mainly the consequence of the inherent capability of FPGA to perform dataflow execution in a deep pipelined fashion. As it can be seen, even baseline hardware version is on average 4× faster than software. However, additional optimizations in the proposed hash table caching mechanism substantially increase the speedup. We observed on average 14.3× speed up.

5.3 The Resource Utilization

The hardware resource usage of the baseline and proposed cache-based engines are shown in Table 3. We observed that although, the utilization rates of the Look-Up Table (LUT) and Flip-Flop (FF) are almost similar in both versions, the usage of BRAMs is significantly different. Entirely 62% of available BRAMs are used as the cache that can deal with about 256K entries.

Table 3. Hardware resource utilization rates

	LUT	FF	BRAM
Baseline	128581 (1%)	150123 (2%)	12 (1%)
Cache-based	16368 (1.5%)	163854 (2%)	724 (62%)

6 Related Work

Our design can be seen as a combination of the Ibex engine [17] and the hardware hash table chaining approach [8] with the main contribution of caching. For joining tables, hash joins are the most commonly used approach [19]. However, many examples of other types of table joins exist such as the merge join algorithm [3], the handshake join [16, 21], etc.

Multithreading the build and probe phase engines have shown to offer direct performance benefits [7, 12]. Multithreading can effectively mitigate the DDR access latencies, with the overhead of needing more I/O bandwidth and the additional circuit to manage the concurrent threads. However, this technique can be integrated with the proposed hash table caching mechanism in this paper to achieve a significant throughput.

In [3], the authors design an FPGA prototype that can perform a parallel sort-merge join, making use of a sort tree as a prerequisite. In this work, we implement a hash join that can be inherently faster, as we do not perform any initial sorting step on the input data tables.

In Widx [12], an out of order SPARC v9 processor core is powered with a small core to accelerate the hash join operation with index walkers that walk multiple buckets, concurrently. This technique improves indexing performance of the TPC-H queries by 3.1× on average, while saves on average 83% of energy. Widx is similar to our approach, as it also aims to reduce the overheads of the pointer chasing (walking). However, Widx is a hardware-software codesign that follows a different approach with the proposed hash table caching method in this paper, which is entirely deployed in the hardware.

LINQits [4] accelerates a domain-specific query language called LINQ and is prototyped on a Zynq processor. It compares queries into hardware accelerator templates and for the hash join case, it keeps the hash table in a sparse key table. It keeps the collided hash keys in the Spill Queue. Once reading its current partition is finished, it re-circulates the content of the Spill Queue (and its partition) until all the elements have been processed. Our proposed technique is designed not to require any Spill Queue or rehashing.

Finally, the proposed design could also be used together with the recent research on key-value stores [5, 11, 20]. Key-value stores are kind of unstructured (non-relational) databases, where the hash table is their key comprising component. The proposed hash table caching mechanism can be customized to improve the throughput of the key-value stores, as well.

7 Conclusions

In this paper, we have demonstrated the design of a novel cache-based query processing operations, i.e. hash join and group-by on FPGAs. Our contributions include hash table caching in the hardware and featuring collision, without reverting any software fallbacks. We showed the usefulness of the proposed hash table caching technique to process relevant hash join and group-by kernels in the TPC-H queries, with a maximum of 4.2X speedup over a pipelined baseline. Our experimental results show that we are enabled to both *(i)* use the full capacity of the DDR memory to store complete hash tables, and by employing a "hash table cache", *(ii)* to mitigate the long and irregular latencies of DDR memories, exploiting the fast BRAM resources of FPGA, which in turn significantly improves the performance of the hash join and group-by operations.

Acknowledgments. The research leading to these results has received funding from the European Union's Seventh Framework Program (FP7/2007-2013), for Advanced Analytics for Extremely Large European Databases (AXLE) project under grant agreement number 318633, and from the Ministry of Economy and Competitiveness of Spain under contract number TIN2015-65316-p.

References

1. Bluespec, Inc. http://bluespec.com/
2. Netezza. The Netezza FAST engines framework. http://www.monash.com/uploads/netezza-fpga.pdf
3. Casper, J., Olukotun, K.: Hardware acceleration of database operations. In: Proceedings of the 2014 ACM/SIGDA International Symposium on Field-programmable Gate Arrays, pp. 151–160. ACM (2014)
4. Chung, E.S., Davis, J.D., Lee, J.: LINQits: big data on little clients. ACM SIGARCH Comput. Archit. News **41**, 261–272 (2013)
5. De, A., et al.: Minerva: accelerating data analysis in next-generation SSDs. In: 2013 IEEE 21st Annual International Symposium on Field-Programmable Custom Computing Machines (FCCM), pp. 9–16. IEEE (2013)
6. Dennl, C., Ziener, D., Teich, J.: On-the-fly composition of FPGA-based SQL query accelerators using a partially reconfigurable module library. In: 2012 IEEE 20th Annual International Symposium on Field-Programmable Custom Computing Machines (FCCM), pp. 45–52. IEEE (2012)

7. Halstead, R.J., et al.: FPGA-based multithreading for in-memory hash joins. In: Biennial Conference of Innovative Data Systems Research (CIDR) (2015)
8. Halstead, R.J., et al.: Accelerating join operation for relational databases with FPGAs. In: 2013 IEEE 21st Annual International Symposium on Field-Programmable Custom Computing Machines (FCCM), pp. 17–20. IEEE (2013)
9. Hayes, T., et al.: Vector extensions for decision support DBMS acceleration. In: 2012 45th Annual IEEE/ACM International Symposium on Microarchitecture, pp. 166–176. IEEE (2012)
10. He, J., Lu, M., He, B.: Revisiting co-processing for hash joins on the coupled CPU-GPU architecture. Proc. VLDB Endow. **6**(10), 889–900 (2013)
11. István, Z., et al.: A flexible hash table design for 10GBPS key-value stores on FPGAs. In: 2013 23rd International Conference on Field Programmable Logic and Applications, pp. 1–8. IEEE (2013)
12. Kocberber, O., et al.: Meet the walkers: accelerating index traversals for in-memory databases. In: Proceedings of the 46th Annual IEEE/ACM International Symposium on Microarchitecture, pp. 468–479. ACM (2013)
13. Koch, D., Torresen, J.: FPGASort: a high performance sorting architecture exploiting run-time reconfiguration on FPGAs for large problem sorting. In: Proceedings of the 19th ACM/SIGDA International Symposium on Field programmable Gate Arrays, pp. 45–54. ACM (2011)
14. Krishnamurthy, R., et al.: Methods and systems for generating query plans that are compatible for execution in hardware. U.S. Patent Application No. 12/168,821, 7 July 2008
15. Mueller, R., Teubner, J., Alonso, G.: Data processing on FPGAs. Proc. VLDB Endow. **2**(1), 910–921 (2009)
16. Oge, Y., et al.: An implementation of handshake join on FPGA. In: 2011 Second International Conference on Networking and Computing (ICNC), pp. 95–104. IEEE (2011)
17. Woods, L., Teubner, J., Alonso, G.: Less watts, more performance: an intelligent storage engine for data appliances. In: Proceedings of the 2013 ACM SIGMOD International Conference on Management of Data, pp. 1073–1076. ACM (2013)
18. Wu, L., et al.: Q100: the architecture and design of a database processing unit. ACM SIGPLAN Not. **49**(4), 255–268 (2014)
19. Zeller, H., Gray, J.: An adaptive hash join algorithm for multiuser environments. In: VLDB, pp. 186–197 (1990)
20. Blott, M., et al.: Achieving 10Gbps line-rate key-value stores with FPGAs. In: Presented as part of the 5th USENIX Workshop on Hot Topics in Cloud Computing (2013)
21. Roy, P., Teubner, J., Gemulla, R.: Low-latency handshake join. Proc. VLDB Endow. **7**(9), 709–720 (2014)
22. Latest version of PostgreSQL 5.3. https://2ndquadrant.com/en/
23. TPC-H benchmark set. http://www.tpc.org/tpch/
24. Hayes, T., et al.: Future vector microprocessor extensions for data aggregations. In: Proceedings of the 43rd International Symposium on Computer Architecture, pp. 418–430. IEEE Press (2016)
25. Arcas-Abella, O., et al.: Hardware acceleration for query processing: leveraging FPGAs, CPUs, and memory. Comput. Sci. Eng. **18**(1), 80–87 (2016)
26. Salami, B., Arcas-Abella, O., Sonmez, N.: HATCH: hash table caching in hardware for efficient relational join on FPGA. In: 2015 IEEE 23rd Annual International Symposium on Field-Programmable Custom Computing Machines (FCCM), p. 163. IEEE (2015)

Distributed Big Data Analysis for Mobility Estimation in Intelligent Transportation Systems

Enzo Fabbiani[1], Pablo Vidal[2], Renzo Massobrio[1(✉)], and Sergio Nesmachnow[1]

[1] Universidad de la República, Herrera y Reissig 565, 11300 Montevideo, Uruguay
{enzo.fabbiani,renzom,sergion}@fing.edu.uy
[2] CONICET–Universidad Nacional de la Patagonia Austral,
Acceso Norte, Ruta 3, 9011 Caleta Olivia, Argentina
pjvidal@uaco.unpa.edu.ar

Abstract. This article describes the application of distributed computing techniques for the analysis of big data information from Intelligent Transportation Systems. Extracting useful mobility information from large volumes of data is crucial to improve decision-making processes in smart cities. We study the problem of estimating demand and origin-destination matrices based on ticket sales and location of buses in the city. We introduce a framework for mobility analysis in smart cities, including two algorithms for the efficient processing of large mobility data from the public transportation in Montevideo, Uruguay. Parallel versions are proposed for distributed memory (e.g., cluster, grid, cloud) infrastructures and a cluster implementation is presented. The experimental analysis performed using realistic datasets demonstrate that significatively speedup values, up to 16.41, are obtained.

Keywords: Distributed computing · Big data · Mobility analysis · Intelligent Transportation Systems

1 Introduction

Nowadays, many complex activities are developed in modern cities, which impose serious challenges to the mobility of citizens [7]. The main mobility issues in dense urban areas are related to public transport systems that are not capable of fulfilling the growing demand for transportation. In order to implement innovative solutions that address this issue, it is necessary to have access to updated information about the mobility of the citizens [2]. In most cities, the information available from public administrations is scarce and outdated, due to the lack of financial and human resources assigned to gathering and managing mobility data. In other cases, data are gathered but are not used for improving the mobility or optimizing public/vehicular transportation. In this scenario, developing improved decision-making processes related to urban mobility becomes mandatory. New smart city technologies are very helpful to offer high quality solutions for this kind of mobility problems.

C.J. Barrios Hernández et al. (Eds.): CARLA 2016, CCIS 697, pp. 146–160, 2017.
DOI: 10.1007/978-3-319-57972-6_11

The paradigm of smart cities proposes taking advantage of information and communication technologies to improve the quality and efficiency of urban services [4]. Intelligent Transportation Systems (ITS) are a key component of smart cities. ITS are defined as those systems integrating synergistic technologies, computational intelligence, and engineering concepts to develop and improve transportation. They are aimed at providing innovative services for transport and traffic management, with the main goals of improving transportation safety and mobility, and also enhancing productivity [18]. ITS allow gathering several data regarding transportation and mobility in the cities [5]. In big urban areas, they generate huge volumes of data that can be processed to extract valuable information about the mobility of citizens.

This article presents a framework to study mobility in the context of smart cities. In order to solve mobility and urban transportation optimization problems it is imperative to understand the mobility patterns of citizens and the demand distribution for public transport. This information is often represented using matrices: (i) origin-destination (OD) matrices indicate the amount of people moving from each point in the city in a given period of time [1]; (ii) demand matrices, measure the number of bus tickets sold between each location in the city. These matrices are often built using data from surveys performed in-situ to passengers and drivers. However, surveys offer only a partial vision of the mobility patterns in the city, are expensive, and need to be performed regularly to get updated information. A different approach to build demand and OD matrices is based on processing real data from ITS, including tickets sold with and without smart cards, GPS data from buses, etc.

We introduce a specific methodology for generating OD and demand matrices using data from ITS to study mobility in smart cities. Taking into account the large computing time demanded when dealing with huge volumes of data, we propose applying distributed computing techniques to speed up the processing. A data-parallel approach is devised to process large datasets on distributed memory parallel architectures (e.g., cluster, grid, and cloud systems). Two specific algorithms are presented, based on real data from the ITS in Montevideo, Uruguay. The proposed approach can easily be extended to any other ITS-related information and scenarios.

The main contributions of the research reported in this article are: (i) we introduce a methodology for OD matrix estimation using smart card information; (ii) we design and implement specific algorithms for processing big data using distributed computing techniques; and (iii) we report an experimental analysis which demonstrates that significant speedup values are obtained, allowing the efficient processing of large datasets.

The article is organized as follows. Section 2 introduces the problem of Big Data analysis for ITS. The proposal of applying distributed computing techniques to accelerate the processing of large volumes of ITS data is described in Sect. 3. The experimental evaluation of the proposed algorithms is reported in Sect. 5. Finally, Sect. 6 presents the conclusions of the research and formulates the main lines for future work.

2   Big Data Analysis for Intelligent Transportation Systems

This section describes the problem of Big Data analysis for building demand and origin-destination matrices. A review of related work is also presented.

2.1   Problem Description

The main challenge faced when generating demand and OD matrices using data from tickets sales is that passengers validate their smart cards when they board but not when they alight the bus. Therefore, while the origin of each trip is known with certainty, it is necessary to estimate the destination. Furthermore, some passengers do not use smart cards to pay for their ticket. Therefore, there are sale records which do not provide information to be used to track several trips made by a single passenger. Specific big data processing algorithms must be designed and implemented for each case.

In this article we focus on generating demand and OD matrices for the city of Montevideo, Uruguay. The city government in Montevideo introduced in 2010 an urban mobility plan to redesign and modernize urban transport in the city [9]. Under this plan, the Metropolitan Transport System (Sistema de Transporte Metropolitano, STM) was created, with the goal of integrating the different components of the public transportation system together. One of the first improvements in STM was to include GPS devices on buses and allow passengers to pay for tickets using a smart card (STM card). Additionally, the complex system of fares was simplified to allow only two different type of tickets: (i) "one hour" tickets, allowing up to 1 transfer within an hour of taking the first bus; (ii) "two hours" tickets, allowing unlimited transfers within 2 h from the moment the ticket is purchased. However, it is not compulsory to use the STM card to buy bus tickets. Passengers may pay with cash directly to the driver. In this case, the ticket is only valid for that trip and no transfers are allowed.

The bus companies that operate in Montevideo are obliged to send bus location and ticket sale data daily to the city authorities. The bus network in Montevideo is quite complex, consisting of 1383 bus lines and 4718 bus stops. In this article we consider the complete dataset of ticket sales and bus location for 2015, comprising nearly 200 GB of data. Bus location data contain information about the position of each bus, sampled every 10 to 30 s. Each location record holds the following information:

- *lineID*, the unique bus line identifier;
- *tripID*, the unique trip identifier for each single trip for a given lineID;
- *latitude* and *longitude*,
- *vehicle speed*;
- *timestamp* of the location; and
- *stopID*, the identifier for the nearest bus stop to the current bus location.

Ticket sales data contain information about sales made with and without STM cards. Each sale record has the following fields:

- *tripID*, as in location data;
- *latitude* and *longitude*,
- *stopID*, as in location data;
- *number of passengers*, since it is possible to buy tickets for multiple passengers at once; and
- *timestamp* of the sale.

Additionally, tickets payed with STM cards have the following fields: unique STM card identifier (cardID) which is hashed for privacy purposes, number of transactions made with that STM card (transactionID), and the last payed transaction (payedID). This allows identifying when a passenger transfers between buses, since transactionID will increment while payedID will remain unchanged. The number of transfers is equal to transactionID−payedID.

2.2   Related Work

Many articles in the related literature have proposed applying statistical analysis for estimating OD matrices and computing several other relevant statistics for ITS. Some approaches applying parallel and distributed computing techniques have also been proposed recently. A review of the main related works is presented next.

A detailed literature review on the use of smart cards in ITS was presented by Pelletier et al. [14]. The review covers the hardware and software needed for the deployment of smart card payment solutions in urban transportation systems as well as the privacy and legal issues that arise when dealing with smart card data. Additionally, the authors identify the main uses for these data, including: long-term planning, service adjustments and performance indicators of the transportation systems. Finally, examples of smart card data usage around the world are reviewed.

Trépanier et al. [20] presented a model to estimate the destination for passengers boarding buses with smart cards, following a database programming approach. Two hypotheses are considered, which are commonly used in many related works: (*i*) the origin of a new trip is the destination of the previous one; (*ii*) at the end of the day users return to the origin of their first trip of the day. Based on these assumptions, the authors propose a method to follow the chain of trips of each user in the system. Those trips for which chaining is not possible (e.g., only one trip in the day for a particular user) are compared with all other trips of the month for the same user, in order to find similar trips with known destination. The experimental evaluation was conducted using real information from a transit authority in Gatineau, Quebec. Two datasets were used, with 378,260 trips from July 2003 and 771,239 trips from October 2003. Results showed that a destination estimation was possible for 66% of the trips. Most trips where destination could not be estimated take place during off-peak hours, where more atypical and non-regular trips are performed. Considering only peak hours, the percentage of trips with their destination estimated improves to about 80%. However, the estimation accuracy could not be assessed due to lack of a second source of data (e.g., automatic passenger count) for comparison.

Wang et al. [21] proposed using a trip-chaining method to infer bus passenger OD from smart card transactions and Automatic Vehicle Location (AVL) data from London, United Kingdom. In the studied scenario, authors needed to estimate both origin and destination of trips. Origins are accurately estimated by searching for the timestamp of each smart card transaction in the AVL records to determine the bus stop of each trip. To estimate destinations, the authors used a similar methodology to that presented by Trépanier et al. [20], chaining trips when possible to infer destinations. Results were compared against passenger survey data from Transport for London, performed every five to seven years for each bus route and including the number of people boarding and alighting at each bus stop. The analysis shows that origins can be estimated for more than 90% of the trips while origin and destinations can be estimated for 57% of all trips. When compared to the survey data, the difference on the estimated destinations were below 4%. Finally, two practical applications of the results are presented. The first one consists of studying the daily load/flow variation to identify locations along each bus route where passenger load is high, as well as underutilized route segments. The second application consists of a transfer time analysis, evaluating the average time that users need to wait for transferring between buses, based on the alighting stop and the AVL data.

Munizaga and Palma [12] presented a similar approach to estimate OD matrices in the multimodal transportation system of Santiago, Chile, where passengers can use their smart cards to pay for tickets at metros, buses or bus stations.

Several proposals have applied distributed computing approaches to process large volumes of traffic data, but few works have dealt with the estimation of demand or OD matrices.

Pioneering works on this topic applied distributing computing to gather traffic data. Sun [17] proposed a client-server model developed in CORBA for collecting traffic counts in real time, to be used for dynamic origin/destination demand estimation. The proposed solution included a CORBA client to extract data from the traffic network, and a CORBA server for storing data in a centralized repository. All the information is processed to be later used in Dynamic Traffic Assignment strategies for the traffic network studied, for the estimation of dynamic OD matrices applying a bi-level optimization framework.

Toole et al. [19] propose combining data from many sources (call records from mobile phones, census, and surveys) to infer OD matrices. The authors combine several existing algorithms to generate OD matrices, assign trips to specific routes, and to compute quality metrics on road usage. Furthermore, a web application is introduced to give simple visualizations of the computed information. The authors mention that computations are performed in parallel, but no parallel model is described and no performance metrics are reported.

Also using mobile phone data, Mellegård [11] proposed a Hadoop implementation to generate OD matrices while keeping users' privacy. However, the experimental analysis is done on synthetic data due to the difficulties on getting real data from mobile operators. Furthermore, no performance metrics are reported, so the advantages of the Hadoop implementation are not clear.

Huang et al. [8] proposed a methodology for offline/online calibration of Dynamic Traffic Assignment systems via distributed gradient calculations. An adaptive network decomposition framework is introduced for parallel computation of traffic network metrics and for parallel simulations, in order to accelerate the computations. Parallel OD demand estimation is proposed as a line for future work, in order to deal with large-scale traffic networks with huge number of OD pairs and sensors.

Our recent work [10] presented a preliminary analysis on using distributed computing techniques to process GPS data from buses. We introduced a Map-Reduce approach for processing historical data to study relevant metrics to assess the quality-of-service of the transportation system in Montevideo, Uruguay. We used the strategy to compute the average speed of buses and to identify troublesome locations, according to the delay and deviation of the times to reach each bus stop. The parallel implementation scaled properly when processing large volumes of input data.

In the present article, we extend our preliminary approach [10] to solve a more complex and computing intensive problem: the estimation of demand and OD matrices for public transportation. Up to our knowledge, this approach has not been previously proposed in the related literature.

3   Mobility Estimation from ITS Smart Card Data

This section presents the proposed methodology for estimating demand and OD matrices taking into account the two kind of transfer trips in Montevideo (explained in Sect. 2). We introduce two models for estimation: the first one for one-way transfer trips and the second one for multiple trips. We present a description of our sequential algorithm for estimating demand and OD matrices. Finally, the parallel implementation with all its components is described.

3.1   Models for Demand and OD Estimation

The model used for estimating OD matrices is based on reconstructing the trip sequence for passengers that use a smart card, following a similar approach to that applied in the related literature [12,20,21]. We assume that each smart card corresponds to a single passenger, so we use the terms *card* and *user* in an indistinct manner. The proposed approach is based on processing each trip, retrieving the bus stop where the trip started, and identifying/estimating the stop where the passenger alighted the bus from the information available.

We identify two different ways of estimating destinations from the data used: *transfer trips* and *direct trips*. The main details for each case are presented next.

Transfer Trips. In a transfer trip, passengers pay for their tickets when boarding the first bus by using a smart card identified by its cardID. Later, they can take one or more buses within the time limits permitted by the ticket, as explained in Sect. 2.1. For each ticket sold, the number of transactions (transactionID) made with that cardID and the last payed transaction (payedID) are recorded. This allows detecting whether a smart card record corresponds to a new trip (payedID is equal to transactionID) or to a transfer between buses (transactionID is higher than payedID). We assume that passengers avoid excessive walking in transfers; we consider that a passenger finishes its first leg at the nearest bus stop to the bus stop where he boards the second leg, and so on. The boarding bus stop for the second leg is recorded in the system, thus we estimate the alighting point from the first bus by looking for the closest bus stop corresponding to that line.

A transfer example is presented in Fig. 1. At 07:42 the passenger takes bus number 1 (green line) at bus stop 12. At this point, we have no information about the destination of the passenger. However, at 08:12 the passenger boards bus number 2 (blue line) by using a transfer, without paying a new ticket. Therefore, we can confidently estimate that the passenger alighted from bus number 1 at bus stop number 1–5 which is the closest bus stop to bus stop 23, where the passenger does the transfer. We have no information about the destination of the second trip. This issue is addressed with the direct trip estimation, described next.

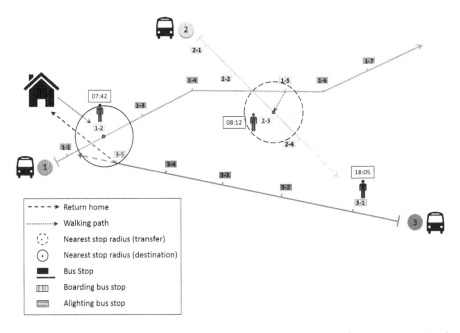

Fig. 1. Demand and OD estimation for transfer and direct trips. (Color figure online)

Direct Trips. We consider direct trips as those that have no bus transfers. We also consider the last leg of a trip with one or more transfers as a direct trip. In both cases, the difficulty lies in accurately estimating a destination point for these trips.

To estimate the destination points we consider two assumptions, which are commonly used in the related literature: (i) passengers start a new trip at a bus stop which is close to the destination of their previous trip; (ii) at the end of the day, passengers return to the bus stop where they boarded the first trip on the same day.

In order to estimate destinations it is necessary to chain the trips made by each passenger on a single day. A preliminary study performed on the sales dataset showed that the best option is to consider each day starting at 04:00, since the lowest number of tickets are sold at that time. This allows considering passengers with different travel patterns, such as those who commute to work during the day and those who work at night.

The model for chaining direct trips of a specific passenger works as follows. We iterate through all the trips done in a 24 h period (from 04:00 to 04:00 on the following day). For each new trip, we try to estimate the alighting point by looking for a bus stop located in a predefined range from the boarding bus stop of the previous trip.

In the example shown in Fig. 1, the passenger takes bus number 3 (red line) at 18:05, to return home. In order to estimate the destination of this trip, we look for the closest bus stop of bus number 3 located within a given search radius from stop number 12, which is the origin of the previous trip. In the example, stop number 35 is the only stop within that radius, so it is chosen as the alighting point for the trip. When no bus stop is found on that radius, the procedure is repeated using a larger radius (two times the original one) to search for bus stops. If no bus stop is found using the larger radius, the origin of the trip is recorded, in order to report the number of unassigned destinations.

3.2   Algorithm for Demand and OD Estimation

We propose a specific methodology for reconstructing the trip sequence for passengers, by estimating the destination points from the information available. The algorithm for estimating trip destinations is described in the flowchart in Fig. 2.

Three phases are identified in the proposed algorithm, which are relevant for building the estimated demand and OD matrices:

Pre-processing. The pre-processing phase prepares the data, filtering those records with incoherent information and classifying records by month per passenger. The algorithm receives as input an unstructured dataset containing raw GPS positions and ticket sales data. Initially, the algorithm discards those sale records that have invalid GPS coordinates; which are not processed for the demand and OD matrices estimation. A sale record has an invalid location when its coordinates are not within the route of the bus corresponding to the sale, with a tolerance of 50 m.

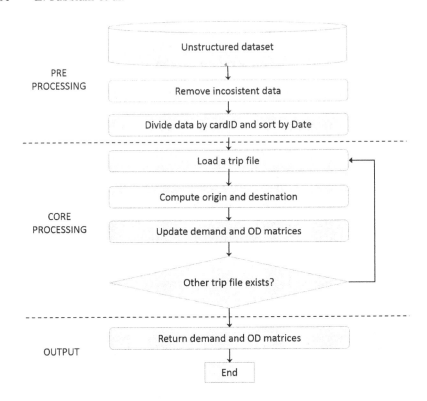

Fig. 2. Flowchart of the algorithm for estimating trip destinations.

Finally, trip records with consistent location information are separated into different files, according to their cardID and then ordered according to their date field. This allows processing the trips of each passenger independently.

Core Processing. In this phase the sales data are processed in order to generate demand and OD matrices. Data are iteratively processed: for each passenger, trips are analyzed considering 24 h periods starting and finishing at 04.00. First, the origin of the trip is recorded. In order to estimate the destination, the models defined in Sect. 3.1 are applied, depending on whether the trip corresponds to a transfer or to a direct trip. Once the origin and the destination are computed, the corresponding values are updated in the demand and OD matrices. The process is repeated until all trip records are processed. In our study, we consider a distance of 500 m for the search radius used when estimating destination of direct trips, as described in Sect. 3.1.

Output. After all records are computed the demand and OD matrices are returned.

4   A Parallel Algorithm for Demand and OD Matrices Estimation

The capability of a traditional sequential algorithm for the estimation of demand and OD matrices is limited by the computational capacity of a single computing element (*node*). High performance computing architectures based on distributed parallel processing principles can achieve a large computational efficiency as well as high scalability for solving complex problems [6].

In this section, we present the parallel model for processing a dataset consisting of many trip files and estimating the demand and OD matrices using a parallel/distributed system.

4.1   Parallel Model

Processing large volumes of data is needed to accurately estimate demand and OD matrices from ticket sales and bus location information. Initial experiments on a reduced portion of the dataset suggest that processing only one month of sales data demands over 18 days of computational time, when using a sequential algorithm in a regular desktop computer (Core i5 x2, 6 GB of RAM, Ubuntu 14.04). Therefore, we propose to run the estimation algorithms in parallel, making use of several computing units. The basic idea of the proposed parallel algorithm is to apply a data-parallel approach, dividing the dataset of sales and GPS records in chunks, following the Bag-of-Tasks (BoT) paradigm [3]. In our case, the BoT corresponds to a set of user trip files. Since each set of trip files are independent, they can be assigned to different compute nodes (slaves) for processing. Using a master-slave architecture seems appropriate since the slave processes do not need to share information with each other.

Figure 3 shows the proposed master-slave model for processing trip data. Initially, the master collects the data to be processed and filters inconsistent records. Next, the master sends the BoT to each slave in the slave pool in order to perform the assigned computation task. Then, each slave node runs the designated estimation procedure. Finally, the master receives the partial results and store them to join and create the final demand and OD matrices.

Two variants of the proposed algorithm were implemented, one for each of the two different estimation procedures presented in Sect. 3.1. Both variants follow the same general approach which is specified in Sect. 4.2.

4.2   Implementation Details

The implemented algorithms were designed using Python 2.7.5. The cross-platform open-source geographic information system QGIS [16] was used to manage geographic information corresponding to bus location and bus stops data.

We applied `dispy` [15] for creating and distributing parallel tasks among several computer nodes. `dispy` is a Python framework that allows executing parallel

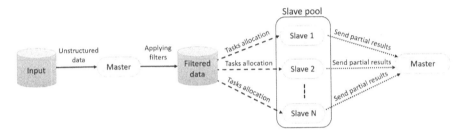

Fig. 3. Diagram of the proposed parallel model for demand and OD matrices estimation.

processes, supporting many different distributed computing infrastructures. The main features of the framework include tasks distribution, load balancing, and fault recovery. The `dispy` framework provides an API for the user to define clusters and schedule jobs to execute on those clusters. Creating a cluster in `dispy` consists of packaging computation fragments (code and data) and specifying parameters that control how the computations are executed, such as which nodes can execute each computation. Figure 4 presents the main methods used with `dispy` to create jobs and assign them to slave nodes in order to estimate demand and OD matrices.

```
# function 'estimationOD'
def estimationOD(tripFile):
    #code for estimating origin-destination
    return pairsOD
#main
if __name__ == '__main__':
    # modules imported, are not available in job computations
    import dispy
    cluster = dispy.JobCluster(estimationOD,depends=[settings,
                               data, visual,...],...more parameters)
    jobs = []
    #Create tasks related with each trip file
    for tripFile in os.listdir(settings.path_to_trip_dataset):
        job = cluster.submit(tripFile)
        jobs.append(job)
        for job in jobs: #Execute jobs into the nodes availables
            job()# waits for job to finish and returns results
            pairsOD = job.result
    for pairs in pairsOD:
      #OD matrix is reconstructed with partial results
      #stored in variable 'pairsOD'
```

Fig. 4. `dispy` script for job creation and distribution.

A list of parameters are needed to set a `dispy` cluster. First of all, the program to execute in each node must be indicated (in our case, the O-D matrix estimation procedure). In addition, the list of nodes available to execute the jobs, and a list of dependencies needed for computation must be specified (in our application the only dependency is the availability of the QGIS software).

Once a cluster is created, jobs can be scheduled to execute at a certain node. `dispy` will execute the job on an available processor in the defined cluster. When a submitted job is called, it returns that job's execution result, waiting until the job is finished if it has not finished yet. After a job is finished the information about the pairs origin-destination found is used to build the OD matrices.

Each slave keeps track of the index of the last file or line processed. Therefore, in case of a system failure it is possible to resume the execution from the last processed record, without the need of starting the process from the beginning.

In our approach, the master creates a set of BoT where each task corresponds to all the trip records of a single passenger. Then, each BoT is distributed using `dispy` across the different slaves to execute the estimation algorithms. It is important to choose the amount of passengers' trip records to assign to each slave in order to optimize the execution time, avoiding costly communications between the slaves and the master. This parameter is configured in the experimental analysis presented in Sect. 5. Finally, the master node distributes tasks to slaves on demand, and obtains the results computed by each slave to gather them to return the final solution.

5   Experimental Analysis

This section describes the experimental analysis performed to assess the efficiency of the parallel algorithms developed. The computational platform used and the problem instances are detailed. Finally, the computational efficiency results are reported and commented.

5.1   Computational Platform

The experimental analysis was performed on an AMD Opteron 6172 Magny Cours processors with 24 cores at 2.26 GHz, 72 GB RAM, with CentOS Linux 5.2 operating system from Cluster FING, the high performance computing infrastructure at Facultad de Ingeniería, Universidad de la República, Uruguay [13].

5.2   Problem Instance and Metrics

Problem Instance. For the experimental analysis, the complete dataset corresponding to the ITS in Montevideo for January 2015 was processed, including ticket sales and bus location data. This dataset holds the mobility information for over half a million smart cards (corresponding to more than 13 million trips).

Computational Efficiency Metrics. In order to evaluate the computational efficiency of the proposed parallel algorithm we evaluate the *execution time* and the *speedup*. If we denote T_m the execution time for an algorithm using m processors, then the speedup is the ratio between the (larger) execution time on one processor T_1 and the (smaller) execution time on m processors T_m. This ratio value is presented in Eq. 1

$$S_m = \frac{T_1}{T_m}. \tag{1}$$

5.3 Results and Discussion

In the proposed master-slave parallel model it is necessary to define the size of the BoT assigned to each slave to compute, in order to have an appropriate load balance and avoid excessive communication between the slaves and the master. Several executions were performed varying the size of the BoT as well as the number of cores used. The experimental results are reported on Table 1. The number of cores (#cores) and the size of the BoT (#BoT) used in each experiment are indicated. Then, for each combination of these values, the best (i.e., minimum), average, and standard deviation of execution time and speedup values are reported for both direct and transfer trips. Execution times are reported in minutes and the results correspond to 5 independent executions of the algorithm using each configuration of #cores and #BoT.

Table 1. Execution time results and performance analysis.

#cores	#BoT	Direct trips		Transfer trips	
		Avg. time $\pm\sigma$ (best)	Speedup	Avg. time $\pm\sigma$ (best)	Speedup
1	1	25920	-	30240	-
16	5000	2092.1 ± 3.4 (2089.6)	12.40	2648.9 ± 3.2 (2645.5)	11.43
16	10000	2372.4 ± 1.8 (2371.1)	10.92	3068.8 ± 3.5 (3063.2)	9.87
24	5000	1582.7 ± 2.4 (1579.4)	16.41	2371.1 ± 2.5 (2368.1)	12.76
24	10000	1858.2 ± 2.1 (1855.9)	13.96	2617.9 ± 3.3 (2614.3)	11.56

The experimental results obtained suggest that the parallel approach is an appropriate strategy for significantly improving the efficiency of the data processing for demand and O-D matrices estimation. Promising speedup values were obtained, up to **16.41** for the direct trips processing and using a BoT of 5000 trips and executing in 24 nodes. These results confirm that the proposed master/slave parallel model allows improving the execution time of the computational tasks by taking advantage of multiple computing nodes.

Furthermore, the computational efficiency results indicate that the size of the BoT (i.e., the amount of passengers' trip data given to each slave to process at once) has a significant impact on the overall execution time of the algorithm.

Execution times were reduced when using the smallest size for the BoT (5000). Further experiments should be performed to assess if using a smaller size for the BoT is still more efficient, and to determine the tradeoff value before the communications between the slaves and the master become more expensive and have a negative impact on the execution time.

Using 24 cores and tasks with the trip data corresponding to 5000 passengers, the proposed strategy allows improving in up to 54.4% the efficiency when compared to using 12 cores and a BoT size of 5000, and up to 57.9% against a sequential algorithm running on a single computing node. This efficiency allows processing the full information of GPS and trip data for one year (more than 130 GB) in 33 days, a significant improvement over the 468 days demanded by a sequential algorithm.

6 Conclusions and Future Work

In this work, we proposed and implemented an efficient estimation method for obtaining demand and origin-destination matrices from real smartcard data of bus ticket sales. The proposed procedure demands estimating the alighting stops, since passengers do not validate the smartcard when getting off the bus. Two different approaches are proposed depending on whether the trip record correspond to a direct trip or to a bus transfer. For the estimations we considered similar assumptions to other works in the related literature.

Due to the large volume of data to be processed, we designed and implemented a parallel version of the estimation algorithm, following the master/slave parallel model. When compared to a sequential algorithm, the proposed parallel model reduces execution time from 56120 to 3954 min and achieves speed up values of 16.41 when using 24 cores in the best case.

We identify three main lines of future work: (i) validate the computed demand and OD matrices using other sources of data, such as surveys; (ii) incorporate machine learning techniques to infer destinations with high accuracy, for example by identifying recurrent destinations of a single passenger; (iii) take advantage of the computed mobility data to address optimization problem that arise in most modern ITS, such as bus route design, bus stop location, bus timetabling, etc.

References

1. Bell, M.: The estimation of an origin-destination matrix from traffic counts. Transp. Sci. **17**(2), 198–217 (1983)
2. Chen, C., Ma, J., Susilo, Y., Liu, Y., Wang, M.: The promises of big data and small data for travel behavior (aka human mobility) analysis. Transp. Res. Part C: Emerg. Technol. **68**, 285–299 (2016)
3. Cirne, W., Brasileiro, F., Sauvé, J., Andrade, N., Paranhos, D., Santos-Neto, E.: Grid computing for bag of tasks applications. In: Proceedings of the 3rd IFIP Conference on E-Commerce, E-Business and EGovernment (2003)
4. Deakin, M., Waer, H.: From Intelligent to Smart Cities. Taylor & Francis, Abingdon-on-Thames (2012)

5. Figueiredo, L., Jesus, I., Machado, J.T., Ferreira, J., de Carvalho, J.M.: Towards the development of intelligent transportation systems. Intell. Transp. Syst. **88**, 1206–1211 (2001)
6. Foster, I.: Designing and Building Parallel Programs: Concepts and Tools for Parallel Software Engineering. Addison-Wesley Longman Publishing Co., Inc., Boston (1995)
7. Grava, S.: Urban Transportation Systems. McGraw-Hill Education, New York (2002)
8. Huang, E., Antoniou, C., Lopes, J., Wen, Y., Ben-Akiva, M.: Accelerated online calibration of dynamic traffic assignment using distributed stochastic gradient approximation. In: 13th International IEEE Conference on Intelligent Transportation Systems, pp. 1166–1171 (2010)
9. Intendencia de Montevideo: Plan de movilidad urbana: hacia un sistema de movilidad accesible, democrático y eficiente (2010)
10. Massobrio, R., Pias, A., Vázquez, N., Nesmachnow, S.: Map-reduce for processing GPS data from public transport in Montevideo, Uruguay. In: 2nd Argentinian Symposium on Big Data (AGRANDA) (2016)
11. Mellegård, E.: Obtaining origin/destination-matrices from cellular network data. Master's thesis (2011)
12. Munizaga, M.A., Palma, C.: Estimation of a disaggregate multimodal public transport origin-destination matrix from passive smartcard data from Santiago, Chile. Transp. Res. Part C: Emerg. Technol. **24**, 9–18 (2012)
13. Nesmachnow, S.: Computación científica de alto desempeño en la Facultad de Ingeniería, Universidad de la República. Rev. Asoc. Ing. Uruguay **61**, 12–15 (2010)
14. Pelletier, M.P., Trépanier, M., Morency, C.: Smart card data use in public transit: a literature review. Transp. Res. Part C: Emerg. Technol. **19**(4), 557–568 (2011)
15. Pemmasani, G.: dispy: distributed and parallel computing with/for Python. http://dispy.sourceforge.net/. Accessed July 2016
16. QGIS Development Team: QGIS Geographic Information System. Open Source Geospatial Foundation (2009). http://qgis.osgeo.org. Accessed July 2016
17. Sun, C.: Dynamic origin/destination estimation using true section densities. Technical report. UCB-ITS-PRR-2000-5, University of California, Berkeley
18. Sussman, J.: Perspectives on Intelligent Transportation Systems (ITS). Springer Science+Business Media, Berlin (2005)
19. Toole, J.L., Colak, S., Sturt, B., Alexander, L.P., Evsukoff, A., González, M.C.: The path most traveled: travel demand estimation using big data resources. Transp. Res. Part C: Emerg. Technol. **58**(Part B), 162–177 (2015)
20. Trépanier, M., Tranchant, N., Chapleau, R.: Individual trip destination estimation in a transit smart card automated fare collection system. J. Intell. Transp. Syst. **11**(1), 1–14 (2007)
21. Wang, W., Attanucci, J., Wilson, N.: Bus passenger origin-destination estimation and related analyses using automated data collection systems. J. Publ. Transp. **14**(4), 131–150 (2011)

Evaluation of a Master-Slave Parallel Evolutionary Algorithm Applied to Artificial Intelligence for Games in the Xeon-Phi Many-Core Platform

Sebastián Rodríguez Leopold[1]([✉]), Facundo Parodi[1], Sergio Nesmachnow[1], and Esteban Mocskos[2,3]

[1] Universidad de la República, Montevideo, Uruguay
{sebastian.rodriguez.leopold,facundo.parodi,Sergion}@fing.edu.uy
[2] Facultad de Ciencias Exactas y Naturales, Departamento de Computación, Universidad de Buenos Aires, Buenos Aires, Argentina
emocskos@dc.uba.ar
[3] Centro de Simulación Computacional para Aplicaciones Tecnológicas, CSC-CONICET, Buenos Aires, Argentina

Abstract. Evolutionary algorithms are non-deterministic metaheuristic methods that emulate the evolution of species in nature to solve optimization, search, and learning problems. This article presents a parallel implementation of evolutionary algorithms on Xeon Phi for developing an artificial intelligence to play the NES Pinball game. The proposed parallel implementation offloads the execution of the fitness function evaluation to Xeon Phi. Multiple evolution schemes are studied to get the most efficient resource utilization. A micro-benchmarking of the Xeon Phi coprocessor is performed to verify the existing technical documentation and obtain detail knowledge of its behavior. Finally, a performance analysis of the proposed parallel evolutionary algorithm is presented, focusing on the characteristics of the evaluated platform.

Keywords: Evolutionary algorithms · Artificial intelligence · Xeon Phi

1 Introduction

Developing an artificial intelligence (AI) is a complex task that requires a high computational effort. Automating this process greatly reduces the human involvement required for its development, but comes with a substantial increase in computational cost [15]. Efficient resource utilization and a high degree of parallelism is necessary to obtain good results in a reasonable time.

In this article, we propose employing the Intel Xeon Phi Many Integrated Core (MIC) architecture for automatic AI generation to play games. Xeon Phi is a massively parallel platform for executing highly parallel tasks, supporting the native execution of x86 software (recompilation is required due

© Springer International Publishing AG 2017
C.J. Barrios Hernández et al. (Eds.): CARLA 2016, CCIS 697, pp. 161–176, 2017.
DOI: 10.1007/978-3-319-57972-6_12

to a different executable file format). Xeon Phi/MIC architecture is offered as a *ready to go* for legacy x86 applications. However, most existing software require modifications in order to achieve acceptable performance [4]. We develop a general framework for parallel Evolutionary Algorithm (EA) in C++, which is capable of evaluating the solutions on Xeon Phi using offload computing technique. In this article, we describe the framework and its application for automating the process of AI generation for games. For solution evaluation, a game emulator was specifically ported to allow its execution on Xeon Phi. The framework and emulator source code are available at https://github.com/Sebarl/Evolutionary-Algorithms-for-NES-Pinball.

A set of micro-benchmarks are performed to understand the behavior of the Xeon Phi platform and offload mechanism. Furthermore, the emulator performance is analyzed through profiling and several distribution strategies for individuals are studied to find the best EA configuration, in order to maximize computational performance. The main contributions of this article are: (*i*) a study of the capabilities of the Xeon Phi through micro-benchmarking; (*ii*) the design and implementation of a framework for EAs to work with the Xeon Phi and (*iii*) porting an existing emulator to the studied architecture.

The article is organized as follows: Sect. 2 explains the architecture and programming models of the Xeon Phi, Sect. 3 reviews the related work about both microbenchmarks for the card and AIs for games. Section 4 reports the results obtained with different micro-benchmark tests executed on the card, while Sect. 5 describes the main concepts about EAs as background for the case study proposed in Sect. 6. The experimental evaluation is reported in Sect. 7, including several profiling tests of the proposed parallel EA. Finally, some conclusions and main lines for future work are drawin in Sect. 8.

2   Xeon Phi Characteristics

This section introduces the main characteristics of the Intel Xeon Phi processor.

Cores. Xeon Phi cores are *in-order* processors based on the original Pentium design (P54C architecture), supporting four hardware threads each. Every core has two pipelines to execute up to two threads in parallel (only one supports the entire instruction set, including vectorization). Each thread, however, cannot issue instructions in two consecutive clock cycles [8, pp. 31–32]. The Xeon Phi lacks many of the present features in current desktop processors: MMX, SSEx and AVX instruction set extensions as well as out-of-order execution. The branch predictor design has limited characteristics also.

A wide vectorization unit is present on each core (512-bit wide, twice as much as AVX 2.0), supporting both float and integer vector operations and fused multiply-add. Most vector operations take four clock cycles. A mask register was added to handle specific conditional branching cases and processing data of different sizes, which could lead to higher successful vectorization rates.

Finally, an Extended Mathematical Unit (EMU) is added to each core, implemented by hardware complex floating point operations based on polynomial approximations. This facility is available only when working with single-precision floating numbers.

Cache and RAM Memory. Two 32 KB 8-way associative L1 caches (for data and instructions) and a 512 KB L2 cache per core are available. L1 cache requests can be performed in back-to-back cycles, while L2 cache requests not.

All cores share their L2 caches to reduce main memory requests using a special protocol to *steal* data from remote L2 cache. This mechanism generates a copy of the remote content in its own L2 cache. If all threads execute the same code in perfect synchronization, the effective L2 memory capacity is 512 KB. However, this capacity depends on the amount of data shared by all cores.

In the legacy Pentium architecture, a cache miss can stall the pipeline. The Xeon Phi can suspend the current thread, running another thread while waiting for memory access. Support for *streaming store* instructions allows writing an entire cache line without reading it first, adding another opportunity to increase memory effective bandwidth.

The Xeon-Phi has six memory controllers supporting 12 GDDR5 channels, providing a maximum theoretical combined bandwidth of 5GT/s (240 GB/s) at 2500 Mhz.

Bus. The bus is a bidirectional ring composed of three sub-rings: (i) *Data block ring* (64 bytes wide, used for data transfer), (ii) *Address ring* (for read/write commands and memory addresses), (iii) *Control ring* (acknowledgment packets). To comply with bandwidth requirements, the last two are duplicated. Ring access is managed by special controllers (ring stops). The ring connects the cores, memory controllers, L2 cache controllers and a Tag Directory (TD) divided in subdirectories (DTDs), used for remote cache access. This configuration is shown in Fig. 1.

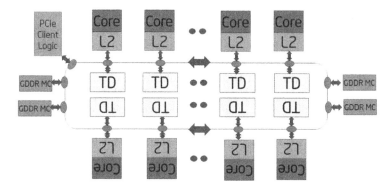

Fig. 1. Xeon Phi architecture: three rings interconnect the cores and support sharing L2 cache contents using a Tag Directory (TD) structure.

When faced with a L2 cache miss, a core sends a message to the TD to seek the line in remote L2 caches. If found, the TD responds indicating which core holds it and another message is sent to the corresponding core requesting the line. This core sends the copy and awaits an acknowledgment. If the data is not present in any cache, a message is sent to a memory controller to fetch the data from RAM. As it can be seen, memory access is a complex procedure, introducing additional overhead compared with conventional multicores.

Execution Environment and Programming Models. Xeon Phi executes a custom flavor of Linux, ported to the MIC architecture. As the card has no non-volatile memory, the memory board has to be shared with the operating system and filesystem, reducing the memory available for applications.

As many standard libraries have been ported to the MIC, the process of porting applications to Xeon Phi is soften. Both `C++` and `Fortran` are supported [8, p. 10]. However, not all the existing APIs are supported, requiring manual porting in some cases.

There are two main programming models available on Xeon Phi: (*i*) *offload*, which executes a main task on the host that send some work to the card. The PCIe maximum bus capacity of 8 GB/s [14] may become a bottleneck in this model, and (*ii*) *native*, which executes the application entirely on the coprocessor.

The offload model is used when specific parallel subroutines are identified, requiring only localized code changes or adding compiler directives. On the other hand, adapting an application for native execution requires global changes and strong redesign focusing on parallel exploitation.

3   Related Work

Fang et al. [4] developed micro-benchmarks to test Xeon Phi, some of which were used to test our cards in Sect. 4. Furthermore, they compared their results against published datasheets showing several differences. Fang et al. [5] also proposed a micro-benchmarking methodology for Xeon Phi, developing mechanisms to mitigate and control potential interfering factors generated by hardware constraints, operative system effects, and compiler optimizations.

Some articles have proposed EAs for optimization of game AIs. Hausknecht et al. [7] presented a survey of neuro-evolution algorithms for learning to play 61 different Atari-2600 games. The proposed strategies outperformed several planning and temporal-difference algorithms in most games, as well as human players in three of them. Murphy proposed Learnfun and Playfun [9], a general approach to optimize NES games. Learnfun infers the game objectives by analyzing a human player recording and Playfun plays the game applying a local search based on backtracking and a set of possible moves inferred from the recording. It yielded mixed results, performing remarkable well on multiple NES games while falling short in others. The author uses a master-slave approach to subdivide the search.

Up to our knowledge, no previous proposals about parallel models for EAs using the Xeon Phi architecture have been presented in the related literature.

We contribute with a first approach using hardware acceleration to improve the performance of the master-slave model for parallel EAs.

4   Xeon Phi Micro-Benchmarking

This section introduces a study of the specifics of the microarchitecture used by the Xeon Phi 31S1P. These tests are performed to understand the details of the target architecture, in order to explain the exhibited behavior of our case study when executed on the card. We modified the code employed in `MIC-Meter` [4] to work with the maximum number of threads in our computing platform (228). All tests were compiled using the Intel 2015 suite, version 15.0.3 20150407.

4.1   Maximum Achievable Throughput

The coprocessor used in this paper exhibits a theoretical instruction throughput of 1003.2 GFlops (approximately 1 TFlop) for double-precision numbers.

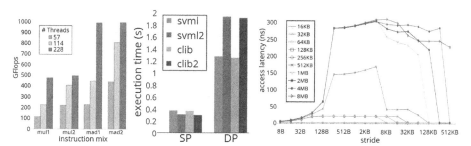

Fig. 2. Throughput   **Fig. 3.** EMU performance   **Fig. 4.** Memory access latency

Figure 2 shows the achieved throughput of two operations and its two-stream variants. The `MAD` (fused multiply add) operation obtains twice the performance of the simple multiplication as the former execute two operations in one cycle.

Using one thread per core generates very poor results (instructions are issued in alternate cycles), whereas 2 threads doubled the throughput. Furthermore, using 3 and 4 threads yields considerable improvement, as vector arithmetic operations have a latency of 4 cycles. For this same reason, the execution of two independent instruction streams yields better performance than using one when running less than 4 threads. The theoretical maximum of 1 TFlop is achieved using 228 threads and `MAD` operations only, being an artificial result.

4.2   Extended Mathematical Unit

Figure 3 shows the execution times for complex arithmetic functions on different implementations (clib, intrinsics) and precisions. No visible difference is observed between both implementations. Double-precision operations show cycle counts between 3.5 and 6.5 times larger than its single-precision counterparts (instead of just doubling cycle count). This shows a considerable boost when using the EMU.

4.3   Memory Bandwidth and Access Latency

Maximum theoretical bandwidth is 4012.8 GB/s for read and write operations to L1 cache memory (70.4 GB/s per core). Testing yielded 31.2 GB/s (read) and 27.63 GB/s (write) when executing the test in a single core, providing an aggregated 1778.4 GB/s and 1574.91 GB/s bandwidth between all cores, using a single-thread test. It could be possible to achieve 3556.8 GB/s and 3149.82 GB/s for read and write respectively using two threads. Even then, these values do not reach the theoretical maximum, being 11% and 21.5% below 4012.8 GB/s.

Figure 6 shows the read and write bandwidth for main memory with different thread counts. Read operations peak at 166.15 GB/s. Write speed peak is 77.46 GB/s. Both are below the theoretical maximum of 240 GB/s. Write speed can be improved using *streaming stores*, though it still is lower than 166 GB/s.

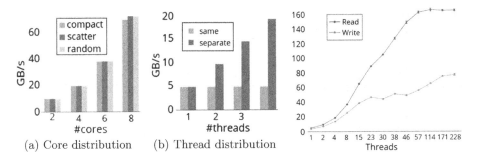

(a) Core distribution   (b) Thread distribution

Fig. 5. Ring interconnect performance study

Fig. 6. Main memory read and write bandwidth vs. thread count

Latency of all components in the memory hierarchy is tested by repeated access to arrays of different size using varying strides. Figure 4 shows the results, suggesting L1 latency is 2.74 ns (3 cycles), L2 latency is 22 ns (24 cycles) and main memory latency is 300 ns (300 cycles).

L2 remote access varies around 250 cycles (between 16.7% less than access to main memory) as presented by Fang et. al [4]. It should be noted that latency varies considerably depending on the distance between cores.

4.4   Bidirectional Ring Interconnect and Offload Latency

A series of tests were performed measuring the obtained bus bandwidth while variating both the thread distribution and amount run on the available cores.

As it can be seen in Fig. 5(a), all different distributions obtained similar performance, noting a small slowdown when using 8 threads located closely together.

This suggests a saturation of the bus, but is negligible (cores are symmetric in practice). However, Fig. 5(b) shows that, no matter how many, executing threads in the same core obtains approximately 4.88 GB/s of bandwidth, indicating that thread contention in a core serializes memory requests.

Code offloading latency was estimated (initialization and tear-down of offload execution) obtaining an average of 189.4 ms (in 100 independent executions).

5   Evolutionary Algorithms

Evolutionary Algorithms (EAs) are non-deterministic methods that emulate the evolutionary process of species in nature to solve optimization, search, and other related problems [2, 10]. In the last thirty years, EAs have been successfully applied to optimization problems underlying many real and complex applications.

An EA (Algorithm 1) is an iterative technique (each iteration is called a *generation*) that applies stochastic operators on a pool of individuals (the population P). Every individual in the population encodes a solution for the problem. The initial population is generated randomly or by using a specific heuristic for the problem (line 2). An evaluation function associates a fitness value to every individual, indicating its suitability to the problem (line 4). The search is guided by a probabilistic selection-of-the-best technique (for both parents and offspring) to tentative solutions of higher quality (line 5). Iteratively, solutions are modified by the probabilistic application of *variation operators* (line 6) like the *recombination* of parts from two individuals or random changes (*mutations*).

The stopping criterion usually involves a fixed number of generations or execution time, a quality threshold on the best fitness value, or the detection of a stagnation situation. Specific policies are used to select the groups of individuals to recombine (the *selection* method) and to determine which new individuals are inserted in the population in each new generation (the *replacement* criterion). The EA returns the best solution found in the iterative process.

Algorithm 1. Schema of an Evolutionary Algorithm

1: t ← 0 {generation counter}
2: **initialize**($P(0)$)
3: **while** not stopcriteria **do**
4:     **evaluate**(P(t))
5:     parents ← **selection**(P(t))
6:     offspring ← **variation operators**(parents)
7:     P(t+1) ← **replacement**(offspring, P(t))
8:     t = t + 1
9: **end while**
10: **return** best solution ever found

Parallel implementations allow improving the efficiency of EAs. By using several computing elements, parallel EAs allow reaching high quality results in a reasonable execution time even for hard-to-solve optimization problems [1].

The *master-slave* model for parallel EAs applies a functional decomposition approach. The evaluation of the fitness function is the main candidate to perform in parallel when solving hard optimization problems, since it usually requires larger computing time than the application of the variation operators. A master-slave parallel EA is organized in a hierarchic structure: a master process performs the evolutionary search, while it controls a group of slave processes that evaluate the fitness function and/or apply the variation operators.

The parallel EA proposed in this article for the pinball game follows a two-level parallel approach and the master-slave model is used for solution evaluation. Our main contribution consist of novel implementation to perform the parallel evaluation of solutions by following a multithreading approach on Xeon Phi.

6   A Master-Slave Parallel EA for Playing Pinball on Xeon-Phi

This section presents the proposed EA executing on the Xeon Phi, the implemented framework and the ported emulator.

6.1   Solution Description

The case study pertains the evolution of an artificial intelligence (AI) that plays the game Pinball for the Nintendo Entertainment System (NES) console. This has been successfully performed using traditional hardware in our previous work [13]. Fitness evaluation is expensive as it simulates an entire match, making it a prime target for execution on the Phi due to its massive parallel architecture. We model a pinball game with two screens (*stages*): (*i*) the upper half of the playfield (UP stage); and (*ii*) the lower half (DOWN stage). The most relevant features of the proposed EA are presented next.

Solution Encoding. The solution is encoded as an array of 23 *genes*. Each gene represents one trigger zone or one extra parameter required by the AI. Trigger zones are defined by the stage it is in (i.e. UP or DOWN), the position of its center in the screen, its radius, and the action to perform when the ball enters it. Valid actions for a trigger zone are either move the left, right, or both flippers. There are 3 extra parameters: the amount of frames to wait with the plunger compressed before releasing the ball into the playfield, the number of frames the ball must stay in the same position before assuming it got stuck, and the amount of frames to stay inactive waiting for the ball to get unstuck. Figures 7 and 8 present an example of a solution encoding.

Fitness Function. The fitness values are computed considering the linear aggregation function $f = score + balls \times 10000$. The values of *score* and *remaining balls* are determined by emulating the game and applying the AI module to decide the action performed in each frame, using the information encoded in the individual. As each evaluation is independent, parallelizing the fitness evaluation is simple using OpenMP.

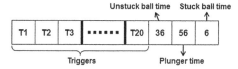

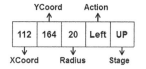

Fig. 7. Solution encoding.   **Fig. 8.** Trigger encoding

Population Initialization. The initial population is generated by applying an ad-hoc randomized method for building AI configurations. Twelve points are selected (three points for each flipper, in each stage), whose positions are randomly selected to fit in the area reachable by the corresponding flipper. The remaining eight points are located randomly anywhere on the playable area, four per each stage. The extra parameters are initialized with a random value chosen uniformly in the range $[0, 150]$.

Selection and Replacement. We apply the Stochastic Universal Sampling selection operator, providing balanced tradeoff between selection pressure and diversity [2]. For replacement, we use the traditional (μ, λ) evolution model. In each generation, elitism is used to keep the best individual in every island.

Recombination. We used an uniform crossover operator that swaps genes in even positions between two parents to form two offspring.

Mutation. A special mutation operator was developed, taking into account the structure of each gen: (i) with a probability of 0.5, selecting a trigger zone $(X, Y, Radius)$ and modify each value applying a Gaussian mutation; (ii) with a probability of 0.33, modifying the action to perform, using a uniform distribution to select between the other two options; and (iii) with a probability of 0.167 the stage is switched, applying a bit flip mutation. For the extra parameters, a standard Gaussian mutation is applied.

Parallel Model. The proposed EA follows a two-level approach: both the evolution process within every subpopulation and the evaluation of every individual are executed in parallel. In this article we focus on the main details of the master-slave model applied for solution evaluation in Xeon Phi.

6.2   Framework Description

The proposed EA framework for Xeon Phi was developed in C++, based on the design of the Watchmaker [3] framework. This development effort was required due to the lack of support for the Xeon Phi on existing solutions, the difficulty of modifying existing implementations to achieve our goals, and support for offload-enabled code being only for C++ and `Fortran`. The offload model was selected to leverage the higher host clock rate and better memory access for the evolutionary framework, as the framework lacks enough parallelism for the card.

The implementation is modular and extensible, supporting multiple paradigms and configurations. In particular, parallel evaluation of the entire population on the card is supported. Both a simple evolution model (simple genetic algorithm) and a subpopulations model is implemented. Multiple interfaces are defined to easily specify a problem and the way it must be solved. Moreover, generic implementations are provided for some of them.

Offload support is provided by a specialized evolutionary engine, implemented as follows: (*i*) when evaluation is required, the entire population is serialized, appended into a vector; (*ii*) the population vector is sent to the coprocessor using offload; (*iii*) offloaded code divides the individuals between threads using an OpenMP `omp for` directive, the results are returned as a new vector; and (*iv*) the results are mapped to each individual, resuming evolution.

This serialization/deserialization process adds an overhead to the offload step. However, the resulting code is much faster than sending each individual to the card separately (better usage of the PCIe bus and less time spent in setup/teardown, including processing done by the offload daemon on the card: *coi-daemon*), effectively optimizing the process (high performance gains where perceived after its implementation). Moreover, this greatly reduces the amount of simultaneous connections to the Xeon Phi to one per concurrent island. Said connections are limited (usually a low fixed number, less than available cores).

The framework is optimized to reduce its memory consumption and CPU utilization as much as possible. Pointers are used to simplify crossover, mutation and migration operations. Low level functions are preferred throughout the framework to reduce computational cost. The amount of existing functions are reduced to minimize the overhead related to function calls. In particular, function inlining is preferred. OpenMP is used to parallelize island execution and individual evaluation. Taking into account the achieved performance by the framework, NES emulator emerges as the bottleneck.

6.3   NES Emulator Description

Each pinball match is simulated using the open source NES emulator *FCEUX* [6]. We modified the FCEUX implementation to include the AI module and to port it to Xeon Phi. In order to achieve acceptable performance most non-essential features were removed, stripping the emulator only to the core functions required to run the simulation (CPU, cartridge, and partial PPU -Picture Processing Unit- emulation). Compiling the emulator for the card is no minor point, considering the lack of support from the Intel suite for most basic components of a typical Linux environment. For example, *zlib* has not been ported. Attempting to compile such dependencies was an exercise in futility. The solution was to depend only on glibc and similar libraries, losing capabilities in the process. In our case, this downgrade was intentional (to improve performance), but in most applications this could be unacceptable.

The produced executable is single threaded (as it is running a CPU emulation, which is sequential in nature, and also not vectorizable due to the dependency on prior states). Its performance is quite poor for low memory performance shown in Sect. 4. To achieve substantial performance gains, a high quantity of parallel instances is needed.

7 Experimental Evaluation

This section describes the calibration process of the implemented solution and presents the results. We begin with a profiling of the FCEUX emulator to better understand its performance on the card. Then we analyze the obtained results after testing multiple configurations of the algorithm.

7.1 Emulator Performance

This subsection reports a comprehensive study of the inner workings of the FCEUX emulator, executing both on the coprocessor and on a desktop computer.

Cache Usage and Vectorization. Cache usage was examined using *Valgrind* [12] on a desktop computer. The results showed minimal misses in any cache level, corresponding to the initial load of the emulator and ROM. In particular, the L1 cache exhibited miss rates of 0% (for instructions) and 0.7% (for data). We conclude that no useful optimization can be done with respect to cache efficiency.

Vectorization reports generated by the Intel compiler indicate that several functions were vectorized successfully. However, the main CPU emulation function was not vectorized, due both to its complexity and its dependency on state generated by previous calls. This function dominates computational time (more than 60%), which is reasonable as the modified emulator does little more than simulating the CPU. Evidently, this impacts negatively on performance, as most computations executed cannot use the vectorization unit.

Profiling. We used the VTune profiler on both the coprocessor and a desktop computer to compare different performance metrics.

Desktop Profiling. We performed a complete performance analysis of the application to expose bottlenecks and other standard code problems, which are relevant for the Xeon Phi implementation, due to the heavy resource limitations.

The profiling results show a large rate of branch misprediction (~19%). The impact on the overall performance is important, as the pipeline must be flushed and populated again with the correct branch. This problem is amplified in the Xeon Phi architecture, as it includes a weaker branch predictor. Nevertheless, this result is reasonable considering that a full CPU is being emulated, including branching, IRQs, and other low level events, through multiple *if* statements. The cart (ROM) reading function also showed a high misprediction rate, impacting performance negatively as it is the second most expensive function (26.2% of execution time).

Instruction starvation is also quite high: the control unit had no instructions to send to the execution pipeline in 13.6% of the CPU cycles. Most starvation is probably caused by misprediction: many pipeline flushes combined with an executable size of 1 MB imply that only a fraction of the code resides on L1 cache and misprediction may require reading instructions from RAM.

Regarding execution stalls, no microinstruction was available to execute 9.1% of the time. This means that most instruction starvation events were followed by execution stalls, wasting resources being idle. A portion of this idle time is spent loading the game ROM file, or the emulator (including external libraries).

In total, 96 million function calls were performed, consuming 4 ms (representing 0.68% of total execution time). This high volume of calls comes mostly from repeated calls in the main loop to the CPU emulation function. Taking into account the low time spent invoking functions against the very high volume of calls, no substantial optimization can be done to improve this metric.

Only six locking events were found during the application lifetime: five over the ROM and AI configuration files, and one over an unknown object, probably a dynamic library. 43 µs were spent waiting for lock acquisition. We do not find any space left for further optimizations. Cache tests reported similar results as Valgrind, with negligible miss rates.

Other considered metrics include a CPI of 0.7, indicating that every instruction takes 0.7 clock cycles to execute in average, even when branch misprediction and pipeline stalls are taken into account. This suggests that the problems found before are partially overcame by improved efficiency in other areas.

Xeon Phi Profiling. The results obtained in the Xeon Phi profiling support previous findings relating slow memory access, made evident by a considerably higher *self time* of the emulated NES RAM memory read/write functions (negligible on desktop to a sizable chunk of the total time on the Xeon Phi). Average time to fulfill cache requests was quite high (around 593.2 cycles for a L1 miss). However, L1 hit rate was 99.5% evidencing once again very low memory access speeds. The average value is much worse than the one obtained on the benchmark, suggesting that realistic loads attain lower performances. As the emulator is loaded from scratch for each simulation, these results fare poorly for FCEUX, as every load time is extended. Furthermore, as the executable and ROM file are small (1 MB and less than 50 KB respectively), this aspect cannot be easily further optimized.

The reported CPI per hardware thread was 3.459, quite high for Xeon Phi. The process with higher CPI (12.455) is vmlinux, out of our control. Considering only the other top six most expensive operations (accounting for 95.73% of the execution time), the CPI is 2.380, closer to the theoretical minimum (2.0).

7.2   Computational Platform

The experimental analysis was performed on DELL PowerEdge R720 servers with 64 GB of DDR3 RAM and two Intel Xeon E5-2650 processors, each with 8 cores working at 2 GHz and 2 MB of L2 cache. Each server has an Intel Xeon

Phi 31S1P with 57 cores working at 1.1 GHz, 28.5 MB of L2 cache (512 KB per core), and 8 GB of GDDR5 RAM. All machines are hosted at Cluster FING, Universidad de la República, Uruguay [11].

7.3   Methodology for the Experimental Evaluation

In order to find the best work distribution and number of threads, we conducted a two-stage experimental analysis. In the first stage, four different settings of the parallel EA were studied, using 200 threads for evaluation: *(i)* five independent processes with 40 individuals each, *(ii)* one process with 200 individuals, *(iii)* one process with five subpopulations of 40 individuals each, and *(iv)* one process with two subpopulations of 100 individuals each. In the second stage we studied the number of threads, using the best setting of the previous stage. We analyzed using 55, 110, 165 and 220 threads.

In all cases, ten independent experiments were performed, accounting for the stochastic nature of EAs. The EA executed for 100 generations, using a crossover probability of 0.9 and mutation 0.1. All simulations used a game instance running for 4000 frames.

7.4   Results

Table 1 reports the execution time results for the configuration tests of the evolutionary pinball AI on Xeon Phi. It presents average elapsed time and average fitness and their respective standard deviations (σ) for different combinations of: number of independent EAs executed (#EA), number of subpopulations in each EA (#SP) and the number of individuals in each subpopulation (PSP).

Table 1. Results of EA configuration tests

#EA	#SP	PSP	Time (minutes)		f	
			Avg	σ	Avg	σ
5	1	40	50.16	3.37	61928	8971.2
1	1	200	51.99	0.50	65186	9444.2
1	5	40	54.71	1.56	65447	7271.8
1	2	100	56.13	1.03	67740	7921.2

According to the results reported in Table 1, the fastest configuration used five independent evolutionary processes, because no synchronizations are performed. However, it also computed the lowest average fitness values. Using subpopulations produced a significant time increase, due to synchronization between them. Taking into account both computational cost and results quality, we opted for the second configuration using a single population of 200 individuals. This configuration must wait for all individuals to be evaluated before producing the next generation. Since not all emulations require the same time, last ones cannot

#T	time (minutes)	
---	avg	σ
55	181.47	2.18
110	93.63	0.62
165	65.68	0.93
220	50.20	0.31

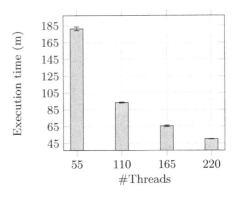

Fig. 9. Scalability: impact of the amount of threads on execution time.

use all the available computational resources, reducing performance. All configurations consume near 80 MB of RAM on the card and 300 MB on the host.

Figure 9 shows the results of the scalability analysis, reporting the average time spent and standard deviation (σ) when using different number of threads ($\#T$). The results show a doubling in performance when going from 55 to 110 threads. This is coherent with not being able to execute instructions from each thread on successive cycles. Using 165 and 220 threads show less improvement, but still achieve better performance. The best results were obtained with 220 threads (4 threads per core). This is expected, since each thread performs several memory accesses to load the game from main memory, and thus is desirable to have other threads available to execute during load operations.

Further details of the experimental analysis and results are reported at the project website www.fing.edu.uy/inco/grupos/cecal/hpc/GAIA.

8   Conclusions and Future Work

This article presents the design, implementation, and evaluation of a parallel EA on Xeon Phi. The proposed EA applies a two-level parallel model including a master-slave approach using an offloading technique. The parallel EA is applied for the automatic generation of an AI for the NES Pinball game.

We found that existing frameworks were difficult to adapt or cannot work with offloading code as they were not written in C or Fortran. For this reason, a new framework was built from scratch, considering performance and offload support. For solution evaluation, a NES emulator was ported to the MIC architecture, requiring multiple modifications to perform acceptably on the coprocessor. From this experience, we conclude that obtaining a good performance on the Xeon Phi is far more complex than recompiling code.

A number of issues arose during development. Vectorization could not be fully used, due to state dependencies for the emulator code. Although memory requirements are low, Xeon Phi memory performance impacted negatively on the efficiency, consuming a larger execution time than on a desktop computer. Moreover, being a single-threaded application, the emulator showed poor performance on the Xeon Phi. Profiling suggested that there is little room for improvement on the emulator. Offload code faced limitations on concurrent offload executions and setup/teardown time. This problem was solved by grouping solutions.

The presented case study (parallel EA for AI in games) exhibited its best performance when executing many parallel tasks with low synchronization. The results indicated that there is a trade-off between total execution time and solution quality. The scalability analysis demonstrated that using 220 threads yielded the best performance. Using up to 110 threads shows a doubling in performance, while further thread count increases produce a smaller boost. This improvement arises from the availability of a thread to execute when another awaits for reading operations to conclude, reducing idle time.

The EA framework has an acceptable performance using offload, suggesting that other Xeon Phi-friendly EA problems may achieve larger speedups.

The main lines of future work include replacing the FCEUX emulator with a JIT-compiler variant and reducing the need of emulation by employing caching techniques to avoid evaluating the same individual twice. An asynchronous master-slave model could exploit individuals that are inserted (and used) faster than others, providing a different exploration pattern and an improved efficiency.

References

1. Alba, E., Luque, G., Nesmachnow, S.: Parallel metaheuristics: recent advances and new trends. Int. Trans. Oper. Res. **20**, 1–48 (2013)
2. Bäck, T., Fogel, D., Michalewicz, Z. (eds.): Handbook of Evolutionary Computation. Oxford University Press, Oxford (1997)
3. Dyer, D.: Watchmaker Framework for Evolutionary Computation. http://watchmaker.uncommons.org/. Accessed 08 2016
4. Fang, J., Sips, H., Zhang, L., Xu, C., Che, Y., Varbanescu, A.: Test-driving Intel Xeon Phi. In: Proceedings of the 5th ACM/SPEC International Conference on Performance Engineering, pp. 137–148. ACM (2014)
5. Fang, Z., Mehta, S., Yew, P.C., Zhai, A., Greensky, J., Beeraka, G., Zang, B.: Measuring microarchitectural details of multi-and many-core memory systems through microbenchmarking. ACM Trans. Archit. Code Optim. **11**(4), 55 (2015)
6. FCEUX Community: The all in one NES/Famicom Emulator, August 2015. http://www.fceux.com/web/home.html
7. Hausknecht, M., Lehman, J., Miikkulainen, R., Stone, P.: A neuroevolution approach to general Atari game playing. IEEE Trans. Comput. Intell. AI Games **6**(4), 355–366 (2014)
8. Jeffers, J., Reinders, J.: Intel Xeon Phi Coprocessor High-performance Programming. Newnes, Oxford (2013)
9. Murphy, T.: The first level of super mario bros. is easy with lexicographic orderings and time travel. In: Proceeding of 7th Annual SIGBOVIK Conference, pp. 112–133 (2013)
10. Nesmachnow, S.: An overview of metaheuristics: accurate and efficient methods for optimisation. Int. J. Metaheuristics **3**(4), 320–347 (2014)

11. Nesmachnow, S.: Computación científica de alto desempeño en la Facultad de Ingeniería, Universidad de la República. Revista de la Asociación de Ingenieros del Uruguay, no. 61, pp. 12–15 (2010)
12. Nethercote, N., Seward, J.: Valgrind: a framework for heavyweight dynamic binary instrumentation. In: Proceedings of ACM SIGPLAN 2007 Conference on Programming Language Design and Implementation, pp. 89–100 (2007)
13. Parodi, F., Rodríguez Leopold, S., Iturriaga, S., Nesmachnow, S.: Optimizing a pinball computer player using evolutionary algorithms. In: XVIII Latin-Iberoamerican Conference on Operations Research (2016)
14. PCI-SIG: PCI Express Base Specification, Revision 2.1, March 2009
15. Simpson, R.: Evolutionary Artificial Intelligence in Video Games. University of Minnesota (2012)

A Software Framework for 2D Mesh Based Simulations in Discrete Time with Local Interaction

Sergio A. Gélvez C.$^{(\boxtimes)}$, Gabriel Pedraza, and Carlos J. Barrios H

High Performance and Scientific Computing Centre,
Universidad Industrial de Santander, Bucaramanga, Colombia
sergio.gelvez@correo.uis.edu.co, {gpredraza,cbarrios}@uis.edu.co

Abstract. Some features shared by families of natural phenomena may be exploited for the process of implementation of software simulation tools. An analogy of this situation is the experimentation in manufacturing, where the products are designed by organisations in a way that it is possible to exploit commonality in components and process. This work aims to exploit commonality in some simulation problems in order to create a software framework allowing the reusing of code to reduce effort in the implementation. The proposed framework shall include the core components for the simulation of varied phenomena. The interested researchers can use parts of the framework and then adapt the remaining components to their specific simulation problems. After this discussion, a test case is proposed from previous works related to lava flow simulations showing experimental results. Some guidelines for the design of the framework are presented, as well as a discussion about them.

Keywords: Modelling · Scientific software frameworks · Components

1 Introduction

Many natural phenomena share some features allowing the classification in families. In order to study and analyse those phenomena, researchers develop simulation tools, and in many cases those tools are solving partial differential equations (PDE) using some numerical method. However, even if those simulation tools are close conceptually, the software produced by different researchers can be very different are not easily shared between them due to the use of different programming languages, libraries (targeting different execution flows in the platforms), the experience of research developing software, etc.

On the other hand, simulation tools solving PDE are computational expensive and the execution platform must be powerful computers (supercomputers) or high performance computing (HPC) platforms. Nevertheless, developing software in a HPC platform is a challenging work, mathematicians or engineers must not only have skills in mathematics and numerical methods but also in software development in HPC. In addition, HPC platforms are currently very

© Springer International Publishing AG 2017
C.J. Barrios Hernández et al. (Eds.): CARLA 2016, CCIS 697, pp. 177–187, 2017.
DOI: 10.1007/978-3-319-57972-6_13

heterogeneous (multi-CPU, CPU-GPU, multiGPUs, etc.) and they use different programming models and technologies like OpenMP, MPI, CUDA, OpenACC, etc. Weak skills in programming models can produce poor performance simulation tools even if the mathematical model and numerical solution are sound.

The framework proposed in this paper aims to create simulation tools for the time discrete 2D spatially distributed phenomena targeting two main goals: (1) reduce development time and (2) produce high quality software. To achieve those goals, the framework exploits the commonalities of phenomena and uses a technique known in the software engineering community as Software Product Families (SPF). A software product family provides a basis of components that can be reused in different software products sharing the main core functionality but having some variabilities among them. In a SFP basic components are then very well known and tested, assuring the quality of the product family. Therefore, the proposed software framework has a set of high quality components that treat the complexity of the execution platform, or the numerical method implementation, allowing the researchers to avoid this complexity, asking them only for main computation components.

The paper is organized as follows, in the first section, the initially studied phenomenon is described to identify the key features that define its family. The second section shows an analysis of variability in the solution. In the next section, a proposal of software framework for simulation of phenomena in the discussed family is introduced. Finally, a discussion over the case study implemented using the framework is shown with its performance evaluation. Finally, conclusions based in the performance evaluation results and the use of the framework for the case of study are presented along with the future work.

2   Model Description

This work aims to exploit features that are common to the modelling of several natural phenomena in order to propose a software framework that allows the reusing of source code and the streamlining of the design method for simulation problems arisen from the study of said phenomena. This proposal was inspired on a Master in Computer Science project concerned with the simulation of lava flows [5] using Cellular Automata as the spatial foundation and implemented over hybrid architectures using GPGPU, and thus, we are primarily concerned with problems that use a 2D feature mesh and discrete time.

An n-dimensional mesh can be defined as the discretisation of a 2D geometric domain into smaller shapes. The most common type is the squared mesh, in which a rectangular shape is divided into small squares of uniform size. Many physical problems can be discretised in squared meshes, at least at great levels of abstraction. On the other hand, a discrete time model is one that takes measurements or reports values at discrete intervals of time, for instance from t_i to t_{i+1}. Natural phenomena usually exhibit continuous behaviour, but in order to create and operate the model, abstractions must be made [10].

The base problem, explained in detail in [5], had a 2D mesh composed of cells of attributes, physical quantities relevant to the simulation process. Also, the model was used in a workflow starting from the reading of mesh data and other parameters, such as crater positioning and rates of extrusion, lava temperature and so on. The tables show the data fields in every cell (Table 1) and the parameters read at the start-up of the simulation process (Table 2).

Table 1. Cell data structure.

Data field	Name description
Thickness	Thickness of the lava layer in the cell
Temperature	Average temperature of lava in the cell
Altitude	Average altitude of the cell
isVent	Indicator of whether a cell contains a crater or not
Yield	Value of the Tensile Yield Strength for the cell
Viscosity	Value of Viscosity for the cell
Exits	Number of lava exits (intermediate step)
InboundV	Lava volume introduced to cell in time t
OutboundV	Lava volume extracted from cell in time t
InboundQ	Heat quantity introduced to dell in time t

Table 2. Parameters read at simulation start-up.

Parameter	Value	Source
Altitude file	{ file }	File
Crater file	{ file }	File
Extrusion temperature	1500	Command line
Extrusion rate	0.15	Command line
Cell width and height	1	Command line
Max rows	1024	Command line
Max cols	1024	Command line
Crater number	1	Command line
Time steps	3600	Command line

The initial reading, including parameters, is the first stage in a pipeline that represents the entire simulation process. We have identified the stages that compose the process and we summarise them in Fig. 1.

Those stages have to be completed in sequence to produce a simulation result, and are also regarded as common to this type of problem. In the literature, there are certainly examples of diverse phenomena which share the 2D mesh with local interaction and discrete time range, such as wildfire spreading [13],

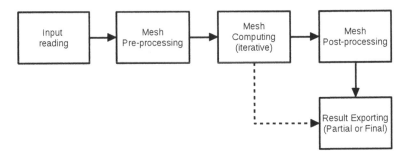

Fig. 1. Stages of the simulation workflow.

cloud dynamics [11], seismic dynamics [7], fluid dynamics [1], earthquakes [2], and many more [3,4,6,12].

Our proposal aims to create a structure in which diverse specific simulation problems can fit and thus, save efforts from the scientists involved in the simulation process.

In the specific case of the lava flow simulation model, the first stage consisted in the reading of a square matrix from a text file, with fixed maximum columns, and another file detailing the position of the craters within the matrix. After that, the initial values of all fields in each cell were calculated and the computing of the mesh for time t_1 started. That calculation was conducted using the methodology from Miyamoto and Sasaki [9]. After that, partial results were reported, and the next step in time, t_i, was calculated. When the process reached the maximum number of time steps, it stopped. That solution inspired the creation of a more general process that allowed quicker deployment of solutions for simulation problems of that type. We needed a path to identify the variability in the solution and exploit it to create a software framework to simplify the development process of that type of simulations.

3   Analysis of Variability and Generalisation of Components

There are several degrees of freedom in terms of variability in the solution described in the preceding sections, and this work we focused on two: Variability in sub-processes in each stage and variability of hardware platform in which the process in general is run. For instance, in the first case, it could have a different pre-processing stage for each of the simulations that can be run using this general processes, and the same can be said about each stage. Perhaps, the simplest case would be just writing different instances of the Result Reporting stage to export the results to several different visualisation formats.

About the second case, it is possible to have different implementations of each stage because the use of several platforms are desired. In the case of our example model, GPGPU are used in the form of NVIDIA CUDA, on one or several GPUs, but we could have used other parallel programming models. This multiple implementation approach certainly improves the applicability of the software solution developed.

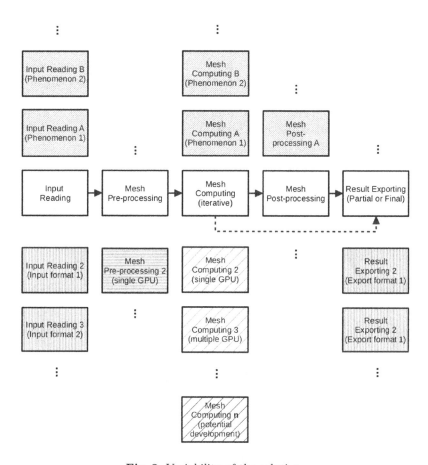

Fig. 2. Variability of the solution.

The Fig. 2 shows several cases of variability exhibited by the solution. Down from the stages (in the vertical center of the figure), the variability generated by the hardware platform is shown. Up from the stages, we can observe variability due to the different phenomenon simulated. In those cases, the variability generates alternative implementations of the stages. The selected implementation for each stage are then assembled in a pipeline creating a whole and particular implementation of the solution. Also, in a few stages, namely Input reading and Results reporting, the variability is produced by the existence of several data formats, and multiple implementation of those stages can be made.

4   Proposed Framework

The previously defined stages can be translated in different implementations, which in turn generate different software components. For a specific simulation, the interested scientists must provide an implementation of selected components, and the framework is coupled with those, creating a complete simulation program. The amount of work by the scientist is thus reduced, provided that the problem is of the type compatible with the framework. The components that can be customised are initially the Input reading, the Result reporting and the Mesh computing; those are very specific to the phenomena studied and mandatory to the process, and also subjected to the most variability of all. A graphical explanation of the situation is presented on Fig. 3.

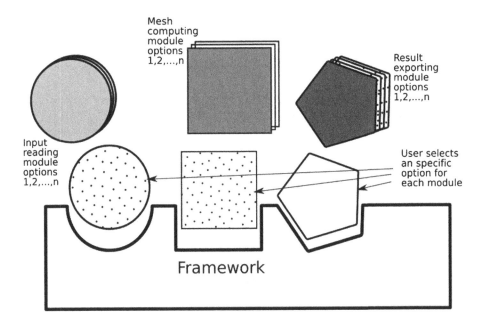

Fig. 3. Framework and sample modules.

For the assembly of a particular solution, the modules are assembled at compilation time, and the simulation program emerges complete from the process. In the first version of the work, the components are created using C syntax, given the fact that CUDA(c) is used, and CUDA C (the language in which the GPU instructions are passed) is based on C. The process is summarized in Fig. 4.

Different degrees of freedom in terms of variability to define the scope of the framework are considered. First, platform variability, addressed to the implementation of the solution in multi-CPU X86, simple GPU and multi GPU based architectures. Also, the numerical variability, which is the name used to describe

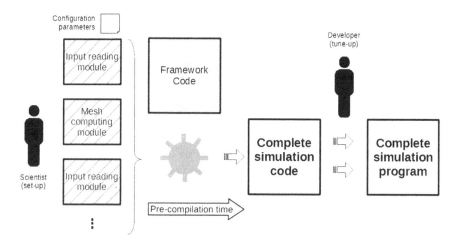

Fig. 4. Development of the solution using the framework.

variability in the mathematical method used to simulate the phenomenon, cellular automata (used in the model inspiring the work) and finite differences (being the most popular) being the initial methods to take in consideration. And finally, algorithm variability, which refers to partitioning and load balance algorithms specifically. The first comparison is between what can be called a naïve approach and an algorithm that exploits previously calculated data, to try and reduce the communications between processing elements.

As mentioned before, the first example constructed using this model of implementation was the Lava flow model [5]. A discussion about an implementation will be shown in the next section.

5   Case Study: Lava Flows in a 2D Mesh Using Cellular Automata

5.1   Automata Definitions

The model is based on the Navier-Stokes equations from fluid dynamics; it also includes the heat transfer equations. Since a Cellular Automata will be used as a tool for managing the geometry of the problem, the transition rules must be defined from the equations applied to a Bingham fluid. The equations are then discretised, according to Miyamoto and Sasaki [9]. The flux from a cell to one adjacent to it is:

$$\Delta V = \frac{\rho S_y h_c^2 w}{3\eta} \left[\left(\frac{h}{h_c} \right)^3 - \frac{3}{2} \left(\frac{h}{h_c} \right)^2 + \frac{1}{2} \right] \Delta t \qquad (1)$$

where the parameters are:

S_y = Yield strength (Bingham fluid parameter)
η = Viscosity
h_c = Critical thickness
w = Cell width
ρ = Density
ΔV = Transferred volume

The critical thickness is the value of thickness in which the force applied by the gravity to the fluid allows the breaking of the cohesion of the molecules of the fluid, and thus, the material stops behaving as a solid and start flowing, as a fluid. This value depends on the viscosity and yield strength. In addition, the model only loses heat due to radiation. Transmission to the ground and convection are negligible. Transfer of heat due to flux is taken into account. The full definition of the automata can be studied more thoroughly in the original work [5].

The cell set is defined as 1024 rows by 1024 columns, each one with the fields in Table 1 in page 179. The craters are read from the file and put in place at the start of the simulation.

The computing of the cell values for a time step t are:

- Read altitude data.
- Initialise the values of fields for every cell.
- For each cell, obtain the critical thickness of every adjacent, then determine which cells transfer material.
- Calculate the value of the flux with Eq. 1.
- Add all fluxes and their corresponding heat transfer.
- Calculate heat loss due to radiation

After all these operations time step t is over and time $t + 1$ starts. This process is reapeated for all time steps according to input parameters.

5.2   Hardware Architecture Used

The machine used for the simulation comprises 16 computing nodes. The specifications of the nodes are summarised in the Table 3. The GPU specifications are summarised in Table 4.

5.3   Scenarios and Experiment

For the simulations, a set of mapping where used. They are presented in Table 5, on page 185. A fixed set of parameters was used.

Table 3. Test node specifications.

Specification	Value
CPU	2 x Intel(R) Xeon(R) CPU E5645 @ 2.40GHz
CPU Cores	6
Threads	2 x Core
Total cores	24
Total memory	107471960 kB (104 Gb)
GPU	8 x NVIDIA Tesla M2075

Table 4. Test node GPU specifications.

Specification	Value
GPU	NVIDIA Tesla M2075
Cores	448
Memory bandwidth	150 Gb/s
Memory	6 Gb GDDR5
Memory speed	1.55 GHz
Performance (Single precision)	1.03 TFlops
Performance (Double precision)	515 GFlops
Architecture	Fermi
Compute capability	2.0

Table 5. Mappings for the testing.

Name	Description
cuda	1 GPU
cuda_normal_multi	Multiples GPU (2, 4, 8)

5.4   Analysis of Results

Due to space constrains, all data is available on request to the authors.

The average running time is presented for the three scenarios, along with others that use pinned zero copy memory in Fig. 5. From the data it can be concluded that:

– The speedup values are greater than 1 for two mappings.
– Pinned memory is slower for this solution.
– Multi GPU mappings have times with a decreasing trend according to the number of GPU used, which is positive.

Also, in the original work, we concluded that the main problem with the performance was the memory transactions [5]. The memory copy was slower that the computing in all cases according to the data obtained.

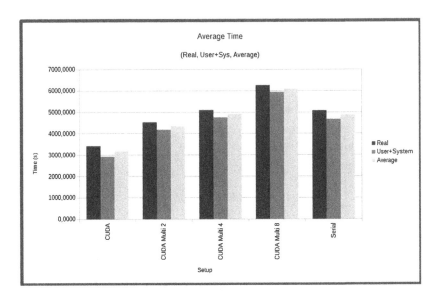

Fig. 5. Average times.

The framework proposed will allow us to continue testing more quickly and on different platforms. At the moment only one specific phenomenon was tested, but the variability over platform was shown.

6   Conclusions

The specific solution implemented has performanced problems arisen from the characteristics of its memory transactions. It is a problem that must be researched more profoundly, and an aid to testing in the form of a reproducibility tool would be very welcome. The framework proposed could help in that regard.

An exploitable variability was shown, and the first steps in addressing it have been taken. The structure of the solution is compatible with the process described in the third chapter. More solution applicable to different phenomena must be used.

The component based architecture seems adequate to treat this type of problem. More testing is required, but the results of the first implementation is promising.

Acknowledgments. Experiments presented in this paper were carried out using the GridUIS-2 experimental testbed, being developed under the Universidad Industrial de Santander (SC3UIS) High Performance and Scientific Computing Centre, development action with support from UIS Vicerrectoria de Investigación y Extension (VIE-UIS) and several UIS research groups as well as other funding bodies (http://www.sc3.uis.edu.co).

References

1. Abarbanel, H., Case, K., Despain, A., Dyson, F., Freedman, M., Max, C., Nelson, D., Rothaus, O.: Cellular automata and parallel processing for practical fluid-dynamics problems, September 1990
2. Akishin, P.G., Altaisky, M.V., Antoniou, I., Budnik, A.D., Ivanov, V.V.: Simulation of earthquakes with cellular automata (1998). http://dx.doi.org/10.1155/S1026022698000247
3. Avolio, M.V., Di Gregorio, S., Mantovani, F., Pasuto, A., Rongo, R., Silvano, S., Spataro, W.: Simulation of the 1992 Tessina landslide by a cellular automata model and future hazard scenarios. JAG **2**(1), 41–50 (2000)
4. D'ambrosia, D., Spataro, W., Iovine, G.: Parallel genetic algorithms for optimising cellular automata models of natural complex phenomena: an application to debris flows. Comput. Geosci. **32**, 861–875 (2006)
5. Gelvez Cortes, S.A.: Problemas Computacionales Asociados a la Construcción de Modelos de Simulación Basados en Autómatas Celulares en Paralelo. Caso de Estudio: Evaluación de Amenazas Asociadas a Flujos de Lava Volcánica como Fluído Bingham. Master's thesis (2015)
6. Ilachinski, A.: Cellular Automata, a Discrete Universe, 1st edn. World Scientific Publishing Co., Pte. Ltd., Singapore (2001)
7. Leamy, M.J.: Application of cellular automata modeling to seismic elastodynamics. Int. J. Solids Struct. **45**(17), 4835–4849 (2008). http://www.sciencedirect.com/science/article/pii/S0020768308001832
8. Mazzariol, M., Gennart, B.A., Hersch, R.D.: Dynamic load balancing of parallel cellular automata. In: Proceedings SPIE Conference, Parallel and Distributed Methods for Image Processing IV 4118, pp. 21–29, July 2000
9. Miyamoto, H., Sasaki, S.: Simulating Lava flows by an improved cellular automata method. Comput. Geosci. **23**, 283–292 (1997)
10. Pearson, R.: Discrete-Time Dynamic Models. Oxford University Press, Oxford (1999)
11. da Silva, A.R., Gouvêa Jr., M.M.: Cloud dynamics simulation with cellular automata. In: Proceedings of the 2010 Summer Computer Simulation Conference, SCSC 2010, pp. 278–283. Society for Computer Simulation International, San Diego (2010). http://dl.acm.org/citation.cfm?id=1999416.1999451
12. Talia, D.: Parallel cellular algorithms and programs (2006)
13. Trunfio, G.A., D'Ambrosio, D., Rongo, R., Spataro, W., Di Gregorio, S.: A new algorithm for simulating wildfire spread through cellular automata. ACM Trans. Model. Comput. Simul. **22**(1), 6:1–6:26 (2011). http://doi.acm.org/10.1145/2043635.2043641

A GPU Parallel Implementation of the RSA Private Operation

Nareli Cruz-Cortés[1]($\boxtimes$), Eduardo Ochoa-Jiménez[2], Luis Rivera-Zamarripa[1], and Francisco Rodríguez-Henríquez[2]

[1] Centro de Investigación en Computación del Instituto Politécnico Nacional, Mexico City, Mexico
nareli@cic.ipn.mx, lrivera_a13@sagitario.cic.ipn.mx
[2] Computer Science Department, CINVESTAV, Mexico City, Mexico
jochoa@computacion.cs.cinvestav.mx, francisco@cs.cinvestav.mx

Abstract. The implementation of the RSA private operation tends to be expensive since its computationally complexity is cubic with respect to the bit-size of its private key. As a consequence, considerable effort has been put into optimizing this operation. In this work, we present a parallel implementation of the RSA private operation using the Single Instruction Multiple Thread (SIMT) threading model of Graphics Processor Unit (GPU) platforms. The underlying modular arithmetic is performed by means of the Residue Number System (RNS) representation. By combining these two approaches, we present a GPU software library that achieves high-speed timings for the RSA private operation when using 1024-, 2048- and 3072-bit secret keys.

Keywords: RSA · Residue number system · GPUs · CUDA

1 Introduction

In 1977, Rivest, Shamir and Adleman famously presented the RSA algorithm [14], which is as of today, the most popular crypto-scheme for key exchange establishment and digital signatures on Internet information security applications. Moreover, most of the Internet certificates currently in use are verified using an RSA public key, and a number of certificate authorities only issue RSA certificates.

For example, RSA is frequently executed in communication protocols such as the Transport Layer Security (TLS) protocol [5]. Indeed, in a client-server TLS session, the client may apply the RSA public operation and the server's public key to encrypt a secret and then send it to the server. Then, the server decrypts this information using its own private key and the RSA private key operation. After that, the client and the server use this shared secret to derive a session key that can be utilized to perform bulk encryption, message authentication and other relevant cryptographic operations.

© Springer International Publishing AG 2017
C.J. Barrios Hernández et al. (Eds.): CARLA 2016, CCIS 697, pp. 188–203, 2017.
DOI: 10.1007/978-3-319-57972-6_14

Until recently, RSA-1024 has been overwhelmingly used to secure Internet communications. Nevertheless, in [3], the US-based National Institute of Standards and Technology (NIST) recommended that as early as the year 2010, cryptographic systems achieving a security level of 80 bits should be deprecated; from 2010 until 2030 a security level of at least 112 bits should be enforced, and a minimum of 128-bit security level was recommended from the year 2030 and beyond. From the current state-of-the-art on integer factorization algorithms, it is believed that those three security levels can be instrumented via RSA using secret keys with bit-lengths of 1024, 2048, and 3072 bits, respectively.

Hence, in order to perform an urgently needed migration to higher levels of security, it would be required to achieve highly-optimized implementations of the RSA cryptosystem and its associated building blocks, so that the key exchange operation as well as the signing and signature verification of documents can be executed at a speed that is able to cope with Internet's high-volume data exchange.

Graphic Processing Units are massively parallel processors consisting of hundreds or even thousands of cores. This contrasts with contemporary general-purpose CPUs, which can only host at most tens of cores. It is then conceivable that taking advantage of the massively parallel architecture of the GPUs, one can speed up several computations where high computing power is required. A chief example of this, is the efficient implementation of cryptographic applications. Some cryptographic algorithms that have been implemented recently using GPUs include the Advanced Encryption Standard, RSA and Elliptic Curve Cryptography to name but just a few.

In this work, a high performance parallel RSA implementation using private key lengths of 1024, 2048 and 3072 bits, is presented. We targeted a GPU GeForce GTX Kepler architecture TITAN card, that executes at a clock speed of 876 MHz. Our library uses the Residue Number System (RNS) arithmetic representation, which is especially suited for fine-grained parallel computations. The experimental results achieved by our library outperform the ones presented in [17] by 19.3% and by 18.5% for the RSA-1024 and RSA-2048 private operations, respectively.

The remainder of this paper is organized as follows. In Sect. 2, the mathematical and algorithmic definitions used throughout this work are presented. This includes the RSA main algorithms, the RNS operand representation and associated arithmetic operations, and a high level overview of the GPU architecture. In Sect. 3, we present a description of a fine-grained level parallelization that takes advantage of the Single Instruction Multiple Thread (SIMT) model for the efficient computation of the RNS integer multiplication, the RNS modular reduction and the RSA main exponentiation. In Sect. 4, an evaluation of the performance of our RSA library and its comparison against related works is presented. Finally, in Sect. 5 we draw some concluding remarks and discuss future work directions.

2   Preliminaries

In this section, a brief overview of the RSA cryptosytem is given in Subsect. 2.1. Then, the residue number system and related arithmetic operations are described in Subsect. 2.2. Finally, in Subsect. 2.3 we discuss some relevant properties and characteristics of the GPU architecture.

2.1   RSA Cryptosystem

RSA is one of the most famous public key cryptosystems suitable for both, encryption and digital signature. It consists of three main algorithms.

First, the key generation algorithm produces the public and private keys, by constructing an ℓ-bit modulo $N = p \cdot q$, where p and q are $\ell/2$-bit randomly chosen prime numbers that should meet some standard security properties. The public key is the tuple composed by the modulo N and the public exponent e that is generally chosen as the integer $2^{16} + 1$. The private key consist of p, q, N and the private exponent $d = e^{-1} \mod \phi(N)$, where $\phi(\cdot)$ represents the Euler's totient function, and hence, $\phi(N) = (p-1) \cdot (q-1)$. Except for the public modulus N, all these parameters must be kept secret.

Depending on the context, the RSA public operation can be used either for data encryption or signature verification. Similarly, the RSA private operation can be used for data decryption or for performing the digital signature of a message. In the case of a message signature, given the private key and a message m, the signature s is computed as $s = H(m)^d \mod N$, where $H(\cdot)$, is a cryptographic hash function that produces a unique fingerprint of the message m in the integer range $[1, N - 1]$. Signature verification consists of checking whether $H(m') = v$, where v is computed as $v = s^e \mod N$, using the signee's public key (N, e), the received signature s, and the received message m'. The RSA security guarantees lie in the computationally hardness of the integer factorization problem.

The Chinese Remainder Theorem. The RSA private operation is the most costly operation of this cryptosystem, involving a modular exponentiation using an ℓ-bit private exponent d, with $\ell \geq 1024$. On the other hand, the encryption/verification RSA public operation is generally considered negligible, since the public exponent e is generally chosen as $2^{16} + 1$, which is a small 17-bit prime with Hamming weight two.

Hence, it is important to find ways to perform the modular exponentiation by the secret exponent d as efficiently as possible. One useful approach for attaining this aim, is to make use of the Chinese Remainder Theorem, which allows us to trade an ℓ-bit modular exponentiation by the computation of two $\ell/2$-bit modular independent exponentiations, which can be performed in parallel. Using this method, the exponentiation $s = H(m)^d \mod N$, can be equivalently computed as,

$$s = (I_q \cdot (s_p - s_q) \mod p) \cdot q + s_q,$$

where the parameters s_p, s_q, and I_p are computed as, $s_p = H(m)^{d \bmod (p-1)} \bmod p$, $s_q = H(m)^{d \bmod (q-1)} \bmod q$, and, $I_q = q^{-1} \bmod p$.

2.2   Residue Number System

In most crypto-schemes, the efficiency of the main computations is bounded by the computationally costs associated to the underlying arithmetic operations, which directly affect the performance of the high level cryptographic primitives. For example, when performing the addition of multi-word integers, any output carry produced at a given word addition, must be sequentially propagated to the remaining most significant words. Unless specific measures are put in place, this situation will limit the overall performance of the arithmetic library being developed.

Mainly due to its parallel-friendly nature, during the last few decades many researchers have adopted the Residue Number System (RNS), which is particularly useful for performing fast arithmetic over large integers.

The foundations of the RNS approach lie in the Chinese Remainder Theorem. Its operation can be described as follows. Let us consider the set $\mathcal{B} = (p_1, p_2, \ldots, p_n)$, composed of n pairwise co-prime k-bit moduli selected as integers near to 2^k (the reason for this choice will be explained in the next section), which is called the RNS-basis, where k is normally chosen to have the same value of the processor's word-size.

Let us define $P = \prod_{i=1}^{i=n} p_i$, and let p be an odd prime such that $p < P$. A large integer x, can be represented by the n-tuple $X = (x_1, x_2, \ldots, x_n)$, where each x_i is the residue $x \bmod p_i$, which will be written in the rest of this paper as, $x_i = |x|_{p_i}$. Provided that the number x is in the range $[0, P-1]$, the RNS representation as defined above is unique.

Let x and y be two large multi-word integers with $x, y < P$, which can be represented as two RNS operands $X = (x_1, x_2, \ldots, x_n)$ and $Y = (y_1, y_2, \ldots, y_n)$ using the RNS-basis $\mathcal{B}$, with $x, y < P$. The RNS addition and multiplication are performed through addition and multiplication over each component of X and Y as,

$$X \oplus Y = (|x_1 + y_1|_{p_1}, |x_2 + y_2|_{p_2}, \ldots, |x_n + y_n|_{p_n}),$$
$$X \otimes Y = (|x_1 \cdot y_1|_{p_1}, |x_2 \cdot y_2|_{p_2}, \ldots, |x_n \cdot y_n|_{p_n}).$$

The RNS number system is particularly interesting because it distributes the overall arithmetic computation over several small moduli whose size in bits is frequently chosen to match the word-size of the target platform. In this way, one can trade the computation of a single arithmetic operation involving two large operands, by the calculation of n independent smaller modular operations that use the moduli in the set $\mathcal{B}$, which happens to be independent and needs no synchronization among them due to the fact that there is no carry propagation among the n modular operations [1,2].

RNS Modular Reduction. In the case of RSA modular exponentiation, all multiplications must be carried out modulo N. Therefore, after performing an RNS multiplication, the result obtained must be reduced modulo N. In order to obtain a valid RNS representation of a multiplication result, which is greater than P, we use a redundant RNS-basis containing $2n$ moduli. Furthermore, to perform an RNS modular reduction, we adopted the method introduced by Bernstein in [4], as explained by Jeljeli in [10] (see also [9]). We selected this approach mainly because it allows us to perform the reduction without having to convert the RNS number to its integer representation. In the following, we closely follow the description given in [9,10].

Let us assume that one wants to find the reduction of a large integer x modulo an n-word integer N. Let us also assume that the RNS vector X represents the integer x using an n−moduli RNS-basis, where each modulo has a bit-length of k bits, and where k is the GPU's wordsize. An strategy to perform the modular reduction of $x \bmod N$, can be found from the CRT reconstruction equation given as,

$$X = \left| \sum_{i=1}^{n} \gamma_i \cdot P_i \right|_P \; , \text{ where } \gamma_i \triangleq \left| x_i \cdot P_i^{-1} \right|_{p_i} \text{ and } P_i \triangleq P/p_i.$$

We can write X as,

$$X = \sum_{i=1}^{n} \gamma_i \cdot P_i - \alpha \cdot P, \text{ with } \alpha = \left\lfloor \sum_{i=1}^{n} \frac{\gamma_i}{p_i} \right\rfloor$$

and, since $\gamma_i < p_i$, we have that $0 \le \alpha < n$. Then, if we assume that α is known, we can define $Z \triangleq \sum_{i=1}^{n} \gamma_i \cdot |P_i|_N - |\alpha \cdot P|_N$, which is congruent to $x \bmod N$, as required. In order to determine the value of α we use the fact that $p_i \approx 2^k$. Hence, we can approximate γ_i/p_i using only the s most significant bits of $\gamma_i/2^k$. The α approximation is computed using,

$$\alpha \triangleq \left\lfloor \sum_{i=1}^{n} \frac{\left\lfloor \frac{\gamma_i}{2^{k-s}} \right\rfloor}{2^s} + \Delta \right\rfloor ,$$

where s is an integer in the range $[1, k]$ and $0 < \Delta < 1$ an error correcting parameter. The modular reduction by N of a vector $X = (x_1, x_2, \ldots, x_n)$ as described above is carried out as shown in Algorithm 1.

It must be pointed out that Algorithm 1 does not give the exact result of the operation $x \bmod N$, but rather, it produces a multiple of the reduction that is bounded by $n2^k N$. This situation implies that the cardinality of the RNS basis $\mathcal{B}$, must be increased from n moduli to $2n$ moduli, so that the condition, $N \cdot n2^k N < (1 - \delta)P$, holds [9,10].

From the programming point of view, notice also that in the execution of Algorithm 1, all the modular operations can be evaluated in parallel, except for the Step 6, where a *broadcast* operation of all the γ_j's is required.

Algorithm 1. RNS modular reduction algorithm [10]

Precomputation: // Performed in the CPU

1 RNS vector $\left|P_j^{-1}\right|_{p_j}$ for $j \in \{1, \ldots, n\}$

2 Table of RNS vectors $|P_i|_N$ for $i \in \{1, \ldots, n\}$

3 Table of RNS vectors $|\alpha \cdot P|_N$ for $\alpha \in \{1, \ldots, n-1\}$

  Input: RNS vector X, the number of moduli in the RNS-basis (n), the
  RNS-basis $\mathcal{B}$, and the parameters k, s and Δ.
  Output: RNS vector Z, such that its integer representation $z \equiv x \mod N$.

  Computation   :   // Performed in the GPU

4 **for** *each* Thread j **do**

5 $\quad \gamma_j \longleftarrow \left| x_j \cdot \left|P_j^{-1}\right|_{p_j} \right|_{p_j}$

6 Broadcast of the γ_j's by all the threads

7 **for** *each* Thread j **do**

8 $\quad z_j \longleftarrow \left| \sum_{i=1}^{n} \gamma_i \cdot \left| |P_i|_N \right|_{p_j} \right|_{p_j}$

9 $\quad \alpha \longleftarrow \left\lfloor \sum_{i=1}^{n} \dfrac{\left\lfloor \dfrac{\gamma_i}{2^{k-s}} \right\rfloor}{2^s} + \Delta \right\rfloor$

10 $\quad z_j \longleftarrow \left| z_j - \left| |\alpha \cdot P|_N \right|_{p_j} \right|_{p_j}$

RNS to Integer Form Conversion. As it was mentioned above, it is possible
to convert back an RNS vector to its integer form by using the CRT recovering
formula,

$$x = \left| \sum_{i=1}^{n} \left| x_i \cdot P_i^{-1} \right|_{p_i} \cdot P_i \right|_P .$$

2.3   GPU Architecture

Originally, Graphics Processing Units (GPU) cards were hardware blocks optimized to perform a small set of graphical operations. In 2006, NVIDIA introduced the CUDA architecture, which is a parallel computing platform for GPUs
that defines the threading model, calling function conventions and, memory hierarchy for CUDA programmers. CUDA applications manage concurrency through
streams, which are a sequence of commands executed in an order fixed by the
programmer. In this work, we used a GPU with the Kepler architecture, which
is briefly explained next.

A Kepler architecture for GPU cards has hundreds if not thousands of
Streaming Multiprocessors (SM) blocks running concurrently. Each SM is composed by 12 groups of 16 cores. The SMs employ the Single Instruction Multiple
Thread (SIMT) programming model, where each core can execute a sequential
thread, but all cores inside of a group execute the same instruction at the same

time. Under the SIMT model, the basic computation and resource allocation unit is a thread, and a program code is executed in groups of 32 concurrent threads, known as a *warp*. In a SM, the execution of an integer o single-precision instruction on an entire warp takes two clock cycles. There is a small cache memory attached to each SM that is shared among its cores. This cache memory is a low-latency block of memory having an access latency close to that of the registers. In a Kepler GPU card, the shared memory has a size of 64 KB, which can be reconfigured by the programmer. For example, a valid configuration could be to allocate 48 KB for the software data cache and 16 KB for the hardware data cache.

The threads are grouped into blocks, which in turn are grouped into a grid. All threads within a grid execute the same code of a kernel until it completes its execution. Threads in a block are partitioned into warps whose threads run concurrently. During the kernel invocation, a programmer can configure the amount of share memory, the number of threads in a block and the number of blocks in a grid, among other features [17]. There is however an upper bound on the size of blocks. In the case of the GPU Kepler architecture, this upper bound is 1024 threads or 32 warps.

The programming model on GPU platforms consists of code sequences called kernels. Generally, each kernel completes its execution before the execution of the next one begins. This behavior is accomplished by using an implicit synchronization barrier between any two kernels. On the other hand, since the SMs are asynchronously executed in parallel, a GPU can simultaneously execute multiple independent kernels. However, the GPU cards do not support synchronization mechanisms among SMs. This limitation implies that several classic parallel programming techniques cannot be applied for this kind of architectures. Besides, given the fact that the GPU threads can create other threads, a nested parallelism is supported on GPU cards. Notice however that the threads executed on a SM can not share results with the threads running on another SM.

3   Implementation

In this section, we first give a brief description of the GPU assembly instructions used in this work. Then, we present a short overview of the modular arithmetic implementation aspects that should be taken into account when targeting a GPU card. Finally, we report several implementation aspects and the optimization techniques used to obtain a faster and more efficient parallel RSA modular exponentiation.

3.1   PTX Assembly Instructions

In order to improve the performance of the RNS arithmetic, we used CUDA PTX, which provides a stable programming model and instruction set for general purpose parallel programming [13]. In particular, the following assembly instructions are heavily used in our library,

- **addc**: This instruction adds two 32/64 bits values taking into account the carry-in bit and producing a carry-out bit.
- **subc**: It subtracts one value from another, each one of 32/64 bits, considering the borrow-in bit and producing a borrow-out bit.
- **mul.lo**: It multiplies two 32/64 bits values and it returns $x_i \times y_i \bmod 2^k$, where x_i and y_i are both non-negative integers, and k is typically selected to be the GPU word size.
- **mul.hi**: It multiplies two 32/64 bits values and it returns $x_i \times y_i / 2^k$, where x_i and y_i are both non-negative integers.
- **mad.(hi,lo).cc**: It multiplies two 32/64 bits values, extracts the higher or lower half of the result, and adds a third 32/64 bits value with carry-out.

The above described instructions helped us to get a better performance, because we can reduce the number of instructions used in the integer arithmetic, since some instructions can handle an implicit carry/borrow. In addition, we can use PTX in order to have more control over arithmetic operations, which allows us to avoid the so-called thread *divergence* during the execution of the program code.[1]

On the other hand, there exist special data types in CUDA that allow us to store values bigger than the GPU register sizes. For example, the uint2 data type is a small 2-element vector that permits to independently store the most significant half and the least significant half of a 64-bit integer. In this way, we can achieve an efficient access and a fast computation over the data using PTX instructions, which are directly executed over registers and shared memory.

3.2   Basic RNS Modular Arithmetic on GPU

As it was mentioned in Subsect. 2.2, the basic operations in RNS are: $x_i + y_i$, $x_i - y_i$, $x_i \times y_i$, as well as the modular reduction by the set of moduli p_i. The addition, subtraction and multiplication operations were performed using the native GPU assembly instructions, which were described in the previous subsection. Aiming to perform an efficient modular reduction by p_i, we selected pseudo-Mersenne co-prime numbers to construct the RNS-basis $\mathcal{B}$. Those co-prime numbers have the form $p_i = 2^k - c_i$, where c_i is a small integer and k is the GPU register size. Typically, the modular reduction is done through integer division, but this is unnecessary when dealing with pseudo-Mersenne numbers moduli. Indeed, for this special class of moduli, the modular reduction can be done efficiently with a small number of additions and multiplications, by means of the following procedure. Let $t_i = x_i \circ y_i$, where $\circ$ stands for an addition, a subtraction or a multiplication operation. Then, one can write t_i as,

$$t_i = t_{iL} + 2^k \times t_{iH}.$$

---

[1] A thread divergence occurs when the threads do not execute the same instruction at the same time. Thread divergence is an important limiting factor in the exploitation of the parallelism of a program and therefore it must be avoided as much as possible.

Where, t_{iL} denotes the k least significant bits and t_{iH} the k most significant bits of t_i. Since, $2^k \equiv c_i \bmod p_i$, it follows that $t_i \equiv t_{iL} + c_i \times t_{iH} \bmod p_i$. So, we can compute the modular reduction of t_i as, $|t_i|_{p_i} = t_{iL} + c_i \times t_{iH}$. However, one must take into account that if the resulting t_i still is greater than p_i, then one should repeat the previous procedure until $t_i < p_i$. In our case, this can provably be done after no more than two reductions provided that the c_i are sufficiently small.

Given the fact that the basic RNS operations are independent of each other, one can perform all the computations in parallel as shown in Fig. 1. Hence, the implementation of basic operations was done launching n concurrent execution threads, each one of them handling each one of the n co-prime numbers contained in the RNS-basis.

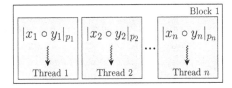

Fig. 1. Parallel implementation of RNS basic modular operations.

$\mathcal{B}$ **Size Selection.** As it has been mentioned, it is necessary to construct a basis $\mathcal{B}$ to work with the operands in the RNS representation. In principle, the size of $\mathcal{B}$ should be $2n$, where n is the number of moduli needed to represent an operand. This would imply that in order to deal with operands of 512, 1024 and 1536 bits we should construct bases containing 16, 32 and 48, 64-bit coprime moduli, respectively. However, in order to avoid thread divergence and to better exploit the inherent parallelism of the GPU platforms, we found experimentally that better performance results were obtained using bases with a cardinality of 32, 36 and 64 co-prime moduli, for 512-, 1024- and 2048-bit operands, respectively.

3.3 RNS Modular Multiplication on GPU

Let X and Y be two integer numbers represented in RNS as $(x_1, x_2, ..., x_n)$ and $(y_1, y_2, ..., y_n)$, respectively. To compute the RNS modular multiplication $X \otimes Y \bmod N$, where N is the module used in the RSA exponentiation, we need to carry out an RNS integer multiplication, followed by an RNS modular reduction with respect to the modulus N. On a GPU platform, these operations can be performed in an efficient manner as described next.

RNS Integer Multiplication. First, we assign to each thread a pair of operands, which is actually the same strategy used to compute the Step 5 of Algorithm 1.

In this way, each warp executes the same instruction, avoiding the computationally costly divergence among threads. The multiplication is performed in a redundant way, that is, we launch n blocks, which compute the same RNS multiplication $X \otimes Y$, as shown in Figs. 2(a) and (b). The idea here is to avoid to perform a costly synchronization phase at each integer multiplication. Moreover, the data can be broadcasted for being processed in the modular reduction phase (See Step 6 of Algorithm 1). Further, the threads can access each coordinate of the operands X and Y in an efficient way. This is due to the feature that each operand is allocated on contiguous segments of memory. Once that each thread completes its processing, it stores the result on a register, avoiding the access to the global memory, which would be expensive. As a general strategy, we strive for allocating all the operands in the shared memory or registers of the GPU as much as possible. This strategy further help us to reduce the system's overall latency.

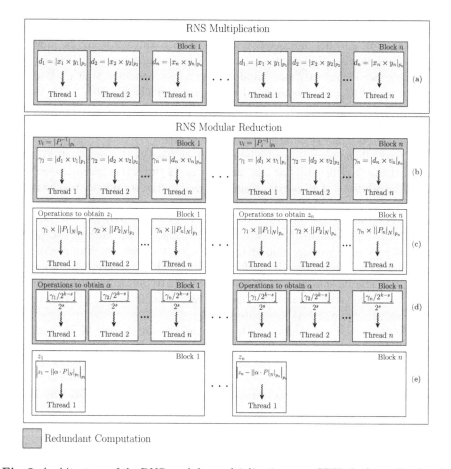

Fig. 2. Architecture of the RNS modular multiplication on a GPU platform. For details on the computation of the RNS modular reduction the reader is referred to Algorithm 1

RNS Modular Reduction. When all the threads have completed the X by Y multiplication, the next step is to perform a modular reduction by N, by performing the procedure shown in Algorithm 1. This algorithm requires the pre-computation of several values, which are preprocessed in the CPU hosting the GPU card, and then they are sent from there to the GPU. The first of such parameters is the vector $|P_i^{-1}|_{p_i}$ with n entries. The next one is the table $|P_i|_N$, which allows to perform the modular reduction by N, without leaving the RNS representation. As this table and this vector can be used at any time by the threads, it was decided to store them in the shared memory region. Finally, the table containing the values of $\alpha \cdot P_i$, is required in step 10 of Algorithm 1, in order to obtain a correct modular reduction. This table is mapped to the texture memory, due to the fact that only some few threads have access to this data and thus, we estimated that this design decision can help us to obtain a better memory access performance.

Step 8 of Algorithm 1 is the most computationally intensive task of the reduction procedure. In step 8, for each modulo p_i in the base $\mathcal{B}$, one must perform n multiplications modulo p_i and $n-1$ additions modulo p_i. Therefore, to compute all operations in parallel one needs n blocks with n threads each, as shown in Fig. 2(c). By following this strategy, in Step 8 one can perform n RNS modular multiplications concurrently as desired. Nevertheless, one must wait until all the threads of each block have completed their execution. Hence, if $n > 32$, then a explicit barrier must be placed in order to synchronize the threads of each block. This will help us to achieve a correct addition of the partial results. This barrier was implemented using standard CUDA commands.

Once that all the partial results by each block have been processed, we must add all of them. To this end, one can use a set of 32 threads (a warp), which will compute the addition of all partial results. These partial results are placed in the shared memory because its better performance. An approach that implements the addition of all the partial results efficiently, uses a collaborative strategy as proposed in [7]. This means that each thread carries out the sum of two partial results without any overlap among them. Figure 3 shows an example of how four threads can collaboratively perform this addition operation for an eight-entry vector. The basic idea is that the additions are performed using a binary addition tree. This collaborative addition is also used in Step 9 of Algorithm 1 in a redundant way, which is illustrated in Fig. 2(d).

Finally, in Step 10 of Algorithm 1, only one thread of each block performs the subtraction and saves the final result of the modular multiplication into the global memory (see Fig. 2(e)). This helps us to avoid that several threads compete to write into the same memory address. To improve the performance of one thread, we used the texture memory, due to its superior efficiency in the scenario when irregular memory access patterns occur.

3.4 RNS Modular Exponentiation

The specialized literature describes many methods for computing the modular exponentiation efficiently. The square-and-multiply method is probably the most

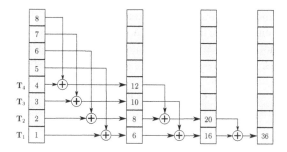

Fig. 3. Example of a binary addition tree performed by four threads on a eight-entry vector.

intuitive of all of them. However, the expected number of modular multiplications for an ℓ-bit modular exponentiation is of about $\frac{3\ell}{2}$ multiplications.[2] This number of multiplications can be further reduced by scanning multiple exponent bits instead of just one exponent bit per iteration. A method that uses this approach is the fixed-window method, which requires in average $\lfloor \frac{\ell}{w} \rfloor$ multiplications and $\ell - 1$ squarings, where w denotes the quantity of bits to be scanned at each iteration. In our work we used the m-ary method with $w = 4$, which allows us to get a better balance between memory usage and performance.[3]

In a modular exponentiation several modular multiplications of the form $X \otimes Y \bmod N$ are required. However, the procedure mentioned in the previous section only performs one single modular multiplication (redundantly). Since in the case of the exponentiation thousands of modular multiplications are needed, one must instrument a control in the block execution. Each block helps to compute an element of the resulting vector and becomes the input for the next iteration. Therefore, we must have a barrier so that each block of threads waits until all the threads have completed the processing of their data. Otherwise, the program will start receiving inconsistent values that will be out of synchrony.

In this work, the barrier mechanism as proposed in [16] was adopted. The general idea of this barrier is that each block sets a flag within an input vector, while a block of threads is in charge of verifying that all blocks have set these input flags. Once that all the processing blocks have set their own input flag, a different block sets an extra output flag in an output vector. It is only until then that the system can safely assume that all the blocks have completed their share of data processing.

The mechanism just described, allows us to perform one single modular exponentiation. However, the use of the CRT technique as described in Sect. 2.1, requires the computation of two independent modular exponentiations for the RSA private operation. In order to solve this issue, one can use *streams*, where

---

[2] Henceforth, we are assuming that the cost of one integer squaring is the same of an integer multiplication.

[3] We stress that the fixed-window method requires the precomputation of up to 2^w values.

each stream is in charge of running a different kernel. Processing data in streams allows the concurrent computation of both exponentiations.

Furthermore, notice that the loading of data from the CPU host to the GPU card using streams, can be performed in an asynchronously fashion by using the CUDA native instruction *cudaMemcpyAsync*. This allows for a concurrent code execution between the CPU host and the kernel, which yields a better performance.

4   Results and Comparison

In this section, the latency achieved by our library is reported along with a performance comparison with other related works. All of our experiments were performed in the GeForce GTX TITAN GPU card, which runs at 0.88 GHz. The software platform and programming model used was CUDA 6.5.

4.1   Related Work

Several works that address the efficient computation of the RSA operations over GPU platforms have been reported recently. All of these works make use of the Chinese Remainder Theorem trick to speedup the RSA computation.

In 2007, Moss *et al.* [11] presented one of the first RSA implementations over GPU platforms, using an NVIDIA 7800-GTX GPU card. The authors implemented a 1024-bit RNS integer multiplication by means of floating-point instructions. Their implementation shows an excessively large latency. Later in 2008, Szerwinski and Güneysu [15] reported an RSA implementation using an NVIDIA 8800 GTS GPU card. They used RNS arithmetic over 1024-bit and 2048-bit integers, and CRT for RSA decryption. The performance of their library achieved a latency of 144 ms and 849 ms, for RSA-1024 and RSA-2048, respectively. In 2011, Neves and Araujo [12] presented an RSA-1024 implementation using an NVIDIA GT200 GPU card, reporting a latency of 70 ms. Their implementation made use of the Montgomery multiplication and the CRT technique for decryption. In the same year, Jang *et al.* [8], proposed a parallel implementation using the Separated Operand Scanning Montgomery multiplication variant, targeting an NVIDIA GTX580 GPU card. Their implementation achieved a latency of 3.8 ms for RSA-1024, and 13.83 ms for RSA-2048 decryption. In 2014, Zheng *et al.* [18] reported an RSA implementation over an NVIDIA GTX TITAN GPU, which used the Montgomery multiplication method and the CRT technique. Their GPU library achieved a latency of 22.47 ms for RSA-2048. Since the authors exploited the floating point arithmetic unit of GPU platforms, their code appears to be more complex than other integer based implementations, and it seems that cannot be easily implemented in generic GPU platforms. In the same year, Fadhil and Younis [6] using an Nvidia GeForce GT630M GPU card presented an RSA implementation, which showed a latency of 2.78 ms for RSA-2014, 9.27 ms for RSA-2048 and 23.62 ms for RSA-3072.

Even more recently, Yang *et al.* [17], reported an RSA implementation based in the Montgomery multiplier that once again used the CRT technique. The authors present their results over an NVIDIA GT 750 GPU card. To our knowledge, the library presented in [17], reports the fastest RSA implementation over a GPU platform before this work, with a latency of 2.6 ms and 6.5 ms for RSA-1024 and RSA-2048, respectively.

4.2   Comparison

We measured the latency of the RSA private operation for key lengths of 1024, 2048 and 3072 bits, which corresponds to security levels of 80, 112 and 128 bits, respectively. Table 1 reports the latency achieved by our library for the RSA private operation implementation, by taking the average of the time required to perform 3,000 RSA decryptions.

Table 1. RSA private operation latency (in milliseconds) obtained by our library.

RSA bit length	Number of threads	Latency [ms]
1024	32×32	2.1
2048	36×36	5.3
3072	64×64	9.7

Table 2 shows a comparison of our library against several selected works reported in the open literature. The speedup that is shown in parenthesis compares each GPU library against our own sequential implementation of the RSA private operation using only one thread. From the timings reported in Table 2, it can be seen that our implementations have better latency for RSA-1024, RSA-2048 and RSA-3072 than the next fastest implementation by an acceleration factor of 1.23, 1.22 and 5.16, respectively.

Table 2. Performance comparison of several recent GPU libraries implementing the RSA private operation.

Work	GPU	@ GHz	Latency in ms (Speedup)		
			RSA-1024	RSA-2048	RSA-3072
Sequential	GTX TITAN	0.88	736.5	1857.6	8685.8
Neves *et al.* [12]	GT 200	1.24	70 (10.5)	-	-
Jang *et al.* [8]	GTX 580	1.54	3.8 (193.8)	13.8 (134.6)	-
Zeng *et al.* [18]	GTX TITAN	0.83	-	22.4 (82.9)	-
Fadhil *et al.* [6]	GT 750	0.8	2.8 (263.0)	17.2 (108)	50.1 (173.3)
Yang *et al.* [17]	GT 750	0.96	2.6 (283.2)	6.5 (285.7)	-
This work	**GTX TITAN**	0.88	**2.1 (350.7)**	**5.3 (350.4)**	**9.7 (895.4)**

5   Conclusion

In this paper, we present a parallel modular multiplication using an RNS representation of the operands that has been specially tailored for its implementation on GPU cards. This multiplication was used to implement the RSA private operation at the security levels recommended by NIST. Our implementation takes advantage of the GPU characteristics and the SIMT programming model. The performance of our software was further improved by assembly level programming along with the usage of techniques that avoid divergence during the computations, prevent the serial execution of the program code and allow the usage of contiguous segments of memory. The performance achieved by our library yields faster timings than previous works that implemented the RSA private operation on GPU platforms using key lengths of 1024, 2048 and 3072 bits.

Nevertheless, the authors of this work also implemented RSA-1024, RSA-2048 and RSA-3072 on a Haswell processor running at 2.6 GHz. As it turns out, our CPU implementation of the RSA private operation is considerably faster than the RSA GPU library described here. Hence, we arrive to the same conclusion mentioned by Yang et al. in [17], i.e., a GPU implementation of RSA can only be competitive compared with its CPU library counterpart, in those scenarios where many RSA signature/decryption operations must be performed in batch. The reason for this is that the massive parallelism available in a GPU card allows for the concurrent computation of many independent RSA exponentiations (a situation that would not be possible in a CPU platform).

Considering the characteristics of the latest generation of GPU cards, it is now possible to use native 64-bit integer arithmetic. Hence, a natural future work would be to code a GPU library that takes advantage of this new instruction set. In addition, it is important to design an RSA library that exhibits a first line of defense against so-called side channel attacks.

References

1. Bajard, J.C., Didier, L.S., Kornerup, P.: An RNS montgomery modular multiplication algorithm. IEEE Trans. Comput. **47**(7), 766–776 (1998). http://dx.doi.org/10.1109/12.709376
2. Bajard, J., Imbert, L.: A full RNS implementation of RSA. IEEE Trans. Comput. **53**(6), 769–774 (2004)
3. Barker, E.: Recommendation for key management, NIST special publication 800–57 part 1 revision 4. Technical report, Gaithersburg, MD, United States, January 2016. http://nvlpubs.nist.gov/nistpubsSpecialPublications/NIST.Spp.800-57pt1r4.pdf
4. Bernstein, D.J.: Multidigit modular multiplication with the explicit Chinese remainder theorem. Technical report (1995)
5. Dierks, T., Rescorla, E.: The Transport Layer Security (TLS) protocol version 1.2, RFC 5246. Network Working Group, IETF (2008). https://tools.ietf.org/html/rfc5246#section-8.1.1
6. Fadhil, H.M., Younis, M.I.: Parallelizing RSA algorithm on multicore CPU and GPU. Int. J. Comput. Appl. **87**(6), 15–22 (2014)

7. Harris, M.: Optimizing parallel reduction in CUDA. Technical report, nVidia (2008). http://developer.download.nvidia.com/assets/cuda/files/reduction.pdf
8. Jang, K., Han, S., Han, S., Moon, S., Park, K.: SSLShader: cheap SSL acceleration with commodity processors. In: Proceedings of the 8th USENIX Conference on Networked Systems Design and Implementation, NSDI 2011, pp. 1–14. USENIX Association, Berkeley (2011)
9. Jeljeli, H.: Accélérateurs logiciels et matériels pour l'algèbre linéaire creuse sur les corps finis. Ph.D. thesis, Inria Nancy - Grand Est, LORIA - ALGO - Department of Algorithms, Computation, Image and Geometry, July 2015. https://hal.inria.fr/tel-01178931
10. Jeljeli, H.: Accelerating iterative SpMV for the discrete logarithm problem using GPUs. In: Koç, Ç.K., Mesnager, S., Savaş, E. (eds.) WAIFI 2014. LNCS, vol. 9061, pp. 25–44. Springer, Cham (2015). doi:10.1007/978-3-319-16277-5_2
11. Moss, A., Page, D., Smart, N.P.: Toward acceleration of RSA using 3D graphics hardware. In: Galbraith, S.D. (ed.) Cryptography and Coding 2007. LNCS, vol. 4887, pp. 364–383. Springer, Heidelberg (2007). doi:10.1007/978-3-540-77272-9_22
12. Neves, S., Araujo, F.: On the performance of GPU public-key cryptography. In: 2011 IEEE Proceedings of the 22nd International Conference on Application-Specific Systems, Architectures and Processors, ASAP 2011, Santa Monica, CA, USA, pp. 133–140 (2011)
13. nVidia: Parallel thread execution ISA v5.0, application guide. Technical report, September 2016. http://docs.nvidia.com/cuda/pdf/ptx_isa_5.0.pdf
14. Rivest, R.L., Shamir, A., Adleman, L.: A method for obtaining digital signatures and public-key cryptosystems. Commun. ACM **21**(2), 120–126 (1978)
15. Szerwinski, R., Güneysu, T.: Exploiting the power of GPUs for asymmetric cryptography. In: Oswald, E., Rohatgi, P. (eds.) CHES 2008. LNCS, vol. 5154, pp. 79–99. Springer, Heidelberg (2008). doi:10.1007/978-3-540-85053-3_6
16. Xiao, S., Feng, W-C.: Inter-block GPU communication via fast barrier synchronization. In: 2010 IEEE Proceedings of the International Symposium on Parallel Distributed Processing, IPDPS 2010, Atlanta, GA, pp. 1–12 (2010)
17. Yang, Y., Guan, Z., Sun, H., Chen, Z.: Accelerating RSA with fine-grained parallelism using GPU. In: Lopez, J., Wu, Y. (eds.) ISPEC 2015. LNCS, vol. 9065, pp. 454–468. Springer, Cham (2015). doi:10.1007/978-3-319-17533-1_31
18. Zheng, F., Pan, W., Lin, J., Jing, J., Zhao, Y.: Exploiting the floating-point computing power of GPUs for RSA. In: Chow, S.S.M., Camenisch, J., Hui, L.C.K., Yiu, S.M. (eds.) ISC 2014. LNCS, vol. 8783, pp. 198–215. Springer, Cham (2014). doi:10.1007/978-3-319-13257-0_12

Reducing the Overhead of Message Logging in Fault-Tolerant HPC Applications

Esteban Meneses[1,2(✉)]

[1] National Advanced Computing Collaboratory, National High Technology Center,
San Jose, Costa Rica
esteban.meneses@acm.org
[2] School of Computing, Costa Rica Institute of Technology, Cartago, Costa Rica

Abstract. With the exascale era within reach, the high performance computing community is preparing to embrace the challenges associated with extreme-scale systems. Resilience raises as one of the major hurdles in making those systems usable for the advance of science and industry. Message logging is a well-known strategy to provide fault tolerance, one that is promising due to its ability to avoid global restart. However, message-logging protocols may suffer considerable overhead if implemented for the general case. This paper introduces a new message-logging protocol that leverages the benefits of a flexible parallel programming paradigm. We evaluate the protocol using a particular type of applications and demonstrate it can keep a low performance penalization when scaling up to 128,000 cores.

Keywords: Resilience · Fault tolerance · Message logging

1 Introduction

The imminent arrival of extreme-scale supercomputers sometime next decade will provide scientists and engineers with the right tool to accelerate fundamental discoveries in the grand challenges of several disciplines. From cosmological simulations of the origin of the universe to drug design for personalized medicine, our understanding of nature heavily depends on the ability to efficiently exploit the massive computational power of those machines. However, with an exascale machine already in sight, reliability stands out as one of the major obstacles in reaching a productive supercomputing system [2,10]. Considering the gigantic number of components that must be assembled into extreme-scale systems, failure rate will undoubtedly increase. Addressing the resilience challenge is crucial to the advance of science and industry.

The High Performance Computing (HPC) community has traditionally relied on rollback-recovery strategies to provide fault tolerance for large-scale simulations. One technique that has recently gained some attention is message logging, which seems promising given its lower energy consumption in a faulty environment [9]. Message logging, however, incurs some performance overhead due to

© Springer International Publishing AG 2017
C.J. Barrios Hernández et al. (Eds.): CARLA 2016, CCIS 697, pp. 204–218, 2017.
DOI: 10.1007/978-3-319-57972-6_15

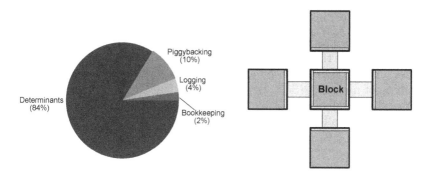

(a) Contribution of each factor to message-logging performance penalty.

(b) Communication structure in LULESH.

Fig. 1. Performance cost of determinants in LULESH. The main source of the performance penalty of message logging with LULESH comes from determinants. The communication structure of LULESH, however, suggests there is a way to avoid determinants altogether.

the additional mechanisms that ensure a correct recovery. One of those mechanisms is called *determinants*, which are in charge of storing all information about non-deterministic events.

Determinants play a major role in the performance penalization of message logging. Figure 1(a) presents the breakdown of that overhead in an experiment. Using 1,024 cores on Stampede supercomputer at Texas Advanced Computing Center (TACC), and the LULESH benchmark, we examine the four sources of performance loss for a traditional message-logging protocol. *Bookkeeping*, a mechanism to avoid duplicate messages, contribute with little over 2%. *Logging*, or storing outgoing messages in main memory, represents about 4%. *Piggybacking*, or the overhead of adding additional information, contributes with 10%. Finally, *Determinants*, or the cost of creating, storing, sending, and acknowledging determinants, is the dominant contributor of performance overhead with 84%. On the other hand, Fig. 1(b) shows why that overhead can be dramatically reduced. The program LULESH comes from a big family of codes collectively referred to as *stencils*. These programs work on a multidimensional grid by applying an operation to each element. The usual data partition algorithm splits the grid into *blocks*. In Fig. 1(b) we observe a two-dimensional grid and a block with all its neighbors. As the computation progresses the blocks exchange the border elements with each neighbor in every iteration before proceeding to apply the transformation of its own elements of the grid. High-level script languages provide a mechanism to express this type of computation explicitly, but more importantly, in a very simple way. Therefore, using that information, new message-logging protocols may take advantage of simple and deterministic communication patterns to avoid creating unnecessary determinants.

The focal points of this paper are:

- A description of a particular kind of programs and high level programming language constructs that exposes the determinism in communication (Sect. 3).
- The design of *fast message-logging*, a protocol that removes all determinants in this type of programs (Sect. 4).
- A comparative evaluation between simple causal message-logging and fast message-logging is offered (Sect. 5).

2 Background

Rollback-recovery is the most popular strategy to build resilient applications in HPC. In the usual form, called checkpoint/restart, a program starts execution and periodically stores its global state. If a failure strikes the system (failures are assumed to be permanent), the application rolls back to the previous checkpoint and resumes from that point. If messages are also stored, then the failure of one component only requires the rollback of the tasks running on that component. Messages can be replayed to the recovering element until it reaches a consistent state with the rest of the system. Therefore, in most of HPC implementations, message logging requires checkpoints to be taken at global synchronization points and messages to be stored at the sender side.

There are several variants of message logging [3], which differ in the way they handle *determinants*. Since message logging provides local rollback (i.e. only the failed tasks must roll back to the previous checkpoint), certain non-deterministic decisions must be stored to provide a consistent recovery. Determinants represent those decisions and protocols become piece-wise deterministic. Figure 2(a) shows an example of a protocol called simple causal message-logging [7]. Assume an application is composed by several tasks, from A to D. Message reception is, in general, non deterministic. Therefore, every message reception will generate a determinant. For instance, message m_1 from B to C generates determinant $\#m_1$. That determinant stores the order in which message m_1 was received at C and it will be necessary for recovery as long as other events in the system causally depend on that. Therefore, determinant $\#m_1$ will be piggybacked on outgoing messages from C until an acknowledgment a_i confirms the determinant has been safely stored somewhere else. The simple causal message logging protocol tolerates a single task failure but works in the general case. More advanced message-logging protocols bank on certain properties of HPC applications to reduce the number of determinants generated. For instance, a program may show *send determinism* [4] if the sequence of send events is always the same for every valid execution. Such program may use a protocol that avoids creating some determinants and thus reduces the overhead of the protocol.

In the parallel-objects programming model, an application is decomposed into objects, also called *chares*. Objects export a list of *entry* methods that other objects may call remotely through messages. Therefore, execution is always message driven. Each message contains the object recipient and the name of the method to be invoked, much like Active Messages [11]. The system is represented

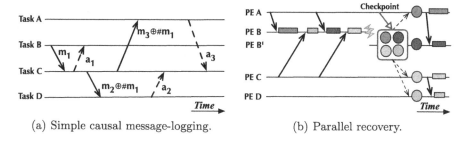

(a) Simple causal message-logging.   (b) Parallel recovery.

Fig. 2. Message logging leverages the overdecomposition property of the parallel-objects programming model.

by a set of *processing entities* (PE) interconnected through a fast network that does not guarantee FIFO ordering. The number of objects usually exceeds the number of PEs in the system and the environment is said to be *overdecomposed*. The ratio between objects and PEs is called *virtualization ratio*. Since the location of an object is irrelevant to the programmer, a smart runtime system may decide to migrate objects between PEs. Some goals of migration include load balancing, proactive fault tolerance, and reduction of power consumption. The parallel-objects model has been implemented into Charm++ [5], a C++ language extension. It is precisely overdecomposition what gives parallel objects an edge on message logging. As shown in Fig. 2(b), if PE B holds 4 objects (represented by the colored circles), the recovery of PE B (replaced by B') can be done concurrently. This is called *parallel recovery* and entails migrating objects in the recovering PE to other PEs during recovery.

In this paper we explore a scripting language that makes the control flow explicit. This is a language extension to Charm++ that provides certain structure and tame the relative flexibility in which messages can be processed at their destination in the parallel-objects model. These extra constructs in the language are referred as SDAG or *structured dagger*. Using programs written in SDAG, we aim to reduce the number of determinants generated in the program and reduce the total execution-time overhead of message-logging.

3   Removing Determinants in Parallel Programs

We assume the underlying machine is formed by a set Σ of PEs. We assume the network is reliable but does not ensure FIFO ordering in the delivery of messages between any pair of PEs. The application is decomposed into a set Γ of objects. We assume there is no shared memory in the program and the only mechanism to exchange information is via message passing. In particular, the objects of the application are *reactive* and execute a method upon the reception of a message. This asynchronous mechanism provides a message-driven execution of the program. All message sends are asynchronous, including the contributions to reductions.

In the parallel-objects model, each message has a *type*, determined by the particular method that gets triggered when it is received. Thus, it is possible to distinguish between two messages based on their type. Furthermore, messages of the same type can also be differentiated by the particular combination of sender object and receiver object. Finally, each message may carry a *tag* (called *reference number* in SDAG) that is used to decide whether to process a message at reception. The tag can be used to further separate two otherwise identical messages. The combination of type, sender, receiver, and tag is an essential component of a message-logging infrastructure.

The parallel-objects model is able to express a wide variety of parallel programs. In particular, it is very well suited for a class of programs named as *stencil codes*. These programs are iterative kernels that update elements on a grid in a very structured way. Partial differential equations (PDEs) are a good source for this type of codes. Usually, to numerically solve a PDE, a discretized version of the space is required. The space can thus be represented by a grid or mesh. Other types of stencil codes are used in image processing, computational fluid dynamics, and other kinds of scientific simulations. The nature of stencil codes consists of applying an operation to all the points in the grid until some convergence criteria is met or after certain number of iterations have been completed. In a parallel implementation of this type of codes, the whole grid is split into *blocks*. Each processing element holds a subset of the blocks. The computation proceeds by iteratively exchanging some values between neighboring blocks, applying an operation over the elements in the blocks and following to the next step. Most of the time, the values exchanged between blocks correspond to the neighboring elements of each block. The communication is very structured and does not change during the execution. The name *stencil* actually comes from the fixed pattern in which message exchange takes place. A program formulated in the parallel-objects model is shown in Fig. 3(a).

Two types of objects are shown: `Main` and `Block`. The former orchestrates the execution of the total number of iterations in the program. It initially broadcasts the message `start` to all blocks (line 5). The latter represents each block and handles exchanging messages between all the blocks. Each iteration starts by sending the ghost elements to the neighbors (line 15). Then, each block must keep track of how many ghost-element messages it has received. Once the counter has reached the total number of neighbors, the block proceeds to apply the computation to its elements. At the end of every iteration (line 23), all the set of blocks contribute to a reduction that returns the control to `Main`. The cycle starts again until the total number of iterations is completed. Note that the reduction after each iteration is inevitable in this model. Since the channels are not FIFO in delivering the messages, then it is possible for a couple of messages between neighboring blocks to go out-of-order. Therefore, a synchronization must be used to avoid such scenario. The reduction effectively separates messages from consecutive iterations.

The very nature of the parallel-objects model offers a lot of flexibility in the way the parallel program executes. It does, however, introduce concerns

```
1   class Main{
2     Collection<Block> blocks;
3     method main(){
4       iter = 0;
5       blocks.start();
6     }
7     method reduction(){
8       iter++;
9       if(iter <= TOTAL)
10        blocks.start();
11    }
12  }
13  class Block{
14    method start(){
15      sendGhostElems();
16    }
17    method ghostElems(msg){
18      copyElems(msg);
19      counter++;
20      if(counter == neighbors){
21        counter = 0;
22        compute();
23        contribute(Main::reduction);
24      }
25    }
26  }
```

(a) Two-dimensional stencil code.

```
1   class Main{
2     Collection<Block> blocks;
3     method main(){
4       blocks.start();
5     }
6   }
7   class Block{
8     method start(){
9       for(iter=1; iter<=TOTAL; iter++){
10        sendGhostElems();
11        overlap[neighbors]{
12          when ghostElems[iter](msg)
13            copyElems(msg);
14        }
15        compute();
16      }
17    }
18  }
```

(b) High-level script for 3(a).

Fig. 3. Program structure of a two-dimensional stencil code. Each block exchanges the ghost elements with its neighbors in each step. There is an asynchronous barrier after each iteration in (a). Its high-level script counterpart in (b) removes the synchronization reduction after each iteration, and handles message reordering by tagging each message with an iteration number.

regarding the order in which messages are going to be received. The counter in Fig. 3(a) reflects the palliative effort in the program to allow concurrency but avoid erroneous receptions. The same effect can be achieved through a high-level script language that expresses the control dependencies between certain types of events. Additionally, this script language must retain the advantages of the reactive characteristic of objects in the program. To illustrate the way a high-level description would work with the same example as in Fig. 3(a), we show the new version of the code in Fig. 3(b).

The high-level script in Fig. 3(b) features various grammatical constructs that alleviate the issues a programmer faces when writing code in the parallel-objects model. The main difference between the two versions of the code resides in the fact that the control mechanism is moved away from the Main object. The only responsibility of the Main object is to spawn the start of the program (line 4). The number of iterations is controlled by the Block objects (line 9). Each iteration will consist in sending the ghost elements to the neighboring blocks, followed by the reception of messages and the computation code. The first grammatical construction is the overlap region that allows the execution of its enclosing statements in any order. If the statements are all the same, it may be specified as a parameter. For instance, the overlap construct in Fig. 3(b) (line 11) has neighbors as a parameter, meaning it allows the reception of the ghostElems messages in any order. This clearly expresses the structure of the code, that requires the ghost data from all the neighbors before performing the computation. The second grammatical construct is the when statement that specifies a message type and a tag (line 12). In the example the message type corresponds to the transmission of ghost elements and the tag matches the iteration number. Using tagging removes the need of a synchronization call after every iteration, because it separates messages from different iterations with otherwise equal type, sender and receiver.

The code in Fig. 3(b) makes explicit the messages that must be received before the computation can take place. It defines the control dependencies in the program. Given that message receptions are specified in the code, this high-level description promotes a *receiver centric* view of the program. However, it still retains the flexibility of the model by allowing different reception orderings via the overlap construct. Permitting different sequences of message receptions may be a source of non-determinism. However, if the behavior of the program is the same, regardless of the reception order of messages within an overlap region, then we say the statements in the region *commute* and any ordering in the reception of those messages is always correct. Note that different sequences of message receptions may lead to a different order of message emissions. However, a different order in the sending of messages is natural in the system model. The receiver has to ensure that messages are actually processed in the right order.

Expressing more clearly the control and data dependencies in the program not only permits eliminating artificial synchronization calls, but effectively removing determinants. The reason of existence of determinants is to guarantee a consistent recovery. Therefore, determinants ensure messages are received in the same order during recovery as they were before the failure. Additionally, the combination of $\langle sender, receiver, ssn \rangle$ is used in discarding duplicate messages. In the stencil code for the two-dimensional stencil of Fig. 1(b), it is possible to avoid the generation of determinants if a high-level script is used. Figure 3(b) shows that a Block would receive the four messages from its neighbors in every iteration before computing and sending out the messages for the next iteration. If a block α would be recovering, then the high-level structure of the code would order all the messages being resent from the other objects. No determinants are required to guarantee a successful recovery. The other objects should, nevertheless, discard duplicate messages.

Using the stencil code as an example, we provide a list of conditions for the total elimination of determinants in a program expressed in a high-level language:

1. **Unique messages.** It should be possible to uniquely identify each message. Besides the combination of $\langle sender, receiver \rangle$, each messages should be tagged with a $msgID$ that will tell apart otherwise identical messages. For instance, the $msgID$ may be a composition of message type and iteration number. That particular combination would make messages unique in stencil codes.

2. **Commutative overlap regions.** The statements in `overlap` regions must commute.
3. **Explicit causal ordering.** The program must make explicit the causal order between two messages.

In addition, if determinants disappear from the message-logging layer, it must be guaranteed that all internal structures in the runtime system are still correct. This includes all the data structures for load balancing, checkpointing, collective communication operations, etc.

4   Fast Message-Logging Protocol

Using the insight from the previous section and the background work of Sect. 2, we present a new breed of message-logging protocols. We name it *fast message-logging* because it focuses on accelerating the three sources of overhead in a resilience solution: forward path, checkpointing, and recovery. This is brief justification about why it is fast message-logging:

Fast forward-path. By removing determinants from an execution, it reduces the slowdown of message-logging. According to Fig. 1(a) determinants are the main source of overhead, so eliminating them should bring the performance overhead to a minimum.

Fast checkpoint. It uses local checkpoint to avoid checkpoint-time congestion in the file system. This reduces the robustness of the system, but just by a tiny margin, given that most failure in HPC systems only involve a single node [8].

Fast recovery. It uses parallel recovery to accelerate the recovery of the failed components.

The fast message-logging protocol only generates message identifiers and does not create determinants. At send time, the tuple $\langle sender, receiver, msgID \rangle$ is used to label each message. This information will be used to eventually ignore messages if they are repeated. It relies on the high-level scripting infrastructure to buffer early messages and to deliver them in a correct order for the program. This way, there is a clear separation of concerns with respect to the functions that must be executed during recovery. Figure 4(a) show the way this protocol achieves a separation of concerns between the layers in the software stack. The bottom layer stands for the message-logging protocol that is in charge of reacting to a failure. That layer is in charge of performing two tasks. The first task is to replay the messages to the failed objects. The second task is to suppress duplicates during recovery based on the tuple $\langle sender, receiver, msgID \rangle$. The top layer is the high-level language infrastructure that guarantees the consistency in the state of the failed objects by delivering the messages in the correct order.

We call the type of programs that comply with all the conditions to remove all the determinants *receive deterministic*. Even when receives and sends may not be deterministic, the state of the objects will nevertheless be the same. Figure 4(b) shows a Venn diagram with the relationships between piece-wise deterministic, send-deterministic and receive-deterministic programs.

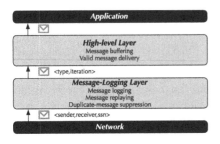

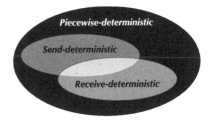

(a) Separation of concerns with the fast message-logging protocol.

(b) Relationships between piecewise, send and receive determinism.

Fig. 4. Fast message-logging protocol. The functionalities of the protocol are split with the high-level scripting infrastructure. The type of programs that can run with this protocol overlap send-determinism and require piece-wise determinism.

4.1 Algorithmic Description

The fast message-logging algorithm assigns a message identifier $msgID$ to each message. There are various sources for this identifier. If the application is send-deterministic, the protocol may assign a sender sequence number (ssn) to each message based on the combination $\langle sender, receiver \rangle$. If the application is a receive-deterministic stencil, the $msgID$ can be the concatenation of iteration and message type. Otherwise, the message type and the tag associated with that message will form the identifier for the message.

There are a handful of major data structures that keep the protocol correct. The structure idTable returns the $msgID$ for each message and combination of $\langle sender, msg, receiver \rangle$. For each of the cases explained above, that structure will return a unique identification for each message. The structure dupTable determines whether a message is a duplicate or not. Again, depending on the properties of the application, this structure can be optimized to improve performance. The structure msgLog stores all messages sent between the PEs. Finally, a couple of lists keep track of objects that have been distributed to other PEs for parallel recovery. If an object α resides in a PE A that crashes, α might be sent to other PE B for recovery. In that case, we refer to α as an *emigrant* from the perspective of A and as an *immigrant* from the perspective of B. The sets listImmigrants and listEmigrants store the list of objects in each category, respectively.

Algorithm 1 presents the main procedures of the fast message-logging protocol. Procedures SEND and RECEIVE describe the process for sending and receiving a message, correspondingly. At the sender side, messages must carry the combination $\langle sender, receiver, id \rangle$. All messages are stored in the message log. The reception of a message includes verifying that the message is not a duplicate. Once this is ensured, the message is passed to the layers above to be correctly processed. This may include buffering the message, forwarding the message to other PE or delivering the message to the application.

Algorithm 1. FASTMESSAGELOGGING

```
 1: procedure SEND(α, msg, β)                              ▷ Object α sends msg to object β
 2:     id ← idTable.getID(α, msg, β)
 3:     msg.id ← id
 4:     msg.sender ← α
 5:     msg.receiver ← β
 6:     msg.incarnation ← IncarnationNumber
 7:     if α.PE ≠ β.PE then
 8:         msgLog.add(msg)                                ▷ Storing remote message
 9:     end if
10:     NetworkSend(msg)
11: end procedure
12: procedure RECEIVE(α, msg, β)                           ▷ Object β receives msg from object α
13:     num ← msg.incarnation
14:     if OldIncarnation(num) then
15:         DiscardOld(msg)                                ▷ Ignoring old message
16:     end if
17:     flag ← dupTable.getFlag(α, β, msg.id)
18:     if flag then
19:         DiscardDuplicate(msg)                          ▷ Ignoring repeated message
20:         return
21:     end if
22:     Process(msg)                                       ▷ Forward to high-level layer
23: end procedure
24: procedure CHECKPOINT                                   ▷ Called at PE A
25:     Send all objects α in listImmigrants
26:     Wait for all objects α in listEmigrants
27:     ckptMsg ← {}
28:     msgLog.clean()
29:     for all objects α do
30:         ckptMsg.add(α.state)
31:         NetworkSend(ckptMsg)
32:     end for
33: end procedure
34: procedure RESTART(A)                                   ▷ Received at every PE except for A
35:     for all objects α in A do
36:         Send all messages bound to α in msgLog
37:     end for
38: end procedure
39: procedure RECOVERY                                     ▷ Called at PE A
40:     for all objects α in A do
41:         Distribute α to a PE in {A₁, A₂, ..., A_P}
42:         Add α to listEmigrants
43:     end for
44: end procedure
```

Fast message-logging relies on globally coordinated synchronized checkpoint. The programmer uses global synchronization points in the application to trigger the checkpoint calls. Procedure CHECKPOINT presents the steps included in the checkpoint process. First, all immigrant objects are send back to their original PEs. These objects may have been migrated to a PE for parallel recovery purposes. Next, a PE waits for all its emigrant objects to arrive. The message log is cleaned up and a new checkpoint message is built with the state of all the objects. Once a failure has been detected, the runtime system notifies the rest of the PEs about the crash of one PE. Let us assume PE A fails. The failure notification activates RESTART in other PEs, which replay the messages in msgLog bound to objects in PE A. Concurrently, PE A executes RECOVERY to distribute all its objects to as many PEs are involved in parallel recovery. The set $\{A_1, A_2, \ldots, A_P\}$ stands for the set of other P PEs helping the recovery of A.

5 Experimental Results

In order to understand the performance penalization imposed by the fast message-logging protocol, we examined three stencil codes: Wave2D, Jacobi3D and LULESH. These programs were implemented in SDAG to decrease execution time (since barriers between iterations are not needed anymore) and allow the possibility of removing determinants.

We first examine the effect of virtualization ratio on each program. Recall from Sect. 2 that virtualization ratio stands for the average number of objects per PE. For this experiment, each PE is a core. Figure 5 presents the results on 1,024 cores of Intrepid supercomputer at Argonne National Laboratory (ANL). Each data point reflects the average of 5 repetitions of the same experiment. Wave2D in Fig. 5(a) seems to manifest that Wave2D benefits from virtualization. In fact, the performance of the program stays within a 5% difference up to 32 objects per core. A similar behavior occurs in Jacobi3D in Fig. 5(b), except in this case the program is always slightly slowed down by virtualization. Again, the average iteration time stays within a 10% margin up to 32 objects per core. Finally, Fig. 5(c) accepts a higher virtualization ratio without a significant performance degradation. Even 128 objects per core stays within a 3% margin. Having a high virtualization ratio is beneficial for applications in view of the eminent thermal variation of future systems. With more objects per core, it is possible to obtain a better load balance in case some of the PEs have to be slowed down to reduce their temperature.

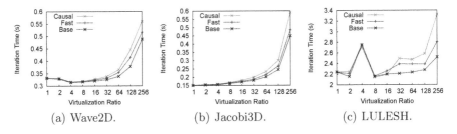

(a) Wave2D.   (b) Jacobi3D.   (c) LULESH.

Fig. 5. Effect of virtualization ratio on performance. Stencil codes admit a high virtualization ratio without sacrificing a significant portion of its performance.

Using a virtualization ratio of 32 for Wave2D and Jacobi3D and 128 for LULESH, we ran 5 times each program and compared the results between fast message-logging and simple causal message-logging. The results are presented in Fig. 6 and offer the relative performance overhead when compared with the base Charm++. The figure shows a weak-scale experiment on Intrepid from 1K to 16K cores. For Wave2D, Fig. 6(a) shows that fast message-logging is able to halve the performance across all the spectrum. Figure 6(b) tells about a more beneficial scenario for the fast protocol with Jacobi3D. The most dramatic difference appear with LULESH. Figure 6(c) shows the big difference determinants can make in message-logging. As the program scales the difference between the fast

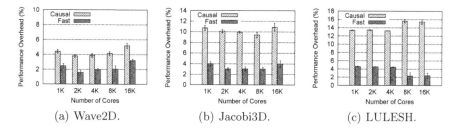

Fig. 6. Performance overhead of fast message-logging. It approximately reduces performance overhead to a half when compared with causal message-logging.

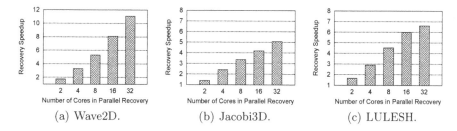

Fig. 7. Parallel recovery in fast message-logging. The more cores are used to recover, the faster the recovery.

and causal variants increases to the point where the overhead of fast message-logging is around 15% of the overhead of causal.

An important feature of the fast message-logging protocol is it ability to work in conjunction with parallel recovery. Section 2 introduced parallel recovery. The more PEs help in recovery, the faster it is expected the failed PE will catch up with the rest of the system. There are, however, a couple of considerations to keep in mind. First, the number of PEs helping in recovery cannot exceed the virtualization ratio. Second, it is possible to have diminishing returns with the addition of more PEs. This latter effect results stems from the fact that more PEs involve sending more remote messages and potentially hitting network bottlenecks. Figure 7 shows for the 3 applications the speedup in recovery when the number of PEs helping ranges from 2 to 32. Wave2D offers the best scenario for parallel recovery. This is due to its relatively simple communication characteristics. Therefore, spreading the objects to more PEs results in a greater speedup. Both Jacobi3D and LULESH present moderate speedup levels during recovery.

Figure 8 offers an overall demonstration of the advantages of using fast message-logging. This scenario corresponds to a large-scale run where the number of cores varies from 8K to 128K on Intrepid. Additionally, it represents a strong-scale test, that stresses even more the message-logging protocol. Figure 8(a) shows the overhead in the forward path can always be kept low. Whereas causal message-logging has an overhead that goes up to approximately 20%, fast message-logging has an overhead lower than 4%. Checkpoint time is measured in milliseconds.

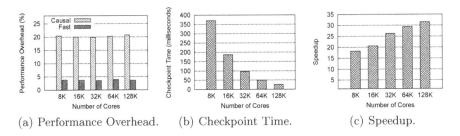

(a) Performance Overhead.   (b) Checkpoint Time.   (c) Speedup.

Fig. 8. Large strong-scale experiment with LULESH. Fast message-logging keeps a low performance overhead, fast checkpoint and fast recovery, compared to checkpoint/restart.

Table 1. Average statistics on messages and determinants per iteration.

Program	Remote messages	Generated determinants	Piggybacked determinants	Determinants per message
Wave2D	72.90	144.40	317.59	4.36
Jacobi3D	141.10	214.80	870.78	6.17
LULESH	3181.85	4295.55	32411.52	10.19

Figure 8(b) offers the checkpoint time as the program is scaled. Based on the runtime-level checkpoint and in-memory checkpoint, the dump of the state of an application is fast. Finally, the speedup over checkpoint/restart is reported in Fig. 8(c). For this case, the program runs for two checkpoint periods (for an arbitrary checkpoint interval), with a failure injected in the second one. The speedup reported in the figure corresponds to the total execution time of fast message-logging versus checkpoint/restart.

Table 1 presents statistics about the number of messages and determinants in different programs collected on Intrepid with 1,024 cores and with the same configuration as in Fig. 6. The causal message-logging protocol was used to collect the data. The table shows the number of instances per iteration, averaged across all cores. LULESH has the highest numbers, because it has a more complex communication graph (neighbors in 3 dimensions) and a higher virtualization ratio (128 compared to 32). The higher number of messages is proportional to the number of determinants generated. In Table 1 there are more determinants than messages, explained by the fact that local messages generate determinants too. The number of piggybacked determinants also grows as the number of messages. The ratio of determinants piggybacked over determinants generated provide an idea on the number of copies each determinant has in the system. Although causal message-logging only requires one copy of each determinant to be safely stored, usually several more copies are logged in the system. Finally, the last row in Table 1 reports the average number of determinants piggybacked per message. This quantity directly dictates the performance overhead of causal message-logging. Not surprisingly, more determinants piggybacked per message implies a higher performance overhead (supported by the results in Fig. 6).

6   Related Work

The seminal work on send determinism [4] provided a clear insight on the futility of creating determinants for all message receptions. Protocols based on that property rely on FIFO channels. We removed that assumption to use the asynchronous execution model of Charm++. However, to tame the excessive flexibility in the order of message reception, we relied on high level programming language constructs. The send-determinism protocol requires to replay the causally-dependent messages in a synchronized fashion, which hampers the ability of message-logging to achieve a faster recovery. By using a reception control mechanism, fast message-logging is able to receive all messages at once and completely sort them in a valid program order. The large scale simulator *BigSim* [12] used parallel discrete event simulation (PDES) to make predictions on the performance of scientific codes for supercomputers. Since BigSim is based on POSE (a framework for PDES), it would allow speculative simulation of different threads of events. In that regard, programs that allow only one possible execution sequence would find a very efficient simulation. In BigSim, *linear order parallel programs* are a special kind of codes for which messages are processed in exactly one order. A scalable replay system was designed based on an algebraic framework to store partial-order dependencies in message-passing programs [6]. That framework improves on most replay algorithms, which make minimal assumptions about the programming model. If some deterministic decisions can be extracted from the programming model, the framework incorporate them into the number of determinants that must be stored. The management of determinant of the fast message-logging protocol presented in this paper is a particular case in that algebraic framework. A new design of the message-logging layer for Open MPI [1] revealed a vast amount of determinants that are not necessary to guarantee a safe recovery. By interposing a message-logging substrate between the application and the network layer, this new design is able to create matchings of events posted by the application and arrival events coming from the network. Matchings may be deterministic if the expected sender and the actual sender of the message are the same. Use of wildcards will create non-deterministic matches. By logging only non-deterministic matches, this design is able to dramatically reduce the number of determinants.

7   Conclusion and Future Work

This paper examines the major source of performance overhead in traditional message-logging protocols. By leveraging the infrastructure of a flexible parallel programming paradigm, a new strategy was proposed. The *fast* message-logging protocol addresses the 3 main sources of overhead by removing unnecessary determinants, checkpointing in memory, and recovering in parallel. The experimental results with typical stencil codes demonstrate the impact of this protocol. The tests scaled up to 128,000 cores. In the future, we plan to devise new protocols for particular types of applications where communication patterns are somehow regular and general-case expensive assumptions can be removed. We also plan to use message-tagging to implement the protocol in MPI.

Acknowledgments. This work was partially supported by a machine allocation on the XSEDE under award ASC050039N, and by a machine allocation on Argonne Leadership Computing Facility awarded by the U.S. Department of Energy under contract DE-AC02-06CH11357.

References

1. Bouteiller, A., Bosilca, G., Dongarra, J.: Redesigning the message logging model for high performance. Concurr. Comput.: Pract. Exp. **22**(16), 2196–2211 (2010)
2. Cappello, F., Geist, A., Gropp, W., Kale, S., Kramer, B., Snir, M.: Toward exascale resilience: 2014 update. Supercomput. Front. Innov. **1**(1), 5–28 (2014)
3. Elnozahy, E.N., Alvisi, L., Wang, Y.-M., Johnson, D.B.: A survey of rollback-recovery protocols in message-passing systems. ACM Comput. Surv. **34**(3), 375–408 (2002)
4. Guermouche, A., Ropars, E., Brunet, E., Snir, M., Cappello, F.: Uncoordinated checkpointing without domino effect for send-deterministic MPI applications. In: IPDPS, pp. 989–1000 (2011)
5. Kalé, L., Krishnan, S.: CHARM++: a portable concurrent object oriented system based on C++. In: Paepcke, A. (ed.) Proceedings of OOPSLA 1993, pp. 91–108. ACM Press, New York (1993)
6. Lifflander, J., Meneses, E., Menon, H., Miller, P., Krishnamoorthy, S., Kale, L.: Scalable replay with partial-order dependencies for message-logging fault tolerance. In: Proceedings of IEEE Cluster 2014, Madrid, Spain, September 2014
7. Meneses, E., Bronevetsky, G., Kale, L.V.: Evaluation of simple causal message logging for large-scale fault tolerant HPC systems. In: 16th IEEE DPDNS in 25th IEEE IPDPS, May 2011
8. Meneses, E., Ni, X., Kale, L.V.: A message-logging protocol for multicore systems. In: Proceedings of the 2nd Workshop on Fault-Tolerance for HPC at Extreme Scale (FTXS), Boston, USA, June 2012
9. Meneses, E., Sarood, O., Kale, L.V.: Energy profile of rollback-recovery strategies in high performance computing. Parallel Comput. **40**(9), 536–547 (2014)
10. Snir, M., Wisniewski, R.W., Abraham, J.A., Adve, S.V., Bagchi, S., Balaji, P., Belak, J., Bose, P., Cappello, F., Carlson, B., Chien, A.A., Coteus, P., DeBardeleben, N., Diniz, P.C., Engelmann, C., Erez, M., Fazzari, S., Geist, A., Gupta, R., Johnson, F., Krishnamoorthy, S., Leyffer, S., Liberty, D., Mitra, S., Munson, T., Schreiber, R., Stearley, J., Hensbergen, E.V.: Addressing failures in exascale computing. IJHPCA **28**(2), 129–173 (2014)
11. von Eicken, T., Culler, D., Goldstein, S., Schauser, K.: Active messages: a mechanism for integrated communication and computation. In: Proceedings of the 19th International Symposium on Computer Architecture, Gold Coast, Australia, May 1992
12. Zheng, G., Kakulapati, G., Kalé, L.V.: BigSim: a parallel simulator for performance prediction of extremely large parallel machines. In: 18th International Parallel and Distributed Processing Symposium (IPDPS), Santa Fe, New Mexico, p. 78, April 2004

Dense and Sparse Matrix-Vector Multiplication on Maxwell GPUs with PyCUDA

Francisco Nurudín Álvarez, José Antonio Ortega-Toro, and Manuel Ujaldón[✉]

Computer Architecture Department, ESTI Informática, University of Málaga,
Bulevar Louis Pasteur, s/n. Campus Teatinos, 29071 Malaga, Spain
ujaldon@uma.es

Abstract. We present a study on Matrix-Vector Product operations in the Maxwell GPU generation through the PyCUDA python library. Through this lens, a broad analysis is performed over different memory management schemes. We identify the approaches that result in higher performance in current GPU generations when using dense matrices. The found guidelines are then applied to the implementation of the sparse matrix-vector product, covering structured (DIA) and unstructured (CSR) sparse matrix formats. Our experimental study on different datasets reveals that there is room for little improvement in the current state of the memory hierarchy, and that the expected Pascal GPU generation will get a major benefit from our techniques.

1 Introduction

Latest developments in scientific computing have taken advantage of new, more efficient hardware and higher level, easier to work with environments. On the hardware end, one of the most notable improvements has come from the adoption of GPUs (Graphics Processing Units) as general purpose processors using SIMD (Single Instruction Multiple Data) parallelism on virtually every area of science. Fields as diverse as medicine or astrophysics and everything in between have witnessed enormous speed-ups in execution time by using those manycore processors [6].

In terms of environments and platforms, the Python programming language has established itself as one of the most commonly used for scientific computing. Its high level of abstraction and rich library ecosystem eases designing complex systems. Furthermore, the language can easily be interfaced with more performant implementations when needed. As such, libraries like NumPy [1] or SciPy [3] include optimized native implementations with Python module interfaces.

One of the most common APIs for GPU programming is CUDA [4], designed by NVIDIA for their hardware. Research conducted with CUDA has been steadily growing since it was first announced, and it is nowadays a robust ecosystem. In Python, we can take advantage of the CUDA API by using the PyCUDA library [2]. With it, we can harness the power of the GPU from the clear and powerful high level abstraction of the language.

© Springer International Publishing AG 2017
C.J. Barrios Hernández et al. (Eds.): CARLA 2016, CCIS 697, pp. 219–229, 2017.
DOI: 10.1007/978-3-319-57972-6_16

As scientific computing empowers researchers to produce valuable work, basic operations have to be adjusted to emerging platforms. One such operation is the Matrix-Vector product (MV product hereon), with which the M *times* 1 vector resulting from the dot product between a M × N matrix and a N × 1 vector is computed. The MV product is one of the most basic operations in science, used for example when solving systems of linear equations. Our study will be tailored to analyze this operation in current GPU hardware, testing whether older implementation schemes still result in peak performance.

The MV product, and in general any operation related to matrices, can be studied depending on how dense a matrix is. In case it is primarily populated by zeros, a different data structure may be used to increase space and time efficiency. When using a structure of the sort we will be using a sparse matrix. There exist multiple different sparse matrix formats, some of which exploit diverse structures and patterns, like only storing diagonals, others are unstructured [10]. Our study on the MV product will cover dense matrices as well as structured and unstructured sparse matrices.

This paper is organized as follows. Section 2 describes related work. Section 3 outlines the MV product from a CUDA perspective. Section 4 presents a set of candidate implementations for the MV product together with a discussion focused on memory management and some performance numbers, allowing us to derive guidelines on CUDA program design in newer architectures. From these guidelines we will pivot towards studying the sparse MV product operation in Sect. 5, showing a set of implementations and linking them to what we have previously learnt. Using data from real world scientific datasets, Sect. 6 provides a performance analysis of those implementations, discussing the suitability of each approach for the sparsity cases. Finally, we will sum up the knowledge gained with some brief conclusions.

2   Related Work

Linear algebra operations are always a must when proving the suitability of a hardware platform for scientific computing, with the matrix multiplication and the MV product as two flagship algorithms. Those early days of the GPUs were not an exception [5], and soon later, Nvidia developed its own cuSPARSE library, where those operations were also efficiently implemented using sparse matrices. The arrival of Maxwell GPU generation has propelled CUDA hardware to a unified memory model that has shortened the gap between CPU and GPU programming [8], and the next generation of Pascal GPUs will bring 3D Memory to make this model closer to what actually can be found on chip [9]. We expect these hardware enhancements to play a decisive role for future scalability of implementations like the ones performed along our work. In the meantime, Table 1 outlines the GPU and graphics card used along our experiments.

In 2016, a new competitor of GPUs has also entered the HPC arena. Accelerators based on Intel Xeon Phis have gained momentum with the advent of Knights Landing (KNL) [9], after Knights Corner (KNC), which was somehow

Table 1. Characterization of the GPU hardware used along our experimental analysis.

GPU model	GeForce GTX 980 (Maxwell GPU)
Number of cores	2048
Core speed	1126 MHz
Peak performance (GFLOPS)	4612
Memory size	4 GB
Memory speed	7000 MHz
Memory interface	GDDR5
Memory width	256 bits
Memory bandwidth	224 GB/s
PCI express (to CPU)	3.0 ×16

disappointing in performance. A recent approach to benefit from those platforms within our context has been published by Maeda and Takahashi [7], where they compare KNC versus GPUs in terms of performance even on clusters composed of multi-sockets and 64 MPI processes. It remains to be seen what the results would be in KNL, as we also have great expectations for our implementations when the new GPUs of the Pascal generation be released next year by Nvidia.

3   Matrix-Vector Product in CUDA

As we discussed in the introduction, both matrix multiplication and the MV product are elementary problems when working on parallel architectures. Developing a working implementation of either of them is a common way of getting accustomed to manycore parallelism. However, and because of the nature of both problems, achieving peak performance requires the programmer to aptly manage memory.

Codes in multicore environments can be classified as either compute bound or memory bound. In the case of a compute bound code, performance depends on the way the actual computation is approached. On the other hand, performance of a memory bound code depends how data accesses needed for the computation are managed. Empirical studies have shown that, across scientific computing as a whole, the majority of codes are memory bound.

The MV product is an eminently memory-bound kernel (that is, a GPU program). To perform the computation, for either dense or sparse matrices, a kernel will only perform a handful of operations per datum. Given this nature, the work of a CUDA programmer will rest on manually managing data to fully exploit locality, by appropriately using shared memory. Furthermore, the programmer will also need to adjust the global memory accesses in a way that takes full advantage of memory coalescing.

Due to its definition as a problem, the MV product is a good testing ground to challenge hypotheses. Particularly, it can be seen as a reasonable scenario to study and tackle different memory management approaches. Indeed, this will be the focus given throughout the rest of this work: to study some long held notions about memory optimizations in CUDA.

4   Memory Management Schemes

In this section we present a set of approaches towards implementing the dense MV product. Those approaches will be centered on the effect of different memory management schemes to work with such a memory bound problem. We first introduce a distinction on the approaches, depending on whether they focus on the underlying data structures or memory spaces used to store data, the management of locality through caching or the communication with global memory.

With that classification in mind, we introduce the following set of approaches:

- **Data structure or memory space related**
  - Using texture memory (K1)
  - Using constant memory to store the vector (K2)
  - Using __restrict__ annotated memory (K3)
- **Locality related**
  - Performing intro-block sum reductions (K4)
- **Global memory communication related**
  - Using vector data types (K5)

Those approaches were studied both disjointly and combined where possible. The experimental results, in terms of performance, were compared to a native CPU implementation in NumPy and a naive CUDA kernel with shared memory caching for the data on the vector. Said caching was applied from the first moment, as it was understood that the vector could be used by several threads within the block. Without caching, kernel performance was worse than the native CPU implementation of NumPy Fig. 1. The obtained performance speed-ups, relative to the basic cache kernel, are shown in Tables 2 and 3.

Approaches shown in K1, K2, K3 and K5 can, in general, be applied to almost any problem. In Fig. 2 we show a comparison showing the effect of the different data structure or memory space related approaches.

Table 2. Kernel execution times (in ms) for different matrix sizes with respect to the basic vector-cached kernel.

Matrix size	K1	K2	K3	K4	K5
512×4096	0.278	0.257	0.270	0.224	0.159
32768×512	0.946	0.895	0.875	0.958	0.467
9600×4096	3.094	2.510	2.711	2.191	1.558
8192×8192	6.634	5.613	5.785	3.818	3.252

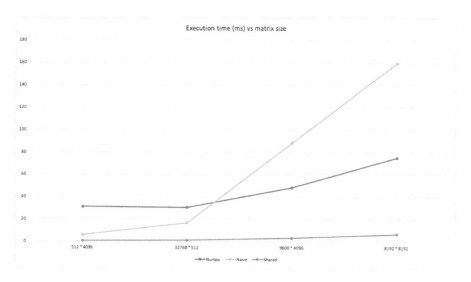

Fig. 1. Comparison between NumPy (middle), a naive kernel with no shared memory usage (upper) and the basic, vector-cached kernel using shared memory (lower).

Table 3. Kernel speed-up for different matrix sizes with respect to the basic vector-cached kernel.

Matrix size	K1	K2	K3	K4	K5
512 × 4096	0.953	1.031	0.981	1.183	1.667
32768 × 512	1.080	1.142	1.168	1.067	2.188
9600 × 4096	0.996	1.228	1.137	1.407	1.979
8192 × 8192	0.993	1.174	1.139	1.725	2.026

Table 4. Kernel execution times (in ms) for different matrix sizes with respect to the basic vector-cached kernel on combined approaches.

Matrix size	K1, 5	K3, 5	K4, 5	K1, 4, 5	K3, 4, 5
512 × 4096	0.169	0.177	0.127	0.128	0.128
32768 × 512	0.460	0.478	0.566	0.566	0.565
9600 × 4096	1.589	1.803	1.261	1.270	1.264
8192 × 8192	2.915	3.239	2.204	2.203	2.203

From the previous results, we implemented several kernels combining compatible different approaches. The results for the combined approaches are shown in Tables 4 and 5.

It must be noted that in both Tables 4 and 5 we discriminated against approach K2 (using constant memory). This was in order to focus the analysis on global memory accesses which could be factored into any problem. Constant

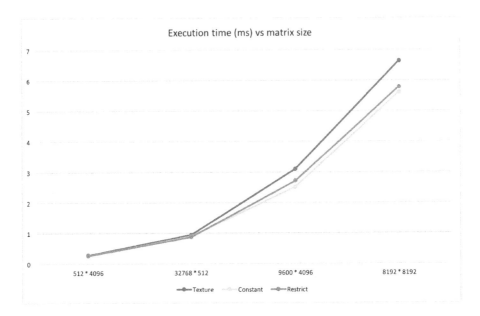

Fig. 2. Comparison in terms of execution times between the memory-space related approaches.

Table 5. Kernel speed-up for different matrix sizes with respect to the basic vector-cached kernel on combined approaches.

Matrix size	K1, 5	K3, 5	K4, 5	K1, 4, 5	K3, 4, 5
512 × 4096	1.568	1.497	2.087	2.070	2.070
32768 × 512	2.222	2.138	1.806	1.806	1.809
9600 × 4096	1.940	1.710	2.445	2.428	2.439
8192 × 8192	2.260	2.034	2.989	2.990	2.990

memory usage restricted to data which would fit in the space reserved for it, which on Maxwell GPUs amounts to up to 64 KB.

From these results we can see that optimizations related to specific memory spaces, such as K1 and K3, do not affect performance greatly. In particular, texture memory usage (K1 + K5) increases execution times with respect to plain vector types (K5), while *read-only* memory (K3) has a marginal effect. The comparison between the combinations of K1, K3 and K5 can be seen in Fig. 3.

Vector data types (K5), in particular when combined with problem specific optimizations (such as intro-block reductions, K4), produce the best results. Figure 4 shows the small difference made by applying approaches K1 and K3 to the combination of K4 and K5.

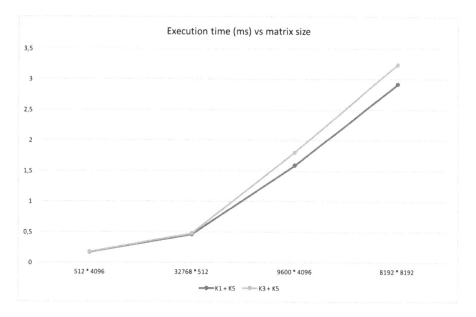

Fig. 3. Comparison in terms of execution times between the memory-space related approaches combined with vector types.

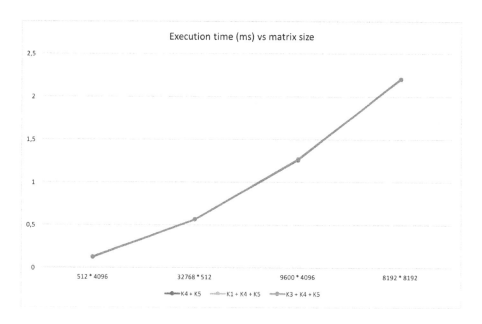

Fig. 4. Comparison in terms of execution times with the combined approaches using a problem-specific optimization, intrablock reductions (K4).

From these results we can see that on Maxwell GPUs peak performance can be achieved by combining vector operations with problem specific caching approaches. Texture memory usage degrades performance slightly, while constant memory and `__restrict__`-labelled memory produce subtle performance gains.

5   Sparse Matrix-Vector Product

For an implementation of the sparse MV product (SpMV hereon), the first challenge to address is to find a format for the sparse data which attain the best performance on the GPU. We have chosen two formats for our experiments: DIA (diagonal) as representative of structured matrices, where only diagonals are considered and stored. CSR (Compressed Sparse Row), as general format for unstructured matrices, where data are stored consecutively as traversed horizontally on a `Data` vector, followed by a `Column` vector which stores the column index for each data, and a `Row` vector which counts the elements per row in an accumulative manner. That way, `Data` and `Column` are the size of the nonzeros and `Row` is the size of the number of rows in the matrix plus one.

For the particular case of these two formats, performance concerns are mostly related to the way data are uploaded when accessing compressed data.

On DIA sparce matrices, our implementation expects the matrix diagonals to be stored in column-major order. This benefits data coalescing when accessing single values of the matrix. CSR matrices, where elements are coupled with their indexed positions, are directly transferred to the GPU.

In terms of the kernels themselves, we give a high level overview of how they compute the results. In the case of the SpMV product with DIA matrices, each thread computes the dot product of a row with the vector. Shared memory caching is used to manage the offsets of the diagonals. On the CSR kernel, each separate concurrent processing unit (called a warp) works on a single matrix row. Shared memory caching is used to both manage the indices of the nonzero elements and the warp-level reduction.

It must be noted that the implementation of the CSR kernel relies on fixed warp size, with 32 threads being grouped on Maxwell GPUs. Furthermore, the kernel works on the assumption that each warp execution remains independent from each other, though for implementation purposes synchronization barries have been used. The effect of those in terms of performance has been measured and does not go beyond factors from 2% to 10% in the execution time depending on the data input.

Kernel variations using either texture memory or read-only memory labelled as so with `__restrict__` were also developed. Approaches using vector datatypes to better alleviate global memory accesses can be considered too.

6   Experimental Results

Our implementation was tested against matrices from several scientific domains. The chosen matrices display several different data layouts, from which we expected clear differences in terms of suitability to our SpMV implementations. A quick overview of the matrices is shown in Table 6:

Table 6. Overview of the matrices used along our experimental study.

Name	Number of nonzeros	Average elements/row	Dimensions	Origin
WATT1	11360	6.1	1856 × 1856	Petrol Engineering
MBEACXC	49920	100	496 × 496	Economics
LNSP3937	25407	6.5	3937 × 3737	Fluid Models
BCSSTK13	42943	42	2003 × 2003	Structural Engineering
PSMIGR3	543162	170	3140 × 3140	Inter-Country Migration
SHERMAN 3	20033	4	5005 × 5005	Oil Simulation
MCFE	24382	32	765 × 765	Astrophysics
BCSPWR10	13571	4.1	5300 × 5300	Power Networks

A test batch using the dataset was prepared. The kernel execution times for each matrix and kernel used, along with the relative performance when using either texture or read only memory against the basic implementation, are shown in Tables 7 and 8.

Overall, results using texture memory are disappointing as speeds-ups are negative on average. We believe texture memory is not as good as it used to be in previous GPU generations, as Nvidia aims to the new 3D memory in Pascal GPUs and tries to foster unified memory in the API versus, say, the old school.

On the other hand, benefits using read-only memory are lower than 10% in most of the cases (but always on the positive territory), and we see encouraging

Table 7. Kernel execution times (in ms) for different SpMV implementations depending on the sparse format used for representing the sparse matrix. The T suffix stands for the implementation using texture memory and the R suffix stands for the one using read-only memory.

Matrix used	DIA	DIA-T	DIA-R	CSR	CSR-T	CSR-R
WATT1	0.053	0.062	0.053	0.058	0.064	0.054
MBEACXC	0.350	0.343	0.345	0.056	0.064	0.054
LNSP3937	0.074	0.081	0.073	0.057	0.068	0.056
BCSSTK13	0.827	0.822	0.826	0.057	0.067	0.054
PSMIGR3	2.016	1.996	2.008	0.104	0.089	0.078
SHERMAN3	0.056	0.063	0.055	0.059	0.070	0.058
MCFE	0.113	0.117	0.112	0.052	0.061	0.051
BCSPWR10	2.594	2.564	2.589	0.059	0.069	0.059

Table 8. Kernel speedups for the SpMV kernels when using either texture memory or read-only memory.

Matrix used	DIA-T	DIA-R	CSR-T	CSR-R
WATT1	0.855	1.000	0.906	1.074
MBEACXC	1.020	1.014	0.875	1.037
LNSP3937	0.914	1.014	0.838	1.018
BCSSTK13	1.006	1.001	0.851	1.056
PSMIGR3	1.010	1.004	1.169	1.333
SHERMAN3	0.889	1.018	0.843	1.017
MCFE	0.966	1.009	0.852	1.020
BCSPWR10	1.012	1.002	0.855	1.000

results (33% gains on CSR format) when the sparse matrix is populated with nonzeros, that is, for the most dense representative of our data set.

In general, there is a trade-off in our study: We focus on sparse matrices containing a small number of nonzeros, but GPUs are happy with high data volumes. That way, either our sparse matrix is huge or has to be densely populated for the critical size of our data set to be attained.

7 Conclusions

This paper has analyzed performance of two related memory bound problems, Matrix Vector product and Sparse Matrix Vector product, on a GPU belonging to the fourth generation of Nvidia, the Maxwell architecture. In both cases, approaches relying on either texture, read only or constant memory have resulted in slim performance benefits and, at times, slightly longer execution times.

SpMV kernels have produced mixed results. In particular, DIA kernels proved themselves unfit for most matrices. For them to be performant, the structure must be as tight as possible. This was not the case on most matrices, even when their overall structure was diagonal-based, because certain unstructured elements caused the number of diagonals to greatly grow. Performance on the CSR kernels was stable throughout the dataset, with execution times that outpaced the MV kernels on sparse matrices. In that regard, results were as expected, and more encouraging as the matrix is more densely populated with spare

As future work, we plan to run our experiments on Pascal GPUs using unified memory and Stacked DRAM to quantify the benefits of the new memory, which will bring a remarkable lift in latency and bandwidth, along with energy savings, which will be worth to be measured as well.

Acknowledgements. This work was supported by the Junta de Andalucía of Spain under Project of Excellence P12-TIC-1741. We also thank Nvidia for hardware donations under GPU Education Center 2011–2016, GPU Research Center 2012–2016 and CUDA Fellow 2012–2016 Awards.

References

1. The NumPy library website. http://www.numpy.org
2. The pyCUDA library website. https://developer.nvidia.com/pycuda
3. The SciPy library website. http://www.scipy.org
4. Cuda books. http://developer.nvidia.com/cuda-books, April 2012
5. Bell, N., Garland, M.: Efficient sparse matrix-vector multiplication on cuda. Technical report, Nvidia Technical report NVR-2008-004, Nvidia Corporation (2008)
6. GPGPU: General-Purpose Computation Using Graphics Hardware (2009). http://www.gpgpu.org
7. Maeda, H., Takahashi, D.: Parallel sparse matrix-vector multiplication using accelerators. In: Gervasi, O., et al. (eds.) ICCSA 2016. LNCS, vol. 9787, pp. 3–18. Springer, Cham (2016). doi:10.1007/978-3-319-42108-7_1
8. NVIDIA Corporation: NVIDIA GeForce GTX 980 Whitepaper. Technical report (2015)
9. Ujaldón, M.: HPC accelerators with 3D memory. In: 19th IEEE International Conference on Computational Science and Engineering (CSE 2016), August 2016
10. Zlatev, Z.: Computational Methods for General Sparse Matrices, vol. 65. Kluwer Academic Publishers, Holland (1991)

HPC Applications and Simulations

Enhancing Energy Production with Exascale HPC Methods

Rafael Mayo-García[1]([⊠]), José J. Camata[2], José M. Cela[3],
Danilo Costa[2], Alvaro L.G.A. Coutinho[2],
Daniel Fernández-Galisteo[1], Carmen Jiménez[1],
Vadim Kourdioumov[1], Marta Mattoso[2], Thomas Miras[2],
José A. Moríñigo[1], Jorge Navarro[1], Philippe O.A. Navaux[4],
Daniel de Oliveira[5], Manuel Rodríguez-Pascual[1], Vítor Silva[2],
Renan Souza[2], and Patrick Valduriez[6]

[1] Centro de Investigaciones Energéticas Medioambientales y Tecnológicas,
Madrid, Spain
rafael.mayo@ciemat.es
[2] COPPE/Federal University of Rio de Janeiro, Rio de Janeiro, Brazil
[3] Barcelona Supercomputing Center-Centro Nacional de Supercomputación,
Barcelona, Spain
[4] Universidade Federal do Rio Grande do Sul (UFRGS), Porto Alegre, Brazil
[5] Fluminense Federal University, Niterói, Brazil
[6] Zenith Team, Inria and LIRMM, Montpellier, France

Abstract. High Performance Computing (HPC) resources have become the key actor for achieving more ambitious challenges in many disciplines. In this step beyond, an explosion on the available parallelism and the use of special purpose processors are crucial. With such a goal, the HPC4E project applies new exascale HPC techniques to energy industry simulations, customizing them if necessary, and going beyond the state-of-the-art in the required HPC exascale simulations for different energy sources. In this paper, a general overview of these methods is presented as well as some specific preliminary results.

1 Introduction

New energy sources, if untapped, might become crucial in the mid-term. Intensive numerical simulations and prototyping are needed to assess their real value and improve their throughput. The impact of exascale HPC and data intensive algorithms in the energy industry is well established in the U.S. Department of Energy document "Synergistic Challenges in Data-Intensive Science and Exascale Computing" [1], for example.

The High Performance Computing for Energy (HPC4E) project, whose kick-off was in February, 2016, aims to provide these new exascale HPC and data intensive algorithms to three energy sources: wind energy, biomass, and oil. To do so, several European and Brazilian institutions are closely working, fostering in this way a collaboration that can be extended to other countries in Latin America as the computational

C.J. Barrios Hernández et al. (Eds.): CARLA 2016, CCIS 697, pp. 233–246, 2017.
DOI: 10.1007/978-3-319-57972-6_17

solutions provided will be useful to many scientific and industrial fields as well as to other software and middleware developers.

Moreover, the current collaboration embraces both public and private companies who are leaders in their respective sector. The industrial sector is formed by REPSOL, Iberdrola Renovables Energía, TOTAL, and PETROBAS. Regarding the public sector, Brazilian (COPPE/UFRJ, LNCC, ITA, UFRGS, UFPE) and European (BSC-CNS, INRIA, UNLAC, CIEMAT) institutions belonging to the HPC and the energy fields are represented.

As previously stated, the main objective of HPC4E is to develop beyond-the-state-of-the-art high performance simulation tools that can help the energy industry to respond future energy demands and also to carbon-related environmental issues using the state-of-the-art HPC systems. This Brazilian-European collaboration also aims at improving the usage of energy using HPC tools by acting at many levels of the energy chain for different energy sources:

– Exploitation: In wind energy (respond to demand peaks, output prediction)
– Efficiency: In biomass-derived fuels (develop more efficient and renewable fuels, reduce green-house gas emissions, reduce hydrocarbon dependency and fuel cost)
– Exploration: In wind energy (resource assessment) and in hydrocarbons (improve available reserves, explore with less financial and environmental risk).

Another main objective is to improve the cooperation between energy industries, guaranteeing that the Technology Readiness Levels (TRL) of the particular project technologies will be very high.

2   A New Architecture for the Exascale Challenge

The project will set up a disruptive exascale computer architecture to study the mapping and optimization of the codes proposed for each energy domain on novel architectures for exascale, as well as developments in the underlying software infrastructure. In order to properly test this infrastructure, the porting, tuning, and testing efforts of the different simulations codes will be previously carried out. Specifically, four lines of action will be pursued.

The selected computing kernels of the codes coming from the energy sector will be optimized for architectures based on accelerators. The goal will be to optimize the performance but keeping a high degree of portability. The ratio flops/watt obtained in each platform will be analyzed. The main target architecture platforms are those based on Xeon Phi and NVIDIA GPUs, but other platforms based on embedded processors will be also analyzed. To guarantee the maximum portability of the codes we will use programing models and tools like openCL, ompSs and BOAST.

The selected kernels will be also ported to architectures based on symmetric multicore processors with NUMA memory. The goal will be to optimize the performance. The main target architectures will be Intel, AMD and SGI, but also new platforms based on ARM processors will be analyzed. Thus, the key point will be the load balancing and data placement, taking into account new scheduling algorithms able to improve locality too.

The management of the MPI level parallelism in the codes coming from the energy sector will be guaranteed for achieving a high scalability of the applications in HPC clusters with millions of cores: The main topics to be analyzed will be: creation of tools for migration of running parallel tasks inside clusters; hierarchical MPI structures to manage coupled multiphysic problems; parallel I/O optimization; design of efficient check-pointing strategies; and, fault tolerance strategies at MPI level.

Last, performance analysis will be focused on the performance analysis of the different applications and kernels. The proper environments and tools (Paraver, Triva, Ocelotl, TAU, etc.) will be deployed to analyze all the parallel levels in the applications. Inside a computational node roof-line analyses will be done to understand the bottlenecks of the architectures. At the cluster level, network traffic, I/O traffic and load balancing will be analyzed to guarantee the application scalability. Also performance prediction tools will be used to analyze the potential benefits of architecture or algorithm modifications. Different proposal of exascale architectures will be studied for the selected applications as well.

2.1   Some Results: Integrating Checkpointing Techniques into Slurm

Slurm is a workload manager designed for Linux clusters of all sizes. Among the plethora of available LRMSs, SLURM is currently one of the most advanced ones, and the most commonly used by the Top500 supercomputers. Thus, any improvement on its behavior will deeply impact the HPC community.

DMTCP (Distributed Multi Threaded Checkpointing) transparently checkpoints a single-host or distributed computation in user-space. It supports the commonly used OFED API for InfiniBand, as well as its integration with various implementations of MPI. It is specially suitable to be used in environments with legacy applications, as it does not oblige to modify their code to include checkpoint directives (as application-level checkpoint libraries) or to re-compile them (as most other system-level libraries). Instead, it acts as an additional software layer between the application and the Operating System, being able to save its status and restore it in the same -or on a different- computational resource.

Both Slurm and DMTCP are Open Source solutions. This allows examining their insights and perform enhancement required for this work.

SLURM is designed to be easily extended with third party plugins. In particular, it already counts with plugins to support checkpoint libraries and perform some basic operations like checkpoint and restart. The performed work consists on the development of a driver serving as a bridge between SLURM and DMTCP APIs. This way, Slurm scheduling algorithms and user-level commands will be able to transparently perform these operations.

As the number of cores composing HPC resources grows, applications are being required to run with an increasing degree of parallelism. However, the Mean Time To Failures (MTTF) of the hardware components (from coolers to memories or random issues) does not grow as fast as the number of resources, so the probability of one or more tasks being affected by a failure increases. In addition, the higher number of tasks composing a job, the higher computational and economic loss.

Thus, in order to achieve the objectives of this project, it is mandatory to increase the robustness and fault tolerance of the developed software. With the proposed software stack, based on Slurm+DMTCP plus their coupling, any job can be checkpointed and restarted transparently to the user and the job itself.

3 Algorithms and Solvers for Exascale Computations

Innovative computational algorithms well suited to the numerical simulation of complex phenomena on exascale architectures will be introduced. These refer to numerical schemes for Partial Differential Equations (PDE), sparse linear solvers, adaptivity, and data management.

Particularly the first topic is concerned with scalable implementations of high order schemes for wave propagation models. The second topic will develop and demonstrate the benefits of generic (i.e. algebraic) parallel solvers for large sparse linear systems of equations. The third topic addresses mesh and (local) time-step adaptive algorithms in order to optimize the use of computational resources. The fourth topic focuses on leveraging techniques to support simulation data management as required by the pre- and post-processing steps involved in highly complex simulations.

Regarding scalable high order numerical schemes, two families of innovative high order finite element methods and a family of (standard and mimetic) finite difference schemes will be considered for both time-domain and frequency domain. These numerical schemes exhibit a high level of parallelism. In particular, they are well suited to a mixed coarse grain/fine grain (MIMD/SIMD) parallelization targeting many-core (Xeon Phi/GPU) systems. First, we will implement and demonstrate the benefits of a recently designed class of high order multiscale methods. The common core approximation framework is the Multiscale Hybrid-Mixed (MHM) methods combined with Discontinuous Galerkin (DG) or Stabilized Continuous Galerkin (SCG). For frequency-domain problems, we will perform the same analysis with the so called hybridized DG formulations that drastically reduce the number of globally coupled degrees of freedom. Both types of solvers (i.e. time-domain and frequency-domain) are linked to the simulation/inversion framework for subsurface imaging proposed in the geophysics domain.

With respect to scalable sparse linear solvers, the goal is to provide state of the art parallel solvers for spare linear systems of equations or numerical schemes adopted in the simulation software associated to the applications coming from the energy field. Both direct and hybrid direct/iterative solvers will be considered. Regarding the former solver type, the PaStiX software [2] will be adopted. It is based on a supernodal approach and has been implemented on top of various runtime systems enabling an efficient use of heterogeneous manycore platforms. The hybrid iterative/direct strategy will be made available through the MaPHyS software [3] that implements algebraic domain decomposition ideas and relies in parallel on parallel sparse direct solvers such as PaStiX for each subproblem. On top of those two solvers, Krylov subspace methods are implemented either for the iterative refinement steps of PaStiX or to solve the reduced Schur complement system in MaPHyS. Finally, the high performance dense linear algebra kernels on which those solvers are relying will also be part of the project but no specific action is foreseen on it. This software stack will be made available through a coherent and flexible API where the matrices can be provided by the application in various formats such as centralized or distributed, assembled or unassembled.

Optimal numerical schemes for PDEs involve adapting the grids in space and time to minimize errors in the simulation. The activity on this topic will then be to explore libraries to support adaptivity such as the libMesh library [4]. libMesh provides a framework for the numerical simulation of partial differential equations using arbitrary unstructured discretization on serial and parallel platforms. Adaptive time stepping controlling strategies will be also studied. The objective here is to demonstrate the applicability of such strategies to large-scale parallel computations of the simulation of polydisperse mixtures typically found in the geological processes.

Big Data management and analysis of numerical simulations will be explored by the use of three systems: SimDB, UpsilonDB and Chiron. The first is being designed to manage spatial-temporal time series predictive data from numerical simulations, represented as a multidimensional array. The second system, UpsilonDB, is currently an early stage prototype aiming at managing the uncertainty on numerical simulation data, integrated with the probabilistic database system MayBMS. UpsilonDB supports simulation post-processing analysis. Chiron is a scientific workflow management system focused on managing scientific dataflow with provenance data support. Chiron strong support in data analytics at runtime allows for dynamic configuration fine-tuning, including uncertainty quantification data steering.

4   Atmosphere for Energy

The fundamental knowledge barriers to further progress in wind energy are defined as scientists' understanding of atmospheric flows, unsteady aerodynamics and stall, turbine dynamics and stability, and turbine wake flows and related array effects. The use of computational fluid dynamics (CFD) large-eddy simulation (LES) models to analyze atmospheric flow in a wind farm capturing turbine wakes and array effects requires exascale HPC systems.

In this way, microscale atmospheric models are based on CFD solvers adapted to simulate the Atmospheric Boundary Layer (ABL) in order to approach two fundamental wind energy problems: analysis (mainly focused on wind resource assessment and wind farm design) and forecast (mainly focused on short-term prediction for wind farm dispatch to the electricity network). The study of both problems will lead to key aspects concerning microscale modelling simulations, as standalone CFD models or in connection with mesoscale models, by developing dynamical and statistical downscaling strategies. All models, methods and techniques developed for analysis will be tuned to produce short-term online forecasts of the wind farms output.

The objective is then to have the CFD models ready to exascale systems in order to overcome the present limitations and increase the accuracy on the evaluation of technical and economic feasibility of wind farms.

Regarding dynamical downscaling in order to assess wind resource, CFD models must account for the coupled effects of complex terrain, Coriolis forces, thermal stability, presence of forests, and wind turbines. Modifications need to be made to the RANS/LES CFD models including turbulent closures for ABL. The objective is to characterize the accuracy of the different ABL-CFD models, the numerical stability (robustness) and the convergence behavior of their HPC implementation.

The statistical downscaling approach will be complementary to the dynamical downscaling. Statistical downscaling models will be developed using local observations and large scale circulation and wind fields in the wind farm region.

A compilation of the available data and an evaluation of the quality issues that might affect the succeeding analyses will be accomplished. For this purpose is necessary to identify an appropriate metrics that account for the deviations in the wind power production predictions. Transfer functions between wind and wind power should be determined and serve as reference to translate the wind into wind power estimates for the rest of analyses.

On the other side, in order to efficiently plug wind farm power production to a distribution electricity network it is mandatory a forecast of the power production that allows the network operator to manage the electricity resources. In this sense, wind power short-term prediction within hourly to daily time scales is of fundamental importance. The models, methods and techniques developed for wind farm modelling will be tuned to produce short-term online forecasts of the wind farms output. Efficient use of HPC resources is critical to have these forecasts online. We will develop a forecast based on dynamical and statistical downscaling strategies.

4.1   Improving CFD Microscale Models

In order to achieve such an improvement, the following actions will be made:

- For RANS/LES models, study the turbulence closure models for ABL simulations as an alternative to the existing parametrizations.
- Implementation of a canopy model [5].
- Validate the HPC implementation using experimental data from the New European Wind Atlas project (ERA-Net).
- Wind farm modelling: Currently, farm models simulate downwind effects of rotors by extracting axial momentum at the turbines. In this simplistic approach, the rotor characteristics are incorporated trough velocity-independent drag coefficients obtained from tunnel experiments. This tasks aims to characterize numerically the downwind effects of rotors by solving complex turbulent rotating flows.

4.2   Dynamical Downscaling Strategies

Boundary conditions for solving wind flow on microscale domains typically assume steady and homogeneous over the computational inflow. These limitations can be overcome by dynamically coupling microscale CFD models with mesoscale simulations, furnishing initial and time-dependent boundary conditions at the computational boundaries. The following will be made:

- Blending between mesoscale (WRF) and CFD computational meshes in order to have consistent terrain information (topography and roughness) at the computational margins. The topography will be interpolated in such a way that it will be coincident with the CFD resolution in the inner zone and coincident with the mesoscale (WRF) over the boundaries.
- Initial condition and time-dependent CFD boundary conditions consistent with the mesoscale outputs that will drive the CFD model through boundary conditions.
- Study the use of nudging strategies based on introducing a force term over the momentum equation in the CFD model close to the boundary in order to enhance consistency between models near the boundaries.
- Validate the methodologies for different site conditions, onshore and offshore, considering benchmark validation cases from other projects such as IEA-Task 31 [6] Wakebench and FP7-NEWA [7].

4.3   Some Results: WRF Model Coupled to Large-Eddy Simulations

Model (WRF) is a tool for multiscale atmospheric simulations that can be coupled to other methods, such as CFDs. In this case, turbulence-resolving Large-Eddy Simulations (LES) have been executed with WRF in real cases with a mesoscale resolution (grid cell size ~ 10 km). Specifically, 6 different domains have been simulated with a 3D unit-cell composed of $121 \times 121 \times 95$ inner points through nested simulations in which the mesoscale domains drive the LES domains.

In order to determine how the system computationally evolves, a fixed total wall-time of 2 h has been set. Thus, the WRF-LES calculi with the WRF MPI-based 3.6.1 version have been executed on an increasing number of processors in order to determine how much time of an atmospheric phenomenon can be simulated in such a period of 2 h. As can be seen in Table 1, moving from 8 to 24 processors a linear behavior is obtained as the total of simulated phenomenon is multiplied by a factor of 3, but the simulation looses this behavior as the number of processors increases even more, getting a time of simulation multiplied by ~ 6.4 when the number of processors has been increased by a factor of 12.

Table 1. WRF-LES computational behavior.

Number of processors	8.	24	48	96
Time of the simulation obtained	00:07:41	00:25:50	00:35:29	00:45:40

This experiment has been performed in a cluster composed of Blade nodes Dual Xeon quad-core 3.0 GHz (2 GB per core) solutions proposed as part of HPC4E are needed in order to better achieve a performance capable of exploiting the coming Exascale supercomputers.

5 Biomass for Energy

Another important challenge is to develop a validated, predictive, multi-scale, combustion modeling capability to optimize the design and operation of evolving fuels. The next exascale HPC systems will be able to run combustion simulations in parameter regimes relevant to industrial applications using alternative fuels, which is required to design efficient furnaces, engines, clean burning vehicles and power plants.

Thus, in order to obtain a thorough understanding of the effects of fuel variability on energy utilization of biomass-derived gaseous fuels, a coupled approach which covers three distinct areas of development will be employed: generation of chemical kinetic mechanisms for biomass-derived fuels, integration of the schemes into a CFD code, and creation of efficient algorithms for data exchange that can run efficiently in HPC platforms.

The activities include analyzing the physical characteristics of bio-syngas flames, assessment of performance in practical systems and providing an optimized industrial guideline for biomass derived gaseous fuel compositions and performance. The application scenario corresponds to industrial devices of the energy sector: stationary gas turbines, furnaces and portable combustion devices.

Generation of detailed chemical schemes that reproduce accurately the oxidation of biomass-derived gaseous fuels will be developed and assessed via detailed chemical kinetic mechanisms that can predict the oxidation process and species formation with certain level of accuracy. Several well-established mechanisms (GRI 3.0, San Diego, Leeds, etc.) will be examined and compared for different fuel compositions and the accuracy at predicting reference species and radicals will be provided for different operating conditions. These mechanisms are the starting point for reduction or tabulation techniques.

Also, development of skeleton and reduced chemical schemes for biomass combustion for engine operating conditions will be carried out. The use of detailed chemical mechanisms imposes an important limitation for practical applications of turbulent combustion. These mechanisms include slow and fast chemical reactions involving a large number of species leading to a highly costly numerical problem. Besides, the effects of turbulence and flow strain also contribute to a complex interaction between chemistry and fluid mechanics that has to be accurately reproduced by CFD codes. In order to reduce the stiffness of the chemical problem, skeleton and reduced mechanisms will be developed, such that it can be integrated into a multiphysics code. The reduction technique will be based on flame-generated manifolds (FGM) and quasy-steady state (QSS) approximation for operating conditions of interest.

For studying the combustion dynamics of laboratory flames and comparing it with available data an integration of the chemical schemes developed in the previous points and the corresponding validation using benchmarking cases will be performed. Several cases using experimental data of laboratory flames will be investigated and the effects of fuel variability on the flame dynamics will be investigated.

Regarding industrial applications of biomass fuels in practical systems, numerical simulation of an industrial engine burning biomass will be carried out. Different operating conditions and fuel compositions will be examined. The activities will be focused on providing details of the system performance to develop industrial guidelines for the use of biomass derived gaseous fuels.

Last, applications of biomass-derived gaseous fuel combustion in portable reformers for hydrogen production will be explored as well. Limitations to the miniaturization of hydrogen production reformers are linked to the large surface to volume ratio, which enhances heat losses through the walls. Additional measures, such as heat recirculation, catalytic combustion, reactant preheating etc., are needed to sustain their proper operation. The activities will consist in numerical studies of the stability of combustion in small size reformers, with the objective of improving the understanding of their operation and determining the stable and more efficient regimes as a function of the fuel composition. The reduced chemical mechanisms developed in the aforementioned paragraphs, as well as the use of HPC shall be essential to this large parametric numerical investigation.

5.1 Some Results: Dynamics of Combustion Regimes in Small Confined Chambers

A thorough parametric study of the combustion regimes associated to the intrinsic instabilities of flames in confined chambers is addressed in the context of the small size reformers. Direct Numerical Simulation (DNS) of a reactive fuel mixture with Arrhenius kinetics is carried out in a classical configuration known as Hele-Shaw cell (i.e., two parallel plates separated by a narrow gap). The stability of the solution depends on:

- The ratio of the thermal to molecular diffusivity of the fuel, through the Lewis number.
- The thermal expansion, through the heat release parameter.
- The buoyant convection term.
- The heat losses through the walls.

Biomass-derived gaseous fuel combustion in portable reformers suffers for the same instabilities, depending on the characteristic parameters of the mixture. A complete parametric study requires the use of the HPC techniques proposed above.

6 Geophysics for Energy

The third energy sector is related to oil as an energy source. Huge computational requirements arise from full wave-form modelling and inversion of seismic and electromagnetic data. By taking into account the complete physics of waves in the subsurface, imaging tools are able to reveal information about the Earth's interior with unprecedented quality. Nevertheless, actual wave physics has a high cost in terms of computational intensity, which can only be matched by using the exascale HPC systems.

In this sense, the capacity for imaging accurately the Earth's subsurface, on land and below the sea floor is a challenging problem that has significant economic implications in terms of resource management, identification of new energy reservoirs and storage sites, as well as their monitoring through time. As recoverable deposits of petroleum become harder to find, the costs of drilling and extraction increase accordingly. Thus, the oil and gas industry needs more detailed imaging of underground geological structures in order to find the best representation of the subsurface in terms of which model sticks better to the data recorded during acquisition surveys. This involves research based on advanced methods combining mathematics, geophysics and scientific computing. Such multidisciplinary collaboration is essential to the design of numerical simulation codes capable of delivering the clearest possible picture of the subsurface.

The data types involved in geophysical imaging are mostly seismic (acoustic or elastic) and electromagnetic. Modern imaging techniques (RTM, FWI, ...) rely on intensive usage of full 3D physical modeling engines. Hence, in order to attain results in a reasonable time, these engines must use, as efficiently as possible, the fastest hardware architectures in a massively parallel way. On top of that, the larger and more complex the scenarios become, techniques which attain results with low computational complexity or few degrees of freedom become preferable.

The main goal is, then, to attain the sharpest possible images of the subsurface with the best possible quantitative content (i.e. parameter estimation, uncertainty analysis) in the shortest possible time. In addition, in the exascale era, power efficiency is becoming ever more a crucial factor in establishing the usability of HPC in industrial applications. The main developments will involve geophysical inversion of elastic and electromagnetic waves using high-order structured and unstructured computational grid types. Test-driven code development will allow us to put a special focus on having detailed comparisons and benchmarks between all possible approaches in the most realistic scenarios. Architecture-oriented programming optimizations are expected to play a crucial role in establishing cost/accuracy/complexity relationships which will help to delineate the future directions of geophysical imaging in the exascale era.

Specific sub-objectives will be: development and optimization of high-order finite-element schemes for 3D elastodynamics; development and optimization of classical extrapolation schemes in 3D; uncertainty estimation of petrophysical quantities; synthetic benchmarking of exascale geophysical problems; and, industry validation.

6.1 Some Results: Uncertainty Quantification in Seismic Imaging Using Chiron SWfMS

A computational simulation usually involves the execution of complex programs chained in a coherent flow. This flow of simulation programs may be modeled as a scientific workflow [8]. A scientific workflow is an abstraction that allows scientists to specify a set of activities and a data flow between them [8]. Each activity is associated to a simulation program, which is responsible for the consumption of a set of input data and the production of another set of output data. Many of the experiments modeled as scientific workflows have to process a large volume of data, thus requiring the effective usage of HPC environments allied to parallelization techniques, such as data parallelism or parameter sweep [9]. In order to support the modeling and execution of scientific workflows in HPC environments, parallel Scientific Workflow Management Systems (SWfMS) [8] were developed, such as Chiron [10]. To foster the workflow parallelism, the activities of workflows can be subdivided in smaller tasks, known as activations [10].

Although these SWfMS execute on large amounts of HPC resources, as the workflow becomes increasingly complex, they tend to execute for weeks or even several months depending on the amount of input data and the availability of computational resources. This way, it is fundamental for scientists of any domain to be aware of the execution status in order to analyze if the current execution complies with some pre-defined quality and performance criteria. Based on this information steering [11], scientists may decide if they have to interfere in the execution (also known as dynamic workflows) or pause the workflow execution to change parameter values or even change the original workflow specification. These facilities allow scientists to perform debugging, partial results analysis or to identify failures as early as they happen as online analysis of scientific workflows. This paper presents a real workflow modeled for Uncertainty Quantification (UQ) in seismic imaging using Chiron.

Reverse Time Migration (RTM) is a standard algorithm for producing accurate images of subsurfaces that help to improve the decision process in the Oil and Gas Industry. However, the use of this algorithm becomes challenging with high dimensional uncertain input due to computational costs. In this context, we present in this study a workflow using Chiron adapted for Uncertainty Quantification (UQ) in seismic imaging. Taking advantage of an optimized RTM code previously developed [12], we consider a framework which allows the uncertainty quantification on the output of a large scale computation managed by Chiron. This approach is non-intrusive, since we use the deterministic simulation of our optimized RTM code, and couple dimension reduction with sparse grid stochastic collocation.

6.1.1 Chiron SWfMS for Managing Provenance in UQ Domain

Chiron [13] is a parallel SWfMS that aims at supporting users to model, execute, and monitor scientific workflows in cluster environments. With this purpose, Chiron uses workflow algebra SciWfA [11] to rule all workflow activities and represents consumed and produced data as relations. This workflow algebra uses a set of operators (Map, Filter, Reduce, SplitMap, SRQuery, and MRQuery) to be associated with workflow activities. Workflow activities (i.e., invocation of scientific programs) are considered operands, while consumed and produced data are also operands.

Therefore, each activity is associated to an operator, which is composed of input (data consumption) and output (data production) relations. Following this workflow algebra, Chiron is able to manage the dataflow generation at the physical (i.e., file flow) and logical (i.e., data element flow) levels from parallel execution of scientific workflows, as presented in [14]. Chiron captures and stores provenance and performance data at runtime on a database. Then, users can run queries in provenance database to analyze domain-specific data and performance execution data at runtime. Chiron presents a provenance data model that follows W3C PROV recommendations, known as

PROV-Df [14]. Chiron's parallel engine distributes activations to the available computing resources using a client-server architecture. Figure 1 presents the architecture for Chiron's engine.

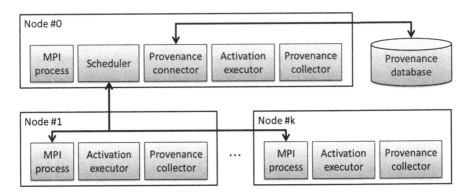

Fig. 1. Architecture for the Chiron's engine.

To enable the communication between available computing resources, Chiron employs Message Protocol Interface (MPI) for Java [15] to exchange messages between those computing resources. To access performance, we coupled the Tuning and Analysis Utilities (TAU) to Chiron. With this, we can collect and visualize the usual performance execution data (MPI operations, scientific programs) plus transactions in the provenance database.

6.1.2   Preliminary Results

Considering the application for UQ in seismic imaging, we modeled and executed a scientific workflow for this domain using Chiron SWfMS (Fig. 2). As an experimental evaluation, this workflow was executed in the Endeavour cluster, an Intel Linux Cluster based on 51,000+ cores with Intel Xeon E5-2697v2 (Ivy Bridge) processors and an Intel Xeon Phi Coprocessor 7110 (MIC Architecture).

Then, as preliminary results, we obtained the workflow elapsed times presented in Table 2, when we vary the number of cores and the stochastic collocation interpolation level (consequently, the number of solver invocations or tasks) to evaluate the scalability of this workflow using Chiron. With those results, we observed that the sequential workflow elapsed time does not increase in the same proportion as we vary the number of stochastic collocation (SC) points. Further, TAU helped to identify potential performance bottlenecks associated to the parallel workflow execution. Thus, we observed that Chiron presents a non-negligible overhead due to the MPI communication and the query processing using a centralized DBMS. For this reason, we are improving Chiron to support provenance data management using a decentralized DBMS or modifying the query execution plan of some provenance transactions.

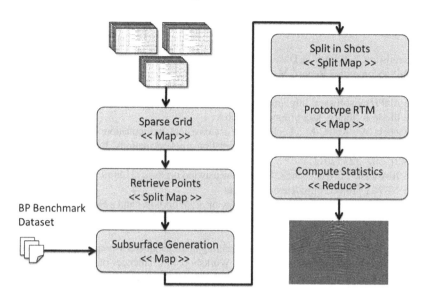

Fig. 2. Scientific workflow for UQ in seismic imaging using Chiron.

Table 2. Experimental results for executing the UQ in seismic imaging workflow.

Number of nodes	Number of cores	Interpolation level	SC points	Workflow elapsed time (minutes)
1	16	1	17	47.18
2	32	2	145	305.15
4	64	3	849	1,758.70

7 Conclusions

The HPC4E project is developing new technologies that will allow the proper exploitation of exascale infrastructures. In this sense, scalability issues and resilience are some of the most important ones.

The solutions proposed are being applied to the energy sector; specifically, to the wind energy, combustion and biogas fields. All of them are transversal ones and can be extrapolated and used by other scientific and technological areas.

Acknowledgments. The research leading to these results has received funding from the European Union's Horizon 2020 Programme (2014-2020) under the HPC4E Project (www. hpc4e.eu), grant agreement no 689772, the Spanish Ministry of Economy and Competitiveness under the CODEC2 project (TIN2015-63562-R), and from the Brazilian Ministry of Science, Technology and Innovation through Rede Nacional de Pesquisa (RNP). Computer time on Endeavour cluster is provided by the Intel Corporation, which enabled us to obtain the presented experimental results in uncertainty quantification in seismic imaging.

References

1. Synergistic Challenges in Data-Intensive Science and Exascale Computing, DOE ASCAC Data Subcommittee Report, March 2013
2. The PaStiX software. http://pastix.gforge.inria.fr
3. The MaPHyS software. http://maphys.gforge.inria.fr
4. The libMesh library. http://libmesh.github.io/
5. Sogachev, A., Kelly, M., Leclerc, M.Y.: Consistent two-equation closure modelling for atmospheric research: buoyancy and vegetation implementations. Bound.-Layer Meteorol. **145**(2), 307–327 (2012)
6. The IEA-Task 31 Wakebench. http://www.ieawind.org/task_31.html
7. The NEWA project. http://euwindatlas.eu/
8. Deelman, E., Gannon, D., Shields, M., Taylor, I.: Workflows and e-Science: an overview of workflow system features and capabilities. Future Gener. Comput. Syst. **25**(5), 528–540 (2009)
9. Walker, E. Guiang, C.: Challenges in executing large parameter sweep studies across widely distributed computing environments. In: Workshop on Challenges of Large Applications in Distributed Environments, Monterey, California, USA, pp. 11–18 (2007)
10. Ogasawara, E., Dias, J., Oliveira, D., Porto, F., Valduriez, P., Mattoso, M.: An algebraic approach for data-centric scientific workflows. Proc. VLDB Endow. **4**, 1328–1339 (2011)
11. Mattoso, M., Dias, J., Ocaña, K.A.C.S., Ogasawara, E., Costa, F., Horta, F., Silva, V., de Oliveira, D.: Dynamic steering of HPC scientific workflows: a survey. Future Gener. Comput. Syst. **46**, 100–113 (2015)
12. Costa, D.L., Coutinho, A.L., Silva, B.S., Silva, J.J., Borges, L.: A trade-off analysis between high-order seismic RTM and computational performance tuning. In: 1st Pan-American Congress on Computational Mechanics, Buenos Aires, Argentina, pp. 955–962 (2015)
13. Ogasawara, E., Dias, J., Silva, V., Chirigati, F., Oliveira, D., Porto, F., Valduriez, P., Mattoso, M.: Chiron: a parallel engine for algebraic scientific workflows. Concurr. Comput. **25**(16), 2327–2341 (2013)
14. Silva, V., de Oliveira, D., Valduriez, P., Mattoso, M.: Analyzing related raw data files through dataflows. Concurr. and Comput.: Pract. Exp. **28**(8), 2528–2545 (2016)
15. Carpenter, B., Getov, V., Judd, G., Skjellum, A., Fox, G.: MPJ: MPI-like message passing for Java. Concurr.: Pract. Exp. **12**(11), 1019–1038 (2000)

Three-Dimensional CSEM Modelling on Unstructured Tetrahedral Meshes Using Edge Finite Elements

Octavio Castillo-Reyes[✉], Josep de la Puente, and José María Cela

Computer Applications in Science and Engineering, Barcelona Supercomputing Center, Torre Girona, C/ Jordi Girona, 29, 08034 Barcelona, Spain
{octavio.castillo,josep.delapuente,josem.cela}@bsc.es
http://www.bsc.es

Abstract. The last decade has been a period of rapid growth for electromagnetic methods (EM) in geophysics, mostly because of their industrial adoption. In particular, the marine controlled-source electromagnetic method (CSEM) has become an important technique for reducing ambiguities in data interpretation in hydrocarbon exploration. In order to be able to predict the EM signature of a given geological structure, modelling tools provide us with synthetic results which we can then compare to real data. On the other hand and among the modelling methods for EM based upon 3D unstructured meshes, the Nédélec Edge Finite Element Method (EFEM) offers a good trade-off between accuracy and number of degrees of freedom, i.e. size of the problem. Furthermore, its divergence-free basis is very well suited for solving Maxwell's equation. On top of that, we present the numerical formulation and results of 3D CSEM modelling using the Parallel Edge-based Tool for Geophysical Electromagnetic Modelling (PETGEM) on unstructured tetrahedral meshes. We validated our experiments against quasi-analytical results in canonical models.

Keywords: CSEM · Geophysics · Edge Finite Element · High performance computing

1 Introduction

The electromagnetic methods (EM) are an established tool in geophysics, finding application in many areas such as hydrocarbon and mineral exploration, reservoir monitoring, CO2 storage characterization, geothermal reservoir imaging, water prospecting, and many others. In particular, the marine Controlled-Source Electromagnetic Method (CSEM) has become an important technique for reducing ambiguities in data interpretation in hydrocarbon exploration. In the traditional configuration, the sub-seafloor structure is explored by emitting low frequency signals from a high-powered electric dipole source towed close to the seafloor. By studying the received signal, subsurface structures can be detected at scales from a few tens of meters to depths of several kilometers [2].

C.J. Barrios Hernández et al. (Eds.): CARLA 2016, CCIS 697, pp. 247–256, 2017.
DOI: 10.1007/978-3-319-57972-6_18

In order to be able to predict the electromagnetic signature of a given geological body, modelling tools provide us with synthetic results which we can compare to real data. These tools require a discretisation method in order to obtain an accurate solution to the physical governing equations. As principal discretisation techniques arise the Finite Difference Method (FDM) and Finite Element Method (FEM). In geophysics electromagnetic modelling, the FDM is still the most widely employed discretisation scheme and one of the most practical and highly efficient parallel codes was developed in [1]. However, the main disadvantage of FDM is its incapacity to work with unstructured grids, which limit its use in scenarios where irregular and complex geology has a significant influence on measurements, e.g., a model with strong seabed bathymetry where an imprecise representation could lead to false interpretations.

On the other hand, the FEM supports completely unstructured tetrahedral meshes as well as local refinement, which enabling the representation of complex structures and thus improving the solution accuracy. Nevertheless, standard FEM does not correctly take into account all the physical properties of vector fields. In fact, there are three main problems when nodal-based FEM is employed to represent vector fields, namely, occurrence of spurious solutions, inconvenience of imposing boundary conditions at materials interfaces and the difficulty in treating conducting and dielectric edges and corner [11].

Finally, Edge Finite Element Method (EFEM) is free of all the previously mentioned shortcomings because of its use of so-called vector basis functions that assign degrees of freedom (DOFs) to the edges. As a consequence, EFEM meets inherent requirements in geophysical electromagnetic modelling, namely, offers unstructured meshing support, has the ability to eliminate spurious solutions and is claimed to yield accurate results because it's divergence-free basis is well suited for solving Maxwell's equations.

On top of that, we have developed a 3D CSEM tool based upon EFEM for parallel computational architectures: Parallel Edge-based Tool for Geophysical Electromagnetic Modelling (PETGEM). To overcome problems related to the spatial singularity at the source, we have employed a secondary field formulation of Maxwell's equations in their diffusive form, namely, the electric field is decomposed into primary and secondary fields. In order to represent complex geological bodies, we use unstructured tetrahedral meshes as these are the easiest to use for very large domains and because offer a good trade-off between accuracy and number of degrees of freedom, i.e. size of the problem.

PETGEM is a Python code for the scalable solution of EM on tetrahedral meshes. It supports parallelism on shared-memory platforms. As result, PETGEM allow users to specify edge-based variational forms of $H(curl)$ for the simulation of electromagnetic fields in real 3D CSEM surveys with high accuracy, reliability and efficiency.

In this paper we present the numerical formulation and results of 3D CSEM modelling using PETGEM. It is divided as follows: Sect. 2 describes the numerical formulation of 3D CSEM and its role as exploration tool. Section 3 shortly describes the theory associated to EFEM for CSEM applications. In Sect. 4 we validated our experiments against quasi-analytical results in canonical models. The last section is dedicated to conclusions and future work.

2   CSEM Problem

Controlled-source Electromagnetic Method (CSEM) is a type of geophysical strategies to study the subsurface electrical conductivity distribution with an ample range of applications. CSEM techniques can be divided into two groups depending on the domain in which collected data is interpreted: time domains (TDEM) and frequency domains (FDEM). In the case of oil prospecting, marine CSEM surveys are done predominantly using FDEM [13].

In marine 3D CSEM, also referred as seabed logging [9] or CSEM, a deep-towed electric dipole transmitter is used to produce a low frequency electro-magnetic signal (primary field) which interacts with the electrically conductive Earth and induces eddy currents that become sources of a new electromagnetic signal (secondary field). The two fields, the primary and the secondary, add up to a resultant field, which is measured by remote receivers placed on the seabed. Since the electromagnetic field at low frequencies, for which displacement currents are negligible, depends mainly on the electric conductivity distribution of the ground, it is possible to detect thin resistive layers beneath the seabed by studying the received signal [14]. Operating frequencies of transmitters in CSEM may range between 0.1 and 10 Hz, and the choice depends on the dimensions of a model. In most studies, typical frequencies vary from 0.25 to 1 Hz, which means that for source-receiver offsets of 10–12 km, the penetration depth of the method can extend to several kilometres below the seabed [10, 14].

The main disadvantage of CSEM is its relatively low resolution compared to seismic imaging. Therefore, CSEM is often used in conjunction with seismic surveying as the latter helps to constrain the resistivity model. Figure 1 depicts the CSEM.

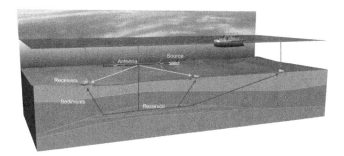

Fig. 1. Controlled-Source Electromagnetic Method (CSEM)

3D CSEM is nowadays a well-known geophysical prospecting tool in the offshore environment and a commonplace in industry, examples of that can be found in [2,6–8,16]. 3D CSEM modelling is typically solved in frequency domain, which involves the numerical solution of Maxwell's equations in stationary regimes for heterogeneous anisotropic electrically conductive domains. As already mentioned, CSEM surveys generally work with low frequency electromagnetic fields ($\sim$1 Hz) because the electric conductivity of the geological structures is much larger than their dielectric permittivity. As a consequence, in an unbound domain Γ, the electric field can be obtained by solving Maxwell's equations in their diffusive form:

$$\nabla \times \mathbf{E} = i\omega\mu_0\mathbf{H}, \tag{1}$$

$$\nabla \times \mathbf{H} = \mathbf{J}_s + \tilde{\sigma}\mathbf{E}, \tag{2}$$

where we have omitted the harmonic time dependence $e^{-i\omega t}$, where ω is the angular frequency, μ_0 the free space magnetic permeability, $\mathbf{J}_s$ the distribution of source current, $\tilde{\sigma}\mathbf{E}$ the induced current in the conductive Earth, and $\tilde{\sigma}$ the electrical conductivity which is assumed isotropic for simplicity.

In numerical approximations of EM fields there are two main drawbacks. The first one is the inevitable spatial singularity at the source. The second is the grid refinement requirements in order to capture the rapid change of the primary field [3]. In order to mitigate these issues, we used a secondary field approach where the total electric field $\mathbf{E}$ is obtained as:

$$\mathbf{E} = \mathbf{E}_p + \mathbf{E}_s, \tag{3}$$

$$\tilde{\sigma} = \tilde{\sigma}_s + \Delta\tilde{\sigma}, \tag{4}$$

where subscripts p and s represent a primary field and secondary field respectively. For a general layered Earth model, $\mathbf{E}_p$ can be computed semi-analytically by using Hankel transform filters. Based on this decomposition and following the work by [15] the equation for $\mathbf{E}_s$ is:

$$\nabla \times \nabla \times \mathbf{E}_s + i\omega\mu\tilde{\sigma}\mathbf{E}_s = -i\omega\mu\Delta\sigma\mathbf{E}_p, \tag{5}$$

where the electrical conductivity σ is a function of position that is allowed to vary in 3D, whereas the vacuum permeability μ is set to the free space value μ_0. We set homogeneous Dirichlet boundary conditions, $\mathbf{E}_s = 0$ on $\partial\Gamma$. The range of applicability of this conditions can be determined based on the skin depth of the electric field [17].

3   Edge Finite Element Method

For the computation of $\mathbf{E}_s$, we have implemented the Nédélec EFEM which uses vector basis functions defined on the edges of the corresponding elements. This vector basis functions are divergence-free but not curl-free [11]. Thus,

EFEM naturally ensures tangential continuity and allows normal discontinuity of $\mathbf{E}_s$ at material interfaces. In our approach we used unstructured tetrahedral meshes because of their ability to represent complex geological structures such as bathymetry or reservoirs, as well as the local refinement capability in order to improve the solution accuracy. Figure 2 shows the tetrahedral Nédélec elements (lowest order) together with their node and edge indexing.

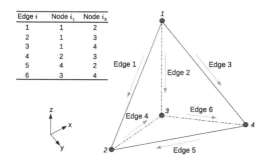

Fig. 2. Tetrahedral Nédélec edge element with node/edge indexing.

We assign the tangential component of the secondary electric field to the edges in the mesh. Therefore, all components of the electric field at a point $\mathbf{x}$ located inside a tetrahedral element e can be obtained as follows:

$$\mathbf{E}^e(\mathbf{x}) = \sum_{i=1}^{6} \mathbf{N}_i^e(\mathbf{x}) E_i^e, \tag{6}$$

where $\mathbf{N}_i^e$ are the vector basis functions associated to each edge i and E_i^e their degrees of freedom. Considering the node and edge indexing in Fig. 2, the vector basis functions can be expressed as follows:

$$\mathbf{N}_i^e = (\lambda_{i1}^e \nabla \lambda_{i2}^e - \lambda_{i2}^e \nabla \lambda_{i1}^e) \ell_i^e, \tag{7}$$

where subscripts $i1$ and $i2$ are the first and second nodes linked to the i-th edge, λ_i^e are the linear nodal basis functions, and ℓ_i^e is the length of the i-th edge of the element e.

By substituting expression (6) into (5), and using Galerkin's approach, the weak form of the original differential equation becomes:

$$Q_i = \int_{\Omega} \mathbf{N}_i \cdot [\nabla \times \nabla \times \mathbf{E}_s - i\omega\mu\tilde{\sigma}\mathbf{E}_s + i\omega\mu\Delta\tilde{\sigma}\mathbf{E}_p]dV. \tag{8}$$

The compact discretized form of (8) is obtained after applying the Green's theorem:

$$[K_{jk}^e + i\omega\tilde{\sigma}_e M_{jk}^e] \cdot \{E_{sk}\} = -i\omega\mu\Delta\tilde{\sigma}_e R_k^e, \tag{9}$$

where K^e and M^e are the elemental stiffness and mass matrices, which can be calculated either analytically or numerically [11], and R_k^e requires numerical integration. Our formulation does not require to calculate the jacobian matrix because the construction of elemental matrices is performed in real space. The interested reader may find a rigorous mathematical development of K^e and M^e in [4,5,11],

In our experiments, the numerical solution of the system of linear equations was obtained using a quasi-minimum residual (QMR) method without preconditioner.

4   Results

We validated our EFEM formulation and PETGEM solution against the quasi analytical results of the canonical model by [6]. PETGEM code is developed as open-source at Computer Applications in Science & Engineering (CASE) of the Barcelona Supercomputing Center - Centro Nacional de Supercomputación. The interested reader may find a comprehensive description about PETGEM design and capabilities in [5].

The model described in [6] consists in four-layers: 1000 m thick seawater (3.3 S/m), 1000 m thick sediments (1 S/m), 100 m thick oil (0.01 S/m) and 1400 m thick sediments (1 S/m). Our computational domain is a $[0, 3500]^3$ m cube. Figure 3 shows a 3D view of the unstructured tetrahedral mesh for the halfspace $y > 1750$, with the color scale representing the electrical conductivity σ for each layer.

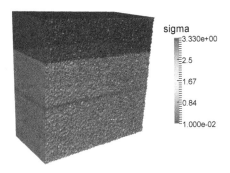

Fig. 3. Unstructured tetrahedral mesh for $y > 1750$. (Color figure online)

For this model we used a 1 Hz x-directed dipole source as in [4], which is located at $z = 975$ m, $x = 1750$ m and $y = 1750$ m. The receivers are aligned to the source position along its orientation, directly above the seafloor ($z = 990$). In order to validate the approach, we have prepared a set of hierarchically refined meshes to verify the convergence of the obtained solution. For all cases, the mesh has been locally refined around the source region.

Figure 4 shows a comparison of the x-component of total electric field between our EFEM solution and the quasi-analytical solution obtained with the WHAM tool [12]. In Fig. 4 it is easy to see the effect of our imperfect absorbing boundaries which can be mitigated by enlarging the domain with element sizes increasing logarithmically outwards from the zone of interest. The total electric field in Fig. 4 was calculated using a mesh with $\approx$ 12 millions of edges (degrees of freedom).

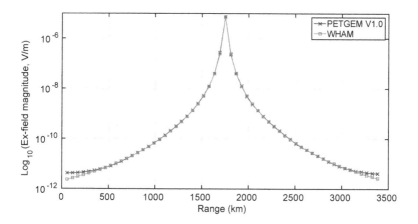

Fig. 4. Total electric field comparative for x-component.

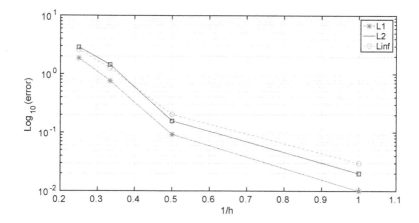

Fig. 5. Convergence order in L^1, L^2 and L^{inf} norm.

Using WHAM as reference solution and excluding those receivers closest to the boundaries, we have quantified the errors in our resulting electric fields by means of the L^1, L^2 and L^{inf} for our set of meshes, as plotted in Fig. 5. Degrees of freedom, mesh spacing and errors for each mesh are depicted in Table 1. We can observe the expected linear convergence in our scheme for all error norms and mesh sizes.

Table 1. Summary of results for convergence test.

	DOFs	$h(m)$	L^1	L^2	L^{inf}
Mesh 1	6.17×10^4	2.0×10^2	2.8447×10^{-7}	2.5059×10^{-7}	2.4939×10^{-7}
Mesh 2	4.36×10^5	1.0×10^2	1.6652×10^{-7}	$1.0365 \times 10{-7}$	9.0489×10^{-8}
Mesh 3	3.43×10^6	5.0×10^1	1.2859×10^{-7}	8.9955×10^{-8}	7.3234×10^{-8}
Mesh 4	1.19×10^7	3.3×10^1	1.5615×10^{-8}	8.3129×10^{-8}	7.0474×10^{-8}

Finally, in Table 2 we include some information about the algorithmic effort using a QMR solver for all cases.

Table 2. Summary of results for a QMR solver.

	Iterations	$||r||$
Mesh 1	1776	9.9777×10^{-7}
Mesh 2	3468	9.9703×10^{-7}
Mesh 3	5512	9.7994×10^{-7}
Mesh 4	8986	1.8174×10^{-6}

4.1 Conclusions

We have studied the feasibility of 3D CSEM modelling on unstructured tetra-hedral meshes using Nédélec EFEM. The formulation is interesting because of its low degree of freedom count and natural divergence-free property. We have employed a secondary field formulation to overcome problems related to the spatial singularity at the source. In our examples, a simple QMR solver was sufficed to obtain accurate solutions. Our formulation was validated against a canonical model of an off-shore hydrocarbon reservoir. The PETGEM solution of this model shows a good agreement with the quasi-analytical results in canonical models. The numerical results also demonstrate convergence to the reference solution. Thus, we conclude that our modelling scheme is capable of computing reliable results for 3D CSEM scenarios. Future work will aim at including other features such as seafloor bathymetry and anisotropy to the scheme as well as comparing the behaviour of the PETGEM with other modelling approaches for CSEM.

Acknowledgments. Authors of this work has received funding from the European Union's Horizon 2020 research and innovation programme under the Marie-Sklodowska Curie grant agreement No. 644202.

The research leading to these results has received funding from the European Union's Horizon 2020 Programme (2014–2020) and from Brazilian Ministry of Science, Technology and Innovation through Rede Nacional de Pesquisa (RNP) under the HPC4E Project (www.hpc4e.eu), grant agreement No. 689772.

Authors gratefully acknowledge the support from the Mexican National Council for Science and Technology (CONACyT). Numerical tests in this work were performed on the MareNostrum supercomputer of the Barcelona Supercomputing Center - Centro Nacional de Supercomputación (www.bsc.es).

References

1. Alumbaugh, D., Newman, G., Prevost, L., Shadid, J.: Three-dimensional wideband electromagnetic modeling on massively parallel computers. Wiley Online Libr. **1**, 1–23 (1996)
2. Boulaenko, M., Hesthammer, J., Vereshagin, A., Gelting, P., Davies, R., Wedberg, T.: Marine CSEM Technology – The Luva Case. Houston Geological Society (2007)
3. Cai, H., Xiong, B., Han, M., Zhdanov, M.: 3D controlled-source electromagnetic modeling in anisotropic medium using edge-based finite element method. Comput. Geosci. **73**, 164–176 (2014)
4. Castillo-Reyes, O., de la Puente, J., Puzyrev, V., Cela, J.M.: Edge-based electric field formulation in 3D CSEM simulations: a parallel approach. In: Proceedings of the 6th International Conference and Workshop on Computing and Communication. IEEE (2015)
5. Castillo-Reyes, O., de la Puente, J., Modesto, D., Puzyrev, V., Cela, J.M.: Parallel tool for numerical approximation of 3D electromagnetic surveys in geophysics. Computacin y Sistemas, Thematic Issue: Topic Trends Comput. Res. Catalonia **20**(1), 29–39 (2016)
6. Constable, S., Weiss, C.: Mapping thin resistors and hydrocarbons with marine EM methods: insights from 1D modeling. Geophysics **71**(2), G43–G51 (2006)
7. Constable, S., Srnka, L.J.: An introduction to marine controlled-source electromagnetic methods for hydrocarbon exploration. Geophysics **72**(2), WA3–WA12 (2007)
8. Constable, S.: Ten years of marine CSEM for hydrocarbon exploration. Geophysics **75**(5), 75A67–75A81 (2010)
9. Eidesmo, T., Ellingsrud, S., MacGregor, L.M., Constable, S., Sinha, M.C., Johansen, S.E., Kong, F.N., Westerdahl, H.: Sea bed logging (SBL), a new method for remote and direct identification of hydrocarbon filled layers in deepwater areas. First Break: Soc. Exploration Geophysicists **20**(3), 144–152 (2002)
10. Hanif, N., Hussain, N., Yahya, N., Daud, H., Yahya, N., Noh, M.: 1D modeling of controlled-source electromagnetic (CSEM) data using finite element method for hydrocarbon detection in shallow water. In: Proceedings of the International MultiConference of Engineers and Computer Scientists (2011)
11. Jianming, J.: The Finite Element Method in Electromagnetics. Wiley, Hoboken (2002)
12. Key, K.: 1D inversion of multicomponent, multifrequency marine CSEM data: methodology and synthetic studies for resolving thin resistive layers. Geophysics **74**, F9–F20 (2009)

13. Key, K.: Marine electromagnetic studies of seafloor resources and tectonics. Surveys Geophys. **33**(1), 135–167 (2012)
14. Koldan, J.: Numerical solution of 3-D electromagnetic problems in exploration geophysics and its implementation on massively parallel computers. Polytechnic University of Catalonia (2013)
15. Newman, G., Alumbaugh, D.: Three-dimensional induction logging problems, Part 2: a finite-difference solution. Geophysics **67**(2), 484–491 (2002)
16. Orange, A., Key, K., Constable, S.: The feasibility of reservoir monitoring using time-lapse marine CSEM. Geophysics **74**(2), F21–F29 (2009)
17. Puzyrev, V., Koldan, J., de la Puente, J., Houzeaux, G., Vázquez, M., Cela, J.M.: A parallel finite-element method for three-dimensional controlled-source electromagnetic forward modelling. Geophys. J. Int. (2013). ggt027

A Parallel Evolutionary Approach to the Molecular Docking Problem

Daniel Espinosa-Galindo, Jesús A. Fernández-Flores, Inés A. Almanza-Román,
Rosaura Palma-Orozco, and Jorge L. Rosas-Trigueros[(✉)]

Laboratorio Transdisciplinario de Investigación en Sistemas Evolutivos de la Escuela,
Superior de Cómputo del Instituto Politécnico Nacional,
Av. Juan de Dios Bátiz esq. Av. Miguel Othón de Mendizábal,
07738 Mexico City, Mexico
jlrosas@ipn.mx

Abstract. The ligand-protein molecular docking is an unsolved problem in Bioinformatics consisting in determining the way in which two such molecules bind in nature, depending on their structure and interaction. The solution of this problem is one of the core aims of Bioinformatics and the basis for the rational drug design process. Through the use of evolutionary and parallelization techniques, a new approach is presented, consisting of a threaded implementation of an island model genetic algorithm. The results show a mixed outcome, with an aided search version achieving quick and accurate predictions, while the more ambitious free search proposal still does not produce acceptable results. Additional advantages of the software obtained are cross-platform nature, reasonable performance on average consumer hardware and ease of use.

Keywords: Bioinformatics · Evolutionary Computing · Parallel Computing · Docking

1 Introduction

The molecular docking of drugs to protein structures is a key step in the rational approach to drug development. When binding certain small ligands to some larger biomolecules, great physical changes may occur; the docked conformation shows a complementarity both chemical and geometrical [1]. The molecular docking problem is defined as the process of searching ligands that bind to a protein in a geometrically and energetically acceptable way to both molecules. It has been formulated as an energy optimization problem through the possible ligand-protein conformations.

Specialized docking prediction algorithms can be used to face this problem. Any such algorithm would focus on finding the protein-ligand bound conformation with a minimum of free energy, and do so in a computable time. This is relevant given the nature of the experiment: the number of possible bound complexes is usually too large to perform an exhaustive search in a reasonable amount of time.

C.J. Barrios Hernández et al. (Eds.): CARLA 2016, CCIS 697, pp. 257–268, 2017.
DOI: 10.1007/978-3-319-57972-6_19

Some of the first molecular docking prediction systems used the Fast Fourier Transform to achieve an efficient representation of the search space [2]. More recently, other systems have employed biochemical knowledge of the docking process to assess the predictions; these systems include representations of the molecules' shape and physicochemical information [3].

In present day, molecular docking is usually approached as an optimization problem. From the molecular structure of two biomolecules, the protein and the ligand, the most stable bound conformation is to be found. This implies that the free energy of the docked conformation is a global minimum. Hence, an intuitive heuristic becomes an option to find the naturally occurring conformation.

On one hand, a scoring function has to selectively discriminate valid from invalid conformations, based on their total free energy. This function is to be minimized by an exploratory algorithm, at which point the predicted docking conformation has been found. Since in nature a protein-ligand pair tends to always find the same conformation, an ideal exploratory algorithm for this end would need to robustly obtain the global optimization of the objective function.

The presented work aims to propose a solution to the docking problem from an approach in which both the protein and the ligand are considered rigid. This rigidity is, however, not far from some cases that appear in living organisms, for example, in transport proteins or neurotransmitters [4]. The proposed solution is a computational tool to predict the ligand to protein molecular docking, considering certain geometrical and energetical restrictions through the use of evolutionary and parallelization techniques.

2   Methodology

The proposed docking tool consists in a modular multiplatform system implemented in the Python 2.7 platform. It is distributed as an add-on to the popular molecular structure visualization program PyMOL [5]. As an auxiliary tool, the de-facto molecular dynamics simulation package, GROMACS [6], is used to obtain the energy of the complex in any given conformation. The search for the solution that provides the minimum energy is then performed by a Genetic Algorithm (GA) following the Age Layered Population Structure (ALPS) model [7], which presents a parallel nature and accomodates the requirements of the problem.

2.1   Docking Problem Representation

The molecular docking problem is commonly seen as an exploratory optimization problem in a five dimensional real-valued space. Three of the variables correspond to the translation of one of the molecules with respect to the other, while the remaining two represent the relative rotation of the molecules with respect to a reference [8].

The system receives, as a description of the problem, the atomic structures of the molecules to be docked, along with a topology file required by GROMACS to compute the free energy.

The problem is encoded then as a five-value floating precision array, as described before. A typical Python installation uses floating precision of 53 bits, which would give a total of $(2^{53})^6 \approx 5.34 \cdot 10^{95}$ possible combinations. This high precision permits to explore practically all of the search space, and makes evident the impossibility to exhaustively search for the best solution since the amount of them approaches a googol.

As mentioned earlier, the scoring function to be minimized is derived from the potential energy in a given proposed state given that the bound conformation that appears in nature has the minimum energy. The energy is obtained by generating the atomic structure corresponding to the proposed conformation to then perform the potential energy calculation through *pipe* Inter-Process Communication (IPC) to GROMACS binaries.

2.1.1 Limiting Exploration to Preidentified Cavities

The prediction system was initially developed aiming for a more limited search, in which a set of previously identified cavities of the protein is given as an input. The format of the input file is as stablished by external binding site prediction tool LISE [9]. This version of the system is thoroughly documented in the full report [10], although the current focus of development is around an autonomous free search.

2.1.2 Scoring Function Tuning

In some cases, the algorithm tended to return predictions where the molecules were so far away from each other, there were no unfavorable interactions between them, thus returning very low potential energy values when the predictions were obviously not useful. For this reason, a penalty was introduced, which is simply added to the potential energy. It relates the distance between the molecules as follows:

$$\text{penalty}_{\text{pair}} = \frac{\exp(\pi s_{\text{pair}})}{\text{score}_{\text{cavity}}}, \tag{1}$$

where s_{pair} is the distance between the pair of molecules and $\text{score}_{\text{cavity}}$ is the score assigned to the cavity, which by definition from LISE is of an exponential order. This penalty is ignored on the free search implementation where there is no concept of cavities.

2.1.3 Energy Calculations

The energy calculations were performed using the GROMACS molecular dynamics package. This package emulates the physical interactions observed in nature through Lagrangian Mechanics equations. Given that they all provide just an approximation, it is important to select a set of parameters and equations appropriate to the problem at hand. This is done through the selection of a force field and the correct description of the molecules' topology.

During the validation of the project, most of the ligand description files were obtained from the Automated Topology Builder (ATB) [11], so the default force

field on the system is a modified GROMOS 54A7 as used by ATB. GROMOS
54A7 parameters for the proteins were obtained using GROMACS.

2.2   Optimization Algorithm: ALPS GA

Given the nature of the problem and the importance of finding consistently the
global optimum, an adequate optimization algorithm would need to be robust
and exhaustive, additionally to the implicit concerns for efficiency and correctness. For this reasons the Age Layered Population Structure (ALPS) model was
selected.

ALPS was designed with the goal of reducing premature convergence and has
shown to achieve better, more consistent results than other techniques. It differs
from other Evolutionary Algorithm models in that it segregates the population
into multiple layers using a novel measure of age, and reduces premature convergence by introducing a new group of randomly generated individuals at regular
intervals. This approach can be thought of as combining multiple, independent
search runs that are done sequentially into a single, multi-layered meta-run [7].

The ALPS model contemplates executing a population-based optimization
technique in several semi-independent *layers*, each with its own population. An
age concept is introduced, describing the number of iterations for which the
information of each solution has been present. Individuals born from recombination have the age of their older parent, while the ones created randomly start
with age 0; for each iteration that they remain as candidate solutions, their age
increases by 1.

The population is then arranged in islands according to age limits. Each layer
holds solutions up to a certain age in its population and when a solution reaches
the limit, it migrates to the next layer. During the population recombination
phase of each iteration in a layer, the candidate solutions to be combined are
taken from the union of the populations of the current layer and the previous
one.

The genetic algorithm, on the other hand, is a canonical GA. The algorithm
starts from a randomly generated population of individuals which encode a candidate solution in an array-like manner. Each iteration begins with the selection
of individuals to be used as parents on the recombination stage. Lastly, the population is replaced from the original parents population and the newly created
one, and used as a starting point for the next generation.

Figure 1 shows the overall sequence of steps of the algorithm. The main interactions with the actual population layers are shown as the non-continuous lines;
dotted for read and dashed for write operations. It is worth noting that in the
first layer, since it has no previous layer to select parents from, the population
ages uniformly and periodically migrates in its entirety during redistribution; at
this point a new fully random one is generated.

The parameters in Table 1 were set empirically as they were found performing
best during testing, since the main focus of the project is currently development
rather than refining. This considering, in the following order, computation time,
diversity across layers and within the population islands, feasibility to be run on

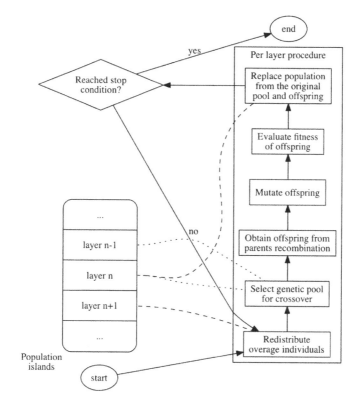

Fig. 1. Flowchart of the optimization algorithm.

consumer hardware, previous theoretical calculations, and quality of resulting predictions. They can be manually reset through a configuration file.

Among the most particular ones is the age limit on the first layer age^0_{max}. This is relevant since, as mentioned previously, when it is reached, the population is replaced by new randomized individuals and thus implies the rate at which fully random information is introduced to the algorithm. It is important to keep this relatively low in order to avoid stagnation when reaching a population with a locally optimum feature set.

Also, this parameter along with the overall aging distribution scheme $scheme_{aging}$ gives the actual limits on all the layers. Besides being used by the ALPS model, these limits influence the selection pressure on each layer, as detailed in Sect. 2.2.1. The available distribution schemes are: linear, polynomial, exponential and Fibonacci, as proposed in the literature [7]. The number of layers to be run n_{layers} can be seen as a derived parameter to be set accordingly to the desired age bounds and iteration hard limit $iter_{max}$.

In addition to this ALPS specific parameters, the quality of the results is heavily dependent on the population size μ, but so is the computation time. On the other hand, the remaining standard GA parameters, mutation rate,

Table 1. Variable parameters for ALPS GA.

Parameter	Description
age_{max}^0	Age limit for the first layer (layer zero)
μ	Number of individuals in each population
$rate_{mutation}$	Rate at which mutations occur in the recombination stage
$ratio_{crossover}$	Ratio of the members of the population obtained from crossover
$scheme_{aging}$	Age distribution scheme to be used
$iter_{max}$	Iteration hard limit for the algorithm
n_{layers}	Number of ALPS layers to be parallelly executed

$rate_{mutation}$, and crossover ratio, $rate_{crossover}$, tend to have more standard values for multi-modal, multi-dimensional, global optimization problems like the one at hand (about 0.15 and 0.8 respectively) [12].

There is a complex interaction between these concepts in the algorithm, and the probability of finding the global optimum relies on fitting the ALPS specific parameters along with the population size, according to the search space and computation time requirements.

2.2.1 Selection

The selection method used is the tournament selection, chosen due to its low computational complexity and the ease to adjust the selective pressure or elitism by simply varying the tournament size. A varying pressure is used in each layer to generate greater variety in the first layers and a more elitist selection as approaching to the last one.

From the literature [13], once the best possible solution exists in the population of a GA with tournament selection, a method for calculating the takeover time is known. This is the number of iterations needed for the best solution to take over the entire population, i.e., the population consists solely of clones of this best individual. The desired takeover time $t_{takeover}$ is given by

$$t_{takeover} = \frac{1}{\ln n_{tourn}}(\ln \mu + \ln(\ln \mu)), \qquad (2)$$

where n_{tourn} is the number of individuals to participate in each tournament. Then, the variable pressure is achieved by proposing a desired takeover time in function of both the age limit in the layer, age_{max}, and the overall iteration limit, $iter_{max}$, leading to

$$t_{takeover} = \frac{iter_{max}}{age_{max}}. \qquad (3)$$

This results in a relaxed, high diversity selection in the lower levels and a more elitist selection throughout each of the higher layers. Also, the quotient balances each layer's requirements with the limit of iterations actually available to explore the search space.

From (2), the required tournament size for each layer is

$$n_{\text{tourn}} = (\mu \ln \mu)^{t_{\text{takeover}}^{-1}} = (\mu \ln \mu)^{\frac{\text{age}_{\max}}{\text{iter}_{\max}}}. \tag{4}$$

2.2.2 Replacement

From the reviewed replacement methods [10], the proposed version, $\lambda + q\mu$, was selected. The parameter $\text{ratio}_{crossover}$ is used to define the proportion of individuals to be taken in an elitist manner from the original population as $q = 1 - \text{ratio}_{crossover}$, while the rest are obtained from crossover.

2.2.3 Parallel Implementation

Being an island population model, ALPS has a parallel nature. Each population layer executes a semi-independent version of a GA with eventual migrations between layers. In this work, the layers were implemented as threads.

As shown in Fig. 1, there are only two kinds of interaction between population layers: when taking the pool of individuals from which selection occurs; and when redistributing the layer population according to its age limit. To maintain consistency, thread synchronization at this points had to be added. This was achieved through an event-oriented approach, described in pseudocode in Algorithm 1.

Algorithm 1. Per layer ALPS GA parallel execution

---

    while not STOPCONDITION() **do**
        $pool \leftarrow thisLayer.population +$ COPY($prevLayer.population$)
3:      **signal** $event :: copied$
        $offspring \leftarrow$ REPRODUCE($pool$)
        $offspring \leftarrow$ MUTATE($offspring$)
6:      SORT($offspring$)   ▷ calculate and sort individuals according to score
        wait $event :: copied$ **from** $nextLayer$
        wait $event :: replaced$ **from** $prevLayer$
9:      $thisLayer.population \leftarrow$ ELITISM($offspring, thisLayer.population$)
        REDISTRIBUTE($thisLayer.population$)
        signal $event :: replaced$
12: **end while**

By far, the most computationally costly stage of the algorithm happens at line 6, since the score of each individual is calculated at each time it is required during the sorting. The proposed synchronization allows for this step to run fully in parallel while ensuring the uniform execution of all threads.

2.3 Technical Details

The prevalent Python implementation, CPython comes with a severe limitation on threaded applications due to its Global Interpreter Lock (GIL). The GIL prevents execution of Python bytecode by several threads at once, since CPython's memory management is not thread-safe. I/O operations block and can be effectively parallelized on threaded applications, being the main use of such approach [14].

The main workaround to exploit muli-core systems with Python consists in using multiple processes as opposed to threads; using the `multiprocessing` module instead of `thread`. One drawback is that independent processes do not typically share a state and the information passing between them must happen through explicit messaging, which can add up to a considerable IPC overhead.

The alternative used in the present work is to use Python to run specialized and fast extensions or external programs that can be executed in parallel outside the Python interpreter. The internal representation of the atomic structures is handled with the Bioinformatics package `Biopython` [15], which in turn uses C/Fortran scientific computing extension `NumPy`. Also, as mentioned in Sect. 2, for each GA fitness evaluation, the proposed atomic structure is outputted as a file for the software GROMACS to perform the energetic analysis. This two considerations allow for more efficient resource usage in multi-threaded environments.

On the other hand, interfacing through file system to GROMACS implies a heavy I/O load and can lead to a storage access bottleneck. This issue is easily circumvented with the use of a form of in-memory file system, e.g., open source `tmpfs` on GNU/Linux or Dataram's *RAMDisk* on Windows. Since the prediction software works on the host platform temporary directory, it would suffice to point this directory to the in-memory file system, also sparing the storage device of unnecessary wear.

3   Results

To evaluate the validity of the predictions, the system was tested with a set of four well studied cases on the aided search implementation. The free search version was tested only with one of the test cases, "The Geometry of the Reactive Site and of the Peptide Groups in Trypsin, Trypsinogen and its Complexes with Inhibitors", which is available in the Protein Data Bank with the identifier 3PTB [16]. Both the presented software and an equivalent sequential implementation were executed in an 8 core desktop PC running Windows 10 Pro with a native GROMACS installation.

As anticipated, the aided search implementation shows dramatically better both execution times and results accuracy, with three out of four cases reaching the expected results within 0.01 RMSD (root mean-square deviation). Furthermore, the tests were ran 10 times to ensure the desired robustness and all of them outputted very similar results. Results and convergence data are available in a previous work [10].

The variable parameters for the ALPS GA (listed in Table 1) were set mainly empirically as shown in Table 2.

Figure 2 shows the evolution of the score of the best individual throughout the execution of the free search version. This test, under the mentioned conditions,

Table 2. Values for the variable parameters in Table 1.

Parameter	Value
age^0_{max}	3
μ	35
$rate_{mutation}$	0.1
$ratio_{crossover}$	0.8
$scheme_{aging}$	Fibonacci
$iter_{max}$	200, 25 for aided
n_{layers}	10, 4 for aided

was executed only once and only for this case. Several other not documented runs were required to set the parameters to their current values and all had a tendency to similarly stray from the desired outcome, although in different directions.

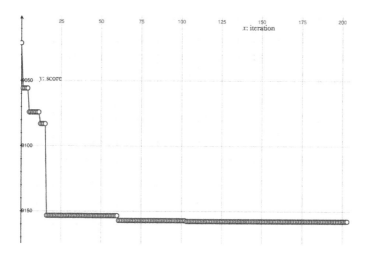

Fig. 2. Convergence plot for the 3PTB test case.

The proposed docking conformation is shown in Fig. 3, along with the one observed in nature. The backbone of the protein is represented as a wireframe, while the full atomic structure of the ligand is shown for both conformations.

To gauge the performance gain of a parallel implementation, the presented system was compared to a sequential implementation of the free search version, as described by Table 3. The computation time was almost threefold in the sequential variant, while only averaging at 8% less CPU usage than the parallel free search. Both resulted, as expected, in similar predictions, although not

Fig. 3. Visualization of the predicted docked conformation (green, left) and the expected one (orange, right) for the 3PTB test case. (Color figure online)

sufficiently accurate. The aided search version, on the other hand, predicted the expected conformation using dramatically less time and resources (see Table 2).

Table 3. Performance evaluation of both versions of system against equivalent sequential implementation.

Metric	Aided search	Free search	Free search (seq.)
Execution time	18 m 37 s	3 h 53 m 24 s	11 h 00 m 20 s
Average CPU usage	16%	22%	14%
Best score	−9124 kJ/mol	−9133 kJ/mol	−9157 kJ/mol

It is notable that the prediction for this test case did not produce the expected outcome. Furthermore the scores for the free search show lower values than for the aided search, despite this last one being much more accurate. This fact indicates that the scoring function as presented in Sect. 2.1.2 is no longer appropriate for the problem when releasing the constraint of exploring a predefined small cavity.

4   Conclusions

Molecular docking is a key unsolved problem in Bioinformatics with important applications in modern drug design. The present work incorporates knowledge from diverse disciplines, mainly Evolutionary Computing, Operating Systems, Parallel Computing, Computer Graphics and Bioinformatics to propose an efficient solution to this well defined problem within Biology.

Results were mixed, with the free search version underperforming. While this is currently the primary aim of the project, the aided search alternative displays an effectiveness of 75% accurate predictions. Being an auxiliary system, that rate of success is quite satisfactory and can be a great aid to assess the viability of a proposed drug. The software allows for quick assessments when performing in a drug screening kind of scenario, given that the target protein structure has to be previously processed by LISE or otherwise analyzed.

Work remains to be done in the objective function, since it currently does not seem to fully reflect the behavior observed in nature. The introduction of some local search using Molecular Dynamics simulations is also being considered to refine the free search process.

Performance on the other hand is better than originally expected, even when running on modest hardware [10]. Convergence is fast and robust, finding consistently the best considered solution throughout several executions, thanks to the ample search achieved with the methods presented. The reduction in the execution time of the parallel variant is within the expected; since the layers do not start simultaneously, the intuitive expectation of an ideal ten fold performance gain would not be realistic.

References

1. Teodoro, M.L., Philips, G.N., Kavraki, L.E.: Molecular docking: a problem with thousands of degrees of freedom. IEEE Int. Conf. Robot. Autom. **8**(1), 960–966 (2001)
2. Bajaj, C., Chowdhury, R., Siddavanahalli, V.: F2Dock: fast Fourier protein-protein docking. IEEE/ACM Trans. Comput. Biol. Bioinform. **8**(1), 45–58 (2011)
3. Geppert, T., Proschak, E., Schneider, G.: Protein-protein docking by shape-complementarity and property matching. J. Comput. Chem. **31**(9), 1919–1928 (2010)
4. Klotz, I.M.: Protein interactions with small molecules. Acc. Chem. Res. **7**, 162–168 (1974)
5. PyMOL. http://www.pymol.org/pymol. Accessed 2016
6. Páll, S., Abraham, M.J., Kutzner, C., Hess, B., Lindahl, E.: Tackling exascale software challenges in molecular dynamics simulations with GROMACS. In: Markidis, S., Laure, E. (eds.) EASC 2014. LNCS, vol. 8759, pp. 3–27. Springer, Cham (2015). doi:10.1007/978-3-319-15976-8_1
7. Hornby, G.S.: The age-layered population structure (ALPS) evolutionary algorithm, July 2009
8. Garzon, J.I., Lopz-Blanco, J.R., Pons, C., Kovacs, J., Abagyan, R., Fernandez-Recio, J., Chancon, P.: FRODOCK: a new approach for fast rotational protein-protein docking. Struct. Bioinform. **25**(19), 2544–2551 (2009)
9. Xie, Z.-R., Hwang, M.-J.: Ligand binding site prediction using ligand interacting and binding site-enriched protein triangles. Bioinformatics **28**, 1579–1585 (2012)

10. Espinosa-Galindo, D., Fernndez-Flores, J., Almanza-Romn, I.A., Rosas-Trigueros, J.L., Palma-Orozco, R.: Sistema de acoplamiento molecular. Escuela Superior de Cmputo del Instituto Politcnico Nacional, Ciudad de Mexico, Mexico (2016)
11. An Automated force field Topology Builder (ATB) and repository: version 1.0
12. Baker, J.E.: Genetic algorithms and their applications. In: Proceedings of the First International Conference on Genetic Algorithms, pp. 101–111 (1985)
13. Goldberg, D.E., Deb, K.: A comparative analysis of selection schemes used in genetic algorithms. Found. Genet. Algorithms 1, 69–93 (1991)
14. GlobalInterpreterLock. https://wiki.python.org/moin/GlobalInterpreterLock. Accessed 10 July 2016
15. Cock, P., Antao, T., Chang, J., Bradman, B., Cox, C., Dalke, A., Friedberg, I., Hamelryck, T., Kauff, F., Wilczynski, B., Hoon, M.: Biopython: freely available Python tools for computational molecular biology and bioinformatics. Bioinformatics 25, 1422–1423 (2009)
16. The Geometry of the Reactive Site and of the Peptide Groups in Trypsin, Trypsinogen and its Complexes with Inhibitors. http://www.rcsb.org/pdb/explore/explore.do?structureId=3ptb. Accessed 14 Oct 2015

Deep Learning Applied to Deep Brain Stimulation in Parkinson's Disease

Pablo Guillén[(✉)]

Center for Advanced Computing and Data Systems, CACDS,
University of Houston, Houston, TX, USA
pgrondon@uh.edu

Abstract. In order to better model complex real-world data such as biomedical signals, one approach is to develop pattern recognition techniques and robust features that capture the relevant information. In this paper, we use deep learning methods, and in particular multilayer perceptron, to build an algorithm that can predict subcortical structures of patients with Parkinson's disease, based on microelectrode records obtained during deep brain stimulation. We report on experiments using a data set involving 52 microelectrode records for the structures: zona incerta, subthalamic nucleus, thalamus nucleus, and substantia nigra. The results show that the combination of features and deep learning produces 99.2% precision of detection and classification on the average of the subcortical structures under study. In conclusion, based on the high precision obtained in the classification, deep learning could be used to predict subcortical structure, and mainly the subthalamic nucleus for neurostimulation.

1 Introduction

Human information processing mechanisms (e.g. vision and speech) suggest the need of deep architectures for extracting complex structure and building internal representation from rich sensory inputs. For example, human speech production and perception systems are both equipped with clearly layered hierarchical structures in transforming information from the waveform level to the linguistic level and vice versa. It is natural to believe that the state of the art can be advanced in processing these types of media signals if efficient and effective deep learning algorithms are developed. Biomedical signals processing systems with deep architectures are composed of many layers of nonlinear processing stages, where each lower layer's outputs are fed to its immediate higher layer as the input. The concept of deep learning originated from artificial neural network research. Multilayer perceptron with many hidden layers is a good example of the models with deep architectures [1].

Deep learning techniques have been applied to a wide variety of problems in recent years [2–7]. In many of these applications, algorithms based on deep learning have surpassed the previous state-of-art performance. At the heart of all deep learning algorithms is the domain independent idea of using hierarchical layers of learned abstraction to efficiently accomplish high-level task. Deep learning allows computational models that are composed of multiple processing layers to learn representations of data with multiple levels of abstraction. Deep learning discovers intricate structure in

© Springer International Publishing AG 2017
C.J. Barrios Hernández et al. (Eds.): CARLA 2016, CCIS 697, pp. 269–278, 2017.
DOI: 10.1007/978-3-319-57972-6_20

large data sets by using the backpropagation algorithm to indicate how a machine should change its internal parameters that are used to compute the representation in each layer from the representation in the previous layer [1].

Parkinson disease (PD) is thought to affect at least 100 persons in every 100,000. The cardinal symptoms of tremor, bradykinesia, postural instability, and rigor result in substantial disability for patients with PD. During the course of the disease, up to 50% of patients will have symptoms refractory to medication and will experience drug-induced dyskinesias. Over activity of the globus pallidus internus (GPi) and the subthalamic nucleus (STN) is believed to be part of the pathophysiologic mechanism of PD. PD is a chronic progressive neurodegenerative disorder affecting multiple brain circuits leading to motor symptoms such as bradykinesia, rigidity, resting tremor, and loss of postural reflexes [8]. PD also has non-motor manifestations such as neuropsychiatric symptoms, cognitive abnormalities, autonomic disorders, and sleep [9].

PD is primary related to substantia nigra degeneration and, thus, dopamine insufficiency. L-DOPA as a precursor of dopamine is the standard medication in PD. However, disease progression causes L-DOPA therapy efficiency decay (on-off symptom fluctuation), and neurologists often decide to classify patients for DBS (Deep Brain Stimulation) surgery.

DBS [10] is considered a safe and well-tolerated surgical procedure to alleviate PD and other movement disorders symptoms along with some psychiatric conditions. Over the last few decades DBS has been shown to provide remarkable therapeutic effect on carefully selected patients. DBS improves motor functions and therefore quality of life. To date, one main target has emerged in PD patients: the subthalamic nucleus.

DBS involves the surgical implantation of electrodes into deep structures of the brain to modulate brain circuitry in an effort to restore normal physiological function. DBS has been used effectively for the treatment of movement disorders, including PD, Essential tremor (ET), and dystonia, as well as for psychiatric disorders such as obsessive-compulsive disorder (OCD). In addition, DBS may exert its influence via the correction of aberrant neuronal activity. For example, in the setting of DBS for the treatment of PD, the loss of dopamine, which is known to be largely responsible for the pathophysiology of the disease, results in changes in the underlying activity of cells within the basal ganglia [11].

The exact placement of the stimulator is fundamental for the sensory and motor effects specific to the subthalamus, since small deviations can affect adjacent structures and generate side effects [12]. Technological development has allowed a higher display resolution for the imaging processing of these types of structures [13]. Also, the development of recording systems for the spontaneous or induced electrical activity of such structures, allows defining more accurately their position limits, anatomic relationships with adjacent structures and behavior in relation to the movement or symptoms of Parkinsonism components, which turns in a suitable situation in order to safely establish and characterize the affected area. The risk of errors in the localization of the surgical target for deep brain electrical stimulation requires the use of some form of intraoperative neurophysiological monitoring to confirm the correct destination during surgery. The purpose of the development and implementation of techniques of classification for the processing microelectrode records (MER) is of great importance today, as it allows the surgical team to determine the optimal location of the lesion or DBS [14, 15].

In this paper we build a set of features each of which measure different signal characteristics, quantify neuronal activity inherent in the subcortical structures, and allows their localization for greater accuracy during DBS. Next, a machine learning algorithm for supervised classification based on deep learning is used with the values of the obtained features, and we show that deep learning can identify and predict with high precision any of the subcortical structures (4 classes): Thalamus (TAL), zona incerta (Zi), subthalamic nucleus (STN) and substantia nigra (SNR).

2 Materials and Methods

2.1 Dataset

Intra-operative microelectrode records were acquired in Parkinsonian patients, awake and unmedicated, subject to deep brain implantation under electrostimulation. Five Parkinsonian patients (4 males and 1 female) aged between 55 ± 6 years old participated voluntarily assuming previously signed consent. Microelectrode records were made using the ISIS MER Inomed system, which is used to obtain an optimal location of the destination (target) through deep brain stimulation. Visualization of neural data started 10 mm on the target data. Each 1 mm a new location was created if the distance between the microelectrode and the destination point was greater than 3 mm. For distances less than 3 mm, the locations were created every 0.5 mm. Specialists in neurosurgery and neurophysiology labeled the obtained signals using the MER system. The acquisition time for each record was 2 s with a sampling frequency of 24 kHz (24,000 samples per second). In total, the database comprises 52 micro recordings, 13 for each of the subcortical structures: Thalamus nucleus (TAL), Zona Incerta (Zi), Subthalamic nucleus (STN) and Substantia Nigra (SNR). These surgical procedures were performed at the Institute of Epilepsy and Parkinson in Pereira, Colombia.

2.2 Features

In the following we present the features to extract the information contained in each of the MER for the different subcortical structures under study.

Curve Length. This feature is useful to know the stability of the values of a signal. If in a given interval, the value of this feature is low, it is an indicative that the signal is stable, otherwise the signal is unstable. Equation (1) defines the calculation of this feature:

$$L = \sum_{i=1}^{N-1} |x_{i+1} - x_i| \tag{1}$$

where each x_i corresponds to a sample in the dataset $X = (x_1, x_2, \ldots, x_N)$.

Threshold. Computation of the threshold is based in the calculation of the deviation of the data in order to know how scattered they are in given window of size N. Threshold is calculated as follows:

$$g = \frac{3}{N-1}\sqrt{\sum_{i=1}^{N}(x_i - \overline{X})^2} \tag{2}$$

where $\overline{X}$ is the mean of the dataset.

Peaks. The number of peaks that a given signal has is determined by:

$$\kappa = \frac{1}{2}\sum_{i=1}^{N-2} max\{0, |sgn[x_{i+1} - x_i] - sgn[x_{i+2} - x_{i+1}]|\} \tag{3}$$

where

$$max(a,b) = \begin{cases} a & \text{if} & a > b \\ b & \text{if} & a < b \\ a\,o\,b & \text{if} & a = b \end{cases}$$

$$sgn(x) = \begin{cases} 1 & \text{if} & x > 0 \\ 0 & \text{if} & x = 0 \\ -1 & \text{if} & x < 0 \end{cases}$$

Root Mean Square. It is defined as the square root of the mean of the squares of the values of the signal. The root mean square (also known as quadratic mean) is determined by:

$$d = \sqrt{\frac{\sum_{i=1}^{N} x_i^2}{N}} \tag{4}$$

Average Nonlinear Energy. The average nonlinear energy is computed as:

$$ANE = \frac{1}{N-2}\sum_{i=2}^{N-1}(x_i^2 - x_{i-1}x_{i+1}) \tag{5}$$

Zero Crossings. The amount of zero crossings k for a given signal is determined through the formula:

$$k = \frac{1}{2}\sum_{i=1}^{N-1} |sgn(x_{i+1}) - sgn(x_i)| \tag{6}$$

2.3   Deep Learning

The concept of deep learning originated from artificial neural network research. Multilayer perceptron with many hidden layers is a good example of the models with deep architectures. Unlike the neural networks of the past, modern deep learning has cracked the code for training stability and generalization and scale on big data. It is often the algorithm of choice for highest predictive accuracy, as deep learning algorithms performs quite well in a number of diverse problems.

There are several theoretical frameworks for deep learning, and here we summarize the feedforward architecture used by H20 [16]. Multilayer perceptron (MLP) are feed-forward neural networks with architecture composed of the input layer, the hidden layer and the output layer. Each layer is formed from small units known as neurons. Neurons in the input layer receive the input signals X and distribute them forward to the rest of the network. In the next layers, each neuron receives a signal, which is a weighted sum of the outputs of the nodes in the previous layer. Inside each neuron, an activation function is used to control the input, (Fig. 1 shows an example). Such a network determines a non-linear mapping from an input vector to the output vector, parameterized by a set of network weights, which are referred to as the vector of weights W. The first step in approximating the weight parameters of the model is finding the appropriate architecture of the MLP, where the architecture is characterized by the number of hidden units, the type of activation function, as well as the number of input and output variables. The second step estimates the weight parameters using the training set. Training estimates the weight vector W to ensure that the output is as close to the target vector as possible. The structure of a MLP network is shown in Fig. 2. This basic framework of MLP neural networks can be used to accomplish deep learning task. Deep learning architectures are models of hierarchical feature extraction, typically involving multiple levels of nonlinearity.

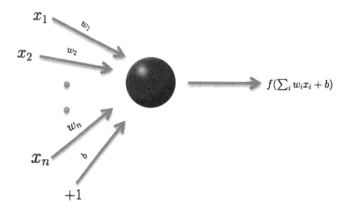

Fig. 1. The function f represents the nonlinear activation function used throughout the network and the bias b represents the neuron's activation threshold.

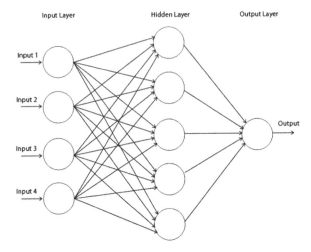

Fig. 2. Structure of an architecture multilayer perceptron.

2.4   Tools

The features described before were implemented in Matlab R2015, and the Library H20 [16] was used in order to perform the classification through deep learning.

3   Results

As mentioned before when we presented the database, each record was acquired for 2 s at a sampling frequency of 24 kHz, which leads to each record having 48,000 samples. If we consider a trajectory of 13 records for each of the subcortical structures: Thalamus nucleus (TAL), Zona Incerta (Zi), Subthalamic nucleus (STN) and Substantia Nigra (SNR), the final trajectory is made up of 52 records and has a total of 2,496,000 samples. Next, the final trajectory is divided into windows 4992 consecutive samples and for each of these windows the six features are determined, yielding a total of 500 instances (patterns) by feature. The decomposition described above is presented in matrix form as follows (Fig. 3):

$$
X = \begin{matrix} & V_1 & V_2 & \cdots & \cdots & V_p \\ X_1 & \\ X_2 & \\ \vdots & \\ \vdots & \\ X_n & \end{matrix}
\begin{bmatrix}
x_{11} & x_{12} & \cdots & \cdots & x_{1p} \\
x_{21} & x_{22} & \cdots & \cdots & x_{2p} \\
\vdots & \vdots & \ddots & \cdots & \vdots \\
\vdots & \vdots & \cdots & \ddots & \vdots \\
x_{n1} & x_{n2} & \cdots & \cdots & x_{np}
\end{bmatrix}
$$

Fig. 3. Feature matrix.

Once the feature matrix is assembled, we proceed to label the first 125 instances as Class 1, which correspond to the Thalamus; the next 125 instances as Class 2, corresponding to Zona Incerta; the following 125 instances as Class 3, representing the Subthalamic nucleus; and finally, the last 125 instances as Class 4, corresponding to the Substantia Nigra. In our approach, we train a MLP on a set of randomly selected features, approximately 60%, extracted from the feature matrix, then approximately 20% are used as the validation set, and approximately 20% are used as the testing set. The purpose of this training is to learn the multilayer architectures by simple stochastic gradient descent. The backpropagation procedure to compute the gradient of an objective function with respect to the weights of a multilayer stack of modules is nothing more than a practical application of the chain rule for derivatives. The key insight is that the gradient of the objective with respect to the input of a module can be computed by working backward from the gradient with respect to the output of that module. The backpropagation equation can be applied repeatedly to propagate gradients through all modules, starting from the output at the top (where the network produces its prediction) all the way to the bottom (where the external input is fed) [1]. Multilayer feedforward neural networks consist of many layers of interconnected neuron units, starting with an input layer to match the feature space, followed by multiple layers of nonlinearity, and ending with a linear regression or classification layer to match the output space. The weights linking neurons and biases with other neurons fully determine the output of the entire network, and finally learning occurs when these weights are adapted to minimize the error on labeled training data. To go from one layer to the next, the weighted sum of their inputs from the previous layer pass the result through a non-linear function. At the present, the most popular non-linear function is the rectified linear unit (ReLU). Variable epochs correspond to the numbers of passes over the training data set. Table 1 shows the size of the architecture multilayer perceptron and parameters used on the experiments to evaluate the classification.

Table 1. Parameters of the architecture multilayer perceptron.

Variables	Parameters
Input	500
Hidden	(32,32,32)
Output	4
Activation function	ReLU
Loss function	Mean squared error
Epochs	1000000

Tables 2 and 4 show the output report by H20 on train data and validation data, respectively, and Tables 3 and 5 show their confusion matrices.

We can see that the results in the training set and validation set are consistent with the architecture and variables used for classification.

Table 2. Precision reported on train data.

Deep learning
** Reported on train data. **
MSE: 2.19526e-11
R^2: 0.9999

Table 3. Confusion matrix on train data.

Class_2	Class_1	Class_3	Class_4	Error	Rate
77.0	0.0	0.0	0.0	0.0	0/77
0.0	77.0	0.0	0.0	0.0	0/77
0.0	0.0	79.0	0.0	0.0	0/79
0.0	0.0	0.0	73.0	0.0	0/73
77.0	77.0	79.0	73.0	0.0	0/306

Table 4. Precision reported on validation data.

Deep learning
** Reported on validation data. **
MSE: 0.0098
R^2: 0.9925

Table 5. Confusion matrix on validation data.

Class_2	Class_1	Class_3	Class_4	Error	Rate
23.0	0.0	0.0	0.0	0.0	0/23
0.0	22.0	0.0	0.0	0.0	0/22
1.0	0.0	23.0	0.0	0.0416	1/24
0.0	0.0	0.0	33.0	0.0	0/33
24.0	22.0	23.0	33.0	0.0098	1/102

The testing set is used to predict the variable CLASS, which contains labels for each class (Class 1, Class 2, Class 3, and Class 4), and a predictive accuracy of 99.2% for the different classes is obtained.

4   Conclusions

In this paper we investigated the use of deep learning for the classification and prediction of subcortical structures of patients with Parkinson's disease, based on microelectrode records (MER), obtained during deep brain stimulation (DBS).

We proposed six types of input features and a corresponding architecture to precisely predict subcortical structures. First, we showed that the network can learn surprisingly well. Second, we showed that the network can classify the different subcortical structures with high efficiency, and finally, a high precision is achieved in the task of predicting the different classes.

Our experiments indicate that a deep learning approach in combination with input features, has the potential to capture subcortical structures patterns, which may boost the classification performance. These investigations could be further improved in future studies by carrying out more exhaustive searches for the parameters in the architectures. Moreover, the overall performance of these systems could be further improved.

We conclude that deep learning could be used to monitor in real time the location of subcortical structures, reducing the uncertainty that exists during surgery, and representing a valuable support tool for neurosurgeons and electrophysiologists during electrical stimulation and deep brain electrode implantation for the treatment of parkinsonian patients.

Acknowledgments. This work was funded by Center for Advanced Computing and Data Systems, CACDS, at the University of Houston, Houston, TX, USA.

References

1. LeCun, Y., Bengio, Y., Hinton, G.: Deep learning. Nature **521**, 436–444 (2015)
2. Langkvist, M., Karlsson, L., Loutfi, A.: A review of unsupervised feature learning and deep learning for time series modeling. Pattern Recogn. Lett. **42**, 11–24 (2014)
3. Yu, D., Deng, L.: Deep learning and its applications to signal and information processing. IEEE Signal Process. Mag. 45–54 (2011)
4. Langkvist, M., Karlsson, L., Loutfi, A.: Sleep stage classification using unsupervised feature learning. Adv. Artif. Neural Syst. 1–9 (2012)
5. Yuste, R.: From the neuron doctrine to neural networks. Nat. Rev. Neurosci. **16**(8), 487–497 (2015)
6. Rubinov, M.: Neural networks in the future of neuroscience research. Nat. Rev. Neurosci. **16**(12), 767 (2015)
7. Yamins, D., DiCarlo, J.J.: Using goal-driven deep learning models to understand sensory cortex. Nat. Neurosci. **19**(3), 356–365 (2016)
8. Jankovic, J.: Parkinson's disease: clinical features and diagnosis. J. Neurol. Neurosurg. Psychiatry **79**(4), 368–376 (2008)
9. Chaudhuri, K., Schapira, A.: Non-motor symptoms of Parkinson's disease: dopaminergic pathophysiology and treatment. Lancet Neurol. **8**(5), 464–474 (2009)
10. Okun, M.: Deep-brain stimulation for Parkinson's disease. New Engl. J. Med. **367**(16), 1529–1538 (2012)
11. Galvan, A., Devergnas, A., Wichmann, T.: Alterations in neuronal activity in basal ganglia-thalamocortical circuits in the parkinsonian state. Front. Neuroanat. **9**(5), 1–21 (2015)
12. Shin-Yuan, C., Sheng-Huang, L., Shinn-Zong, L.: Subthalamic nucleus deep brain stimulation for Parkinson's disease – an update review. Tzu Chi Med. J. **17**(4), 205–212 (2005)

13. Pollo, C., Vingerhoets, F., Pralong, E., Ghika, J., Maeder, P., Meuli, R., Thiran, J., Villemure, J.: Localization of electrodes in the subthalamic nucleus on magnetic resonance imaging. J. Neurosurg. **106**, 36–44 (2007)
14. Guillén, P., Martínez-de-Pisón, F., Sánchez, R., Argaez, M., Velásquez, L.: Characterization of subcortical structures during deep brain stimulation utilizing support vector machines. In: 33rd Annual International Conference of the IEEE Engineering in Medicine and Biology Society (EMBC 2011), Conference Proceedings, Boston, MA, USA (2011)
15. Guillén, P., Barrera, J., Martínez-de-Pisón, F., Argaez, M., Velásquez, L.: Data mining in the process of localization and classification of subcorticals structures. In: EATIS, Conference Proceedings, Valencia, España (2012)
16. Aiello, S., Click, C., Roark, H., Rehak, L.: Machine Learning with Python and H20. H20, Gravesend (2016). Edited by Lanford, J.

Computational Simulation of the Hemodynamic Behavior of a Blood Vessel Network

Nathan Weinstein[1], Alejandro Aviles[1,2,3], Isidoro Gitler[1],
and Jaime Klapp[1,2(✉)]

[1] ABACUS-Laboratorio de Matemática Aplicada y Cómputo de Alto Rendimiento,
Departamento de Matemáticas, Centro de Investigación y de Estudios Avanzados
CINVESTAV-IPN, Carretera México-Toluca Km 38.5, La Marquesa,
52740 Ocoyoacac, Estado de México, Mexico
jaime.klapp@inin.gob.mx
[2] Departamento de Física, Instituto Nacional de Investigaciones Nucleares (ININ),
Carretera México-Toluca S/N, La Marquesa, 52750 Ocoyoacac,
Estado de México, Mexico
[3] Consejo Nacional de Ciencia y Tecnología, Av. Insurgentes Sur 1582,
Ciudad de México, Mexico

Abstract. During development, blood vessel networks adapt to gradual changes in the oxygen required by surrounding tissue, shear stress, and mechanical stretch. The possible adaptations include remodeling the vessel network and thickening the walls of blood vessels. However, the treatment of several vascular diseases including cerebral arteriovenous malformations, arteriosclerosis, aneurysms, and vascular retinal disorders, may lead to abrupt changes that could produce hemorrhage or other problems. Modeling the hemodynamic behavior of a blood vessel network may help assess or even diminish the risks associated with each treatment. In this work, we briefly describe the radiological studies available to study the anatomy and hemodynamics of a patient. We then describe the segmentation, smoothing, healing, skeletonyzation, and meshing processes that are needed to obtain an initial model for the numerical simulations. Additionally, we state some important concepts about blood rheology and blood vessel elasticity. Further, we include a system of equations to describe the interaction between flowing blood and the elastic blood vessels.

1 Introduction

The circulatory system allows the existence of large multicellular organisms, by actively transporting oxygen, nutrients and the cellular and molecular components of the immune system [1]. During development, the vascular network must adapt to the changing requirements of the body. At least three processes allow the vascular network to adapt: vasculogenesis, angiogenesis [2] and arteriogenesis [3]. Vascular network adaptation depends on the coordinated response of several signaling pathways [4]. Genetic, epigenetic or developmental changes may lead to vascular disease or oncogenesis. Surgical treatment of several vascular diseases may lead to abrupt changes which may result in hemorrhage or other problems.

© Springer International Publishing AG 2017
C.J. Barrios Hernández et al. (Eds.): CARLA 2016, CCIS 697, pp. 279–288, 2017.
DOI: 10.1007/978-3-319-57972-6_21

Hemodynamic models may help assess and minimize the risks associated with several vascular diseases and their treatment, including: aneurysms [5], atherosclerosis [6,7], vascular retinal disorders [8,9] and arteriovenous malformations [10–12]. Hemodynamic modeling is also helpful in understanding cancer treatment [13]. Additionally, studying the interaction between shear stress, mechanosensors and molecular signaling pathways may enable us to understand the development of the circulatory system during embriogenesis [14] and during the aging process [15,16].

Modeling the hemodynamic behavior of a blood vessel network is a complex, multistep process. In this work, we describe our approach, in particular we aim to include a careful mathematical description of the topology of the blood vessel network, blood rheology and blood vessel elasticity.

2   Creating a Model of a Blood Vessel Network

Obtaining a detailed geometrical model of a part of the circulatory system of a patient, is a complex multistage process that transforms certain relevant medical

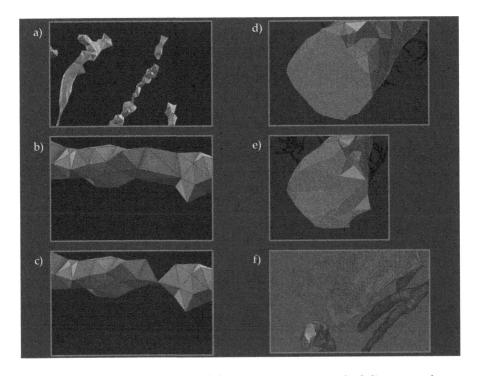

Fig. 1. The mesh healing process: *(a)* Connection or removal of disconnected components, *(b)* Segment of an artery after removing a non manifold, *(c)* Segment of an artery with a non-manifold, in this case a cross section with no area, *(d)* Cross section of an artery, used as a boundary of the model after flattening, *(e)* Boundary artery cross section before flattening, and *(f)* Cross section of an artery after the meshing process.

images into a curated 3D surface or volumetric mesh that can be used as the base geometry to simulate the hemodynamic behavior of the blood vessel network. In Fig. 1 we show screen shots of the mesh healing process that we carried out using the program Blender to process the brain arterial network surface mesh from the MIDA atlas [17], and in Fig. 2 we show a screen shot of the resulting initial model. The most common methods used to obtain medical vascular images are: Computed Tomography Angiography (CTA) [18], Magnetic Resonance Angiography (MRA) [19], and Digital Subtraction Angiography (DSA) [20,21].

Segmentation of medical images requires two main processes: vessel surface extraction and vessel surface construction. The former involves dividing a volume containing the vascular network into voxels, and identifying all the voxels that conform the blood vessels; while the latter defines a 3D surface that forms the boundary of the blood vessel network. The VMTK [22], and MITK [23] publicly available C++ frameworks contain many tools that allow segmentation. Current segmentation techniques produce surface meshes that require non-manifold removal (Fig. 1b and c), connecting dangling segments (Fig. 1a), flattening boundary regions (Fig. 1d and e) filling holes, surface smoothening, skeletonyzation, circle or ellipse fitting, and other time consuming procedures. Recent advances in automated blood vessel segmentation, may allow in the near

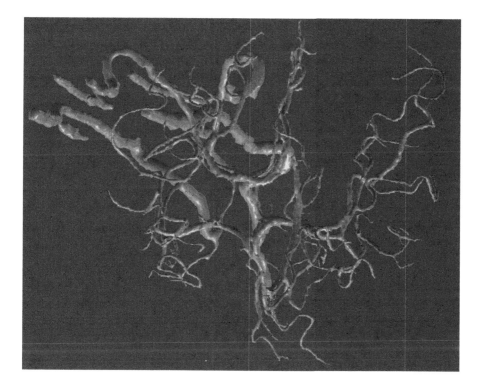

Fig. 2. A screen shot of our model of the brain arteries after processing

future, the reconstruction of patient-specific vascular networks ready for hemo-dynamic simulation in a timely manner [24]. Validating the accuracy of the reconstructed surface is another important challenge for which other techniques have been developed recently [25].

If the model is going to be used to simulate computationally the hemody-namic behavior of the blood vessel network using the finite element numeri-cal integration method, the volume enclosed in the 3D surface mesh needs to be divided into smaller sub-domains, made up of geometric primitives such as hexahedra and tetrahedra (Fig. 1f). Unstructured mesh generation is usu-ally achieved using the Advancing Front technique (AFT), Octree methods, and Voronoi Delaunay based methods [26]. Meshes composed entirely of hexahedra usually allow higher efficiency and robustness during a computational hemo-dynamic simulation, for which some interesting algorithms have been recently developed [27,28].

3   Simulating the Hemodynamic Behavior of a Blood Vessel Network

3.1   Blood Rheology

Blood is composed of plasma, red blood cells, leukocytes, and platelets. In order for blood flow to commence, it is necessary to apply stress surpassing a certain threshold. This critical stress is referred to as the yield stress of blood, if less than the yield stress is applied to a blood film, the response will be elastic. The viscosity of blood is mainly affected by the erythrocyte volume fraction. However, erythrocyte deformability, leukocyte and platelet count, temperature, glucose concentration, pH, and other factors also affect blood viscosity. Blood exhibits shear thinning, in part because erythrocytes are able to form aggregate structures called rouleaux, which are formed at sufficiently small shear rates. As the shear rate increases, the rouleaux structures break up into increasingly smaller pieces. At sufficiently high shear rates, the erythrocytes are fully dispersed [29].

Blood cells cause two interesting effects on capillary blood flow [30]. First, when blood flows into a capillary from a vessel with a larger diameter, the average hematocrit of the capillary blood is smaller than that of the blood flowing through the larger blood vessel. This is referred to as the Fåhrus effect, and it strengthens as the diameter of the capillary decreases [31,32].

Blood cells move towards the center of the vessel, leaving plasma at the wall of the vessel and decreasing the viscosity of blood. The effect strengthens as the diameter of the tube decreases (only if the vessel diameter is between 10 and 300 μm). This is called the Fåhrus - Lindqvist effect. [29,30].

The Herschel-Bulkley model is a very convenient model to describe blood because it is possible to include both the yield stress and the shear-thinning behavior of blood [33,34].

The constitutive equation of the Herschel-Bulkley model is:

$$\tau = \tau_0 + k\dot{\gamma}^n, \tag{1}$$

where τ is the shear stress, $\dot{\gamma}$ the shear rate, τ_0 the yield stress, k the consistency index, and n the flow index.

3.2 Blood Vessel Elasticity

Understanding the elasticity of blood vessels is necessary in order to estimate the risk of blood vessel rupture and hemorrhage in different parts of a blood vessel network, and to pinpoint the areas where the highest risk exists. Blood vessels are composed of three main layers separated by two layers of elastic material, the innermost, *tunica intima* is a single layer of endothelial cells, the middle layer, *tunica media* is a layer of muscle cells that is much thicker in arteries than it is in veins of a similar diameter, and the outermost layer, *tunica externa* or *tunica adventitia* is a layer of connective tissue which contains elastin and collagen fibers. Blood vessels react to the usual changes in flow and shear stress by undergoing elastic deformation. Two important characteristics of elastic materials are the elastic modulus and the elastic limit. The elastic modulus is the amount of force per unit area needed to cause a certain amount of deformation. The elastic limit is the stress beyond which permanent deformation of the material will take place. Furthermore, blood vessels are made of non isotropic rubber-like materials, the slope of the stress-strain curve increases with stress, meaning that they become progressively more difficult to stretch, such that the elastic modulus increases with applied force [35].

4   Blood Fluid-Vessel Wall Interactions

In this section we shall consider regions in which the blood behaves as a fluid. Under this assumption, its evolution can be described by the continuity and Euler equations

$$\frac{\partial \rho}{\partial t}(\mathbf{x}, t) + \nabla_i(\rho v^i) \quad = 0, \tag{2}$$

$$\rho \frac{\partial v^i}{\partial t}(\mathbf{x}, t) + \rho(v^j - w^j)\nabla_j v^i = \nabla_j T^{ij}, \tag{3}$$

where sum over repeated indexes is implicit. Here ρ is the mass density of the blood fluid, $\mathbf{v}$ its velocity field, and the stress tensor $\mathbf{T}$ is composed of two terms: the isotropic fluid pressure P and the Cauchy stress tensor, for which we use the constitutive equation

$$T^{ij} = P\delta^{ij} + \mu \left(\nabla^i v^j + \nabla^j v^i \right), \tag{4}$$

providing the blood fluid with shear, and possibly bulk, viscosity. In Newtonian fluids one assumes a constant shear viscosity coefficient. The further assumption of incompressible fluids leads to $\nabla \cdot \mathbf{v} = 0$, instead of Eq. (2). The set of Eqs. (2), (3) and (4) are the well-known Navier-Stokes equations.

   We note that the total time derivative in Euler equation further introduces an arbitrary velocity $\mathbf{w}$. This scheme is essentially a choice of reference frame, and is generically referred as an Arbitrary Lagrangian Eulerian (ALE) method. In situations as the one we are concerned, it is very useful to let $\mathbf{w}$ be the velocity of the blood vessel at the interface, such that the boundary conditions are easily defined as we shall do below.

Vessel walls are usually modeled as elastic materials with linear response. Several options exist in the literature, here we follow an approach similar to the one developed in [36,37]. In Fig. 3 we show the geometry of a small section of the vessel network. We consider local cylindrical coordinates along the main axis $\hat{\mathbf{z}}$ of the vessel. When the vessel is relaxed, the radius at fixed z and angle θ coordinates is denoted by R_0. This radius is deformed to R as the evolution takes place. We are interested in an equation for the deformation

$$\eta(z,\theta,t) \equiv R(z,\theta,t) - R_0(z,\theta).$$ (5)

Since R_0 depends on the vessel configuration only, it is an input for the problem and does not enter into the equations as a dynamical variable. The thickness of the vessel h_0 is neglected, such that we are considering it as a two dimensional surface with unit normal vector $\hat{\mathbf{n}}(z,\theta,t)$. As described above, we demand its velocity to be

$$\mathbf{w} = \frac{\partial \eta}{\partial t} \hat{\mathbf{R}}.$$ (6)

The fluid exerts a force per unit area upon the vessel given by $\mathbf{T} \cdot \hat{\mathbf{n}}$, and possibly additional external forces. Then, for a wave-like behavior, the simplest choice is

$$\frac{\partial^2 \eta}{\partial t^2}(z,\theta,t) + b\frac{\partial \eta}{\partial t} + c\eta = H,$$ (7)

where b and c are positive constants linked to the elastic properties of the vessel, as the Young's and elasticity moduli. The first derivative should appear because of the observational fact that given a small deformation to the vessel, the system is relaxed to its original configuration after a short time period, thus b acts as a damping restoring coefficient. Actually, this elastic relaxation time is small compared to the evolution characteristic time of the system, thus the coefficient b should be large enough. If we decide to simply neglect all other terms depending on η we obtain the standard equations of a linear elastic media.

The term H is the total force per unit mass along the $\hat{R}$ direction, and it is composed by the stress and pressure forces exerted by the blood and the external pressure force, such that the balance gives

$$H = \frac{1}{\rho_v}\left[\nabla^j(P - P_{\text{ext}}) + \mu\nabla_i(\nabla^i v^j + \nabla^j v^i)\right]\hat{n}_j,$$ (8)

where ρ_v is the mass density of the vessel wall. Since there is also a tension along the z direction, we have to add constitutive dynamic terms to Eq. (7). This is easily done by considering a second order derivative along z. Furthermore, we should note that the angular symmetry considered so far leads to numerical instabilities—for example, a localized small deformation is instantaneously reflected along a whole constant z ring. Thus, our final equation is

$$\frac{\partial^2 \eta}{\partial t^2}(z,\theta,t) - a_z \frac{\partial^2 \eta}{\partial z^2} - a_\theta \frac{\partial}{\partial \theta}\left(\frac{\partial \eta}{\partial \theta} + c_\theta \eta\right) + b\frac{\partial \eta}{\partial t} + c\eta = H, \qquad (9)$$

where the coefficients are also a_θ, c_θ and a_z are linked to the viscoelasticity properties of the vessel blood.

The equations for the whole system are (2), (3), (4), (8), and (9) subjected to appropriate boundary conditions given below. Note that the interaction among the vessel and the blood is given by the force H only, although it appears in the equations also through $\mathbf{w}$ because of the choice of the reference frame in the ALE formalism.

4.1 Boundary Conditions

We use Dirichlet boundary conditions for the Γ^W region (See Fig. 3) by putting $\mathbf{v} = \mathbf{w}$. This means that at the interface of the fluid with the structure, the velocity of the fluid relative to the velocity of the structure at each point is zero. We also use Dirichlet for Γ^{in} by defining which is the input velocity. This cannot be obtained for the problem itself, one should use it as an input or include in the model the entire circulatory system.

For the region Γ^{out} we use Neumann boundary conditions. Specifically, we set $\mathbf{T} \cdot \mathbf{n} = 0$, with $\mathbf{n}$ the unit normal vector to the boundary. This means that the force over a particle at the boundary due to stresses in the output direction is zero. It is a reasonable assumption because (1) the viscous forces only act perpendicular to the motion; and (2) the pressure in the immediate left part of the boundary is equal to the pressure on the immediate right part of the boundary, which should be the case because the boundary Γ^{out} is fictitious.

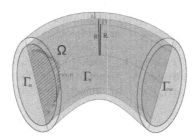

Fig. 3. Section of a blood vessel: Ω is the interior and it is the region in which the fluid flows, Γ^W is where the area in contact with the elastic blood vessel and it is a piece of the boundary of Ω, the thickness of the blood vessel is h_0. The other pieces are the boundaries Γ^{in} and Γ^{out}, which are fictitious and chosen only for numerical purposes. It is important to note that η is the deformation vector of the structure, and it depends on the spatial and time coordinates.

5   Conclusion

Simulating the hemodynamic and elastic behavior of a patient-specific model of a vascular network is a multidisciplinary task. One of the greatest challenges is to build a model and analyze it sufficiently fast to help vascular surgeons. Having an initial, general model of a human circulatory network that can be adapted to represent a patient-specific vascular network and developing the right high performance computing tools is an important part of the solution. However, vascular networks are biological systems that change continuously and allow the circulatory system to adapt to changing demands. Formation of new blood vessels (vasculogenesis), capillary network remodeling (angiogenesis) and increasing the diameter of blood vessels (arteriogenesis) are the main biological processes that allow blood vessel networks to adapt. The molecular regulatory network involved in the control of vascular adaptation interacts with shear stress and circumferential stress through several different mechanoreceptors. Understanding vascular remodeling will allow us to simulate not only what happens during a vascular surgery but also during the recovery process until hopefully homeostasis is reached. This is especially important when treating congenital diseases such as arteriovenous malformations [38].

Acknowledgements. This work was supported by ABACUS, CONACyT grant EDOMEX-2011-C01-165873. The numerical simulations for this work were performed in the Abacus I supercomputer.

References

1. Monahan-Earley, R., Dvorak, A., Aird, W.: Evolutionary origins of the blood vascular system and endothelium. J. Thromb. Haemost. **11**(s1), 46–66 (2013)
2. Kässmeyer, S., Plendl, J., Custodis, P., Bahramsoltani, M.: New insights in vascular development: vasculogenesis and endothelial progenitor cells. Anat. Histol. Embryol. **38**(1), 1–11 (2009)
3. Chillo, O., Kleinert, E.C., Lautz, T., Lasch, M., Pagel, J.-I., Heun, Y., Troidl, K., Fischer, S., Caballero-Martinez, A., Mauer, A., et al.: Perivascular mast cells govern shear stress-induced arteriogenesis by orchestrating leukocyte function. Cell Rep. **16**(8), 2197–2207 (2016)
4. Simons, M., Gordon, E., Claesson-Welsh, L.: Mechanisms and regulation of endothelial VEGF receptor signalling. Nat. Rev. Mol. Cell Biol. **17**(10), 611–625 (2016)
5. Voß, S., Glaßer, S., Hoffmann, T., Beuing, O., Weigand, S., Jachau, K., Preim, B., Thévenin, D., Janiga, G., Berg, P.: Fluid-structure simulations of a ruptured intracranial aneurysm: constant versus patient-specific wall thickness. Comput. Math. Methods Med. **2016**, 1–8 (2016). Article ID 9854539
6. Brown, A.J., Teng, Z., Evans, P.C., Gillard, J.H., Samady, H., Bennett, M.R.: Role of biomechanical forces in the natural history of coronary atherosclerosis. Nat. Rev. Cardiol. **13**(4), 210–220 (2016)
7. Morbiducci, U., Kok, A.M., Kwak, B.R., Stone, P.H., Steinman, D.A., Wentzel, J.J., et al.: Atherosclerosis at arterial bifurcations: evidence for the role of haemodynamics and geometry. Thromb. Haemost. **115**(3), 484–492 (2016)

8. Gelfand, B.D., Ambati, J.: A revised hemodynamic theory of age-related macular degeneration. Trends Mol. Med. **22**(8), 656–670 (2016)
9. Causin, P., Guidoboni, G., Malgaroli, F., Sacco, R., Harris, A.: Blood flow mechanics and oxygen transport and delivery in the retinal microcirculation: multiscale mathematical modeling and numerical simulation. Biomech. Model. Mechanobiol. **15**(3), 525–542 (2016)
10. White, A., Smith, F.: Computational modelling of the embolization process for the treatment of arteriovenous malformations (AVMs). Math. Comput. Model. **57**(5), 1312–1324 (2013)
11. Busch, K.J., Kiat, H., Stephen, M., Simons, M., Avolio, A., Morgan, M.K.: Cerebral hemodynamics and the role of transcranial doppler applications in the assessment and management of cerebral arteriovenous malformations. J. Clin. Neurosci. **30**, 24–30 (2016)
12. Golovin, S., Khe, A., Gadylshina, K.: Hydraulic model of cerebral arteriovenous malformations. J. Fluid Mech. **797**, 110–129 (2016)
13. Penta, R., Ambrosi, D., Quarteroni, A.: Multiscale homogenization for fluid and drug transport in vascularized malignant tissues. Math. Models Methods Appl. Sci. **25**(01), 79–108 (2015)
14. Chen, Q., Jiang, L., Li, C., Hu, D., Bu, J.-W., Cai, D., Du, J.-L.: Haemodynamics-driven developmental pruning of brain vasculature in zebrafish. PLoS Biol. **10**(8), e1001374 (2012)
15. Humphrey, J.D., Harrison, D.G., Figueroa, C.A., Lacolley, P., Laurent, S.: Central artery stiffness in hypertension and aging a problem with cause and consequence. Circ. Res. **118**(3), 379–381 (2016)
16. Yu, H., Huang, G.P., Yang, Z., Liang, F., Ludwig, B.: The influence of normal and early vascular aging on hemodynamic characteristics in cardio-and cerebrovascular systems. J. Biomech. Eng. **138**(6), 061002 (2016)
17. Iacono, M.I., Neufeld, E., Akinnagbe, E., Bower, K., Wolf, J., Oikonomidis, I.V., Sharma, D., Lloyd, B., Wilm, B.J., Wyss, M., et al.: MIDA: a multimodal imaging-based detailed anatomical model of the human head and neck. PLoS ONE **10**(4), e0124126 (2015)
18. Fujiwara, H., Momoshima, S., Akiyama, T., Kuribayashi, S.: Whole-brain CT digital subtraction angiography of cerebral dural arteriovenous fistula using 320-detector row CT. Neuroradiology **55**(7), 837–843 (2013)
19. Wright, S.N., Kochunov, P., Mut, F., Bergamino, M., Brown, K.M., Mazziotta, J.C., Toga, A.W., Cebral, J.R., Ascoli, G.A.: Digital reconstruction and morphometric analysis of human brain arterial vasculature from magnetic resonance angiography. Neuroimage **82**, 170–181 (2013)
20. Davis, B., Oberstar, E., Royalty, K., Schafer, S., Strother, C., Mistretta, C.: Volumetric limiting spatial resolution analysis of four dimensional digital subtraction angiography (4D-DSA). In: SPIE Medical Imaging, pp. 94121B–94121B. International Society for Optics and Photonics (2015)
21. Lescher, S., Gehrisch, S., Klein, S., Berkefeld, J.: Time-resolved 3D rotational angiography: display of detailed neurovascular anatomy in patients with intracranial vascular malformations. J. NeuroInterv. Surg., 1–8 (2016). neurintsurg-2016
22. Antiga, L., Piccinelli, M., Botti, L., Ene-Iordache, B., Remuzzi, A., Steinman, D.A.: An image-based modeling framework for patient-specific computational hemodynamics. Med. Biol. Eng. Comput. **46**(11), 1097–1112 (2008)

23. Nolden, M., Zelzer, S., Seitel, A., Wald, D., Müller, M., Franz, A.M., Maleike, D., Fangerau, M., Baumhauer, M., Maier-Hein, L., et al.: The medical imaging interaction toolkit: challenges and advances. Int. J. Comput. Assist. Radiol. Surg. **8**(4), 607–620 (2013)

24. Hsu, C.-Y., Schneller, B., Alaraj, A., Flannery, M., Zhou, X.J., Linninger, A.: Automatic recognition of subject-specific cerebrovascular trees. Magn. Reson. Med. **77**, 398–410 (2016)

25. Klepaczko, A., Szczypiński, P., Deistung, A., Reichenbach, J.R., Materka, A.: Simulation of MR angiography imaging for validation of cerebral arteries segmentation algorithms. Comput. Methods Programs Biomed. **137**, 293–309 (2016)

26. Du, Q., Wang, D.: Tetrahedral mesh generation and optimization based on centroidal voronoi tessellations. Int. J. Numer. Methods Eng. **56**(9), 1355–1373 (2003)

27. Li, Y., Liu, Y., Xu, W., Wang, W., Guo, B.: All-hex meshing using singularity-restricted field. ACM Trans. Graph. (TOG) **31**(6), 177 (2012)

28. Hu, K., Zhang, Y.J.: Centroidal voronoi tessellation based polycube construction for adaptive all-hexahedral mesh generation. Comput. Methods Appl. Mech. Eng. **305**, 405–421 (2016)

29. Fedosov, D.A., Noguchi, H., Gompper, G.: Multiscale modeling of blood flow: from single cells to blood rheology. Biomech. Model. Mechanobiol. **13**(2), 239–258 (2014)

30. Rai, V., Rathore, D.S.: Analysis of viscosity of non-newtonian flow in blood vessels. Int. J. Res. Comput. Eng. Electron. **3**(6), 1–6 (2015)

31. Barbee, J.H., Cokelet, G.R.: The fahraeus effect. Microvasc. Res. **3**(1), 6–16 (1971)

32. Albrecht, K., Gaehtgens, P., Pries, A., Heuser, M.: The fahraeus effect in narrow capillaries (id 3.3 to 11.0 μm). Microvasc. Res. **18**(1), 33–47 (1979)

33. Sankar, D., Hemalatha, K.: Pulsatile flow of Herschel-Bulkley fluid through catheterized arteries-a mathematical model. Appl. Math. Model. **31**(8), 1497–1517 (2007)

34. Priyadharshini, S., Ponalagusamy, R.: Biorheological model on flow of herschel-bulkley fluid through a tapered arterial stenosis with dilatation. Appl. Bionics Biomech. **2015**, 1–12 (2015). Article ID 406195

35. Zheng, X., Ren, J.: Effects of the three-dimensional residual stresses on the mechanical properties of arterial walls. J. Theor. Biol. **393**, 118–126 (2016)

36. Crosetto, P., Reymond, P., Deparis, S., Kontaxakis, D., Stergiopulos, N., Quarteroni, A.: Fluid-structure interaction simulation of aortic blood flow. Comput. Fluids **43**(1), 46–57 (2011)

37. Tricerri, P., Dedè, L., Deparis, S., Quarteroni, A., Robertson, A.M., Sequeira, A.: Fluid-structure interaction simulations of cerebral arteries modeled by isotropic and anisotropic constitutive laws. Comput. Mech. **55**(3), 479–498 (2015)

38. Buell, T.J., Ding, D., Starke, R.M., Crowley, R.W., Liu, K.C.: Embolization-induced angiogenesis in cerebral arteriovenous malformations. J. Clin. Neurosci. **21**(11), 1866–1871 (2014)

Scaling Properties of Soft Matter in Equilibrium and Under Stationary Flow

Armando Gama Goicochea[✉]

División de Ingeniería Química y Bioquímica, Tecnológico de Estudios
Superiores de Ecatepec, Av. Tecnológico s/n, 55210 Ecatepec
Estado de México, Mexico
agama@alumni.stanford.edu

Abstract. A brief review is presented of the scaling of complex fluids, polymers and polyelectrolytes in solution and in confined geometry, in thermodynamical, structural and rheology properties using equilibrium and non-equilibrium dissipative particle dynamics simulations. All simulations were carried out on high performance computational facilities using parallelized algorithms, solved on computers using both central and graphical processing units. The scaling approach is shown to be a unifying axis around which general trends and basic knowledge can be gained, illustrated through a series of case studies.

Keywords: Scaling · Polymers · Polyelectrolytes · Radius of gyration · Couette flow · Viscosity · Friction coefficient

1 Introduction

Scaling is one of the most cherished concepts in physics and its applications to soft matter have been as successful as in other areas of physics. At the heart of it is the idea that if a system is self-similar and it is not under the influence of long range interactions, then it should display properties whose general behavior is invariant under scale transformations. A superb account of it is de Gennes's treatise [1], where he uses simple concepts to arrive at profound and general scaling laws for polymers under various circumstances. This could be accomplished in part because of the advanced state of the experimental efforts to understand the nature of complex fluids. Searching for scaling is important also from a practical perspective, because quantitative predictions can be made about systems of vastly different chemical composition.

A few decades ago, there were also fundamental theoretical developments, such as the renormalization group [2] and fractal geometry [3], which led to a robust understanding of scaling, particularly in physics. At the time Ref. [1] was written, molecular simulation was still a novel tool and there were only a few works focused on testing scaling laws. The advent of modern computers, with fast processors, efficient architecture and optimum algorithms have made of molecular simulation an indispensable research tool, one that has become commonplace both in academia and in the productive sector [4].

C.J. Barrios Hernández et al. (Eds.): CARLA 2016, CCIS 697, pp. 289–313, 2017.
DOI: 10.1007/978-3-319-57972-6_22

When testing scaling laws using molecular simulation, one faces the challenge of reducing finite size effects that could potentially mask the underlying scaling phenomena. Doing so means performing numerical simulations on systems of increasing size, such that the phenomenon under study can be traced over considerable changes of scale, which in turn requires longer simulation time. If one uses atomistically detailed models [5], this task quickly becomes prohibitive or impractical due to the relatively long range of basic interaction models such as the Lennard-Jones potential. Since all simulations are of finite size, one must cut the range of the interactions using some criterion, which may lead to artifacts unless large systems are considered [5].

In addition to the so-called long range corrections employed when the interactions are long-ranged [5], there is also a systematic approach that helps simulate large systems using moderately sized simulation boxes. Such approach, generally termed "coarse-grained" models [6], typically consists of integrating out some degrees of freedom, yielding effective interactions that can be thought of as potentials of mean force rather than basic interactions. What one loses in atomic-scale detail is gained in mesoscopic-scale information and in savings in computational time. Among the most successful and popular coarse-grained methods is the one known as dissipative particle dynamics [7] (DPD), introduced originally to study the rheology of colloidal suspensions. Once its statistical mechanics foundations were correctly laid out [8], the potential and versatility of DPD was quickly recognized and it became widely applied to model systems as diverse a proteins [9], surfactants and polymers in solution [10], biological membranes [11], paints [12] and even to phenomena such as thrombosis [13]. The DPD model is now well known among practitioners of numerical simulation; there are various reviews available that detail its foundations and some of its most successful applications [14–16]. Therefore, for the sake of brevity, only what is pertinent shall be presented here; the reader is referred to the cited reviews for additional details.

In this work revisit some of the recent work carried out by our group on scaling properties of soft matter systems such as polymers in solution and under confinement, polymer brushes and polyelectrolytes in equilibrium and under stationary flow, using DPD. In Sect. 2 the essentials of the DPD model are presented briefly, followed in Sect. 3 by the scaling of the interfacial tension in mixtures of organic liquids and water. Section 4 is devoted to the scaling of polyelectrolytes under different solvent conditions, while Sect. 5 focuses on various scaling features of polymer brushes. Results on the scaling of polymer brushes under flow can be found in Sect. 6. In Sect. 7 the scaling of polymers in two dimensions are revisited. The conclusions are laid out in Sect. 8. Emphasis is placed on the discussion of physical ideas; for simulation details and additional information the reader is referred to the original articles.

2   Models and Methods

The DPD model is based on the integration of the internal degrees of freedom of groups of atoms used to construct the DPD particles or beads whose motion is solved through the integration of Newton's second law of motion, following an algorithm that is essentially the same as the one used in atomistic simulations [5]. The conservative interaction between DPD particles is a linearly decaying, short range force:

$$\mathbf{F}_{ij}^C = \begin{cases} a_{ij}(1 - r_{ij})\hat{\mathbf{r}}_{ij} & r_{ij} \leq r_c \\ 0 & r_{ij} > r_c \end{cases}, \qquad (1)$$

where a_{ij} is a strength of the interaction, which determines the thermodynamics of the system, and r_C is the cutoff distance that sets the length scale of the interactions. Notice that the force remains finite even when the centers of mass of two interacting particles overlap, meaning that DPD particles can in principle occupy the same space at the same time. However, this does not occur in practice because the interaction strength a_{ij} is at least $25\,k_B T / r_C$ or larger, therefore there is a very large energy cost involved in the full overlap of DPD particles. This was not originally recognized when electrostatic interactions were introduced into the DPD model [17], as it was believed that the soft nature of the DPD beads containing charges would lead to the formation of ionic pairs of infinite electrostatic energy, which is of course unphysical. In Sect. 4 I show this is not really a problem, and point charges can in fact be used in DPD leading to correct and artifact-free conclusions.

The short range nature of the force in Eq. (1) is the key to the mesoscopic reach of DPD and its capability of produce simulations with observation times of the order of tens of microseconds, setting it at least three orders of magnitude apart from its all – atom counterparts [4]. It is also the reason why one can do away with long range corrections and why finite size effects in DPD are minimal [18]. Yet, what is perhaps more advantageous is the DPD thermostat: the local viscosity of the fluid is modeled as a dissipative force, whose energy dissipation is invested into local Brownian motion, modeled by a random force. As is customary when these types of forces are present, one must make sure that the fluctuation-dissipation theorem is obeyed; doing so in DPD leads to a relation between the strengths of the dissipative (γ) and random (σ) forces given by $k_B T = \frac{\sigma^2}{2\gamma}$, which sets up the thermostat [8]. All forces are pairwise additive, leading to global momentum conservation. The conservative $\left(\mathbf{F}^C\right)$, dissipative $\left(\mathbf{F}^D\right)$, and random $\left(\mathbf{F}^R\right)$ forces acting between any two particles i and j, placed a distance r_{ij} apart must be integrated in finite time steps to yield the momenta and positions of all particles:

$$\dot{\mathbf{p}}_i = \sum_{j \neq i} \mathbf{F}_{ij}^C + \sum_{j \neq i} \mathbf{F}_{ij}^D + \sum_{j \neq i} \mathbf{F}_{ij}^R. \qquad (2)$$

All forces between particles i and j are zero beyond a finite cutoff radius r_c, which is usually also chosen as $r_c \equiv 1$. The natural probability distribution function of the DPD model is found to be that of the canonical ensemble [8], where N (the total particle number), V, and T are kept constant, although it is equally possible to solve the system using a Monte Carlo algorithm [4] under various ensembles of interest [18–20]. Polymer chains can be constructed following the Murat-Grest bead-spring linear chain model [21], while surfaces can either be introduced using effective force fields [19, 22] or by freezing layers of particles [23]. The chemical composition of the DPD particles is incorporated into the value chosen for the conservative interaction strength, a_{ij}, see

Eq. (1), usually obtained from the Flory-Huggins solution theory [24]. Full details and several applications of DPD can be consulted in recently published reviews [14–16].

3 Interfacial Tension Scaling

The pioneering work of Widom and collaborators [25, 26] established that the interfacial tension between two liquids at finite temperature, $\sigma(T)$, could be expressed as

$$\sigma(T) = \sigma_0 \left(1 - \frac{T}{T_C} \right)^{\mu},$$ (3)

where T_C is the critical temperature at which the interface becomes unstable, σ_0 is a system-dependent constant, and μ is the scaling exponent, whose currently accepted value is $\mu = 1.26$ [27]. On the other hand, the correlation length of the phases, ξ, ignoring logarithm corrections, can be written as

$$\xi(T) = \xi_0 \left(1 - \frac{T}{T_C} \right)^{-\nu},$$ (4)

where ξ_0 is also system depending and ν is the scaling exponent. Its value for the three – dimensional Ising model is $\nu = 0.63$ [28]. The energy of the liquid mixture, $k_B T$, can be expressed as the product of the interfacial tension times the area defined by the correlation length, which is generalized in d dimensions as ξ^{d-1}; mathematically, $k_B T \sim \sigma(T) \xi^{d-1}$. As the system approaches its critical point $k_B T \to k_B T_C$, which must be temperature-independent; combining then Eqs. (3) and (4) yields the following hyperscaling relationship between the scaling exponents in those equations [26]:

$$\mu = (d - 1)\nu.$$ (5)

To test Eq. (5) one must first device a model to introduce the temperature dependence into the DPD framework. The first work to accomplish that is due to Mayoral and Gama Goicochea [29], where temperature changes are introduced through the temperature dependence of the conservative interaction strength, a_{ij}, see Eq. (1). The dependence of a_{ij} on temperature is in turn obtained from the dependence of the Flory-Huggins parameter on temperature by means of the solubility parameters. Equation (5) was tested in 3D for mixtures of organic solvents (dodecane, benzene and hexanol) and water using this procedure, at several temperatures [30]. The results for the interfacial tension as a function of reduced temperature are shown in Fig. 1, along with the best fit to the scaling function given by Eq. (3). First, it is reassuring to find that the predictions of the DPD simulations for the interfacial tension collapse on a single curve despite the different chemical composition of the systems, i.e., there is scaling. Secondly, the scaling exponent obtained from the simulations is $\mu = 1.2$, which is close to the universality accepted value for 3D liquids, $\mu = 1.26$.

The natural correlation length in these mixtures can be defined as the thickness of the interface between the immiscible liquids, and by tracing its change with varying

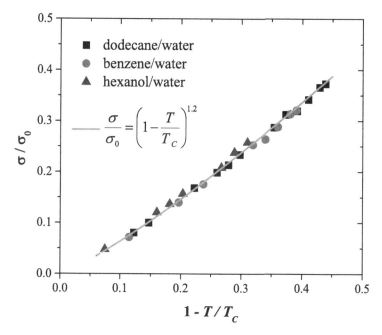

Fig. 1. Normalized interfacial tension as a function of reduced temperature for three mixtures of organic solvents with water. The solid line represents the best fit to Eq. (3), with $\mu = 1.2$. The value of σ_0 is 81.8 for dodecane/water, 71.9 for benzene/water and 57.3 for hexanol/water. Adapted from Ref. [30].

temperature one can compare to the predictions of Eq. (4) [30]. Figure 2 displays the evolution of the correlation length at different temperatures, for the particular case of the mixture of hexanol (red data) and water (blue data). The correlation length is found to grow with increasing temperature, as expected; in fact, it should be infinite when the system reaches the critical temperature, as usual for several critical properties.

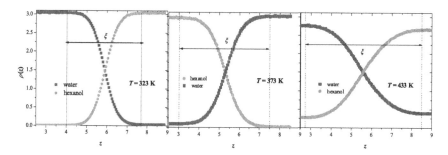

Fig. 2. Concentration profiles of the water/hexanol interface at three different temperatures. The thickness of the interface, labelled as ξ in the panels shown in the figure, is defined as the correlation length of the system, see Eq. (4). Adapted from Ref. [30]. (Color figure online)

Following the same procedure for the mixtures water-benzene and water-dodecane leads to reasonable collapse of all data on a single curve, as seen in Fig. 3. The solid line in Fig. 3 is the fit to Eq. (4), with $v = 0.63$, in agreement with the value expected for the 3D Ising model [28]. The average value for v found from the data shown in Fig. 3 is $v = 0.67$, hence $\mu = 2\xi = 1.34$. The prediction from Eq. (5) for $d = 3$ is $\mu = 2\xi = 1.26$ for the Ising model in 3D, therefore our simulations confirm Widom's hyperscaling relation, Eq. (5), at least for $d = 3$.

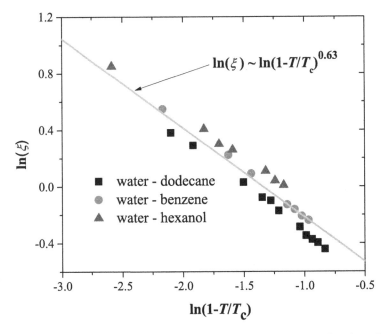

Fig. 3. Correlation length in mixtures of organic solvents with water, as a function of reduced temperature. The solid line is the best fit to Eq. (4), with critical exponent $v = 0.63$; see text for details. Adapted from Ref. [30].

It is important to ask why the interfacial tension of 3D liquids modeled with DPD appears to belong to the 3D Ising universality class [28]. A simple argument can be provided to supply such an interpretation. The Ising model can be equally applied to spin up/spin down sites (its original purpose) as to occupied/empty sites, or equally well to (site occupied by liquid 1)/(site occupied by liquid 2) systems, see illustration in Fig. 4. This is precisely what occurs at the interface between immiscible liquids, as shown by the region where ξ is defined in Fig. 2. In addition to DPD, this equivalence is expected to hold for other interaction models, as long as they are short-ranged, so that next-nearest neighbor interactions can be neglected.

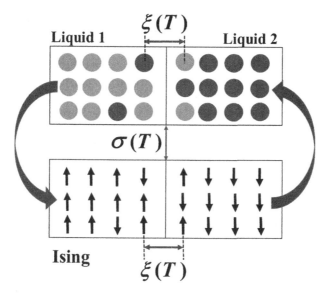

Fig. 4. An illustrative interpretation of the reason why the interfacial tension between liquids predicted by DPD belongs to the 3D Ising universality class. Adapted from the Table of Contents graphic of Ref. [30].

4   Scaling of the Radius of Gyration of Polyelectrolytes

Early work by Flory and others [1] led to the conclusion that the characteristic length of a polymer in solution, its radius of gyration R_g, obeys a scaling law in terms of its polymerization degree, N. Such scaling law is given by

$$R_g = N^v, \tag{6}$$

where v is the scaling exponent. Flory arrived at the conclusion that $v = 3/(d+2)$ using insightful yet simple arguments [1]; this relation is found to hold reasonably well in experiments and simulations, except for $d = 3$, where renormalization group calculations yield the universally accepted value $v = 0.588$ [31]. Following de Gennes's analogy between polymer statistics and critical phenomena [1], an equivalence can be expressed between the proximity of temperature to the critical point (see Eq. (4)), in critical phenomena, and the polymerization degree of large polymers, see Eq. (6):

$$N \sim 1/|1 - T/T_C|. \tag{7}$$

If such analogy holds for the relation between the interfacial tension scaling exponent μ, see Eq. (3), and the scaling exponent of a polymer's radius of gyration v, see Eq. (6), then Eq. (5) in two dimensions (2D) reads simply $\mu = v$. Now, if the correlation length of a mixture of immiscible liquids in 2D follows Ising's universality class in 2D, where $v = 1$ [28], then $\mu = 1$. If, on the other hand, v obeys the scaling expected for the gyration radius of polymers in solution under good – solvent conditions, then

$v = 3/4$, and applying Widom's hyperscaling relation, Eq. (5), one should find that $\mu = 3/4$ also. Research is under way to test these scaling relations and find out which limit applies.

The two leading arguments usually provided to understand scaling properties in polymers are, on the one hand, the self-similar structure of polymers on different scales, and on the other, the absence of long range interactions. The latter is not fulfilled in polyelectrolytes, which are electrically charged polymers. However, experiments [32] and theories [33] have determined that, under special circumstances polyelectrolytes do show scaling characteristics. To help understand recent experiments such as those performed on DNA molecules under changing ionic concentration [34], our group has performed extensive DPD simulations of polyelectrolytes, searching for scaling properties.

Electrostatics in DPD was introduced first in [17] following a simple idea: let every charged particle carry a spatially decaying distribution of charge so that when such distribution is integrated over volume one obtains the full charge carried by the DPD particle. This charge-distribution method was employed to predict the changes in the radius of gyration of a single polyelectrolyte immersed in a theta solvent (all non-electrostatic interactions are equal) while increasing the ionic strength [35]; the results are presented in Fig. 5. For both polyelectrolytes, the short (a) and larger one (b), there appears a minimum in the radius of gyration as the ionic strength is increased, with the minimum being dependent upon N. It is however noteworthy that re-expansion of the polyelectrolyte is found when the ionic strength is increased beyond that where the minimum R_g is obtained, regardless the polymerization degree. This phenomenon, which has been observed in experiments [36] and is confirmed by simulations that use interactions different from those used by DPD [37] has been interpreted as being due to charge inversion clouds around the charged monomers on the polyelectrolyte chain [35].

Solvent quality is found to play a major role in determining the radius of gyration of polyelectrolytes. Although most simulations and analytic theories are developed for good-solvent conditions under the assumption that is the experimentally relevant case, this assumption is increasingly challenged in several industrial application [38]. Therefore, simulations of the relatively short polyelectrolyte ($N = 32$) were performed for the three solvent conditions to determine its gyration radius at increasing ionic strength; the results can be found in Fig. 6. To change solvent quality one needs only modify the strength of the maximum conservative DPD force, see Eq. (1) and the legend in Fig. 6. As expected, the radius of gyration of the polyelectrolyte dissolved in a poor solvent is considerable smaller than in any other case, see black triangles in Fig. 6. The influence of electrostatics is not enough to overcome the short range interactions and full re-expansion of the polyelectrolyte after it has collapse is not observed. By contrast, theta- and good-solvent conditions (circles and squares in Fig. 6, respectively) lead to essentially the same radius of gyration. One important difference is that the contraction–re-expansion phenomenon found in theta-solvent is less pronounced when the polyelectrolyte is under good-solvent conditions, since by its very definition, it is the solvent that leads to the largest possible polyelectrolyte configuration. The reader is referred to [35] for further details and discussion.

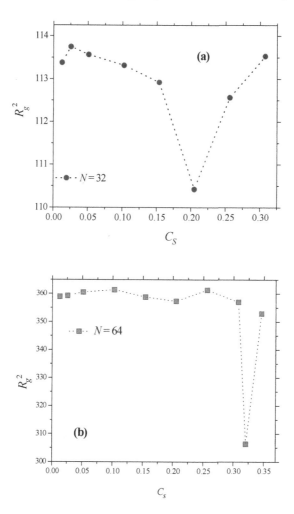

Fig. 5. Radius of gyration for a polyelectrolyte immersed in a theta solvent as a function of the salt (NaCl) concentration of valence (4:1) for (a) polymerization degree $N = 32$, and (b) for $N = 64$. Axes are shown in reduced DPD units; lines are only guides for the eye. Adapted from Ref. [35].

Performing a series of simulations for increasing polymerization degree, it is possible to extract the exponent ν defined in Eq. (6), *if* such scaling exists for polyelectrolytes. What is found is that in fact such scaling *does* exist and the value of the scaling exponent can be larger than it is for neutral polymers [1]. Before attempting to understand why scaling behavior is obtained when long range interactions are present, let us first consider a somewhat alternative approach to incorporate electrostatics to the DPD model. As announced in Sect. 2, here I briefly review very recent work [39] on the use of point charges (rather than charge distributions) in conjunction with Ewald sums, and its application to the prediction of the scaling exponent ν for polyelectrolytes. Let us first recall, see Eq. (1), that DPD particles are "soft", thus they can overlap completely. Since

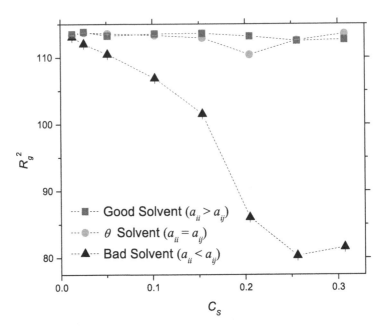

Fig. 6. Radius of gyration for the polyelectrolyte with $N = 32$ as a function of ionic strength, under conditions of different solvent quality. The latter is modified through the conservative DPD interaction strength, see Eq. (1), as indicated in the legend. All quantities are reported in reduced DPD units. Adapted from [35].

the electrostatic interaction blows up when the particles overlap, Groot [17] envisaged a way to prevent this from happening. He argued that using distributions of charge, with an appropriately modified force interaction when particle overlapping began to occur, was sufficient to avoid such artifact. Using distributions of charge means that one must provide a mean to solve Poisson's equation for those distributions, which cannot be accomplished exactly, and some ansatz must be used to calculate the full electrostatic interactions and forces. Although this research program is useful and leads to correct results, it suffers from its need to resort to interpolating formulas to solve Poisson's equations. Our approach [39] begins with the realization that DPD particles are only really soft for the smallest coarse-graining degree, i.e., the grouping of one solvent molecule per DPD particle, which is not as useful as larger coarse-graining degrees to model soft matter at the mesoscopic level. Since increasing the coarse-graining degree is tantamount to "hardening" the DPD particles, which in turn makes full particle overlap improbable, it is then unnecessary to use charge distributions and point charges can instead be used. For these one can use the full machinery of the Ewald sums, without relying on electrostatic potential energy ansatz [5].

To see how good the point-charge approach can be in DPD, Fig. 7 shows a diagram displaying the percentage of ionic pairs formed when the coarse-graining degree (N_m) and point charge strength are increased. The "hardening" of the DPD particle increases if N_m is increased, while increasing the charge requires also of harder DPD particles to avoid the formation of artificial ionic pairs.

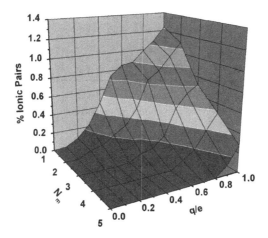

Fig. 7. Three-dimensional diagram for point charges in DPD, illustrating the formation of ionic pairs, as a function of the coarse-graining degree N_m and the value of the point charge q. All simulations were run on GPU's. Adapted from [39].

Using point charges and following a procedure similar to that described in the discussion of Fig. 6, long simulations were carried out for polyelectrolytes of increasing polymerization degree under theta- and good-solvent conditions. The results are shown in Fig. 8, where only the value of the scaling exponent v is reported, for brevity. However, the reader is made aware that each point in Fig. 8 represents a series of simulations for a polyelectrolyte chain of increasing polymerization degree, so that a R_g vs N curve could be generated and the scaling exponent extracted from a linear fit (in a log-log plot). Therefore the need to perform large simulations in relatively short times led us to implement our code so that it could be executed in fast graphical processing units (GPU). The scaling exponent is reported in Fig. 8 as a function of the salt content. The dashed line is the expected value of the scaling exponent for three-dimensional neutral polymers in good solvent, namely $v = 0.588$ [31], while the dot – dashed line is Flory's prediction, $v = 0.6$ [1]. For theta – solvent conditions in $3D$ one expects $v = 0.5$ for neutral polymers, which is not obtained for polyelectrolytes, as Fig. 8 clearly shows. The scaling for polyelectrolytes in theta solvent is close to the scaling expected for neutral polymers under good-solvent conditions, while polyelectrolytes in good solvent scale like ideal neutral polymers. This can be interpreted as thinking that electrostatic interactions modify solvent quality as well as neutral ones do. That the scaling exponent is larger for polyelectrolytes than for polymers may perhaps be expected also, since electrostatic repulsion between neighboring charged monomers along the polyelectrolyte chain would lead to a more stretched out configuration. What might not be obvious is why scaling is obtained despite the presence of electrostatics, as Fig. 8 shows. Once polyelectrolytes are introduced, even at zero ionic strength, counter ions must also be added to the system, to keep it globally neutral. Those counter ions tend to group around charged monomers in the polyelectrolyte, screening the charges in it and effectively reducing the range of the electrostatic interaction. Then, the same arguments used for scaling in neutral

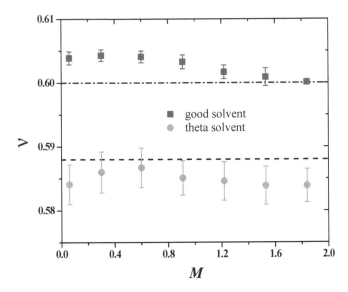

Fig. 8. The scaling exponent of the radius of gyration as a function of polymerization degree, ν, see Eq. (6) obtained for a polyelectrolyte chain of increasing size, as a function of increasing ionic strength (M). The dashed and dot – dashed lines are included as reference to the currently accepted value for neutral polymers in good solvent in 3D (n = 0.588) and Flory's prediction. All simulations were performed on GPU cards, using the SIMES code [41]. Adapted from [39].

polymers can be recalled. This is admittedly an overly simplified view, one that does not take into account important aspects such as the change in the persistence length with charge, Kuhn's length, Manning's condensation, and the solvent's permittivity change with charges [40]. Although important for a full understanding of polyelectrolytes in solution, those aspects are not as fundamental in yielding scaling characteristics as the shortening of the interaction length, while preserving self-similarity on different scales. The rest of this chapter is devoted to results for neutral systems.

5   Scaling Properties of Polymer Brushes in Equilibrium

When polymer chains are grafted on a surface and the grafting sites are closer to each other than the radius of gyration of the polymers in solution, they form arrangements that resemble brushes. They are known to display some scaling properties that depend on parameters such as grafting density, polymerization degree, and of course solvent quality. They are also important from a technological point of view, since polymer brushes can be very effective as colloidal dispersion stabilizers when used as coats on colloidal particles, such as in paints [12]. Polymer brushes also constitute excellent lubricating tools, able to reduce friction between brush-coated surfaces by three-orders of magnitude [42]. Since those works are well known [43], I shall focus here on a less known but increasingly important type of polymer brushes: biological polymer brushes. One particular example that draws our attention is the case of biological brushes on the surface of healthy and cancerous human cervix epithelial cells. Various types of physical probes have been able to detect linear protuberances in the form of brushes covering the surfaces of cells [44]. Those brushes are complex entities, described as microvilli, microridges and cilia, thought to be made of filaments of acting. Experiments using atomic force microscopy (AFM) detected different mechanical response between the surface of cancerous and healthy cells [45], with those differences being attributed to the brushes.

Using DPD simulations, most of those results have been interpreted and are now understood [46]. In particular, the force exerted by the mesoscopic tip of an AFM on the surface of healthy epithelial cervical cells covered with biological brushes has been correctly predicted, as shown in Fig. 9. Notice also that both experiments and numerical predictions are found to be in agreement with the polymer brush scaling law proposed by Alexander and de Gennes, which can be written as

$$F \sim F_0 e^{-2\pi h/L}, \tag{8}$$

when $0.2 \leq h/L \leq 0.9$, see [47]. In Eq. (8) F_0 is a constant expressed in terms of the thermal energy, the radius of curvature of the AFM tip, and the brushes grafting density [45]. The force decays linearly on a semi-log scale, with slope proportional to the reduced brush thickness (h/L), as Fig. 9 illustrates. The physical arguments that lead to the scaling predicted by Eq. (9) can be stated as follows: as the brush is compressed, the local osmotic pressure is increased. This contribution must compete with the attractive elastic energy stored in the polymer chains, leading to the scaling law in Eq. (8) [1]. This accuracy of DPD simulations in capturing scaling behavior in polymer brushes is not accidental as it has been found to be successful in other applications, see for example [22]. Additional examples are displayed in Fig. 10.

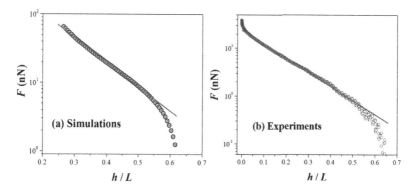

Fig. 9. Force applied by an AFM probe to the surface of normal cervical epithelial cells covered by biological brushes as predicted by DPD simulations [46] (a), and determined experimentally [45], (b). The solid line is the best fit to the Alexander-de Gennes's brush scaling law, see text for details. The x-axis was normalized by the average size of the unperturbed brushes. Adapted from the supplementary information of Ref. [46].

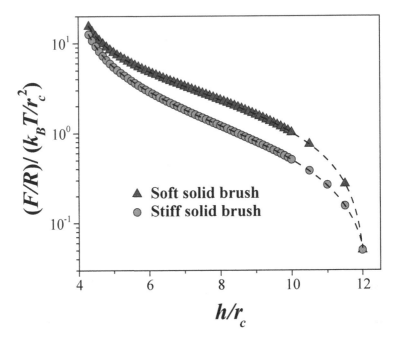

Fig. 10. Force applied by a mesoscopic sized tip of an AFM per its radius of curvature, as a function of the distance between the surface of cancerous epithelial cervical cells and the AFM's tip, obtained from DPD simulations [46]. Solid triangles correspond to brushes made up of chains where each monomer is joined to its neighbors by soft springs. Solid circles correspond to brushes with stiff springs; chains' heads in both soft and stiff brushes are fixed on the surface of the cell, thereby their label as "solid". Dashed lines are the fits to the Alexander-de Gennes scaling adapted to a three-length brush, as found in experiments [45], see text for details. Adapted from the supplementary information of Ref. [46].

The results of DPD simulations presented in Fig. 10 (solid symbols) along with their fit to the Alexander-de Gennes scaling law (dashed lines) correspond to a model cancerous epithelial cell covered by brushes of three different lengths and grafting densities [46]. The model was constructed following experimental findings on that type of cell, which showed that cancerous cervical epithelial cells were covered by a thick small brush, coexisting with less dense, medium sized chains; the micrographs also displayed a rare, much less dense and much larger third brush [45]. Fitting the surface force to a three-brush Alexander-de Gennes scaling force, given by

$$\frac{F}{R} / \left(\frac{k_B T}{r_c^2} \right) = A_1 e^{-(x-x_0)/L_1} + A_2 e^{-(x-x_0)/L_2} + A_3 e^{-(x-x_0)/L_3} + B \qquad (9)$$

yields the dashed lines shown in Fig. 10. Obviously, the predictions are in excellent agreement with the scaling and with the experimental trends. In Eq. (9) the lengths of the three different brushes are labelled L_i, x_0 is the complete three-length brush maximum compression, and A_i and B are adjustable constants [46]. The values of all these parameters obtained from regression analysis are also in excellent agreement with the model parameters used in the simulations; for full details the reader is referred to [46].

It is satisfying to find that physical models such as the DPD model and its thermostat are successful in reproducing complex phenomena occurring in many-body systems, such as those representing biological brushes. The fundamental reasons behind this success are found in the DPD model interactions, which despite the fact they are short range, they still lead to a non-vanishing second virial coefficient [24]. This sets the DPD model ahead of mean-field theories, where chain-chain interactions and even solvent interactions are neglected. There are weak but finite DPD interactions between chains in brushes, an aspect that several popular scaling theories neglect [48], one that is fundamental in capturing many-body collective phenomena, as typically required for scaling laws to work.

6 Scaling Properties of Polymer Brushes Under Flow

Scaling laws of dynamical properties of polymer brushes have been developed, some of which are briefly discussed in this section, particularly with focus on brushes under stationary, Couette flow [49]. Important technological applications demand fundamental knowledge of the properties of polymer brushes under flow, such as those where brushes are used as friction reducing agents [50]. Basic research in this direction has helped the plastic industry design better and more efficient schemes for the production of plastic bags, for example, so that users can separate the sheets of their plastic bags more easily when they go grocery shopping [51]. No less important is the basic understanding of the mechanisms that give rise to scaling trends even when polymer brushes are subjected to flow. In what follows I show some results our group has obtained regarding the scaling of dynamical properties of polymer brushes, with focus on two measurable quantities: viscosity of a fluid composed of polymer brushes under flow, and the friction coefficient between those opposite brushes and the solvent.

The setup of the simulations reported in this section is as follows. Polymer chains are grafted by one of their ends to parallel surfaces placed at the ends of the simulation box in the z-direction, see Fig. 11. Those ends, represented by blue beads in Fig. 11, are subjected to an external force that makes them move to the right (top surface in Fig. 11) with constant velocity v_0, while the beads grafted to the bottom surface move to the left with constant velocity $-v_0$. This setup leads to a linear velocity gradient for all particles confined within the pore of width D shown in Fig. 11; this type of stationary flow is known as Couette flow [49]. The shear rate in this situation is defined as $\dot{\gamma} = 2v_0/D$, which is constant since the velocity of the grafted beads and the spacing between the surfaces are constant. The viscosity can then be expressed as follows:

$$\sigma = \eta\dot{\gamma}, \tag{10}$$

where $\sigma = \langle F_x \rangle / A$ is the shear stress on the sample, given by the mean force on the particles along the x direction divided by the transversal area of the surfaces, see Fig. 11.

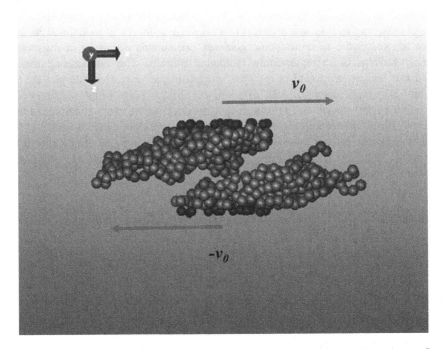

Fig. 11. Snapshot of the simulation cell used to model polymer brushes under stationary flow. Blue beads represent the ends of the brushes grafted on the surfaces (not shown), which are moved by an external force so that they move at constant speed v_0 to the right (upper surface) or to the left (lower surface). The rest of the polymer chains are shown in ochre beads; the solvent particles are not shown for simplicity. (Color figure online)

The coefficient of friction can also be obtained from the simulation setup shown in Fig. 11, as the ratio of the average force along the x direction to the average force along the z direction, i.e. perpendicularly to the wall, as given by

$$\mu = \langle F_x \rangle / \langle F_z \rangle. \tag{11}$$

Non Newtonian fluids, and polymer fluids usually belong to this category, are those with viscosities that depend on the applied shear rate, as given by Eq. (10). Shear thinning behavior is found in many polymer liquids, namely their viscosity is reduced when shear rate is increased. There is a critical shear rate, $\dot{\gamma}^*$, below which the fluid behaves as a Newtonian fluid. For values larger than $\dot{\gamma}^*$ shear thinning behavior sets in. In fact, it is possible to define a universal dimensionless number, the so-called Weissenberg number [52], We, given by $We = \dot{\gamma}/\dot{\gamma}^*$ so that $We \geq 1$ signals non Newtonian behavior.

Figure 12 shows the results of several DPD simulations, performed on brushes of different polymerization degree, subjected to increasing flow under theta-solvent conditions. The idea behind those simulations was to determine if characteristics such as increasing polymer length eventually lead to size-free physical trends. Let us first focus

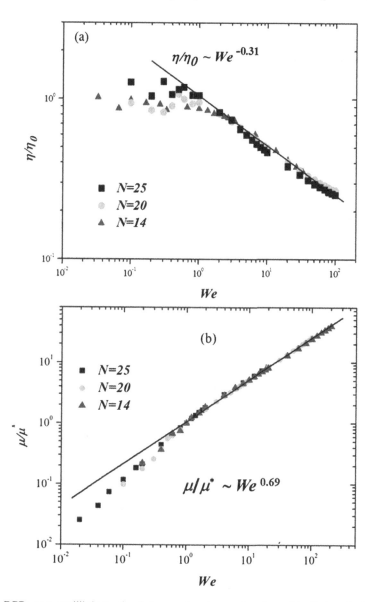

Fig. 12. DPD non-equilibrium simulations of polymer brushes. (a) Reduced dynamical viscosity as a function of the Weissemberg number (*We*) for polymer brushes of three different lengths, as indicated by the legend. The solid line represents the fit to the scaling model proposed by Galuschko *et al.* [52]. (b) Reduced friction coefficient between brushes of increasing polymerization degree as a function of *We*. Notice scaling behavior is captured for both properties when *We* > 1, as indicated by the solid lines. Adapted from [54].

on panel (a) in Fig. 12, where the dynamic viscosity of brushes—at the same grafting density for all cases reported in Fig. 12—is shown as a function of increasing Weissenberg number, *We*. Predictions of simulations of polymer brushes in theta-solvent conditions under increasing shear flow rate show that scaling behavior *is* obtained for the viscosity of polymer brushes regardless the polymerization degree, where the scaling exponent is found to be equal to $\zeta = -0.31$ on a log-log scale, see Fig, 12(a).

The reduced coefficient of friction for the same polymer brushes as those reported in Fig. 12(a) is shown in Fig. 12(b), as a function of *We*. Once again, scaling trends independent of the polymerization degree are obtained once $We \geq 1$, with the scaling exponent being $\kappa = 0.69$. Remarkably, universal curves are obtained for all polymerization degrees modeled [52], and a relationship can be established between the scaling exponents of the viscosity and the friction coefficient, yielding the equation (see [52])

$$\kappa - \zeta = 1, \tag{12}$$

where $\kappa = 0.69$ and $\zeta = -0.31$ for polymers under theta-solvent conditions [54]. Simulations carried out by other groups using different model interactions for polymers under good solvent conditions yield values for these scaling exponents given by $\kappa = 0.57$, and $\zeta = -0.43$ [52], which are clearly different from those obtained for brushes in theta solvent. However, it is most remarkable that Eq. (12) is equally fulfilled, regardless the solvent quality. Scaling behavior is obtained for polymer brushes under strong confinement $(D \ll R_g)$ and Couette flow $(We \gg 1)$ because chains are strongly stretched along the shear direction, giving rise to a situation where flow plays the role of an external field whose role is mostly brush alignment [52]. Therefore, for large N and under strong flow and confinement, polymers appear again to be self-similar and scaling ensues. Under those conditions, the brushes whose scaling is reported in Fig. 12 behave like polymer melts, for which the scaling exponent ν, see Eq. (6), is $\nu = 0.5$. Then, it can be shown [52] that $\mu/\mu_0 = \langle F_x(\dot{\gamma}) \rangle / \langle F_x(\dot{\gamma}^*) \rangle = N/N^{-0.5}$, and that $N \sim We^{6/13}$ which combined yield $\mu/\mu_0 = We^{9/13} = We^\kappa$, or $\kappa \approx 0.69$; using Eq. (12) one gets $\zeta = -0.31$, in excellent agreement with the results shown in Fig. 12 [54].

Before leaving this section I comment briefly on the scaling of polymer brushes under flow when there are also free chains of the same type of polymers that make up the brushes. This is not only of academic interest but it is also important in plastic sheet production, where polymers are injected into the plastic matrix (which later will constitute the plastic sheet) so that they migrate to the surfaces of the matrix during the extrusion process. As the plastic cools, more and more polymer chains migrate, forming brushes, thereby reducing friction between sheets and energy consumption. However, some chains get desorbed and get trapped between opposite sheets, creating a complex confined fluid, one that includes free polymer chains, polymer brushes, and solvent particles. The question then arises as to whether those free chains help reduce the coefficient of friction (COF) or not. Figure 13 illustrates the process just described, where the COF and the viscosity are reported also. Notice that in this case the variable is not the shear rate but the polymer chains' grafting density, Γ [55]. The results shown in the center of Fig. 13 have been found to be in excellent agreement with experiments performed in both academia and in the private sector [56], but since the focus of this chapter is on scaling properties, I invite the interested reader to review Ref. [55], and references therein.

In Fig. 14, I show the average force along the direction perpendicular to the surfaces on which polymer chains are grafted, as a function of their grafting density under

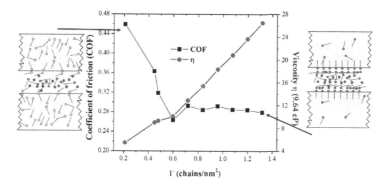

Fig. 13. Schematics of the polymer chains migration (green molecules) to the surfaces of the plastic matrix (orange colored sheets), where they form brushes as the plastic cools. Some chains are desorbed and form free aggregates, interacting with the brushes and the solvent (red particles). Couette flow is applied and the COF (black squares) and viscosity (red circles) are calculated at increasing brush grafting density (Γ). Adapted from the Table of Contents Graphic of Ref. [55]. (Color figure online)

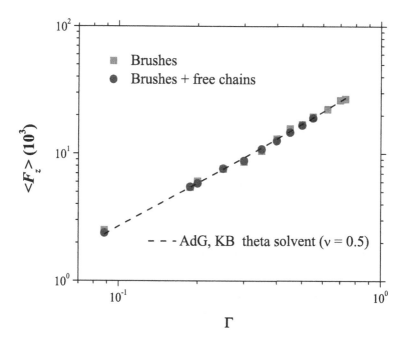

Fig. 14. Average force along the direction perpendicular to the confinement of polymer brushes (red squares), and brushes plus free chains (blue circles) as a function of polymer grafting density, under constant Couette flow, obtained using DPD simulations. The dashed line is the fit to the Alexander-de Gennes (AdG) [47] and Kreer-Balko (KB) [53] scaling laws, see Eqs. (13) and (15), respectively. Adapted from [55]. (Color figure online)

theta solvent conditions. Notice the scale on both axes is logarithmic. The squares are results of DPD simulations where only brushes are subjected to constant Couette flow; the circles correspond to DPD simulations of brushes and free polymer chains under flow. It is tempting to apply the Alexander-de Gennes (AdG) scaling law to this case, even though it was not derived for brushes under flow. For the present purposes, let us write the AdG law as follows:

$$\langle F_z \rangle = A k_B T f(a, D, N) \Gamma^y, \tag{13}$$

$$y = \frac{3v}{3v - 1}. \tag{14}$$

In Eq. (13) A is the surfaces' transversal area, and f is a function that depends on the polymer's monomer size, a, the distance between surfaces, D, and the polymerization degree, but it does not depend on Γ; therefore it is not shown here, for simplicity. The exponent y depends on the familiar exponent v. For theta-solvent polymers, $v = 0.5$ and $y = 3$. Another scaling theory, proposed recently, is that of Kreer and Balko's (KB) [53], which predicts that

$$\langle F_z \rangle = A k_B T g(a, D, N) \Gamma^{y'}, \tag{15}$$

$$y' = \frac{2 + 5v}{3(3v - 1)}. \tag{16}$$

The function g in Eq. (15) depends on the same variables as function f in Eq. (13), although they are different functions. However, their explicit form is not relevant to the present discussion. What is important is to note that y and y' are both equal to 3 for $v = 0.5$, even though they are based on different assumptions. The dashed line in Fig. 14 is the fit to a function $\sim \Gamma^3$, which indicates that there is scaling for these systems, and that the presence of free chains does not change the scaling properties of the compression force of polymer brushes in a theta solvent.

The fact that Eqs. (13) and (15) lead to the same scaling exponent means that chain-chain interaction and brush interdigitation (allowed by KB but not by AdG) are not the principal factors that give rise to scaling, under theta conditions. Other aspects define the scaling for these systems, such as the compression (D) and the polymerization degree. The fact that both systems (only brushes and brushes plus free chains) are under flow does not affect the scaling either. The physical reason is to be found in the fact that D does not change. Differences in scaling behavior between equilibrium and non-equilibrium simulations of polymer brushes are expected to occur for the force along the x direction, but that is beyond the scope of the present work.

7 Scaling in Lower Dimensions

Lastly, I present some results for scaling of polymers in two dimensions (2D), with particular emphasis on the scaling of their disjoining or solvation pressure Π [57]. When fluids are confined, the component of the pressure tensor along the direction normal to the confinement (P_N) is in general different from other components; in particular, it is different from the unconfined, bulk pressure (P_B). Such difference is precisely Π; it is important because it can be used as a means to gauge colloidal stability since Π is proportional to the free energy difference between the bulk and confined systems, see for example [58]. It can be measured using a surface force apparatus, or with AFM [47]. In systems with varying concentration of a given component, the disjoining pressure should be proportional to the osmotic pressure π. The latter was shown a long time ago [59] to obey the following scaling relation:

$$\pi \sim c^{\frac{vd}{vd-1}}, \tag{17}$$

where c is the monomer concentration, d the spatial dimension, and v the scaling exponent of the Flory radius. Given the fact that π and Π are related, one should expect that the latter obeys a scaling law as well.

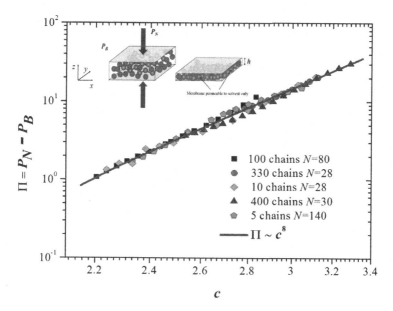

Fig. 15. Grand Canonical Monte Carlo simulations of polymer confined on quasi 2D space using the DPD interaction model. The y axis is the disjoining pressure and the x axis represents the polymers' monomer concentration. The symbols represent data for chains of various polymerization degrees, as indicated by the legend. The solid line is the fit to Eq. (18) with $v_{2d} = 4/7$; see text for details. Both axes are reported in reduced DPD units. The cartoon in the upper left corner shows the simulation setup; red beads are solvent particles and blue beads are monomers that make up the chains. Adapted from [60]. (Color figure online)

For polymer chains under strong confinement along the z direction, see schematic representation in the inset in Fig. 15, the chains are effectively restricted to move on a quasi-2D plane. Following arguments similar to those used by des Cloiseaux to obtain Eq. (17) [59], but with the most important difference that the separation between surfaces, h, remains small but finite, the author and Pérez showed in [60] that Π scales as

$$\frac{\Pi}{k_B T} \sim c^{2v_{2d}/(2v_{2d}-1)}, \qquad (18)$$

where v_{2d} represents the value of the ubiquitous Flory's scaling exponent v in 2D (see Eq. (6)), whose value depends not only on d but also on solvent quality. The scaling of Π proposed in Ref. [60] and shown in Eq. (18), the first ever reported for the disjoining pressure, was tested with DPD simulations of a fixed number of polymer chains under increasing confinement (reducing h, see diagram in Fig. 15). By reducing the spacing between the surfaces, the volume is reduced and monomer concentration, c, can be increased. This renders the simulation of several polymer concentrations unnecessary, since with a fixed number of chains one can sweep over several monomer concentration values.

When the distance between the surfaces is reduced, the fluid confined may not be in the same state of thermodynamic equilibrium, unless the chemical potential between it and the surrounding fluid is kept constant. This restriction means that simulations of confined fluids must be performed in the Grand Canonical ensemble, where in addition to volume and temperature, the chemical potential must also be kept constant [61]. Failure to do so may lead to vastly different predictions between constant-density simulations and constant chemical potential simulations, see [62]. Figure 15 shows the results of Monte Carlo simulations in the Grand Canonical ensemble for a fluid containing polymer chains and solvent particles, interacting through DPD forces [19], under theta-solvent conditions. Only solvent particles are exchanged between the confined fluid and the virtual reservoir.

The different symbols in Fig. 15 correspond to chains for different polymerization degree, ranging from $N = 28$ up to $N = 128$; once again it is quite remarkable to find all data collapse into a single curve, signaling that scaling occurs. The solid line in Fig. 15 corresponds to the best fit to the function $\Pi \sim c^8$; comparing this exponent with the one predicted by Eq. (18) yields $v_{2d} = 4/7$. This is precisely the same value predicted by other scaling theories for two-dimensional polymers under theta-solvent conditions [63, 64]. Simulations performed for quasi-2D chains under good solvent conditions (not reported here for brevity) of the disjoining pressure for polymers of various polymerization degrees yield the commonly accepted value, $v_{2d} = 3/4$ [1]. Therefore, the scaling law predicted by Gama Goicochea and Pérez in [60], Eq. (18), is very robust. For more discussion about the implications of this scaling, as well as full for details of its derivation and of the simulations whose results are shown in Fig. 15, see Ref. [60]. For fractal scaling of cluster aggregation, see for example Ref. [65].

8 Conclusions

The physicist Thomas A. Witten once wrote *"Why should a physicist be interested in polymers? They do not hold the key to vast resources of energy like atomic nuclei. They do not defy intuition with ultrasmall dissipation like superconductors and superfluids. They do not reveal subtle new nonabelian symmetries as do subatomic particles. Nor do they hold secrets about the origin or fate of the universe"* [66]. This is indeed true, yet as Witten himself goes on to argue in [66], polymers constitute a most important field of study, for polymer liquids display properties that can be understood using powerful analogies with critical phenomena; they have motivated the development of sophisticated experimental techniques; they are commonplace in modern society, and if that was not enough, even biological matter can be thought of and understood as polymer liquids.

The study of polymers fluids, and soft condensed matter in general, has benefited in recent decades from numerical simulations, which are ever faster, adaptable to model systems of ever increasing complexity and, with costs of powerful processors becoming more competitive, accessible to a wider number of scientists worldwide. Here I have focused on reviewing the modeling of scaling properties of soft matter systems using in particular the technique known as dissipative particle dynamics, carried out by our group. However, all scaling properties reported here are independent of the technique used; some have been obtained by other groups using different models or measured in various experiments. The fact that the same scaling exponents are found in chemically different compounds, using vastly different techniques is gratifying for those using such techniques, and it is also a beautiful example of the unifying concept of scaling in physics.

Acknowledgments. The author wishes to thank his collaborators, with whom most of the results reported here were obtained, in particular: F. Alarcón, S. J. Alas Guardado, M. A. Balderas Altamirano, J. Barroso – Flores, R. Catarino Centeno, J. S. Hernández Fragoso, J. D. Hernández Velázquez, J. Klapp, R. López – Esparza, R. López – Rendón, E. Mayoral, S. Mejía – Rosales, C. Pastorino, R. Patiño Herrera, E. Pérez, G. Pérez – Hernández, Z. Quiñones, E. Rivera – Paz, K. A. Terrón – Mejía, J. Vallejo and M. A. Waldo. Educational discussions with E. Blokhuis and I. Sokolov are also gratefully acknowledged. For computational resources the author is indebted to ABACUS, where some calculations were run; to the high performance cluster Yoltla at UAM – Iztapalapa; to Universidad de Sonora for access to the Ocotillo cluster at their High Performance Computational Area; to the CNS supercomputing facilities at IPICyT, to the Olinka cluster at UAEM, and to the Laboratorio Nacional de Caracterización de Propiedades Fisicoquímicas y Estructura Molecular Supercómputo Universidad de Guanajuato. For technical support at the IFUASLP, J. Limón is also acknowledged. This work was supported in part by project Proinnova – CONACYT, through grant 231810.

References

1. de Gennes, P.G.: Scaling Concepts in Polymer Physics. Cornell University Press, New York (1979)

2. Cardy, J.: Scaling and Renormalization in Statistical Physics. Cambridge University Press, Cambridge (1997)
3. Mandelbrot, B.: The Fractal Geometry of Nature. Freeman, New York (1983)
4. Frenkel, D., Smit, B.: Understanding Molecular Simulation. Academic Press, San Diego (2002)
5. Allen, M.P., Tildesley, D.J.: Computer Simulation of Liquids. Oxford University Press, New York (1989)
6. Brini, E., Algaer, E.A., Ganguly, P., Li, C., Rodríguez-Ropero, F., van der Vegt, N.F.A.: Soft Matter **9**, 2108 (2013)
7. Hoogerbrugge, P.J., Koelman, J.M.V.A.: Europhys. Lett. **19**, 155 (1992)
8. Español, P., Warren, P.: Europhys. Lett. **30**, 191 (1995)
9. Vishniakov, A., Talanga, D.S., Neimark, A.V.: J. Phys. Chem. Lett. **21**, 3081 (2012)
10. Groot, R.D.: Langmuir **16**, 7493 (2000)
11. Groot, R.D., Rabone, K.L.: Biophys. J. **81**, 725 (2001)
12. Gama Goicochea, A.: Competitive adsorption of surfactants and polymers on colloids by means of mesoscopic simulations. In: Klapp, J., Medina, A. (eds.) Experimental and Computational Fluid Mechanics. Environmental Science and Engineering, pp. 147–155. Springer, Cham (2014). doi:10.1007/978-3-319-00116-6_10
13. Filipovic, N., Kojic, M., Tsuda, A.: Philos. Trans. A Math. Phys. Eng. Sci. **366**, 3265 (2008)
14. Murtola, T., Bunker, A., Vattulainen, I., Deserno, M., Karttunen, M.: Phys. Chem. Chem. Phys. **11**, 1869–1892 (2009)
15. Pastorino, C., Gama Goicochea, A.: Dissipative particle dynamics: a method to simulate soft matter systems in equilibrium and under flow. In: Klapp, J., Ruíz Chavarría, G., Medina Ovando, A., López Villa, A., Sigalotti, L. (eds.) Selected Topics of Computational and Experimental Fluid Mechanics. Environmental Science and Engineering, pp. 51–79. Springer, Cham (2015). doi:10.1007/978-3-319-11487-3_3
16. Moeendarbary, E., Ng, T.Y., Zangeneh, M.: Int. J. Appl. Mech. **02**, 161 (2010)
17. Groot, R.D.: J. Chem. Phys. **118**, 11265–11277 (2003)
18. Velázquez, M.E., Gama Goicochea, A., González-Melchor, M., Neria, M., Alejandre, J.: J. Chem. Phys. **124**, 084104 (2006)
19. Gama Goicochea, A.: Langmuir **23**, 11656 (2007)
20. Willemsen, S.M., Vlugt, T.J.H., Hoefsloot, H.C.J., Smit, B.: J. Comp. Phys. **147**, 507 (1998)
21. Murat, M., Grest, G.S.: Phys. Rev. Lett. **1989**, 63 (1074)
22. Gama Goicochea, A., Alarcón, F.: J. Chem. Phys. **134**, 014703 (2011)
23. Goujon, F., Malfreyt, P., Tildesley, D.J.: Soft Matter **6**, 3472 (2010)
24. Groot, R.D., Warren, P.B.: J. Chem. Phys. **107**, 4423 (1997)
25. Widom, B.: J. Chem. Phys. **43**, 3892–3897 (1965)
26. Widom, B.: In: Domb, C., Green, M.S. (eds.) Phase Transitions and Critical Phenomena. Academic, New York (1972)
27. Binder, K.: Monte Carlo calculation of the surface tension for two- and three-dimensional lattice-gas models. Phys. Rev. A **25**, 1699–1709 (1982)
28. Goldenfeld, N.: Lectures on Phase Transitions and the Renormalization Group. Westview Press, New York (1992)
29. Mayoral, E., Gama Goicochea, A.: J. Chem. Phys. **138**, 094703 (2013)
30. Mayoral, E., Gama Goicochea, A.: Soft Matter **10**, 9054 (2014)
31. Le Guillou, J.C., Zinn-Justin, J.: Phys. Rev. B **21**, 3976–3998 (1980)
32. Konop, A.J., Colby, R.H.: Macromolecules **32**, 2803 (1999)
33. Dobrynin, A.V., Colby, R.H., Rubinstein, M.: Macromolecules **28**, 1859 (1995)
34. Sim, A.Y.L., Lipfert, J., Herschlag, D., Doniach, S.: Phys. Rev. E **86**, 021901-1 (2012)

35. Alarcón, F., Pérez-Hernández, G., Pérez, E., Gama Goicochea, A.: Eur. Biophys. J. **42**, 661 (2013)
36. Wong, G.C.L., Pollack, L.: Ann. Rev. Phys. Chem. **61**, 171 (2010)
37. Hsiao, P.-Y., Luijten, E.: Phys. Rev. Lett. **97**, 148301 (2006)
38. Gama Goicochea, A., Briseño, M.: J. Coat. Technol. Res. **9**, 279 (2012). doi:10.1007/s11998-011-9364-8
39. Terrón-Mejía, K.A., López-Rendón, R., Gama Goicochea, A.: J. Phys. Condens. Matter **28**, 425101 (2016). http://dx.doi.org/10.1088/0953-8984/28/42/425101
40. Stigter, D.: Biophys. J. **69**, 380 (1995)
41. Visit: http://www.simes.uaemex-labs.org.mx/
42. Klein, J., Kumacheva, E., Mahalu, D., Perahia, D., Fetters, L.J.: Nature **370**, 634 (1994)
43. Advincula, R., Brittain, W.J., Caster, K.C., Rühe, J. (eds.): Polymer Brushes. Wiley-VCH, Weinheim (2004)
44. Wang, X., Shah, A.A., Campbell, R.B., Wang, K.-T.: Appl. Phys. Lett. **97**, 263703 (2010)
45. Iyer, S., Gaikwad, R.M., Subba-Rao, V., Woodworth, C.D., Sokolov, I.: Nature Nanotech. **4**, 389 (2009)
46. Gama Goicochea, A., Alas Guardado, S.J.: Sci. Rep. **5**, 13218 (2015). doi:10.1038/srep13218
47. Israelachvili, J.N.: Intermolecular and Surface Forces, 3rd edn. Academic Press, San Diego (2011)
48. Milner, S.T., Witten, T.A., Cates, M.E.: Europhys. Lett. **5**, 413 (1988)
49. Macosko, C.W.: Rheology Principles, Measurements, and Applications. Wiley-VCH, Weinheim (1994)
50. Shuler, C.A., Janorkar, A.V., Hirt, D.E.: Polym. Eng. Sci. **44**, 2247 (2004)
51. Allen, C.M., Drauglis, E.: Wear **14**, 363 (1969)
52. Galuschko, A., Spirin, L., Kreer, T., Johner, A., Pastorino, C., Wittmer, J., Baschnagel, J.: Langmuir **26**, 6418 (2010)
53. Kreer, T., Balko, S.M.: ACS Macro Lett. **2**, 944 (2013)
54. Gama Goicochea, A., Mayoral, E., Klapp, J., Pastorino, C.: Soft Matter **10**, 166 (2014)
55. Gama Goicochea, A., López-Esparza, R., Balderas Altamirano, M.A., Rivera-Paz, E., Waldo, M.A., Pérez, E.: J. Mol. Liq. **219**, 368–376 (2016)
56. Rivera, E., Quiñones, Z., Waldo, M.A.: Private communication
57. Derjaguin, B.V.: Theory of Stability of Colloids and Thin Films. Plenum Publishing Corporation, New York (1979)
58. van Dongen, P.G.J., Ernst, M.H.: Phys. Rev. A **32**, 670 (1985)
59. des Cloizeaux, J.: J. Phys. (Paris) **36**, 281 (1975)
60. Gama Goicochea, A., Pérez, E.: Macromol. Chem. Phys. **216**, 1076 (2015). doi:10.1002/macp.201400623
61. Huang, K.: Statistical Mechanics. Wiley, New York (1987)
62. Balderas Altamirano, M.A., Gama Goicochea, A.: Polymer **52**, 3846 (2011). doi:10.1016/jpolymer.2011.06.015
63. Duplantier, B., Saleur, H.: Phys. Rev. Lett. **59**, 539 (1987)
64. Kremer, K., Lyklema, J.W.: Phys. Rev. Lett. **54**, 267 (1985)
65. Kolb, M.: Phys. Rev. Lett. **53**, 1653 (1984)
66. Witten, T.A.: Polymer solutions: a geometric introduction. In: Daoud, M., Williams, C.E. (eds.) Soft Matter Physics, pp. 261–288. Springer, Heidelberg (1999)

On Finite Size Effects, Ensemble Choice and Force Influence in Dissipative Particle Dynamics Simulations

Miguel Ángel Balderas Altamirano[1,2], Elías Pérez[1],
and Armando Gama Goicochea[1,2(✉)]

[1] Instituto de Física, Universidad Autónoma de San Luis Potosí,
Avenida Álvaro Obregón 64, 78000 San Luis Potosí, San Luis Potosí, Mexico
agama@alumni.stanford.edu
[2] División de Ingeniería Química y Bioquímica, Tecnológico de Estudios
Superiores de Ecatepec, Av. Tecnológico S/N, 55210 Ecatepec,
Estado de México, Mexico

Abstract. The influence of finite size effects, choice of statistical ensemble and contribution of the forces in numerical simulations using the dissipative particle dynamics (DPD) model are revisited here. Finite size effects in stress anisotropy, interfacial tension and dynamic viscosity are computed and found to be minimal with respect to other models. Additionally, the choice of ensemble is found to be of fundamental importance for the accurate calculation of properties such as the solvation pressure, especially for relatively small systems. Lastly, the contribution of the random, dissipative and conservative forces that make up the DPD model in the prediction of properties of simple liquids such as the pressure is studied as well. Some tricks of the trade are provided, which may be useful for those carrying out high-performance numerical simulations using the DPD model.

Keywords: DPD · Finite size effects · Surface tension · Solvation pressure · Viscosity · Conservative · Dissipative · Random forces

1 Introduction

Molecular Dynamics (MD) simulation is now a popular multidisciplinary research tool in science, which consists essentially of solving Newton's second law of motion for fluids made up of many particles using computers in discret time steps to calculate properties of interest. Some systems can be easily modeled as a pure homogeneous fluid, but some others require the modeling of complex interactions competing with one another, as is the case in biological systems with many molecules interacting in solution such as proteins, viruses or molecular chaperones [1–3]. Computer evolution in recent years has already brought many opportunities for the modeling not only of toy models but also of useful realistic problems. It must be borne in mind though that all simulations are necessarily subject to a number of choices, such as the size of the cell and the time step, model interactions, and thermodynamic conditions under which the

© Springer International Publishing AG 2017
C.J. Barrios Hernández et al. (Eds.): CARLA 2016, CCIS 697, pp. 314–328, 2017.
DOI: 10.1007/978-3-319-57972-6_23

simulations are performed. Therefore, some guidelines must be followed to make those choices judiciously [1].

Choosing a box size depends on finding a compromise between the smallest size that requires the least time to complete the calculations, and the largest number of particles one can calculate to capture realistic behavior found in experiments. Another issue is time; some proteins need at least a few seconds to unfold; nowadays MD can simulate 100 ns with little effort, but much work is still required to go beyond that. To tackle these problems of scale, some techniques have been proposed that can increase the size or the observation time of the simulations. One of those techniques is known as Dissipative Particle Dynamics (DPD) [2], which is very similar in its essence to MD, namely solving the forces acting in many particle systems to obtain their momenta and positions. The difference between them comes from the choice of the model forces and of the thermostat. While MD requires usually of conservative forces only, DPD adds a dissipation force and a randomly fluctuating force to its structure, given respectively by

$$F_{ij}^{D} = -\gamma \omega^{D}(rij)\left[\hat{r}_{ij}.v_{ij}\right]\hat{r}_{ij}, \tag{1}$$

$$F_{ij}^{R} = \sigma \omega^{R}(rij)\varepsilon_{ij}\hat{r}_{ij}, \tag{2}$$

where $r_{ij} = r_i - r_j$, $r_{ij} = \left|r_{ij}\right|$, $\hat{r}_{ij} = r_{ij}/r_{ij}$, r_{ij}, is the relative position vector between particles i and j, σ is the noise amplitude, γ is the viscous force amplitude and $v_{ij} = v_i - v_j$ is the relative velocity between the particles, with $\varepsilon_{ij} = \varepsilon_{ji}$ being random numbers with Gaussian distribution between 0 and 1, and unit variance. The weight functions ω^D and ω^R are related as follows:

$$\omega^{D}\left(r_{ij}\right) = \left[\omega^{R}\left(r_{ij}\right)\right]^{2}. \tag{3}$$

The spatial dependence of the weight function can be freely chosen, as long as Eq. (3) is fulfilled; for computational convenience only, $\omega^R = \left(1 - \frac{r_{ij}}{r_C}\right)$. The constants in Eqs. (1) and (2) must obey the fluctuation–dissipation theorem, which yields [3]:

$$k_B T = \frac{\sigma^2}{2\gamma}, \tag{4}$$

where k_B is Boltzmann's constant and T the absolute temperature. When one chooses a value for those two constants the temperature is immediately set, thereby defining a built-in thermostat.

MD simulations usually resort to using the Lennard–Jones potential to model van der Waals type forces, complemented with the Coulomb equation for electrostatics to account correctly for the interactions of atoms and molecules. DPD on the other hand incorporates a repulsive (F_{ij}^C) conservative, linearly decaying force, see Eq. (5) below, which comes with some advantages: being a short range force, it makes its calculation between pairs of particles more efficiently performed by computers because the force changes little with distance and dies off beyond a cutoff distance. Secondly, the particles are represented by beads without internal structure, where the strength of the force between beads is obtained from the grouping of several atoms or even molecules of the fluid, through a coarse-graining procedure based on the chemical nature of the beads [4]. The conservative force is given by

$$F_{ij}^C = a_{ij}\left(1 - \frac{r_{ij}}{r_C}\right);$$

(5)

a_{ij} is the interaction parameter between DPD particles i and j; r_C is the cutoff radius, beyond which all interactions become equal to zero. It is because of the choice of force law given by Eq. (5) that DPD is a mesoscopic simulation technique. There are, of course, capabilities that one may need for applications and which DPD does not possess; one of those is that the repulsive nature of the forces leads to the absence of the so-called van der Waals loop in the pressure–volume phase diagram, hence liquid–gas transitions cannot be modeled with DPD. Also, the presence of the dissipative force yields simulations that cannot be performed at constant energy, which is necessary for the simulation of heat transport. However, both of those disadvantages have been circumvented [5, 6], at the cost of decreasing the computational efficiency and simplicity of the method. For more details about the DPD methodology and applications see, for example, Refs. [7–10].

In this brief review we summarize recent results on the effects of the finite size of the simulation box on the prediction of properties such as the stress tensor anisotropy, interfacial tension, dynamic viscosity and disjoining pressure, under various statistical ensembles. Also, we discuss the role of the dissipative, random and conservative forces in the calculation of the pressure of simple fluids, as well as their dependence on the size of the time step and of the size of the simulation box.

2   Finite Size Effects in Equilibrium and Dynamic Properties

A very popular application of MD is for the prediction of interfacial and surface tension. To accomplish that one needs to calculate the components of the pressure tensor; if the interface between the fluids is perpendicular to the z axis the interfacial tension is obtained as:

$$\gamma = L_z\left[\langle P_{zz}\rangle - \frac{1}{2}\left(\langle P_{xx}\rangle + \langle P_{yy}\rangle\right)\right],$$

(6)

where $\langle P_{xx}\rangle$, $\langle P_{yy}\rangle$ and $\langle P_{zz}\rangle$ are the diagonal components of the pressure tensor, averaged over time or over an ensemble. If one models a homogeneous liquid with periodic boundary conditions in all directions, where no interfaces are expected to appear, the quantity defined by Eq. (6) can no longer be called an "interfacial" tension; it is only a measure of the stress anisotropy. To test the influence of finite size on the interfacial tension, Gama Goicochea and co-workers carried out simulations of a mixture of two immiscible model liquids as a function of the size of the simulation box using the standard DPD model, and using the Monte Carlo (MC) method under the $NP_{zz}T$ ensemble [11]. In this ensemble the component of the pressure tensor which is perpendicular to the interface separating the liquids (P_{zz}) remains constant, in addition to N and T. The comparison between both methods is shown in Fig. 1; asterisks on quantities indicate they are expressed in reduced DPD units.

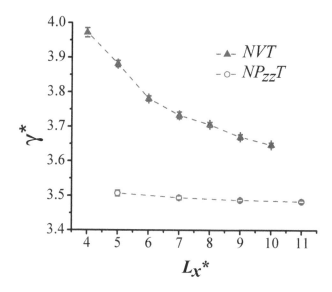

Fig. 1. Interfacial tension results for a mixture of two DPD fluids, obtained from simulations carried out in the *NVT* (filled triangles) and $NP_{zz}T$ (open circles) ensembles. The error bar sizes, shown in the figure, are of the order of the size of the symbols. Except for the choice of ensemble, both series of simulations have identical interaction parameters. The lines are only guides to the eye. All quantities are reported in reduced DPD units. Adapted from Ref. [11].

As seen in Fig. 1, the choice of ensemble is very important when seeking to keep finite size effects to a minimum in the prediction of interfacial tension with DPD. Using standard DPD, that is, a dynamics that solves the equation of motion for the forces in Eqs. (1), (2) and (5) in the canonical ensemble (*NVT*) leads to strong dependence of γ^* on box size. This is to be contrasted with the choice of MC in the $NP_{zz}T$ ensemble, where γ^* remains almost constant even for the smallest boxes. The difference between the γ^* predictions at the smallest and largest boxes amounts to less than two percent, while the time required to carry out the simulations at those two sizes differ by about eighty percent! For this application, it turns out that $NP_{zz}T$ is a better ensemble to simulate the interfacial tension than *NVT* because it is the one that more closely resembles the experimental conditions under which the interfacial tension is measured. Full details on this calculation of the interfacial tension between two simple liquids can be found in Ref. [11], where the stress tensor anisotropy for a pure liquid with periodic boundary conditions was also calculated; it is shown in Fig. 2.

The stress anisotropy shown in Fig. 2 should be exactly equal to zero for a single liquid with no interfaces, as occurs for simulation boxes with periodic boundary conditions. However, numerical simulations as well as experiments are subject to finite size restrictions, which may introduce artifacts that shadow the value of the property in

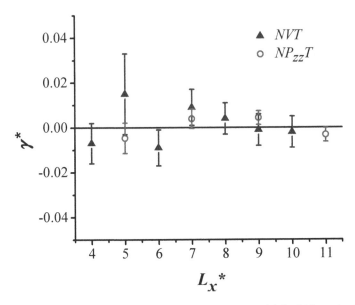

Fig. 2. Stress anisotropy results for a pure, monomeric DPD model liquid in a simulation box with periodic boundary conditions using the *NVT* (filled triangles) and $NP_{zz}T$ (open circles) ensembles, as a function of box size. For a one phase system such as this γ^* is expected to be zero (solid horizontal line) because there is no interface. Axes are in reduced DPD units. Adapted from Ref. [11].

the thermodynamic limit. Although the values of γ^* are small for both sets of data, those obtained with the $NP_{zz}T$ ensemble are closer to zero than those for the *NVT* ensemble. Also, as the box size is increased the stress anisotropy becomes closer to zero for both ensembles, meaning that finite size effects are negligible, as expected.

An attractive conservative force can be added to the original DPD interactions, leading to a method that can predict liquid–vapor transitions [12]. Such term arises from the calculation of the local average density around each particle, giving rise to a conservative force that can be expressed as

$$F_{ij}^C = a_{ij}w^C\left(r_{ij}\right)\hat{e}_{ij} + b_{ij}\left(\rho_i + \rho_j\right)w_\rho\left(r_{ij}\right)\hat{e}_{ij}, \tag{7}$$

where the first term is the usual repulsive interaction, see Eq. (5), and the second is the attractive contribution. The average local density around particle i is $\bar{\rho}_i = \sum_{j\neq i} w_\rho(r_{ij}, R_d)$, b_{ij} is the strength of the attractive force, and w_ρ is a weight function given by

$$w_\rho\left(r_{ij}, R_d\right) = \frac{15\left(1 - r_{ij}/R_d\right)^2}{2\pi R_d^3}, \tag{8}$$

where R_d is the range of the weight function $w_\rho\left(r_{ij}, R_d\right)$. The addition of the second term in Eq. (7) leads to a total conservative interaction that changes considerably with

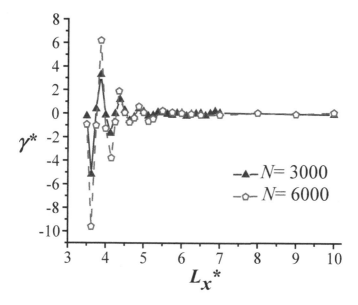

Fig. 3. Stress anisotropy for a one component DPD fluid with attractive and repulsive interactions as a function of box side length, L_x^*. Results are shown for $N = 3000$ (filled triangles) and for $N = 6000$ (open pentagons); for both the density is $\rho^* = 3$. Lines are guides to the eyes. Both axes are represented in reduced DPD units. Adapted from [11].

relative inter particle distance; this in turn produces oscillations in the pressure tensor components, as seen in Fig. 3.

The systems whose stress anisotropy are shown in Fig. 3 are pure, monomeric liquids with periodic boundary conditions at two values of the particle number, hence γ^* should be equal to zero. Yet one sees strong oscillations for both cases, at very small boxes, being larger for the largest number of particles (open pentagons in Fig. 3). Two salient features in Fig. 3 demand comments: first, for boxes which are still relatively small, e.g. $L_x^* = 5$, finite size effects in γ^* are minimal and are once again negligible for moderately sized boxes. Therefore, even with the inclusion of an attractive term to the original conservative DPD term finite size effects are much smaller than those found in other interaction models. The origin of this feature can be traced back to the fact that the forces, even that in Eq. (7) are short ranged. Secondly, one should note that the oscillations in Fig. 3, which come of course from oscillations in the components of the pressure tensor, have the same period for both systems. They originate from the basic interactions of the model and appear in all structural and thermodynamic properties of the fluid, such as in the radial distribution function and density profile, with the same period. This exponentially decaying oscillatory behavior is found in three-dimensional fluids interacting through short range potentials at high density, as predicted by the Fisher–Widom conjecture [12, 13]. Full simulation details can be found in [11].

Let us now proceed to review the influence of finite size effects in non-equilibrium properties, particularly in the dynamic viscosity. To do so the following system was set up [14]: polymer chains were grafted at high density on parallel surfaces on the faces of the simulation cell perpendicular to the z axis; the solvent monomers were added explicitly also. To establish stationary Couette flow, a constant velocity was imprinted to the "heads" of the polymer chains grafted on the surface and an equal in magnitude but opposite in direction velocity was added to the grafted heads on the opposite surface. This setup forms a constant velocity gradient for the particles confined by the pore defined by the surfaces, along the z axis, which allows one to calculate the viscosity η as follows [15]:

$$\eta = \frac{\langle F_x(\dot{\gamma}) \rangle / A}{\dot{\gamma}}. \tag{9}$$

In Eq. (9) $\dot{\gamma}$ is the shear rate, which is given as $\dot{\gamma} = 2v/D$, where v is the constant velocity applied to the grafted polymer heads, and D is the distance between the surfaces, which is constant as well. The square area of each surface is A and $\langle F_x(\dot{\gamma}) \rangle$ is the mean force along the direction of the flow (x) that the particles on the surfaces experience, averaged over time for all particles. Figure 4 shows the dependence of the viscosity on the size of the simulation cell [14]. The difference between the value of the viscosity predicted for the smallest box and the largest one amounts to less than

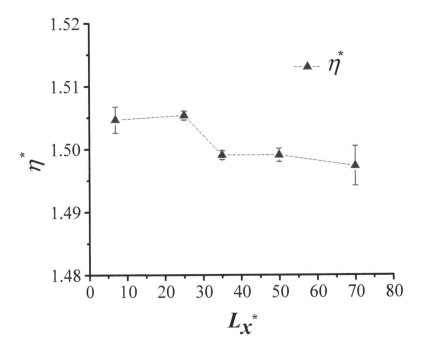

Fig. 4. Finite size effect in the viscosity, η^*, of polymer brushes on parallel walls. The symbol L_x^* represents the size of the simulation box in the x direction, which is equal to that in the y direction, L_y^*. In all cases, $L_z^* = 7$, the shear rate is $\dot{\gamma} = 0.28$, and the grafting density is $\Gamma^* = 0.30$. All quantities are reported in reduced DPD units. The line is only a guide to the eye. Adapted from [14].

0.5 percent only, showing once again that finite size effects are negligible in DPD even in the calculation of non–equilibrium properties. For additional discussion and computational details the reader is referred to [14].

3   Influence of the Statistical Ensemble Choice in the Prediction of Pressure of Confined Fluids

Confined complex fluids are important for various reasons, among which is the need to understand how the internal structure of the confined fluid depends on its basic interactions and on the characteristics of the confinement. Additionally, from an industrially relevant point of view, many nanotechnology applications of confined fluids such as in the design of new stimuli–responsive materials and in the fabrication of plastic sheets require detailed knowledge of properties such as the stability of fluids confined by surfaces. One key property of fluids under reduced symmetry conditions is the so called "disjoining" or solvation pressure Π, defined as [16]

$$\Pi(z) = [P_{ZZ}(z) - P_B], \tag{10}$$

where P_{zz} is the component of the pressure tensor along the z axis, assuming that the confining walls are placed on the xy plane, and P_B is the bulk pressure of the fluid, i.e., its pressure when it is not confined by the surfaces. If the fluid is not confined all diagonal components of the pressure tensor are equal to the bulk pressure and $\Pi = 0$. Therefore, the disjoining pressure is a useful gauge of the stability of the confined fluid because if $\Pi > 0$ the walls are kept apart and stability ensues. If, however, $\Pi < 0$ this signals attraction between the surfaces and the fluid becomes unstable.

The calculation of equilibrium properties of fluids under confinement usually requires the implementation of the Grand Canonical (GC) ensemble, where the chemical potential must be kept constant, in addition to the volume and the temperature. This is necessary to ensure that the confined fluid is in chemical and thermal equilibrium with the virtual bulk fluid that surrounds the former fluid, and the mechanism used to reach equilibrium is through the exchange of particles between confined and bulk fluids. Implementing the GC ensemble requires performing averages over spatial configurations rather than averages over time, which in turn means one must carry out Monte Carlo simulations [17] instead of MD simulations. Implementing the DPD model interaction in the Grand Canonical Monte Carlo (GCMC) algorithm [18] allows one to test the influence of ensemble choice in the predicted value of Π for DPD fluids.

Figure 5 shows the comparison between the predictions of Π under the canonical ensemble (NVT) and under the GC ensemble for a simple monomeric fluid confined by structureless walls as a function of the simulation box size. The difference between those two approaches is striking at small to medium box sizes, becoming negligible only for the largest boxes. Moreover, the ergodic theorem states that the value of a property in equilibrium obtained from averages over time (as in NVT) must be the same as the value of it obtained from averages over configurations (as in GCMC) [20]. This is clearly not the case here, except for the largest boxes, as Fig. 5 shows. It should be stated at the outset that this is not a shortcoming of the DPD model, since similar results have been obtained for other models [21]. The reason for the discrepancy of predictions between those two ensembles lies in the fact that the NVT ensemble does not allow for the density fluctuations that the fluid undergoes when it is compressed, which bring also pressure fluctuations, while the GC ensemble does. That is why the pressure grows as the fluid is compressed under NVT conditions in Fig. 5, while fluctuations appear when pressure is calculated using the GCMC method [19]. Experiments on fluids under confinement using the surface force apparatus or atomic force microscopy confirm the predictions under the GC ensemble [22].

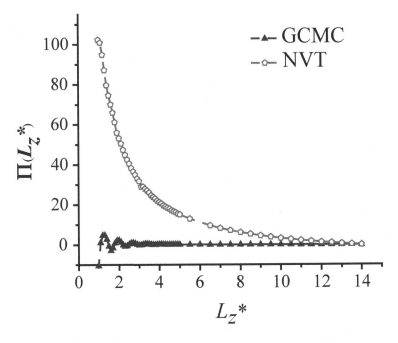

Fig. 5. Comparison of the solvation or disjoining pressure of a pure monomeric confined fluid as a function of box size obtained at fixed chemical potential (GCMC, filled triangles), and a fixed density (NVT, empty pentagons). The interaction parameters, density and temperature are the same for both systems. Both axes are represented in reduced DPD units. Adapted from [19].

There is of course a caveat: by their very construction, GCMC simulations are considerably more computationally intensive than MD simulations, regardless the interaction model [17], which in practical terms means that more computer time is required to predict properties in equilibrium with GC simulations. To try to get the best of both worlds, Balderas Altamirano and Gama Goicochea proposed a simple method to improve the speed of simulations of confined fluids without losing accuracy [19]. It consists of performing GCMC simulations at high confinement, keeping track of the average particle number; when that average is almost constant; which typically occurs after a few simulation blocks have been completed, the GCMC simulations are stopped. Then, that average particle number is inserted into the faster, NVT dynamics simulations, which are run until equilibrium is reached at a fraction of the computational cost [19]. The results, shown in Fig. 6, demonstrate that this simple method works very well, since the faster DPD simulations carried out under the canonical ensemble (NVT, empty pentagons in Fig. 6) reproduce the predictions of the disjoining pressure obtained from GCMC simulations (solid triangles in Fig. 6). The NVT data follow closely those from GCMC even for the smallest boxes, capturing the oscillation amplitudes and periods. For full details and additional applications, see [19].

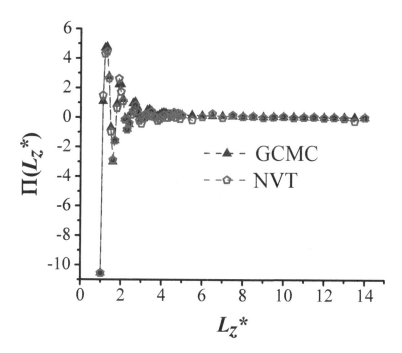

Fig. 6. Comparison of the disjoining pressure of a confined monomeric liquid obtained at constant chemical potential (filled triangles; see GCMC curve in Fig. 5) with that obtained using standard DPD (NVT, empty pentagons) after having chosen the density of the latter to match the average density obtained at the same box volume from GCMC simulations. The scales on both axes are reported in reduced DPD units. Adapted from [19].

4 Influence of the Conservative, Dissipative and Random DPD Forces on the Virial of Simple Fluids

In this section we review the influence that factors such as the size of the time step used in the integration of the equation of motion, simulation box size and strength of dissipation and Brownian motion have on the DPD force contributions to the virial calculation in simple liquids [23]. The focus is on the calculation of the virial only,

324   M.Á. Balderas Altamirano et al.

because it is a popular method used to calculate the pressure in numerical simulations [24], as follows:

$$P = \rho k_B T + \frac{1}{3V}\left\langle \sum_{j>i} \vec{F}_{ij} \cdot \vec{r}_{ij} \right\rangle,$$ (11)

where P is the pressure of the homogeneous fluid, ρ its density and the brackets represent average over time. The contribution of each DPD force is calculated separately to study the influence of the above mentioned factors to the virial. Let us start with the influence of the time step while keeping the size of cell fixed; Fig. 7(a) shows the effect that increasing the time step has on the random force contribution to the virial, as a function of the simulation time, where N is the number of times the equation of motion is solved numerically. Clearly, the random force contribution is very small, and quickly becomes negligible, independently of the choice of time step. This occurs because the random force is basically white noise. The dissipative force contributes very little to the virial also, as Fig. 7(b) shows, but in this case it requires longer simulation time, specially if the time step is very small, see the blue line in Fig. 7(b),

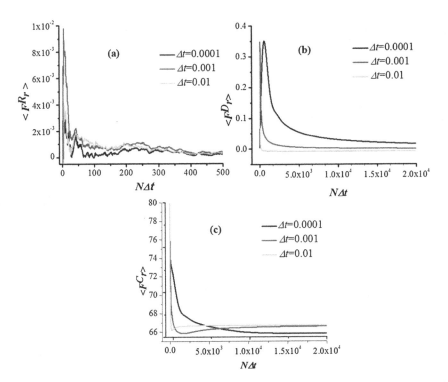

Fig. 7. The virial contribution of (a) the random, (b) dissipative and (c) conservative forces for a DPD simple fluid as a function of time, for three choices of the integration time step. For the conservative force the interaction constant was chosen as $a_{ij} = 78.3$. The fluid is made up of 3000 identical particles in a cubic box with volume $V = 10 \times 10 \times 10$. All axes are shown in reduced DPD units. N is the number of times the dynamics is solved. Adapted from [23].

where more than twenty thousand integrations of Newton's second law are needed for this artifact to become zero. It can be shown [23] that if the dissipative force is coupled to a random force, as occurs in the DPD model, the contribution of the former to the pressure – and to all equilibrium properties of the fluid – becomes zero, given a long enough period of time. The question is how long is long enough, but luckily if a relatively large time step is used, e.g. $\Delta t = 0.01$ the contribution of the dissipative force to the virial is zero almost immediately after the simulation has begun. When equilibrium is reached, only the conservative force should contribute to the virial, and this is indeed confirmed by Fig. 7(c).

Another variable of interest is the size of the simulation cell, whose influence on the virial is broken down into the three contributions shown in Fig. 8. In all cases the time step was set at $\Delta t = 0.01$, the box is cubic and the fluid density is fixed to 3, as in previous cases. Except for the small fluctuations that appear in the random force contribution to the virial in Fig. 8(a), what can be concluded from the results shown in Fig. 8 is that the size of the simulation box does not affect the contribution of the DPD forces to the virial as the simulation time evolves. This is expected because of the short range nature of the DPD forces and because the virial contributions are traced as functions of time.

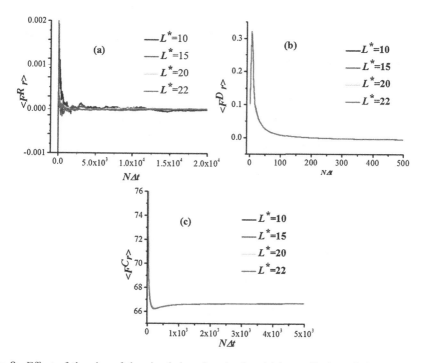

Fig. 8. Effect of the size of the simulations box in the virial contribution of the (a) random, (b) dissipative and (c) conservative forces for a DPD fluid as a function of time, for four values of the volume of the cubic box with the side length L^*. The conservative force constant is $a_{ij} = 78.3$. The fluid density is kept equal to $\rho^* = 3$ and the integration time step is chosen as $\Delta t = 0.01$ in all cases. All quantities are shown in reduced DPD units. Adapted from [23].

As a last case study we explore the dependence of the virial on the simulation time for four different values of the constants defining the strength of the dissipative and random forces in DPD, namely γ and σ in Eqs. (1) and (2), respectively. For this part of the work, the volume of the cell, as the density and the time step are fixed in all simulations [23]. Increasing these constants makes the fluid more viscous and the DPD thermostat comes into play to invest that increase into more Brownian motion.

As Fig. 9 shows, the more viscous the DPD fluid becomes, the less important the non conservative interactions are with respect to their contributions to the virial as the numerical simulation evolves in time. Even for the least viscous fluid (blue line in Fig. 9), the dissipative and random forces contributions to the virial are very small and the pressure can be accurately obtained from the conservative force contribution only. Moreover, the simulation running time required to remove artifacts contributing to the pressure from the dissipative and random forces is of the order of 3×10^4 except for the least viscous fluid, which is only of academic interest. As Fig. 9(c) shows, for long enough simulations only the conservative force is important in the calculation of the

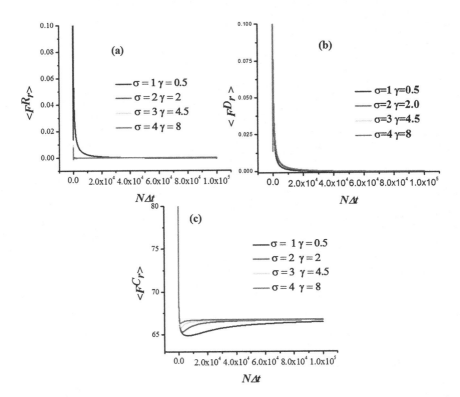

Fig. 9. Effect of varying the strength of the random (σ) and dissipative (γ) forces in the contribution to the virial of the (a) random, (b) dissipative and (c) conservative forces for a monomeric DPD fluid as functions of time. In all cases the temperature is $T^* = 1$, the conservative force constant is $a_{ij} = 78.3$, and the fluid density is kept equal to $\rho^* = 3$, while the integration time step was chosen as $\Delta t = 0.001$ in all cases. All quantities are reported in reduced units; adapted from [23].

pressure through the virial, except for the least viscous fluid. The same trends are expected to hold for other thermodynamic and structural properties in equilibrium.

5 Conclusions

No technique is without shortcomings and DPD is no exception, but in this contribution we have focused on reporting some tricks of the trade that practitioners of numerical simulations might find useful, especially when it comes to trying to optimize computational efforts. By judiciously choosing parameters and scales, users of DPD can benefit from the fact that its mesoscopic reach and the simplicity of its interactions can be helpful tools to derive novel information on soft matter systems.

Acknowledgments. MABA thanks PRODEP DSA/103.5/15/3894 and CA – Ingeniería de Procesos Químicos y Ambientales. MABA and AGG thank the Centro Nacional de Supercomputo (IPICYT) and the High Performance Computation Area of the Universidad de Sonora, for allocation of computer time; J Limón (IF UASLP) is acknowledged for technical support. AGG would like to thank JD Hernández Velázquez, J. Klapp, E. Mayoral and C. Pastorino for important discussions.

References

1. Allen, M.P., Tildesley, D.J.: Computer Simulation of Liquids. Clarendon, Oxford (1987)
2. Hoogerbrugge, P.J., Koelman, J.M.V.A.: Simulating microscopic hydrodynamic phenomena with dissipative particle dynamics. Europhys. Lett. **19**, 155–160 (1992)
3. Español, P., Warren, P.: Statistical Mechanics of Dissipative Particle Dynamics. Europhys. Lett. **30**, 191–196 (1995)
4. Groot, R.D., Warren, P.B.: Dissipative particle dynamics: bridging the gap between atomistic and mesoscopic simulation. J. Chem. Phys. **107**, 4423–4435 (1997)
5. Dinsmore, A.D., Warren, P.B., Poon, C.K., Yodh, A.G.: Fluid Solid transition on walls in binary hard sphere mixtures. Europhys. Lett. **40**, 337–342 (1997)
6. Mackie, A., Bonet Avalos, J., Navas, V.: Dissipative Particle Dynamics with energy conservation: Modeling of heat flow. Europhys. Lett. **40**, 337–342 (1999)
7. Pastorino, C., Gama Goicochea, A.: Dissipative particle dynamics: a method to simulate soft matter systems in equilibrium and under flow. In: Klapp, J., Ruíz Chavarría, G., Medina Ovando, A., López Villa, A., Sigalotti, L. (eds.) Selected Topics of Computational and Experimental Fluid Mechanics. ESE, pp. 51–79. Springer, Cham (2015). doi:10.1007/978-3-319-11487-3_3
8. Moeendarbary, E., Ng, T.Y., Zangeneh, M.: Dissipative Particle Dynamics: Introduction, methodology and complex flui applications - a review. Int. J. App. Mech. **1**, 737–763 (2009)
9. Lu, Z.Y., Wang, Y.L.: An introduction to Dissipative Particle Dynamics. Methods Mol. Biol. **924**, 617–633 (2013)
10. Fuchslin, R.M., Fellermann, H., Ericksson, A., Ziock, H.J.: Coarse graining and scaling in Dissipative Particle Dynamics. J. Chem. Phys. **130**(214102), 1–8 (2009)
11. Velázquez, M.E., Gama Goicochea, A., Gonzalez Melchor, M., Neria, M., Alejandre, J.: Finite Size effects in dissipative particle dynamics simulations. J. Chem. Phys. **124**, 084104 (2006)

12. Warren, P.B.: Vapor liquid coexistence in many body Dissipative Particle Dynamics. Phys. Rev. E **68**, 066702 (2003)
13. Fischer, M.E., Widom, B.: Decay of Correlations in Linear Systems. J. Chem. Phys. **50**, 3756–3772 (1969)
14. Gama Goicochea, A., Mayoral, E., Klapp, J., Pastorino, C.: Nanotribology of biopolymer brushes in aqueous solution using dissipative particle dynamics simulations: an application to PEG covered liposomes in a theta solvent. Soft Matter **10**, 166 (2014)
15. Makosco, C.: Rheology principles, measurements and applications. VCH J. Phys. Chem. Lett. **7**, 1836–1844 (1994)
16. Derjaguin, B.V., Churaev, N.V.: In Fluid International Phenomena. Wiley, New York (1986)
17. Frenkel, D., Simt, B.: Understanding Molecular Simulation. Academic Press, UK (2016)
18. Gama Goicochea, A.: Adsorption and Disjoining Pressure Isotherms of Confined Polymers using Dissipative Particle Dynamics. Langmuir **23**, 11656–11663 (2007)
19. Balderas Altamirano, M.A., Gama Goicochea, A.: Comparison of mesoscopic solvation pressure at constant density and constant chemical potential. Polymer **52**, 3846 (2011)
20. McQuarrie DA, Statistical Mechanics (Harper & Row, New York)
21. Xiao, C., Rowlison, J.S.: The solvation pressure in a system of fixed density. Mol. Phys. **73**, 937 (1991)
22. Israelachvilli, J.N.: Molecular and Surfaces Forces. Academic Press, Netherlands (2011)
23. Gama Goicochea, A., Balderas Altamirano, M.A., Hernández, J.D., Pérez, E.: The role of the dissipative and random forces in the calculation of the pressure of simple fluids with dissipative particle dynamics. Comput. Phys. Commun. **188**, 76–81 (2015)
24. Goldstein, H.: Classical Mechanics. Addison Wesley, Nueva York (1980)

Ab initio DFT Calculations for Materials in Nuclear Research

E. Mayoral[1(⊠)], A. Rey[2], Jaime Klapp[1,3], A. Gómez[1],
and M. Mayoral[4]

[1] Instituto Nacional de Investigaciones Nucleares (ININ),
Carretera México-Toluca S/N, La Marquesa, 52750 Ocoyoacac,
Edo de Mexico, Mexico
{estela.mayoral,jaime.klapp,
armando.gomez}@inin.gob.mx
[2] Department of Chemical Engineering, McGill University,
Montreal, QC H3A 2B2, Canada
alejandro.rey@mcgill.ca
[3] Abacus-Laboratorio de Matemática Aplicada y Cómputo de Alto Rendimiento,
Departamento de Matemáticas, CINVESTAV-IPN,
Carretera México-Toluca Km 38.5, La Marquesa, 52740 Ocoyoacac,
Estado de México, Mexico
[4] MTrip, 1117 Sainte-Catherine West 601, Montreal, QC H3B 1H9, Canada

Abstract. Currently, high performance computing is a very important tool in material science. The study of materials at the microscopic level for obtaining macroscopic properties from the behavior at atomic level is a big challenge, even more when a large number of atoms are involved in the analysis. One of the most important open source codes capable of performing *ab initio* density functional theory (DFT) calculations with many hundreds of atoms at low computational cost is the SIESTA code. This code is able to perform self-consistent electronic structure simulations based on DFT for very complex materials. The performance of this code is tested in this work by applying it to the study of typical core structural materials used in nuclear reactors such as Zr and Zircaloy-2. These materials are commonly used for the cladding of the fuel rods used in Light Water Reactors (LWR) and CANDU reactors. First-principles calculations for Zr, Zircalloy-2 and modified structures of them were performed with microstructural defects in order to analyze material damage. Adsorption energy of I_2 on Zr (0 0 0 1) surfaces as a function of the distance is also presented. Results showed how this kind of simulations can be carried out for large systems at a relatively cheap computational cost.

1 Introduction

Nowadays, the need to have alternative options to produce clean and sustainable energy is one of the problems of paramount importance at the global level. Nuclear energy is one of the main alternatives for obtaining clean energy on a large scale. This power source guarantees electricity supply and reduces pollutant emissions by producing electricity on a constant basis with stable and predictable prices. Currently, operating

© Springer International Publishing AG 2017
C.J. Barrios Hernández et al. (Eds.): CARLA 2016, CCIS 697, pp. 329–339, 2017.
DOI: 10.1007/978-3-319-57972-6_24

nuclear reactors provide about 11.5 percent of the world's electricity. In a nuclear reactor the fuel is located in the core where the nuclear fission reactions occur. The materials used in the core are called *"core structural materials"*. One of the options in order to improve the competence of the existing nuclear power plants is the increase in the burn-up of the nuclear fuel (a measure of how much energy is extracted from the fuel and it is related directly to the time that the fuel is in the reactor core). In order to increase the efficient use of the fuel, it is desired that the fuel remains inside the reactor as much time as possible (several years or fuel cycles), i.e., to be subject to high burn-up. This strategy leads to lower fuel costs, fuel storage expenses as well as the amount of waste for final disposal. Nevertheless, higher burn-ups jeopardize the materials performance of reactor fuels, reactor components and reactor vessels due to the high loads affecting the fuel (pressure, temperature, radiation, etc.). The core structural materials in a nuclear reactor are those used to contain the fuel in rods, to keep together the fuel assemblies as well as the materials to build the control rods, core monitoring instruments and their support structures. These structural materials must preserve their functionality to maintain the integrity of the fuel, rods and fuel assemblies, preventing the release of radioactive materials from the fuel to the coolant and in the worst case to the environment. Aiming to increase the efficient operation of nuclear reactors (to operate with higher burn-ups), new improved materials-able to resist radiation and withstand irradiation conditions and extreme temperatures and pressures are required. Therefore, the design of new materials with adequate characteristics to support the operating conditions involved in nuclear processes is one of the main challenges in the design of new nuclear technologies.

Zirconium is the most widely used material for the fuel cladding and gathering structure in nuclear reactors because of its low neutron capture cross-section. Other important properties are good corrosive and mechanical properties that have led to its use preferably over stainless steels. Even though the high purity in zirconium produces very good resistance to corrosion in water, the use of alloys is required to enhance the resistance to high temperatures. The main alloying elements used are tin, nickel, iron and chromium because they have very low neutron absorption. Zircaloy-2 is a Zirconium-based alloy containing 1.2–1.7% Sn, 0.07–0.20% Fe, 0.05–0.15% Cr and 0.03–0.04% Ni and is employed as the cladding for Light Water (LWR) and CANDU reactors fuel rods, as well as for other reactor uses such as the pressure tubes in CANDU reactors.

On the other hand, it is well known that numerical simulation and computational materials science are nowadays an important complement in the comprehensive study and design of new materials (Wimmer et al. 2010). These kinds of tools are very significant, especially when hazardous materials or processes are involved as in the case of nuclear research area. For these applications, it is important to avoid as much as possible the use of radioactive sources. Reducing experimental essays in order to decrease high-level waste and the exposition to hazardous material is mandatory; the possibility of designing new materials and predicting their properties in nuclear research in a safer manner and at low cost is a challenge, thus, numerical modeling seems to be a promissory option. Specifically, simulation and modeling applied to the study of radiation damage make available novel fundamental insights into the microstructural evolutions that go on for the small period of time related to the radiation damage cascades. Additionally, not only is the understanding at atomic scale fundamental in the design of new materials in the nuclear area, but also allows the prediction of properties in a quantitative way. Mechanical, thermal, electrical, optical, magnetic and chemical properties are some of the main characteristics that need to be known in order to have real applications in engineering and to solve technological problems in an effective way.

Ab initio DFT calculations have become a very popular technique to study the behavior of molecules and condensed materials at a microscopic scale. However, one of the main limitations in this kind of studies is the high computational cost needed to deal with big systems, so new methodologies must be developed in this area. An alternative is the use of high performance computational resources and the optimization of codes running in different platforms (CPUs and GPUs). The SIESTA code (Spanish Initiative for Electronic Simulations with Thousand of Atoms) is one of the most important open source codes capable of performing *ab initio* DFT calculations with many hundreds of atoms at low computational cost (Ordejon et al. 1996; Soler et al. 2002). The SIESTA code is able to perform self-consistent electronic structure simulations based on DFT for very complex materials. Using this code (available at http://www.uam.es/siesta) a large number of atoms have been studied using modest computational resources. This approach has been capable of suggesting the effect of impurities, defects and composition in different properties of solid materials and alloys. It has been applied in different systems like surfaces, nano-materials, ceramics, alloys, amorphous semiconductors, biological molecules among others (Sánchez-Portal et al. 2004).

In this work the performance of this code is applied to the study of typical core structural materials used in nuclear reactors. First-principles calculations for Zr, Zircalloy-2 and modified structures of them with microstructural defects were performed in order to analyze material damage. The adsorption energy of I_2 on Zr (0 0 0 1) surface as a function of the distance is also presented.

2 Schrodinger by Schrödinger

Considering the size and complexity of the materials that are analyzed, all simulations were performed using the SIESTA code, which is based in linear-scaling, or $O(N)$ methods that scales the computing time and memory linearly with the increase of the number of atoms N, in contrast with the standard approaches that scale proportionally to the cube of the number of atoms in the system. This allows to obtain very accurate *ab initio* simulations of systems with a considerable size at a relative low computational cost (Bowler and Miyazaki 2012). Among quantum mechanical methods the most reliable and also the most computationally demanding are the fully self-consistent density functional theory methods (DFT). The use of these methods requires solving the Schrodinger equation and the determination of the self-consistent Hamiltonian, which usually requires a large amount of computing resources. The method inside the SIESTA code (Soler et al. 2002) allows the use of self-consistent DFT to simulate big systems (thousands of atoms) in $O(N)$ iterations. The DFT methodology used is based in a flexible linear combination of atomic orbitals (LCAO) basis set and multiple-Z plus polarization basis which allows the use of minimal basis sets, fast calculations and a combination of *ad-hoc* set of parameters depending on the needed accuracy and the available computing resources. The Born-Oppenheimer approximation is used as core approximation as well as the treatment of exchange and correlation terms and the use of pseudopotentials. The introduction of norm-conserving pseudopotentials is useful to allow the expansion of the pseudo-charge density on a uniform spatial grid. SIESTA reads them as semilocal and after that, semilocal form is transformed to non-local form as is proposed by Kleinman and Bylander (Kleinman and Bylander 1982). Double-Z plus polarization basis set is used as the standard basis because it usually balances convergence and reasonable computational cost. It makes the combination of multiple-Z polarization basis sets and semicore states a good technique in the case of alkali and some transition metals. The total Energy is calculated using Kohn-Sham approximation (Kohn and Sham 1965). The program is a totally self-consistent implementation of DFT and uses Kohn-Sham approach to calculate the electronic structures of molecules and condensed phases simultaneously with the total energy and derivatives of atomic positions, which are related to the total energy for the optimization of crystal structures.

In this work the basis sets chosen were numerical double zeta plus polarization, with this we consider the possibility that the atom orbital could be polarized by the molecular interactions (Hu et al. 2013). The exchange correlation function of Perdew-Burke-Ernserh (Perdew J.P. et al. 1997), and the Troulier-Martins pseudopotentials for all atoms in the system (Troullier and Martins 1991) are also used.

3   Results

3.1   Adsorption of I_2 on Zr Surfaces

Comprehension of the microscopic factors that produce fracture in core structural materials such as Zirconium alloys is of fundamental importance in the design and study of materials for nuclear power plants. An important process is the one known as Pellet-Clad Interaction (PCI), which can occur through power transients in nuclear plants. In PCI it is supposed that the main responsible in the detriment of the Zr structure is the iodine produced during the fission process which induces stress corrosion cracking (SCC).

The mechanism involved in SCC includes dissociation, adsorption and diffusion of I_2 in contact with the Zr structures. In this section, the adsorption process using *ab initio* DFT calculations is explored with the SIESTA code and the methodology described in the previous section.

The *hcc* Zr structure is modeled using 78 atoms in a cell. The surface corresponds with the (0 0 0 1). The initial structure was relaxed and the total energy calculated obtaining $E_T[Zr] = -8359.93672$ eV. Figure 1 shows the relaxed structure for the system studied.

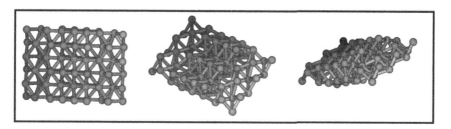

Fig. 1. *hcc* Zirconium relaxed structure.

The adsorption process was modelled considering one I_2 molecule attached at the Zr (0001) surface. This study requires that the I_2 be able to relax to its most favourable arrangement and then the bond distances connecting the Iodine with the Zirconium surface contracted and stretched to model the process of bond rupture and creation. To do this, in the simulation the position of the I and the Zr atoms which are attached each other are fixed whereas the rest of the atoms are allowed to relax.

The adsorption energy E_{ads} of $I_2 + Zr \rightarrow I$ - Zr - I was obtained using the expression

$$E_{ads} = \frac{E[I/Zr] + E[Zr] + nE[I_2]}{2n},\qquad(1)$$

where E[I/Zr] is the energy of the I-Zr-I system, E[Zr] = −8359.9367 eV is the energy of the pure Zirconium structure and E[I_2] = −2346.43186 eV is the energy of I_2 gas phase molecule calculated in this work. n is the number of I_2 molecules in the system. The results for different reaction coordinates are shown in Table 1. The computed adsorption energy is E_{ads} = 610 kJ/mol in good agreement with previous results reported in literature (Wimmer et al. 2010) indicating strong chemical affinity of iodine and Zirconium.

In Table 1 and Fig. 2, x is the reaction coordinate and is related to the height of the center of mass of the I-I atoms; x = 1 refers to the adsorbed iodine atoms at a height of 4.5509 Å and x = 0 corresponds to the undissociated I_2 molecule at a height of 12.1711 Å; x > 1 corresponds with the diffusion of the I in the Zr structure.

Table 1. Total energy for the I-Zr-I system E[I/Zr], relative reaction coordinate and adsorption energy E_{ads} calculated for different distances D.

D [Å]	E[I/Zr] [kJ/mol]	Reaction Coordinate (x)	E_{ads} [kJ/mol]
1.64045	−10687.8184	1.38194444	−554.2801
4.55092	−10693.7056	1	−610.8922
8.99601	−10698.8260	0.41666667	−363.8731
12.17107	−10702.8313	0	−170.6443

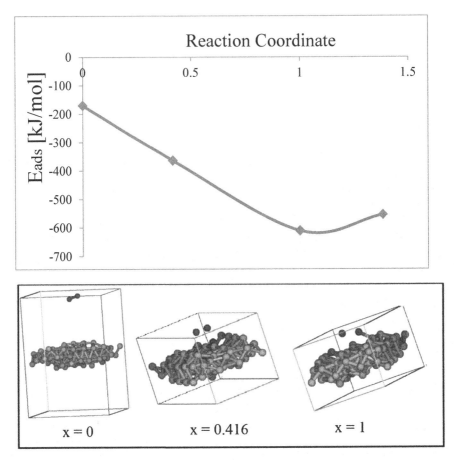

Fig. 2. Computed energy profile of the dissociation of an I_2 molecule on a Zr (0001) surface and final structures.

3.2 Microstructural Defects: Vacancies in Zr Structures

Micro-structural defects are the responsible of the changes in material properties for materials exposed to radiation. The simplest natural defects are the vacancies. In nuclear damage, these defects occur when an atom in a material is hit by a high energetic particle and knocked it out of its lattice site. This initial knock-on atom and the recoiling particle produce further collisions with new atoms causing the displacement of other atoms or distortions. All these distortions produce changes in the mechanical properties. In this section the *ab initio* calculations results are presented for the energies of the vacancies defects. Formation energies of defects in Zr structures were calculated using the total energies of perfect and defected supercells. *ab initio* calculations of the total energies are performed using the SIESTA atomic-orbitals within GGA. The electronic configuration for Zr is $[Kr]4d^2 5s^2$, the core electrons were replaced by Troullier-Martins pseudopotentials; valence electrons were described by a double- polarized DZP basis set with cutoff radii of 3.04 a.u. for the 5s and 2.65 a.u. for the 4d orbitals. Six structures with different number of vacancies V = 1, 2, 3, 4, 10 and 20 were studied. The cells contained 78 Zr atoms for the perfect structure minus the removed vacancy atom in each case. The total energies of the cells for each system were optimized for the atomic positions until all forces were lower than 0.005 eV/Å. Every one of the Zr atoms except for the corner atoms of the supercell were permitted to locate their lowest energy position. Relaxed structures are shown in Fig. 3.

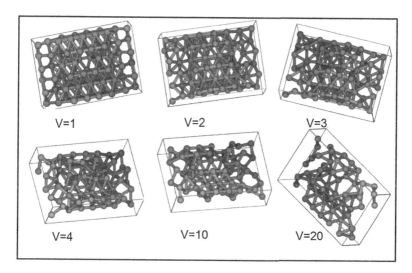

Fig. 3. Relaxed structures for Zirconium with vacancies (V = 1, 2, 3, 4, 10 and 20).

The vacancy formation energies E_v can be obtained by the cohesive energies of the initial E_{coh}^1 and final system E_{coh}^2 and is defined as:

$$E_v \equiv (N - 1) \cdot (E_{coh}^1 - E_{coh}^2). \tag{2}$$

It is assumed that the total potential energy, E_1, in the perfect Zr crystal has reached the cohesive state and also E_2 in the vacancy-formed structure after the relaxation, then

$$E_1 = \sum_i^N E_i \equiv N \cdot E_{coh}^1, \tag{3}$$

$$E_2 = \sum_i^{N-1} E_i \equiv (N - 1) \cdot E_{coh}^2 \tag{4}$$

$$E_v \equiv E_2 - \frac{N - 1}{N} \cdot E_1, \tag{5}$$

where N is the number of atoms in the simulation box (Verite et al. 2013). It is important to point out that E_v is not just the difference between E_1 and E_2. Both energies were calculated for supercells of identical size. The results are shown in Table 2 and Fig. 4.

Table 2. Total energies obtained for Zr structures with vacancies V = 1, 2 3, 4, 5, 10 and 20.

V	E(eV)
0	−8359.93672
1	−8254.75205
2	−8147.10783
3	−8040.74528
4	−7933.69248
10	−7285.39938
20	−6200.15237

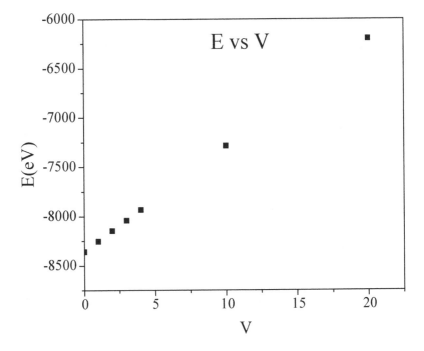

Fig. 4. Total energies obtained for Zr structures as a function of the vacancies V = 1, 2 3, 4, 5, 10 and 20.

As it can be seen, the total energies of a supercell are on the order of 10^4 eV and the formation energy is just a few eV. For this reason calculations of formation energies are hard to converge and high performance computing is required. The E_v obtained for Zr was E_v = 1.9940 eV, which it is in good agreement with the experimental evidence from positron annihilation spectroscopy which leads to $H_f^{exp} \geq 1.5\ eV$ (Verite et al. 2007).

3.3   Impurities and Alloys

Zirconium is one of the most used materials in core nuclear reactors due to its low neutron capture cross-section, good mechanical properties and its resistance to corrosion. Even so, to improve the resistance to elevated temperatures the use of alloys is necessary. The most important alloying elements used are Sn, Ni, Fe and Cr due to its low neutron absorption. Zircaloy-2 is a Zirconium-based alloy containing 1.2–1.7% Sn, 0.07–0.20% Fe, 0.05–0.15% Cr, and 0.03–0.04% Ni. Because the stoichiometric quantities of these atoms are small, its inclusion in a Zirconium structure for *ab initio* calculations implies the use of many atoms. In this part of the work structures with 250 atoms including n atoms of Sn (n_{Sn} = 1, 2, 3, 10) and $250-n_{Sn}$ atoms of Zirconium were built. Total energies for each system were calculated performing *ab initio* calculations. The electronic configuration for Zr is $[Kr]4d^2 5s^2$ and for Sn is $[Kr]\ 4d^{10}\ 5s^2\ 5p^2$ the core electrons were replaced by Troullier-Martins pseudopotentials and valence electrons were described by a double-polarized DZP basis set. The cutoff radii of Zr were 3.04 a.u. for the 5s and 2.65 a.u. for the 4d orbitals. For the Sn the cutoff radii used were 2.4 a.u. for 5s and 2.46 a.u. for 5p orbitals. The total energies of the systems were optimized for the atomic positions until all forces were smaller than 0.005 eV/Å. Every one of the Zr atoms but the corner atoms of the supercell were permitted to locate their lowest energy position. Relaxed structures are shown in Fig. 5. Even though differences in energy are obtained, a more exhaustive comprehension involving different configurations and bigger systems is necessary in order to understand the effect of the presence of Sn (Table 3).

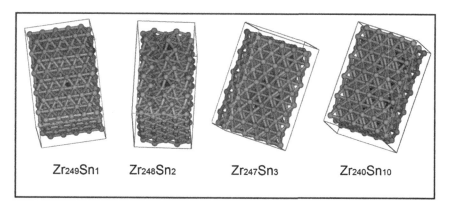

| $Zr_{249}Sn_1$ | $Zr_{248}Sn_2$ | $Zr_{247}Sn_3$ | $Zr_{240}Sn_{10}$ |

Fig. 5. Relaxed structures for $Zr_x Sn_y$ alloys structures.

Table 3. Total energies calculated for $Zr_x Sn_y$ alloys structures.

$Zr_x Sn_y$	Total energy (eV)
$Zr_{250}Sn_0$	−26584.31579
$Zr_{249}Sn_1$	−26585.98849
$Zr_{247}Sn_3$	−26589.57301
$Zr_{240}Sn_{10}$	−26601.46296

4 Conclusions

In this work, it was shown with some examples, the necessity of the use of high performance computing (HPC) in nuclear material science because of the combination of the required high accuracy and the large number of atoms to study this kind of systems makes the calculations very demanding. The use of the SIESTA code applied in the study of typical core structural materials used in nuclear reactors such as Zr, Zr_xSn_y alloys, and modified structures with microstructural defects was presented. Results showed how this kind of simulations can be carried out for large systems at a relatively cheap computational cost. Nevertheless, for more advanced studies such as the design of materials needed for fourth-generation nuclear technology and upcoming fusion reactors that must hold up operating conditions, with temperatures in the range of 500–1000°C and exposure damage of $\sim$ 30–100 dpa more computational resources will be necessary. Numerical modeling simulations using HPC are necessary to reduce exposure to radioactive material, supporting the analysis, optimization, control, good operation, and innovation of materials for the design of new nuclear technologies.

Acknowledgements. This work was partially supported by ABACUS, CONACyT grant EDOMEX-2011-C01-165873. The calculations for this paper were performed in the Cinvestav-Abacus supercomputer.

References

Bowler, D., Miyazaki, T.: Methods in electronic structure calculations. Rep. Prog. Phys. **75**, 036503 (2012)

Hu, H., Reven, L., Rey, A.D.: Ab initio study of 6-mercapto-hexane SAMs: effect of Au surface defects on the monolayer assembly. Mol. Simul. **39**(4), 292–298 (2013)

Kleinman, L., Bylander, D.M.: Efficacious form for model pseudopotentials. Phys. Rev. Lett. **48**, 1425 (1982)

Kohn, W., Sham, L.J.: Self-consistent equations including exchange and correlation effects. Phys. Rev. **140**, A1133 (1965)

Ordejon, P., Artacho, E., Soler, J.M.: Self-consistent order-N density-functional calculations for very large systems. Phys. Rev. B **53**, R10441(R) (1996)

Perdew, J.P., Burke, K., Ernserhof, M.: Generalized gradient approximation made simple. Phys. Rev. Lett. **77**, 3865 (1997). Erratum Phys. Rev. Lett. 78, 1396

Sánchez-Portal, D., Ordejón, P., Canadell, E.: Computing the properties of materials from first principles with SIESTA. In: Kaltsoyannis, N., McGrady, J.E. (eds.) Principles and Applications of Density Functional Theory in Inorganic Chemistry II. Structure and Bonding, vol. 113, pp. 103–170. Springer, Heidelberg (2004)

Soler, J.M., Artacho, E., Gale, J.D., Garcia, A., Junquera, J., Ordejon, P., Sanchez-Portal, D.: The SIESTA method for ab initio order-N materials simulation. J. Phys.: Condens. Matter **14**, 2745–2779 (2002)

Troullier, N., Martins, J.L.: Efficient pseudopotentials for plane-wave calculations. Phys. Rev. B. **43**, 1993 (1991)

Verite, G., Domain, C., Fu, C., Gasca, P., Legris, A., Willaime, F.: Self-interstitial defects in hexagonal close packed metals revisited: evidence for low-symmetry configurations in Ti, Zr, and Hf. Phys. Rev. B **87**, 134108 (2013)

Verite, G., Willaime, F., Fu, C.: Anisotropy of the vacancy migration in Ti, Zr and Hf hexagonal close-packed metals from first principles. Solid State Phenom. **129**, 75–81 (2007)

Wimmer, E., Najafabadi, R., Young Jr., G.A., Ballard, J.D., Angeliu, T.M., Vollmer, J., Chambers, J.J., Niimi, H., Shaw, J.B., Freeman, C., Christesen, M., Wolf, W., Saxe, P.: Ab initio calculations for industrial materials engineering: successes and challenges. J. Phys.: Condens. Matter **22**, 384215 (2010)

Super Free Fall of a Liquid Frustum in a Semi-infinite Cone

Áyax Torres[1]([✉]), Salomón Peralta[1], Abraham Medina[1], Jaime Klapp[2,3], and Francisco Higuera[4]

[1] SEPI ESIME Azcapotzalco, Instituto Politécnico Nacional,
Av. de las Granjas 682, Col. Santa Catarina, Azcapotzalco,
02250 Mexico City, Mexico
higherintellect@hotmail.com, peraltasalomon@hotmail.com,
abraham_medina_ovando@hotmail.com
[2] Departamento de Física, Instituto Nacional de Investigaciones Nucleares,
Ocoyoacac, Estado de México, Mexico
jaime.klapp@hotmail.com
[3] ABACUS-Centro de Matemáticas Aplicadas y Cómputo de Alto Rendimiento,
CINVESTAV-IPN, La Marquesa, 52740 Ocoyoacac, Estado de México, Mexico
[4] Escuela Técnica Superior de Ingenieros Aeronáuticos,
Plaza del Cardenal Cisneros 3, 28040 Madrid, Spain

Abstract. In this paper we have analyzed theoretically the super free fall of a near inviscid mass of liquid, which fills partially a small section of a very long vertical conical pipe. Through the use of a one-dimensional inviscid model, we describe the simultaneous and pecular motion of the two interphases of the liquid.

Keywords: Flow in quasi-one-dimensional system · Flows in pipes and nozzles · Navier-stokes equations

1 Introduction

Recently, it has been shown that the upper free surface of a liquid column filling a cylindrical pipe of short length, but increasing radius, reaches super free fall [1–3]. In fact, it was demonstrated that when a liquid column, in a slowly expanding conical pipe is suddenly released from the rest, by opening abruptly its bottom exit and all liquid is exhausted from the tube, the upper free surface reaches initially a super gravitational acceleration, then the acceleration becomes sub-gravitational, and finally it turns back to terminate at exactly gravitational acceleration as required [2]. In the case of pipes with a sudden expansion (interconnected pipes at different radii) the upper free surface can achieve persistent accelerations several times larger than the gravity acceleration g, and the acceleration is larger for smaller levels of filling in the upper pipe [3]. All the previous rich dynamics in confined systems contrast with those where an initially confined mass of liquid is suddenly released to the ambient due to the explosion

© Springer International Publishing AG 2017
C.J. Barrios Hernández et al. (Eds.): CARLA 2016, CCIS 697, pp. 340–345, 2017.
DOI: 10.1007/978-3-319-57972-6_25

of a water-filled rubber-balloon [4]. Thus, such a mass of liquid falls initially, and thereafter, it disintegrates into smaller droplets. Incidentally, the super free fall in liquids also recalls the purely-mechanical problem of the super free fall of the tip of chains falling under the gravity action in two main configurations: a vertically hanging chain released from rest and an horizontally folded chain [5]. In this work we analyze theoretically, based on a slender slope approximation, the problem of the super free fall of a specific volume of low viscosity liquid contained in a conical pipe of very large length which is supposed to be released from the rest at any part of it. Since the mass of liquid never leaves the pipe, we conceptualize such configuration as a liquid slice in a semi infinite cone. This simple system allows us to predict the dynamic behavior of both upper and lower free interfaces, during the overall history of the flow (while the liquid slice does not desintegrates due to their extreme thinness). In the last part of this communication we discuss the realization of a qualitative experiment to visualize the dynamic evolution of the liquid slice. Finally, we give the main conclusions.

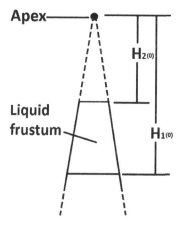

Fig. 1. Scheme of an idealized semi-infinite cone. The liquid frustum is bounded by $H_{1(0)}$ and $H_{2(0)}$.

2 Theory

Ideally, a semi-infinite conical pipe model has an infinite length and consequently, in any part of this pipe and under this configuration the radius is always increasing downwards along the flow direction. Here, we consider a finite volume of quiescent liquid confined at any part of the semi-infinite vertical cone by conforming a conical frustum (*i.e.*, a cone initially sliced by two horizontal parallel planes), both interfaces of the frustum are opened to the atmosphere at $z = H_{2(0)}$ and $z = H_{1(0)}$, respectively. Subindex (0) indicates initial positions. A scheme of the problem can be seen in Fig. 1. These two distances are taken in reference to the apex of the cone. This quasi-unidirectional model of motion of a liquid volume contained in a semi-infinite tube obeys the mass and momentum conservation equations.

$$\frac{1}{z^2}\frac{\partial}{\partial z}(z^2 u) = 0, \tag{1}$$

$$\rho\left(\frac{\partial u}{\partial t} + u\frac{\partial u}{\partial z}\right) = \frac{\partial P}{\partial z} + \rho g, \tag{2}$$

where z is the vertical distance measured downward from the apex of the cone, t is the time, u and P are the velocity and pressure of the liquid, ρ is the density of the liquid, g is the gravitational constant, and viscous effects have been neglected. Let $H_1(t)$ and $H_2(t)$ denote the position of the lower and upper surfaces at anytime during the movement. Then $u = dH_1/dt$, $P = P_a$ at $z = H_1$, and $u = dH_2/dt$, $P = P_a$ at $z = H_2$,

$$u = 0,\ H_1 = H_{1(0)},\ H_2 = H_{2(0)}\ \text{at}\ t = 0, \tag{3}$$

where P_a is the pressure outside the liquid and surface tensions have been neglected.

Equation (1) can be immediately integrated to give

$$u = \frac{dH_1}{dt}\frac{H_1^2}{z^2} = \frac{dH_2}{dt}\frac{H_2^2}{z^2}. \tag{4}$$

From the second equality, after using the initial condition (3), we obtain

$$H_1^3 - H_2^3 = H_{1(0)}^3 - H_{2(0)}^3, \tag{5}$$

which expresses the condition of conservation of the liquid volume.

Carrying equation (4) into the momentum equation (2), integrating the resulting equation from $z = H_1$ to $z = H_2$ and using the boundary conditions (3) for the pressure, we find, after some algebra

$$\frac{d^2 H_2}{dt^2} = \frac{H_1}{h_2}g + \frac{1}{2}\left(\frac{dH_2}{dt}\right)^2\left(\frac{1}{H_1} + \frac{H_2}{H_1^2} + \frac{H_2^2}{H_1^2} - \frac{3}{H_2}\right), \tag{6}$$

which is obtained by integrating (2) between $z = H_2$ to a generic value of z.

Introducing the dimensionless variables

$$\xi = \frac{H_2}{H_{1(0)} - H_{2(0)}},\quad \eta = \frac{H_1}{H_{1(0)} - H_{2(0)}},\quad \tau = t\sqrt{\frac{g}{H_{1(0)} - H_{2(0)}}}. \tag{7}$$

Equations (5) and (6) take the dimensionless form:

$$\eta^3 - \xi^3 = 1 + 3\xi_0\left(1 - \xi_0\right), \tag{8}$$

$$\frac{d^2\xi}{d\tau^2} = \frac{\eta}{\xi} + \frac{1}{2}\left(\frac{d\xi}{d\tau}\right)^2\left(\frac{1}{\eta} + \frac{\xi}{\eta^2} + \frac{\xi^2}{\eta^3} - \frac{3}{\xi}\right). \tag{9}$$

with

$$\xi = \xi_0,\quad \frac{d\xi}{d\tau} = 0\ \text{at}\ z = 0. \tag{10}$$

Now this final solution depends on the single dimensionless parameter

$$\xi_0 = \frac{H_{2(0)}}{H_{1(0)} - H_{2(0)}}. \tag{11}$$

3   Numerical Procedure

To obtain a numerical solution, after eliminating η by using Eq. (8), the resulting nonlinear second order equation (9) can be simply broken in a set of two stiff ordinary differential equations which will be numerically integrated by using Gill's method [7]. This method was developed from the general theory given by Kutta [8] and was chosen for this work because it is capable to reach fourth-order accuracy with the use of minimum storage registers. As mentioned in Blum [8] the two advantages of implementing Gill's method are: first, it only requires $3n + B$ storage registers whereas the standard Runge-Kutta method requires $4n + B$, where n refers to the number of coupled first-order differential equations and B is a constant; second, under Gill's method scheme the computation can be arranged and the rounding errors can be reduced significantly.

The celebrated subroutine introduced by White [6] was rewritten into a convenient from under the Fortran®95 standard, and the resulting project was compiled with the Absoft Pro Fortran®16.0.2 which is suitable to handle the proper irrational constants of Gill's method $e.g.$, $A = \sqrt{\frac{1}{2}} = 1.7071067811865475244$ with an explicit length declaration.

In order to estimate the development of the interphase acceleration we have chosen the next ΔH value at $\tau = 0$: $\xi(0) = 0.2$ and $\eta(0) = 1.2$. Those initial conditions were measured from the apex to every single interface conforming the height of the liquid frustum.

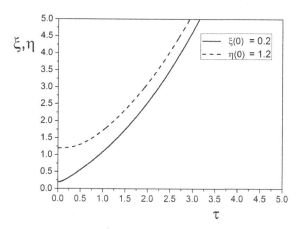

Fig. 2. Spatial evolution of both non-dimensional upper and lower free surfaces at initial conditions of filling $\xi_0 = 0.2$ and $\eta_0 = 1.2$.

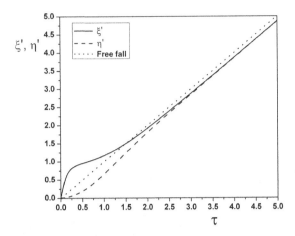

Fig. 3. Evolution of both upper and lower free interfaces $\dot{\xi}$ and $\dot{\eta}$ as a function of time.

As seen in Fig. 2 each free interface presents a similar behavior when this liquid column is suddenly released from the rest; it is apparent that the distance between interfaces decreases until a minimum distance is reached. According to Figs. 3 and 4 it is possible to conclude that at the beginning of the movement the upper free surface ξ starts to move faster than η and at later stages of the movement, both surfaces ξ and η will reach the pure free fall acceleration.

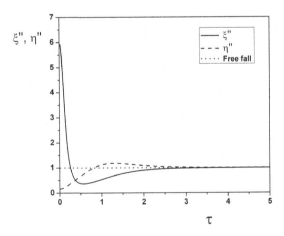

Fig. 4. Evolution of both, upper and lower interface acceleration as a function of time at initial conditions of filling $\xi_0 = 0.2$ and $\eta_0 = 1.2$.

4   Conclusions

The theoretical model based on the slender slope theory presented here, predicts the behavior of the free interfaces that conform a liquid frustum, which ideally lies in any part of a semi infinite cone and its suddenly released from the rest. The method used for the numerical computations reported here was originally designed in order to use efficiently every single storage space of the memory unit of the machine.

Acknowledgments. This work has been partially supported by the Instituto Politécnico Nacional (México), through projects SIP 20121347 and SIP 20120286, and by the Consejo Nacional de Ciencia y Tecnología (CONACyT) under the project CONACyT-EDOMEX-2011-C01-165873. The calculations for this work were performed in the Abacus I supercomputer.

References

1. Villaermaux, E., Pomeau, Y.: Super free fall. J. Fluid Mech. **642**, 147 (2010)
2. Torres, A., Medina, A., Higuera, F.J., Weidman, P.D.: On super free fall. J. Fluid Mech. **642**, 147–157 (2013)
3. Treviño, C., Peralta, S., Torres, A., Medina, A.: Super free fall of an inviscid liquid through interconnected vertical pipes. Europhys. Lett. **112**(1) (2015). Article no. 14002
4. Vollmer, M., Mollman, K.-P.: Is there a maximum size of water drops in nature? Phys. Teach. **51**(7), 400–402 (2013)
5. Virga, E.G.: Chain paradoxes. Proc. R. Soc. Lond. **471** (2015). Article no. 20140657
6. White, F.M.: Viscous Fluid Flow. McGraw-Hill, New York (2006)
7. Gill, S.: A process for the step-by-step integration of differential equations in an automatic digital computing machine. Math. Proc. Camb. Philos. Soc. **47**, 96–108 (1951). Cambridge University Press
8. Blum, E.K.: A modification of the Runge-Kutta Fourth Order Method. http://www.ams.org

A Particle Method for Fluid-Structure Interaction Simulations in Multiple GPUs

Julián Becerra-Sagredo[1]([✉]), Leonardo Sigalotti[2], and Jaime Klapp[1,3]

[1] ABACUS-Laboratorio de Matemática Aplicada y Cómputo de Alto Rendimiento,
Departamento de Matemáticas, Centro de Investigación y de Estudios Avanzados
CINVESTAV-IPN, Carretera México-Toluca Km 38.5, La Marquesa,
52740 Ocoyoacac, Estado de México, Mexico
juliansagredo@gmail.com

[2] Departamento de Ciencias Básicas, Universidad Autónoma Metropolitana Campus
Azcapotzalco, Avenida San Pablo Xalpa 180, Azcapotzalco,
Reynosa Tamaulipas, 02200 D.F., Mexico, Mexico

[3] Departamento de Física, Instituto Nacional de Investigaciones Nucleares,
La Marquesa Ocoyoacac s/n, 52740 Ocoyoacac, Estado de México, Mexico

Abstract. This chapter is a presentation of the programming philosophy behind a novel numerical particle method for the simulation of the interaction of compressible fluids and elastic structures, specifically designed to run in multiple Graphics Processing Units (GPUs). The code has been developed using the CUDA C Application Programming Interface (API) for fine-grain parallelism in the GPUs and the Message Passing Interface library (MPI) for the distribution of threads in the Central Processing Units (CPUs) and the communication of shared data between GPUs. The numerical algorithm does not use smoothing kernels nor weighting functions for the computation of differential operators. A novel approach is used to compute gradients using averages of radial finite differences and divergences using Gauss' theorem by approximations based on area integrals around local spheres around each particle. The interactions of the particles inside the fluid are modelled using the isothermal, compressible Navier-Stokes equations and a simple equation of state. The elastic material is modelled using inter-particle springs with damping. Results show the potential of the method for the simulation of flows in complex geometries.

1 Introduction

The simulation of fluids interacting with elastic structures has a broad number of applications in engineering, medicine and architecture. Aerodynamic design, thermodynamic cycles in motors, containment of fluids and blood flow, to name a few, can be described using the compressible Navier-Stokes equations for the fluid dynamics, combined with linear elasticity theory for the mechanics of solid boundaries. The computational tools designed for the numerical integration of the governing equations have therefore been the focus of a large research effort.

© Springer International Publishing AG 2017
C.J. Barrios Hernández et al. (Eds.): CARLA 2016, CCIS 697, pp. 346–358, 2017.
DOI: 10.1007/978-3-319-57972-6_26

The most general problem requires the handling of complex dynamic geometries, the two way coupling of the forces in the fluid and the solid, and often, the resolution or approximation of turbulent flows.

In aerodynamic design, early works were focused on the use of finite differences or finite volume formulations using curvilinear grids [1–4]. This description can be useful for static boundaries but unpractical for moving or elastic ones. Mathematically, the grid orientation is an important factor to reduce numerical errors due to the lack of multidimensionality of the dimensional splitting technique, producing mesh-dependent solutions. Another partially successful technique is the use of vortex methods [5–7]. These were successful in describing the flow around boundaries for simple grids in Cartesian, cylindrical and spherical coordinates, for incompressible flows reaching Reynolds numbers of several thousands, and providing insight into turbulent flow control with actuators [8]. Nevertheless, the description of more general boundaries was challenged by the need of accurate interpolations near the complex interphase.

A promising technique to deal with complex geometries is the finite element method [9–12]. This technique has been the focus of many works, specially in blood flow simulations [13]. A clear advantage of this technique is the use of triangular or tetrahedral elements able to handle any boundary's geometric complexity. The mesh can be adaptive and able to follow moving boundaries. The elasticity of solid boundaries can be coupled to the fluid pressure for compressible or incompressible flows. Many libraries are available for the simulation of fluid-structure interactions using finite elements [16,17]. But one must keep in mind that the generation of the grids is not trivial and can be quite time consuming. Also, the equations are expressed in weak form and solved implicitly in time, what generates a large non-symmetrical system of linear equations to be solved using GMRES [14], a solver that is difficult to implement with fine grain parallelism [15].

Another technique is the use of Smoothed Particle Hydrodynamics (SPH) [18–22]. In this technique, the equations are discretized following the fluid element's trajectories and derivatives are approximated using the superposition of interpolation kernels for every particle. Some of the advantages of this technique are that there is no need to generate grids and that it naturally follows moving boundaries. Given the purely Lagrangian formulation, the fluid moves with the boundary velocity right at the interphase. If the domains are compressed or even the volume vanishes in some regions, like in the case of flow in pistons, the particles are able to leave the domain entirely and fill newly open spaces. The streamlines can be sketched using the particles' trajectories and simple equations of state can be used to simulate quasi-incompressible flows.

Hybrid techniques have been developed, combining both finite elements and particle trajectories, using a finite element grid that is advected at the boundary [23]. In fact, there is no alternative to this description because necessarily the mesh must follow the boundary. In this case, the generation of the mesh is a problem to be considered. A full Lagrangian description is out of the question for the most general case given that in the presence of vorticity, the grids get highly deformed producing a badly conditioned mass matrix.

During the last decade, the graphics processing unit (GPU) has surpassed the performance of the central processing unit (CPU) in floating point operations per second and local memory transfer velocity [24,25], and the trend is going to continue. The GPUs double their performance approximately every year while the CPUs do it every two years [26]. Therefore, the hardware has become an important factor in the design of fluid flow solvers. They must be designed or adapted to run entirely inside the GPU, with minimum communications with the CPU. This is because the velocity of memory transfers from CPU to GPU is several orders of magnitude slower than the internal memory transfers of the GPU, which can work entirely with L2-cache shared memory.

Considering all the factors, we have collected new ideas for the simulation of fluid-structure interactions using several GPUs. We are motivated to do it because our group has access to Abacus I, a supercomputer with one hundred Tesla K40 GPUs, providing 1200 GB of RAM and 288 000 cores of 745 MHz. In this chapter we describe the programming philosophy and the algorithms necessary for the implementation of a novel particle method running entirely inside a set of GPUs, associated to one another through a corresponding set of CPU threads using the Message Passing Interface library (MPI), and communicating by data transfers between the corresponding CPUs using MPI non-blocking send and receive functions. The particle method is entirely Lagrangian and different from an SPH because it does not use a smoothing particle kernel nor radial weighting functions. It has some similarities to the Moving Particle Semi-implicit method (MPS) [27], but in general, the approximations and search of neighbors are completely new. Its main characteristic is that it computes derivatives using averaged radial finite differences using approximations of area integrals on adaptive spheres around each particle, complemented with the divergence theorem when necessary. It is explicit in time, not requiring the inversion of a linear system of equations. It considers compressible fluids, closing the system using an equation of state for the pressure. The elastic boundary is simulated using another set of particles kept together with forces approximated by springs and damps. The two sets of particles are coupled using the forces of the fluid pressure and the velocity of the elastic surface. The results show the potential of the method to handle complex geometries.

2 Fluid Particles

Consider a Newtonian, compressible fluid with density ρ, pressure P and viscosity μ, kept at a constant temperature T, for simplicity but without loss of generality, which motion is described by the velocity vector $\boldsymbol{v}$. The material derivative $D/Dt = \partial/\partial t + \boldsymbol{v} \cdot \nabla$ is the chain rule for the total derivative in time, describing the variations along the trajectories of the fluid elements given by $d\boldsymbol{x}/dt = \boldsymbol{v}$.

The system of equations describing its dynamics are given by the conservation of mass

$$\frac{D\rho}{Dt} = -\rho \nabla \cdot \boldsymbol{v}, \tag{1}$$

and Newton's second law

$$\rho\frac{D\boldsymbol{v}}{Dt} = -\nabla P + \mu\nabla^2\boldsymbol{v}, \tag{2}$$

closed by an equation of state relating the density and the pressure $P = P(\rho, T)$. We consider moving solid boundaries where the fluid velocity is set to the solid velocity $\boldsymbol{v} = \boldsymbol{v}_s$. The equation of state

$$P = \frac{\rho}{3} \tag{3}$$

is used for simplicity during this work.

3   Solid Particles

The solid is represented by particles which conserve mass, subject to linearly elastic, spring like forces and damping. The conservation of mass in the solid is given by

$$\frac{D\rho_s}{Dt} = -\rho_s\nabla \cdot \boldsymbol{v}_s. \tag{4}$$

Newton's second law for the forces in the solid is given by

$$\rho_s\frac{D\boldsymbol{v}_s}{Dt} = \boldsymbol{f}_s, \tag{5}$$

where $\boldsymbol{f}_s$ is the sum of the elastic, friction and pressure forces, such that $\boldsymbol{f}_s = \boldsymbol{f}_e + \boldsymbol{f}_f + \boldsymbol{f}_p$.

4   Discretization

The discretization of the system could be done by seeding particles inside the fluid domain as desired, keeping them at a minimum distance between each other, denoted by h_{min}. We have chosen to seed the boundary with particles, either by a given boundary mesh, necessary for complex geometries, or using a level set function. If the boundary is provided by a given mesh, the location of the particles must be complemented with the surface's normal vector pointing towards the fluid domain for every boundary particle. These normal vectors are going to be used to determine the interior and exterior of the computational domain by simple weighted dot products with the relative position vector from the surface. If the boundary is given by a level set function, the boundary is seeded with particles and the level set is used to know if any position in space is part of the computational domain. We choose to seed the particles inside the fluid domain using a virtual Cartesian mesh covering the desired volume to mesh, eliminating the points that lie outside. Each location of the virtual Cartesian mesh is tested to be inside of the computational domain, and if so, stored. Figure 1 shows a cylinder seeded with particles using a Cartesian array

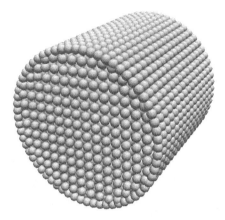

Fig. 1. Initial particle grid for a cylindrical domain. The particles are seeded using a Cartesian array and adjusted near the boundary to keep a minimum distance between particles.

with spacing h and keeping particles at a minimum distance $0.5\,h$ next to the boundary particles.

Once the initial particle positions are given, the fields are initialized for every particle, giving the densities ρ and ρ_s, and the velocities $\boldsymbol{v}$ and $\boldsymbol{v}_s$, at time $t = 0$.

The particle trajectories are solved with second order accuracy in time by setting

$$\boldsymbol{x}_i^{n+1} = \boldsymbol{x}_i^n + \frac{1}{2}(\boldsymbol{v}_i^n + \boldsymbol{v}_i^{n+1})\varDelta t, \qquad (6)$$

where the time is discretized, such that the super-index n denotes the time step $t^n = n\varDelta t$ for $n = 0, 1, ..., N$. This formula provides a second order, explicit integration of the trajectories and is sketched in Fig. 2.

We choose to use a purely Lagrangian formulation where particles are never re-meshed and interpolations are not necessary for advection. This warranties that the transport is exact along the trajectories of the particles with small errors due to the trajectory integration. Additionally, we leave the mollifier kernel concept used in SPH and focus only in computing the derivatives on the right hand side of the equations for the conservation of mass and Newton's second law. All the derivatives are computed using averages of radial finite differences, considering a regular distribution of particles. The approximations will reduce accuracy when the particle field deforms and the corrections to this approximations are the focus of future research. Only first line of sight nearest neighbors are considered in every 26 directions in three dimensions and 8 in two dimensions. The gradient is computed using a vector average of radial finite differences

$$\nabla P_i \approx \frac{D}{N} \sum_{j \neq i} \frac{P_j - P_i}{||\boldsymbol{x}_j - \boldsymbol{x}_i||} (\widehat{\boldsymbol{x}_j - \boldsymbol{x}_i}), \qquad (7)$$

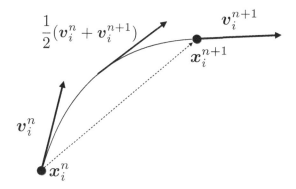

Fig. 2. Second order scheme for the integration of trajectories. The velocity is advanced using the momentum equation and the time-averaged velocity is used to advance the position of the particles.

where D is the number of dimensions and N is the number of nearest neighbor particles. The divergence is computed using Gauss' theorem by

$$\nabla \cdot v_i \approx \frac{A}{V} \sum_{j \neq i} \frac{(v_j + v_i)}{2} \cdot \frac{(x_j - x_i)}{||x_j - x_i||}, \tag{8}$$

where $V = (4/3)\pi R^3$ and $A = 4\pi R^2/N$, are the volume and area of a reference sphere for the calculation of the divergence. The radius R is considered as the averaged half distance to the nearest neighbors. Finally, the Laplacian is the combination of both concepts,

$$\nabla^2 v_i \approx \frac{A}{V} \sum_{j \neq i} \frac{(v_j - v_i)}{||x_j - x_i||}. \tag{9}$$

The model for the friction force consists of a damping factor $\mathcal{D}$ times the square of the velocity magnitude,

$$f_f = -\mathcal{D} v_s^2 \hat{v}. \tag{10}$$

The elastic forces are modelled using springs to the nearest neighbors

$$f_{e,i} = -\sum_{j \neq i} k(||x_j - x_i|| - L_{i,j})(\widehat{x_j - x_i}), \tag{11}$$

where $L_{i,j}$ is the equilibrium length for the spring bonding particles i and j.

The conservation of mass and Newton's second law are advanced as ordinary differential equations over the trajectory of each fluid particle, explicitly in time with a forward Euler method, after evaluating the spatial operators on the right hand side.

Particle methods do not have conservation issues due to advection. Only the inaccurate computation of the sources of compressibility and force can partially affect conservation of the advected quantities. The accurate calculation of

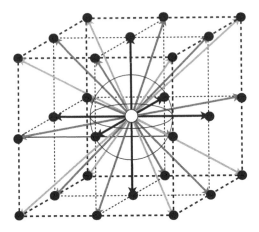

Fig. 3. Scheme for the radial finite differences approximation of the gradient (7), the divergence (8) and the Laplacian (9). The radial finite difference approximations are based on sums of individual difference vectors to the nearest neighbor particles combined with the divergence theorem using a sphere with radius of the average half distance to the neighbors.

gradients and divergences can be affected by a highly deformed particle field. Viscous flows have fluid elements that deform smoothly. Anyway, the computation of individual area weights for each neighbor particle is necessary for accurate approximations of the differential operators. Its detailed analysis and implementation are subjects of future research.

5   Data Structures

The data structure is a list of particles for each CPU process, where the solid particles, which describe also the fluid particles at the boundary, are given at the beginning of the list, followed by the particles in the bulk of the fluid.

A list of nearest neighbors is constructed in order to compute the differential operators in the right hand side of the transport equations for the solid and the fluid. Analogously to Lattice-Boltzmann algorithms, we consider 8 neighboring particles in two dimensions and 26 in three. An initial list is constructed or given. The list is updated after a fixed number of time steps during the numerical integration. The new list is produced following the hypothesis that for every particle, every new neighbor was in the neighbor list of its former neighbors. Algorithm 1 is the pseudo-code for the updating of the list of nearest neighbors $neighborlist(1 : n, 1 : 26)$, where n is the total number of particles in the computational domain. The distance between particles is given by the function $distance(i, j)$ (line 3 and 11). If any particle lies outside a neighboring radius h, its index is tagged to be replaced. The list is double-checked to avoid the repetition of particles (line 14).

```
1: oldneighborlist(i,1:26) = neighborlist(i,1:26)
2: do j from 1 to 26
3: k = oldneighborlist(i,j)
4:    dr = distance(i,k)
5:    if (dr > h) neighborlist(i,k) = -1
6: do j from 1 to 26
7: k = oldneighborlist(i,j)
7:    if (neighborlist(i,k) = -1)
8:       mindr = 10 h
9:       do l from 1 to 26
10:         m = oldneighborlist(i,l)
11:         do o from 1 to 26
12:            p = oldneighborlist(l,o)
13:            dr = distance(i,p)
14:         if (dr < mindr)
15:            inthelist = false
16:            do q from 1 to 26
17:               if (p = neighborlist(i,q)) inthelist = true
18:            if (inthelist = false)
19:               neighborlist(i,j) = p
20:               mindr = dr
```

Algorithm 1. Update list of nearest neighbors.

6   The Programming Model

We use the template code presented in [28] but adapted for a list of particles. The computational domain is geometrically decomposed in a one-dimensional array of M sub-domains. The Message Passing Interface (MPI) library is used to start M threads for the same number of CPU cores. Every CPU thread corresponds to a process to be run in a different GPU. Frequently, each node of the cluster will have one or two GPUs, therefore it is necessary to distribute the M threads in different nodes, such that every process is able to pick at least one exclusive GPU.

Communications between GPUs is achieved loading the necessary GPU data to the local CPU memory, communicating the CPU threads using MPI unblocked but synchronized sends and receives, and loading it back to the GPU. In this implementation, only boundary data is communicated and particles are not transferred between processes. Future versions may contain the transfer of particles between GPUs.

Inside the GPU, operations are threaded over the list of particles, as described in Fig. 4. The list is distributed in a three-dimensional array with power of two dimensions, further subdivided in blocks to be given to the GPU cores. The list of threads will be in general larger than the list of particles. Those threads that do not correspond to a particle perform no work.

The programming model for a single GPU is focused in performing parallel L2 memory reads and a few global memory writes. The *nvcc* compiler is capable

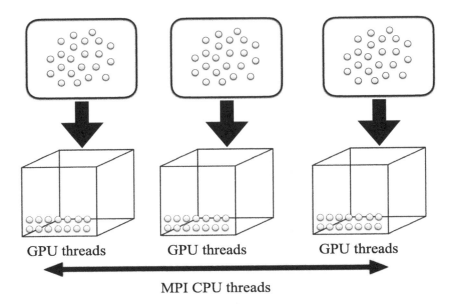

Fig. 4. Scheme of the computational decomposition of the list of particles and its arrangement as GPU threads in a cube. The GPUs are mastered by CPU threads using MPI.

of automatically allocating L2 memory reads if we provide read-only arrays. All numerical operations are done using the registers memory and the results are written back to write-only arrays in global memory.

7   Results

The algorithm is a newly proposed numerical method and the tests are focused in proving its correctness without going into deep analysis of order of convergence. The algorithm has been theoretically designed to be second order for a regular distribution of neighboring particles.

We use an initial Gaussian perturbation in the density

$$\rho(r) = 1.0 + 0.01 \exp^{-r^2/5}, \tag{12}$$

where r is the distance from the center of the domain with dimensions $[15, 15, 15]$, in a quiet Newtonian fluid with viscosity $\mu = 1$.

First we prove that our new radial difference formulas are correct by computing the norm of the pressure gradient and the divergence of the velocity field after a single time step $\Delta t = 0.02$. Figure 5 shows the comparison of the differential operators for a cylindrical domain filled with 250000 particles and a Cartesian 64^3 mesh with finite differences. It shows agreement and even a slight improvement in the case of the divergence.

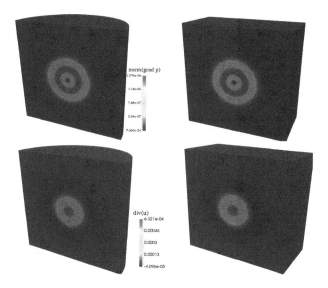

Fig. 5. Comparison of the square of the norm of the pressure gradient (top) and the divergence of the velocity (bottom), for the radial differences scheme using particles in a cylindrical domain (left) and finite differences in a cube (right). Both domains are shown cut in half by a plane normal to the x-axis.

We simulate the acoustic wave resulting from the Gaussian initial condition in a cylinder filled with 250000 particles. We compare it with a second order semi-Lagrangian scheme [29] in a 64^3 cube. Figure 6 shows agreement between the schemes even though the reflection of the waves is different for the square domain and the cylinder. Therefore, only early stages of the wave are compared.

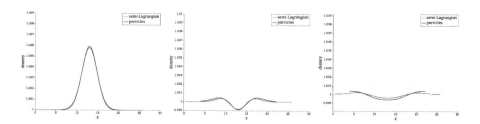

Fig. 6. Comparison of the acoustic wave for the newly proposed particle method with 250000 particles and a semi-Lagrangian scheme [29] for a 64^3 domain. From left to right we can see the density along the y-axis for times $t = 0.2$, $t = 0.6$ and $t = 1.2$.

We have run the code for one, two and four GPUs Tesla C2070. The results for a small run consisting of a thousand time steps are presented in Fig. 7. The runs show strong scalability in the vertical direction and weak scalability in the horizontal direction. The weak scalability shows a small penalty due to the communication between GPUs. The objective of running in many GPUs is not the acceleration of the code, although it is possible to observe significant acceleration in the case of two GPUs compared to one. Nevertheless, we note that for the case of four GPUs, the acceleration is much less and extrapolating we can see that many more GPUs would not achieve significant acceleration. The point is that runs in several GPUs must be focused in the simulation of very large problems or with high resolutions. The GPUs are very fast processing units that should be exploited at maximum with the lowest number of communications possible. The use of several GPUs must be evaluated using the weak scalability concept where larger problems are run in the approximately same computational time, shown in Fig. 7 in the horizontal direction.

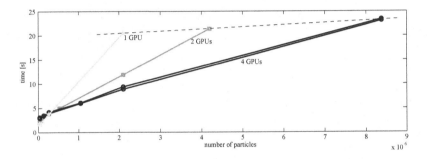

Fig. 7. Weak (horizontal) and strong (vertical) scalability of the domain decomposition scheme for the list of particles using MPI communication between GPUs. The two black curves correspond to one- and two-dimensional domain decomposition.

8 Conclusion

We presented a programming model using domain decomposition with message passing for computations using multiple GPUs adapted to a list of particles. This particle template code has been filled with a novel numerical method. The numerical method consists of a particle method for the integration of transport equations along material trajectories of fluid elements. The fluid elements are defined by the location of the particles. The equations are solved in time using a second order mid-point integration scheme for the positions of the particles and a first order explicit Euler integration for the velocity and density. The pressure is obtained explicitly using an equation of state. Averages of radial derivatives combined with the divergence theorem are used for the approximation of the spatial differential operators at the right hand side of the transport equations. These differences have been used in different forms in other works but never in the form presented here. We take the nearest neighbors in the 26 principal Cartesian directions like in a Lattice-Boltzmann scheme. The approximations have been tested to be second order accurate for a regular, Cartesian distribution of particles, and are expected to loose accuracy as the particle field distorts. Moment conservation for the area covered by the neighbors around each particle will be explored to keep the accuracy regular for any configuration of the neighbors. The list of particles is complemented with a list of nearest neighbors, updated after a fixed number of time steps with a local search scheme. The results of the acoustic waves inside a cylinder meshed with a Cartesian array of particles show the potential of the code to solve problems in complex geometries without the need of complex mesh generators. For complex geometries, the boundary node positions and normal vectors pointing to the fluid must be provided.

Acknowledgements. This work was partially supported by ABACUS, CONACyT grant EDOMEX-2011-C01-165873. The calculations for this work have been performed in the Abacus I supercomputer.

References

1. Steger, J.L.: On application of body conforming curvilinear grids for finite difference solution of external flow. Appl. Math. Comput. **10–11**, 295–316 (1982)
2. Karki, K.C., Patankar, S.V.: Calculation procedure for viscous incompressible flows in complex geometries. Numer. Heat Transfer **14**(3), 295–307 (1988)
3. LeVeque, R.J.: Finite Volume Methods for Hyperbolic Problems. Cambridge Texts in Applied Mathematics. Cambridge University Press, Cambridge (2002)
4. Bijl, H., Wesseling, P.: A unified method for computing incompressible and compressible flows in boundary-fitted coordinates. J. Comput. Phys. **141**(2), 153–173 (1998)
5. Leonard, A.: Vortex methods for flow simulation. J. Comput. Phys. **37**(3), 289–335 (1980)
6. Cottet, G.H., Koumoutsakos, P.D.: Vortex Methods: Theory and Practice. Cambridge University Press, Cambridge (2000)
7. Ploumhans, P., Winckelmans, G.S., Salmon, J.K., Leonard, A., Warren, M.S.: Vortex methods for direct numerical simulation of three-dimensional Bluff body flows: application to the sphere at Re = 300, 500 and 1000. J. Comput. Phys. **178**(2), 427–463 (2002)
8. Koumoutsakos, P.: Active control of vortex-wall interactions. Phys. Fluids **9**(12), 3808–3816 (1997)
9. Strang, G., Fix, G.: An Analysis of the Finite Element Method. SIAM, Wesley-Cambridge Press, Philadelphia (1973)
10. Kuzmin, D., Hämäläinen, J.: Finite Element Methods for Computational Fluid Dynamics: A Practical Guide. Computational Science & Engineering. SIAM, Philadelphia (2014)
11. Löner, R., Morgan, K., Peraire, J., Zienkiewicz, O.C.: The free-lagrange method. In: Fritts, M.J., Crowley, W.P., Trease, H. (eds.) Recent developments in FEM-CFD. Lecture Notes in Physics, pp. 236–254. Springer, Heidelberg (2005)
12. Schweitzer, M.A.: Generalizations of the finite element method. Cent. Eur. J. Math. **10**(1), 3–24 (2012)
13. Taylor, C.A., Hughes, T.J.R., Zarins, C.K.: Finite element modeling of blood flow in arteries. Comput. Methods Appl. Mech. Eng. **158**(1), 155–196 (1998)

14. Saad, Y., Schultz, M.H.: GMRES: a generalized minimal residual algorithm for solving nonsymmetric linear systems. SIAM J. Sci. Stat. Comput. **7**, 856–869 (1986)

15. Ziane Khodja, L., Couturier, R., Glersch, A., Bahi, J.M.: Parallel sparse linear solver with GMRES method using minimization techniques of communications for GPU clusters. J. Supercomput. **69**(1), 200–224 (2014)

16. Whiting, C.H., Jansen, K.E.: A stabilized finite element method for the incompressible Navier-Stokes equations using a hierarchical basis. Int. J. Numer. Methods Fluids **35**(1), 93–116 (2001)

17. Quarteroni, A.: Numerical Models for Differential Problems. Springer, Heidelberg (2009)

18. Monaghan, J.J.: Smoothed particle hydrodynamics. Annu. Rev. Astrophys. **30**, 543–574 (1992)

19. Monaghan, J.J.: Smoothed particle hydrodynamics. Rep. Prog. Phys. **68**(8), 1703–1760 (2005)

20. Antoci, C., Gallati, M., Sibilla, S.: Numerical simulation of fluid-structure interaction by SPH. Comput. Struct. **85**(11), 879–890 (2007)

21. Sigalotti, L.D.G., Klapp, J., Rendon, O., Vargas, C.A., Peña-Polo, F.: On the kernel and particle consistency in smoothed particle hydrodynamics. J. Appl. Numer. Math. **108**, 242–255 (2016)

22. Sigalotti, L.D.G., Rendon, O., Klapp, J., Vargas, C.A., y Campos, K.: A new insight into the consistency of Smoothed Particle Hydrodynamics. arXiv:1644200 [physics.com-ph] 21 August 2016

23. Donea, J., Huerta, A.: Finite Element Flow Problems. Wiley, Hoboken (2003)

24. Nickolls, J., Dally, W.J.: The GPU computing era. IEEE Micro **30**(2), 56–69 (2010)

25. Keckler, S.W., Dally, W.J., Khailany, B., Garland, M., Glasco, D.: GPUs and the future of parallel computing. IEEE Micro **31**(5), 7–17 (2011)

26. NVIDIA CUDA C Programming Guide, version 7.5, Nvidia (2015)

27. Koshizuka, S., Oka, Y.: Moving particle semi-implicit method for fragmentation of incompressible fluid. Nucl. Sci. Eng. **123**, 421–434 (1996)

28. Becerra-Sagredo, J., Mandujano, F., Málaga, C., Klapp, J., Teresa, I.: A template for scalable continuum dynamic simulations in multiple GPUs. In: Gitler, I., Klapp, J. (eds.) ISUM 2015. CCIS, vol. 595, pp. 473–484. Springer, Cham (2016). doi:10.1007/978-3-319-32243-8_33

29. Becerra-Sagredo, J.T., Málaga, C., Mandujano, F.: Moments preserving and high-resolution semi-Lagrangian advection scheme. SIAM J. Sci. Comput. **38**(4), A2141–A2161 (2016)

Scheduling Algorithms for Distributed Cosmic Ray Detection Using Apache Mesos

Germán Schnyder[1(✉)], Sergio Nesmachnow[1], Gonzalo Tancredi[1], and Andrei Tchernykh[2]

[1] Universidad de la República, Montevideo, Uruguay
{german.schnyder,sergion}@fing.edu.uy, gonzalo@fisica.edu.uy
[2] CICESE Research Center, Ensenada, Baja California, Mexico
chernykh@cicese.mx

Abstract. This article presents two scheduling algorithms applied to the processing of astronomical images to detect cosmic rays on distributed memory high performance computing systems. We extend our previous article that proposed a parallel approach to improve processing times on image analysis using the Image Reduction and Analysis Facility IRAF software and the Docker project over Apache Mesos. By default, Mesos introduces a simple list scheduling algorithm where the first available task is assigned to the first available processor. On this paper we propose two alternatives for reordering the tasks allocation in order to improve the computational efficiency. The main results show that it is possible to reduce the makespan getting a speedup = 4.31 by adjusting how jobs are assigned and using Uniform processors.

Keywords: Image processing · Distributed memory · Containers · Mesos · Scheduling

1 Introduction

Hubble Space Telescope (HST) is not only an astronomical observatory but also an excellent cosmic ray detector. Because HST is above the Earth's atmosphere and therefore not protected against low-energy cosmic rays, and crosses the Van Allen radiation belts, HST is an unique particle detector. Since cosmic ray flux is affected by the strength of the magnetic field, detectors of HST detectors sample different conditions of the magnetic field, which can be used to compare to magnetic field strength, gamma ray flux and other geophysical data measured by the geomagnetic observatories. HST dark frames (or just *darks*) are suitable for cosmic ray studies because they are acquired with closed shutters so only cosmic ray events are recorded. HST results will complement that of the existing cosmic rays detectors on ground and space. Launch of the HST predate geomagnetic satellites by more than a decade; its 26 years of low altitude cosmic-ray detection provide high-resolution observations of the geomagnetic field. We propose [1] to analyze the full darks dataset to calculate the flux of cosmic rays above Earth's

© Springer International Publishing AG 2017
C.J. Barrios Hernández et al. (Eds.): CARLA 2016, CCIS 697, pp. 359–373, 2017.
DOI: 10.1007/978-3-319-57972-6_27

surface and estimate variations in the external magnetic field, thereby complementing geophysical observatory measurements. By combining HST results with measurements of solar activity, cosmic ray flux on Earth's surface, and geomagnetic data, our analysis will contribute to understating external magnetic field variations.

A two-phases workflow is needed to process the images: first, extracting the noise from the images; and second, processing the noise to understand if there are connected components that can be understood as cosmic rays impacts. For the first phase, there is a widely used scientific package named IRAF (Image Reduction and Facility [2]). IRAF includes several utilities for manipulating images in the open standard digital file format Flexible Image Transport System (FITS). For the second phase, several algorithms have been proposed to detect every stroke in the dark and determine if it is a cosmic ray or some anomaly (e.g. a damaged pixel). This step is basically about finding connected components on the image and estimating the cosmic ray inner energy. In addition, this step also determines the exact point of impact based on the instruments logs, regarding the telescope position.

In our previous article [3], we proposed an approach for improving the performance of image analysis on distributed memory High Performance Computing systems through Apache Mesos. In this work, we extend our approach to consider two scheduling algorithms for tasks-to-resource assignment in order to further improve the performance.

Originally, the scheduling of jobs and resources was not analyzed in [3], because the focus of our previous research was to design and implement a parallel approach to distribute the work with the main goal of obtaining the best horizontal scaling possible. Apache Mesos [4] is a resource scheduler that uses internal algorithms for assigning tasks to processing machines based on user specified conditions and the available resources in the computational infrastructure. In our previous proposal, tasks became available from the beginning, and so do the processes used to image processing, resulting in a straightforward workflow. In this work, we propose some tweaks to improve the performance, based on a job scheduling logic and not specifically focusing on horizontal scaling. An evolution from the Mesos default scheduling strategy, to a combination of Longest Processing Time (LPT) and Shortest Processing Time (SPT) scheduling algorithms demonstrates that the total makespan can be minimized on favor of a faster processing pipeline.

The article is organized as follows. Next section describes the problem and our previous approach for image processing. Section 3 presents a review of related works on scheduling jobs over virtualized environments. The proposed methods and scheduling algorithms are described in Sect. 4. After that, Sect. 5 presents the experimental evaluation of the proposed scheduling algorithms and reports the efficiency results. Finally, Sect. 6 presents the conclusions and formulates the main lines for future work.

2   Problem Description

The problem of detecting cosmic rays from HST images is complex and requires a lot of computing effort, especially taking into account that a large dataset of historical images (from the early 1990s) is available. Thus, applying a parallel model either on data or instructions domain is required to complete the processing in reasonable execution times. In this work, we follow a data-parallel approach for distributed memory system using containers, which is described in detail in our previous work [3]. All the images are supposed to be available at the same time on an external database. The processing is performed by a set of worker processes running as Docker containers, managed by Apache Mesos.

The execution environment includes a node executing Marathon [5]. Marathon is a framework for container orchestration and it is a part of the Apache Mesos ecosystem. Marathon is responsible of instantiating the containers, as described on a job configuration file. Each container can be seen as an independent processing node, where every node follows the same logic of obtaining a new image from the repository and processing it. In order to perform this task, each container uses Zookeeper [6] for synchronization: each process must know in advance which images are available to determine which image it should process.

Figure 1 presents a diagram of the proposed architecture. The dotted line indicates what is running inside the Mesos managed environment (i.e. Marathon, containers and Zookeeper); DockerHub (https://hub.docker.com/) is a publicly accessible cloud registry where docker images are stored (for its later retrieval by Marathon); the images repository is where the FITS files reside (a filesystem reachable from the containers); and the output files are the results from the cosmic rays analysis.

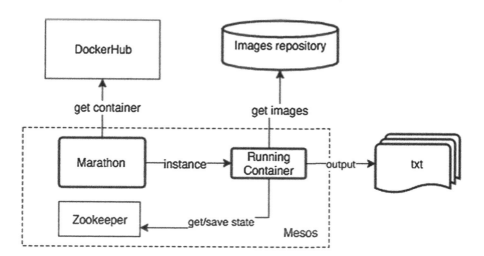

Fig. 1. Architecture for the parallel/distributed processing of HST images to detect cosmic rays using containers.

In order to achieve the goal of obtaining the best horizontal scaling (or, in other words, to perform faster as the number of processing nodes grow in a linear ratio), a solution applying virtualization is proposed. The worker code is packed and distributed through as a Docker container. Docker enables virtualization of an operating system in a lightweight container. As a consequence, Marathon can instantiate as many workers as needed on the execution environment, and the only limitation is given by the physical resources available. Taking into account this last consideration, the system can scale horizontally as much as needed for processing very large datasets (in the case of HST images, more than 10 TB of image data are available, from images taken since the Hubble started operating in 1990).

3   Related Work

This section reviews some relevant and recent related works about improving jobs scheduling in distributed computing systems and virtualized environments using containers.

On the last years, as MapReduce became popular on cloud computing, many researchers started focusing on how to apply Hadoop for image processing (see for example the articles by Golpayegani and Halem [7], or Ali and Kumar [8]). Particularly on the present work, the focus will be over the already established architecture and the objective is to improve the tasks assignment strategies.

Job scheduling has been widely analyzed and developed through the last 40 years. The literature about scheduling algorithms is very large, but in this work we focus on studying simple algorithms that can be integrated easily on Mesos and provide improved execution times. Specifically, we consider the classical algorithms proposed by Adam et al. [9], who studied how to schedule parallel processors to minimize makespan assuming partially ordered tasks. This is not the case on this work, as we work with non-related tasks, but it shows a first approach on comparing execution algorithms that is relevant for our work. Almost at the same time, Coffman and Sethi [10] presented LPT and SPT algorithms applied to job scheduling. Their work is tightly related to the research we propose here, and some of the results presented by Coffman et al. are applied in this article. Based on the already known $O(n \log n)$ algorithm for the execution time for a system with identical processors, from Graham [11]) Coffman et al. demonstrated the efficacy of several heuristics to optimize the mean flow time or the total makespan, separately. Closer in time, Kovács [12] showed how to properly assign jobs to a setup where one processor is faster than the others. His work is also close to our proposal, but the main difference is related to the proportion between fast and slow processors. Finally, Oyetunji [13] defined and used several metrics to analyze performance on scheduling strategies that are useful to explain the algorithms proposed in our article.

Related to Map-Reduce applications for astronomical data processing, Wiley et al. [14] showed how to adapt image co-addition to the MapReduce framework. Image co-addition is a technique that has the objective of getting a high quality image as output, consuming lower resolution images as input. They realized several experiments combining Hadoop and SQL with the result of processing 100.000 images (the equivalent to 300 million pixels) in 3 min. Finally, Singh et al. [15] developed a custom version of MapReduce on python to process astronomical datasets. Their work developed parallel processing recipes for multicore machines for astronomical data processing. These recipes are intended to be used by astronomers with PyIRAF/IRAF knowledge. They compared three different approaches for parallelizing the execution (Pool/Map, Process/Queue and Parallel Python) with the result of Process/Queue being the faster one. This approach involves two FIFO queues (for input of parameters and output of results) that work as pipelines to connect the nodes. This approach is similar to the one we apply in our work, because it does not block the pipeline in anyway, and enables the horizontal scaling based on the number of workers.

Our work combines distributed computing (using data parallelism) and job scheduling algorithms applied to a cosmic ray detection. This approach enables future researchers to focus on data analysis taking advantage of results presented here.

4   Scheduling Algorithms for Cosmic Ray Detection Using Mesos

This section presents the two algorithms proposed for minimizing total execution time of the image processing tasks.

4.1   Architecture for the Parallel Execution

The diagram of the proposed architecture for the parallel execution of the IRAF image processing in our original work [3] was already presented in Fig. 1.

Regarding the scheduling considerations, in our previous work Marathon instantiates the containers as described in the configuration file, and it responsibility is just to keep them running. It does not decide how the tasks are assigned to the workers. Then, by default, tasks are assigned on a non-ordered basis. The first processor that becomes available will get the first image on the list. This can be thought as a straightforward list scheduling algorithm, where no precondition apply neither on the process or the images.

4.2   Scheduling Model

Considering the architecture described in Fig. 2, an improved job scheduling strategy can be devised. The workers have equal ready times, and the wait time for getting tasks assigned is zero (since all the images are available from the beginning).

Given the previous considerations, the scheduling problem can be defined according to the following guidelines:

- Which is the best method for tasks-to-processor assignment in order to minimize the total finishing time when processing a given set of images?
- Is it possible to maximize the throughput of the computational infrastructure used for the processing?

The problem also must take into account that: all tasks are independent, and no precedence requirements are defined; there is no need for preemption; every task runs on a separate worker and job priorities are not considered; all the processors used by workers are identical (or uniform, if needed, as it will be shown on Sect. 4.5).

The mathematical model for the scheduling problem considers the following elements:

- A set of processors $P = \{p_1, \ldots, p_m\}$.
- A set of tasks (images to process) $T = \{t_1, \ldots, t_n\}$.
- A speed function $s : P \rightarrow N^+$, where $s(p_j)$ gives the computing capacity of processor p_j.
- A weight function $w : T \rightarrow N^+$, where $w(t_i)$ gives the computing cost needed to process task t_i.

The objective of the scheduling problem is to find a function $f : T \rightarrow P$ that assigns tasks to processors minimizing w_i/s_j where $f(t_i) = p_j$.

According to the classification by Graham et al. [16], the resulting scheduling problem can be classified as of type $P \parallel C_{max}$.

4.3 Scheduling Strategies

Scheduling problems within type $P \parallel C_{max}$ are proved to be NP-complete [10]. However, the problem complexity can be relaxed imposing some constraints, for example assigning priorities. Thus, the order in which the tasks will be assigned can be determined by either priorities or worker processing speed.

If each image is paired with a priority number, a well-known list scheduling algorithm can be applied to obtain a performance bound below $2 - 1/m$ (being m the number of processors). Particularly, using LPT, the mean performance bound is $\frac{4}{3} - \frac{1}{3} \times m$ [11]. Specifically for this work, the image size works as a priority indicator: the bigger the image size, the bigger the priority.

4.4 LPT-CRD Scheduling Algorithm

The traditional LPT algorithm consists on sorting the tasks (images) in increasing size order and workers (processors) according to their processing power. Under this task ordering logic, tasks with larger processing times are guaranteed to start first, and they are executed by workers running on the fastest processors. We propose an adapted LPT-CRD algorithm, which is the version used for assigning images to workers following the LPT principle.

The pseudocode for the adapted LPT-CRD algorithm applied to cosmic ray detection on astronomical images is shown in Algorithm 1.

The schema for ordering workers (CPUs) and tasks (images) in the LPT-CRD algorithm is graphically presented in the diagram on Fig. 2.

Algorithm 1. Adapted LPT-CRD algorithm for $P \parallel C_{max}$.

begin

    Order tasks $\{t_1, ..., t_n\}$, such that $w(t_1) \geq ... \geq w(t_n)$

    for $i \leftarrow 1$ **to** m **do**

        $c_i := 0$

        `/* proc. `p_i` are assumed to be idle from time `c_i`=0 on        */`

    end

    $j := 1$

    repeat

        $c_k := \min \{c_i\}$

        Assign task t_j to processor p_k at time c_k

        `/* the first non-assigned task from the list is scheduled on`

        `   the first processor that becomes free                */`

        $c_k := c_k + w(t_j)$

        $j := j + 1$

    until $j = n;$ `/* all tasks have been scheduled         */`

end

4.5 Combined CRD Scheduling Algorithm

In Marathon, the processor speed of each worker can be adjusted to a custom value on the task definition. This procedure allows applying a different approach for scheduling, suitable for the paradigm of heterogeneous computing [17]. By adjusting the speed to a different value, the processor speed of each worker can be modified, for maintaining a set of *uniform* workers. By definition, processors are *uniform* if every job that executes on a processor of computing capacity s for t time units completes $s \times t$ units of execution. Assuming this scenario, the main focus is to minimize the *mean flowtime* for the tasks.

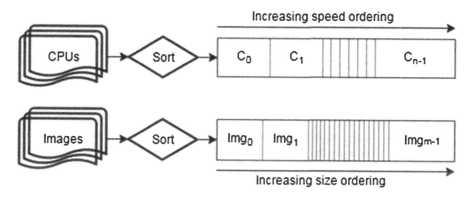

Fig. 2. In LPT-CRD, workers and images are sorted in increasing speed/size order

The *flowtime* is defined as the sum of the finishing times of all tasks (see a formal definition in Sect. 5.2), and the *mean flowtime* is the average flowtime value when considering the number of tasks in execution in a batch. This new version of the scheduling problem is within the class $Q \parallel \sum C_j$. Horowitz and Sahn [18] demonstrated that for the case of minimizing mean flowtime on a system with m processors it is possible to implement an algorithm whose complexity is $O(n \log mn)$.

Algorithm 2 presents the pseudocode of the proposed solution (combined CRD algorithm, CCRD) to solve the problem of maximizing throughput when processing astronomical images for cosmic ray detection. The main idea in CCRD consists in combining the scheduling strategies proposed by the LPT and SPT heuristics.

Algorithm 2. Combined CRD algorithm for $Q \parallel \sum C_j$.

---

begin
 Order tasks $\{t_1, ..., t_n\}$, such that $w(t_1) \geq ... \geq w(t_n)$
 for $i \leftarrow 1$ **to** m **do**
  $c_i := 0$
  `/* proc. `q_i` are assumed to be idle from time `c_i`=0         */`
 end
 j := 1
 l := n
 repeat
  $c_k := \min \{c_i\}$
  if q_k *is a fast processor* **then**
   Assign task t_j to processor q_k at time c_k
   j := j + 1
  else
   Assign task t_{n-j} to processor q_k at time c_k
   l := l - 1
  end
  `/* the first or the last non-assigned task from the list is`
   `scheduled on the first processor that becomes free,`
   `depending on its type                              */`
  $c_k := c_k + w(t_j)$
 until $l = j$; `/* all tasks have been scheduled             */`

end

In CCRD, both workers and images are sorted in increasing order of power/size. At any moment where an idle worker is ready to process, the CCRD algorithm assigns an available image to it. If the worker is running on a fast processor, the algorithm selects the biggest image available. However, if the worker is running on a slow processor, the algorithm selects the smallest image available. Since the images are already sorted by size, this assignment is performed at $O(1)$.

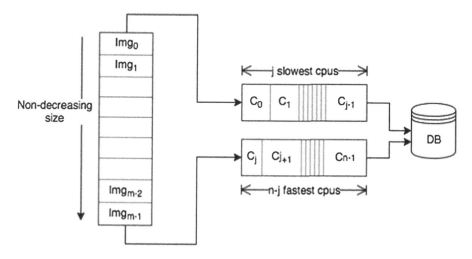

Fig. 3. Proposed schema for minimizing mean flowtime using CCRD algorithm

Figure 3 describes the proposed schema for the CCRD scheduling algorithm. A worker is defined as "slow" if its processing power is 60% of available processing power, and "fast" if it is 100%. Mesos determines the available processing power based on the underlying infrastructure and the Marathon tasks requirements. These values are arbitrary, the percentage defining a slow processor can be anyone below 100%, actually. The maximum must be 100% though, because the code to execute is not parallel at instruction level and running it on more than one processor has no positive impact on performance.

Finding the optimum ratio between the values for fast and slow processors speed, in terms of makespan and mean flowtime minimization, is an interesting theoretical issue, which we propose as the focus for a future line of work. This further analysis should also consider studying the optimum number of nodes of each type. In this article, for the sake of simplicity, we establish as of five of each type, making a total of 10 workers, which provides a realistic description of a parallel system in the studied architecture.

The details about how to indicate Marathon to instantiate both the slow and fast processors are presented in the codes shown in Figs. 4 and 5, respectively. In addition to processing speed, the configuration file must also include the instance count (i.e., in the setup used in this work, five slow processors and five fast processors) and the memory resources to be used. Both type of workers are configured with enough memory to guarantee that every image can be manipulated and the analysis can be performed without any memory issues. Finally, there are several other settings that are required by Marathon (e.g., container URL at Dockerhub, environment variables, etc.). We do not report the details here because these settings are not directly related to the scheduling problem.

```
{
  "id": "slow_worker",
  "cpus": 0.6,              //CPU percentage to be reserved
  "mem": 512.0,             //RAM to be reserved
  "instances": 5           //number of nodes to instantiate
}
```

Fig. 4. Sample code of a Marathon task definition for slow processors (as those using 60% of CPU)

```
{
  "id": "fast_worker",
  "cpus": 1.0,              //CPU percentage to be reserved
  "mem": 512.0,             //RAM to be reserved
  "instances": 5           //number of nodes to instantiate
}
```

Fig. 5. Sample code of a Marathon task definition for fast processors (as those using 100% of CPU)

5   Experimental Evaluation

This section presents the experimental evaluation of the proposed scheduling algorithms compared to the original efficiency results [3].

5.1   Computational Platform

The experimental evaluation was executed using the same machine configuration, even when considering different configurations for the Marathon jobs in the proposed scheduling algorithms. The CPU processing power was capped to the same maximum value (equivalent to 8 processors). The host computer used to perform the tests is a *c4.4xlarge* instance from the EC2 Amazon Web Services (AWS) cloud, with 16 cores running Ubuntu 14.04, Intel Xeon E5-2666 v3 at 2.90 GHz, with a disk of 200 GB and 30 GB of memory.

5.2   Metrics

Performance Metrics. The standard *speedup* and *computational efficiency* metrics are used for the comparison between the sequential model and the parallel execution based on containers running in Mesos. In this context, the speedup is defined as the ratio between the total processing time between the sequential execution time (T_1) and the parallel execution time (T_N) when using a specific number of N computing elements, as defined by Eq. 1 below. The efficiency is the normalized value of the speedup, according to the number of computing elements used, as defined by Eq. 2.

$$S_N = \frac{T_1}{T_N}, \qquad (1) \qquad E_N = \frac{S_N}{N}. \qquad (2)$$

Finally, an *acceleration* metric is reported, to evaluate the relative improvement (in execution time) obtained when comparing a two algorithms as defined by

$$acceleration_{AB} = \frac{executiontime(Algorithm_A)}{executiontime(Algorithm_B)} \qquad (3)$$

Scheduling Evaluation. When considering the time spent to execute all tasks within a job, the most usual metrics to optimize are the *makespan* and the *flowtime* [19]. The makespan is a relevant objective to evaluate the resource utilization; it is defined as the time spent from the moment when the first task begins execution to the moment when the last task is completed. The flowtime evaluates the sum of the tasks finishing times, and it is important from the point-of-view of the users, since it reflects the response time of a computational system for a set of submitted tasks [20].

5.3 Scheduling Improvements Results

Table 1 reports the total makespan when evaluating the computing times for the three schedulers proposed (the default scheduler in Mesos [3], LPT-CRD for identical processors with ordering, and combined CRD for uniform processors with ordering). The table also reports the values of the acceleration, speedup, and computational efficiency metrics. The analysis is performed using different number of images in a job (100, 500, and 1000 images), following the Bag-of-Tasks (BoT) paradigm for distributed computing [21]. In our case, the BoT corresponds to a set of images. Since images are independent, they can be assigned to different workers for processing, according to the BoT model.

The results in Table 1 show that both LPT-CRD and Combined CRD algorithms performed better than the default scheduling strategy. Also, differences become more significant as the image dataset grows. For instance, on the 100 images dataset the speedups are 2.83 and 3.41 (for LPT-CRD and CCRD respectively), but goes up to 4.17 and 4.31 when the dataset size is ten times bigger. Its noticeable a minor speedup on the 500 images dataset, but this value is still better than the execution time provided by the default scheduling algorithm in Mesos. In addition, the acceleration achieved is reported as a measurement of performance improvement. On this regard, the proposed algorithms also performed better than the default scheduling, and increasing as the datasize grows, showing a good scalability behavior. The proposed scheduling strategies allows executing faster the processing.

Table 2 reports the total flowtime when evaluating the computing times for the three schedulers proposed, and also the computational metrics evaluated.

Table 1. Makespan results and computational efficiency analysis for the proposed scheduling algorithms over different datasets, according to the BoT model.

# images	Execution time (s)		Acceleration	Speedup	Efficiency
	Default	Improved			
LPT-CRD algorithm					
100	346	644	0.54	2.83	0.28
500	2382	1705	1.40	1.69	0.17
1000	5180	3438	1.51	4.17	0.42
Combined CRD algorithm					
100	346	533	0.65	3.41	0.34
500	2382	1710	1.39	1.69	0.17
1000	5180	3326	1.56	4.31	0.43

Table 2. Flowtime results and computational efficiency analysis for the proposed scheduling algorithms over different datasets, according to the BoT model.

# images	Execution time (s)		Acceleration	Speedup	Efficiency
	Default	Improved			
LPT-CRD algorithm					
100	186.26	327.44	0.57	2.83	0.28
500	996.83	864.52	1.15	1.69	0.17
1000	2127.65	1739.53	1.22	4.17	0.42
Combined CRD algorithm					
100	186.26	242.67	0.77	3.41	0.34
500	996.83	850.20	1.17	1.69	0.17
1000	2127.65	1708.33	1.25	4.31	0.43

Similarly to the makespan evaluation, results in Table 2 indicate that the proposed algorithms computed significantly improved results when considering the mean flowtime as optimization metric. For both scheduling algorithms, the acceleration increased as the images datasets became bigger. As reported in the results, the acceleration grew slower than the makespan acceleration. This behavior could be analyzed on a future line of work, answering why makespan acceleration grows faster than flowtime acceleration. Since the reported acceleration grows as the images dataset size increases, it can be concluded that both strategies performed better than the default scheduling in terms of flowtime.

Figure 6 graphically summarizes the main results of the computational efficiency analysis for LPT-CRD and Combined CRD on different image datasets when compared with the default Mesos scheduling algorithm.

Figure 6 indicates that both algorithms performed faster than the default scheduling strategy for all the tested datasets. The graphics show that there are slight differences between LPT-CRD and CCRD, and the speedup increases as the dataset size increases. Regarding acceleration, Fig. 6 illustrates how it increased over the image dataset size, but slowing its pace. Further tests should be run to generalize this behavior for bigger image datasets as the ones proposed to analyze in the project "Geophysics using Hubble Space Telescope".

From the obtained results, we conclude that the scheduling improvements are convenient to process the full set of images (10 TB) available from HST. Either LPT-CRD or CCRD execute much faster than the original version. A processing that would eventually take months could be computed in days or even hours, depending on the behavior of the speedup on the dataset size.

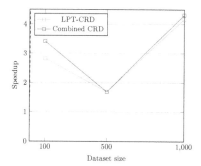
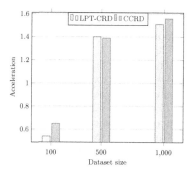

Fig. 6. Computational efficiency analysis for LPT-CRD and Combined CRD on different image datasets

6   Conclusions and Future Work

In this work, we improve an existent distributing computing architecture using Apache Mesos and Docker for processing images within the project "Geophysics using Hubble Space Telescope". We proposed using adapted LPT and SPT algorithms, combined with different processors, for scheduling. According to the metrics used for performance evaluation (makespan and mean flowtime), the proposed schedulers improved over the traditional one in Mesos. The main results indicate that the total makespan can be reduced up to 35% (acceleration 1.56), and the mean flowtime can be reduced 20% (acceleration 1.25) when using five fast workers, five slow workers and a dataset of 1000 images.

The main contribution of this article is that including some adjustments on the algorithms for job scheduling, an Apache Mesos based architecture can perform better regarding makespan and flowspan metrics. This performance improvement contributes to reducing times in astronomical images processing tasks.

The main lines of current and future work are related to exploring the utilization of different CPU speeds according to the heterogeneous computing model,

for example having different levels of speed and generalizing the results of the present work from two levels (slow and fast) to many levels. Finding the optimum ratio between slow and fast processing speeds, and the best configuration in terms of how many workers of each type obtains minimizes the total makespan is another line for further improving the proposed scheduling algorithms.

References

1. Tancredi, G., Cromwell, G., Deustua, S., Gonzalez, G., Nesmachnow, S., Schnyder, G.: Geophysics using Hubble Space Telescope. Hubble Space Telescope Cycle 24 approved proposal (2016)
2. NOAO: IRAF Project Home Page, July 2016. http://iraf.noao.edu/
3. Schnyder, G., Nesmachnow, S.: Improving the performance of cosmic ray detection using Apache Mesos. In: International Supercomputing Conference in México (2016)
4. The Apache Software Foundation: Mesos, July 2016. http://mesos.apache.org/
5. Mesosphere Inc.: Marathon: a cluster-wide init and control system for services in cgroups or Docker containers, July 2016. https://mesosphere.github.io/marathon/
6. The Apache Software Foundation: Apache ZooKeeper, July 2016. http://zookeeper.apache.org/
7. Golpayegani, N., Halem, M.: Cloud computing for satellite data processing on high end compute clusters. In: International Conference on Cloud Computing (2009)
8. Ali, M., Kumar, J.: Implementation of image processing system using handover technique with map reduce based on big data in the cloud environment. Int. Arab J. Inf. Technol. **13**(2), 326–331 (2016)
9. Adam, T.L., Chandy, K.M., Dickson, J.R.: A comparison of list schedules for parallel processing systems. Commun. ACM **17**(12), 685–690 (1974)
10. Coffman, E.G., Sethi, R.: Algorithms minimizing mean flow time: schedule-length properties. Acta Informatica **6**(1), 1–14 (1976)
11. Graham, R.L.: Bounds on multiprocessing timing anomalies. SIAM J. Appl. Math. **17**(2), 416–429 (1969)
12. Kovács, A.: Tighter approximation bounds for LPT scheduling in two special cases. J. Discret. Algorithms **7**(3), 327–340 (2009)
13. Oyetunji, E.O.: Some common performance measures in scheduling problems: review article. Res. J. Appl. Sci. Eng. Technol. **1**(2), 6–9 (2009)
14. Wiley, K., Connolly, A., Gardner, J., Krughoff, S., Balazinska, M., Howe, B., Kwon, Y., Bu, Y.: Astronomy in the cloud: using MapReduce for image co-addition. Publ. Astron. Soc. Pac. **123**(901), 366–380 (2011)
15. Singh, N., Browne, L.M., Butler, R.: Parallel astronomical data processing with Python: recipes for multicore machines. Astron. Comput. **2**, 1–10 (2013)
16. Graham, R., Lawler, E., Lenstra, J., Kan, A.: Optimization, approximation in deterministic sequencing, scheduling: a survey. Ann. Discret. Math. **5**, 287–326 (1979)
17. Eshaghian, M.: Heterogeneous Computing. Artech House, Norwood (1996)
18. Horowitz, E., Sahni, S.: Exact and approximate algorithms for scheduling nonidentical processors. J. ACM **23**(2), 317–327 (1976)
19. Nesmachnow, S.: Parallel multiobjective evolutionary algorithms for batch scheduling in heterogeneous computing and grid systems. Comput. Optim. Appl. **55**(2), 515–544 (2013)

20. Leung, J., Kelly, L., Anderson, J.: Handbook of Scheduling: Algorithms, Models, and Performance Analysis. CRC Press Inc., Boca Raton (2004)
21. Cirne, W., Brasileiro, F., Sauvé, J., Andrade, N., Paranhos, D., Santos-Neto, E.: Grid computing for bag of tasks applications. In: Proceedings of 3rd IFIP Conference on E-Commerce, E-Business and E-Government (2003)

The IMPETUS Project: Using ABACUS for the High Performance Computation of Radiative Tables for Accretion onto a Galaxy Black Hole

José M. Ramírez-Velasquez[1,2](✉), Jaime Klapp[2,3], Ruslan Gabbasov[4],
Fidel Cruz[5], and Leonardo Di G. Sigalotti[1,5]

[1] Centro de Física, Instituto Venezolano de Investigaciones Científicas (IVIC),
Apartado Postal 20632, Caracas 1020A, Venezuela
josem.ramirez@gmail.com

[2] ABACUS-Laboratorio de Matemática Aplicada y Cómputo de Alto Rendimiento,
Departamento de Matemáticas, Centro de Investigación y de Estudios Avanzados
CINVESTAV-IPN, Carretera México-Toluca Km 38.5, La Marquesa, 52740
Ocoyoacac, Estado de México, Mexico
jaime.klapp@hotmail.com

[3] Departamento de Física, Instituto Nacional de Investigaciones Nucleares (ININ),
Carretera México-Toluca Km. 36.5, La Marquesa,
52750 Ocoyoacac, Estado de México, Mexico
ruslan.gabb@gmail.com

[4] Instituto de Ciencias Básicas e Ingenierías, Universidad Autónoma del Estado de
Hidalgo (UAEH), Ciudad Universitaria, Carretera Pachuca-Tulancingo km. 4.5 S/N,
Colonia Carboneras, 42184 Mineral de la Reforma, Hidalgo, Mexico
fidelcru@gmail.com

[5] Área de Física de Procesos Irreversibles, Departamento de Ciencias Básicas,
Universidad Autónoma Metropolitana-Azcapotzalco (UAM-A), Av. San Pablo 180,
02200 Mexico City, Mexico
leonardo.sigalotti@gmail.com,
http://www.abacus.cinvestav.mx/impetus

Abstract. We present the intensive calculations of digital tables for the
radiative terms that appear in the energy and momentum equations used
to simulate the accretion onto supermassive black holes (SMBHs) at the
centers of galaxies. Cooling and heating rates are presented, calculated
with a Spectral Energy Distribution constructed from: an accretion disk
plus an X-ray power-law and an accretion disk plus a Corona. The electronic structures of atoms, the photoionization cross-sections, and the
recombination rates are treated in great detail. With the recent discovery of outflows originating at sub-parsec scales, these tables may provide
a useful tool for modeling gas accretion processes onto a SMBH.

Keywords: Accretion · Supermassive black hole · Galaxies: feedback ·
Evolution galaxy formation · Observational black hole

© Springer International Publishing AG 2017
C.J. Barrios Hernández et al. (Eds.): CARLA 2016, CCIS 697, pp. 374–386, 2017.
DOI: 10.1007/978-3-319-57972-6_28

1   Introduction

Nowadays it is believed that at the centers of all active galaxies (AGNs) reside a compact, super-massive object (supermassive black hole, SMBHs) that empowers its immediate surrounding with radiative energy. This radiation and its temporal evolution have been the subject of studies from radio to γ-rays, allowing in parallel the exploration of systems that involve compact objects, e.g., supernova remnants, X-ray binary stars, accretion onto SMBHs, and also their impact on the large-scale structure of the Universe, unprecedentedly.

The radiative energy transfer component, and the related astrophysical processes, are computed by the balance between heating ($\mathcal{H}$) and cooling ($\mathcal{C}$) agents. Sometimes these rates are computed using analytical prescriptions in order to save computational costs. However, improvements in computational facilities and numerical algorithms have allowed to substitute this strategy by detailed photoionization computations that are in principle limitation-free over a wide range of physical conditions.

Specifically, advanced codes like CLOUDY [12] and XSTAR [16], permit the computation of non-equilibrium thermodynamics, including their ionization, molecular states, level populations, and kinetic temperatures from low densities up to $\sim 10^{15}$ cm^{-3}, and temperatures from the cosmic microwave background (CMB) scale upto 10^{10} K. We recall that the electronic structure of atoms, the photoionization cross-sections, the recombination rates, and the grains and molecules are treated in detail by these codes.

Some of the major processes like for example: (i) photoionization/recombination, (ii) collisional ionization/3-body recombination to all levels, and (iii) collisional and radiative processes between atomic levels, are included in CLOUDY, so we expect to be taken into account the main spectral features in IR (infrared), UV (ultraviolet) and X-rays, and therefore objects in local thermodynamic equilibrium (LTE) are modeled self-consistently [11]. Inner-shell processes are also considered, including the radiative one [11]. On the other hand, analytical formulas for the heating and cooling rates have been widely used. For instance, previous work on accretion onto SMBHs in the centers of galaxies (active galactic nuclei, AGNs) by [26–28], and [4] have made use of [6] analytical formulas for the heating and cooling rates, which are limited to temperatures in the range $10^4 \lesssim T \lesssim 10^8$ K and ionization parameters ($\xi = L/[n_H r^2]$) in the interval $1 \lesssim \log(\xi) \lesssim 5$.

In this chapter, we develop a methodology and present tabulated values that account for highly detailed photoionization calculations together with the underlying microphysics to provide a platform for use in existing radiation hydrodynamics codes based either on Smoothed Particle Hydrodynamics (SPH) or Eulerian methods. Using the Cinvestav-ABACUS supercomputing facilities, we have run a very extensive grid of photoionization models using the most up-to-date version of CLOUDY (v 13.03), which allows us to pre-visualize physical conditions for a wide range of distances, from four Schwarzschild radii ($\approx 4r_{\text{Sch}}$) to $r \lesssim 34,000 r_{\text{Sch}}$ ($r_{\text{Sch}} = \frac{2GM_{BH}}{c^2}$), densities ($10^{-2} \lesssim n_H \lesssim 10^9$ cm^{-3}), and temperatures ($10^2 \lesssim T \lesssim 10^9$ K) around SMBHs in AGNs.

Active galaxies may be playing a key role in the regulation of the growth of their SMBHs [3,9,14,31]. In cosmology, and specifically in the standard model (i.e., Λ-Cold Dark Matter), the interplay between inflows and outflows are components that may be establishing the possible relationship between the grow of the SMBHs and the bulk kinematics properties of their host galaxies [13,19]. Theoretical and observational pieces of information are supporting such scenario. The equations of gravitohydrodynamics put theoretical constrains [7,18,23,24] on observations, where a lack of spatial resolution from kpc to pc is present. This is why a prescribed sub-grid is employed to solve this lack of resolution. Having X-ray luminosities high enough to overcome the gravitational escape velocities, combined with continuum and spectral lines opacities, outflows produced at sub-parsec scales are observed. This is why the calculations of the present tables provide a tool to solve the problem of accretion onto SMBHs in the center of galaxies at sub-parsec scales. In addition, two Spectral Energy Distributions (SEDs) and three ways of breaking up the luminosity between the disk and the X-ray components are presented. On average, these runs take about 200 min using $\approx$4000 cores ($\approx$13.3k CPU hours) of the Cinvestav-ABACUS supercomputer.

Examples of hydrodynamics codes using CLOUDY as their radiative modules can be found in evolution of HII regions, photoevaporation of the circumstellar disks, and cosmological minihaloes. Reference [32] invokes an SPH-based magnetohydrodynamics (MHD) code with CLOUDY for the simulation of the photoevaporation of the hot-Jupiter atmospheres. Moreover, [22] and [25] combine a finite-volume MHD code with CLOUDY to simulate planetary nebulae.

The symbols appearing through the manuscript have the standard meaning: $G \equiv$ Newtonian gravitational constant, $c \equiv$ speed of light, $m_e \equiv$ electron mass, $M_{BH} \equiv$ black hole mass, $h \equiv$ Planck's constant, $\sigma_T \equiv$ Thompson scattering cross-section, and $T \equiv$ temperature.

2   The Geometrically Thin, Optically Thick Disk Used in the SEDs

An accretion disk with dissipation $D(r)$ has a luminosity

$$L_{\text{disk}} = 2\pi \int_{r_{iD}}^{\infty} D(r)rdr = \frac{1}{2}\frac{\eta G M_{BH}\dot{M}}{r_{iD}}, \tag{1}$$

which is half of the accretion luminosity $L_{\text{a}} = \eta \dot{M}_{\text{a}}c^2$. For an optically thick disk L_{disk} radiates as a blackbody, its temperature $T_{bb}(r)$ as a function of distance is given by

$$\sigma_{\text{SB}}T_{bb}^4 = \frac{1}{2}D(r), \tag{2}$$

where σ_{SB} is the Stefan-Boltzmann constant and the factor $\frac{1}{2}$ enters because only one side of the disk is considered. Using the form of $D(r)$ for a viscous accretion disk, we have that

$$T_{bb}(r) = T_{\mathrm{iD}} \left(\frac{r}{r_{\mathrm{iD}}} \right)^{-3/4} \left[1 - \left(\frac{r_{\mathrm{iD}}}{r} \right)^{1/2} \right]^{1/4}, \tag{3}$$

where

$$T_{\mathrm{iD}} = \left(\frac{3\eta G M_{BH} \dot{M}}{8\pi r_{iD}^3 \sigma_{\mathrm{SB}}} \right)^{1/4}. \tag{4}$$

In our SEDs we use $M_{BH} = 10^8\ M_\odot$, $\dot{M}_a = 1.6\ M_\odot\ \mathrm{yr}^{-1}$, and $r_{\mathrm{iD}} = 3r_{\mathrm{Sch}}$ ($\approx r_{\mathrm{ISCO}}$ for a non-rotating SMBH). Hence, in the inner ring of the disk $T_{bb}(r_{\mathrm{iD}}) = 1.35 \times 10^5$ K, while in the outer part, i.e., for $r_{\mathrm{oD}} = 10r_{\mathrm{Sch}}$, the temperature would be $T_{bb}(r_{\mathrm{oD}}) = 4.50 \times 10^4$ K. In Fig. 1 we show the initial system we are proposing to solve.

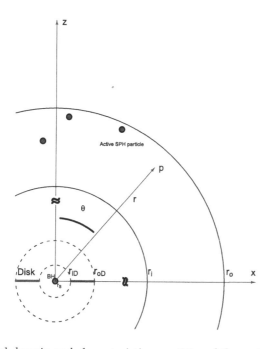

Fig. 1. Spatial domain and characteristic quantities of the system under study. BH is the position of the SMBH at the origin. Distances are properly scaled by the Schwarzschild r_{Sch}. The inner and outer SS disk radii are denoted r_{iD} and r_{oD}. Every SPH particle will be active if it is inside the domain given by r_{i} and r_{o}. Precomputed physical quantities as cooling, heating rates and radiative accelerations, are given to a particle located at point p, at a distance r from the SMBH.

3   Parameters and Computed Ionic Fractions

We have included the following elements: H, He, C, N, O, Ne, Na, Mg, Al, Si, S, Ar, Ca, and Fe. The abundances have been taken from [15] and we have neglected the effects of grains and molecules. Our grid of CLOUDY's models for the calculation of the heating and cooling rates and the radiative acceleration uses the following physical parameters with their respective resolution: $\theta = 0 \ldots \pi/2$ with $\Delta\theta = \pi/10$; $\log_{10}(n_H) = -2 \ldots 9$ [cm^{-3}] with $\Delta\log_{10}(n_H) = 0.1$; $\log_{10}(r) = 14 \ldots 18$ [cm] ($\approx 3.4 \times [1 - 10^4]$ r_{Sch}) with $\Delta\log_{10}(r) = 1$; and $\log_{10}(T) = 2 \ldots 9$ [K] with $\Delta\log_{10}(T) = 0.1$.

In order to look inside the cooling/heating tables we use a conventional bisection method, where for each SPH particle (or Eulerian cell) with coordinates (r_i, θ_i, ϕ_i) and density ρ_i, the functions $\mathcal{C}(\rho_i, T_i)$ and $\mathcal{H}(\rho_i, T_i)$ are linearly interpolated within the temperature interval $T_{\min} \leq T_i \leq T_{\max}$ (cloudy cell: abstract non-thermal equilibrium multidimensional unit, see Fig. 2). [12] discuss in great detail the numerical algorithm and the atomic databases used by CLOUDY. Here we shall only describe the calculation of the level populations and refer the interested reader to [12] (and references therein) for technical details.

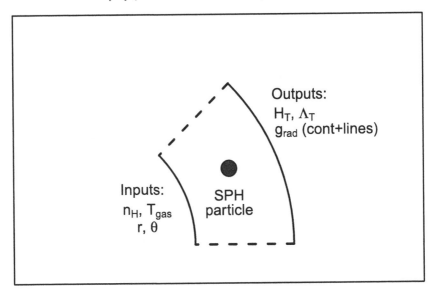

Fig. 2. Abstract non-thermal equilibrium multidimensional unit cell (cloudy cell), which is able to return pre-computed physical conditions, that is, $\mathcal{H}$, $\mathcal{C}$, $\mathbf{g}_{\text{Cont}}^{\text{rad}}$, $\mathbf{g}_{\text{Grav}}^{\text{rad}}$, $\mathbf{g}_{\text{Elec}}^{\text{rad}}$, $\mathbf{g}_{\text{Line}}^{\text{rad}}$, and $\mathbf{g}_{\text{Total}}^{\text{rad}}$ for given values of the hydrogen number density n_H, temperature T, distance to the source r, and incident angle θ.

Radiative and collisional processes contribute to the evolution of the level populations such that

$$\frac{db_n}{dt} = \frac{db_n}{dt}\bigg|_{\text{rad}} + \frac{db_n}{dt}\bigg|_{\text{col}}, \tag{5}$$

where b_n is the departure coefficient given by

$$b_n = \frac{n_n}{P_n^* n_e n_{\text{ion}}}, \tag{6}$$

n_n is the actual population of the level, n_e and n_{ion} are, respectively, the electron and ion number density, and P_n^* is the LTE relative population density for level n defined as

$$P_n^* = \frac{n_n^*}{P_n^* n_e n_{ion}} = \frac{g_n}{g_e g_{ion}} \left(\frac{m_n^*}{m_{ion}} \frac{h^2}{2\pi m_e kT} \right)^{3/2} \exp\left(\frac{\chi_n}{kT} \right). \tag{7}$$

Here $g_n = 2n^2$ is the hydrogenic statistical weight of level n, n_n^* is the LTE population of level n, $g_e = 2$ is the electron statistical weight, g_{ion} is the ion statistical weight, which is equal to 1 or 2 for H- or He-like species, respectively, and χ_n is the ionization potential of level n. The other symbols are: the electron mass, m_e, the Planck constant, h, and the temperature, T.

The collisional term in Eq. (5) can be written as

$$\left. \frac{db_n}{dt} \right|_{col} = \sum_l b_l C_{nl} + \sum_u \frac{P_u^*}{P_n^*} b_u C_{un}$$

$$-b_n \left[\sum_l C_{nl} + \sum_u \frac{P_u^*}{P_n^*} C_{un} + C_{nk}(1 - b_n^{-1}) \right], \tag{8}$$

where the summations are taken over the upper and lower levels and the C_{ij} are the collisional rates in units of s^{-1}. The first, second, and third terms of the above equation are, respectively, the collisional excitation from the lower levels to level n, the collisional de-excitation to level n from higher levels, and the term for destruction processes. The collisional ionization rate, C_{nk}, is multiplied by a factor that takes into account the effects of collisional ionization and three-body recombination.

The radiative contribution term in Eq. (5) can be written as

$$\left. \frac{db_n}{dt} \right|_{rad} = \sum_l \frac{P_l^*}{P_n^*} b_l A_{nl} \frac{g_n}{g_l} \eta_{nl} \gamma_{nl} +$$

$$\sum_u \frac{P_u^*}{P_n^*} b_u (A_{un}\beta_{un} + A_{un}\eta_{un}\gamma_{un}) +$$

$$\frac{\alpha_{rad} + \alpha_{ind}}{P_n^*} - b_n \times \tag{9}$$

$$\left[\sum_l (A_{nl}\beta_{nl} + A_{nl}\eta_{nl}\gamma_{nl}) + \sum_u A_{un}\frac{g_u}{g_n}\eta_{un}\gamma_{un} + \Gamma_n \right],$$

where A_{ij} is the transition probability, $\eta_{ij} \equiv J_\nu(ij)/(2h\nu_{ij}^3/c^2)$ is the continuum occupation number of the transition ij, with $J_\nu(ij)$ being the mean intensity of the ionizing continuum at the line frequency ν. The first of the two escape probabilities, β, is a two-side function, which takes into account line scattering and escape

$$\beta(\tau, T) = \frac{\beta(\tau) + \beta(T - \tau)}{2}, \tag{10}$$

where τ is the optical depth of the point in question and T is the total optical depth. The escape probability, $\gamma_{ij}(\tau)$, accounts for the fraction of the primary continuum penetrating up to τ and inducing transitions between level i and j.

The photoionization rate, Γ_n, from level n that appears in Eq. (9) is given by

$$\Gamma_n = 4\pi \int_{\nu_0}^{\infty} \frac{J_\nu}{h\nu} \sigma(\nu) d\nu, \tag{11}$$

and the induced recombination rate (cm^3 s^{-1}) is defined as

$$\alpha_{\mathrm{ind},n} = P_n^* 4\pi \int_{\nu_0}^{\infty} \frac{J_\nu}{h\nu} \sigma(\nu) \exp\left(-\frac{h\nu}{kT}\right) d\nu. \tag{12}$$

Spontaneous radiative recombination rates, α_{rad}, are calculated as in [2] and [1].

In summary, we have added terms which correspond to induced upward transitions from lower levels, spontaneous and induced downward transitions from higher levels, spontaneous and induced capture from the continuum to the level, and destruction of the level by radiative transitions and photoionization. The ionic emission data is taken from CHIANTI [8] and was recently revised by [17].

4   The Tables

The tables are available to the public at the following link: www.abacus. cinvestav.mx/impetus. They are plain ASCII files (my1Part_OUT.txt) stored in the directories simul_i_j/, where the index i corresponds to a value of the number density (n_H) and j corresponds to a value of the incident angle θ. For example, the sub-directory simul_1_1/ contains the ASCII text, with 12 columns (to be explained below), of the first density ($i \equiv 1, n_H = 10^{-2}\,\mathrm{cm}^{-3}$) and first angle ($j \equiv 1, \theta = 0$) in our grid. Moreover, in directory simul_101_6/, one can find the calculations for $n_H = 10^8\,\mathrm{cm}^{-3}$ and $\theta = \pi/2$.

Each main directory is provided with an ASCII file nH_SED1_mod_11.txt, where it is easy to see the values of i and j corresponding to a given density and angle. Inside this file we can find:

1. Column1: Index i.
2. Column2: Index j.
3. Column3: Number density $\log_{10}(n_H)$ [in cm^{-3}].
4. Column4: Incident angle θ [in radians].
5. Column5: Initial radius $\log_{10}(r)$ [in cm].
6. Column6: Final radius $\log_{10}(r)$ [in cm].

We now describe in more detail the content of the ASCII file my1Part_OUT.txt. There are twelve (12) columns inside:

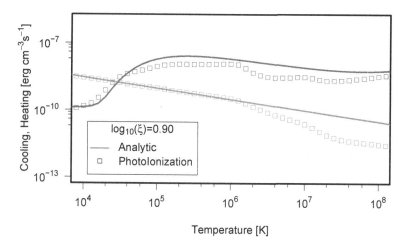

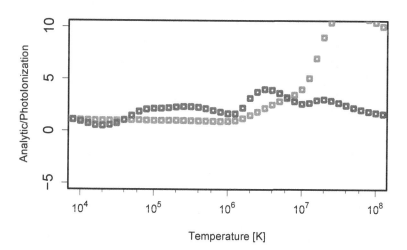

Fig. 3. Comparison between Blondin's analytical formulas (solid lines) and the detailed photoionization calculations (squares). The upper panel shows the cooling (blue) and heating (red) rates as a function of temperature. The same SED has been used for both models (a bremsstrahlung with $T_X = 1.16 \times 10^7$ K). A luminosity $L = f_X L_{\rm Edd}$ with $f_X = 0.5$ and a number density $n_H = 10^7 \, {\rm cm}^{-3}$ were used for these plots. The ionization parameter ξ was calculated for a distance of 3.2 pc from the source. The lower panel shows the analytic/photoionization ratio. (Color figure online)

1. Column1: Incident angle θ [in radians].
2. Column2: Number density $\log_{10}(n_H)$ [in cm^{-3}].
3. Column3: Distance from the BH $\log_{10}(r)$ [in cm].
4. Column4: Temperature $\log_{10}(T)$ [in K].
5. Column5: Total cooling rate $\log_{10}(\mathcal{C})$ [in erg cm^{-3}s^{-1}].
6. Column6: Total heating rate $\log_{10}(\mathcal{H})$ [in erg cm^{-3}s^{-1}].

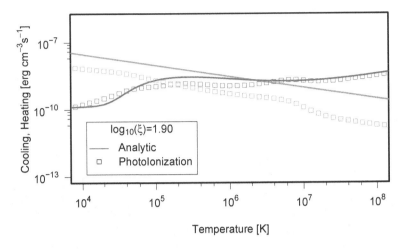

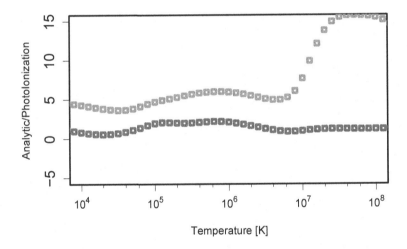

Fig. 4. Comparison between Blondin's analytical formulas (solid lines) and the detailed photoionization calculations (squares). The upper panel shows the cooling (blue) and heating (red) rates as a function of temperature. The same SED has been used for both models (a bremsstrahlung with $T_X = 1.16 \times 10^7$ K). A luminosity $L = f_X L_{\mathrm{Edd}}$ with $f_X = 0.5$ and a number density $n_H = 10^7$ cm^{-3} were used for these plots. The ionization parameter ξ was calculated for a distance of 1 pc from the source. The lower panel shows the analytic/photoionization ratio. (Color figure online)

7. Column7: Acceleration due to continuum $\mathbf{g}_{\mathrm{Cont}}^{\mathrm{rad}}$ [in cm s^{-2}].
8. Column8: Acceleration due to gravity $\mathbf{g}_{\mathrm{Grav}}^{\mathrm{rad}}$ [in cm s^{-2}].
9. Column9: Total acceleration outwards $\mathbf{g}_{\mathrm{Total}}^{\mathrm{rad}}$ [in cm s^{-2}].
10. Column10: Acceleration due to electron scattering $\mathbf{g}_{\mathrm{Elec}}^{\mathrm{rad}}$ [in cm s^{-2}].
11. Column11: Acceleration due to spectral lines $\mathbf{g}_{\mathrm{Line}}^{\mathrm{rad}}$ [in cm s^{-2}].
12. Column12: Force multiplier M_t [dimensionless].

Two versions of the tables are made available: a short version and a full one. The short version contains only the my1Part_OUT.txt file, the illuminating SED at $r = 10^{14}$ cm (the my1contFile_OUT_14 file), and the ionic fractions at $r = 10^{16}$ cm (the my1Part_OUT_frac.txt file). On average, the short version of the Tables (e.g. SED1, $f_{disk} = 0.95$ and $f_X = 0.05$) occupies ∼47 MB. The full version contains the full output (my1Part_OUT.out) from CLOUDY, which is useful to explore features related to the calculations in deeper detail. Each uncompressed directory has, on average, a size of ∼32 GB. Multiplying by six this size leads to ∼200 GB for the full version of the tables. A summary of the short and full versions and their location can be found in Table 1.

Table 1. Short and full$^{(a)}$ versions of the table files

Calc	File name	Size (MB)
I	New_DB_SED1_1_short.gz	47
II	New_DB_SED1_2_short.gz	47
III	New_DB_SED1_3_short.gz	47
IV	New_DB_SED2_1_short.gz	47
V	New_DB_SED2_2_short.gz	47
VI	New_DB_SED2_3_short.gz	47

The main webpage of the project is: http://www. abacus.cinvestav.mx/impetus.
(a) The full version of the tables can be accessed by request to the corresponding author.

5   Discussion and Concluding Remarks

How the contributions of several physical mechanisms (in addition to Doppler effects and cooling by expansion), impact the rates, are displayed in Fig. 3. Low-ionization species are important to low-to-intermediate temperatures. The Unresolved Transition Array (UTA, [5,21] and also see [30] for an observational point of view), is among the main heating (also cooling) agents contributing to the rates (≈20%). Highly ionized species of iron $Fe^{+17} - Fe^{+24}$ and H− and He-like ions of $O^{+7}-O^{+8}, C^{+4}-C^{+5}$ become relevant in the range $10^4 \lesssim T \lesssim 10^6$ K. At $\log_{10}(\xi) \sim 0.90$ photoionization heating due to O^{+7} contributes close ≈20%. Closer to the SMBH (see Fig. 4), at $\log_{10}(\xi) \sim 1.90$, heating by Compton processes dominate the range $6.3 \times 10^6 \lesssim T \lesssim 3.2 \times 10^9$ K. The inclusion of the Sobolev optical depth in our calculations, made the equilibrium temperature cooler at high temperatures, compared with cooling rates where these effects are not taken into account.

Reference [4] discusses in detail three-dimensional SPH simulations of accretion onto a SMBH, using the heating and cooling rates proposed by [6,20]. Some of their runs take longer to reach a steady state compared to the Bondi accretion. When analyzing radiative properties in the $T - \xi$ plane, the authors find many particles following the equilibrium temperature ($\mathcal{L} = 0$) and discuss where and when artificial viscosity play a dominant role over radiative heating.

From the observational point of view, having available tabulated values of heating and cooling rates and radiative accelerations at sub-parsec scales, may be important for our understanding of several types of astrophysical flows. For instance, high-energy features [10,33], observed throughout the signature of ~ 1000 km s^{-1} molecules and $\sim 0.2c$ highly ionized gas outflows [29], may indicate locations of ~ 900 r_{Sch}. In luminous quasars [34], again, spectral features of ~ 6 keV, are clear evidence of Fe XXV and Fe XXVI in the flows, which could be located at $\sim 10^{15}$–10^{16} cm, for another application of these tables. It is therefore clear that a quantitative analysis of the heating and cooling agents operating in these kinds of astrophysical environments are key aspects to the understanding of the radiation hydrodynamical processes governing the accretion onto SMBHs. We have provided the files my1Part_OUT.het and my1Part_OUT.col as part of the tables, where the default ≈ 10 agents are given by CLOUDY. The interested reader may request the modified 100 agent files to the corresponding author. A strict comparison between theoretical models and simulations is beyond the scope of the tables presented here. At present, such simulations are under preparation.

Acknowledgments. IMPETUS is a collaboration project between the ABACUS-Centro de Matemáticas Aplicadas y Cómputo de Alto Rendimiento of Cinvestav-IPN, the Centro de Física of the Instituto Venezolano de Investigaciones Científicas (IVIC), and the Área de Física de Procesos Irreversibles of the Departamento de Ciencias Básicas of the Universidad Autónoma Metropolitana–Azcapotzalco (UAM-A) aimed at the SPH modeling of astrophysical flows. The project is supported by ABACUS under grant EDOMEX-2011-C01-165873, by IVIC under the project 2013000259, and by UAM-A through internal funds. JMRV thanks the hospitality, support, and computing facilities of ABACUS, where this work was done.

References

1. Badnell, N.R.: Dielectronic recombination of Fe 3p^q ions: a key ingredient for describing X-ray absorption in active galactic nuclei. ApJ **651**, L73–L76 (2006)
2. Badnell, N.R., O'Mullane, M.G., Summers, H.P., Altun, Z., Bautista, M.A., Colgan, J., Gorczyca, T.W., Mitnik, D.M., Pindzola, M.S., Zatsarinny, O.: Dielectronic recombination data for dynamic finite-density plasmas. I. Goals and methodology. A&A **406**, 1151–1165 (2003)
3. Barai, P.: Large-scale impact of the cosmological population of expanding radio galaxies. ApJ **682**, L17–L20 (2008)
4. Barai, P., Proga, D., Nagamine, K.: Smoothed particle hydrodynamics simulations of black hole accretion: a step to model black hole feedback in galaxies. MNRAS **418**, 591–611 (2011)
5. Behar, E., Sako, M., Kahn, S.M.: Soft X-ray absorption by Fe^{0+} to Fe^{15+} in active galactic nuclei. ApJ **563**, 497–504 (2001)

6. Blondin, J.M.: The shadow wind in high-mass X-ray binaries. ApJ **435**, 756–766 (1994)
7. Ciotti, L., Ostriker, J.P.: Cooling flows and quasars. II. Detailed models of feedback-modulated accretion flows. ApJ **551**, 131–152 (2001)
8. Dere, K.P., Landi, E., Mason, H.E., Monsignori Fossi, B.C., Young, P.R.: Chianti - an atomic database for emission lines. A&AS **125**, 149–173 (1997)
9. Fabian, A.C.: The obscured growth of massive black holes. MNRAS **308**, L39–L43 (1999)
10. Faucher-Giguère, C.-A., Quataert, E.: The physics of galactic winds driven by active galactic nuclei. MNRAS **425**, 605–622 (2012)
11. Ferland, G.J., Korista, K.T., Verner, D.A., Ferguson, J.W., Kingdon, J.B., Verner, E.M.: CLOUDY 90: numerical simulation of plasmas and their spectra. PASP **110**, 761–778 (1998)
12. Ferland, G.J., Porter, R.L., van Hoof, P.A.M., Williams, R.J.R., Abel, N.P., Lykins, M.L., Shaw, G., Henney, W.J., Stancil, P.C.: The 2013 release of cloudy. Rev. Mex. Astron. Astrofis. **49**, 137–163 (2013)
13. Gebhardt, K., Bender, R., Bower, G., Dressler, A., Faber, S.M., Filippenko, A.V., Green, R., Grillmair, C., Ho, L.C., Kormendy, J., Lauer, T.R., Magorrian, J., Pinkney, J., Richstone, D., Tremaine, S.: A relationship between nuclear black hole mass and galaxy velocity dispersion. ApJ **539**, L13–L16 (2000)
14. Germain, J., Barai, P., Martel, H.: Anisotropic active galactic nucleus outflows and enrichment of the intergalactic mediumI. I. Metal distribution. ApJ **704**, 1002–1020 (2009)
15. Grevesse, N., Asplund, M., Sauval, A.J., Scott, P.: The chemical composition of the sun. Astrophys. Space Sci. **328**, 179–183 (2010)
16. Kallman, T., Bautista, M.: Photoionization and high-density gas. ApJS **133**, 221–253 (2001)
17. Landi, E., Del Zanna, G., Young, P.R., Dere, K.P., Mason, H.E.: CHIANTI-an atomic database for emission lines. XII. Version 7 of the database. ApJ **744**, 99 (2012)
18. Li, Y., Hernquist, L., Robertson, B., Cox, T.J., Hopkins, P.F., Springel, V., Gao, L., Di Matteo, T., Zentner, A.R., Jenkins, A., Yoshida, N.: Formation of z~6 quasars from hierarchical galaxy mergers. ApJ **665**, 187–208 (2007)
19. Magorrian, J., Tremaine, S., Richstone, D., Bender, R., Bower, G., Dressler, A., Faber, S.M., Gebhardt, K., Green, R., Grillmair, C., Kormendy, J., Lauer, T.: The demography of massive dark objects in galaxy centers. AJ **115**, 2285–2305 (1998)
20. Mościbrodzka, M., Proga, D.: Thermal and dynamical properties of gas accreting onto a supermassive black hole in an active galactic nucleus. ApJ **767**, 156 (2013)
21. Netzer, H.: The iron unresolved transition array in active galactic nuclei. ApJ **604**, 551–555 (2004)
22. Niederwanger, F., Öttl, S., Kimeswenger, S., Kissmann, R., Reitberger, K.: 3D radiative transfer models of planetary nebulae with CRONOS and CLOUDY. In: Asymmetrical Planetary Nebulae VI Conference, p. 67, April 2014
23. Novak, G.S., Ostriker, J.P., Ciotti, L.: Feedback from central black holes in elliptical galaxies: two-dimensional models compared to one-dimensional models. ApJ **737**, 26 (2011)
24. Ostriker, J.P., Choi, E., Ciotti, L., Novak, G.S., Proga, D.: Momentum driving: which physical processes dominate active galactic nucleus feedback? ApJ **722**, 642–652 (2010)
25. Öttl, S., Kimeswenger, S., Zijlstra, A.A.: Ionization structure of multiple-shell planetary nebulae. I. NGC 2438. A&A **565**, 87 (2014)

26. Proga, D.: Dynamics of accretion flows irradiated by a quasar. ApJ **661**, 693–702 (2007)
27. Proga, D., Kallman, T.R.: Dynamics of line-driven disk winds in active galactic nuclei. II. Effects of disk radiation. ApJ **616**, 688–695 (2004)
28. Proga, D., Stone, J.M., Kallman, T.R.: Dynamics of Line-driven disk winds in active galactic nuclei. ApJ **543**, 686–696 (2000)
29. Ramírez, J.M.: Physical and kinematical properties of the X-ray absorber in the broad absorption line quasar APM 08279+5255. A&A **489**, 57–68 (2008)
30. Ramírez, J.M., Komossa, S., Burwitz, V., Mathur, S.: Chandra LETGS spectroscopy of the quasar MR 2251-178 and its warm absorber. ApJ **681**, 965–981 (2008)
31. Salpeter, E.E.: Accretion of interstellar matter by massive objects. ApJ **140**, 796–800 (1964)
32. Salz, M., Banerjee, R., Mignone, A., Schneider, P.C., Czesla, S., Schmitt, J.H.M.M.: TPCI the PLUTO-CLOUDY Interface. A versatile coupled photoionization hydrodynamics code. A&A **576**, 21 (2015)
33. Tombesi, F., Meléndez, M., Veilleux, S., Reeves, J.N., González-Alfonso, E., Reynolds, C.S.: Wind from the black-hole accretion disk driving a molecular outflow in an active galaxy. Nature **519**, 436–438 (2015)
34. Vignali, C., Iwasawa, K., Comastri, A., Gilli, R., Lanzuisi, G., Ranalli, P., Cappelluti, N., Mainieri, V., Georgantopoulos, I., Carrera, F.J., Fritz, J., Brusa, M., Brandt, W.N., Bauer, F.E., Fiore, F., Tombesi, F.: The XMM deep survey in the CDF-S. IX. An X-ray outflow in a luminous obscured quasar at z~1.6. ArXiv e-prints, September 2015

Database of CMFGEN Models
in a 6-Dimensional Space

Janos Zsargó[1], Celia Rosa Fierro[2(✉)], Jaime Klapp[2,3], Anabel Arrieta[4],
Lorena Arias[4], and D. John Hillier[5]

[1] Escuela Superior de Física y Matemáticas, Instituto Politécnico Nacional,
Av. Instituto Politécnico Nacional S/N, Edificio 9, 07738 Mexico City, Mexico
jzsargo@esfm.ipn.mx

[2] ABACUS-Laboratorio de Matemática Aplicada y Cómputo de Alto Rendimiento,
Departamento de Matemáticas, Centro de Investigación y de Estudios Avanzados
CINVESTAV-IPN, Carretera México-Toluca Km 38.5, La Marquesa, Ocoyoacac,
Estado de México 52740, Mexico
celia.fierro.estrellas@gmail.com

[3] Instituto Nacional de Investigaciones Nucleares, Carretera México-Toluca Km.
36.5, 52750 Ocoyoacac, Estado de México, Mexico

[4] Universidad Iberoamericana, Prolongación Paseo de la Reforma 880,
01219 Mexico City, Mexico

[5] Departament of Physics and Astronomy and Pittsburgh Particle Physics,
Astrophysics, and Cosmology Center (PITT PACC), University of Pittsburgh,
3941 Ohara Street, Pittsburgh, PA 15260, USA

Abstract. We present a database of 25,000 atmospheric models (which
is to grow to a grand total of 75000 models by the conclusion of the
project) with stellar masses between 9 and $120 \, M_\odot$, covering the region
of the OB main sequence and W-R stars in the H-R diagram. The models were calculated using the ABACUS I supercomputer and the stellar
atmosphere code CMFGEN. The parameter space has 6 dimensions: sur-
face temperature of the star, also called the effective temperature (T_{eff}),
luminosity (L), metallicity (Z), and three stellar wind parameters, the
exponent (β) of the wind velocity law, the terminal velocity (V_∞), and
the volume filling factor (F_{cl}). For each model, we also calculate synthetic
spectra in the UV (900–2,000 Å), optical (3,500–7,000 Å), and near IR
(10,000–30,000 Å) ranges. For comparison with observations, the synthetic spectra were rotationally broaden using ROTIN3, by covering the
range between 10 and 350 km s^{-1} with steps of 10 km s^{-1}, resulting a
library of 1,575,000 synthetic spectra.

1 Introduction

Stellar atmospheric models are valuable tools for improving our understanding of stellar, galactic, and cosmic evolution. Comparisons of observational data
with synthetic spectra allow us to learn more about the chemical composition
and the physical conditions in the atmospheres and winds of stars. However,
the numeric codes that are able to compute the atomic populations assuming nonlocal thermodynamic equilibrium (NLTE) and incorporate the effects

© Springer International Publishing AG 2017
C.J. Barrios Hernández et al. (Eds.): CARLA 2016, CCIS 697, pp. 387–392, 2017.
DOI: 10.1007/978-3-319-57972-6_29

of the line-blanketing, e.g., TLUSTY (Hubeny and Lanz 1995), FASTWIND (Santolaya-Rey et al. 1997; Puls et al. 2005), and CMFGEN (Hillier and Miller 1998), are very microprocessor-time consuming and require a large amount of memory to run. Furthermore, these computational requirements strongly depend on the initial conditions that are utilized at the beginning of the simulations.

One can alleviate these problems by creating a grid of pre-calculated models to provide suitable initial conditions for future modeling. Such grids also allow the rapid and crude analysis of a large number of stars. Unfortunately, the necessary number of models in the grid increases exponentially with the number of input parameters that are taken into account; therefore, only supercomputers allow the production of realistic grids in reasonable time.

In the course of this project, we generate a mega-grid of atmospheric models by using the program CMFGEN on the supercomputer ABACUS-I of the ABACUS Centre for Applied Mathematics and High Performance Computing of CINVESTAV, México. The grid covers a six-dimensional space with different values of the main parameters of the star, wind and chemical composition.

2   CMFGEN

CMFGEN (Hillier 2013; Hillier and Miller 1998) is a sophisticated and widely-used non-LTE stellar atmosphere code. It models the full spectrum and has been used successfully to model O & B stars, W-R stars, luminous blue variables, and even supernova. The code determines the temperature, ionization structure, and level populations for all elements in the stellar atmosphere and wind. It solves the spherical radiative transfer equation in the co-moving frame in conjunction with the statistical equilibrium equations and radiative equilibrium equation. The hydrostatic structure can be computed below the sonic point; allowing the simultaneous treatment of spectral lines formed in the atmosphere, the stellar wind, and in the transition region between the two. Such features make it particularly well suited to the study of massive OB stars with winds. However, there is a price for such sophistication, a CMFGEN simulation takes anywhere between 24 and 36 hours of microprocessor time to finish.

For atomic models, CMFGEN utilizes the concept of "super levels", by which levels of similar energies are grouped together and treated as a single level in the statistical equilibrium equations (see Hillier and Miller 1998 and references therein). The stellar models in this project include 28 explicit ions of the different elements as function of their T_{eff}. Table 1 summarizes the levels and super levels included in the models. The atomic data references are given in Herald and Bianchi (2004).

To model the stellar wind, CMFGEN requires values for the mass loss rate ($\dot{M}$), terminal velocity (V_∞), β parameter, and the *volume filling factor* of the wind (F_{cl}). The profile of the wind speed is modeled by a beta-type law (Castor et al. 1975)

$$\mathbf{v}(\mathbf{r}) = v_\infty \left(1 - \frac{r}{R_*}\right)^\beta.$$ (1)

Table 1. Super levels/levels for the different ionization stages included in the models.

Element	I	II	III	IV	V	VI	VII	VIII
H	20/30	1/1	...	...	...	...	...	...
He	45/69	22/30	1/1	...	...	...	...	...
C	...	40/92	51/84	59/64	1/1	...	...	...
N	...	45/85	41/82	44/76	41/49	1/1	...	...
O	...	54/123	88/170	38/78	32/56	25/31	1/1	...
Si	...	...	33/33	22/33	1/1	...	...	...
P	...	...	...	30/90	16/62	1/1	...	...
S	...	...	24/44	51/142	31/98	28/58	1/1	...
Fe	...	...	104/1433	74/540	50/220	44/433	29/153	1/1

The β parameter controls how the stellar wind is accelerated to reach the terminal velocity (see Fig. 1), while the volume filling factor F_{cl} is used to introduce the effects of optically thin clumping in the wind (see Sundqvist et al. (2014) and references therein).

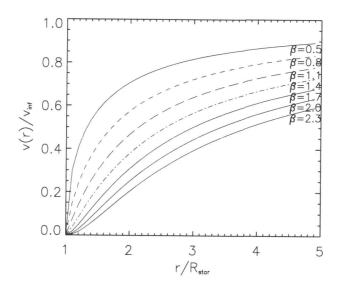

Fig. 1. Examples of beta-type velocity laws.

2.1 Synthetic Spectra

The auxiliary program CMF_FLUX of the CMFGEN package (Hillier 2013) computes the synthetic observed spectrum in the observer's frame which is one of the most important output of our models. To simulate the effects of rotation on the spectral lines, the synthetic spectra are also rotationally broadened using the program ROTIN3 which is part of the TLUSTY package (Hubeny and Lanz 1995).

For each model in the grid, we calculate the normalized spectra in the UV (900–3,500 Å), optical (3,500–7,000 Å), and IR (7,000–40,000 Å) range; then, we apply rotation by sampling the range between 10 and 350 km s^{-1} with steps of 10 km s^{-1}. This process results a library with a total of 1,575,000 synthetic spectra.

3   The Model Grid

The main parameters of a model atmosphere are the luminosity (L) and the effective temperature (T_{eff}) whose values allow to place the star in the H–R diagram. In order to constrain appropriately the input parameters, we use the evolutionary tracks of Ekström et al. (2012) calculated with solar metallicity (Z=0.014) at the zero age of the main sequence (ZAMS). For any track, each point corresponds to a star with specific values of T_{eff}, luminosity (L) and stellar mass (M). We calculated several models along each track with the approximate steps of 2,500 K in T_{eff}, while the stellar radius and log g were calculated to get the L and M corresponding to the track.

The elements included in our models are H, He, C, N, O, Si, P, S, and Fe. The values of H, He, C, N, and O were taken from the Tables of Ekström et al. (2012). For consistency, we assumed the solar metallicity reported by Asplund et al. (2009) for the Si, P, S, and Fe in all models.

The grid is organized as a hypercube data in dimensions which correspond to T_{eff}, L, β, F_{cl}, Z, and V_{∞}. The plane generated by T_{eff} and L is the H-R diagram (Fig. 2, *Top*); the values of these variables are restricted by evolutionary tracks. The third dimension is the β parameter of the stellar wind for which we use the values of $\beta = 0.5, 0.8, 1.1, 1.4, 1.7, 2.0, 2.3$ (Fig. 2, *Bottom left*). Models with different values of T_{eff}, L and β populate a data cube. Each value of $F_{cl} = 0.05, 0.30, 0.60, 1.0$ generates a similar cube, which they are aligned one after another in a fourth dimensional space. We have two values of metallicity, solar and solar enhanced by rotation. This 5-dimensional arrangement generates a plane populated with data cubes (Fig. 2, *Bottom right*). Finally, for V_{∞} we use two values, a low ($V_{\infty} = 1.3 V_{esc}$) and a high ($V_{\infty} = 2.1 V_{esc}$) velocity model, where the escape velocity (V_{esc}) has the usual meaning. The result is a 6-dimensional arrangement.

This arrangement only populates regions of the H-R diagram where nature form stars, and does not produce non-physical models. If needed, we can interpolate between models to achieve better fits to the observed spectra.

4   Summary

We present a mega grid of, "soon to be" 75,000 stellar atmospheric models calculated with the CMFGEN package. These models cover the region of the HR

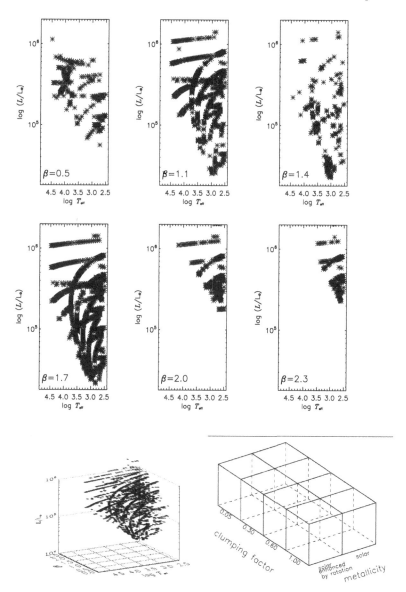

Fig. 2. Organization of the grid as a 5-dimensional hypercube. *Top:* T_{eff}-Luminosity planes with different values of β parameter. *Bottom Left:* Data cube with the models contained in the six planes. *Bottom Right:* Plane formed by cubes similar to that shown on the left, the dimensions of these are different values of the *volume filling factor* with two different metallicities.

diagram populated by OB main sequence and W-R stars with masses between 9 and 120 $M_\odot$. The grid provides UV, visual, and IR spectra for each model.

We use T_{eff} and luminosity values that correspond to the evolutionary traces of Ekström et al. (2012); furthermore, we sample seven values of β, five values of the clumping factor and two different metallicities and terminal velocities. This generates a 6-dimensional hypercube of stellar atmospheric models which we intend to release to the general astronomical community as a free tool for analyzing OB stars.

Acknowledgments. All models and their synthetic spectra were calculated by the cluster Abacus I. The authors express their acknowledgement for the resources, expertise and the assistance provided by "ABACUS" Centre of Applied Mathematics and High Performance Computing ABACUS-CINVESTAV, CONACyT-EDOMEX-2011-C01-165873 Project. J. Zsargo acknowledges CONACyT CB-2011-01 No. 168632 grant for support.

References

Asplund, M., Grevesse, N., Sauval, A.J., Scott, P.: ARA&A **47**, 481 (2009)
Castor, J.I., Abbott, D.C., Klein, R.I.: ApJ **195**, 157 (1975)
Ekström, S., Georgy, C., Eggenberger, P., Meynet, G., et al.: A&A **537**, 146 (2012)
Herald, J.E., Bianchi, L.: ApJ **609**, 378 (2004)
Hillier, D.J., Miller, D.: ApJ **496**, 407 (1998)
Hillier, D. J., CMFGEN Manual (2013)
Hubeny, I., Lanz, T.: ApJ **439**, 875 (1995)
Puls, J., Urbaneja, M.A., Venero, R., et al.: A&A **435**, 669 (2005)
Santolaya-Rey, A.E., Puls, J., Herrero, A.: A&A **323**, 488 (1997)
Sundqvist, J.O., Puls, J., Owocki, S.P.: A&A **568**, A59 (2014)

Cosmography with the Hubble Rate: The *Eis* Approach

Jaime Klapp[1,2(✉)], Alejandro Aviles[1,2,3], and Orlando Luongo[4,5,6,7]

[1] Departamento de Física, Instituto Nacional de Investigaciones Nucleares (ININ),
Carretera México-Toluca S/N, La Marquesa, 52750 Ocoyoacac,
Estado de México, Mexico
jaime.klapp@inin.gob.mx

[2] ABACUS-Laboratorio de Matemática Aplicada y Cómputo de Alto Rendimiento,
Departamento de Matemáticas, Centro de Investigación y de Estudios Avanzados
CINVESTAV-IPN, Carretera México-Toluca Km 38.5, La Marquesa,
Ocoyoacac, Estado de México 52740, Mexico

[3] Consejo Nacional de Ciencia y Tecnología,
Av. Insurgentes Sur 1582, Ciudad de México, Mexico

[4] Department of Mathematics and Applied Mathematics, University of Cape Town,
Rondebosch 7701, Cape Town, South Africa

[5] Astrophysics, Cosmology and Gravity Centre (ACGC), University of Cape Town,
Rondebosch 7701, Cape Town, South Africa

[6] Dipartimento di Fisica, Università di Napoli "Federico II",
Via Cinthia, 80126 Napoli, Italy

[7] Istituto Nazionale di Fisica Nucleare (INFN), Via Cinthia, 80126 Napoli, Italy

Abstract. The statefinder parameters characterize the expansion history of the Universe in a model independent way. The standard method to estimate them is named Standard Cosmography (SC). In this paper we show how these estimations turn out to be highly biased and the standard deviations of their probability distributions very large. The *Eis* method was tailored to minimize these drawbacks. Here, with the aid of mock supernovae catalogs, we show how our new method works, and that it surpasses the performance of SC for both the bias and dispersion of the estimated statefinders.

1 Introduction

Currently, the most accepted paradigm to describe the evolution of the Universe since very early times is the Lambda Cold Dark Matter (ΛCDM) model. It relies mainly on the premises that the Einstein's field equations are valid, and that the Universe is highly homogeneous and isotropic when averaging over very large scales (about above $150\,\mathrm{Mpc}$). It also assumes the Standard Model of particle physics, thus the energy-matter content includes baryons, photons, and neutrinos. Nevertheless, to accurately explain several different astronomical and cosmological observations the model adds two ingredients of unknown fundamental description which comprises about 96% of the whole energy content: the cosmological constant driving the accelerated expansion of the universe; and

© Springer International Publishing AG 2017
C.J. Barrios Hernández et al. (Eds.): CARLA 2016, CCIS 697, pp. 393–405, 2017.
DOI: 10.1007/978-3-319-57972-6_30

the cold dark matter, which is responsible of the clustering of matter due to its gravitational self-attraction and very small negligible velocity dispersion, and for which the Jeans length scale is zero.

Although the cosmological constant suffers from the magnitude and cosmic coincidence problems [1–3], it is well motivated as the minimal modification to the theory of General Relativity consistent with the principle of general covariance. Actually, any other extension introduces additional degrees of freedom, either to the metric or as new scalar or vector fields. In this sense, the nature of the dark matter is perhaps more intriguing: today observations are consistent with several particle physics models, and are not able to tell if the dark matter is really cold. The success of the ΛCDM is remarkable in the early universe (see, for example, Figs. 1 and 3 in [4]), but it is still not very well tested in the late times, where there is large room for an evolving dark energy and several behaviors for the dark matter. Other possibilities are the existence of a unified fluid for the whole dark sector [5–7], or that the laws of gravity are different at large scales [8–10].

It is for these reasons that parameters that encapsulate different aspects of cosmology without calling any specific model are very useful. Among several treatments, *cosmography-on the background*, or simply cosmography, attempts to reconstruct the expansion history of the Universe in a model independent way. To do so, it introduces a set of parameters called *statefinders*, which characterize the expansion rate of the Universe. In other words, the main objective of cosmography is to reconstruct the Hubble diagram as model independent as possible. Cosmography is a "top-down" approach to cosmology that deduces its kinematics directly from observations; in contrast to a "bottom-up" approach, that assumes the dynamics of a given model from the very beginning [11].

To measure the statefinders parameters, several frameworks have been considered: fits with Standard Cosmography (SC) [12–14], expansions on different functions of redshift z [15,16], Padé rational approximants [17–19], Gaussian process cosmography [11,20], and principal component analysis [21,22], among others. However, beyond the estimation of the first statefinder parameter, q_0, none of these approaches turn out to be totally satisfactory.

In this work we show how the estimated statefinders in SC are biased and have very large standard deviations non-tolerable for current and future observations. We also show a model proposed by us in [23] which considerably reduces the bias and the dispersion of the estimations. The rest of the paper is organized as follows: in Sect. 2 we review the basics aspects of cosmography; in Sect. 3 we introduce the *Eis* method for cosmography; in Sect. 4 we show the performed numerical analysis; finally, we present our conclusions in Sect. 5.

2   Cosmography as a Tool for Studying the Universe's Background Evolution

The isotropy and homogeneous condition restricts the spacetime to have constant space 3-dimensional Ricci curvature, thus the metric should take the

Friedmann-Robertson-Walker (FRW) form[1] [24]

$$ds^2 = g_{\mu\nu}dx^\mu dx^\nu = -dt^2 + a(t)\gamma_{ij}dx^i dx^j. \tag{1}$$

The γ tensor is the metric of the three dimensional space-like foliations, and it can take only three forms: euclidean, hyperbolic, or spherical. In the following we will assume it euclidean, since it is preferred by observations; see, for example [4]. Therefore, the only metric freedom is the scale factor $a(t)$. It encodes the cosmic background evolution in such a way that two points that are separated by a physical distance ℓ_i at some time t_i, will be separated by a distance $\ell(t) = a(t)\ell_i/a(t_i)$ at a time t. This property also implies that its normalization is irrelevant, by convention it is set equal to 1 nowadays, $a(t_0) = 1$ (hereafter a subindex "0" denotes present time quantities). The time-like geodesics of the FRW metric are the curves with spatial coordinates x^i fixed, and their proper time coincides with the coordinate time t. These geodesics correspond to observers that see the isotropic and homogeneous Universe; that is, the free-fall observers are comoving with the background expansion.

Einstein's equations lead to the Friedmann and continuity equations,

$$H^2 = \frac{8\pi G}{3}\sum_i \rho_i \tag{2}$$

and

$$\dot{\rho}_i + 3H(1 + w_i)\rho_i = 0, \tag{3}$$

respectively. Here, $H(t) \equiv \dot{a}/a$ is the Hubble factor, the subindex i labels the different matter-energy components, ρ_i refers to their energy densities, and w_i the equations of state parameters, such that the pressures are given by $P_i = w_i\rho_i$. For incoherent relativistic components $w_r = 1/3$, for cold dark matter and baryons $w_m = 0$, while for dark energy $w_\Lambda \simeq -1$ (being exactly -1 for a cosmological constant). If we further define the density abundance parameters $\Omega_i = 8\pi G\rho_{i0}/3H_0^2$, Friedmann and continuity equations lead to

$$H^2 = H_0^2 \left(\Omega_m a^{-3} + \Omega_\Lambda G(a)\right)^{1/2}, \tag{4}$$

where the function $G(a)$ gives the evolution of dark energy,

$$G(a) = \exp\left[-3\int_a^1 \frac{1 + w_\Lambda(a')}{a'}da'\right]. \tag{5}$$

Note that $G(a)$ goes to 1 as a goes to 1, and that $G(a) = 1$ in the case of a cosmological constant. By evaluating Eq. (4) at the present time, it follows that $\Omega_m + \Omega_\Lambda = 1$. Since we are concerned in studying late times, we have included no radiation contributions into the Friedmann equation, which become negligible.

---

[1] Greek letters denote space time coordinates, while Latin letters refer only to space coordinates. Summation over repeated indices is implicit.

Relativistic components should be considering for the early Universe, when $a \ll 1$. Furthermore, the effects of baryons and dark matter are degenerated in the background evolution: they enter the equations through the combination $\Omega_b + \Omega_{dm} = \Omega_m$.

In this work we are interested in comparing the expansion history of the Universe against supernovae type Ia observations. The fittings should be performed by comparing against the distance modulus

$$\mu(z) = 5 \log \left(\frac{d_L(z)}{\text{Mpc}} \right) + 25, \qquad (6)$$

which is the quantity inferred by observations [25]. Here $z = 1/a - 1$ is the cosmological redshift, such that at present time $z_0 = 0$. For a flat FRW spacetime, the luminosity distance d_L can be written as

$$d_L(z) = (1 + z) \int_0^z \frac{dz'}{H(z')}. \qquad (7)$$

For example, using the Joint Light-curve Analysis (JLA) supernovae compilation, in [26] it is found that the content of matter is $\Omega_m = 0.295 \pm 0.034$, by assuming the ΛCDM model.

Cosmography considers the fewest number of assumptions as possible. Its basic premise is that the background cosmology is well described by a FRW universe, at least at very large scales. Lying on this assumption, an expansion of the scale factor $a(t)$ in Taylor series about an arbitrary cosmic time t_* is provided:

$$a(t) = \sum_{n=0}^{\infty} \frac{1}{n!} \frac{d^n a(t)}{dt^n} \bigg|_{t=t_*} \Delta t^n = a_* \sum_{n=0}^{\infty} \frac{1}{n!} \frac{1}{a_* H_*^n} \frac{d^n a(t)}{dt^n} \bigg|_{t=t_*} (H_* \Delta t)^n, \qquad (8)$$

where $a_* = a(t_*)$, $H_* = H(t_*)$, and $\Delta t \equiv t - t_*$. From this expansion we define the hierarchy of statefinders, the first three of them are given by

$$q(t) \equiv -\frac{1}{aH^2} \frac{d^2 a}{dt^2}, \quad j(t) \equiv \frac{1}{aH^3} \frac{d^3 a}{dt^3}, \quad s(t) \equiv \frac{1}{aH^4} \frac{d^4 a}{dt^4}. \qquad (9)$$

These definitions are the most used in the literature, but slightly differ from the originals in [13]. In this work we concentrate only in the statefinders at the present time, that is in q_0, j_0, and s_0. Cosmography including up to 5 statefinders parameters has been studied in [16].

Relations between the statefinders and the parameters of a given cosmological model may be obtained in principle. For example, for the wCDM model, which is a dark energy model with constant w_Λ, it is found

$$q_{0,w\text{CDM}} = \frac{1}{2} + \frac{3}{2} w_\Lambda (1 - \Omega_m),$$

$$j_{0,w\text{CDM}} = 1 + \frac{9}{2} w_\Lambda (1 + w_\Lambda)(1 - \Omega_m), \qquad (10)$$

$$s_{0,w\text{CDM}} = -\frac{7}{2} - \frac{81}{4} w_\Lambda (1 - \Omega_m) - \frac{9}{4} w_\Lambda^2 (16 - 19\Omega_m + 3\Omega_m^2)$$

$$- \frac{27}{4} w_\Lambda^3 (3 - 4\Omega_m + \Omega_m^2).$$

For $w_\Lambda = -1$ we obtain $j_0 = 1$ and that s_0 can be written as a function of q_0 only. Thus, one statefinder and the Hubble factor are sufficient to characterize the expansion history at late times in the ΛCDM model.

Thereafter, in the case of the SC method, we expand the luminosity distance in terms of the statefinder parameters in a Taylor series as

$$\tilde{d}_{L(SC)}(z; q_0, j_0, s_0, \dots) = z + \frac{1}{2}(1 - q_0)z^2 + \frac{1}{6}(-1 + q_0 + 3q_0^2 - j_0)z^3$$
$$+ \frac{1}{24}\left(2 + 5j_0 - 2q_0 + 10j_0 q_0 - 15q_0^2 - 15q_0^3 + s_0\right)z^4 + \cdots, \tag{11}$$

where a tilde means that we have factorized a constant factor H_0^2, such that $d_L = \tilde{d}_L/H_0^2$. By using Eqs. (6) and (11), we may compare against the observed modulus distance data, finding the best fits and probability distributions of the statefinder parameters.

3   The *Eis* Method

As we shall see in Sect. 4, the statefinders parameters turn out to be highly biased estimated by SC. Therefore in [23] we have proposed three methods that improve the estimation of parameters. Here we are interested in the *Eis* method; it expands directly the Hubble function in Taylor series about redshift $z = 0$,

$$E(z) \equiv \frac{H(z)}{H_0} = \sum_i \frac{1}{i!} E_i z^i, \tag{12}$$

with $E_i = H^{(i)}(z)/H_0|_{z=0}$. Relations between these *eis* parameters and the statefinders q_0, j_0 and s_0 are giving by

$$\begin{aligned}
E_0 &= 1, \\
E_1 &= 1 + q_0, \\
E_2 &= -q_0^2 + j_0, \\
E_3 &= 3q_0^2 + 3q_0^3 - j_0(4q_0 + 3) - s_0.
\end{aligned} \tag{13}$$

Thereafter, we use the expansion (12) directly into the luminosity distance expression (7). That is, we define

$$\tilde{d}_L^{(n)}(z) \equiv (1 + z) \int_0^z \left(\sum_{i=0}^n \frac{1}{i!} E_i z'^i\right)^{-1} dz'. \tag{14}$$

At low redshifts not all of the powers in the $E(z)$ expansion are important. Thus, in order to speed up the numerical computations, we estimate the *eis* parameters in a hierarchical way by splitting Eq. (14) in redshift bins as

$$\tilde{d}_L(z; E_1, E_2, E_3) = \begin{cases} \tilde{d}_L^{(1)}(z) & z < z_{low} \\ \tilde{d}_L^{(2)}(z) & z_{low} < z < z_{mid} \\ \tilde{d}_L^{(3)}(z) & z_{mid} < z < z_{high}. \end{cases} \tag{15}$$

For $z > z_{high}$ we expand in Taylor series the integrand of $\tilde{d}_L^{(3)}(z_k)$ up to z^3 and analytically perform the integration. This last step is recommended, otherwise the tails of the probability distributions become very noisy.

That is, for a single supernova at redshift z_k in a given catalog, we use $\tilde{d}_L^{(1)}(z_k)$ if $z_k < z_{low}$, $\tilde{d}_L^{(2)}(z_k)$ if $z_{low} < z_k < z_{mid}$, and $\tilde{d}_L^{(3)}(z_k)$ if $z_{mid} < z_k < z_{high}$, and numerically integrate Eq. (15). Our preliminar numerics hinted us that a good choice for the redshift cuts is $z_{low} = 0.05$, $z_{mid} = 0.4$, and $z_{high} = 0.9$ The numerical outcomes of this particular binning does not significatively differ from those obtained by a direct application of Eq. (14), but the speeding-up in computational time is about a factor of 2.5. We refer to the method of Eq. (15) as the *Eis* method.

4 Numerical Analysis

We build simulated catalogs of supernovae Ia to test the performance of the *Eis* and SC methods. On each of these simulations we take 740 data distributed with the same redshifts and Gaussian errors of the observed peak magnitudes (~ 0.12) as in the JLA compilation [26]. This catalog has a large amount of low redshift supernovae providing a good inference of E_1, acting as a leverage for a better estimation of the rest of *eis* parameters, and it does not go too far in redshift as the Union2.1 compilation does [27], where expansions on redshift z about $z = 0$ may not converge [15].

By modifying the publicly available code CosmoMC [28], we are able to draw the likelihood and posterior probability distributions for the statefinder parameters.[2] Our approach relies on a Monte Carlo Markov Chain (MCMC) Metropolis-Hastings algorithm [29,30] in order to find the best fits and confidence intervals of the *eis* parameters distributions. For each mock, and for each model, we run 8 Markov chains and the convergence is assumed when the Gelman-Rubin parameter R [31] falls below the threshold 1.01. Finally, from the *eis* estimations, we derive the statistics for the statefinders.

4.1 The Simulated Data

The simulated data set consists in 100 mock catalogs in which each one of the 740 supernovae is obtained from fiducial ΛCDM models with the abundance parameters Ω_m's realizations of a Gaussian distributed variable with mean 0.30 and standard deviation of 0.034. Further, we fix the Hubble constant to $H_0 = 70$ km/s/Mpc. This is irrelevant because supernovae data alone cannot estimate the Hubble constant. Therefore, in the numerical analysis we internally marginalize the combination $5\ln(c/H_0) + M_b$ as described in [32]. That is, in a single catalog, for each supernova at redshift z_k we give the modulus distance a value $\mu_k = \mu(z_k; \Omega_{m\,k} \in \mathcal{N}(0.30, 0.034))$. We choose the redshifts z_k to take the same values as in the JLA compilation, spanning a range $z \in (0.01, 1.3)$.

---

[2] The module to CosmoMC we use is available at https://github.com/alejandroaviles/EisCosmography.

One may assume that the underlying, *true*, cosmology of the dispersed simulated data sets is the same for all of them, and given by $\Omega_m = 0.3$; see, *e.g.* [33]. Nevertheless, this approach is not very accurate because the true cosmology is actually unknown for each catalog. Thus, in order to analyze how good the fits are, we must compare against ΛCDM fittings to the same simulations. These fits lead to the average value $\langle \hat{\Omega}_m \rangle = 0.307$, a dispersion $\sigma_{\hat{\Omega}_m} = 0.036$, and the average of the standard deviations $\langle \sigma_{\Omega_m} \rangle = 0.012$, for the 100 mocks.

In Fig. 1 we show the 68% and 96% confidence regions of the derived statefinders for a single one of our simulated catalogs, both for the SC (red) and the *Eis* (blue) methods, revealing that the dispersions are smaller for *Eis*, most notably for the parameter s_0. In Fig. 2 we show the q_0-s_0 2D joint posterior. The solid black line is the graph of the function $s_0 = -2 - 3q_0$, this corresponds to the allowed region in ΛCDM, and may be derived by setting $w_\Lambda = -1$ in Eq. (10). We notice that SC does not follow this degeneracy, while *Eis* does it properly, even inside its 0.68 confidence region.

Complementing Fig. 1, in Table 1 we show the 1-dimensional marginalized posterior intervals for the same simulated data. The average statistics of the standard deviations and mean posterior of the 100 simulated catalogs, for both cosmography methods, are shown in Table 2.

We conclude that the *Eis* method improves the standard deviations of the statefinders estimations from those obtained by using SC.

4.2 Bias on the Estimators

We adopt the relation

$$b_\theta \equiv \hat{\theta} - \theta_{\text{true}} \tag{16}$$

as the definition of the bias of an estimator $\hat{\theta}$, where θ_{true} is the true value of the parameter θ. For the estimated $\hat{\theta}$ we use the mean value of the posterior distribution obtained from the MCMC analysis. As explained above, we do not know the true values of the parameters, but since we have constructed the simulated data from a fiducial ΛCDM model, we shall assume that the ΛCDM provides unbiased estimations for them. That is, we use $\theta_{\text{true}} = \hat{\theta}_{\Lambda\text{CDM}}$.

The bias does not provide a complete information of how well $\hat{\theta}$ estimates θ. For this reason, it is convenient to use complementary statistics. Thus, we consider the risk statistic [34,35]

$$risk(\theta) = \sqrt{\sigma_\theta^2 + b_\theta^2}, \tag{17}$$

which penalize the bias with the standard deviation. Furthermore, for the whole set of parameters, following [34,36], we compute the bias statistics

$$\Delta\chi^2 = \mathbf{b}^T \mathbf{F} \mathbf{b}, \tag{18}$$

which roughly quantifies the slip from the χ^2-statistics due to bias. Here $\mathbf{F}$ is the reduced Fisher matrix for the estimated parameters and $\mathbf{b} = (b_{E_1}, b_{E_2}, b_{E_3})$ is the bias vector for *eis* parameters.

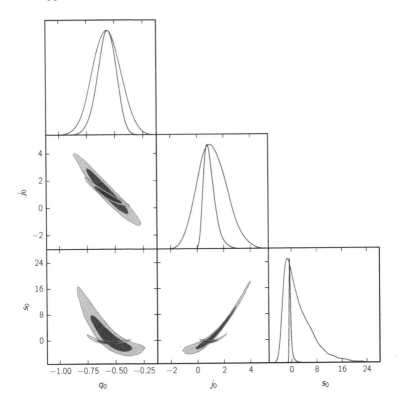

Fig. 1. Triangle plots for the estimated statefinder parameters using *Eis* (blue) and Standard Cosmography methods (red). Figure taken from [23]. (Color figure online)

A smaller $\Delta\chi^2$ does not imply a smaller bias, this can be noted for the case of one single parameter, for which $\Delta\chi^2 = b_\theta^2/\sigma_\theta^2$. Therefore, we additionally compute the figure of merit (FoM), that we define as

$$\text{FoM} = \frac{4\pi}{3} \frac{1}{\sqrt{\det \mathbf{F}}}. \tag{19}$$

Because of the numerical factor $4\pi/3$, the FoM coincides with the volume of the 3-dimensional ellipsoid defined by the covariance matrix.

We perform the four statistics for each simulated catalog. In Table 2 we show the average values of the bias and risk for the statefinder parameters. It can be noted that in these 1-parameter bias tests, *Eis* performs better than SC.

For the whole 3-dimensional bias statistics, the average values over the 100 simulated catalogs for $\Delta\chi^2$ and FoM are

$$
\begin{array}{llll}
\text{SC:} & \langle\Delta\chi^2\rangle = 0.806, & \text{FoM} = 0.1226. \\
\textit{Eis:} & \langle\Delta\chi^2\rangle = 2.121, & \text{FoM} = 0.0108. & (20)
\end{array}
$$

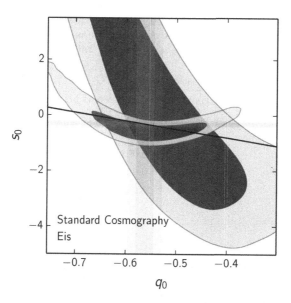

Fig. 2. Zoom of the q_0-s_0 contour plot of Fig. 1. We also show the region allowed by the flat ΛCDM model (solid line) and the ΛCDM confidence intervals (horizontal and vertical shadows). Figure taken from [23].

For $\nu = 3$ parameters, the 1σ contour is $\Delta\chi^2 \leq 3.53$ [36], thus for both methods, on the average, the true value is well inside this region, but we note SC is able to do it because the volume of its error ellipsoid, or FoM, is very large in comparison with *Eis*.

From this statistical analysis we conclude that SC is highly biased, and this is reduced considerably by the *Eis* method. In [23] we performed further statistics with catalogs based on fiducial CPL dark energy models [37,38] to show that this holds beyond ΛCDM.

Table 1. Marginalized 1 estimations for one of our simulated catalog. We show the means of the posterior distributions and the 0.95 confidence intervals. A complete table for the 100 catalogs, as well as one for the *eis* parameters, can be found in https://github.com/alejandroaviles/EisCosmography. Table modified from [23].

Method	q_0	j_0	s_0	$\Delta\chi^2$	FoM
Eis	$-0.567^{+0.150}_{-0.173}$	$0.960^{+0.906}_{-0.773}$	$-0.318^{+1.134}_{-0.727}$	0.923	0.0107
SC	$-0.568^{+0.240}_{-0.241}$	$1.161^{+2.155}_{-2.086}$	$2.147^{+9.443}_{-6.395}$	0.920	0.1201
ΛCDM	$-0.562^{+0.033}_{-0.033}$	1	$-0.313^{+0.098}_{-0.098}$	–	–

Table 2. Averaged statistics for the 100 simulated catalogs. We show, from up to bottom, the mean of the estimations, the mean of the standard deviations, the standard deviations of the estimations, the bias, and the risk. Table modified from [23].

Statistic	Eis	SC
$\langle \hat{q}_0 \rangle$	-0.542	-0.543
$\langle \sigma_{q_0} \rangle$	0.082	0.124
$\sigma_{\hat{q}_0}$	0.060	0.057
$\langle b_{q_0} \rangle$	-0.003	-0.004
$\langle risk(q_0) \rangle$	0.082	0.125
$\langle \hat{j}_0 \rangle$	0.938	1.144
$\langle \sigma_{j_0} \rangle$	0.439	1.095
$\sigma_{\hat{j}_0}$	0.074	0.063
$\langle b_{j_0} \rangle$	-0.062	0.144
$\langle risk(j_0) \rangle$	0.450	1.106
$\langle \hat{s}_0 \rangle$	-0.432	1.985
$\langle \sigma_{s_0} \rangle$	0.590	4.424
$\sigma_{\hat{s}_0}$	0.361	0.545
$\langle b_{s_0} \rangle$	-0.050	2.367
$\langle risk(s_0) \rangle$	0.628	5.018

5   Conclusions

In this work we have emphasized the importance of constraining the kinematics of the Universe through the use of model independent procedures, which do not *a priori* assume the validity of a particular cosmological model. This is the case of cosmography.

With the use of simulated supernova Type Ia catalogs we showed that the statefinder parameters are not accurately estimated by SC. We estimated the bias for cosmologies close to the cosmological concordance model showing that these are very large, making standard cosmography useless for future cosmological observations. To overcome this problem, we showed a new method, recently proposed by us in [23], which consists on directly perform the analysis with the expansion of the Hubble function; furthermore, we estimated their derivatives in a hierarchical manner, in which the order of the expansion depends on the redshift of a single data. This procedure speeds-up the computations by a factor of 2.5 in average. This is mainly due to the convergence of MCMC chains, which is attained within a less number of steps. We showed how this new method performs better than the standard approach both in the dispersion and the bias of the estimations.

We made publicly-available a module to the code CosmoMC that perform the MCMC numerical analysis for the cosmographic methods of this work at https://github.com/alejandroaviles/EisCosmography. There, we also uploaded all the simulated data as well as further tables and statistical files.

The case of fitting theoretical models by using the statefinders has attracted attention recently, it has been argued that the impossibility for the statefinders to constrain general models poses questions about its usefulness [33,39,40]. We differ from this point of of view: suppose we have a theoretical model $\mathcal{M}(\Psi; \alpha_i)$ with Ψ denoting the fields of the model and α_i its free parameters. For $\mathcal{M}$ to be a well defined model, each realization of the parameters, subjected to initial conditions, should give a unique Hubble diagram; and given that, it is as simple as taking derivatives to find the statefinders in that model. Thereafter, one can make comparisons to the measured statefinders, and accept or reject the realization α_i; clearly, one can restart the procedure with a new realization of the parameters, although at this point it may be a better idea to fit directly to the data. That is, to fit a general class of models, say *e.g.* the whole class of $f(R)$ theories, using the statefinders is not always possible at least some extra assumptions are considered [41]. Although doable, the main objective of cosmography is not to constrain theoretical models; instead, it is to reconstruct the Hubble diagram as model independent as possible.

Acknowledgements. This work was partially supported by ABACUS, CONACyT grant EDOMEX-2011-C01-165873. The numerical calculations in this paper made use of the ABACUS-I supercomputing of the Centro de Matemáticas Aplicadas y Cómputo de Alto Rendimiento, CINVESTAV-ABACUS.

References

1. Weinberg, S.: The cosmological constant problem. Rev. Mod. Phys. **61**, 1–23 (1989)
2. Bianchi, E., Rovelli, C.: Why all these prejudices against a constant? (2010)
3. Martin, J.: Everything you always wanted to know about the cosmological constant problem (but were afraid to ask). C.R. Phys. **13**, 566–665 (2012)
4. Ade, P.A.R., et al.: Planck results-XIII. Cosmological parameters (2015)
5. Bento, M.C., Bertolami, O., Sen, A.A.: Generalized Chaplygin gas, accelerated expansion and dark energy matter unification. Phys. Rev. **D66**, 043507 (2002)
6. Aviles, A., Cervantes-Cota, J.L.: Dark degeneracy and interacting cosmic components. Phys. Rev. **D84**, 083515 (2011). [Erratum: Phys. Rev. **D84**, 089905 (2011)]
7. Aviles, A., Cruz, N., Klapp, J., Luongo, O.: Emerging the dark sector from thermodynamics of cosmological systems with constant pressure. Gen. Relet. Gravit. **47**(5), 63 (2015)
8. Capozziello, S.: Curvature quintessence. Int. J. Mod. Phys. **D11**, 483–492 (2002)
9. Carroll, S.M., Duvvuri, V., Trodden, M., Turner, M.S.: Is cosmic speed - up due to new gravitational physics? Phys. Rev. **D70**, 043528 (2004)
10. Dvali, G.R., Gabadadze, G., Porrati, M.: 4-D gravity on a brane in 5-D Minkowski space. Phys. Lett. **B485**, 208–214 (2000)
11. Shafieloo, A., Kim, A.G., Linder, E.V.: Gaussian process cosmography. Phys. Rev. **D85**, 123530 (2012)
12. Weinberg, S.: Gravitation and Cosmology: Principles and Applications of the General Theory of Relativity. Wiley, New York (1972)

13. Sahni, V., Saini, T.D., Starobinsky, A.A., Alam, U.: Statefinder: a new geometrical diagnostic of dark energy. JETP Lett. **77**, 201–206 (2003). [Pisma Zh. Eksp. Teor. Fiz. **77**, 249 (2003)]

14. Alam, U., Sahni, V., Saini, T.D., Starobinsky, A.A.: Exploring the expanding universe and dark energy using the statefinder diagnostic. Mon. Not. Roy. Astron. Soc. **344**, 1057 (2003)

15. Cattoen, C., Visser, M.: The Hubble series: convergence properties and redshift variables. Class. Quantum Gravity **24**, 5985–5998 (2007)

16. Aviles, A., Gruber, C., Luongo, O., Quevedo, H.: Cosmography and constraints on the equation of state of the universe in various parametrizations. Phys. Rev. **D86**, 123516 (2012)

17. Gruber, C., Luongo, O.: Cosmographic analysis of the equation of state of the universe through Padé approximations. Phys. Rev. **D89**, 103506 (2014)

18. Aviles, A., Bravetti, A., Capozziello, S., Luongo, O.: Precision cosmology with Padé rational approximations: theoretical predictions versus observational limits. Phys. Rev. **D90**, 043531 (2014)

19. Zhou, Y.-N., Liu, D.-Z., Zou, X.-B., Wei, H.: New generalizations of cosmography inspired by the Padé approximant. Eur. Phys. J. C **76**(5), 281 (2016)

20. Nair, R., Jhingan, S., Jain, D.: Exploring scalar field dynamics with Gaussian processes. JCAP **1401**, 005 (2014)

21. Qin, H.-F., Li, X.-B., Wan, H.-Y., Zhang, T.-J.: Reconstructing equation of state of dark energy with principal component analysis (2015)

22. Feng, C.-J., Li, X.-Z.: Probing the expansion history of the universe by model-independent reconstruction from supernovae and gamma-ray burst measurements. Astrophys. J. **821**, 30 (2016)

23. Aviles, A., Klapp, J., Luongo, O.: Toward unbiased estimations of the statefinder parameters. arXiv:1606.09195

24. Wald, R.M.: General Relativity. Chicago Univ. Press, Chicago (1984)

25. Copeland, E.J., Sami, M., Tsujikawa, S.: Dynamics of dark energy. Int. J. Mod. Phys. **D15**, 1753–1936 (2006)

26. Betoule, M., et al.: Improved cosmological constraints from a joint analysis of the SDSS-II and SNLS supernova samples. Astron. Astrophys. **568**, A22 (2014)

27. Suzuki, N., et al.: The Hubble space telescope cluster supernova survey: V. Improving the dark energy constraints above $z > 1$ and building an early-type-hosted supernova sample. Astrophys. J. **746**, 85 (2012)

28. Lewis, A., Bridle, S.: Cosmological parameters from CMB and other data: a Monte Carlo approach. Phys. Rev. **D66**, 103511 (2002)

29. Metropolis, N., Rosenbluth, A.W., Rosenbluth, M.N., Teller, A.H., Teller, E.: Equation of state calculations by fast computing machines. J. Chem. Phys. **21**, 1087–1092 (1953)

30. Hastings, W.: Monte Carlo samping methods using Markov chains and their applications. Biometrika **57**, 97–109 (1970)

31. Gelman, A., Rubin, D.B.: Inference from iterative simulation using multiple sequences. Stat. Sci. **7**, 457–472 (1992)

32. Goliath, M., Amanullah, R., Astier, P., Goobar, A., Pain, R.: Supernovae and the nature of the dark energy. Astron. Astrophys. **380**, 6–18 (2001)

33. Busti, V.C., de la Cruz-Dombriz, A., Dunsby, P.K., Sáez-Gómez, D.: Is cosmography a useful tool for testing cosmology? Phys. Rev. **D92**, 123512 (2015)

34. Kendall, M., Stuart, A., Ord, J.: Advanced Theory of Statistics. Oxford University Press, New York (1987)

35. Linder, E.V.: Like vs. like: strategy and improvements in supernova cosmology systematics. Phys. Rev. **D79**, 023509 (2009)
36. Press, W.H., Teukolsky, S.A., Vetterling, W.T., Flannery, B.P.: Numerical Recipes in C: The Art of Scientific Computing, 2nd edn. Cambridge University Press, New York (1992)
37. Chevallier, M., Polarski, D.: Accelerating universes with scaling dark matter. Int. J. Mod. Phys. **D10**, 213–224 (2001)
38. Linder, E.V.: Exploring the expansion history of the universe. Phys. Rev. Lett. **90**, 091301 (2003)
39. de la Cruz-Dombriz, A.: Limitations of cosmography in extended theories of gravity. In: 11th International Workshop on the Dark Side of the Universe (DSU 2015), 14–18 December 2015, Kyoto, Japan (2016)
40. Saez-Gomez, D.: Testing the concordance model in cosmology with model- independent methods: some issues (2016)
41. Aviles, A., Bravetti, A., Capozziello, S., Luongo, O.: Updated constraints on f(R) gravity from cosmography. Phys. Rev. **D87**(4), 044012 (2013)

Author Index

Printed in the United States
By Bookmasters